Lecture Notes in Artificial Intelligence　　5459

Edited by R. Goebel, J. Siekmann, and W. Wahlster

Subseries of Lecture Notes in Computer Science

T0223374

Wenjie Li   Diego Mollá-Aliod (Eds.)

Computer Processing of Oriental Languages

Language Technology for the Knowledge-based Economy

22nd International Conference, ICCPOL 2009
Hong Kong, March 26-27, 2009
Proceedings

 Springer

Series Editors

Randy Goebel, University of Alberta, Edmonton, Canada
Jörg Siekmann, University of Saarland, Saarbrücken, Germany
Wolfgang Wahlster, DFKI and University of Saarland, Saarbrücken, Germany

Volume Editors

Wenjie Li
The Hong Kong Polytechnic University
Hung Hom, Kowloon, Hong Kong
E-mail: cswjli@comp.polyu.edu.hk

Diego Mollá-Aliod
Macquarie University
Sydney NSW 2109, Australia
E-mail: diego@ics.mq.edu.au

Library of Congress Control Number: Applied for

CR Subject Classification (1998): I.2.6-7, F.4.2-3, I.2, H.3, I.7, I.5

LNCS Sublibrary: SL 7 – Artificial Intelligence

ISSN   0302-9743
ISBN-10   3-642-00830-5 Springer Berlin Heidelberg New York
ISBN-13   978-3-642-00830-6 Springer Berlin Heidelberg New York

springer.com

© Springer-Verlag Berlin Heidelberg 2009
Printed in Germany

Typesetting: Camera-ready by author, data conversion by Scientific Publishing Services, Chennai, India
Printed on acid-free paper   SPIN: 12643370   06/3180   5 4 3 2 1 0

Preface

The International Conference on the Computer Processing of Oriental Languages (ICCPOL) series is hosted by the Chinese and Oriental Languages Society (COLCS), an international society founded in 1975. Recent ICCPOL events have been held in Hong Kong (1997), Tokushima, Japan (1999), Seoul, Korea (2001), Shenyang, China (2003) and Singapore (2006).

This volume presents the proceedings of the 22nd International Conference on the Computer Processing of Oriental Languages (ICCPOL 2009) held in Hong Kong, March 26-27, 2009. We received 63 submissions and all the papers went through a blind review process by members of the Program Committee. After careful discussion, 25 of them were selected for oral presentation and 15 for poster presentation. The accepted papers covered a variety of topics in natural language processing and its applications, including word segmentation, phrase and term extraction, chunking and parsing, semantic labelling, opinion mining, ontology construction, machine translation, information extraction, document summarization and so on.

On behalf of the Program Committee, we would like to thank all authors of submitted papers for their support. We wish to extend our appreciation to the Program Committee members and additional external reviewers for their tremendous effort and excellent reviews. We gratefully acknowledge the Organizing Committee and Publication Committee members for their generous contribution to the success of the conference. We also thank the Asian Federation of Natural Language Processing (AFNLP), the Department of Computing, The Hong Kong Polytechnic University, Hong Kong, the Department of Systems Engineering and Engineering Management, The Chinese University of Hong Kong, Hong Kong, and the Centre for Language Technology, Macquarie University, Australia for their valuable support.

January 2009

Wenjie Li
Diego Molla

Organization

ICCPOL 2009 was organized by the The Hong Kong Polytechnic University, The Chinese University of Hong Kong and City University of Hong Kong

Honorary Chairs

Bonnie Dorr
University of Maryland, USA (2008 President, ACL)

Jong Hyeok Lee
POSTECH, Korea (President, COLCS)

Elizabeth D. Liddy
Syracuse University, USA (Chair, ACM SIGIR)

Jun-Ichi Tsujii
University of Tokyo Japan (President, AFNLP)

Conference Chairs

Qin Lu
The Hong Kong Polytechnic University, Hong Kong

Robert Dale
Macquarie University, Australia

Program Chairs

Wenjie Li
The Hong Kong Polytechnic University, Hong Kong

Diego Molla
Macquarie University, Australia

Local Organizing Chair

Grace Ngai
The Hong Kong Polytechnic University, Hong Kong

Local Organizing Committee

Gaoying Cui
The Hong Kong Polytechnic University, Hong Kong

You Ouyang
The Hong Kong Polytechnic University, Hong Kong

Publication Chairs

Chunyu Kit
City University of Hong Kong, Hong Kong

Ruifeng Xu
City University of Hong Kong, Hong Kong

Program Committee

Tim Baldwin	University of Melbourne, Australia
Sivaji Bandyopadhyay	Jadavpur University, India
Hsin-Hsi Chen	National Taiwan University, Taiwan
Keh-Jiann Chen	Academia Sinica, Taiwan
Key-Sun Choi	Korea Advanced Institute of Science and Technology, Korea
Guohong Fu	Heilongjiang University, China
Choochart Haruechaiyasak	National Electronics and Computer Technology Center, Thailand
Xuanjing Huang	Fudan University, China
Kentaro Inui	Nara Institute of Science and Technology, Japan
Seung-Shik Kang	Kookmin University, Korea
Chunyu Kit	City University of Hong Kong, Hong Kong
Olivia Oi Yee Kwong	City University of Hong Kong, Hong Kong
Sobha L.	Anna University - KBC, India
Wai Lam	The Chinese University of Hong Kong, Hong Kong
Jong-Hyeok Lee Pohang	University of Science and Technology, Korea
Sujian Li	Peking University, China
Haizhou Li	Institute for Infocomm Research, Singapore
Wenjie Li	The Hong Kong Polytechnic University, Hong Kong
Ting Liu	Harbin Institute of Technology, China
Qun Liu	Chinese Academy of Sciences, China
Qing Ma	Ryukoku University, Japan
Diego Molla	Macquarie University, Australia
Masaaki Nagata	NTT Communication Science Laboratories, Japan
Manabu Okumura	Tokyo Institute of Technology, Japan
Jong Cheol Park	Korea Advanced Institute of Science and Technology, Korea
Sudeshna Sarkar	Indian Institute of Technology Kharagpur, India
Yohei Seki	Toyohashi University of Technology, Japan
Jian Su	Institute for Infocomm Research, Singapore
Zhifang Sui	Peking University, China
Le Sun	Chinese Academy of Sciences, China
Bin Sun	Peking University, China
Thanaruk Theeramunkong	Sirindhorn International Institute of Technology, Thailand
Takehito Utsuro	University of Tsukuba, Japan
Vasudev Varma	International Institute of Information Technology, India

Yunqing Xia	Tsinghua University, China
Ruifeng Xu	City University of Hong Kong
Min Zhang	Institute for Infocomm Research, Singapore
Tiejun Zhao	Harbin Institute of Technology, China
Hai Zhao	City University of Hong Kong, Hong Kong
Guodong Zhou	Suzhou University, China
Jingbo Zhu	Northeastern University, China

Hosted by

Chinese and Oriental Languages Computer Society (COLCS)

Supported by

Asian Federation of Natural Language Processing (AFNLP)
Department of Computing, The Hong Kong Polytechnic University
Department of Systems Engineering and Engineering Management, The Chinese
    University of Hong Kong
Centre for Language Technology, Macquarie University, Australia

Table of Contents

Regular Papers

Posters

A Density-Based Re-ranking Technique for Active Learning for Data Annotations

Jingbo Zhu[1], Huizhen Wang[1], and Benjamin K. Tsou[2]

[1] Natural Language Processing Laboratory, Northeastern University, Shenyang, P.R. China
{zhujingbo,wanghuizhen}@mail.neu.edu.cn
[2] Language Information Sciences Research Centre, City University of Hong Kong
rlbtsou@cityu.edu.hk

Abstract. One of the popular techniques of active learning for data annotations is uncertainty sampling, however, which often presents problems when outliers are selected. To solve this problem, this paper proposes a *density-based re-ranking* technique, in which a density measure is adopted to determine whether an unlabeled example is an outlier. The motivation of this study is to prefer not only the most informative example in terms of uncertainty measure, but also the most representative example in terms of density measure. Experimental results of active learning for word sense disambiguation and text classification tasks using six real-world evaluation data sets show that our proposed density-based re-ranking technique can improve uncertainty sampling.

Keywords: active learning, uncertainty sampling, density-based re-ranking, data annotation, text classification, word sense disambiguation.

1 Introduction

In machine learning approaches to natural language processing (NLP), supervised learning methods generally set their parameters using labeled training data. However, creating a large labeled training corpus is expensive and time-consuming, and is often a bottleneck to build a supervised classifier for a new application or domain. For example, building a large-scale sense-tagged training corpus for supervised word sense disambiguation (WSD) tasks is a crucial issue, because validations of sense definitions and sense-tagged data annotation must be done by human experts [1].

Among the techniques to solve the knowledge bottleneck problem, active learning is a widely used framework in which the learner has the ability to automatically select the most informative unlabeled examples for human annotation [2][3]. The ability of the active learner can be referred to as *selective sampling. Uncertainty sampling* [4] is one of popular selective sampling techniques, and selects the most uncertain unlabeled examples for human annotation from the learner's viewpoint. In recent years, uncertainty sampling has been widely studied in natural language processing applications such as word sense disambiguation [5][6], text classification (TC) [4][7], statistical syntactic parsing [8], and named entity recognition [9].

W. Li and D. Mollá-Aliod (Eds.): ICCPOL 2009, LNAI 5459, pp. 1–10, 2009.

The motivation behind uncertainty sampling is to find some unlabeled examples near decision boundaries, and use them to clarify the position of decision boundaries [7]. Experimental results show that some selected unlabeled examples (i.e. near decision boundaries) have high uncertainty, but can not provide much help to the learner, namely outliers. Uncertainty sampling often fails by selecting such outliers [10]. There are some attempts done in previous studies [7][9][10][11]. Cohn *et al.* [11] and Roy and McCallum [10] proposed a method that directly optimizes expected future error on future test examples. However, in real-world applications, their methods are almost intractable due to too high computational cost for selecting the most informative example from a large unlabeled pool. Shen *et al.* [9] proposed an approach to selecting examples based on informativeness, representativeness and diversity criteria. However, it is difficult to sufficiently determine those coefficients automatically. Perhaps there are different appropriate coefficients for various applications. Zhu *et al.* [7] proposed a sampling by uncertainty and density technique in which a new uncertainty measure called density*entropy is adopted. But because the density*entropy uncertainty measure is based on posterior probabilities produced by a probabilistic classifier thus may not work for active learning with non-probabilistic classifiers such as support vector machines (SVMs).

To solve this outlier problem, this paper presents a new *density-based re-ranking* approach based on an assumption that an unlabeled example with high density degree is less likely to be an outlier. It is noteworthy that our proposed re-ranking technique can be applied to active learning with probabilistic or non-probabilistic classifiers, and is easy to implement with very low additional computational cost. Experimental results of active learning for WSD and TC tasks on six evaluation data sets show that our proposed re-ranking method outperforms traditional uncertainty sampling.

2 Active Learning Process

Active learning is a two-stage process in which a small number of labeled samples and a large number of unlabeled examples are first collected in the initialization stage, and a closed-loop stage of query (i.e. selective sampling process) and retraining is adopted. The general active learning process can be summarized as follows:

Procedure: General Active Learning Process
Input: initial small training set L, and pool of unlabeled data set U
Use L to train the initial classifier C
Repeat
- Use the current classifier C to label all unlabeled examples in U
- Using uncertainty sampling technique to select the most uncertain unlabeled example from U, and ask oracle H for labeling
- Augment L with this new labeled example, and remove it from U
- Use L to retrain the current classifier C
Until the predefined stopping criterion SC is met.

Fig. 1. General active learning process with uncertainty sampling

In this study, we are interested in uncertainty sampling [4] for pool-based active learning, in which an unlabeled example x with maximum uncertainty is selected for human annotation at each learning cycle. The maximum uncertainty implies that the current classifier (i.e. the learner) has the least confidence on its classification of this unlabeled example. The key is how to measure uncertainty of each unlabeled example x. The well-known *entropy* is a popular uncertainty measurement widely used in previous studies on active learning [5][8][12]. The uncertainty measurement function based on the entropy can be expressed as below:

$$H(x) = -\sum_{y \in Y} P(y \mid x) \log P(y \mid x) \tag{1}$$

Where $P(y|x)$ is the a posteriori probability. We denote the output class $y \in Y = \{y_1, y_2, ..., y_k\}$. $H(.)$ is the uncertainty measurement function based on the entropy estimation of the classifier's posterior distribution.

3 Density-Based Re-ranking

To explain the motivation of our study in this paper, here we first give an exemplar figure as follows.

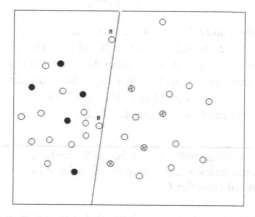

Fig. 2. An example of two points A and B with maximum uncertainty at the ith iteration

In uncertainty sampling scheme, these examples near decision boundaries are viewed as the cases with the maximum uncertainty. Fig. 2 shows two unlabeled examples A and B with maximum uncertainty at the ith learning cycle. Roughly speaking, there are three unlabeled examples near or similar to B, but, none for A. We think example B is more representative than example A, and A is likely to be an outlier. Adding B to the training set will thus help the learner more than A.

The motivation of our study is that we prefer not only the most informative example in terms of uncertainty measure, but also the most representative example in terms of density measure. The density measure can be evaluated based on how many examples there are similar or near to it. An example with high density degree is less likely to be an outlier.

In recent years, N-best re-ranking techniques have been successfully applied in NLP community, such as machine translation [13], syntactic parsing [14], and summarization [15]. Based on above motivation, we propose a density-based re-ranking technique for active learning as follows. To our best knowledge, there has been no attempt to use re-ranking technique for active learning.

In most real-world applications, the scale of unlabeled corpus would be very large. To estimate the density degree of an unlabeled example x, we adopt a K-Nearest-Neighbor-based density (KNN-density) measure [7]. Given a set of K (i.e. =20 used in our comparison experiments) most similar examples $S(x)=\{s_1, s_2, ..., s_K\}$ of the unlabeled example x, the KNN-density DS(.) of example x is defined as:

$$DS(x) = \frac{\sum_{s_i \in S(x)} \cos(x, s_i)}{K} \qquad (2)$$

The traditional cosine measure is adopted to estimate the similarity between two examples, that is

$$\cos(w_i, w_j) = \frac{w_i \bullet w_j}{\|w_i\| \cdot \|w_j\|} \qquad (3)$$

where w_i and w_j are the feature vectors of the examples i and j.

In our density-based re-ranking scheme, a baseline learner[1] based on uncertainty sampling is used to generate N-best output from the unlabeled pool U at each learning iteration. The re-ranking stage aims to select the unlabeled example with maximum density degree from these N candidates. The procedure of active learning with density-based re-ranking can be summarized as follows:

Procedure: Active Learning with Density-based Re-ranking
Input: initial small training set L, and pool of unlabeled data set U
Use L to train the initial classifier C
Repeat
- Use the current classifier C to label all unlabeled examples in U
- Using uncertainty sampling technique to select N most uncertain unlabeled examples from U
- Select the unlabeled example with maximum density (i.e. estimated by Equation (2)) from these N candidates, and ask oracle H for labeling.
- Augment L with this new labeled example, and remove it from U
- Use L to retrain the current classifier C
Until the predefined stopping criterion SC is met.

Fig. 3. Active learning with density-based re-ranking

---

[1] The baseline learner can be implemented in case of SVM-based classifiers (Shen *et al.* 2004).

4 Evaluation

4.1 Deficiency Measure

To compare density-based re-ranking technique with traditional uncertainty sampling method, *deficiency* is a statistic developed to compare performance of active learning methods globally across the learning curve, which has been used in previous studies [16][7]. The deficiency measure can be defined as:

$$Def_n(AL, REF) = \frac{\sum_{t=1}^{n} (acc_n(REF) - acc_t(AL))}{\sum_{t=1}^{n} (acc_n(REF) - acc_t(REF))} \qquad (4)$$

where acc_t is the average accuracy at t^{th} learning iteration. REF is a baseline active learning method, and AL is an active learning variant of the learning algorithm of REF. n refers to the evaluation stopping points (i.e. the number of learned examples). Smaller deficiency value (i.e. <1.0) indicates that AL method is better than REF method. Conversely, a larger value (i.e. >1.0) indicates a negative result. In the following comparison experiments, the REF method (i.e. the baseline method) refers to as entropy-based uncertainty sampling.

4.2 Evaluation Data Sets

In the following sections, we will construct some comparison experiments of active learning for word sense disambiguation and text classification tasks, using six publicly available real-world data sets as follows.

- **Word sense disambiguation task:** Three publicly available real-world data sets are used in this task: *Interest, Line* and *OntoNotes* data sets. The *Interest* data set consists of 2369 sentences of the noun *"interest"* with its correct sense manually labeled. The noun *"interest"* has six different senses in this data set. Interest data set has been previously used for WSD study [17]. In *Line* data set, each instance of line has been tagged with one of six WordNet senses. The Line data set has been used in some previous studies on WSD [18]. The *OntoNotes* project [1] uses the WSJ part of the Penn Treebank. The senses of noun words occurring in OntoNotes are linked to the Omega ontology [19]. In this experiment, we focus on 10 most frequent nouns[2] previously used for active learning on WSD task [12]: *rate, president, people, part, point, director, revenue, bill, future,* and *order*.
- **Text classification task:** Three publicly available natural data sets are used in this active learning comparison experiment: *Comp2a, Comp2b* and *WebKB* data sets. The Comp2a consists of *comp.os.ms-windows.misc* and *comp.sys.ibm.pc. hardware* subset of 20-NewsGroups. The Comp2b data set consists of *comp.graphics* and *comp.windows.x* categories from 20-NewsGroups. The WebKB dataset was widely used in text classification research. Following previous studies [20], we use the four most populous categories: *student, faculty, course* and *project*. These data sets have been previously used in active learning for text classification [10][16]. We first processed all data sets by running a stop word list.

---

[2] See http://www.nlplab.com/ontonotes-10-nouns.rar

4.3 Experimental Settings

We utilize a maximum entropy (ME) model [21] to design the basic classifier for WSD and TC tasks. The advantage of the ME model is its ability to freely incorporate features from diverse sources into a single, well-grounded statistical model. A publicly available ME toolkit[3] was used in our experiments.

To build the ME-based classifier for WSD, three knowledge sources are used to capture contextual information: *unordered single words in topical context, POS of neighboring words with position information,* and *local collocations,* which are the same as the knowledge sources used in [22]. In the design of text classifier, the maximum entropy model is also utilized, and no feature selection technique is used.

In the following comparison experiments, the algorithm starts with a initial training set of 10 labeled examples, and selects the most informative example at each learning iteration. A 10 by 10-fold cross-validation was performed. All results reported are the average of 10 trials in each active learning process.

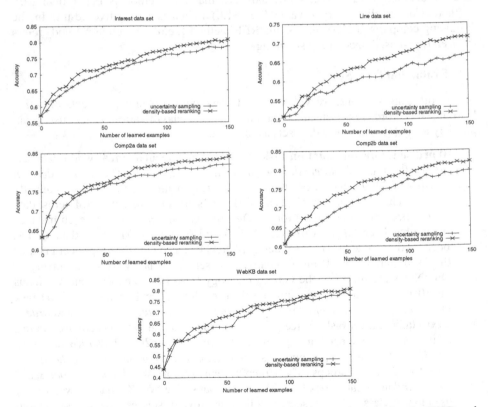

Fig. 4. Effectiveness of various selective sampling techniques in active learning for WSD and TC tasks on five evaluation data sets such as *Interest, Line, Comp2a, Comp2b* and *WebKB*. Note that evaluation results on OntoNotes data set are given in Table 1

---

[3] See http://homepages.inf.ed.ac.uk/s0450736/maxent_ toolkit.html

4.4 Experimental Results

Fig. 4 and Table 1 show results of various active learning methods for WSD and TC tasks on six data sets. We aim to analyze the effectiveness of our proposed density-based re-ranking technique, comparing to uncertainty sampling scheme[4] [4]. Fig. 4 depicts that re-ranking method constantly outperforms uncertainty sampling on these five data sets (i.e. the results on OntoNotes are shown in Table 1). The reason is because the KNN-density criterion can effectively avoid selecting the outliers that often cause uncertainty sampling to fail. In other words, density-based re-ranking technique prefers to choose an unlabeled example with maximum density which is less likely to be an outlier.

Seen from results on 10 subsets of OntoNotes shown in Table 1, re-ranking method in most cases only achieves slightly better performance than uncertainty sampling. The anomaly lies on *revenue* subset of OntoNotes, for which a worse deficiency than baseline uncertainty sampling is achieved by re-ranking method. From Table 1 we can see that those words in OntoNotes have very skewed sense distributions. In general, a supervised WSD classifier is designed to optimize overall accuracy without taking into account the class imbalance distribution in a real-world data set. The result is that

Table 1. Average deficiency values achieved by various active learning methods on all evaluation data sets. The REF method is the uncertainty sampling. The stopping point is 150. 'NA' indicates 'not applicable'. The **boldface** numbers indicate that the corresponding method obtained a worse performance than REF method.

Data sets		Uncertainty sampling	Density-based re-ranking
Interest		NA	0.75
Line		NA	0.54
Comp2a		NA	0.66
Comp2b		NA	0.62
WebKB		NA	0.79
OntoNotes	rate	NA	0.94
	president	NA	0.98
	people	NA	0.94
	part	NA	0.94
	point	NA	0.78
	director	NA	0.89
	revenue	NA	**1.51**
	bill	NA	0.85
	future	NA	0.97
	order	NA	0.83

---

[4] In above comparison experiments, we also evaluated random sampling scheme in which a candidate in each learning cycle is chosen at random from the unlabeled pool U. Experimental results show that random sampling works worst.

the classifier induced from imbalanced data tends to overfit the predominant class and to ignore small classes [12]. Seen from results on *revenue* data set, the classifier already achieves 95.8% accuracy using the initial small training data, and only makes 0.6% accuracy improvement during active learning process. In such anomaly situation the density-based re-ranking method seems to have possibly caused negative effects on active learning performance.

5 Discussion

Our density-based re-ranking technique can be applied for committee-based sampling [3] in which a committee of classifiers (always more than two classifiers) is generated to select the next unlabeled example by the principle of maximal disagreement among these classifiers. In this case, the baseline learner is a committee of classifiers. From top-m candidates outputted by this baseline learner, the density-based re-ranking technique selects one with maximum density degree for human annotation.

From experimental results of batch mode active learning, we found there is a redundancy problem that some selected examples are identical or similar. Such situation would reduce representative ability of these selected examples. We plan to study the redundancy problem when applying density-based re-ranking technique for batch mode active learning in our future work.

Furthermore, we believe that a misclassified unlabeled example may convey more information than a correctly classified unlabeled example that is closer to the decision boundary. We think it is worth stduying how to consider misclassification information and density criterion together for the selection of informative and representative unlabeled examples during active learning process.

Zhu and Hovy [12] studied the class imbalance issue for active learning, and found that using resampling techniques such as over-sampling or under-sampling for class imbalance problem can possibly improve the active learning performance. It is worth studying in the future work how to combine the best of density-based re-ranking and resampling technique for active learning.

6 Conclusion and Future Work

In this paper, we addressed the outlier problem of uncertainty sampling, and proposed a density-based re-ranking method, in which a KNN-density measure is considered to select the most representative unlabeled example from N most uncertain candidates generated by a baseline learner for human annotation at each learning cycle. Experimental results on six evaluation data sets show that our proposed density-based re-ranking technique can improve active learning over uncertainty sampling. In future work, we will focus on how to make use of misclassified information to select the most useful examples for human annotation, and applying our proposed techniques for batch mode active learning with probabilistic or non-probabilistic classifiers.

Acknowledgments. This work was supported in part by the National 863 High-tech Project (2006AA01Z154), the Program for New Century Excellent Talents in

University (NCET-05-0287), Microsoft Research Asia Theme Project (FY08-RES-THEME-227) and the National Science Foundation of China (60873091).

References

1. Eduard, H., Marcus, M., Palmer, M., Ramshaw, L., Weischedel, R.: Ontonotes: The 90% Solution. In: Proceedings of the Human Language Technology Conference of the North American Chapter of the ACL, poster session (2006)
2. David, C., Atlas, L., Ladner, R.: Improving generalization with active learning. Machine Learning 15(2), 201–221 (1994)
3. Seung, H.S., Opper, M., Sompolinsky, H.: Query by committee. In: Proceedings of the Fifth Annual ACM Conference on Computational Learning Theory, pp. 287–294. ACM Press, New York (1992)
4. Lewis David, D., Gale, W.A.: A sequential algorithm for training text classifiers. In: Proceedings of the 17th annual international ACM SIGIR conference on Research and development in information retrieval, pp. 3–12 (1994)
5. Jinying, C., Schein, A., Ungar, L., Palmer, M.: An empirical study of the behavior of active learning for word sense disambiguation. In: Proceedings of the main conference on Human Language Technology Conference of the North American Chapter of the Association of Computational Linguistics, pp. 120–127 (2006)
6. Seng, C.Y., Ng, H.T.: Domain adaptation with active learning for word sense disambiguation. In: Proceedings of the 45th annual meeting on Association for Computational Linguistics, pp. 49–56 (2007)
7. Jingbo, Z., Wang, H., Yao, T., Tsou, B.: Active Learning with Sampling by Uncertainty and Density for Word Sense Disambiguation and Text Classification. In: Proceedings of the 22nd International Conference on Computational Linguistics, pp. 1137–1144 (2008)
8. Min, T., Luo, X., Roukos, S.: Active learning for statistical natural language parsing. In: Proceedings of the 40th Annual Meeting on Association for Computational Linguistics, pp. 120–127 (2002)
9. Dan, S., Zhang, J., Su, J., Zhou, G., Tan, C.-L.: Multi-criteria-based active learning for named entity recognition. In: Proceedings of the 42nd Annual Meeting on Association for Computational Linguistics (2004)
10. Nicholas, R., McCallum, A.: Toward optimal active learning through sampling estimation of error reduction. In: Proceedings of the Eighteenth International Conference on Machine Learning, pp. 441–448 (2001)
11. Cohn David, A., Ghahramani, Z., Jordan, M.I.: Active learning with statistical models. Journal of Artificial Intelligence Research 4, 129–145 (1996)
12. Jingbo, Z., Hovy, E.: Active learning for word sense disambiguation with methods for addressing the class imbalance problem. In: Proceedings of the 2007 Joint Conference on Empirical Methods in Natural Language Processing and Computational Natural Language Learning, pp. 783–790 (2007)
13. Ying, Z., Hildebrand, A.S., Vogel, S.: Distributed language modeling for N-best list reranking. In: Proceedings of the 2006 Conference on Empirical Methods in Natural Language Processing, pp. 216–223 (2006)
14. Michael, C., Koo, T.: Discriminative reranking for natural language parsing. In: Proceedings of 17th International Conference on Machine Learning, pp. 175–182 (2000)
15. Eduard, H., Lin, C.-Y.: Automated Text Summarization in SUMMARIST. In: Maybury, M., Mani, I. (eds.) Advances in Automatic Text Summarization. MIT Press, Cambridge (1998)

16. Schein Andrew, I., Ungar, L.H.: Active learning for logistic regression: an evaluation. Machine Learning 68(3), 235–265 (2007)
17. Tou, N.H., Lee, H.B.: Integrating multiple knowledge sources to disambiguate word sense: an exemplar-based approach. In: Proceedings of the Thirty-Fourth Annual Meeting of the Association for Computational Linguistics, pp. 40–47 (1996)
18. Claudia, L., Towell, G., Voorhees, E.: Corpus-Based Statistical Sense Resolution. In: Proceedings of the ARPA Workshop on Human Language Technology, pp. 260–265 (1993)
19. Andrew, P., Hovy, E., Pantel, P.: The Omega Ontology. In: Proceedings of OntoLex 2005 - Ontologies and Lexical Resources, pp. 59–66 (2005)
20. Andrew, M., Nigam, K.: A comparison of event models for naïve bayes text classification. In: AAAI 1998 workshop on learning for text categorization (1998)
21. Berger Adam, L., Vincent, J., Della Pietra, S.A.D.: A maximum entropy approach to natural language processing. Computational Linguistics 22(1), 39–71 (1996)
22. Keok, L.Y., Ng, H.T.: An empirical evaluation of knowledge sources and learning algorithm for word sense disambiguation. In: Proceedings of the ACL 2002 conference on Empirical methods in natural language processing, pp. 41–48 (2002)

CRF Models for Tamil Part of Speech Tagging and Chunking

S. Lakshmana Pandian and T.V. Geetha

Anna University, Department of Computer Science and Engineering,
Patel Road, Chennai-25, India
lpandian72@yahoo.com, rctamil@annauniv.edu

Abstract. Conditional random fields (CRFs) is a framework for building probabilistic models to segment and label sequence data. CRFs offer several advantages over hidden Markov models (HMMs) and stochastic grammars for such tasks, including the ability to relax strong independence assumptions made in those models. CRFs also avoid a fundamental limitation of maximum entropy Markov models (MEMMs) and other discriminative Markov models based on directed graphical models, which can be biased towards states with few successor states. In this paper we propose the Language Models developed for Part Of Speech (POS) tagging and chunking using CRFs for Tamil. The Language models are designed based on morphological information. The CRF based POS tagger has an accuracy of about 89.18%, for Tamil and the chunking process performs at an accuracy of 84.25% for the same language.

Keywords: Conditional Random Fields, Language Models, Part Of Speech (POS) tagging, Chunking.

1 Introduction

POS-tagging is the process of assigning part of speech tags to natural language text based on both its root words and morpheme parts. Identifying POS-tags in a given text is an important task for any Natural Language Application. POS tagging has been developed using statistical methods, linguistic rules and hybrid of statistical and rule based methods. The statistical models are the HMMs [1], MEMMs [2] and CRFs [3]. These taggers work well when large amount of tagged data is used to estimate the parameters of the tagger. However, for morphologically rich languages like Tamil requires additional information like morphological roots and the possible tags for the words in the corpus to improve the performance of the tagger. *Chunking or shallow parsing* is the task of identifying and segmenting the text into syntactically correlated word groups like noun phrase, verb phrase etc. It is considered as an intermediate step towards full parsing. This paper presents the exploitation of CRFs for POS tagging and Chunking of Tamil languages with the help of morphological information that can be obtained from morphological analyzer. In Tamil languages, the availability of the tagged corpus is limited and so most of the techniques suffer due to data sparseness problem. In addition, a different approach and set of features are required to tackle the partial free word order nature of the language. This paper is organized as follows. The

W. Li and D. Mollá-Aliod (Eds.): ICCPOL 2009, LNAI 5459, pp. 11–22, 2009.
© Springer-Verlag Berlin Heidelberg 2009

next section explains the related work in POS tagging and chunking of natural language text. The section 3 explains briefly about how CRF can be exploited in this work. In Section 4, we explain how morphological features are vital in identifying the POS tagging of word and in sequencing the related phrases. The section 5 explains the language specific models for POS tagging and chunking. The methodology for training the designed models are described in section 6. The section 7 explains the evaluation of the model by comparing a baseline CRF model and our morpheme feature based model. Finally, we conclude and address future directions of this work.

2 Related Work

POS tagging is essentially a sequence labelling problem. Two main machine learning approaches have been used for sequence labeling. The first approach is based on k-order generative probabilistic models of paired input sequences, for example HMM [4] or multilevel Markov Models [5]. The second approach views the sequence labeling problem as a sequence of a classification problem, one for each of the labels in the sequence. CRFs bring together the best of generative and classification models. Like classification models, they can accommodate many statistically correlated features of the inputs, and they are trained discriminatively. But like generative models they can trade off decisions at different sequence positions to obtain globally optimal labeling. Lafferty [6] showed that CRFs overwhelms related classification models as well as HMMs on synthetic data and on POS-tagging task. Among the text chunking techniques, Fei Sha [3] proposed a Conditional Random Field based approach (how the work differs). There are also other approaches based on Maximum entropy [7], memory-based etc. Pattabhi et al [8] presents a transformation based learning (TBL) approach for text chunking for three of the Indian languages namely Hindi, Bengali and Telugu.

Many techniques have been used to POS tag English and other European language corpora. The first technique to be developed was rule-based technique used by Greene and Rubin in 1970 to tag the Brown corpus. Their tagger (called TAGGIT) used context-frame rules to select the appropriate tag for each word. It achieved an accuracy of 77%. Interest in rule-based taggers has re-emerged with Eric Brill's tagger that achieved an accuracy of 96%. The accuracy of this tagger was later improved to 97.5% [9]. In the 1980s more research effort went into taggers that used hidden Markov models to select the appropriate tag. Such taggers include CLAWS; it was developed at Lancaster University and achieved an accuracy of 97% [10].

In Brill's tagger, rules are selected that have the maximum net improvement rate that is based on statistics. More recently, taggers that use artificial intelligence techniques have been developed. One such tagger [11] uses machine learning, and is a form of supervised learning based on similarity-based reasoning. The accuracy rates of this tagger for English reached 97%. Also, neural networks have been used in developing Part-of-Speech taggers. The tagger developed at the University of Memphis [12] is an example of such a tagger. It achieved an accuracy of 91.6%. Another neural network tagger developed for Portuguese achieved an accuracy of 96% [13].

The sequential classification approach can handle many correlated features, as demonstrated in work on maximum-entropy [14] and a variety of other linear classifiers, including winnow [15], AdaBoost [16], and support-vector machines [17]. Furthermore, they are trained to minimize some function related to labeling error, leading to smaller error in practice if enough training data are available. In contrast, generative models are trained to maximize the joint probability of the training data, which is not as closely tied to the accuracy metrics of interest if the actual data was not generated by the model, as is always the case in practice. In this work we use CRF++ tool [18] and morphological analyzer for both POS tagging and chunking for Tamil.

3 Conditional Random Fields

Conditional random fields (CRFs) are undirected graphical models developed for labeling sequence data [19]. CRFs directly model $p(x \mid z)$, the *conditional* distribution over the hidden variables x given observations z. This model is different from generative models such as Hidden Markov Models or Markov Random Fields, which apply Bayes rule to infer hidden states [20]. CRFs can handle arbitrary dependencies between the observations z, which gives them substantial flexibility in using high-dimensional feature vectors.

The nodes in a CRF represent hidden states, denoted $x = \langle x_1, x_2, \ldots, x_n \rangle$, and data, denoted z. The nodes x_i, along with the connectivity structure represented by the undirected edges between them, define the conditional distribution $p(x \mid z)$ over the hidden states x. Let C be the set of cliques (fully connected subsets) in the graph of a CRF. Then, a CRF factorizes the conditional distribution into a product of *clique potentials* $\phi_c(z, x_c)$, where every $c \in C$ is a clique in the graph and z and x_c are the observed data and the hidden nodes in the clique c, respectively. Clique potentials are functions that map variable configurations to non-negative numbers. Intuitively, a potential captures the "compatibility" among the variables in the clique: the larger the potential value, the more likely the configuration.

Using clique potentials, the conditional distribution over hidden states is written as

$$p(x \mid z) \quad = \quad \frac{1}{Z(z)} \prod_{c \in C} \phi_c(z, x_c) \tag{1}$$

where $Z(z) = \sum_{x} \prod_{c \in C} \phi_c(z, x_c)$ is the normalizing partition function.

The computation of this partition function can be exponential in the size of x. Hence, exact inference is possible for a limited class of CRF models only. Potentials $\phi_c(z, x_c)$ are described by log-linear combinations of *feature functions* f_c i.e,

$$\phi_c(z, x_c) \quad = \quad \exp(w_c^T . f_c(z, x_c)) \tag{2}$$

where w_c^T is called as a weight vector.

$f_c(z, x_c)$ is a function that extracts a vector of features from the variable values. Using feature functions, we rewrite the conditional distribution (1) as

$$p(x \mid z) = \frac{1}{Z(z)} \exp\left\{ \sum_{c \in C} w_c^T \cdot f_c(z, x_c) \right\} \tag{3}$$

4 Approach for POS Tagging and Chunking

4.1 POS Tagging

The main parts of speech in Tamil are:

1. Noun: A noun in Tamil is a name or a word that describes a person, thing, idea, abstract, action and place. Traditionally the Noun class in Tamil is subdivided into derivatives (that is, nouns derived from verbs, nouns derived from other nouns, and nouns derived from particles) and primitives (nouns not so derived). These nouns could be further sub-categorized by number and case. The noun can be classified as Noun, Pronouns, Relatives, Demonstratives and Interrogatives Nominal noun, pronominal noun, verbal noun.

2. Verb: The verb classification in Tamil by its tenses and aspects, person, number and gender. The Verb tag can be sub-categorized into Imperative, Finite Verb, Negative finite verb and permissive. Further sub-categorization of the Verb class is possible using number, person and gender.

3. Other class: This includes: Adjective, Adverbs, Prepositions, Conjunctions, Interrogative, Demonstrative Particles, Intensifier and Interjections.

The tag set has five main tags namely Noun, Verb, Adjective, Adverb, Particles The subcategories of the five main categories contains 131 tags.

The verbs have been sub-categorized by 'type' (perfect, imperfect, imperative), person, number and gender, and the tag name reflects this sub categorization. For example, the word அவன் வருகிறான் *[avan varukiRAn]* " he [Pronoun] comes", which is a perfect verb in the second person masculine plural form, has the tag VPSg3M. An indicative imperfect second person feminine singular verb such as அவள் எழுதிக்கொண்டிருக்கிறாள் "she [singular, feminine] are writing" would be tagged VISg3FI.

Similarly, personal pronouns are tagged for number, person and gender. As well as personal pronouns, there are relative and demonstrative pronouns, which are also classed by number and gender. Nouns are classed by number (compare பறவை, பறவைகள், meaning "a bird", and "books"). Foreign and proper nouns receive separate tags. The category of others includes prepositions, adverbs and conjunctions, all of which appear in Tamil either as individual words, or as suffix attached to the word. Others are interjections, exceptions and negative particles. Dates, numbers, punctuations and abbreviations are also tagged separately. Dates are classified as either a Tamil date such as சித்திரை [ciththirai] which is the first month in the Tamil calendar.

The approach that was used in this work for POS tagging is as follows: CRF model (CRF++) is used to perform the initial tagging and then a set of transformation rules is applied to correct the errors produced by CRFs. The baseline CRF model contains the basic word features, whereas the modified CRF model includes morphological information like the root word, all possible pos tags for the words in the corpus, the suffix and prefix information. The modified CRF model is then trained using these updated features. To measure the performance of CRFs against other ML approaches we carried out various experiments using Brant's TnT [3] for HMMs, Maxent for MEMMs. Interestingly HMMs performed as high as CRFs with basic features. We preferred CRFs over HMMs as addition of features like the root words were much easier in CRFs.

4.2 Chunking

Phrase chunking is a process that separates and segments sentences into its sub constituents. The training corpus for chunking is prepared by rule based to mark the chunk labels. The CRF models are trained on the feature templates for predicting the chunking boundary. Finally the chunk labels and the chunk boundary names are merged to obtain the appropriate chunk tag. It is basically HMM+ CRF model for chunking.

Table 1 shows the Phrase chunking for an example sentence in Tamil. The input to the phrase chunker consists of the words in a sentence annotated automatically with part-of-speech (POS) tags. The chunker's task is to label each word with a label indicating whether the word is outside a chunk (O), starts a chunk (B), or continues a chunk (I). For example, the tokens in table 1 would be labelled BIIBBIIIIIBIO.

Table 1. Chunk tagged sentence

words	Transliteration	POS	Chunk
இந்தத்	[intha]	\<adj>	B -NP
தகவலின்	[thakavalin]	\<Ngen>	I-NP
அடிப்படையில்	[atippataiyil]	\<Nloc>	I-NP
போலீசார்	[pOlicAr]	\<noun>	B-NP
அந்தந்த	[andthandtha]	\<Dadj>	B-NP
மாவட்ட	[mAvatta]	\<Madj>	I-NP
போலீஸ்	[pOlish]	\<noun>	I-NP
சோதனைச்	[cOthanaic]	\<adj>	I-NP
சாவடி	[cAvati]	\<noun>	I-NP
மையங்களில்	[maiyangkalil]	\<Nloc>	I-NP
வாகனச்	[vAkanac]	\<adj>	B-NP
சோதனையில்	[cOthanaiyil]	\<Nloc>	I-NP
ஈடுபட்டனர்	[Itupattanar]	\<FV>	O

Tamil Sentence : இந்தத் தகவலின் அடிப்படையில் போலீசார் அந்தந்த மாவட்ட போலீஸ் சோதனைச் சாவடி மையங்களில் வாகனச் சோதனையில் ஈடுபட்டனர்
Translation: Based on this information, police were involved in investigating the vehicles in the centers of District Police check posts

5 Language Specific CRF Models

5.1 POS Tagging

Baseline CRF Model: A template with the following features as mentioned an example in CRF++ tools with a window size 5. This CRF model is considered as a baseline model for POS tagging. The features are

> *1)   The state features are*
> word(-2) ,word(-1), word(0), word(1), word(2)
> *(2) The Transition features*
> *word(-2) / word(-1), word(-1) / word(0), word(0) / word(1), word(1) / word(2),*
> *word(-2) / word(-1) / word(0), word(-1)/word(0)/word(-1), word(0) / word(1) / word(2)*

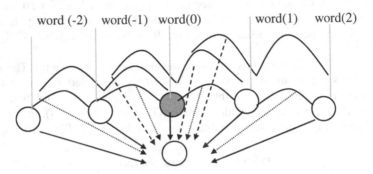

Fig. 1. Baseline CRF model for Tamil Pos tagging

Morpheme featured based CRF Model: Root of a word that can be identified through morphological analyzer provides information about main POS type classification and the further classification can be done by separate CRF model for each main class. The Root types are Numbers; Numbers in words, Date Time, Enpavar[1], Enpathu[1] , En[1], Noun, Pronoun, Interrogative Noun, Adjectival Noun, Non Tamil Noun, Verb, Finite Verb, Negative Finite Verb, Adjective, Demonstrative Adjective, Interrogative Adjective Postposition, Conjunction, Particle, Intensifier, Interjection and Adverb. The CRF model is designed with the following features

> *1)   The state features are*
> *Lost Morpheme part(word(0), previous to the last morpheme part(word(0), Root type(word(0)), Root type(word(-1)) and Root type (word(+1))*
> *2)   The transition features are (Two states)*
> *Root type(word(0)) / Root type (word(-1))*
> *Root type(word(+1)) / Root type (word(0))*
> *Last morpheme part (word(0)) / Lost Morpheme part(word(-1))*
> *Lost Morpheme part(word(+1))/ last morpheme part (word(0))*
> *(Three states)*
> *last morpheme pa t(word(-1)) / Lost Morpheme part(word(0)) / Root type(word(0))*

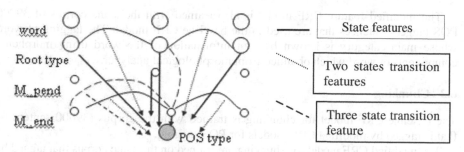

Fig. 2. Morpheme feature based CRF model for Tamil Pos tagging

5.2 Chunking

Baseline CRF Model: The features of base line CRF model are

> *1) State features*
> word(-2), word(-1), word(0), word(1), word(2), POS(-2), POS(-1), POS(0), POS(1), POS(2)
> *2) Transition features*
> word(-1))/ word(0), word(0) / word(1), POS(-2) / POS(-1), POS(-1) / POS(0), POS(0) / POS(1), POS(1) / POS(2),POS(-2))/ POS(-1)/ POS(0), POS(-1)/ POS(0)/ POS(1) and POS(0)/ POS(1) /POS(2)

The window size for baseline CRF is 5 with labeled -2, -1, 0, 1, 2. Word denotes string of characters. POS denotes the Part-of-speech of the word in the corresponding position mentioned in the parameter.

Morpheme featured based CRF Model: In partially free word order languages, the order of words in a single phrase is a sequential one. In this characteristic point of view, the features to be considered in designing a CRF model are its POS type, Last end morpheme component (E_l) and previous to last end morpheme component (E_{l-1}). The size of the window is 5 words. The centre word of the window is considered as zeroth position. The sequence from left to right of 3 words snippet is -1 0 1. The zeroth position word is considered for chunking to tag as B, I or O .The features of designed language specific CRF model for chunking are

> *1) The state features are*
> POS(-1), POS(0), POS(1), E_{l-1}(-1), E_{l-1} (0), E_{l-1} (1) , E_l(-1), E_l (0), E_l (1)
> *2) The transition features*
> POS(-1)/ POS(0) ,POS(0)/ POS(1), , E_{l-1} (-1)/ E_{l-1} (0), E_{l-1} (0)/ E_{l-1} (1), E_l(-1)/ E_l (0), E_l (0) / E_l (1), POS(-1) / POS(0) / POS(1), E_{l-1} (-1)/ E_{l-1} (0)/ E_{l-1} (1) and E_l (-1) / E_l (0))/ P(E_l (1)

6 Training

6.1 POS Tagging

The Baseline CRF model for POS tagging is trained with 39,000 sentences (a mixtures different type of sentences with an average of 13 words per sentence. This corpus is semi automatically POS tagged and manually verified).

The modified feature CRF model is also trained with the same corpus of 39000 POS tagged sentences that are used in the baseline CRF model. The tagging of word whose main category is known by root information of the word using morpheme components of word which obtained from morphological analyzer.

6.2 Chunking

The baseline CRF model for chunking is trained with the corpus (39000 sentences) that is tagged by modified CRF models for POS tagging.

The modified CRF model for chunking are trained on the same corpus that tagged by POS tagging and tested with the same datasets used in the generic CRF model for chunking. The performance comparison between both models is explained in the next section.

7 Evaluation Metric

Evaluation in Information Retrieval makes frequent use of the notation precision and recall. The same metrics can be used for both POS tagging and chunking.

Precision is defined as a measure of the proportion of the selected items that the system got right

$$precision = \frac{No.of\ items\ tagged\ correctly}{No.of\ items\ tagged} \tag{4}$$

Recall is defined as the proportion of the target items that the system selected

$$Re\ call = \frac{No.of\ items\ tagged\ by\ the\ system}{No.of\ items\ to\ be\ tagged} \tag{5}$$

To combine precision and recall into a single measure of over all performance, The F measure is defined as

$$F = \frac{1}{\alpha \times \dfrac{1}{p} + (1 - \alpha) \times \dfrac{1}{R}} \tag{6}$$

where P is precision, R is recall and $\propto$ is factor which determine the weighting of precision and recall. A value of $\propto$ is often chosen for equal weighting of precision and recall. With this $\propto$ value the F measure simplifies to

$$F = \frac{2 \times P \times R}{P + R} \tag{7}$$

The standard evaluation metrics for a chunker are precision P (fraction of output chunks that exactly match the reference chunks), recall R (fraction of reference chunks returned by the chunker), and their harmonic mean, the F measure. The relationships between F score and labeling error or log-likelihood are not direct, so we report both F score and the other metrics for the models we tested.

7.1 POS Tagging Evaluation

The modified feature CRF model is evaluated and compared with the performance of the baseline CRF model. These two models are tested with three test sets. The test sets are prepared by extracting sentences from various Tamil web sites. The sizes of test sets are 18345, 19834 and 18907 words respectively.

Table 2. F-score for Tamil POS tag with baseline CRF model

Test set	No of words (A)	No. of word tagged (B)	No. of words correctly tagged (C)	Precision (P) C / B	Recall (R) B/A	F-Score 2*P*R/ P+R
1	18345	15234	13134	0.8622	0.8304	0.8460
2	19834	17142	14923	0.8706	0.8643	0.8674
3	18907	15921	13835	0.8690	0.8421	0.8553

Table 2 shows the performance of the POS tagging with baseline CRF model. Some of the untagged words are proper names. Three experiments are conducted with test sets. It shows precision, recall and F-Score values for corresponding test sets.

Table 3. F-score for Tamil POS tag with Modified CRF model

Test Set	No of words (A)	No. of word tagged (B)	No. of words correctly tagged (C)	Precision (P) C /B	Recall (R) B/A	F-Score 2*P*R/P +R
1	18345	16498	14371	0.8711	0.8993	0.8850
2	19834	18182	15989	0.8794	0.9167	0.8977
3	18907	16961	15072	0.8886	0.8971	0.8928

The table 3 shows the Performance of the POS tagging with Modified CRF model. The result shows the total POS tagging of 3 test set as used in the previous experiment. The effect of comparison between both CRF model shows that F-score value of modified CRF model for POS tagging increased significantly and Recall metric value of the modified CRF model is predominantly increased as compared with baseline CRF model.

The modified CRF model improves the performance of Tamil POS tagging significantly as compared with baseline. The reason behind this is the modified model depends on the root type and morpheme ends of the word. The POS type of a word in Tamil is strongly depends on the morpheme ends and its root type. The baseline CRF model depends on the words and its sequence but the language is free word order nature. The sequence is not so much important for predicting the POS type of word.

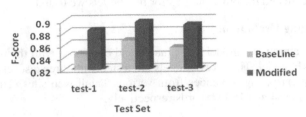

Fig. 3. The F-Score comparison for Tamil POS tagging

7.2 Chunking Evaluation

The modified feature CRF model is evaluated and compared with the performance of the baseline CRF model. These two models are tested with three test sets. The test sets are prepared in two steps semi automatic POS tagging of test set used in the previous pos tagging evaluation. The sizes of test sets are 6342, 6834 and 6521 chunks respectively.

Table 4. F-score for Chunk tag with baseline CRF model

Test set	Actual No of Chunks in test set (A)	No. of chunks tagged by the system (B)	No. of chunks correctly tagged (C)	Precision (P) C /B	Recall (R) B/A	F-Score 2*P*R/ P+R
1	6342	5071	3972	0.7833	0.7996	0.7913
2	6834	5200	4112	0.7908	0.7609	0.7755
3	6521	5100	4051	0.7943	0.7821	0.7882

Table 4 shows the performance of the chunking with baseline CRF model. Three experiments are conducted with separate test set with size of 6342, 6834 and 6521 chunks respectively. It shows precision, recall and F-Score values for corresponding test sets.

Table 5 shows the performance for Tamil chunking with precision, recall and F-Score as metric of modified CRF. The result shows the total chunking of three test corpuses which are already used in baseline model.

Table 5. F-score for Chunk tag with modified CRF model

Test set	Actual No of Chunks in test set (A)	No. of chunks tagged by the system (B)	No. of chunks correctly tagged (C)	Precision (P) C /B	Recall (R) B/A	F-Score 2*P*R/ P+R
1	6342	5612	4443	0.7917	0.8849	0.8357
2	6834	5742	4822	0.8398	0.8402	0.8400
3	6521	5672	4732	0.8343	0.8698	0.8517

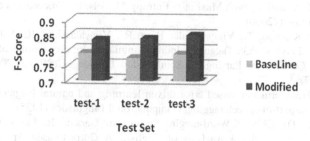

Fig. 4. The F-Score comparison for Tamil Chunking

The baseline CRF model is designed with features of the words, their POS and their sequence in a sentence. In textual point of view, chunking of a word in Tamil depends on the morpheme ends and its root type. Tamil language is free word order nature and morphologically rich. Our CRF model is designed with these language properties in mind. This CRF model with modified feature improves the performance of Tamil chunking significantly as compared with baseline. The graph in figure shows the performance comparison of Modified feature CRF model with baseline CRF model for Tamil Chunking for three difference set of test data.

8   Conclusions and Future Work

The models designed for POS tag and chunking for Tamil using CRF give high performance as compared baseline CRF POS tagging and chunking. The morphological information is very important feature for designing CRF model of languages with free word order or partially free word order characteristic. This work can also be improved by adding error correction module like Transformation based Learning. Also this model can be improved by adding the phrase boundary detection before Chunking process. This work can be extended for semantic tagging like named entity recognition and semantic role labeling.

References

1. Cutting, D., Kupiec, J., Pederson, J., Sibun, P.: A practical part-of-speech tagger. In: Proc. of the 3rd Conference on Applied NLP, pp. 133–140 (1992)
2. Ratnaparkhi, A.: Learning to parse natural language with maximum entropy models. Machine Learning 34 (1999)
3. Sha, F., Pereira, F.: Shallow Parsing with Conditional Random Fields. In: The Proceedings of HLT-NAACL (2003)
4. Freitag, D., McCallum, A.: Information extraction with HMM structures learned by stochastic optimization. In: Proc. AAAI (2000)
5. Bikel, D.M., Schwartz, R.L., Weischedel, R.M.: An algorithm that learns what's in a name. Machine Learning 34, 211–231 (1999)

6. Lafferty, J., McCallum, A., Pereira, F.: Conditional random _elds: Probabilistic models for segmenting and labeling sequence data. In: Proc. ICML 2001, pp. 282–289 (2001)
7. Koeling, R.: Chunking with Maximum Entropy Models. In: Proceedings of CoNLL 2000, Lisbon, Portugal (2000)
8. Pattabhi, R.K., Rao, T., Vijay Sundar Ram, R., Vijayakrishna, R., Sobha, L.: A Text Chunker and Hybrid POS Tagger for Indian Languages. In: Proceedings of the IJCAI 2007 Workshop On Shallow Parsing for South Asian Languages (SPSAL 2007), Hyderabad, India (2007)
9. Brill, E.: Transformation-based error driven learning and natural language processing: A case study in part-of-speech tagging. Computational Linguistics (1995)
10. Garside, R.: The CLAWS Word-tagging System. In: Garside, R., Leech, G., Sampson, G. (eds.) The Computational Analysis of English: A Corpus-based Approach. Longman, London (1987)
11. Daelemans, W., Zavrel, J., Berck, P., Gillis, S.: MBT: A Memory-Based Part ofSpeech Tagger-Generator. In: Proceedings of the Fourth Workshop on Very Large Corpora, Copenhagen, Denmark, pp. 14–27 (1996)
12. Olde, B.A., Hoener, J., Chipman, P., Graesser, A.C.: The Tutoring Research Group A Connectionist Model for Part of Speech Tagging. In: Proceedings of the 12th International Florida Artificial Intelligence Research Society Conference, Menlo Park, CA, pp. 172–176 (1999)
13. Marques, N., Lopes, J.G.: Using Neural Nets for Portuguese Part-of-Speech Tagging. In: Proceedings of the Fifth International Conference on The Cognitive Science of Natural Language Processing, Dublin City University (1996)
14. Ratnaparkhi, A.: Maximum Entropy Model For Natural Language Ambiguity Resolution, Dissertation in Computer and Information Science, University Of Pennslyvania (1998)
15. Punyakanok, V., Roth, D.: The use of classifiers in sequential inference. In: NIPS, vol. 13, pp. 995–1001. MIT Press, Cambridge (2001)
16. Abney, S., Schapire, R.E., Singer, Y.: Boosting applied totagging and PP attachment. In: Proc. EMNLP-VLC, NewBrunswick, New Jersey, ACL (1999)
17. Kudo, T., Matsumoto, Y.: Chunking with. support vector machines. In: Proceedings of NAACL, pp. 192–199 (2001)
18. CRF++: Yet Another Toolkit, http://chasen.org/~taku/software/CRF++
19. Lafferty, J.: Andrew McCallum and Fernando Pereira, Conditional Random Fields: Probabilistic Models for Segmenting and Labeling Sequence Data. In: Proc. of the International Conference on Machine Learning (ICML) (2001)
20. Rabiner, L.R.: A tutorial on hidden Markov models and selected applications in speech recognition. In: Proceedings of the IEEE. IEEE, Los Alamitos (1989) IEEE Log Number 8825949

A Probabilistic Graphical Model for Recognizing NP Chunks in Texts

Minhua Huang and Robert M. Haralick

Computer Science, Graduate Center
City University of New York
New York, NY 10016
mhuang@gc.cuny.edu, haralick@aim.com

Abstract. We present a probabilistic graphical model for identifying noun phrase patterns in texts. This model is derived from mathematical processes under two reasonable conditional independence assumptions with different perspectives compared with other graphical models, such as CRFs or MEMMs. Empirical results shown our model is effective. Experiments on WSJ data from the Penn Treebank, our method achieves an average of precision 97.7% and an average of recall 98.7%. Further experiments on the CoNLL-2000 shared task data set show our method achieves the best performance compared to competing methods that other researchers have published on this data set. Our average precision is 95.15% and an average recall is 96.05%.

Keywords: NP chunking, graphical models, cliques, separators.

1   Introduction

Noun phrase recognition, also called noun phrase chunking (NP chunking), is a procedure for identifying noun phrases (NP chunks) in a sentence. These NP chunks are not overlapping and not recursive [1]; that is, they can not be included in other chunks. Although the concept of NP chunking was first introduced by [1] for building a parse tree of a sentence, these NP chunks provide useful information for NLP tasks such as semantic role labeling or word sense disambiguation. For example, a verb's semantic arguments can be derived from NP phrases and features with syntactic and semantic relations for word sense disambiguation can be extracted from NP phrases.

The methods for classifying NP chunks in sentences have been developed by [2], [3], [4], [5]. Of the methods reported, the best precision is 94.46% and the best recall is 94.60% on the CoNLL-2000 data.

In this paper, we discuss a new method for identifying NP chunks in texts. First, a probabilistic graphical model is built from different perspectives compared with other existed graphical models under two conditional independence assumptions. Moreover, the corresponding mathematical representation of the model is formed. Finally, decision rules are created to assign each word in a sentence to a category (class) with a minimal error. As a consequence, a sentence is

W. Li and D. Mollá-Aliod (Eds.): ICCPOL 2009, LNAI 5459, pp. 23–33, 2009.

attributed to a sequence of categories with the best description. Finally, grouping consecutive words of the sentence with the same assigned specific classes forms a NP chunk.

In experiments on the Penn Treebank WSJ data, our method achieves a very promising result: the average recall is 97.7%, the average of precision is 98.7% and the average of f-measure is 98.2%. Moreover, in experiments on the CoNLL-2000 data, our methods does better than any of the competing techniques: the average recall is 95.24%, the average precision is 96.32%, and the f-measure is 95.83%.

The rest of the paper is structured in the following way. The second section presents the proposed method. The third section demonstrates the empirical results. The fourth section reviews related researches. The fifth section gives a conclusion.

2   The Proposed Method

2.1   An Example

Table 1 shows that an input sentence with it POS tags. Then, by our method, it is assigned to three different categories. Finally, NP chunks are derived from these categories.

2.2   Describing the Task

Let U be a language, V be vocabulary of U, and T be POS tags of V. Let S be a sequence of symbols associated with a sentence, $S = (s_1, ..., s_i, ..., s_N)$,

Table 1. An example NP chunking procedures

Word	POS	Category	NP chunks	Number of chunks
The	DT	C_1	√	1
doctor	NN	C_1	√	
was	VBD	C_2		
among	IN	C_2		
dozens	NNS	C_1	√	2
of	IN	C_2		
people	NN	C_1	√	3
miling	VBG	C_2		
through	IN	C_2		
East	NNP	C_1	√	4
Berline	NNP	C_1	√	
's	POS	C_3	√	5
Gethsemane	NNP	C_1	√	
Church	NNP	C_1	√	
Saturday	NNP	C_3	√	6
morning	NN	C_1	√	

$s_i =< w_i, t_i >$, $w_i \in V$, $t_i \in T$. Let C be a set of categories, $C = \{C_1, C_2, C_3\}$, where C_1 indicates the current symbol is in an NP chunk, C_2 indicates the current symbol is not in an NP chunk, and C_3 starts a new NP chunk. The tasks can be stated as follows:

Given $S = (s_1, ..., s_N)$, we need

1. to find a sequence of categories, $(c_1, ..., c_N)$, $c_i \in C$, with the best description of S;
2. to determine NP chunks based on $(c_1, ...c_N)$.

2.3 Building Probabilistic Graphical Models

Given $S = (s_1, s_2, ..., s_N)$, $C = \{C_1, C_2, C_3\}$, for $s_i \in S$, we want to find $c_i \in C$, s.t.

$$(c_1, c_2, ..., c_N) = \underset{c_1, c_2, ..., c_N}{argmax}\, p(c_1, c_2, ..., c_N | s_1, s_2, ..., s_N)$$

$$p(c_1, c_2, ..., c_N | s_1, s_2, ..., s_N) = p(c_1 | c_2, ..., c_N, s_1, s_2, ..., s_N) \times$$
$$p(c_2 | c_3, ..., c_N, s_1, s_2, ..., s_N) \times$$
$$.... \times$$
$$p(c_N | s_1, s_2..., s_N)$$

Suppose c_i is independent of $c_{j \neq i}$ given $(s_1, s_2, ..., s_N)$. Then, $p(c_1, ..., c_N | s_1, ..., s_N)$ can be represented as Fig 1.

Based the assumption we have made,

$$p(c_1, c_2, ..., c_N | s_1, s_2, ..., s_N) = \prod_{i=1}^{N} p(c_i | s_1, ..., s_N) \tag{1}$$

Assume c_i is independent of $(s_1, .., s_{i-2}, s_{i+2}, .., s_N)$ given (s_{i-1}, s_i, s_{i+1})

$$p(c_1, c_2, ..., c_N | s_1, s_2, ..., s_N) = \prod_{i=1}^{N} p(c_i | s_{i-1}, s_i, s_{i+1}) \tag{2}$$

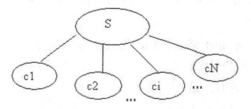

Fig. 1. The graphical model of $p(c_1, ..., c_N | s_1, ..., s_N)$ under the assumption c_i is independent of $c_{j \neq i}$ given $(s_1, s_2, ..., s_N)$

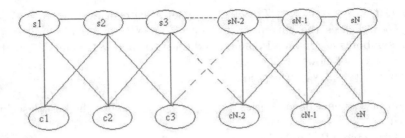

Fig. 2. The probabilistic graphical model of $p(c_i|s_1,...s_N)$ under assumptions c_i is independent of $c_{j\neq i}$ given $(s_1, s_2, ..., s_N)$ and c_i is independent of $(s_1, .., s_{i-2}, s_{i+2}, .., s_N)$ given (s_{i-1}, s_i, s_{i+1})

A probability graphical model for $p(c_1, ..., c_N|s_1, ..., s_N)$ is constructed. Fig 2 shows this model. From this model, a set of $N+1$ cliques[1] is obtained:

$$CIL = \{p(s_1, s_2, c_1), p(s_1, s_2, c_2), ..., p(s_{N-1}, s_N, c_N), p(s_{N-1}, s_N, c_N)\}$$

Moreover, a set of $2N - 3$ separators [2] is received:

$$SEP = \{p(s_1, s_2), ..., p(s_{N-1}, s_N), p(s_2, c_2), ..., p(s_{N-1}, c_{N-1})\}.$$

From this model, according to [6], $p(c_1, .., c_N|s_1, .., s_N)$ can be computed by the product of cliques divided by the product of separators.

Hence:

$$p(c_1, ..., c_N|s_1, ..., s_N)$$
$$\propto \prod_{i=1}^{N} p(s_{i-1}|s_i, c_i)p(s_{i+1}|s_i, c_i)p(s_i|c_i)p(c_i) \tag{3}$$

Differences between Other Graphical Models. What is the different between our model and other graphical models? In Fig 3, we show a HMM[7], a second order HMM[4], a MEMM[7], a CRF[8], and the model of us. For simplicity, we just show the s_i part. These models represent a joint probability $p(s_1, ..., s_N, c_1, ..., c_N)$ or a conditional probability $p(c_1, ..., c_N|s_1, ..., s_N)$ under different conditional independence assumptions. By observing these models, the structure of our model is different from other models. From empirical results on CoNLL-2000 shared task data set, our model can achieve the better performance than HMMs. However, there are no comparisons between our model with $MEMMs$ or $CRFs$.

Making a Decision and Error Estimations. For $S = (s_1, ..., s_N)$, $s_i \in S$, based on (3), we define $M(s_i, c_i)$:

$$M(s_i, c_i)$$
$$= p(s_{i-1}|s_i, c_i)p(s_{i+1}|s_i, c_i)p(s_i|c_i)p(c_i) \tag{4}$$

---

[1] A clique is a maximal complete set of nodes.
[2] $\Gamma = \{\Gamma_1, ..., \Gamma_M\}$ is a set of separators, where $\Gamma_k = \Lambda_k \cap (\Lambda_1 \cup ... \cup \Lambda_{k-1})$.

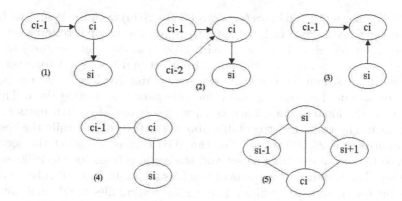

Fig. 3. (1): a HMM model $p(s_1, ..., s_N, c_1, ..., c_n) = \prod_{i=1}^{N} p(s_i|c_i)p(c_i|c_{i-1})$, (2): a second order HMM $p(s_1, ..., s_N, c_1, ..., c_n) = \prod_{i=1}^{N} p(s_i|c_i)p(c_i|c_{i-1}, c_{i-2})$, (3): a MEMM model $p(s_1, ..., s_N, c_1, ..., c_n) = \prod_{i=1}^{N} p(c_i|c_{i-1}, s_i)$, (4): a CRF model $p(c_1, ..., c_N|s_1, ..., s_N) = \prod_{i=1}^{N} p(c_i|s_i)p(c_i|c_{i-1})p(c_{i-1})$, and (5): the model presented by this paper $p(c_1, ..., c_N|s_1, ..., s_N) = \prod_{i=1}^{N} p(s_{i-1}|s_i, c_i)p(s_{i+1}|s_i, c_i)p(s_i|c_i)p(c_i)$

We select C_k for s_i if :

$$p(s_{i-1}|s_i, C_k)p(s_{i+1}|s_i, C_k)p(s_i|C_k)p(C_k) >$$
$$p(s_{i-1}|s_i, C_j)p(s_{i+1}|s_i, C_j)p(s_i|C_j)p(C_j)$$
$$\text{where}: C_j \neq C_k \tag{5}$$

We estimate an error for assigning C_k to s_i by:

$$p(e_{s_i}) = p(s_i \in C_{j \neq k}, C_k) \tag{6}$$

According (5), (6) is minimal.

Term Estimations of the Equation (3). For $S = (s_1, ..., s_N)$, for every $s_i \in S$, $s_i = < w_i, t_i >$, we have $w_i \in V$ and $t_i \in T$. We want to determine $p(s_i|c_i)$, $p(s_{i+1}|s_i, c_i)$, and $p(s_{i-1}|s_i, c_i)$. To make an approximation, we assume that w_i and t_i are independent conditioned on c_i.

$$p(s_i|c_i) = p(w_i|c_i)p(t_i|c_i) \tag{7}$$
$$p(s_{i-1}|s_i, c_i) = p(t_{i-1}|t_i, c_i) \tag{8}$$
$$p(s_{i+1}|s_i, c_i) = p(t_{i+1}|t_i, c_i) \tag{9}$$

3   Empirical Results and Discussions

3.1   Experiment Setup

Corpora and Training and Testing Set Distributions. We have used two corpora in our experiments. One corpus is the CoNLL-2000 shared task data set

[9] while another is the WSJ files (sections $0200-2099$) from the Penn Treebank [10]. For the CoNLL-2000 task data, first, we use the original training set and the testing set (developed by the CoNLL-2000 task data set creators) to test our model. Then, we mix the original training set and testing set together and redistributing based on sentences. We do this by first dividing it into ten parts. Nine parts are used as training data and one part is as testing data. This is done repeatedly for ten times. Each time, we select one of the ten parts as the testing part. The training set contains about $234,000$ tokens while the testing set contains about $26,000$ tokens. For the WSJ corpus, we select the sections from 0200 to 0999 as our training set and the sections from 1000 to 2099 as our testing set. The training set consists of 800 files about $40,000,000$ tokens, while the testing set contains 1000 files . These 1000 testing files are divided into 10 parts as Table 2 shows . Each test contains 100 files and about $5,000,000$ tokens.

Evaluation Metrics. The evaluation methods we have used are precision, recall, and f-measure. Let Δ be the number of s_i which is correctly identified to the class C_k, let Λ be the total number of s_i which is assigned to the class C_k, let Γ be the total number of s_i which truly belongs to the class C_k. The precision is $P_{re} = \frac{\Delta}{\Lambda}$, the recall is $R_{ec} = \frac{\Delta}{\Gamma}$, and the f-measure is $F_{me} = \frac{1}{\frac{\alpha}{P_{re}} + \frac{1-\alpha}{R_{ec}}}$. If we take $\alpha = 0.5$, then the f-measure is $F_{me} = \frac{2*P_{re}R_{ec}}{P_{re}+R_{ec}}$.

3.2   Procedures and Results

For every sentence in the training corpus, we extract noun phrases, no noun phrases, and break point phrases. We form a set of three classes. The class c_1 contains all noun phrases, the class c_2 contains all no noun phrases, and the class c_3 contains all break point phrases.

We estimate $\hat{p}(w_i|c_i)$ (or: $\hat{p}(t_i|c_i)$) by the number of words w_i (or: the number of POS tags t_i) in c_i divided by the total number of words w (or: the total number of POS tags t) in c_i. We estimate $\hat{p}(w_{i+1}|w_i, c_i)$ (or: $\hat{p}(t_{i+1}|t_i, c_i)$) by the number of word phrases $w_i w_{i+1}$ (or: the number of POS tag phrases $t_i t_{i+1}$) in c_i divided by the number of words w_i (or: the number of POS tags t_i) in c_i. We estimate $\hat{p}(w_{i-1}|w_i, c_i)$ (or: $\hat{p}(t_{i-1}|t_i, c_i)$) by the number of word phrases $w_i w_{i-1}$ (or: the number of POS tag phrases $t_i t_{i-1}$) in c_i divided by the number of words w_i (the number of POS tags t_i) in c_i.

Making a Decision on the Testing Set. For a word with its corresponding POS tag in each sentence in the testing set, we assign a class based on (5). In our experiment, we also rewrite (5) into an equivalent mathematical representation as follows. We select C_k for s_i, when:

$$\frac{p(s_{i-1}|s_i, C_k)p(s_{i-1}|s_i, C_k)p(s_i|C_k)p(C_k)}{p(s_{i-1}|s_i, C_j)p(s_{i-1}|s_i, C_j)p(s_i|C_j)p(C_j)} \geq \theta \tag{10}$$

We test precision and recall under different θ.

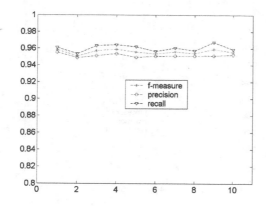

Fig. 4. The testing result for the probabilistic graphical model of $p(c_1, ..., c_N | s_1, ..., s_N)$ on CoNLL-2000 shared task data. X axis represents the ten different testing set. Y axis is a probability value of precision, or recall, or f-measure. Corresponding to each test set, there are three values from up to down in order: recall, f-measure, and precision. Overall, the average precision is 95.15%, the average recall is 96.05%, and the average f-measure is 95.59%.

Results from the CoNLL-2000 Shared Task Data Set. On CoNLL-2000 shared task data, we have tested our model based on (3), (4), and (5). The result is demonstrated in Fig 4.

In the Figure 4, the X axis represents the ten testing sets described in Section 3.1. The Y axis is a probability value that represents precision, or recall, or f-measure accordingly. Corresponding to each number in the X axis, there are three values. The upper value represents a recall, the middle value represents a f-measure, and the lower value represents a precision. By collecting the results for each test, the average precision is 95.15%, the standard deviation for the precision is 0.0020. The average recall is 96.05%, the standard deviation for the recall is 0.0041. And the average f-measure is 95.59%, the standard deviation for the f-measure is 0.0027.

We further test our model by excluding the lexicon (the w_i) and using only the POS tags (the t_i). The test result is shown in Fig 5. Comparing the results we have got in the Fig 4, the average precision is reduced about 3% from 95.15% to 92.27%. The average recall is reduced about 2.4% from 96.05% to 93.76%. And the f-measure is reduced about 3.4% from 95.59% to 92.76%.

Further, we test our model by excluding the POS tags and using only the lexicon. The test result is depicted in Fig 6. Comparing the results to that of Fig 4, the average precision is reduced about 8.9% from 95.15% to 86.42%. The average recall is reduced about 2.8% from 96.05% to 93.35%. And the f-measure is reduced about 6% from 95.59% to 89.75%.

By comparing the three results on the CoNLL-2000 shared task data, we have noticed that if the model is built only on the lexical information, it has the lowest performance of f-measure 89.75%. The model's performance improved 3% in f-measure if it is constructed by POS tags. The model achieves the best

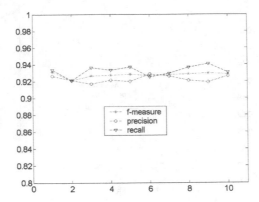

Fig. 5. The testing result for the probabilistic graphical model of $p(c_1, ..., c_N | s_1, ..., s_N)$ on CoNLL-2000 shared task data only contains POS tags. The upper value represents a recall, the middle value represents a f-measure, and the lower value represents a precision. Overall, the average precision is 92.27%, the average recall is 93.76%, and the average f-measure is 92.76%.

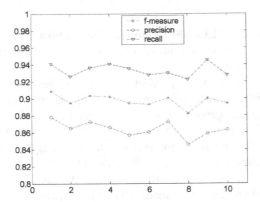

Fig. 6. The testing result for the probabilistic graphical model of $p(c_1, ..., c_N | s_1, ..., s_N)$ on CoNLL-2000 shared task data only contains lexicon. The upper value represents a recall, the middle value represents a f-measure, and the lower value represents a precision. Overall, the average precision is 86.42%, the average recall is 93.35%, and the average f-measure is 89.75%.

performance of 95.59% in f-measure if we are considering both lexicons and POS tags.

Another experiment we have done on the CoNLL-2000 shared task data set is to test the relationship between precision and recall under different θ on our model based on the equation (10). We test our model within the range of $\theta = 0.01$ to $\theta = 160$. The result is shown in Fig 7. The X axis represents different values of precision, while the Y axis represents different values of recall. As θ increasing, the precision increases and the recall decreases. When θ equals 5, the precision

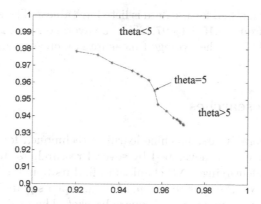

Fig. 7. Precision and recall change as θ changes of the model $p(c_1, ..., c_N | s_1, ..., s_N)$ on CoNLL-2000 shared task data. The X axis represents different values of precision while the Y axis represents different values of recall. The range of θ is from 0.01 to 160.

= the recall = 95.6%. By observing the result, we have noticed if we want to select a higher precision, we can select $\theta > 5$. If we want to select a higher recall, we can select $\theta < 5$.

Results from the WSJ Data Set. The second data set we have experimented is WSJ data of Penn Treebank. The main reason for us to use this data set is that we want to see whether the performance of our model can be improved when it is built on more data. We build our model on a training set which is seven times larger than the CoNLL-2000 shared task training data set (Section 3.1). The

Table 2. The testing result on the WSJ data from the Penn Treebank. The recall, precision, and f-measure obtained for each test of 100 files. The average recall, precision, and f-measure and their standard deviations obtained from 1000 testing files.

Training Corpus	Testing Corpus	Precision	Recall	F-measure
W0200-W0999	W1000-W1099	0.9806	0.9838	0.9822
	W1200-W1299	0.9759	0.9868	0.9814
	W1300-W1399	0.9794	0.9863	0.9828
	W1400-W1499	0.9771	0.9868	0.9817
	W1500-W1599	0.9768	0.9858	0.9814
	W1600-W1699	0.9782	0.9877	0.9829
	W1700-W1799	0.9770	0.9877	0.9824
	W1800-W1899	0.9771	0.9848	0.9809
	W1900-W1999	0.9774	0.9863	0.9819
	W2000-W2099	0.9735	0.9886	0.9806
$\bar{x} = \frac{\Sigma_{x_i \in X} x_i}{|X|}$		0.9773	0.9865	0.9818
$std(x) = \sqrt{\frac{1}{|X|} \Sigma_{x_i \in X} (x_i - \bar{x})^2}$		0.0019	0.0014	0.0008

performance of our method for the data is listed in Table 2. The average precision is increased 2.7% from 95.15% to 97.73%. The average recall is increased 2.8% from 96.05% to 98.65%. The average f-measure is increased 2.7% from 95.59% to 98.2%.

4   Related Researches

Over the past several years, machine-learning techniques for recognizing NP chunks in texts have been developed by several researchers. It starts from [2]. Their method for identifying a NP chunk is to find its boundaries in a sentence. A start point of a NP chunk is represented by an open square bracket while an end point is represented by an closed square bracket. The method calculates the frequencies of brackets between two POS tags to find a pattern. A classifier is trained on the Brown Corpus. The testing result is shown by a set of fifteen sentences with NP chunk annotations.

Ramshaw and Marcus [3] show that NP chunking can be regarded as a tagging task. In their method, three tags (classes) are defined. They are I tag, O tag, and B tag. The first tag indicates that the current word is in a NP chunk. The second tag indicates that the current word is not in a NP chunk. The last tag shows a break point of two consecutive NP chunks. In order to label one of these three tags to each word in a sentence, they design a set of rules based on linguistic hypotheses and use transformation based learning techniques to train the training set in order to obtain a set of ordered rules. Experiments are conducted on the WSJ corpus, sections 02-21 are used for training and section 00 is used for testing. The resulting precision is 93.1%, the recall is 93.5%, and the f-measure is 93.3%.

Molina et al. [4] employ the second-order HMM to identify NP chunks in texts by creating an output tag sequence $C = (c_1, ..., c_N)$ with the best representation for an input sequence $S = (s_1, ..., s_N)$. In order to determine probabilities of state transitions (hidden states), a new training set, which contains POS tags and selected vocabularies, is formed by a transformation function. Experiments are conducted on the CoNLL-2000 task data. The precision is 93.52%, the recall is 93.43%, and the f-measure is 93.48%.

The most recent attempt for identifying NP chunks uses a support vector machine (SVM) [5]. In this method, based on the methodology provided by [3], a set of high dimensional feature vectors are constructed from the training set to represent classes. A new and unknown vector x can be judged by a linear combination function. According to the authors, SVM has achieved the best performance among all the algorithms. The paper shows that SVM can achieve the precision 94.15%, recall 94.29%, and f-measure 94.22% on the CoNLL-2000 task data set.

Our method adopt Ramshaw's idea [3] of assigning different categories to words in a sentence based on whether these words are inside a NP chunk, outside a NP chunk, or start a new NP chunk. Moreover, the information collected for constructing our probabilistic graphical model is based on syntactic (POS tags) and lexical (words) information. Our method tries to find a category chain with the best description of a new input sentence. However, our model assigns a category for a word of the input sentence based on the information of the word, the previous word, and the next word we have met before, which a human often does this in the same way.

5 Conclusions

Identifying noun phrases in a sentence, also called NP chunking, is an important preprocessing task not only for parsing, information extraction, and information retrieval, but also for semantic role labeling and word sense disambiguation. For example, a verb's semantic arguments can be derived from NP chunks and features with syntactic and semantic relations for word sense disambiguation can be extracted from NP chunks. With this motivation, we discuss a probabilistic graphical model for recognize noun phrase patterns in texts. Although this model is constructed under two conditional independence assumptions, it can accurately identify NP chunks in sentences.

References

1. Abney, S., Abney, S.P.: Parsing by chunks. In: Principle-Based Parsing, pp. 257–278. Kluwer Academic Publishers, Dordrecht (1991)
2. Church, K.W.: A stochastic parts program and noun phrase parser for unrestricted text. In: Proceedings of the second conference on Applied natural language processing, pp. 136–143 (1988)
3. Ramshaw, L.A., Marcus, M.P.: Text chunking using transformation-based learning. In: Proceedings of the Third Workshop on Very Large Corpora, pp. 82–94 (1995)
4. Molina, A., Pla, F., Informátics, D.D.S., Hammerton, J., Osborne, M., Armstrong, S., Daelemans, W.: Shallow parsing using specialized hmms. Journal of Machine Learning Research 2, 595–613 (2002)
5. Wu-Chieh, W., Lee, Y.S., Yang, J.C.: Robust and efficient multiclass svm models for phrase pattern recognition. Pattern Recognition 41, 2874–2889 (2008)
6. Bishop, C.M.: Pattern Recognition and Machine Learning. Springer, Heidelberg (2002)
7. MaCallum, A., Freitag, D., Pereira, F.: Maximum entropy markov models for information extraction and segmentation. In: Proceedings of 17th International Conf. on Machine Learning, pp. 591–598 (2000)
8. Lafferty, J., MaCallum, A., Pereira, F.: Conditional random fields: Probabilistic models for segmenting and labeling sequence data. In: Proceedings of 18th International Conf. on Machine Learning, pp. 282–289 (2001)
9. Tjong, E.F., Sang, K.: Introduction to the CoNLL 2000 Shared Task: Chunking. In: Proceedings of CoNLL 2000, pp. 127–132 (2000)
10. Marcus, M.P., Santorini, B., Marcinkiewicz, M.A.: Building a large annotated corpus of english: The penn treebank. Computational Linguistics 19(2), 313–330 (1994)

Processing of Korean Natural Language Queries Using Local Grammars

Tae-Gil Noh, Yong-Jin Han, Seong-Bae Park, and Se-Young Park

Department of Computer Engineering
Kyungpook National University
702-701 Daegu, Korea
{tgnoh,yjhan,sbpark,sypark}@sejong.knu.ac.kr

Abstract. For casual web users, a natural language is more accessible than formal query languages. However, understanding of a natural language query is not trivial for computer systems. This paper proposes a method to parse and understand Korean natural language queries with local grammars. A local grammar is a formalism that can model syntactic structures and synonymous phrases. With local grammars, the system directly extracts user's intentions from natural language queries. With 163 hand-crafted local grammar graphs, the system could attain a good level of accuracy and meaningful coverage over IT company/people domain.

Keywords: Query processing, Local grammars, Korean natural language query, Query understanding.

1 Introduction

When we type something in existing search engines, it takes the form of keywords. That is, for most of commercial search engines, queries are treated as a bag of keywords. It works pretty well for web pages; however the situation is changing with advent of Semantic Web. For example, semantic web applications already enable the users to search like this with a formal query language [1]: "Find who regularly posts on this forum more than once in a week and whose posts are read by more than 20 subscribers." It is difficult to describe this with a set of mere keywords.

Question Answering (QA) is a traditional research area where parsing and understanding of query is important. In recent TREC QA task, one can see various strategies for query processing. In some systems, classical NLP methods of parsing and semantic analysis are used to process queries [2], while others ignore sentence structures and treat a query as a bag of words, and then process it with a classification method [3]. Most systems are somewhere in the middle, combining hand-coded rules, statistical classifiers and partial parsers [4].

The interests on querying over knowledge base are being renewed recently. Various approaches are reported in literature. Zhou et al. [5] used keywords as queries, and built any possible structure among keywords, and then let users select one through a visual interface. Tablan [6] used Controlled Natural Language (CNL) to process formal queries in a natural language form. Kiefer et al. [7] used a form and a visual interface to

W. Li and D. Mollá-Aliod (Eds.): ICCPOL 2009, LNAI 5459, pp. 34–44, 2009.

guide users to compose formal queries. Kaufmann [8] made a usability study on various query methods and concluded that casual users prefer a natural language interface to a menu-guided or a graphical query interface. However he also noted that NL interfaces are generally more difficult to build and less accurate.

Syntactic structures of natural language queries are important. For example, consider two Korean sentences: "대우전자를 합병한 회사는? (What is the company that takes over Daewoo Electronics?)", "대우전자가 합병한 회사는? (What is the company that taken over by Daewoo Electronics?)". In Korean, they have identical nouns and verbs with identical order, but have opposite sentence structures (Object-verb-subject and Subject-verb-object) and opposite meanings. When treating a query as a bag of words, this kind of information is lost. It has to be recaptured somehow by a different method.

The problem of traditional parsing is that it only reveals syntactic structures. Synonymous phrases can be written in different syntactic forms. For example, consider synonymous Korean questions with three different syntactic structures: "그는 어디로 발령받았나요? (Where did he assigned to?)", "그의 발령지를 알고 싶습니다. (I would like to know the location assigned to him.)","이번에 그가 일하게 된 곳은? (The place he will work this time is?)". For traditional parsing, post-processings like semantic analysis, classification or rule heuristic are needed to conclude that the sentences above are asking the same thing.

Local grammar approach is a grammar formalism that can be used to recognize recurring phrases or sentences. A phrase which is recognized by a local grammar not only reveals its syntactic structure, but also its class and possible synonymous phrases. By a well-prepared local grammar, a computer system can directly reveal the intention of a user's natural language message. In this paper, local grammars are adopted to capture patterns of query sentences. The system can process a large number of sentences from finite query types. It is designed to be used as a natural language query interface for a large scale IT ontology.

This article unfolds as follows. Section 2 briefly introduces the local grammar and its graph building process. In Section 3, the parsing system and its processes are described. In Section 4, the experiment and the results are shown, and finally Section 5 has conclusions.

2 Building Local Grammar Graphs for IT Domain

2.1 A Brief Background on the Local Grammar Approach and Its Tools

The notion of "Local grammar" has been devised by Gross [9], where it is for capture semi-frozen phrases or sequences with frozen behavior inside a specific domain (eg. "cloudy with sunny periods", weather forecast domain). The idea is that once local grammars for recurring elements are complete (eg. date expression, personal title expressions, etc), then they can be reused in the description of larger linguistic constructions. It is a bottom-up approach towards a description of a language.

Local grammars are also well-suited for fixed phrases, where some variation in form is possible, but with minimal change in its meaning. In [10] he gives examples like below.

"Bob lost his cool.", "Bob lost his temper.", "Bob lost his self-control.", "Bob blew a fuse.", "Bob blew his cool.", ...

According to Gross, these phrases are synonymous, and they can easily be captured in a local grammar.

The formalism of the local grammar is based on finite state machines. Intex [11], Unitex [12] and recently Outilex [13] are the tools that enable linguists to describe local grammars and lexicon grammars. They not only support the grammar building in a visualized way, but also support various capabilities needed to test language resources, such as morphological analysis, tagging, disambiguation and applying of grammars over corpus.

Local grammars have been successfully used in applications including information extraction [14], named entity localization [15], grammatical structure identification [16]. All of these experiments result in recall and precision rates equaling the state-of-the-art.

In this paper, Unitex is adopted to capture query patterns in local grammars. With Unitex, local grammars are expressed in graphs, and such graphs are called local grammar graphs (LGG).

2.2 Building Local Grammar Graphs for IT Domain

In this section, the building processes of LGGs are briefly described. It starts with gathering of sentences from target domain. Some policy for the modeling is decided, then in a bottom-up fashion, sentences are clustered into groups. Each group is then modeled into local grammar graphs.

As the first step, various questions about people and companies of IT domain are gathered from web forums. Figure 1 shows some of such sentences.

In a bottom-up fashion, the collected questions are modeled into 9 classes and 38 subclasses with policy described below.

1. Exclusion of Yes or No questions.
2. For questions with interrogative words, types of interrogative words are limited to 누구(Who)/무엇(What)/어디(Where)/얼마(How much/large)/몇 N(How many + Noun).
3. Questions with hidden interrogative words are treated in the same way with the questions with interrogative words.
4. Most of the sentences are written in form of active voice. Thus, the basic sentence structure to consider is active.
5. Synonymous expressions among predicate-noun based phrases and simple-verb based phrases should be collected and grouped together.

Policy #5 shows one important aspect to note. In Korean, some classes of nouns can be combined with general do-verb("하다"), or become-verb("되다") to form a new verb. Such nouns are called *predicate nouns*. Examples of predicate-noun based verbs are, "분리되다 (become-separation)", "합병되다 (become-union)", "개발하다 (do-development)". In a given domain, one can also find simple verbs with similar meaning. For above examples, "나누다 (divide)","합쳐지다 (being-merged)" and "만들다

- 마우스를 처음 개발한 사람은? (Who first developed the mouse?)
- 스타크래프트를 만든 사람 이름은 뭐에요? (What is the name of the person who developed game "Starcraft"?)
- SK텔레콤이 금년 인수했던 업체에 대해 알려주세요. (Tell me about the companies that SKTelecom took over this year.)
- 현대모비스는 몇 개의 회사로 구조조정되었습니까? (How many divisions has Hyundai-Mobis been restructured into?)
- 안철수가 개최한 네트워크 보안사업 강화를 위한 간담회는 무엇? (What is the name of the seminar organized by Mr. Ahn Chul-su, about network security enhancement?)
- 구자경이 참석한 LG전자 공장 준공식은 미국 어디? (Where is the new factory located which Mr. Ku-Ja-Kyung participated in its opening?)
- 모토로라가 확장한 공장은 어디에 있나요? (Where is the new factory of Motorola located?)
- LG텔레콤의 수익을 알려주세요. (Tell me about profits of LG Telecom.)
- 삼성전자의 직원 숫자가 얼마나 되는지 알고 싶네요. (I would like to know how many employees Samsung Electronics has.)

Fig. 1. Questions observed from web forums

(make)" are similar simple verbs. Policy #5 states that finding and describing such synonymous phrases for given domain are important.

With this policy, 163 graphs are built to cover 9 classes and 38 subclasses. Figure 2 shows the classes and number of graphs per each class.

In Figure 3, a graph from pattern 4.b is shown as an example. Each box can have a surface form or a lexical code, or a sub-graph. For Korean, the surface form can be either an eojeol[1], or a morpheme. A lexical code is a syntactic/semantic code of lexicon as described in the lexical resource (eg. Noun+animal+living-human). Frequently reappearing linguistic elements are usually captured in a separate graph, and used as a sub-graph. Box "WonderNI" in the figure is a sub-graph that holds asking/wondering expressions. The symbol '#' means that both sides connected by a '#' are morphemes and should be connected to form one eojeol.

Figure 4 shows some sentences generated from the graph of Figure 3. Note that in the graph and the generated text, there are code units like "N+Prod" or "N+Comp". Such code represents a slot that can be filled with lexicon with given attributes. In the system, it is called as a "variable".[2] It usually holds the needed arguments for query patterns. All variable types used in the graphs are listed in Table 1.

3 Query Processing System Based on Local Grammars

3.1 Generating All Possible Sentences

The system first traverses grammar graphs to generate all possible sentences that can be recognized by each grammar. There are two reasons for this. First, it makes match

---

[1] Eojeol is a Korean spacing unit which consists of one or more morphemes.
[2] This "variable" is different with "Unitex graph variable". In Unitex graph, variables exist to capture text segments that can be used in transducer output.

1. IT-Person/Product		2. IT-Company/Product		3. IT-Person/Person	
(a) TheMostFirstPerson	(8 graphs)	(a) TheMostFirstCompany	(8 graphs)	(a) Family	(4 graphs)
(b) Who/ProductName	(5 graphs)	(b) Who/ProductName	(5 graphs)	(b) PersonalRelation	(5 graphs)
(c) PersonName/What	(3 graphs)	(c) CompanyName/What	(2 graphs)	(c) FriendsRivals	(5 graphs)
4. IT-Person/Company		5. IT-Company/Company		6. IT-Person/Activity	
(a) Who/Title	(4 graphs)	(a) Union	(3 graphs)	(a) ConferenceOrganization	(3 graphs)
(b) Who/Affiliation	(6 graphs)	(b) Dis-Union	(3 graphs)	(b) ConferenceParticipation	(3 graphs)
(c) Who/NewPosition	(8 graphs)	(c) Rivals	(1 graphs)	(c) Visit	(6 graphs)
(d) PersonName/Head	(2 graphs)	(d) Cooperation	(1 graphs)	(d) Prize	(3 graphs)
(e) PersonName/Affiliation	(3 graphs)				
(f) PersonName/NewPosition	(6 graphs)				
(g) Title/Salary	(4 graphs)				
7. IT-Company/Activity		8. IT-PersonID		9. IT-Company/ID	
(a) OrgConfOrganization	(3 graphs)	(a) Career/AcademicBackground	(6 graphs)	(a) ContactLocation	(5 graphs)
(b) OrgConfParticipation	(5 graphs)	(b) IDNumberBirthDate	(5 graphs)	(b) HistoryScale	(5 graphs)
(c) Prize	(3 graphs)	(c) PhysicalCharacter	(3 graphs)		
(d) Exhibition	(3 graphs)	(d) AddressEmail	(6 graphs)		
(e) Expansion	(3 graphs)	(e) PersonalInformation	(10 graphs)		
(f) ProjectContract	(3 graphs)				
(g) EconomicProfit	(2 graphs)				

Fig. 2. Query patterns : 9 classes and 38 subclasses

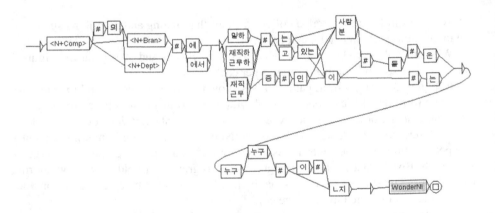

Fig. 3. A sample graph from pattern 4.b

Table 1. Variable Types

Variable Code	Variable Type	Example
N+Comp	Company/Organization name	LG전자(LG Electronics), 삼성(Samsung)
N+Bran	Name of branches	한국지부(Korea Branch), 본사(Headquarter)
N+Dept	Name of departments	기술보증팀(Quality Assurance Team)
N+Title	Titles of people	수석개발자(Lead engineer), 사장(CEO)
N+Peop	Name of a person	이재용(Lee Jaeyong), Bill Gates
N+Loca	Name of locations and places	미국(US), 서울(Seoul), 태국(Thailand)
N+Prod	Name of objects	LCDTV, 아이폰(iPhone), 마우스(mouse)

- N+Comp의 N+Bran에서 일하는 사람들은 누구 누군지 궁금하군요
- N+Comp의 N+Bran에서 일하는 사람들은 누구 누군지 궁금하군여
- N+Comp의 N+Bran에서 일하는 사람들은 누구 누군지 궁금하군염
- N+Comp의 N+Bran에서 일하는 사람들은 누구 누군지 궁금하군용
- N+Comp의 N+Bran에서 일하는 사람들은 누구 누군지 궁금하다
- N+Comp의 N+Bran에서 일하는 사람은 누구인지 궁금
- N+Comp의 N+Bran에서 일하는 사람은 누구인지 궁금…
- N+Comp의 N+Bran에서 일하는 사람은 누구인지 궁금합니다

Fig. 4. A part of sentences generated from Figure 3. They are synonymous sentences with the meaning of "Wonder who is working at N+Branch of N+Company".

method simpler. By generating all sentences, minimal match unit is changed from a morpheme to an eojeol. Thus morphological analysis of the query sentence is not needed at the query time. Result of a morphological analysis can have more than one output for a given eojeol, thus it reveals some ambiguity. Though the ambiguity at this level can be decided effectively, it is better to avoid it.

Another important reason for sentence generation is to process partial matches. As an agglutinative language, Korean can have near free word-order. Even if the modeling of a query is good for the situation, word-order changes or a newly inserted adverb can ruin the perfect match. Modeling all possible word-order change in the graph is not feasible, so partial matching has to be done. Processing partial match is generally a difficult problem related to alignment [18]. In the system, the issue of partial matching is converted into an easier problem with some assumptions described in the next section.

3.2   Building the Eojeol Sequence Table

In this stage, all generated sentences are checked word by word to keep records of eojeol level bi-gram sequences. The method is described in the Figure 5.

1. Pick next pattern. If no more pattern left, ends.
2. Pick each sentence in turn. If no more sentence left, go to step 1.
3. Observe first eojeol, record pattern ID in the table row:START, column:first eojeol.
4. For each i:=[0 to n] where n is number of eojeols
   (a) Observe sequence eojeol[i-1]–eojeol[i], record pattern ID in the table row:eojeol[i-1], column:eojeol[i].
5. Observe last eojeol, record pattern ID in the table row:last eojeol, column:END.
6. Go to step 2.

Fig. 5. Building of Eojeol Sequence Table from Sentences

The idea behind this is simple. If all eojeol sequences in a user query are found in a particular pattern, there would be exactly one sentence in the generated pattern sentences.[3] When the query is not covered completely, the best pattern is chosen that covers most of the query. This is a bi-gram model of eojeols to find the most similar sentence in the pre-generated bag of sentences. By changing the alignment problem into a bi-gram model, some information of word location is lost. However, it is endurable and gives some additional advantages. Inserted adverbs or changing of word-orders which are not modeled in the LGGs can now be treated as partial matches.

In total, 43,640 unique eojeols are observed. With the additional *start* and *end* position, the bi-gram table is a 43,642 by 43,642 table, where each row and column has an observed eojeol and each cell holds graph IDs where a sequence of row eojeol to column eojeol has been observed.

3.3   Query Processing

This section describes how the system uses the sequence table to process user's query. The code is outlined in Figure 6.

At the beginning, each eojeol of the user's query is checked if it can be decomposed with a variable eojeol. If such decomposition is possible, the eojeol is decomposed into variable-eojeol form and its variable value is saved for later processing. The system then process eojeol by eojeol to decide the query pattern. It records simple voting counts from each eojeol sequence. If an eojeol sequence (E_1, E_2) has been observed in two patterns P_a and P_b, this sequence votes for both P_a and P_b. All votes for each pattern are accumulated. Each candidate pattern is checked whether or not it has recognized all the needed arguments for the pattern. If some arguments are missing, the pattern gets no final vote count. When a pattern gets all needed arguments, it gets one additional vote count.

By comparing vote counts, the system chooses one pattern and produces the pattern name and recognized arguments as the output. If a tie happens, the system calls the

1. Check every eojeol for variable-decomposition.
2. For each i := [0 to n-1] where n is number of eojeols
    (a) Check table cell (Eojeol[i-1], Eojeol[i]). Add one count to each observed patternID.
3. For each recorded PatternID
    (a) Check arguments of each candidate. Add one additional count if a candidate has all arguments.
4. Compare candidate Patterns
    (a) If only one candidate has maximum count, select it.
    (b) If not, do step 6.
    (c) Submit it pattern ID and arguments. Ends.
5. Tie-breaker: for all patterns with maximum count, calculate eojeol-IDF value. Select the pattern with higher score.

Fig. 6. Query match process using sequence table lookup

---

[3] This is only true when there are no cycles in the graph and no duplicated eojeols in the pattern sentence. None of the 163 graph has a cycle. Very few eojeols appear twice in a sentence (5 out of 43,640).

tie-breaker. The tie-breaker calculates each eojeol's IDF value by regarding each graph pattern as a document. With this value, the tie-breaker chooses a pattern with higher score.

Here is a simple example of how a query is processed.

- Query : 세상에서 핸드폰을 젤 첨 만든 사람은 누구일까염? (Who first made the cell phone in the world?)
- Eojeols : 세상에서 (in the world), N+Prod를 (N+product), 젤 (the most), 첨 (first), 만든 (have made), 사람은 (person), 누구일까염? (who is?)
- Sequences
  - 세상에서 (in the world) – N+Prod를 (N+Product) (Observed in graph 0, 1, 2, 16, 21)
  - N+Prod를 (N+Product) – 젤 (the most) (Observed in graph 7)
  - 젤 (the most) – 첨 (first) (Observed in graph 0, 1, 2, 3, 4 ...)
  - 첨 (first) – 만든 (have made) (Observed in graph none)
  - 만든 (have made) – 사람은 (person) (Observed in graph 0, 9)
  - 사람은 (person) – 누구일까염? (who is?) (Observed in graph 0, 55, 58, 61)
- Vote
  - 1.a TheMostFirstNPeop : 5 + 1 (argument : N+Prod)
  - 2.a TheMostFirstNComp : 2 + 1 (argument : N+Prod)
  - 1.b WhoProductNamePeop : 1 + 1 (argument : N+Prod)
  - 4.c WhoNewPosition : 1 + 0 (argument : N+Peop missing)
- Vote result : (type : subclass 1.a , argument : 핸드폰/N+Prod)

4   Experiments

The system was implemented in Perl, and tested on a MacOS system with 3.0Ghz intel zeon quadcore CPU. From 163 graphs, 167,298,259 sentences have been generated. It took 30 hours to obtain to 43,642x43,642 eojeol sequence table. With the sequence table, user queries are processed in real time. The experiments were made with two things in mind. How well will our model process sentences for each given pattern? And how much is the coverage of our model in possible queries in this domain?

For the first experiment, three separate individuals were asked to write down questions for each pattern. In the survey form, description of each pattern was written in a plain language with a small number of examples. For each pattern, they were asked to write down several questions with similar meaning. For the second experiment, the questions about IT company and people were sampled from Korean web forum.[4] To test the coverage of our patterns, we only gathered questions posted in the year of 2008 (all graphs were built in 2007). We did not made any other restrictions on selecting of questions. Before doing query process, all entity names and general nouns that can be placed in the variable slots are enlisted in the system's lexical resource.

---

[4] Local web portal called Naver and its question answering forum were selected for sampling.

For the first experiment, three testers produced 484 sentences. After removing duplicated sentences (7 sentences), 477 sentences were left. Out of 477 sentences, the system correctly processed 426 sentences, thus accuracy is 89.3%.

The error types are listed in Table 2. *Out of pattern* implies that the questions are not actually one of 38 subclasses. The examples of this type are Yes/No question, or questions out of pattern's scope (Pattern 8.c is about a person's physical issue like height, weight and blood type. But one of the tester wrote something like "Does he have a hot temper?"). *Unknown synonymous phrase* are the cases where the match fails because of an unlisted expression with similar meaning. For example, the patterns for company "Expanding" should enlist all synonymous verbs, but we could find some missing expressions like "진출하는 (move in)" or "공략하는 (targeting)". *Unknown structure* is similar in effect, but this counts cases with different sentence structure. For example, a noun phrase "합병한 회사 (merged company)" can be expressed in verb phrase form, "회사와 합병했나요? (did they merged with the company?)", but it was not listed in our pattern. Unknown structures can appear not only as a phrase, but also as a full sentence. *Unbreakable tie* cases are where tie breakings are not possible. When two pattern covers exactly the same sequence of words, no tie-breaking is possible. The result shows 12 such cases and it means that some patterns are quite similar or nearly overlapping. If *out of pattern* cases are removed from the set and *unbreakable tie* cases are counted as correct, the result can go up to 92.9% of accuracy.

For the second experiment, 50 sentences were sampled from web forum. The system only processed 32% of them correctly. Most of errors were from unknown type of questions, such as recruiting, stock market related questions, or questions about comparing of two companies. The number of *unknown structure* case is also high, where companies' merging, takeover and profit related questions are more complex than the described patterns. Note that we did not restrict the type of questions in this experiment. Any questions about IT people and IT company written in a sentence were sampled.

Table 2. Results of two experiments

Type	Experiment 1	Experiment 2
Correct	426 (89.3%)	16 (32%)
Out of pattern	6 (1.25%)	18 (36%)
Unknown synonymous phrase	14 (3.28%)	3 (6%)
Unknown structure	10 (2.34%)	8 (16%)
Unbreakable tie (that includes correct one)	12 (2.81%)	2 (4%)
Other errors	9 (2.11%)	3 (6%)
Total	477	50

5 Conclusions

This paper presented a query processing system based on hand-crafted local grammars. By analyzing large number of user questions of the domain, 38 subclasses are modeled with 163 local grammar graphs. Each pattern graph essentially holds all synonymous expressions of the given meaning. A bi-gram model is adopted to handle partial match problem caused by Korean word-order change and free insertion of adverbs. The system showed a good accuracy over given question types, and meaningful coverage over unrestricted queries of the domain. At the best of our knowledge, this is the first system that uses local grammars to understand Korean natural language queries.

A local grammar based approach is well-suited for query understanding. The approach can recognize not only syntactic structures of a sentence but also the class of the sentence in the pre-defined domain, thus effectively extracts the intention of the sentence directly. We will continue our research to produce better models. Future works are including: translating query patterns into actual SPARQL queries and evaluate coverages over the ontology, processing sentences as a combination of more than one LGG patterns, and expanding of query patterns to cover more issues of the domain.

It is easy to think only keywords (and respectively nouns and nouns phrases) are trackable and can be used as a query while sentences are not. However, local grammar-based applications like our research show that if you can restrict the domain, variations of sentences (including verbs and verb phrases) are also trackable, and can be used to understand user's natural language message.

Acknowledgements. This work was supported in part by MIC & IITA through IT Leading R&D Support Project and by the Korean Ministry of Education under the BK21-IT Program.

References

1. John, G.B., Andreas, H., Uldis, B., Stefan, D.: Towards semantically-interlinked online communities. In: Gómez-Pérez, A., Euzenat, J. (eds.) ESWC 2005. LNCS, vol. 3532, pp. 500–514. Springer, Heidelberg (2005)
2. Boris, K., Gregory, M., Sue, F., Daniel, L., Ben, L., Federico, M., Ozlem, U., Muchael, M., Natalie, C., Yuan, L., Alexey, R., Yuan, S., Gabriel, Z.: Question Answering Experiments and Resources. In: The Fifteenth Text REtrieval Conference Proceedings (TREC 2006) (2006)
3. Jimmy, L.: An exploration of the principles underlying redundancy-based factoid question answering. ACM Transactions on Information Systems 25(2) (2007)
4. Nico, S., Jaeongwoo, K., Justin, B., Guido, S., Manas, P., Eric, N.: Semantic Extensions of the Ephyra QA System for TREC 2007. In: The Sixteenth Text REtrieval Conference Proceedings (TREC 2007) (2007)
5. Qi, Z., Cong, W., Miao, X., Haofen, W., Yong, Y.: SPARK: Adapting keyword query to semantic search. In: Aberer, K., Choi, K.-S., Noy, N., Allemang, D., Lee, K.-I., Nixon, L., Golbeck, J., Mika, P., Maynard, D., Mizoguchi, R., Schreiber, G., Cudré-Mauroux, P. (eds.) ASWC 2007 and ISWC 2007. LNCS, vol. 4825, pp. 694–707. Springer, Heidelberg (2007)
6. Valentin, T., Danica, D., Kalina, B.: A natural language query interface to structured information. In: Bechhofer, S., Hauswirth, M., Hoffmann, J., Koubarakis, M. (eds.) ESWC 2008. LNCS, vol. 5021, pp. 361–375. Springer, Heidelberg (2008)
7. Popov, B., Kiryakov, A., Ognyanoff, D., Manov, D., Kirilov, A., Goranov, M.: Towards Semantic Web Information Extraction.In: Proceedings of Human Language Technologies Workshop at 2nd International Semantic Web Conference (ISWC 2003) (2003)

8. Kaufmann, E., Bernstein, A.: How useful are natural language interfaces to the semantic web for casual end-users? In: Proceedings of the Forth European Semantic Web Conference (ESWC 2007) (2007)
9. Maurice, G.: The Construction of local grammars. In: Finite State Language Processings, pp. 329–354. MIT Press, Cambridge (1997)
10. Maurice, G.: Local Grammars and Their Representation by Finite Automata. In: Data, Description, Discourse: Papers on the English Language, HarperCollins, pp. 26–38 (1993)
11. Max, S.: INTEX: an FST toolbox. Theoretical Computer Science 231(1), 33–46 (2000)
12. Sebastien P.: UNITEX 1.2 Manual,
    http://www-igm.univ-mlv.fr/~unitex/manuel.html
13. Olivier, B., Matthieu, C.: Outilex, a Linguistic Platform for Text Processing. In: Proceedings of the COLING/ACL on Interactive presentation sessions, pp. 73–76 (2006)
14. Takuya, N.: Analyzing texts in a specific domain with local grammars: The case of stock exchange market reports. In: Linguistic Informatics - State of the Art and the Future, pp. 76–98. Benjamins (2005)
15. Cvetana, K., Dusko, V., Denis, M., Mickael, T.: Multilingual Ontology of Proper Names. In: Proceedings of the Language and Technology Conference, pp. 116–119 (2005)
16. Oliver, M.: Automatic Processing of Local Grammar Patterns. In: Proceedings of the 7th Annual CLUK Research Colloquium (2004)
17. Jeesun, N.: Constructing Finite-State Graphs for Accurate Recognition of Queries by Natural Languages in Information Retrieval Systems. Journal of Language Sciences 15(1), 39–69 (2008) (in Korean)
18. Gonzalo, N.: A Guided Tour to Approximate String Matching. ACM Computing Surveys 33(1), 31–88 (2001)

Improving the Performance of a NER System by Post-processing, Context Patterns and Voting

Asif Ekbal and Sivaji Bandyopadhyay

Department of Computer Science and Engineering
Jadavpur University, Kolkata-700032
India
asif.ekbal@gmail.com, sivaji_cse_ju@yahoo.com

Abstract. This paper reports about the development of a Named Entity Recognition (NER) system in Bengali by combining the outputs of the two classifiers, namely Conditional Random Field (CRF) and Support Vector Machine (SVM). Lexical context patterns, which are generated from an unlabeled corpus of 10 million wordforms in an unsupervised way, have been used as the features of the classifiers in order to improve their performance. We have post-processed the models by considering the second best tag of CRF and class splitting technique of SVM in order to improve the performance. Finally, the classifiers are combined together into a final system using three weighted voting techniques. Experimental results show the effectiveness of the proposed approach with the overall average recall, precision, and f-score values of 91.33%, 88.19%, and 89.73%, respectively.

Keywords: Named Entity Recognition, Conditional Random Field, Support Vector Machine, Weighted Voting.

1 Introduction

Named Entity Recognition (NER) is an important tool in almost all Natural Language Processing (NLP) application areas including machine translation, question answering, information retrieval, information extraction, automatic summarization etc. The current trend in NER is to use the machine-learning approach, which is more attractive in that it is trainable and adoptable and the maintenance of a machine-learning system is much cheaper than that of a rule-based one. The representative machine-learning approaches used in NER are Hidden Markov Model (HMM) (BBN's IdentiFinder [1]), Maximum Entropy (ME) (New York University's MENE [2]) and Conditional Random Fields (CRFs) [3]. Support Vector Machines (SVMs) based NER system was proposed by Yamada et al. [4] for Japanese. The process of stacking and voting method for combining strong classifiers like boosting, SVM and Transformation Based Learning (TBL), on NER task can be found in [5]. Florian et al. [6] tested different methods for combining the results of four systems and found that robust risk minimization worked best. Munro et al. [7] employed both voting and bagging for combining classifiers. The work reported in this paper differs from that of

W. Li and D. Mollá-Aliod (Eds.): ICCPOL 2009, LNAI 5459, pp. 45–56, 2009.

Wu et al. [5], Florian et al. [6] and Munro et al. [7] in the sense that here, we have conducted a number of experiments to post-process the outputs of the classifiers with the lexical context patterns, which are generated in a semi-automatic way from an unlabeled corpus of 10 million wordforms, and used several heuristics to improve the performance of each classifier before applying weighted voting.

Named Entity (NE) identification and classification in Indian languages in general and in Bengali in particular is difficult and challenging as.

- Unlike English and most of the European languages, Bengali lacks capitalization information, which plays a very important role in identifying NEs.
- Indian person names are more diverse and a lot of these words can be found in the dictionary with specific meanings.
- Bengali is a highly inflectional language providing one of the richest and most challenging sets of linguistic and statistical features resulting in long and complex wordforms.
- Bengali is a relatively free order language.
- Bengali, like other Indian languages, is a resource poor language - annotated corpora, name dictionaries, good morphological analyzers, Part of Speech (POS) taggers etc. are not yet available at the required performance level.
- Although Indian languages have a very old and rich literary history, technological developments are of recent origin.
- Web sources for name lists are available in English, but such lists are not available in Bengali forcing the use of transliteration to develop such name lists.

A pattern directed shallow parsing approach for NER in Bengali is reported in [8]. A HMM based NER system for Bengali has been reported in [9], where additional contextual information has been considered during emission probabilities and NE suffixes are kept for unknown word handling. More recently, the works in the area of Bengali NER can be found in [10] and [11] with the CRF, and SVM approach, respectively. Other than Bengali, the works on Hindi can be found in [12] with CRF, in [13] with a language independent method, in [14] with a hybrid feature set based ME approach and in [15] using MEMM. As part of the IJCNLP-08 NER shared task, various works of NER in Indian languages using various approaches can be found in the proceedings of the IJCNLP-08 workshop on Named Entity Recognition on South and South East Asian Languages (NERSSEAL[1]).

2 Named Entity Recognition in Bengali

We have used a Bengali news corpus [16], developed from the web-archive of a widely read Bengali newspaper for NER. A portion of this corpus containing 200K wordforms has been manually annotated with the four NE tags namely, *Person, Location, Organization* and *Miscellaneous*. We have also used the annotated corpus of 122K wordforms, collected from the IJCNLP-08 workshop on Named Entity Recognition on South and South East Asian Languages (NERSSEAL) data. This data was

---

[1] http://ltrc.iiit.ac.in/ner-ssea-08/proc/index.html

annotated with a fine-grained tagset of twelve tags and collected from the literature, agriculture and scientific domains. We consider only those tags that represent person, location, organization and miscellaneous names (NEA [Abbreviation], NEN [number], NEM [Measurement] and NETI [Time] are considered to belong to the miscellaneous entities). In order to properly denote the boundaries of NEs, four NE tags are further divided into the following forms:

B-XXX: Beginning of a multiword NE, I-XXX: Internal of a multiword NE consisting of more than two words, E-XXX: End of a multiword NE, XXX→PER/LOC/ORG/MISC. For example, the name *sachin ramesh tendulkar* is tagged as *sachin*/B-PER *ramesh*/I-PER *tendulkar*/E-PER. The single word NE is tagged as, PER: Person name, LOC: Location name, ORG: Organization name and MISC: Miscellaneous name. In the final output, sixteen NE tags are directly mapped to the four NE tags.

3 Approaches to NER for Bengali

Incorporating diverse features in an HMM-based NE tagger is difficult and complicates the smoothing typically used in such taggers. In contrast, CRF or SVM based method can deal with the diverse and morphologically complex features of the Indian languages.

In this paper, we have used CRF and SVM frameworks in order to identify NEs from a Bengali text and to classify them into *Person, Location, Organization* and *Miscellaneous*. Lexical context patterns, second best tag of CRF and class decomposition technique of SVM have been used in order to improve the performance of each of the classifiers. Finally, we have combined these post-processed models with the help of three weighted voting techniques.

We have used the C^{++} based CRF++ package (http://crfpp.sourceforge.net) for NER. Support Vector Machines (SVMs) have advantages over conventional statistical learning algorithms, such as Decision Tree, HMM, ME in terms of its high generalization performance independent of feature vector dimension and its ability of learning with all combinations of given features without increasing computational complexity by introducing the *kernel function*. We have used *YamCha* (http://chasen-org/~taku/software/yamcha) toolkit, an SVM based tool for detecting classes in documents and formulating the NER task as a sequential labeling problem. Here, we conducted several experiments with the different degrees of the *polynomial kernel function*. We have used TinySVM-0.07 (http://cl.aist-nara.ac.jp/~taku-ku/software/TinySVM) classifier that seems to be the best optimized among publicly available SVM toolkits.

3.1 Named Entity Features

Experiments have been carried out in order to find out the most suitable features for NER in Bengali. Following are the details of the set of features that have been applied to the NER task:

- Context words: Preceding and following words of a particular word. This is based on the observation that the surrounding words are very effective in the identification of NEs.

- Word suffix and prefix: Word suffix and prefix information are helpful to identify NEs. A fixed length (say, *n*) word suffix/prefix of the current and/or the surrounding word(s) can be treated as feature(s). If the length of the corresponding word is less than or equal to *n-1* then the feature values are not defined and denoted by ND. The feature value is also not defined (ND) if the token itself is a punctuation symbol or contains any special symbol or digit. Another way to use the suffix information is to modify the feature as binary valued. Variable length suffixes of a word can be matched with predefined lists of useful suffixes (e.g., *-babu, -da, -di* etc. for persons and *-land, -pur, -lia* etc. for locations). These features are useful to handle the highly inflective Indian languages like Bengali. The underlying reason is that NEs contain some common prefixes and/or suffixes.
- Named Entity Information (dynamic feature): NE tag(s) of the previous word(s). The NE tag(s) of the previous word(s) is (are) very effective in deciding the NE tag of the current word.
- First word (binary valued): Whether the current token is the first word of the sentence or not. Though Bengali is a relatively free order language, the first position of the sentence often contains the NE. Bengali grammar follows the SOV (Subject-Object-Verb) structure and maximum of the NE(s) generally do appear in the subject position. Also, we have used the newspaper corpus and NEs are generally found in the starting positions of the sentences in the news documents.
- Length of the word (binary valued): Whether the length of the word is less than three or not. This is based on the observation that very short words are rarely NEs.
- Infrequent word (binary valued): A cut off frequency has been chosen in order to consider the infrequent words in the training corpus. The intuition of using this feature is that frequently occurring words are rarely NEs.
- Digit features: Several digit features have been considered depending upon the presence and/or the number of digit(s) in a token (e.g., ContainsDigit, FourDigit, TwoDigit), combination of digits and punctuation symbols (e.g., ContainsDigitAndComma, ConatainsDigitAndPeriod), combination of digits and symbols (e.g., ContainsDigitAndSlash, ContainsDigitAndHyphen, ContainsDigitAndPercentage). These binary valued features are helpful in recognizing miscellaneous NEs such as time expressions, monetary expressions, date expressions, percentages, numbers etc.
- Position of the word (binary valued): Position of the word in a sentence is a good indicator of NEs. Generally, verbs occur at the last position of the sentence. This feature is used to check whether the word is the last word in the sentence.
- Part of Speech (POS) Information: We have used a CRF-based POS tagger [17] that was developed with 26 POS tags, defined for the Indian languages.
- Gazetteer Lists: Gazetteer lists, developed from the Bengali news corpus [16], have been used as the features in each of the classifiers. If the current token is in a particular list, then the corresponding feature is set to 1 for the current and/or the surrounding word(s); otherwise, it is set to 0. The following is the list of gazetteers used in the present work along with the number of entries in each gazetteer:

(1). Organization clue word (e.g., *kong, limited* etc): 94, Person prefixes (e.g., *sriman, sreemati* etc.): 245, Middle names: 1,491, Surnames: 5,288, Common location (e.g., *sarani, road* etc.): 547, Action verb (e.g., *balen, ballen* etc.): 241, Function words: 743, Designation words (e.g., *neta, sangsad* etc.): 947, First names:

72,206, Location names: 7,870, Organization names: 2,225, Month name (English and Bengali calendars): 24, Weekdays (English and Bengali calendars): 14

(2). Common word (521 entries): Most of the Indian languages NEs appear in the dictionary with some other meanings. For example, the word *kamol* may be the name of a person but also appears in the dictionary with another meaning *lotus*, the name of a flower; the word *dhar* may be a verb or also can be the part of a person name. We have manually created a list, containing the words that can be NEs as well as valid dictionary words.

(3). Lexicon (128,000 entries): We have developed a lexicon [18] from the Bengali news corpus in an unsupervised way. The feature 'LEX' has value 0 for those words that appear in the lexicon; otherwise, the value is 1. This feature has been considered, as the words that appear in the lexicon are rarely NEs.

4 Unsupervised Learning of Context Patterns

For English NER, a context pattern induction method through successive learners has been reported in [19]. Here, we have developed a method for generating lexical context patterns from a portion of the unlabeled Bengali news corpus [16]. These are used as the features of the classifiers as well as to post-process the output of each of the classifiers. For this purpose, we have used an unlabeled corpus of 10 million word-forms of the Bengali news corpus [16]. Given a small seed examples and an unlabeled corpus, the algorithm can generate the lexical context patterns in a bootstrapping manner. The seed name serves as a *positive example* for its own NE class, *negative example* for other NE classes and *error example* for non-NEs.

1. Seed List preparation: We have collected the frequently occurring words from a part of this news corpus and the training set to use as the seeds. There are 123, 87, and 32 entries in the person, location, and organization seed lists, respectively.

2. Lexical pattern generation: The unlabeled corpus is tagged with the elements from the seed lists. For example, <Person> sonia gandhi </Person>, <Location> kolkata </Location> and <Organization> jadavpur viswavidyalya </Organization>. For each tag T inserted in the training corpus, the algorithm generates a *lexical* pattern p using a context window of maximum width 6 (excluding the tagged NE) around the left and the right tags, e.g., $p = [l_{-3}l_{-2}\ l_{-1}$ <T> ...</T> $l_{+1}\ l_{+2}\ l_{+3}]$, where, $l_{\pm i}$ are the *context* of p. Any of $l_{\pm i}$ may be a punctuation symbol. In such cases, the width of the lexical patterns will vary. All these patterns, derived from the different tags of the training corpus, are stored in a Pattern Table (or, set P), which has four different fields namely, pattern *id* (identifies any particular pattern), pattern *example* (pattern), pattern *type* (*Person/Location/Organization*) and *relative frequency* (indicates the number of times any pattern of a particular *type* appears in the entire training corpus relative to the total number of patterns generated of that *type*). This table has 27,986 entries, out of which 21,071 patterns are distinct.

3. Evaluation of patterns: Every pattern p in the set P is matched against the same unannotated corpus. In a place, where the context of p matches, p predicts the occurrence of the left or right boundary of name. The POS

information of the words as well as well as some linguistic rules and/or length of the entity have been used in detecting the other boundary of the entity. The extracted entity may fall in one of the following categories:

- *positive example*: The extracted entity is of same NE *type* as that of the pattern.
- *negative example:* The extracted entity is of different NE *type* as that of the pattern.
- *error example*: The extracted entity is not at all a NE.

4. Candidate pattern extraction: For each pattern p, we have maintained three different lists for the *positive, negative* and *error* examples. The *type* of the extracted entity is determined by checking whether it appears in any of the seed lists (person/location/organization); otherwise, its *type* is determined manually. The *positive* and *negative* examples are then added to the appropriate seed lists. We then compute the *accuracy* of the pattern as follows:

$$accuracy(p) = |positive\ (p)|/[|\ positive\ (p)| + |negative\ (p)| + |error(p)|],$$

where, *positive*(p), *negative*(p), and *error*(p) are the positive, negative, and error examples of the pattern p.

A threshold value of *accuracy* has been chosen and the patterns below this threshold value are discarded. A pattern is also discarded if its total *positive count* is less than a predetermined threshold value. The remaining patterns are ranked by their *relative frequency* values. The n top high frequent patterns are retained in the pattern set P and this set is denoted as *Accept Pattern*.

5. Generation of new patterns: All the *positive* and *negative* examples extracted by a pattern p in Step 4 can be used to generate further patterns from the same training corpus. Each new *positive* or *negative* instance (not appearing in the seed lists) is used to further tag the training corpus. We repeat steps 2-4 for each new NE until no new patterns can be generated. The threshold values of *accuracy, positive count* and *relative frequency* are chosen in such a way that in the first iteration of the algorithm at least 5% new patterns is added to the set P. A newly generated pattern may be identical to a pattern that is already in the set P. In such case, the *type* and *relative frequency* fields in the Set P are updated accordingly. Otherwise, the newly generated pattern is added to the set with the *type* and *relative frequency* fields set properly. The algorithm terminates after the 17 iterations and there are 24,073 distinct entries in the set P.

5   Evaluation Results

Out of 200K wordforms, 150K wordforms along with the IJCNLP-08 shared task data have been used for training the models and the rest 50K wordforms have been used as the development data. The system has been tested with a gold standard test set of 35K wordforms. Statistics of the training, development and test sets are given in Table 1.

A number of experiments have been carried out taking the different combinations of the available words, context, orthographic word level features and gazetteers to identify the best-suited set of features in the CRF and SVM frameworks for NER in

Table 1. Statistics of the training, development and test sets

	Training	Development	Test
# of sentences	21,340	3,367	2,501
#of wordforms	272,000	50,000	35,000
#of NEs	22,488	3,665	3,178
#Average length of NE	1.5138	1.6341	1.6202

Table 2. Results of the development set for the *baseline* models (W[i,j]: Words spanning from the ith position to the jth position, i,j<0 denotes the words to the left of the current word and i,j>0 denotes the words to the right of the current word)

Model	Recall (in %)	Precision (in %)	F-Score (in %)	Best set of features
CRF	75. 97	75.45	75.71	W[-2,+2], POS tag of W[-1,0], NE tag of the previous word, Prefixes and suffixes of length upto three characters of the current word and other set of features.
SVM	77.14	75.48	76.30	W[-3,+2], POS tag of W[-1,+1], and other set of features as for CRF.

Bengali. These are defined as the *baseline* models. Results of each model along with the best combination of the feature are shown in Table 2.

Results demonstrate that the SVM based *baseline* system performs best with the f-score value of 76.3% followed by CRF (f-score=75.71%). During all the experiments, we have observed that word context, prefixes, suffixes, POS information, dynamic NE tag(s) and digit features are the most effective features for NER in each of the models. Other features are not so effective but helpful in increasing the overall performance of the NER system. We have conducted various experiments with the several degrees of the *polynomial kernel function* and observed the highest performance with degree 2. The use of gazetteers increases the performance by 4.11%, and 4.45% in the f-score value in the CRF, and SVM, respectively.

5.1 Use of Context Patterns as Features

The high frequency patterns of the *Accept Pattern* set (discussed in section 4) are used as the features of the classifiers. A feature 'ContextInformation' is defined by observing the words in the window [-3, 3] (three words spanning to left and right) of the current word in the following way:

- Feature value is 1 if the window contains any word of the pattern type "*Person*".
- Feature value is 2 if the window contains any word of the pattern type "*Location*".
- Feature value is 3 if the window contains any word of the pattern type "*Organization*".

- Feature value is 4 if the window contains any word that appears with more than one type.
- Feature value is 0 for those if the window does not contain any word of any pattern.

Results of the models that include this feature are presented in Table 3. The use of this feature along with the previously discussed features increase the overall f-score values to **82.69%**, and **83.39%** in the CRF, and SVM based systems, respectively. Thus, these are the improvement of 2.87%, and 2.64% in the f-score values with the use of context features.

Table 3. Results using context features on the development set

Model	Recall (in %)	Precision (in %)	F-Score (in %)
CRF	84.31	81.12	82.69
SVM	84.73	82.09	83.39

5.2 Second Best Tag for CRF

If the best tag given by CRF is "NNE" (other than NE) and the confidence of the second best tag is greater than a particular threshold value then the second best tag is considered as the correct tag. We have carried out a number of experiments for the choice of the threshold value. Evaluation results of the system have shown the improvement in the recall value by 9.08% with the second best tag. But, the choice of second tag decreases the precision values by 2.44%. This resulted in the overall performance improvement in terms of f-score value (by **2.29%**).

5.3 Class Decomposition Technique for SVM

SVM predicts the class depending upon the labeled word examples only. If target classes are equally distributed, the *pairwise* method can reduce the training cost. Here, we have a very unlabeled class distribution with a large number of samples belonging to the class 'NNE' (other than NEs) (Table 1). This leads to the same situation like *one-vs-rest* strategy. One solution to this unbalanced class distribution is to decompose the 'NNE' class into several subclasses effectively. Here, we have decomposed the 'NNE' class according to the POS information of the word. That is, given a POS tagset POS, we produce new $|POS|$ classes, 'NNE-C'$|C \in POS$. So, we have 26 subclasses which correspond to non-NE regions such as 'NNE-NN' (common noun), 'NNE-VFM' (verb finite main) etc. Results have shown the recall, decomposition technique is included in the SVM.

5.4 Voting

Voting scheme becomes effective in order to improve the overall performance of any system. Here, we have combined the models using three different weighted voting techniques. In the literature [20][21], it has been shown that the voted system performs better than any single machine learning based system. In our experiments, in order to obtain higher performance, we have applied weighted voting to the three systems. But before applying weighted voting, we need to decide the weights to be given to the individual system. We can obtain the best weights if we could obtain the accuracy for the 'true' test data. However, it is impossible to estimate them. Thus, we have used following weighting methods in our experiments:

5.4.1 Uniform Weights (Majority voting)
We have assigned the same voting weight to all the systems. The combined system selects the classifications, which are proposed by the majority of the models (including the *baseline* model). If outputs are different, then the output of the SVM based system is selected.

5.4.2 Uniform Weights (Majority voting)
We have assigned the same voting weight to all the systems. The combined system selects the classifications, which are proposed by the majority of the models (including the *baseline* model). If outputs are different, then the output of the SVM based system is selected.

5.4.3 Cross Validation Precision Values
The training data is divided into N portions. We employ the training by using N-1 portions, and then evaluate the remaining portion. This is repeated N times. In each iteration, we have evaluated the individual system following the similar methodology, i.e., by including the various gazetteers, context features, second best tag and the class decomposition technique. At the end, we get N precision values for each of the system. Final voting weight for a system is given by the average of these N precision values. Here, we have considered the value of N to be 10. We have defined two different types of weights depending on the cross validation precision as follows:

(a). Total Precision: In the first method, we have assigned the overall average precision of any classifier as the weight for it.
(b). Tag Precision: In the second method, we have assigned the average precision value of the individual tag as the weight.

Experimental results of the voted system are presented in Table 4. Evaluation results show that the system achieves the highest performance for the voting scheme 'Tag Precision', which considers the individual tag precision value as the weight of the corresponding system. Voting shows an overall improvement of **5.23%** over the CRF based system and **4.08%** over the SVM based system in terms of f-score values.

Table 4. Experimental results of the voted system for the development set

Voting Scheme	Recall (in %)	Precision (in %)	F-Score (in %)
Majority	89.14	85.21	87.13
Total Precision	91.11	87.19	89.11
Tag Precision	92.39	88.13	90.21

5.5 Results on the Test Set

Three models have been tested with a gold standard test set of 35K wordforms. Approximately, 25% of the NEs are unknown in the test set. Results for the *baseline* models have shown the f-score values of 74.56%, and 75.67% in the CRF and SVM models, respectively. Results have demonstrated the improvement in f-scores by 7.68%, and 9.52% in the CRF, and SVM models, respectively, by including the gazetteers, context features, second best tag of CRF and class decomposition technique of SVM.

These two systems are then combined together into a final system by using three weighted voting techniques. Experimental results are presented in Table 5. The system has shown the highest recall, precision, and f-score values of **91.33%**, **88.19%**, and **89.73%**, respectively. Clearly, this is the improvement in performance compared to any individual system.

Table 5. Experimental results of the voted system for the test set

Voting Scheme	Recall (in %)	Precision (in %)	F-Score (in %)
Majority	88.17	85.01	86.56
Total Precision	90.88	87.01	88.9
Tag Precision	91.33	88.19	89.73

5.6 Comparison with Other NER Systems

The most recent existing Bengali NER systems, i.e., HMM based system [9], CRF based system [10] and SVM based system [11] have been trained and tested with the same datasets. Some works in the area of Bengali NER have been reported in the IJCNLP-08 NER shared task. But, comparisons with those works are out of scope because of the following reasons:

- IJCNLP-08 NER shared task was based on a more fine-grained tagset of twelve tags.
- One of the important tasks in the shared task was to identify the nested NEs (i.e., the multiword *mahatma gandhi road* is tagged as the location name and the nested NEs, i.e., *mahatma Gandhi,* and *road* are tagged as the person, and location names, respectively). But here, we concentrate only on the *type* of the maximal NEs.

Evaluation results are presented in Table 6. Results show the effectiveness of the proposed NER model that outperforms the other existing Bengali NER systems by the impressive margins. The system outperforms the HMM based system with **13.45%** f-sore, CRF based system with **8.44%** f-score and SVM based system with **7.77%** f-score. Thus, it has been established that purely statistical approaches cannot always perform well across the domain (here, both training and test sets are collected from the mixed domains). So, post-processing the output of the statistical framework with the context patterns, second best tags and class decomposition technique can yield a reasonably good performance. Results also suggest that combination of several classifiers is more effective than any single classifier.

Table 6. Comparison with other models

Model	Recall (in %)	Precision (in %)	F-Score (in %)
HMM [9]	76.02	73.55	76.28
CRF [10]	82.46	80.17	81.29
SVM [11]	82.98	81.04	81.96
Voted System	91.33	88.19	89.73

6 Conclusion

In this paper, we have developed a NER system for Bengali by combining the CRF and SVM classifiers using weighted voting approach. Performance of each *baseline* classifier has been improved by the lexical context patterns generated from an unlabeled corpus of 10 million wordforms, second best tag of CRF and class decomposition technique of SVM. The proposed approach shows the effectiveness with the reasonably high recall, precision and f-score values. We have shown that the reported system outperforms the other existing Bengali NER systems. This approach can be applicable for NER in other languages, especially for the Indian languages. Future works include investigating how the proposed approach has its effects on each of the NE classes.

References

1. Bikel, Daniel, M., Schwartz, R., Weischedel, Ralph, M.: An Algorithm that Learns What's in Name. Machine Learning (Special Issue on NLP), 1–20 (1999)
2. Bothwick, A.: A Maximum Entropy Approach to Named Entity Recognition. Ph.D. Thesis, New York University (1999)
3. Lafferty, J., McCallum, A., Pereira, F.: Conditional Random Fields: Probabilistic Models for Segmenting and Labeling Sequence Data. In: Proc. of 18th ICML, pp. 282–289 (2001)
4. Yamada, Hiroyasu, Kudo, T., Matsumoto, Y.: Japanese Named Entity Extraction using Support Vector Machine. Transactions of IPSJ 43(1), 44–53 (2003)
5. Wu, D., Ngai, G., Carpuat, M.: A Stacked, Voted, Stacked Model for Named Entity Recognition. In: Proceedings of CoNLL 2003 (2003)
6. Florian, R., Ittycheriah, A., Jing, H., Zhang, T.: Named Entity Recognition through Classifier Combination. In: Proceedings of CoNLL 2003 (2003)
7. Munro, R., Ler, D., Patrick, J.: Meta-learning Orthographic and Contextual Models for Language Independent Named Entity Recognition. In: Proceedings of CoNLL 2003 (2003)
8. Ekbal, A., Bandyopadhyay, S.: Lexical Pattern Learning from Corpus Data for Named Entity Recognition. In: Proc. of 5th ICON, India, pp. 123–128 (2007)
9. Ekbal, A., Naskar, S., Bandyopadhyay, S.: Named Entity Recognition and Transliteration in Bengali. Named Entities: Recognition, Classification and Use, Special Issue of Lingvisticae Investigationes Journal 30(1), 95–114 (2007)
10. Ekbal, A., Haque, R., Bandyopadhyay, S.: Named Entity Recognition in Bengali: A Conditional Random Field Approach. In: Proc. of IJCNLP 2008, India, pp. 589–594 (2008)
11. Ekbal, A., Bandyopadhyay, S.: Bengali Named Entity Recognition using Support Vector Machine. In: Proc. of NERSSEAL, IJCNLP 2008, India, pp. 51–58 (2008)

12. Li, W., McCallum, A.: Rapid Development of Hindi Named Entity Recognition Using Conditional Random Fields and Feature Inductions. ACM TALIP 2(3), 290–294 (2003)
13. Cucerzan, S., Yarowsky, D.: Language Independent Named Entity Recognition Combining Morphological and Contextual Evidence. In: Proc. of the Joint SIGDAT Conference on EMNLP and VLC, pp. 90–99 (1999)
14. Saha, S., Sarkar, S., Mitra, P.: A Hybrid Feature Set based Maximum Entropy Hindi Named Entity Recognition. In: Proc. of IJCNLP 2008, India, pp. 343–349 (2008)
15. Kumar, N., Bhattacharyya, P.: Named Entity Recognition in Hindi using MEMM. Technical Report, IIT Bombay, India (2006)
16. Ekbal, A., Bandyopadhyay, S.: A Web-based Bengali News Corpus for Named Entity Recognition. Language Resources and Evaluation Journal 42(2), 173–182 (2008)
17. Ekbal, A., Haque, R., Bandyopadhyay, S.: Bengali Part of Speech Tagging using Conditional Random Field. In: Proc. of SNLP, Thailand (2007)
18. Ekbal, A., Bandyopadhyay, S.: Web-based Bengali News Corpus for Lexicon Development and POS Tagging. Polibits Journal 37, 20–29 (2008)
19. Niu, C.g., Li, W., Ding, J., Srihari, R.: A Bootstrapping Approach to Named Entity Classification Using Sucessive Learners. In: Proc. of ACL 2003, pp. 335–342 (2003)
20. Erik, F., Sang, T.K.: Noun Phrase Recognition by System Combination. In: Proceedings of ANLP-NAACL 2000, pp. 50–55 (2000)
21. Erik, F., Sang, T.K.: Text Chunking by System Combination. In: Proceedings of CoNLL 2000 and LLL 2000, pp. 151–153 (2000)

Research on Automatic Chinese Multi-word Term Extraction Based on Term Component

Wei Kang and Zhifang Sui

Institute of Computational Linguisitcs, Peking University,
100871 Peking, China
{kangwei,szf}@pku.edu.cn

Abstract. This paper presents an automatic Chinese multi-word term extraction method based on the unithood and the termhood measure. The unithood of the candidate term is measured by the strength of inner unity and marginal variety. Term component is taken into account to estimate the termhood. Inspired by the economical law of term generating, we propose two measures of a candidate term to be a true term: the first measure is based on domain speciality of term, and the second one is based on the similarity between a candidate and a template that contains structured information of terms. Experiments on I.T. domain and Medicine domain show that our method is effective and portable in different domains.

Keywords: Chinese terminology, Automatic terminology extraction, Term component, Unithood, Termhood.

1 Introduction

Automatic term extraction (ATE) has gained the interest of many researchers and has applications in many kinds of NLP tasks, such as Information Retrieval, Information Extraction, and Automatic Domain Ontology Construction in the last few years. There is a variety of previous researches that focus on the linguistic filters, such as adjective-noun or noun-noun sequences to improve precision by ranking their candidates [1]. These methods are limited by the experience of the specialists who manually select the grammatical patterns.

Many researches on ATE focus on methods that are based on statistics. The method of *Mutual Information* [2], *log-likelihood* [3] [4] and *Left/Right Entropy* [5] etc. are widely used. *Mutual Information* and *log-likelihood* measure the unithood from the strength of inner unity, and *Left/Right Entropy* measures the unithood from the strength of marginal variety.

Some studies rely on a combination of linguistic knowledge and statistical association measures. Term extraction is modeled as compound extraction and is formulated as a classification problem in [6]. The mutual information, relative frequency and *Part-of-speech* tags are used as features for compound extraction.

The *C-value* measure is used to get more accurate terms, especially those nested terms in [7]. This empirical approach doesn't take domain speciality of term into account, therefore a comparable numbers of frequent constituents, such as

W. Li and D. Mollá-Aliod (Eds.): ICCPOL 2009, LNAI 5459, pp. 57–67, 2009.

"参考文献" (Reference), "联系地址"(Address) are wrongly recognized. Many researches focus on the statistics between a compound term and its component single-terms recently [8] [9] [10] [11], but their methods seldom consider the fact that terms are prominent key concepts in a subject field.

Based on the domain-specific prominence, a comparative approach for candidate term ranking by comparing their ranks in a thematic corpus and a background corpus is taken in [12].

This paper presents an automatic Chinese multi-word term extraction method based on the unithood and the termhood measure. We test the hypothesis that both the unithood and the termhood can measure whether a candidate is a true term. The unithood is to estimate whether a string is a complete lexical unit, and it is measured by the strength of inner unity and marginal variety. The termhood is to investigate whether the lexical unit is used to refer to a specific concept in a specific domain. Taking term component into account to estimate the termhood, we propose two measures of a candidate term to be a true term: the first measure is based on domain speciality of term, and the second one is based on the similarity between a candidate and a template that contains structured information of terms. Experiments on I.T. domain and Medicine domain show that our method is effective and portable in different domains.

The rest of the paper is organized as follows. Section 2 briefly introduces the idea of our method. Section 3 describes our term extraction algorithm. Section 4 presents the experiments and analysis. Section 5 is the conclusion.

2   The Brief Idea

2.1   Term Component

The economical law of term generating suggests that a majority of multi-word terms consist of the much smaller number of the single-word terms [13]. An economical term system tends to improve the ability of combination of the single-word terms. We call those single-words which are part of multi-word terms "Term Component". Take multi-word term "计算机 控制系统"(Computer Control System) as an example, all of the words "计算机"(Computer), "控制"(Control) and "系统"(System) are term components. From linguistic perspective, a multi-word term can be represented by features of term components.

2.2   The Brief Idea of Termhood Measure Based on Term Component

A term component makes up multi-word terms more contributively when it is domain specific. So, we can make the judgment about how likely it is that a term candidate will be a true term by measuring the term components. When a new multi-word is generated, it tends to be made up of some term components, especially the ones that are domain-specific and have strong ability to make up multi-word terms. The more term components are as part of a candidate, the more likely the candidate to be a true term.

- **The contribution of domain-specific term components to a true term**
When a term component appears frequently in a domain D, and seldom appears in other domains, the term component is prominently domain-specific. Meanwhile, the

candidates that are made up by those term components are domain-specific. For example, the term component "寄存器"(Register) appears frequently in IT domain, so the candidates, such as "通用 寄存器"(General Register), "标志 寄存器"(Flag Register) have strong domain speciality. By comparing ranks of term components in a thematic corpus and a general balanced corpus, we measure how domain-specific are the term components. Furthermore, it is a measure of the termhood of a candidate term.

- **The contribution of term components that contain structure information to a true term**
When a term component has a ability to make up multi-word terms, it means that if the term component tends to appear on the same position of many multi-word terms with a fixed length, a candidate is very likely to be a true term when the term component appears on the same position of the candidate. For example, the term component "数字"(Digital) often appears on the first position of many terms, such as "数字 逻辑 电路"(Digital Logic Circuits) and "数字 电子 技术"(Digital Electronics). Then for a candidate "数字 信号 处理"(Digital Signal Processing), the first word of the candidate is "数字"(Digital), the candidate is very likely to be a true term. So, there is another measure of the termhood of a candidate by using the structure information of term components.

The above two measures of the termhood consider the relation between term components and multi-word terms, and effectively estimate the domain speciality of candidates.

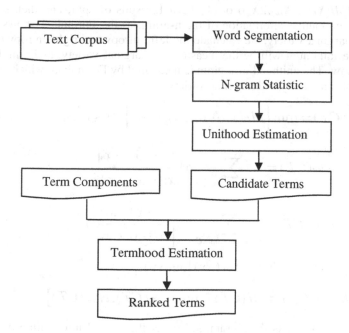

Fig. 1. The workflow of the ATE process

2.3 The Architecture of the ATE Process

The automatic term extraction based on term component contains four major modules, namely Corpus Preprocessing, Unithood Measuring, Term Component Weight Measuring and Termhood Measuring. The preprocessing module includes word segmentation and n-grams frequency count [14]. The unithood measuring module calculates the unithood of n-grams, and obtain candidate word strings whose unithood are above selected threshold. The term component weight measuring module extracts term components from terminology dictionary, and calculates the weight of domain speciality and structure template of term components. The termhood measuring module calculates the termhood of all candidate terms based on the term components. By a combination of unithood and termhood of candidates, score of all the candidates are measured.

The architecture of the ATE process is shown in Figure 1.

3 Algorithm Design

3.1 The Unithood Measurement

The unithood of n-gram is measured on the strength of inner unity and marginal variety [15]. After word segmentation and n-gram frequency counting, the unithood of all n-grams is calculated. The n-grams whose unithood are above a threshold will be selected as candidates.

For an n-gram $X_1...X_iX_{i+1}...X_n$, we can split it into two parts as $X_1...X_i$ and $X_{i+1}...X_n$, and there are n-1 ways to split. On the measure of inner unity, we calculate the mutual information $(MI(X_1...X_iX_{i+1}...X_n))$ of all the n-1 results of split, and then select the minimum as the mutual information of the n-gram, as the Formula 1 shows. On the measure of marginal variety, we calculate the left entropy and right entropy of the n-gram, and the minimum will be the measure of marginal variety, as Formula 2 and Formula 3 show. The unithood of n-gram is measured by Formula 5, which combines the strength of inner unity and marginal variety.

$$MI(CT) = \min_i \left\{ MI(x_1 \cdots x_i, x_{i+1} \cdots x_n) \right\}, (1 \le i < n) . \tag{1}$$

$$e_{left}(CT) = \sum_{u, ux_1 \cdots x_i \cdots x_n \in C} h\left(\frac{|ux_1 \cdots x_i \cdots x_n|}{|x_1 \cdots x_i \cdots x_n|}\right) . \tag{2}$$

$$e_{right}(CT) = \sum_{u, x_1 \cdots x_i \cdots x_n u \in C} h\left(\frac{|x_1 \cdots x_i \cdots x_n u|}{|x_1 \cdots x_i \cdots x_n|}\right) . \tag{3}$$

$$h(x, y) = (xy) \log(xy) . \tag{4}$$

$$Unithood(CT) = MI(CT) * \min \left\{ e_{left}(CT), e_{right}(CT) \right\} . \tag{5}$$

Where, $CT = x_1...x_i...x_n$ is the n-gram, $MI(xy)$ is the mutual information of x and y, $e_{left}(CT)$ and $e_{right}(CT)$ are left/right entropy of x and y, u is the word appears on edge of xy, $|xy|$ is the frequency of xy in corpus C.

3.2 The Termhood Measurement Based on Term Component

The measure of termhood of candidate is based on the domain speciality and structure information of term component. So, we first extract all the term components from the terminological dictionary. Then we calculate the weight of domain speciality and structure template of all the term components.

3.2.1 The Domain Speciality Measure on Termhood

The domain speciality of multi-word terms can be measured by the domain speciality of term component. We rank the term components in a thematic corpus and a general balanced corpus by their frequency in the corpus. A term component is more domain-specific when it ranks much higher in the thematic corpus than in the general balanced corpus [12].

A term candidate is very likely to be a true term when the components of the candidate have prominent domain speciality. This paper applies the domain speciality measure (DS) as shown in Formula 6 and Formula 7.

$$DS(C_i) = G_{rank}(C_i) - T_{rank}(C_i) \ . \tag{6}$$

$$DS(CT) = \sqrt[Len]{\prod_{i=1}^{Len} DS(C_i)} \ . \tag{7}$$

Where C_i is the term component, $G_{rank}(C_i)$ is the rank of C_i in a general balanced corpus, $T_{rank}(C_i)$ is the rank of C_i in the thematic corpus, $DS(CT)$ is the measure of domain speciality of a multi-word candidate, and Len is the number of words that the candidate contains.

3.2.2 The Structure Information Template Measure on Termhood
• **The structure information template of term component**
The multi-word terms are made up with term components; a term component tends to appear on a fixed position of a multi-word term. This paper makes a statistical analysis on the terminological dictionary, and extracts a set of structure information templates $(S(C_i))$ for every term component. Table 1 lists several template and some instances.

• **The method of template matching**
A structure information template of term component has four parts: the term component, the number of words that are on the left of the component (as *Left*), the number of words that are on the right of the component (as *Right*), and the *weight* of the template (frequency of the template in the terminological dictionary). We can measure the weight of a candidate term by template matching, but the templates which are extracted from the terminological dictionary can not contain all the possible structure information of term components. So, we use a template matching method that is based on the similarity between a candidate and the templates to overcome data sparseness.

For a candidate term $CT = C_1...C_i...C_n$, we sign the number of words on the left of C_i as *Left'*, and the number of words on the right of C_i as *Right'*. Formula 8 defines a variable called $Edit_{dist}$. The similarity [16] is defined by Formula 8.

$$Edit_{dist} = |Left - Left'| + |Right - Right'| \tag{8}$$

Table 1. Some structure information templates and their instances

Term component	Template	Weight	Example
驱动器(Drive)	W+驱动器(Drive)	68	软盘 驱动器(Floppy Drive)、磁盘 驱动器(Disk Drive)、磁带 驱动器(Tape Drives)
寄存器(Register)	W+W+寄存器(Register)	273	通用 寄存器 (General Register)、指针 寄存器 (Pointer Register)、标志 寄存器(Flag Register)
数字(Digital)	数字(Digital)+W+W	295	数字 电子 技术 (Digital Electronics)、数字 逻辑 电路 (Digital Logic Circuits)、数字 信号 处理(Digital Signal Processing)

Where the "W" can be any term component.

$$Sim(T) = \frac{1}{1 + Edit_{dist}} \tag{9}$$

Where T is a template, $Sim(T)$ is the similarity between $CT = C_1...C_i...C_n$ and T.

- **The measure of termhood of candidate term**

The algorithm of measuring termhood of a candidate based the structure template (ST) is shown as below:

```
Input:   Candidate term (CT); Length of the CT(Len)
Output:  ST(CT)
Method:  ST(CT) = 1;
         For each term component Cᵢ in CT:{
         ST(Cᵢ) = 0;
         If the template set of Cᵢ is S(Cᵢ) = Φ {
             ST(Cᵢ) = 1};
         Else  Calculate the Left' and Right' of Cᵢ ;
         For each template Tⱼ in S(Cᵢ) {
             Calculate the Left, Right, and weight(Tⱼ) of Tⱼ;
             Calculate the Sim(Tⱼ);
             ST(Cᵢ) = ST(Cᵢ)+Sim(Tⱼ)*weight(Tⱼ); }
         ST(Cᵢ) = ST(Cᵢ) /Len;
         If ST(Cᵢ) < 1, ST(Cᵢ) = 1;
         ST(CT) =ST(CT)* ST(Cᵢ); }
         ST(CT) = (ST(CT))^{1/Len};
```

4 Experiment and Evaluation

This section presents the evaluation of the algorithm. To evaluate the performance of our method, experiments on IT domain and Medicine domain are conducted.

4.1 Data Sets

In I.T. domain, we use the "Encyclopedia of Computer Science and Technology" (ECST) which contains about 2,709K Chinese text to extract multi-word terms. To extract term components of I.T. domain, we use a terminological dictionary which contains about 141,760 terms from the Institute of Computational Linguistics, Peking University. When measuring the domain speciality of term component, the "Xinhua Net" corpus which contains about 80M Chinese text is used as the thematic corpus, and a similar-sized I.T. journal corpus is used as the general balanced corpus.

To evaluate the portability of our method, we conducted an experiment on the Medicine domain. The corpus we use to extract terms is the "Circulatory System Diseases" section of the book "Internal Medicine" (IM) that contains about 405K Chinese text. The term components of Medicine domain is extracted from "MESH" and "Modern Medicine" from the Encyclopedia of China Publishing House. We also use the "Xinhua Net" corpus as the thematic corpus, and use a similar-sized "Modern Medicine" corpus for measure of domain speciality of term components.

We conduct comparing experiments to compare the performance of our method with the method of C-value [7] and the method only using unithood.

The performance is evaluated in terms of precision, recall and F-measure. To evaluate the precision, we select a sample of 100 terms from N terms, where N is the total number of extracted terms. Then we manually check the 100 terms. Recall is hard to evaluate in ATE, we measure the recall of I.T. domain by measuring the recall of the 2,089 terms that appear on the "Content Index" section of the "ECST", while the recall of Medicine domain is measured by the recall of the 475 terms that appear on the "Index" section of the "IM".

Table 2. Result of the DS, ST and Hybrid approaches in I.T. domain

	Precision (%)			Recall (%)			F-measure (%)		
Top	DS	ST	Hybrid	DS	ST	Hybrid	DS	ST	Hybrid
100	80.0	98.0	92.0	0.8	1.2	1.0	1.5	2.5	2.0
500	70.0	96.0	96.0	3.4	4.2	4.0	6.4	8.0	7.6
1000	70.0	90.0	92.0	5.1	6.9	8.0	9.5	12.8	14.8
3000	63.0	82.0	82.0	14.0	14.5	16.3	22.9	24.6	27.2
5000	73.0	71.0	80.0	21.0	19.3	21.9	32.6	30.4	34.4
10000	67.0	69.0	76.0	32.2	30.1	31.7	43.5	41.9	44.8
15000	62.0	48.0	60.0	36.2	37.9	37.4	45.7	42.4	46.1
20000	43.0	53.0	56.0	38.3	44.2	41.8	40.5	48.2	47.9
30000	47.0	41.0	58.0	47.0	52.4	51.1	47.0	46.0	54.3
40000	30.0	46.0	50.0	53.5	56.9	56.9	38.4	50.9	53.2

Table 3. Result of the DS, ST and Hybrid approaches in Medicine domain

	Precision (%)			Recall (%)			F-measure (%)		
Top	DS	ST	Hybrid	DS	ST	Hybrid	DS	ST	Hybrid
100	83.0	94.0	93.0	3.6	6.5	5.5	6.8	12.2	10.3
500	77.0	90.0	93.0	13.7	18.9	17.3	23.2	31.3	29.1
1000	82.0	82.0	86.0	19.6	26.9	22.5	31.6	40.6	35.7
3000	59.0	63.0	67.0	28.0	38.7	35.4	38.0	48.0	46.3
5000	46.0	43.0	47.0	41.7	44.2	44.2	43.7	43.6	45.6

4.2 Experiments on DS and ST Method

In order to evaluate the two measures on termhood: the domain speciality measure (*DS*) and the structure information template measure (*ST*), we conduct two sets of experiments on I.T. and Medicine domain. We build a hybrid method taking both two methods above. Formula 10 shows the hybrid approach:

$$termhood(CT) = \sqrt{DS(CT) * ST(CT)} \tag{10}$$

Where *CT* is the candidate, *DS(CT)* is the domain speciality measure, and *ST(CT)* is the structure template measure. The result of three approaches is shown in Table 2 and Table 3.

Table 2 and Table 3 show that, with the increment of number of ranked terms, we get better recall, though the precision drops, the F-measure improves much. When we select the 30,000 top ranked terms, we get a best performance using the hybrid method with an F-measure of 54.3% in I.T. domain. By using the ST method, we get the best performance with an F-measure of 48.0% in Medicine domain when we select the 3,000 top ranked terms.

Table 4. Result of the Unithood, C-value and Hybrid approaches in I.T. domain

	Precision (%)			Recall (%)			F-measure (%)		
Top	Unithood	C-value	Hybrid	Unithood	C-value	Hybrid	Unithood	C-value	Hybrid
100	32.0	66.0	92.0	0.4	1.6	1.0	0.9	3.1	2.0
500	43.0	65.0	96.0	0.7	6.5	4.0	1.4	11.8	7.6
1000	41.0	58.0	92.0	1.5	11.3	8.0	3.0	19.0	14.8
3000	38.0	63.0	82.0	5.3	23.5	16.3	9.3	34.2	27.2
5000	41.0	56.0	80.0	9.5	30.0	21.9	15.4	39.0	34.4
10000	43.0	39.0	76.0	20.9	40.4	31.7	28.1	39.7	44.8
15000	45.0	36.0	60.0	32.2	43.4	37.4	37.5	39.3	46.1
20000	43.0	25.0	56.0	39.8	46.1	41.8	41.3	32.4	47.9
30000	41.0	34.0	58.0	50.9	51.4	51.1	45.4	40.9	54.3
40000	39.0	28.0	50.0	55.6	55.3	56.9	45.9	37.2	53.2

Table 5. Result of the Unithood, C-value and Hybrid approaches in Medicine domain

Top	Precision (%)			Recall (%)			F-measure (%)		
	Unithood	C-value	Hybrid	Unithood	C-value	Hybrid	Unithood	C-value	Hybrid
100	71.0	79.0	93.0	3.2	5.1	5.5	6.0	9.5	10.3
500	59.0	67.0	93.0	10.7	14.7	17.3	18.2	24.2	29.1
1000	64.0	50.0	86.0	20.0	20.8	22.5	30.5	29.4	35.7
3000	46.0	48.0	67.0	35.6	32.8	35.4	40.1	39.0	46.3
5000	43.0	44.0	47.0	41.1	40.2	44.2	42.0	42.0	45.6

4.3 Comparing Experiments on Unithood, C-Value and the Hybrid

In order to compare the performance of hybrid method, unithood method and the C-value method, two sets of experiments are conducted in I.T. domain and Medicine Domain. The unithood method is the algorithm described in section 3. The C-value [7] is measured as Formula 11.

$$C-value(a) = \begin{cases} \log_2 |a| \cdot f(a) & |a| = \max, \\ \log_2 |a| \cdot f(a) - \dfrac{1}{c(a)} \sum_{i=1}^{c(a)} f(b_i) & otherwise \end{cases} \quad (11)$$

Where a is the candidate string, $|a|$ is the number of words in string a, $f(a)$ is the frequency of occurrence of c in the corpus, $c(a)$ is the set of extracted candidate terms that contain c, b_i is the candidate extracted terms that contain a, $c(a)$ is the number of those candidate terms.

Table 4 and Table 5 show that the hybrid approach improves performance of unithood and c-value notably. The improvement in F-measure is about 10%, and in precision is above 25%. The primary improvement is in precision, due to the measure of domain speciality and structure information template of term component.

Table 6. Top 20 term components of I.T. domain

	TermComponent		TermComponent		TermComponent		TermComponent
1	图形学 (Graphics)	6	寄存器 (Register)	11	遍历(Traversal)	16	数据链(Data Chain)
2	信噪比(Signal-to-Noise)	7	基函数(Primary Function)	12	晶格(Crystal Lattice)	17	子程序 (Subroutine)
3	子句(Clause)	8	单击(Click)	13	点阵(Lattice)	18	倍频 (Frequency Multiplication)
4	导数 (Derivative)	9	字符串(String)	14	例程(Routine)	19	数据区(Data Section)
5	缺省(Default)	10	磁道(Track)	15	述语(Adnex)	20	参数化 (Parameterize)

Table 7. Top 10 templates of I.T. domain

	Template	Instance		Template	Instance
1	W+控制 (Control)+W	计算机 控制 系统 (Computer Control System)	6	W+网络 (Network)	通信 网络 (Communication on Network)
2	程序 (Program)+W+W	程序 设计 语言 (Programming Language)	7	进程 (Process)+W	进程 同步 (Process Synchronization)
3	W+W+系统 (System)	分布式 处理 系统 (Distributed Processing System)	8	W+W+W+语言 (Language)	高级 程序 设计 语 言 (Advanced Programming Language)
4	W+程序 (Program)	并行 程序(Parallel Programming)	9	输入 (Input)+W+W	输入 输出 设备 (Input-Output Device)
5	数字 (Digital)+W+W	数字 逻辑 电路(Digital Logic Circuits)	10	W+数据 (Data)+W	抽象 数据 类型 (Abstract Data Types)

Where the "W" can be any term component.

4.4 Term Components and Structure Information Templates

In addition to extracting terms from corpus, we also build the resource of term components and structure templates, which may be useful in further ATE methods. Table 6, 7 list some of the top term components and templates.

We extract 20,000 term components with 63,000 structure information templates from the I.T. terminological dictionary, and 12,000 term components with 40,000 structure information templates from the Medicine terminological dictionary.

5   Conclusion

This paper proposes an automatic Chinese multi-word term extraction method based on the unithood and the termhood measure. Term components that are extracted from terminological dictionary are taken into account to estimate the termhood. We propose two measures of a candidate term to be a true term: the first measure is based on domain speciality of term component, and the second one is based on the similarity between a candidate and a template that contains structured information of terms. By a combination of unithood and termhood of candidates, score of all the candidates are measured.

Experiments on I.T. domain and Medicine domain show that our method performs better than the unithood method and the C-value method both in precision and recall. The result of experiments on two domains presents that our method is portable in different domains.

Acknowledgments. This work is supported by NSFC Project 60503071, 60873156, 863 High Technology Project of China 2006AA01Z144 and 973 Natural Basic Research Program of China 2004CB318102.

References

1. Dagan, Ido, Church, K.: Termight: Identifying and Translating Technical Terminology. In: Proceedings of the 4th Conference on Applied Natural Language Processing (ANLP), pp. 34–40 (1994)
2. Church, K.W., Hanks, P.: Word Association Norms, Mutual Information and Lexicography. Computational Linguistics 16(1), 22–29 (1990)
3. Dunning, T.: Accurate Methods for the Statistics of Surprise and Coincidence. Computational Linguistics 19(1), 61–75 (1993)
4. Daille, B.: Study and Implementation of Combined Techniques for Automatic Extraction of Terminology. In: The Balancing Act: Combining Symbolic and Statistical Approaches to Language, New Mexico State University, Las Cruces (1994)
5. Patry, A., Langlais, P.: Corpus-based Terminology Extraction. In: 7th International Conference on Terminology and Knowledge Engineering, Copenhagen, Denmark, pp. 313–321 (August 2005)
6. Su, K.-Y., Wu, M.-W., Chang, J.-S.: A Corpus-based Approach to Automatic Compound Extraction. In: Proceedings of the 32nd Annual meeting on Association for Computational Linguistics, Las Cruces, New Mexico, June 27-30, pp. 242–247 (1994)
7. Frantzi, K.T., Ananiadou, S.: Extracting Nested Collocations. In: Proceedings of the 16th Conference on Computational Linguistics, pp. 41–46 (1996)
8. Nakagawa, H., Mori, T.: A Simple but Powerful Automatic Term Extraction Method. In: Proceeding of the 2nd International Workshop on Computational Terminology, Taipei, Taiwan, pp. 29–35, August 31 (2002)
9. Wermter, J., Hahn, U.: Paradigmatic Modifiability Statistics for the Extraction of Complex Multi-word Terms. In: HLT-EMNLP 2005–Proceedings of the 5th Human Language Technology Conference and 2005 Conference on Empirical Methods in Natural Language Processing, Vancouver, Canada, October 6-8, pp. 843–850 (2005)
10. Wermter, J., Hahn, U.: You Can't Beat Frequency (Unless You Use Linguistic Knowledge)–A Qualitative Evaluation of Association Measures for Collocation and Term Extraction. In: Proceedings of the 21st International Conference on Computational Linguistics and 44th Annual Meeting of the ACL, Sydney, pp. 785–792 (July 2006)
11. Deane, P.: A Nonparametric Method for Extraction of Candidate Phrasal Terms. In: Proceedings of the 43rd Annual Meeting of the Association for Computational Linguistics (ACL 2005), Ann Arbor, Michigan, pp. 605–613 (2005)
12. Kit, C.: Corpus Tools for Retrieving and Deriving Termhood Evidence. In: 5th East Asia Forum of Terminology, Haikou, China, December 6, pp. 69–80 (2002)
13. Feng, Z.: An Introduction to Modern Terminology. Language & Culture Press, Beijing (1997)
14. Nagao, M., Mori, S.: A New Method of N-gram Statistics for Large Number of N and Automatic Extraction of Words and Phrases from Large Text Data of Japanese. In: Proceedings of the 15th Conference on Computational Linguistics, vol. 1, pp. 611–615 (1994)
15. Chen, Y.: The Research on Automatic Chinese Term Extraction. Master's thesis of Peking University (2005)
16. Lin, D.: An Information-Theoretic Definition of Similarity. In: Proceedings of the 15th International Conference on Machine Learning, pp. 296–304. Morgan Kaufmann, San Francisco (1998)

A Novel Method of Automobiles' Chinese Nickname Recognition

Cheng Wang, Wenyuan Yu, Wenxin Li, and Zhuoqun Xu

Key Laboratory of Machine Perception,
Peking University, 100871, Beijing, China
{cici,yuwy,lwx,zqxu}@pku.edu.cn

Abstract. Nowadays, we have noticed that the free writing style becomes more and more popular. People tend to use nicknames to replace the original names. However, the traditional named entity recognition does not perform well on the nickname recognition problem. Thus, we chose the automobile domain and accomplished a whole process of Chinese automobiles' nickname recognition. This paper discusses a new method to tackle the problem of automobile's nickname recognition in Chinese text. First we have given the nicknames a typical definition. Then we have used methods of machine learning to acquire the probabilities of transition and emission based on our training set. Finally the nicknames are identified through maximum matching on the optimal state sequence. The result revealed that our method can achieve competitive performance in nickname recognition. We got precision 95.2%; recall 91.5% and F-measure 0.9331 on our passages test set. The method will contribute to build a database of nicknames, and could be used in data mining and search engines on automobile domain, etc.

Keywords: Automobile, nickname recognition, named entity.

1 Introduction

In recent years, the development of technologies makes the communication more convenient and freer. The Internet allows people to publish their own opinions online and discuss with others at liberty, it also makes people's writing style much freer. People always use abbreviations, aliases or some other short and lovely names to replace the original names of some people, some objects, etc. These new names are widely accepted online. We call them nicknames as a whole. The definition of nickname is in Section 3.

Nowadays, more and more people can afford automobiles, so they may need information from others. Thus, the public bulletin board systems (BBS) become one of the most important ways for people who already have or who want to purchase a new automobile to communicate. The famous forums in China such as The Home of automobiles[1], The Pacific Automobile[2] and so on are often divided into some

---

[1] The Home of automobile : http://www.autohome.com.cn/
[2] The Pacific of automobile : http://www.pcauto.com.cn/

W. Li and D. Mollá-Aliod (Eds.): ICCPOL 2009, LNAI 5459, pp. 68–78, 2009.

separate sub forums by different kinds of automobiles. Then, if people want to acquire information of a specific automobile, they can go to the sub forum of each specific type.

However, the free style of writing leads a lot of people to call their automobiles by their nicknames. For instance, they call "马自达六"(Ma Zi Da Six) as "马六" (Ma Six), they call "北斗星" (Bei Dou Xing) as "小星星" (small xing xing), and they call "福克斯"(Fu Ke Si) as "FKS" etc. Thus, we can get the original text, and we can know which automobile the original text describes through the name of the sub forum. But it is difficult for the computer to recognize these nicknames automatically using the general methods of named entity recognition.

Named entities (NE) are broadly distributed in texts, and named entity recognition (NER) plays a significant role in data mining (DM), information extraction (IE), natural language processing (NLP) and many other applications. Previous studies on NER are mainly focused on the recognition of location (LOC), organization (ORG), name of person (PER), time (TIM), and numeral expressions (NUM) in news domain, or other named entity recognition (NER) such as product named entity recognition in business domain and term acronym named entity recognition in biology domain, etc.

Admittedly, the named entity recognition is one of the most effective ways to extract information from texts. However, the general NER may not extract the key information effectively for automobiles' nickname recognition problem. Not only automobiles, other products or some other things have their nicknames. Thus, we decided to do the automobiles' nickname recognition in Chinese text, and establish a database of automobiles' nicknames. The database can be used in data mining, information extraction, search engine, and so on. Finally, we will establish a search engine about the comment and introduction of automobiles. And our algorithm can be extended to other domains which have the same nickname recognition problem.

2 Related Work

The goal of automobile's nickname recognition is to extract the nicknames of the specific automobile from the text.

Eckhard et al.[1] recognized Danish named entities including product names using constraint grammar, but this method was dependent on the specific grammar highly.

Zhang et al. [2] used Hidden Markov Model, the semantic role as linguistic feature and the pattern rules as the combinative points to do Chinese named entity recognition and Zhang et al. [3] used role model to do the Chinese named entity recognition. These methods perform excellently on general NER, but not proper for nickname recognition problem.

Chang et al .[4] presented an algorithm using a statistical learning method to match short/long forms. Sun et al. [5] presented an algorithm for Chinese abbreviations recognition. Okazaki et al. [6] presented a term recognition algorithm to tackle the acronym recognition problem. These methods are not focus on the traditional NER, but also not proper for our problem.

Wentian Company et al.[7] established a search engine of automobile's Chinese comments, however, it only accepts the original automobiles' names as keywords.

3 The Definition of Nickname

Given the original passage, our goal is to recognize the nickname of the automobile from the passage.

A nickname is a name of an entity which is used to replace the original name. A nickname is sometimes considered desirable, symbolizing a form of acceptance, but can also be a form of ridicule. As a concept, it is distinct from both pseudonym and stage name, and also from a title (for example, City of Fountains), although there may be overlap in these concepts.[3] The automobiles' nicknames always mean that people have a close emotional bond to their automobiles or just abbreviations because the original names would be too long to type.

In our research, we defined an automobile's nickname by three parts, and the three parts constitute five different patterns.

The three parts are: prefix, main, postfix, which have been described in the following list Table 1.

The five patterns are: prefix + main, prefix + main + postfix, prefix + postfix, main + postfix, main, which have been described in the following list Table 2.

Table 1. The parts of nickname

Parts	Description	Examples
Prefix(Pre)	Some characters which always appear at the front part of the nicknames of automobiles.	" 小 "(small), " 大 "(big), " 白 "(white)," 红 "(red)," 小红"(small red)
Main(M)	The characters acquire from the original name and the additional information, such as brand.	If the automobile's name is " 宝马 " and the additional information is "BMW" (the brand),the examples are: "宝"," 马", "BMW" (The pinyin of the characters)
Postfix(Post)	Some characters which always appear at the last part of the nicknames of automobiles.	" 子 "(zi)," 儿 " (er), Numbers.

---

[3] Refer to Wikipedia. http://www.wikipedia.org

According to Table 1, we define the patterns of the automobiles' nicknames as below:

Table 2. The patterns of nicknames

Patterns	Examples
Main	"KY" refers "凯越" (Kai Yue); "轩轩" (Xuan Xuan) refers "轩逸" (Xuan Yi);
Prefix + Main	"小轩" (small Xuan) refers "轩逸" (Xuan Yi); "紫轩" (purple Xuan) refers "轩逸" (Xuan Yi); "小白星"(small white Xing) refers "北斗星" (Bei Dou Xing);
Prefix+Main+Postfix	"小Q6" (small Q6) refers "QQ"; "小虫子"(Small Chong Zi) refers "甲壳虫"(Jia Ke Chong);
Prefix + Postfix	"小6" (Small 6) refers "QQ 6"; "小三"(Small 3) refers "马自达三" (Ma Zi Da 3);
Main + Postfix	"轩逸2.0"(Xuan Yi 2.0) refers "轩逸"(Xuan Yi); "虫子"(Chong Zi) refers "甲壳虫"(Jia Ke Chong);

To avoid ambiguity, we stipulate some additional conditions:

1. The type of a specific automobile is a part of the nickname. For instance, "QQ 6" will be tagged as "QQ(M) 6(post)", but will not be tagged as "QQ(M) 6(O)".

2. We have learned from about 4,000 nicknames, and find that people accept the word which has a single Chinese character to describe the automobile as part of the nickname, but they do not accept words which constitute by two or more characters. For instance, "小蓝狮" (Small blue lion, which refers to the car Peugeot) will be tagged as "小(pre)蓝(pre)狮(M)" [Small (pre) blue(pre) lion (M)]; "银灰小狮子" (Silver gray little lion zi) will be tagged as "银(O)灰(O)小(pre)狮(M)子(post)" [Silver(O) gray(O) small(pre) lion(M) zi(post)]. Even though"银灰"(Silver gray) is a word describes the color of the automobile, but it is not formed by a single Chinese character.

Here is a passage which comes from the famous Chinese Automobiles' BBS, "the Home of Automobile". The passage is from the sub forum "标致". The content of this passage is that: "秀秀我的小灰狮子。我的小六到今天，刚好到手一个月" (I want to show my small grey lion zi. I bought my Little Six one month ago.) Because every-one knows the brand of this automobile is a lion, so the main characters are"标","致", "狮". (The Chinese name of the automobile and the lion). So the passage after labeled is that: "秀(O)秀(O)我(O)的(O)小(Pre)灰(Pre)狮(M)子(Post)。我(O)的(O)小(Pre)六(Post)到(O)今(O)天(O)，刚(O)好(O)到(O)手(O)一(O)个(O)月(O)". [I(O) want(O) to(O) show(O) my(O) small(pre) grey(pre) lion(M) zi(post). I(O) bought(O) my(O) Little(pre) Six(post) one(O) month(O) ago(O).]

4 Nickname Recognition

Consider the definition of nickname we defined above, our motivation is making a classification of the characters according to their linguistic features. We designed our algorithm based on Hidden Markov Model, and using Viterbi algorithm to find the best solution.

We defined the state sequence and the observation sequence of HMM in Section 4.1 and 4.2, describe Viterbi algorithm in Section 4.3, and the whole process in Section 4.4.

4.1 The State Sequence

According to the definition of nickname we defined in Section 3, there are only six states. Similar to the parts of nickname, the six states are: prefix, main, postfix, other, before, after, which are listed in Table 3 below. We will assign a corresponding state to each character automatically, and then perform NER.

Table 3. The states of nickname

States	Description	Examples
Prefix(Pre)	Some characters which always appear at the front part of the nicknames of automobiles.	"小"(small), "大"(big), "白"(white),"蓝"(blue),"小白"(small and white)
Main(M)	The characters which acquired from the name and the additional information of the specific automobile	If the automobile's name is "标致" and the additional information is "狮" (Lion, the brand),the examples are: "标","致","狮","BiaoZhi", "Shi",(The pinyin of the characters)
Postfix(Post)	Some characters which always appear at the last part of the nicknames	"子"(zi)," 儿" (er), Numbers.
Before(B)	The neighboring character or word in front of the nicknames	"辆"(the unit of the car in Chinese), "我的" (mine)
After(A)	The neighboring character or word following the nicknames	"KM", "公里"(kilometers)
Others(O)	The characters do not appear in the nicknames	

4.2 The Observation Sequence

Since our definition is very different from a POS or other tag set, we decided not to use the results of the word segmentation as the initial processing. We have just used the characters sequence.

We have defined the observation values as follows.

Because different brands of automobiles have different names and different information, the main characters type is not a fixed set. There may be overlap between the main characters and other types. To eliminate the overlap, we stipulate that if a character belongs to both Main Characters type and Other Characters type, its type is Main Characters.

Table 4. The observations of nickname

Type	Description	Sample
Main Characters (Main)	The characters from the automobile's name and other information.	"BMW", "宝."(Bao)"
Single Adjective (Adj)	The adjectives which have a single character	"白"(white), "大" (big), "胖"(fat)
Letter String (String)	The consecutive letters, include capital letter, lowercase.	"DFZZ", "FKS", "XY"
Numeric String (Num)	The numbers, include Arabic numerals, Roman numerals, Chinese numerals, etc.	"2.0","III"(two),"3000", "六" (six)
Characters indicate tones (tone)	Characters which indicates tones and express some affection	"子"(zi), "儿"(er), "仔"(zi)
Other Characters (Other)	Other Characters	

4.3 Use Viterbi Algorithm to Find the Proper State Sequence

A state set can be viewed as a token tag collection. However, from the point of view of the named entity recognition, a POS tag is always defined by the part-of-speech of a word, while a state in our research is always defined based on linguistic features. A token may represents one or more states, such as "马自达六是辆好车"(Ma Zi Da Six is an excellent automobile) and "我的马自达六千公里了"(My Ma Zi Da have drove six thousands kilometers). The "六" (six) in the former means the type of the automobile while it means the number in the latter. So, in the former, the "六" plays the "postfix" state while it plays the "other" state in the latter.

We have prepared the state set and state corpus. Let us consider the question, given a token sequence, how can we tag a proper state sequence automatically? We have used the Viterbi algorithm to select an optimal state sequence from all the state sequences. The algorithm and its calculation are given below:

After tokenization of original sentences, suppose that T is the token sequence, S is the state sequence for T, and S# is the best choice with the maximum probability. That is,

$$T = (t_1, t_2, ..., t_m),$$

$$S = (s_1, s_2, ..., s_m), m > 0,$$

$$S^\# = \frac{argmax\ P(S|T)}{S} \tag{1}$$

According to the Bayes' Theorem, we can get

$$P(S|T)=P(S)P(T|S)/P(T) \tag{2}$$

For a specific token sequence, P(T) is a constant. Thus, based on E1 and E2, we can get E3:

$$R^{\#} = \frac{argmax}{S} \, P(S)P(T|S) \tag{3}$$

Consider the Hidden Markov Model, we may consider S as the state sequence and T as the observation sequence. The statement sequence is hidden behind the observation sequence, and the S is hidden behind T. Thus, we can use Hidden Markov Model to solve this problem.

$$P(S)P(T|S) \approx \prod_{i=1}^{m} P(t_i|s_i)P(s_i|s_{i-1}),$$

where s_0 is the beginning of the sentence. $\qquad$ (4)

Because of that T is the observation sequence, which is a real sequence we can observe, so *P(T) = 1.*

$$\therefore S^{\#} \approx \frac{argmax}{S} \prod_{i=1}^{m} P(t_i|s_i)P(s_i|s_{i-1}) \tag{5}$$

Because of that the probability are all less than 1, to reduce and avoid the precision error, we decided to use the log probability to replace the original one. That is,

$$S^{\#} \approx \frac{argmax}{S} \prod_{i=1}^{m} \{\ln P(t_i|s_i) + \ln P(s_i|s_{i-1})\} \tag{6}$$

Finally, we can use Viterbi algorithm to solve E6 problem and finish the state tagging.

Next, we will use the sentence "紫轩2.0很好"(The purple Xuan 2.0 is excellent) which used nickname "紫轩2.0" (purple Xuan 2.0) to replace the original name "轩逸" (Xuan Yi) to explain the process of the global optimal selections. After tokenization, the most probable token sequence will be "color(紫) /main(轩) /num(2.0) /other(很) /adj(好)/". Consider that we already calculated the transfer matrix from each state to another state, the impossible transfer has been eliminated.

Consider that some state values and observation values do not have any bond, we use P(t_i|s_i)=-∞ to demonstrate them. During the Viterbi Algorithm, we will not choose these states to calculate the next move if we know they are impossible. This improvement may save a vast amount of time.

Figure 1 shows how the Viterbi Algorithm works, on one simple sentence. The thick arrow means the best transition. Please notice that each arrow (even those arrows we haven't draw on the figure) means a transition from one state to another state. This is the state transition matrix.

After the Viterbi algorithm, we could get the optimal tagged sequence which has a maximum value. In this example, the best state sequence is "我"/O "的" /O "紫"/Pre, "轩"/M, "好"/O. (Mine/O Purple/Pre Xuan/M, is excellent/O).

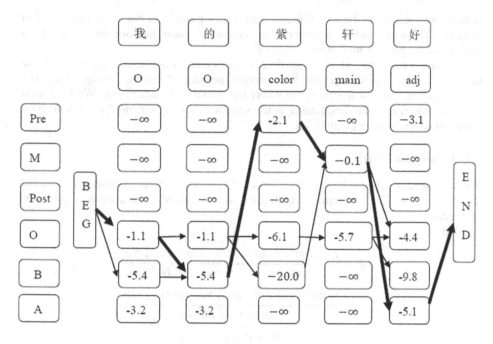

Fig. 1. The state transition of The Viterbi algorithm

4.4 The Work Flow of Chinese Automobile's Nickname Recognition

The steps are listed below:

1. Prepare the data. Separate train set and data set.
2. Train the model.
3. Tokenization sentences.
4. Tag token sequences using Viterbi algorithm. Get the optimal state sequence which has the maximum possibility. (It also can get the top 2-3 results as required and to increase the recall rates of right tokens).
5. Nickname recognized after maximum matching with the specific nickname patterns, the nickname patterns are shown in Table 2.

5 Experiments and Results

5.1 Dataset

Even though the nickname is popular and being used and accepted widely, but we have not found any published dataset which contains information in automobiles' domain. In addition, our definitions are very different from a POS or other tag set. Thus, we have to make the dataset by ourselves.

We have chosen the forum named "The home of Automobile" and "The Pacific Automobile", collected two thousands passages as passage dataset and two thousands sentences as sentences dataset. We assure that each passage in passages dataset has at least one nickname and each sentence in sentences dataset has one nickname. Then we tagged the parts of nicknames artificially.

We have used a part of sentences in sentences dataset as the training set, because the sentences have less noise than the passages, because of that the passages include a lot of paragraphs and some paragraphs may not contain any nicknames. We have used other sentences in sentences dataset as the sentences testing set, used the whole 2000 passages as the passages testing set.

5.2 Evaluation Metric

We have used precision (P), recall (R) and the F-measure (F) to evaluate the result of this experiment. The last term, F, is defined as a weighted combination of precision and recall.

That is,

$$P = \frac{number\ of\ correctly\ recognized\ NE}{number\ of\ recognized\ NE}$$

$$R = \frac{number\ of\ correctly\ recognized\ NE}{number\ of\ all\ NE}$$

$$F = \frac{R \times P \times (1 + \beta^2)}{R + P \times \beta^2}$$

In the formulation above, β is the relative weight of precision and recall. In our experiments, we supposed that precision and recall have equally weight. So we set $\beta = 1$.

5.3 Experiments

We have tested several times, divided the training set and testing set randomly, and the result of precision, recall and F-measure we listed in Table 5 and Table 6 are the average value.

The result reveals that our algorithm performances a little better on sentences than on the passages, because passages usually have more noises. Such as "刚刚去修理我家的刚刚" (My Gang Gang had gone to be repaired just now. In Chinese, "gang gang" means, just now.) The first "刚刚" means just now, it is not a nickname while the second "刚刚" refers to the car "金刚" (Jin Gang).

Table 5. Result on a small training set

Dataset	Amount	Precision	Recall	F-measure
Training Set	500	95.1%	93.2%	0.9414
Test Set by Sentences	1500	93.7%	91.3%	0.9248
Test Set by Passages	2000	92.2%	89.5%	0.9082

Table 6. Result on a large training set

Dataset	Amount	Precision	Recall	F-measure
Training Set	1000	98.1%	96.2%	0.9714
Test Set by Sentences	1000	96.7%	92.3%	0.9445
Test Set by Passages	2000	95.2%	91.5%	0.9331

The result also proved that using 1000 sentences as the training data got better performance than 500 sentences as the training data.

6 Conclusion and Future Research

The experiments we made have proved that our methods of Chinese automobiles' nickname recognition have got a good result. Our algorithm can be used to establish a nickname database. The nickname database can be used to improve other projects on automobiles' domain such as the named entity recognition, information extraction, data mining, search engine, etc.

We think that this algorithm could also expand to other domains, not only in automobiles domain. Not only automobiles have nicknames, many objects all have their own nicknames. We can fine tuning our program and the form of nicknames to make our method can be used on nickname recognition in other domains.

In our future work, we will try to use our theory, model and program on other domains. Finally, we hope that our research on nickname recognition could get a general model.

Acknowledgements

This work is supported by the National Grand Fundamental Research 973 Program of China under Grant No.2007CB310900 and Chun-Tsung scholarship, which was established by Nobel Laureate Professor Tsung-Dao Lee.

Thanks for the technical support from Supertool company, especially from Minghui Wu, Xuan Zhao, Songtao Chi, Yuqian Kong, Pei Liu, Chaoxu Zhang, Jian Gao, Hao Xu, Bingzheng Wei. We are grateful for the help you give us. Thanks for your nice attitude and thanks for the many hours of discussions.

References

1. Bick, E.: A Named Entity Recognizer for Danish. In: Proc. of 4th International Conf. on Language Resources and Evaluation (2004)
2. Zhang, H., Liu, Q.: Automatic Recognition of Chinese Person based on Roles Taging. In: Proc. of 7th Graduate Conference on Computer Science in Chinese Academy of Sciences (2002)
3. Zhang, H., Liu, Q., Yu, H., Cheng, X., Bai, S.: Chinese Named Entity Recognition Using Role Model. Computational Linguistics and Chinese Language Processing (2003)

4. Chang, J.T., Schütze, H.: Abbreviations in biomedical text. In: Ananiadou, S., McNaught, J. (eds.) Text Mining for Biology and Biomedicine, pp. 99–119 (2006)
5. Sun, X., Wang, H., Yuzhang: Chinese Abbreviation-Definition Identification: A SVM Approach Using Context Information. LNCS. Springer, Heidelberg (2006)
6. Okazaki, N., Ananiadou, S.: A Term Recognition Approach to Acronym Recognition. In: Proceedings of the COLING/ACL Main Conference Poster (2006)
7. Qin, B., Lang, J., Chen, Y., He, R., Zhao, Y.: The search engine of Chinese automobile's comments, http://zp.isoche.com/
8. Pierre, J.M.: Mining knowledge from text collections using automatically generated metadata. In: Karagiannis, D., Reimer, U. (eds.) PAKM 2002. LNCS, vol. 2569, pp. 537–548. Springer, Heidelberg (2002)
9. Collins, M., Singer, Y.: Unsupervised Models for Named Entity Classification. In: Proc. of EMNLP/VLC 1999 (1999)
10. Liu, F., Zhao, J., Lv, B., Xu, B., Yu, H.: Product Named Entity Recognition Based on Hierarchical Hidden Markov Model. Journal of Chinese Information Processing (2006)
11. Andrei, M., Marc, M., Claire, G.: Named Entity Recognition using an HMM-based Chunk Tagger. In: Proc. of EACL (1999)
12. Bikel, D., Schwarta, R., Weischedel, R.: An algorithm that learns what's in a name. Machine learning 34, 211–231 (1997)
13. Luo, Z., Song, R.: Integrated and Fast Recognition of Proper Noun in Modern Chinese Word Segmentation. In: Proceedings of International Conference on Chinese Computing (2001)

Fast Semantic Role Labeling for Chinese
Based on Semantic Chunking

Weiwei Ding and Baobao Chang

Institute of Computational Linguistics
Peking University, Beijing, 100871, China
weiwei.ding.pku@gmail.com, chbb@pku.edu.cn

Abstract. Recently, with the development of Chinese semantically annotated corpora, e.g. the Chinese Proposition Bank, the Chinese semantic role labeling (SRL) has been boosted. However, the Chinese SRL researchers now focus on the transplant of existing statistical machine learning methods which have been proven to be effective on English. In this paper, we have established a semantic chunking based method which is different from the traditional ones. Semantic chunking is named because of its similarity with syntactic chunking. The difference is that semantic chunking is used to identify the semantic chunks, i.e. the semantic roles. Based on semantic chunking, the process of SRL is changed from "parsing – semantic role identification – semantic role classification", to "semantic chunk identification – semantic chunk classification". With the elimination of the parsing stage, the SRL task can get rid of the dependency on parsing, which is the bottleneck both of speed and precision. The experiments have shown that the semantic chunking based method outperforms previously best-reported results on Chinese SRL and saves a large amount of time.

Keywords: semantic chunking, Chinese semantic role labeling.

1 Introduction

Semantic Role labeling (SRL) was first defined by Gildea etc. [1]. The SRL task is to identify and classify the semantic roles of each predicate in a sentence. The semantic roles are marked and each of them is assigned a tag which indicates the type of semantic relationship with the related predicate. Typical tags include Agent, Patient, Source, etc and adjuncts such as Temporal, Manner, Extent, etc. Since the arguments can provide useful semantic information, the SRL is crucial to many natural language processing tasks, such as Question and Answering [2] and Machine Translation [3]. With the efforts of many researchers [4, 5], different machine learning methods and linguistics resources are applied to this task, which has made SRL progress fast.

Compared to that on English, however, the research on Chinese SRL is still in its infancy stage. Previous work on Chinese SRL [6, 7, 8] mainly focused on how to transplant the machine learning methods, which has been successful on English. Sun [6] did the preliminary work on Chinese SRL without any large semantically annotated corpus of Chinese. This paper made the first attempt on Chinese SRL and

W. Li and D. Mollá-Aliod (Eds.): ICCPOL 2009, LNAI 5459, pp. 79–90, 2009.

produced promising results. After the PropBank [9, 10] was built, Xue [7] and Xue [8] have produced more complete and systematic research on Chinese SRL.

The architectures of complete SRL systems for Chinese and English are quite similar. They are mostly the "parsing – semantic role identification – semantic role classification" pipeline. The fundamental theory of this architecture is the "linking theory", in which the mapping relationship between the semantic constituents and the syntactic constituents is discussed. In this architecture, all the arguments of the predicate are projected to a syntactic node in the parsing tree. Accordingly, the whole process seems natural: a sentence is firstly parsed, and then all the nodes in the parsing tree are identified whether they are the arguments of the target predicate or not. Finally, the nodes which are recognized as semantic roles are classified into different categories. Unlike the previous "parsing based" architecture, in this paper, a "semantic chunking" method is proposed. We use similar technologies as chunking to identify and classify the semantic roles. With this method, the parsing trees are no longer necessary for SRL, which will greatly reduce the time expense, since parsing is quite a time-consuming task. Also, it can improve the performance of Chinese SRL.

Hacioglu [11] have done the similar work on English with semantic chunking. But their work focused on transplant the widely-used syntactic chunking technology to semantic role labeling. However, only features that are useful to syntactic chunking are not enough for semantic chunking, because the characteristics of the two research objects are different. The results of the experiments had reassured this problem. Besides, semantic chunking has more practical use on Chinese, since both parsers and chunkers on Chinese are not easy to find and the performances are not satisfactory. In our paper, we will try to fully explore useful information for the Chinese semantic chunking to build a robust semantic role labeler without parsers. Besides, we will make comparisons of the time consumption between semantic chunking based methods with previous parser based ones.

The rest of the paper is organized as follows. In section 2, the semantically annotated corpus - Chinese Propbank is discussed. The semantic chunking, which is the main part of this paper is described in section 3. We then apply this method on hand-crafted word segmentation and POS tagging in section 4. The results of the experiments can be found in section 5. Section 6 is the conclusion and future work.

2   The Chinese PropBank

The Chinese PropBank has labeled the predicate-argument structures of sentences from the Chinese TreeBank [9]. It is constituted of two parts. One is the labeled data, which indicates the positions of the predicates and its arguments in the Chinese Treebank. The other is a dictionary which lists the frames of all the labeled predicates. The following is an example from the PropBank.

In this sentence, 宁波港 (the Harbor of Ningbo) is the proto-agent of the verb 利用 (utilize), which is labeled as arg0 in PropBank. 外资 (foreign investments) is the proto-patient, which is labeled as arg1. 多渠道 (in all kinds of channels) is used to describe the method of the investment utilization, so it is labeled as argM-ADV. "argM" shows that this constituent is an argument of modality. "ADV" is a functional tag, which suggests that this constituent is adverbial.

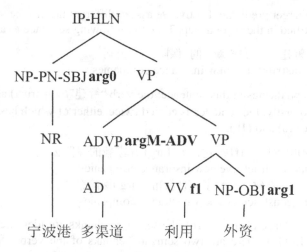

Fig. 1. An example from PropBank[1]

The task of Chinese semantic role labeling of the PropBank data is to identify all the constituents which are the arguments of the predicate and to classify them. There are two types of labels in the PropBank. One is the numbered label which includes arg0, arg1...arg4. The other is argM with functional tags like ADV in the example. Other tags include TMP, which represents the temporal information and EXT, which is the extent, and so on. In this paper, we keep the functional tags, as did Xue [7], since different kinds of argMs describe different kinds of information related to the verb which is quite useful for other NLP tasks.

The PropBank is built on the hand-crafted annotations of the parsing tree from the TreeBank, because the arguments are chunks of words which correspond to the nodes in the parsing trees. With this reason and the mapping theory, it is quite natural to build a classifier to filter the nodes in the parsing trees. However, since the purpose of SRL is just to determine which chunks of words are verb arguments, we can also view SRL as a sequence labeling problem, which leads to the idea of semantic chunking.

3 Semantic Chunking

Semantic chunking is named because of its similarity with syntactic chunking. It is used to identify the "semantic chunks" in a sentence. Some people use the term to express the idea of syntactic chunking exploiting semantic information [12]. However, in this paper, we define the argument constituents of the target predicate as semantic chunks. In other words, the semantic chunks are verb-dependent. With different target verbs, same sentences will have different semantic chunks. The process of semantic chunking is: firstly, we make the same number of copies of the sentence as the number of predicates in it, and for each copy, there is only one predicate which will be the target. Secondly, we use the chunking method to identify the semantic

---

[1] This sentence is from Chinese TreeBank chtb_433.fid.

chunks of the target predicate. Lastly, we assign different tags to the semantic chunks we have identified in the second step. Take the following sentence as an example.

(1) 中国　筹建　　五家新 的 保险　　公司²
(1) China **construct** five **new** insurance companies

There are two predicates in this sentence: the verb "筹建"(construct) and the adjective "新"(new). So firstly, the sentence is copied twice, either of which has only one target predicate, like (1a) and (1b).

(1a) [arg0中国]　　[f1筹建]　　[arg1五家新的保险公司]
China construct five new insurance companies
(1b) 中国　　筹建　　五家 [f1新]的 [arg0保险公司]
China construct five new insurance companies

Then for the sentence (1a) and (1b), the semantic chunks are identified and classified respectively. In (1a), there are two semantic chunks of the verb "筹建"(construct). That is "中国", the arg0 and "五家保险公司"(five insurance companies), the arg1. However in (1b), there is only one chunk. That is "保险公司"(insurance companies), which is the arg0 of the predicate "新"(new). The copies of the sentences, like (1a) and (1b), have no relationship with each other in the last two stages of semantic chunking.

Through the first step of semantic chunking, we solve the problem that arguments of different verbs in the same sentence might overlap, like "五家保险公司" (five insurance companies) in (1a) and "保险公司" (insurance companies) in (1b).

We call the second step the process of semantic chunk identification, and the third step, the process of semantic chunk classification. The semantic chunk identification and classification are done separately instead of simultaneously.

3.1 Semantic Chunk Identification

From the view of functionality, semantic chunk identification (SCI) is equal to the integration of parsing and semantic role identification. The purpose of SCI is to identify which part of the sentence is the potential argument of the target predicate in this sentence.

The semantic chunk identification is also a sequence labeling problem. The first thing we need to do for sequence labeling task is to decide which representation of sequence we shall choose. There are some widely-used representation methods, like IOB1, IOB2, IOE1, IOE2 and start/end. For this paper, we used all these representation strategies to find out which one will work better.

IOB1, IOB2, IOE1, IOE2 belongs to the inside/outside representation. IOB1 was first introduced by Ramshaw [13], and the other three are by Sang [14]. "I" indicates that the current word is inside a chunk and "O" indicates that it's outside the chunk. The differences between the four representations are the different resolutions of the start or end of the chunk.

---

² This sentence is from Chinese TreeBank ctb_030.fid.

IOB1 "B" is used when the current word is a start of a chunk which is immediately following another. IOB2 "B" is used any time when the current word is a start of a chunk. IOE1 "E" is used when the current word is an end of a chunk which is immediately followed by another. IOE2 "E" is used any time when the current word is an end of a chunk.

However, start/end is quite a different representation, and it was first used for Japanese Named Entity Recognition by Uchimoto[3] [15]. There are five signs in start/end representation, which are: B, I, E, O and S. The uses of these signs are:

B the current word is the start of a chunk. I the current word is in the middle of a chunk. E the current word is an end of a chunk. O the current word is outside a chunk. S the current word is a chunk with only 1 word.

From the definitions, we can find that the start/end is the most complex one.

3.2 Semantic Chunk Classification

Semantic chunk classification is quite like semantic role classification. In this stage, the semantic chunks which have been identified previously should be classified into different kinds of arguments, in other words, the labels arg0-4, argM+(functional tags) are assigned to the semantic chunks. However, because we didn't get the parsing tree from the previous stages, many features that are related to the parsing trees can't be used. So we have to explore other features to take its place.

4 Semantic Role Labeling Using Semantic Chunking

In this section, we present a SRL system based on hand-crafted word-segmentation and POS tagging. We removed the parsing information from the Chinese TreeBank and only left the word segmentation and POS information. Since the word segmentation and POS tagging are quite challenging tasks in Chinese, we omit these to focus on the SRL task and make the comparisons with other related systems fair.

4.1 Data

We use Chinese PropBank 1.0 (LDC number: LDC2005T234) in our experiments. PropBank 1.0 includes the annotations for files chtb_001.fid to chtb_931.fid, or the first 250K words of the Chinese TreeBank 5.1. For the experiments, the data of Prop-Bank is divided into three parts. 648 files (from chtb_081 to chtb_899.fid) are used as the training set. The development set includes 40 files, from chtb_041.fid to chtb_080.fid. The test set includes 72 files, which are chtb_001 to chtb_041, and chtb_900 to chtb_931. We use the same data setting with that in [8].

---

[3] There are some differences between the start/end representations in [15] and [16]. We follow the latter one's standard.

[4] http://www.ldc.upenn.edu/Catalog/CatalogEntry.jsp?catelogId=LDC2005T23

4.2 Classifier

In our SRL system, we use the CRF++[5] toolkit as the classifier, since the CRFs have proven effective on the sequence labeling problem [17].

The CRF++ toolkit uses the LBFGS training algorithm which converges much faster but requires more memory and it can output n-best results. It has also distinguished two kinds of feature templates: the unigram template and the bigram template. The unigram and bigram are not about the features, but the output tags. The bigram template can generate more feature functions which will improve the performance but increase the time and space expense. In our system, we take advantage of both to achieve a balance.

4.3 Features for Semantic Chunk Identification

In this section, the feature templates used for semantic chunk identification are presented. With these templates, we can extract thousands of features.

Table 1. Feature Templates for Semantic Chunk Identification

Unigram Feature Templates:	
TargetPredicate	The target predicate in the sentence
Distance0	The distance between the current word and the target verb, using +/- to distinguish whether the current word is located before or after the target verb
Word-1(0, 1)	The previous (current, following) word
POS-1(0, 1)	The previous (current, following) word's POS
TargetOrNot-1(0, 1)	Whether or not the previous (current, following) word is the target predicate
Begin0, Middle0, End0	The current word and the target predicate divide a sentence into three parts: the beginning part, the middle part and the ending part. Each part can be viewed as a series of POS. To avoid data sparseness, we make some simplifications of them. Duplicate patterns of POS or POS strings will be omitted. If the POS string is "N-V-N-V-N-V-N", the simplified form will be "N-V-N". SimpleBegin represents the simplified form of the beginning part, SimpleMiddle the middle part and SimpleEnd the ending part. 0 indicates that it is the current word and the target verb that divided the sentence
Begin-1, Middle-1, End-1	The simplification form of the three parts generated by the previous word and the target predicate
Begin1, Middle1, End1	The simplification form of the three parts generated by the following word and the target predicate
PunctsInMiddle0	The number of punctuations (comma, period, semicolon, colon, interrogation and exclamatory mark) in the middle part between the current word and target predicate.

---

[5] http://sourceforge.net/projects/crfpp/

VerbsInMiddle0	The number of verbs in the middle part between the current word and target predicate.
Bigram Feature Templates:	
Word-1/Word0/Word1	The combination of Word-1, Word0 and Word1. Slash "/" indicates the combination.
Verb-1/Verb0/Verb1	Verb-1 (0,1) feature will be the previous(current, following) word if it is a verb and NULL if not.
VerbPOS-1/ VerbPOS0/VerbPOS1	VerbPOS-1 (0,1) feature will be the POS of the previous(current, following) word if it is a verb and NULL if not.
VerbVector-1/ VerbVector0/ VerbVector1	VerbVector-1 (0,1) is a vector, each dimension of which indicates the amount of a kind of verb POS in the middle part between the target predicate and the previous(current, following) word. Since there are 4 kinds of verbs in the Chinese TreeBank: VV, VA, VC and VE, the VerbVector feature is a 4-dimensional vector. For example, if numbers of VV, VA, VC and VE are 1, 2, 0, 3 respectively, the feature will be (1, 2, 0, 3)
Rhythm-1/Rhythm0/ Rhythm1	Rhythm-1(0, 1) represents the number of Chinese characters (Hanzi) contained in the previous (current, following) word
SemanticCategory0/ TargetPredicate	The combination of the semantic category of the current word and TargetPredicate. The semantic category is extracted from the *Semantic Knowledge-base of Contemporary Chinese* [18]. If the word doesn't appear in the dictionary, the word itself will be the feature
Output-1/Output0	The combination of the previous output and the current output
Distance0/ TargetPredicate	
VerbsInMiddle0/ TargetPredicate	
Word0/POS0/ TargetPredicate	
VerbVector0/ TargetPredicate	
Word0/Distance0/ POS0/TargetOrNot0	

4.4 Features for Semantic Chunk Classification

The features used for semantic chunk classification are listed below. They are quite different from the features used in the semantic role identification task in parser based methods. Since the semantic chunking method doesn't depend on parsing, the parsing-dependent features like "path" cannot be used. We must find some new ones.

Table 2. Feature Templates for Semantic Chunk Classification

Bigram Feature Templates:	
FirstWord	The first word of a chunk.
FirstWordPOS	The POS of FirstWord
LastWord	The last word of a chunk
LastWordPOS	The POS of LastWord
PreviousWord	The word just before a chunk.
PreviousWordPOS	The POS of PreviousWord.
FollowingWord	The word just after a chunk.
FollowingWordPOS	The POS of FollowingWord.
Length	The length of a chunk
Distance	The distance between the chunk and the target predicate
BeforeorAfter	Whether the chunk is before or after the target predicate
VerbSemcat	The semantic category of the target predicate, which is also extracted from the *Semantic Knowledge-base of Contemporary Chinese*
LastWordSemcat	The semantic category of LastWord
TargetPredicate	The target predicate
MiddleWords	The words in the middle of a chunk. Start and end are not included. The feature is NULL if no words are in the middle
MiddlePOS	The POS of the MiddleWords
SimpleMiddle0	It is the same with SimpleMiddle0 in the process of semantic chunk identification
Frames	The target predicate may have several frames in PropBank. The Frames feature is a string consisting of the numbers of the arguments in all the frames of the target predicate. Take the verb "保持"(keep) as an example. It has two frames: one has three arguments, arg1, arg1, arg2; the other has only two: arg0, arg1. The Frames of "保持"(keep) will be C3C2. Detailed information about this feature can be found in [7].
AllFrames	A string consisting of all the frames of the target predicate. For example, the AllFrames feature of the verb "保持"(keep) will be C0x1x2C1x2.
Output-1/Output	The combination of previous and current output
Unigram Feature Templates:	
FirstWord/LastWord	
PreviousWord/PreviousWordPOS	

5 Results and Discussion

The results of semantic chunking based SRL on hand-crafted word segmentation and POS tagging are presented in Table 3. SCI and SCC represent respectively semantic chunk identification and classification. We have used five different representations in our experiments. From the results, we find that start/end performs the best among all the representations. For the in/out representation, results on IOB2/IOE2 are better than those on IOB1/IOE1. Besides, the performance of semantic chunk classification didn't decrease and yet increased a bit compared to semantic role classification in parser-based methods. The highest precision is 94.25%, compared to 94.1% in [8].

Table 3. Results on the hand-crafted word segmentation and POS tagging with different representations

	SCI			SCC	whole
	Precision	Recall	F-value	Precision	F-value
IOB1	69.49%	78.09%	73.54%	94.17%	69.25%
IOB2	71.48%	78.45%	74.80%	94.25%	70.50%
IOE1	70.42%	77.53%	73.81%	94.19%	69.52%
IOE2	72.30%	79.53%	75.74%	94.10%	71.27%
Start/end	73.58%	81.00%	77.11%	94.20%	**72.64%**

Table 4. Amount and labeled performance of the semantic roles of different lengths on test set

length	amount	Recall	Precision	F-value
1	3197	77.20%	87.77%	82.14%
2	1503	79.11%	85.23%	82.06%
3	964	70.44%	79.79%	74.82%
4	644	73.45%	78.83%	76.04%
5	462	71.86%	73.94%	72.89%
6	370	67.57%	76.22%	71.63%
7	236	70.76%	73.25%	71.98%
8	211	64.93%	72.11%	68.33%
9	172	55.81%	65.75%	60.38%
≥10	418	60.93%	62.76%	61.83%

Specifically on the labeled precision of semantic roles of different lengths, we will find that the performance decreases with the growth of length, namely, the number of the words contained in the semantic roles. Table 4 shows the amount, labeled recall, precision and f-value of arguments that have 1 to 9, and 10 or more words. From the table, we can see that the performances decrease sharply if the lengths of the semantic roles are below 8. However, this trend ends when the lengths are 9 and above.

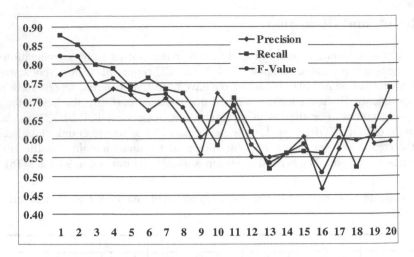

Fig. 2. Detailed labeled performance of different lengths

More intuitive impressions can be acquired in Figure 2, which reveals the more detailed information from the length of 1 to 19, 20 and above. We can see from the figure that with lengths of 1 to 9, the F-value decreases sharply from 80% to 60%, however, from 9 to 20 and above, the F-values are quite stable at around 60%.

To prove that our method is effective, we make a comparison between our system and that in [8], which is the state-of-the-art parsing-based SRL system and has the same data setting as ours. The results are presented in Table 5.

Table 5. Performance Comparison

	The system in [8]	Ours
Precision	**79.5%**	76.31%
Recall	65.6%	**69.31%**
F-value	71.9%	**72.64%**

In this table, we can find that the recall and f-value of our system are higher while the precision is lower. This probably can be explained with the use of parser. Because of the parsing errors, a semantic role sometimes can't correspond to a constituent in a parsing tree, so subsequently; it will never be recognized correctly, which will lower the recall. Oppositely, if a semantic role is correctly recognized as one node in the parsing tree, the rich information provided by the parsing tree will be of great help to identify it and assign the right tag, which would be the reason for the higher precision.

As we mentioned before, the greatest difference between the semantic chunking based methods and parsing based methods is the elimination of the parsing stage, which is a greatly time-consuming task. The comparison of the time consumption on the test set between the two kinds of methods has verified this assertion, which is shown in table 6. We build a simple parsing based SRL system, in which we use the Collins parser. The Collins parser is trained with the model1 presented by Collins [19] on the training set. We also used the head rules for Chinese used by Sun [6]. There are 922 sentences in the test set, and the average length of the sentences in the test set is 26.8 words. The experiment running environment is a server with Pentium Dual-Core 2.8GHz CPU and 2 gigabytes memory.

Table 6. Time Consumption Comparison on test set

Parsing based	SC based
210 hours	**17 seconds**

In table 6, we can find the semantic chunking based method has indeed decreased the time expense sharply, from hours to seconds. It's easy to understand because the time complexity of the algorithm used in Collins parser is $O(n^5)$, which is far behind that of the decoding algorithm of CRFs, whose time complexity is only $O(n)$, and n represents the length of the sentence. And the time gap will increase greatly with the growth of the sentence length. Not only the Collins parser, but other parsers will also require lots of time since the combination possibilities of the syntactic rules in the parsing process increase very fast in amount with the growth of the sentence length.

6 Conclusions and Future Work

In this paper, we have built a completely new SRL system on the Chinese PropBank corpus based on semantic chunking. Instead of classifying the constituents in a parsing tree, we turn SRL into a sequence labeling problem. Besides the elevation of the labeled precision, with the novel method we have presented in this paper, we can greatly reduce the time expense, most of which is consumed during the parsing stage in traditional strategies. Less time consumption is useful especially for large corpora, like the millions of pages from the web.

Previous Research [4, 5] has shown that the great limitation of semantic role labeling is the process of parsing. As far as Chinese is concerned, this limitation is even more prominent. The performance of Chinese SRL on automatic parsing is much worse than that of English while the performances of the two languages through handcrafted parsing are comparable [8]. The semantic chunking based method has provided us another way to try to decrease the limitations of parsing, especially for Chinese that lacks efficient parsers.

In the future, we will explore more features which are related with the SRL task. Other NLP tasks like the named entity recognition, syntactic chunking and more language resources can provide helpful information. Besides the introduction of more linguistic knowledge, it's interesting to consider how to integrate the semantic chunking based and parsing based methods to build a SRL system which has rich syntactic information and consumes less time.

Acknowledgments. This work is supported by National Natural Science Foundation of China under Grant No. 60303003 and National Social Science Foundation of China under Grant No. 06BYY048.

References

1. Gildea, D., Jurafsky, D.: Automatic labeling of semantic roles. Computational Linguistics 28(3), 245–288 (2002)
2. Narayanan, S., Harabagiu, S.: Question answering based on semantic structures. In: The 20th International Conference on Computational Linguistics, Geneva, Switzerland (2004)
3. Boas, H.C.: Bilingual FrameNet dictionaries for machine translation. In: The International Conference on Language Resources and Evaluation, Las Palmas, Spain (2002)
4. Carreras, X., Màrquez, L.: Introduction to the conll-2004 shared task: Semantic role labeling. In: The Eighth Conference on Natural Language Learning, Boston, Massachusetts, USA (2004)
5. Carreras, X., Màrquez, L.: Introduction to the conll-2005 shared task: Semantic role labeling. In: The Nineth Conference on Natural Language Learning, Ann Arbor, Michigan, USA (2005)
6. Sun, H., Jurafsky, D.: Shallow Semantic Parsing of Chinese. In: The Human Language Technology Conference of the North American Chapter of the Association for Computational Linguistics, Boston, Massachusetts, USA (2004)
7. Xue, N., Palmer, M.: Automatic semantic role labeling for Chinese verbs. In: The 19th International Joint Conference on Artificial Intelligence, Edinburgh, Scotland (2005)
8. Xue, N.: Labeling Chinese predicates with semantic roles. Computational linguistics 34(2), 225–255 (2008)
9. Xue, N., Palmer, M.: Annotating the Propositions in the Penn Chinese Treebank. In: The 2nd SIGHAN Workshop on Chinese Language Processing, Sapporo, Japan (2003)
10. Xue, N., Xia, F., Chiou, F., Palmer, M.: The Penn Chinese TreeBank: Phrase Structure Annotation of a Large Corpus. Natural Language Engineering 11(2), 207–238 (2005)
11. Hacioglu, K., Ward, W.: Target word detection and semantic role chunking using support vector machines. In: The Human Language Technology Conference of the North American Chapter of the Association for Computational Linguistics, Edmonton, Canada (2003)
12. Wang, R., Chi, Z., Wang, X., Wu, T.: An algorithm for semantic chunk identification of Chinese sentences. In: The Tenth IASTED International Conference on Intelligent Systems and Control, Cambridge, Massachusetts, USA (2007)
13. Ramshaw, L.A., Marcus, M.P.: Text chunking using transformation-based learning. In: The 3rd Workshop on Very Large Corpora, Cambridge, Massachusetts, USA (2005)
14. Sang, E., Kim, T., Veenstra, J.: Representing text chunks. In: The 38th Annual Meeting of the Association for Computational Linguistics, Hong Kong, China (1999)
15. Uchimoto, K., Ma, Q., Murata, M., Ozaku, H., Isahara, H.: Named Entity Extraction Based on A Maximum Entropy Model and Transformation Rules. In: The 38th Annual Meeting of the Association for Computational Linguistics, Hong Kong, China (2000)
16. Kudo, T., Matsumoto, Y.: Chunking with Support Vector Machines. In: Second Meeting of North American Chapter of the Association for Computational Linguistics, Pittsburgh, USA (2001)
17. Lafferty, J., McCallum, A., Pereira, F.: Conditional Random Fields: Probabilistic Models for Segmenting and Labeling Sequence Data. In: The 18th International Conference on Machine Learning, Williamstown, MA, USA (2001)
18. Wang, H., Zhan, W., Yu, S.: The Specification of The Semantic Knowledge-base of Contemporary Chinese. Journal of Chinese Language and Computing 13(2), 159–176 (2003)
19. Collins, M.: Head-Driven Statistical Models for Natural Language Parsing. Pennsylvania University (1999)

Validity of an Automatic Evaluation of Machine Translation Using a Word-Alignment-Based Classifier

Katsunori Kotani[1], Takehiko Yoshimi[2], Takeshi Kutsumi[3], and Ichiko Sata[3]

[1] Kansai Gaidai University. 16-1 Nakamiya Higashino-cho Hirakata, Osaka, 573-1001 Japan
kkotani@kansaigaidai.ac.jp
[2] Ryukoku Univerisity. 1-5 Yokotani, Seta Oe-cho Otsu, Shiga, 520-2194 Japan
[3] Sharp Corporation 492 Minosho-cho Yamatokoriyama, Nara, 639-1186 Japan

Abstract. Because human evaluation of machine translation is extensive but expensive, we often use automatic evaluation in developing a machine translation system. From viewpoint of evaluation cost, there are two types of evaluation methods: one uses (multiple) reference translation, e.g., METEOR, and the other classifies machine translation either into machine-like or human-like translation based on translation properties, i.e., a classification-based method. Previous studies showed that classification-based methods could perform evaluation properly. These studies constructed a classifier by learning linguistic properties of translation such as length of a sentence, syntactic complexity, and literal translation, and their classifiers marked high classification accuracy. These previous studies, however, have not examined whether their classification accuracy could present translation quality. Hence, we investigated whether classification accuracy depends on translation quality. The experiment results showed that our method could correctly distinguish the degrees of translation quality.

Keywords: machine translation evaluation, translation property, classification.

1 Introduction

The importance of automatic evaluation cannot be overstated. It is necessary to examine translation quality in developing a machine translation system. An automatic evaluation method performed more efficiently than a manual evaluation method. Owing to the advent of automatic evaluation method, we can easily check translation quality.

Even though there have been proposed various evaluation methods, we can classify automatic evaluation methods roughly into two types. One compares machine-generated translations (MTs) with human-generated translations (HTs), i.e., BLEU [5], NIST [6], and METEOR [7]. Under this method, multiple reference translations would yield better evaluation results. The other method evaluates quality of MTs without reference HTs. Comparing with the former method, the latter method is a cheaper method, because there is no need to prepare reference HTs when evaluating MTs. This method evaluates MT quality by analyzing linguistic properties of MTs, i.e., classification-based approaches [1, 2, 3, 4]. This method consists of the following procedures: (i) extracting features for classification from MT and HT sentences, (ii)

W. Li and D. Mollá-Aliod (Eds.): ICCPOL 2009, LNAI 5459, pp. 91–102, 2009.

constructing a classifier using machine learning algorithms based on the features, and (iii) classifying test MT data either into MT-like or HT-like translation. Even though this method requires HTs in constructing a classifier, no more reference HTs are required when evaluating MTs. Regarding (multiple) reference HTs, this method is cheaper and plausible for evaluation of system improvement.

In this paper, we adopted the classification-based evaluation method for English-to-Japanese MT systems. Our classifier was constructed by machine learning algorithms, i.e., Support Vector Machines (SVMs). This classifier examines the degree of literal translation of MTs and HTs, and determines MTs as MT-like or HT-like translations. If the classification accuracy for MTs decreases for HT-like translation, the decrease suggests that a classification method can evaluate the difference of translation quality between a pre-improved MT system and the improved system, as noted by a previous study [1]. This is because "good" MTs are indistinguishable from HTs. A "good" MT sentence should be incorrectly classified into an HT sentence. The previous study [1], however, has not yet assessed their classification method from this viewpoint.

We examined whether the classification accuracy of our proposed method would decrease for fluent translation. In our experiment, the classification accuracy of our method presented statistically significant decrease in the classification accuracy depending on the fluency of translation in four degrees. This dependent relation of classification accuracy with the translation quality suggests that our proposed method should provide valid evaluation results for system improvement. Hence, this method is expected to assist system development.

We further examined the property of our evaluation criteria by comparing our method with a previous automatic evaluation criterion, i.e., METEOR. Through this comparison, we found that our evaluation criterion is stricter than the METEOR-based method.

In the rest of this paper, we introduce related works in section 2. In section 3, we report the experimental design and the results. In section 4 we summarize this paper.

2   Related Works

In this section we will introduce previous studies using machine learning algorithms to classify MTs depending on translation quality.

2.1   Classification-Based Evaluation Methods

Some are expensive methods [8, 9, 10], because these methods need manual evaluation results (manually labeled training examples) to train classifiers. The others [1, 2, 3, 4] need no manual evaluation results. Due to the cost problem, we decided to employ the latter method in this paper.

The latter method treated evaluation of translation quality as a classification problem. This method evaluates translation quality on the basis of the classification results of MTs either into HT-like or MT-like translation. Classification is carried out by examining the linguistic properties of MTs. "Good" translations share a number of properties with HTs, while "bad" translations are dissimilar to HTs and exhibit translation properties specific to MTs.

A study [1] constructed classifiers for Spanish-to-English MTs with decision trees [11]. Classification features consisted of perplexity features and linguistic features, and thus they obtained three types of classifiers: (i) a perplexity-feature-based classifier, (ii) a linguistic-feature-based classifier, and (iii) a classifier based on the both features. These classifiers exhibited the following accuracy: 74.7% accuracy for the classifier (i), 76.5% for the classifier (ii), and 82.9% for the classifier (iii).

Another study [2] adopted SVMs in constructing a classifier for Chinese-to-English MTs. The classification features were combined with (i) n-gram precision of MTs compared with HTs, (ii) the sentence length of MTs and HTs, and (iii) the word error rate of MTs. This classifier achieved 64.4% accuracy.

Another study [3] also employed SVMs, and constructed a classifier for English-to-French MTs. Classification features involved linguistic properties of translation such as subcategorization properties and semantic properties, e.g., finiteness and argument structures. This classifier marked 77.6% accuracy.

The other study [4] constructed a classifier for English-to-Japanese MTs using SVMs. Classification features consisted of word-alignment properties between English sentences and translations (MTs or HTs), i.e., aligned pairs and unaligned words. Their classifier showed 99.4% accuracy.

2.2 Property of Classification Accuracy

Under a classification-based evaluation method, classification accuracy should decrease for better MTs, because the translation is similar to HTs as a previous study [1] suggested. Since a classifier incorrectly classifies "good" MTs into HTs, classification accuracy would decrease. By contrast, classification accuracy should increase for "bad" MTs. Given this property of classification accuracy, we consider that the adequacy of classification-based evaluation should be assessed by checking not only the independent accuracy but also the translation-quality-dependent accuracy.

The previous studies [1, 2, 3, 4], however, did not assess their method from viewpoint of the dependent accuracy. Then, we examined our classification method by checking whether the classification accuracy depends on translation quality, too.

3 Classification Approach

In this section we will introduce our classifier that employed word-alignment distribution as classification features.

3.1 Constructing a Classifier

We constructed a classifier with SVMs, well-known learning algorithms that have high generalization performance [13]. SVMs have an advantage that the algorithms do not depend on the number of classification features. We trained an SVM classifier by taking HTs as positive training examples and MTs as negative examples.

As our classifier is trained with parallel corpora, our method requires neither multiple reference HTs nor manually labeled training examples. Due to these properties, our method should be an inexpensive but effective automatic evaluation metric.

3.2 Classification Features

Literal translation often makes translation unnatural. This unnaturalness should be observed in any type of translation such as English-to-French translation, English-to-Japanese translation. Thus, a human translator used various translation techniques in order to exclude unnatural literal translation if necessary. By contrast, MT systems often provide literal translation even if non-literal translation is required. From viewpoint of system development, it is definitely useful to identify what sort of literal translation makes MTs distinct from HTs.

Let us illustrate such unnatural literal translation here. For instance, a human translator does not provide literal translation for an English nominal modifier "some" in the case of Japanese translation (1c). If the nominal modifier "some" is literally translated into Japanese, a Japanese nominal modifier "ikuraka-no (some)" comes up, as seen in (1b). Actually, the sentence (1b) was obtained with a state-of-the-art MT system.

(1)   a. Source Sentence: Some students came.
       b. MT: Ikuraka-no gakusei-wa ki-ta
          some-GEN student-TOP come-PST
          "Several students came".
       c. HT: Ki-ta   gakusei-mo i-ta
          come-PST student-also ex-ist-PST
          "Some students came".
       (GEN: Genitive case marker, TOP: Topic marker, PST: Past tense marker)

A translator does not provide the literal translation but conveys the meaning of the English nominal modifier with a Japanese existential verb "i-ta (existed)," as in (1c). Both the translations (1b) and (1c) are perfectly grammatical Japanese sentences, but some unnaturalness remains in (1b) due to the literal translation of "some."

To identify the unnatural literal translation, we decided to examine the word-alignment distribution between source sentences and translations, i.e., MTs or HTs. Literal translations maintain lexical properties such as parts of speech, whereas non-literal translations usually lack the parallel lexical properties. Hence, literal translation should be more easily aligned than non-literal translation. This hypothesis seems correct, as we observed MTs and HTs exhibited different word-alignment distributions in section 4.3.

The distinction of alignment distribution is illustrated in the example (2). Sentence (2a) is a source sentence for the word-for-word translation in (2b), i.e., MT, and the natural translation in (2c), i.e., HT.

(2)   a. Source Sentence: Today, the sun is shining.
       b. MT: Kyoo taiyoo-wa kagayai-teiru
          today the-sun-TOP shine-BE(ING)
          "Today the sun is shining".
       c. HT: Kyoo-wa seiten-da
          today-TOP fine-BE
          "It's fine today".
       (BE(ING): Gerundive verb form)

An alignment tool we used in the experiment provides alignment distributions for the example sentences (2) as in Table 1. Here, "align(A, B)" means that an English word "A" and a Japanese word "B" compose an aligned pair, "non-align_eng(C)" means that an English word "C" remains unaligned, and "non-align_jpn(D)" means that a Japanese word "D" remains un-aligned.

Table 1. Alignment distribution for MT (2b) and HT (2c)

	MT (2b)	HT (2c)
1	align(today, kyoo [today])	align(today, kyoo-wa [today-TOP])
2	align(is, teiru [BE-ING])	align(is, da [BE])
3	align(sun, taiyoo [sun])	nonalign_jpn(seiten [fine])
4	align(shining, kagayai [shine])	nonalign_eng(the)
5	nonalign_jpn(wa [TOP])	nonalign_eng(sun)
6	nonalign_eng(the)	nonalign_eng(shining)

From the alignment distribution in (2b) and (2c), we see that the ratio of alignment and non-alignment varies between MTs and HTs. MTs involve more aligned pairs, while HTs involve more non-aligned words. Thus, we consider that the distribution of aligned pairs might reflect MT-likeness, whereas that of non-aligned words could exhibit HT-likeness. Given this property, a word-alignment-based classification should reveal the literal translation properties of MTs.

As alignment distribution exhibits lexical properties of translation, we can add some other features indicating syntactic and discourse properties. However, the experimental results in the next section revealed that alignment distribution-based classification marked sufficiently high classification accuracy. Then, we will employ only alignment distribution as classification features in this paper.

4 Experiments

In this section we will describe our experiment design, and report experimental results.

4.1 Design

In this experiment, we assessed the validity of our evaluation method by examining whether the classification accuracy would depend on the fluency of translation. An adequate classification method should exhibit a low classification accuracy for "good (HT-like)" translation and a high accuracy for "bad (MT-like)" translation. Therefore, we examined the classification accuracy for translation fluency. In addition, we also investigated whether the classification accuracy was influenced by an alignment tool or an MT system. A previous study [4] used an alignment tool developed by Sharp [12]. This tool carries out alignment of (sets of) words using bilingual dictionary/thesaurus and dependency analysis. In order to investigate the influence on classification accuracy by alignment tools, we constructed two classifiers: one used a popular word alignment tool GIZA++ [14], and the other employed Sharp's tool, and compared the classification accuracy of these classifiers. We further investigated the evaluation properties of our method by comparing with an automatic evaluation method, i.e., METEOR. Since METEOR is an improved method of BLEU so as to perform sentence-level evaluation as well as text-level evaluation, we regarded it as an adequate candidate for this comparison.

4.2 Method

We constructed a classifier using a parallel corpus consisting of Reuters' news articles in English and their Japanese translations [15]. We chose this corpus, because the goal of our classifier is to evaluate English-to-Japanese machine translations. As far as we know, there is no publicly available evaluation data for English-to-Japanese machine translation.

Since some pairs of a source sentence and its translation appeared repeatedly in this corpus, the repeated translations were eliminated. Japanese translation of this corpus was taken as HTs. MTs were translation of English source sentences with three state-of-the-art translation systems commercially available in Japan. Consequently, we obtained three sets of translation data (henceforth MTa, MTb and MTc). Each set consisted of 25,800 sentences (12,900 HT and 12,900 MT sentences). Given the general circumstances of MT systems in Japan, these systems should basically adopt a rule-based translation method. However, some parts of the system might implement an example-based translation method.

From these sets of translation data, we derived word-alignment distributions between the source sentences and MTs/HTs, using word-alignment tools, i.e., GIZA++ [14] and Sharp's tool [12]. As a result, we got six types of word-alignment distribution data, i.e., MTa data, MTb data and MTc data. (henceforth, we refer to translation data with alignment distribution as MT data or as HT data). GIZA++ was trained with 12,900 HT and 12,900 MT sentences, and each parameter was assigned a default value. The alignment results consisted of the aligned pairs and non-aligned words. Each alignment instance was taken as a classification feature.

Machine learning was carried out with the TinySVM software [16]. The first order polynomial was taken as a type of kernel function, and the other settings were taken as default settings.

We randomly chose 500 sentences from MTa to examine the classification accuracy of our method for different qualities of translation. These sentences were assessed by three human evaluators (not the authors) whose native language was Japanese. The evaluators assessed both the adequacy and fluency of the sentences, and scored them on a scale from 1 to 4. The evaluation scores were determined with a median value of the scores among the evaluators. Adequacy is defined as to what extent a translated sentence conveys the meaning of the original sentence. Fluency is defined as the well-formedness of a translated sentence, which can be evaluated independently of adequacy.

The evaluation results are shown in Table2. From the results, we found that our MT data involved more problems with respect to the fluency, because more than half of translation was judged to be less fluent (the degrees 1-2). Given this translation property, we decided to examine the fluency of translation.

Table 2. Evaluation Results of MTs

| Degree | Fluency | | Adequacy | |
	N	Relative Frequency (%)	N	Relative Frequency (%)
1	184	38.6	66	13.2
2	208	41.6	177	35.4
3	90	18.0	150	30.0
4	18	3.6	107	21.4

4.3 Translation Data Properties

We examined the word-alignment distributions in MT data and HT data (12,900 sentences for each data). As Table 3 shows, all the MT data involved more aligned words in MTs than HTs. This tendency is observed in both GIZA++-based alignment and Sharp's tool-based alignment. We confirmed the statistic significance of the different alignment distributions between HT and MTs (p<0.05, Chi-square test). We further performed a multi analysis for both alignment tools. This analysis showed that the difference was significant (p< 0.05) between HT and all MTs. This result supports our hypothesis that MT and HT be distinguishable based on word-alignment distribution.

Table 3. Alignment distribution of HT and MT: GIZA++ (G) and Sharp's tool (S)

| Translation | N | | Aligned Pairs (%) | | Non-aligned Words (%) | |
	G	S	G	S	G	S
HT	428402	550851	40.8	24.1	59.2	75.9
MTa	422315	505119	59.0	35.7	41.0	64.3
MTb	414900	502942	57.7	37.1	42.3	62.9
MTc	412683	521049	62.1	36.4	37.9	63.6

4.4 Classification Accuracy

Supposing that machine translation system might affect the classification accuracy, we have examined whether the classification accuracy varies using the three different MT systems in constructing a classifier. In addition, we have compared the classification accuracy using both alignment tools, GIZA++ and Sharp's. These classifiers were constructed using both aligned pairs and non-aligned words as classification features. Before using GIZA++, we segmented Japanese sentences into words.

Table 4. Classification Accuracy (%)

Alignment Tools / MT systems	MTa	MTb	MTc
GIZA++	99.0	98.5	99.6
Sharp's	98.8	99.5	99.6

The classification accuracy for each MT data, i.e., MTa, MTb and MTc data, was examined in five-fold cross validation tests. Table 4 shows the mean classification accuracy for each test. Fairly high classification accuracy was observed in all the MT data and alignment tools. Hence we have concluded that our classification method is robust for MT systems and alignment tools.

4.5 Comparison with a Classifier Based on Syntactic Features

We evaluated our classification method by comparing with a baseline. We set a classifier using syntactic properties as a baseline, because some of the previous studies [1, 3] reviewed in section 2.1 employed the syntactic properties such as the branching properties of the parse tree. Therefore, we decided to compare our alignment-distribution-based classifier with a classifier based on syntactic properties, i.e., dependency relations.

Although this comparison is not so rigorous, we think the comparison can suggest that our method is valid. HTs and MTs were parsed with a Japanese dependency parser CaboCha [17]. The dependency relation between a modifier and a modified phrase was used as a classification feature. The classification accuracy of each MT data was 83.1% (MTa), 82.0% (MTb), and 83.3% (MTc). We set this classification accuracy as the baseline. Our method outperformed the baseline in all cases, exhibiting approximately 20% superiority. Based on these results, we concluded that our word-alignment-based classifiers more accurately distinguish MTs and HTs than dependency-relation-based classifiers.

4.6 Validity of Our Evaluation Method

We examined whether classification accuracy decreases for fluent translation. The classification accuracy was investigated in each fluency degree (1-4) of the evaluation results (500 sentences) as in Table 2. Our method judges a correctly classified translation as less fluent, whereas an incorrectly classified translation as fluent. In this experiment, we checked the classification results of the following classifiers: (i) a classifier based on aligned pairs, (ii) a classifier based on non-aligned words, and (iii) a classifier constructed with both aligned pairs and non-aligned words.

Decrease in classification accuracy was not observed in the classifiers (ii) and (iii). Due to the space limitation, we will omit the results of these classifiers (ii) and (iii). By contrast, classification accuracy decreased in the classifier (i). Table 5 and 6 show the classification accuracy of a GIZA++-based classifier and that of a Sharp's tool-based classifier, respectively. These tables show the number of sentences and the classification accuracy, i.e., the ratio of correctly classified translation (worse translation).

We applied Fisher's exact test to evaluate the statistical significance of the distribution of classification accuracy of these classifiers. Statistically significant difference was found in the classification of the GIZA++ (p=0.07) and in the classification of the Sharp's tool

Table 5. Fluency and Classification Accuracy: Aligned Pairs-based Classifier using GIZA++

Translation Fluency	Correct Classification	Incorrect Classification	Accuracy (%)
1	183	1	99.5
2	204	4	98.1
3	87	3	96.7
4	16	2	88.9

Table 6. Fluency and Classification Accuracy: Aligned Pairs-based Classifier using Sharp's

Translation Fluency	Correct Classification	Incorrect Classification	Accuracy (%)
1	176	8	95.7
2	198	10	95.2
3	78	12	86.7
4	10	8	55.6

($p<0.01$). As classification accuracy decreased in the both classifiers, we considered that there is no great difference between these two results. Thus, the classification accuracy of our evaluation method is expected to decrease between a pre-improved MT system and a post-improved MT system in the course of system development. Therefore, we have concluded that our method is valid for evaluating system improvement.

By comparing the evaluation results between the GIZA++-based method and the Sharp's tool-based method, we found that both methods marked the similar classification results for the influent translation, i.e., fluency degree 1. These methods, however, differed with respect to the evaluation results on the fluency degrees 4. Here, the GIZA++-based method regarded 11.1% of MTs as "good" translation, while the Sharp's tool-based method classified more MTs (44.4%) into "good" translation. Hence, if one has to detect fluent translation as much as possible, the Sharp's tool-based method fits the purpose.

We also found that the classification accuracy seemed independent of the fluency of translation when a classifier was constructed based on non-aligned words as classification features. Non-aligned words represent the distinction between MTs and HTs, while aligned pairs show the similarity of MTs and HTs. Hence, even the classifiers based on non-aligned words, i.e., (ii) and (iii), should have provided more "incorrect" classification for fluent translation. This unexpected result suggests that even fluent MTs should differ from HTs with respect to non-aligned words.

Following this idea, we investigated translation properties of fluent MTs and those of the relevant HTs. This investigation showed that HTs, unlike MTs, conveyed additional information that a source sentence did not literally conveyed. This additional information should be taken as unaligned words, because relevant information does not appear in a source sentence. Due to these non-aligned Japanese words for additional information, even fluent MTs could be judged as MT-like translation under our method. This additional information would result in an adverse effect on the classification based on non-aligned words.

Let us illustrate the explication of contextually salient meaning in HTs. The MT (3b) was evaluated as the highest fluency degree, and the classifiers using non-alignment words judged it as MT. The relevant HT (3c) involves additional information, which cannot be seen in the source sentence (3a). In the HT (3c), a human translator added some contextually salient information, and thus the translation involves additional expressions such as "market player" and "statistics." Since these additional expressions are regarded as non-aligned words, a classifier would distinguish the MT sentence (3b) from the HT sentence (3c).

(3)   a. Source Sentence: Most were expecting an improvement.
       b. MT: Dai-bubun-wa kaizen-o   yokisitei-ta
         most-part-TOP improvement-ACC predict-PST
       c. HT: Ookata-no sijyo-kankeisya-wa doo-toukei-no

Most-GEN market-player-TOP same-statistics-GEN
kaizen-o   yosoosite-iru
improvement-ACC predict-PRES
(ACC: Accusative Case marker, PRES: Present tense marker)

4.7 Property of Our Evaluation Method

Given the validity of our evaluation method, we compared our method with a publicly available metric METEOR, in order to examine the property of our evaluation criterion. We used the word-matching component of METEOR. The component is applicable to Japanese. Reference translation was made up of Japanese translation sentences of Reuters' news articles. Before using METEOR, we segmented Japanese sentences into words.

Our evaluation method is a binary classifier, which judges MTs as "good" (HT-like) or "bad" (MT-like) translation. On the other hand, METEOR determines the translation quality by computing the evaluation scores indicating translation quality as a result of the comparison of MTs with the relevant reference HTs. METEOR represents translation quality with scores ranging from 0.0 to 1.0. In order to compare METEOR with our method, we set a threshold on METEOR score, and we classified MTs into two groups: if a translation marked a higher score than the threshold, it would be judged as "good" translation, and vice versa. If we set a proper threshold between "good" and "bad" translations, the METEOR-based classification should properly classify MTs into the four degrees of fluency, as well as our classification-based method. Here, we set such a threshold for METEOR that the scores would yield as many statistically significant degrees as possible. In order to determine the threshold, we examined the classification results by setting a threshold in every 0.1 from 0.1 to 0.9.

The distribution was significantly different ($p < 0.05$) when the threshold was 0.4, 0.5, and 0.6. We further performed the residual analysis. This analysis showed that the difference was significant in three degrees (fluency degrees 2, 3, and 4) when the threshold was 0.4, and that the difference was significant in two degrees when the threshold was 0.5 and 0.6.

From these results, we decided to compare our classification method with the METEOR-based classification with the threshold 0.4. The classification result under the METEOR-based method is shown in Table 7. Table 7 shows the number of sentences whose METEOR scores were lower/higher than the threshold 0.4. The ratio indicates the rate of lower score sentences, and it parallels with the classification accuracy of our method. The result of the residual analysis for the classification is shown in Table 8.

By comparing the evaluation results between our method (Table 5 and 6) and the METEOR-based method (Table 7), we found that our classification differed from the METEOR-based classification with respect to the evaluation results on the fluency

Table 7. METEOR-based Evaluation (0.4)

Translation Fluency	Correct	Incorrect	Ratio (%)
1	126	58	68.5
2	143	65	68.7
3	42	48	46.7
4	6	12	33.3

Table 8. Residual Analysis Results for METEOR-based Evaluation (0.4)

Translation Fluency	Correct	Incorrect
1	1.80	-1.80
2	2.10*	-2.10*
3	-3.64*	3.64*
4	-2.70*	2.70*

degrees 1 and 4. While the METEOR-based method correctly classified 68.5% of MTs as "bad" translation in the degree 1, our method regarded most MTs (99.5%; 95.7%) as "bad" translation in the degree 1. Hence, if one must never overlook influent translation, our method fits the purpose.

In the case of fluency degree 4, the METEOR-based method regarded more MTs (66.7%) as "good" translation than our method (11.1%; 44.4%). Hence, if one is sure to evaluate fluent translation as fluent, the METEOR-based method is preferable. From this classification property, we found that our method and the METEOR-based method fit the different purposes for the evaluation.

5 Conclusion

We proposed an automatic method of evaluating MTs, which employed neither reference translations for evaluation of new translations nor manually labeled training data for constructing a classifier. Our evaluation metric classifies MTs into either "good" (HT-like) or "bad" (MT-like) translations. The classification is determined based on the word-alignment distributions between source sentences and translations. As we confirmed, the alignment distribution was different between HTs and MTs, and that the classification results depended on the translation quality. In addition, we examined our evaluation property, and found that HT-likeness was a strict evaluation criterion. Given these findings, we conclude that our method is an inexpensive and effective automatic evaluation metric for translation improvement.

This paper leaves several problems unsolved. First, we must examine the classification properties based on non-aligned words. As we saw, additional information in HTs might affect the classification judgment. We will examine the adverse effect from non-aligned words in more detail. Second, our method should be improved by comparing with the previously proposed evaluation method, or with the other classifiers employing the general linguistic features. Thirdly, we will examine our method in other languages, e.g., Chinese. Last but not least, we will examine our method for sentence level evaluation.

References

1. Corston-Oliver, S., Gamon, M., Brockett, C.: A machine Learning Approach to the Automatic Evaluation of Machine Translation. In: Proceedings of the 39th Annual Meeting of the Association for Computational Linguistics, Toulouse, France, pp. 148–155 (2001)
2. Kulesza, A., Shieber, S.M.: A Learning Approach to Improving Sentence-level MT Evaluation. In: Proceedings of the 10th International Conference on Theoretical and Methodological Issues in Machine Translation, Baltimore, Maryland, pp. 75–84 (2004)

3. Gamon, M., Aue, A., Smets, M.: Sentence-level MT Evaluation without Reference Translations: Beyond Language Modeling. In: Proceedings of the 10th European Association for Machine Translation Conference, Budapest, Hungary, pp. 103–111 (2005)
4. Kotani, K., Yoshimi, T., Kutsumi, T., Sata, I., Isahara, H.: A Classification Approach to Automatic Evaluation of Machine Translation Based on Word Alignment. In: Language Forum, vol. 34, pp. 153–168 (2008)
5. Papineni, K.A., Roukos, S., Ward, T., Zhu, W.-J.: Bleu: A Method for Automatic Evaluation of Machine Translation. Technical Report RC22176 (W0109–022). IBM Research Division, Thomas J. Watson Research Center (2001)
6. Doddington, G.: Automatic Evaluation of Machine Translation Quality Using N-gram Co-occurrence Statistics. In: Proceedings of the 2nd Human Language Technology Conference, San Diego, California, pp. 128–132 (2002)
7. Banerjee, S., Alon, L.: METEOR: An Automatic Metric for MT Evaluation with Improved Correlation with Human Judgments. In: Proceedings of the 43th Annual Meeting of the Association for Computational Linguistics, Ann Arbor, Michigan, pp. 65–72 (2005)
8. Quirk, C.B.: Training a Sentence-level Machine Translation Confidence Measure. In: Proceedings of the 4th International Conference on Language Resources and Evaluation, Lisbon, Portugal, pp. 825–828 (2004)
9. Albrecht, J.S., Hwa, R.: A Re-examination of Machine Learning Approaches for Sentence-level MT Evaluation. In: Proceedings of the 45th Annual Meeting of the Association for Computational Linguistics, Prague, Czech Republic, pp. 880–887 (2007)
10. Paul, M., Finch, A., Sumita, E.: Reducing Human Assessment of Machine Translation Quality to Binary Classifiers. In: Proceedings of the 11th International Conference on Theoretical and Methodological Issues in Machine Translation, Skövde, Sweden, pp. 154–162 (2007)
11. Quinlan, J.: C4.5: Programs for Machine Learning. Morgan Kaufmann, San Mateo (1992)
12. Whitelock, P., Poznanski, V.: The SLE Example-Based Translation System. In: Proceedings of the International Workshop on Spoken Language Translation, Kyoto, Japan, pp. 111–115 (2006)
13. Vapnik, V.: Statistical Learning Theory. Wiley Interscience, New York (1998)
14. Och, F.J., Ney, H.: A Systematic Comparison of Various Statistical Alignment Models. Computational Linguistics 29(1), 19–51 (2003)
15. Utiyama, M., Isahara, H.: Reliable Measures for Aligning Japanese-English News Articles and Sentences. In: Proceedings of the 41st Annual Meeting of the Association for Computational Linguistics, Sapporo, Japan, pp. 72–79 (2003)
16. TinySVM, http://chasen.org/~taku/software/TinySVM/
17. CaboCha, http://chasen.org/~taku/software/cabocha/

Lexicalized Syntactic Reordering Framework for Word Alignment and Machine Translation

Chung-chi Huang, Wei-teh Chen, and Jason S. Chang

Institute of Information Systems and Application, National Tsing Hua University,
Hsinchu, Taiwan 300
{u901571,weitehchen,jason.jschang}@gmail.com

Abstract. We propose a lexicalized syntactic reordering framework for cross-language word aligning and translating researches. In this framework, we first flatten hierarchical source-language parse trees into syntactically-motivated linear string representations, which can easily be input to many feature-like probabilistic models. During model training, these string representations accompanied with target-language word alignment information are leveraged to learn systematic similarities and differences in languages' grammars. At run-time, syntactic constituents of source-language parse trees will be reordered according to automatically acquired lexicalized reordering rules in previous step, to closer match word orientations of the target language. Empirical results show that, as a preprocessing component, bilingual word aligning and translating tasks benefit from our reordering methodology.

Keywords: word alignment, machine translation, phrase-based decoder and syntactic reordering rule.

1 Introduction

Researchers have long believed that syntactic analyses of languages will improve natural language processing tasks, such as semantic understanding, word alignment and machine translation. In cross-lingual applications, much work has explicitly introduced grammars/models to describe/capture languages' structural divergences.

[1] is one of the pioneering researches in ordering corresponding grammatical constituents of two languages. Wu devises binary Inversion Transduction Grammar (ITG) rules to accommodate similar (in order) and different (reverse order) word orientations in synchronous bilingual parsing. The constraint imposed by Wu's straight and inverted binary branching rules is better than IBM one without syntactic insights in terms of machine translation (see [2]). On the other hand, [3], given source-language (SL) production rules of arbitrary length, utilizes EM algorithm to distinguish statistically more probable reordered grammatical sequences in target-language (TL) end from others. Recently, ever since Chiang's hierarchical phrase-based machine translation model [4], successfully integrating bilingual grammar-like rewrite rules into MT, more and more researchers have devoted themselves to syntax-based MT system: [5], [6], and [7].

W. Li and D. Mollá-Aliod (Eds.): ICCPOL 2009, LNAI 5459, pp. 103–111, 2009.

Syntactic reordering plays a vital role for modeling languages' preferences in word order in above grammatically motivated systems and has been proved to be quite effective in translation. In [8], they manually craft reordering rules concerning some characteristic differences of SL and TL word orders. These rules are aimed to reorder SL sentences such that new sequences of words better match their TL counterparts. Although better translation quality is obtained, two issues are worth mentioning: there might be exceptions to reordering rules with coarse-grained grammatical labels and their reordering rules are not automatically learnt. To address these issues, in this paper, we propose a framework which automatically acquires lexicalized reordering rules based on a parallel corpus.

The reminder of this paper is organized as follows. Section 2 discusses the reordering framework in detail. Section 3 shows the data sets used and experimental results. At last, Section 4 concludes this paper.

2 Reordering Framework

In this section, we begin with an example to illustrate how lexicalized reordering rules can have positive influence on word aligning and machine translating quality. Thereafter, we elaborate on the proposed automatic reordering framework.

2.1 An Example

Consider an English sentence "After the meeting, Mr. Chang went straight home" and its Mandarin Chinese translation "會議 後 ， 張 先生 直接 回 家". Figure 1 shows the parse tree of the English sentence (we can ignore the '·' between English words for now), and correspondence links between the English words and their Mandarin counterparts.

In Figure 1, there are three crossings among the word alignment links, indicating three instances of reversing of some syntactic constituents during translation process. The first crossing involves the reversal of a prepositional/subordinating word and a

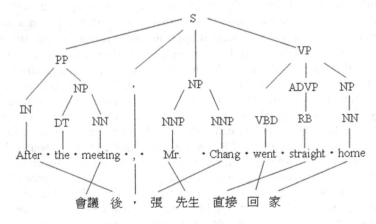

Fig. 1. An example sentence pair

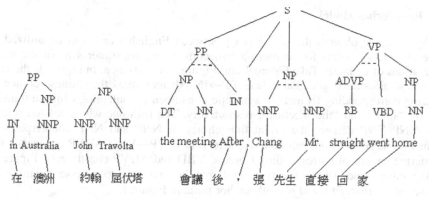

Fig. 2. Counterexamples   **Fig. 3.** Reordered tree with Chinese sentence

noun phrase. The example may lead us to conclude that we should invert all prepositional phrases when encountering IN and NP constituents. However, as indicated by
the counterexample in Figure 2, the reversal of IN and NP under PP does not exist
when the lexical item of IN is "in", and syntactic information alone is not sufficient to
make such a reordering decision, especially, presented with a coarse-grained grammatical label set. Instead, we further need lexical cues of the IN syntactic constituent
(i.e., "after" and "in"). Accompanied with the lexicalized information, we have higher
chance to recognize that, contrast to English, in Chinese, temporal subordinating
conjunctions always appear after the noun phrase. Similarly, for the second crossing,
we need to examine the corresponding word of the first NNP of a proper noun since a
title word (e.g., "President", "Professor", "Mr." and so on) has different ordering
preference in Chinese, compared with the first NNP, proper noun (i.e., John), in Figure 2. [9] and [10] also point out the importance of lexical items in determining word
orders from one language to another.

Encouragingly, it is straightforward to incorporate lexical information into synchronous context-free grammar rules such as ITG rules. Table 1 shows the lexicalized
syntactic reordering rules that apply for the sentence pair in Figure 1. We follow Wu's
notation in [1] by using pointed bracket to depict the inverted order of the corresponding syntactic constituents in two languages and the English words enclosed in parentheses are lexical cues for the constituents. Intuitively, by learning the reordering rules
shown in Table 1, we can easily transform the English tree in Figure 1 into one in
Figure 3, where the horizontal dashed lines imply the subtrees had been inversely
reordered. Note that such reordering rules capture languages' divergences, thus potentially conducive to word alignment and translation.

Table 1. Lexicalized reordering rules

PP→ <IN (After) NP>
NP→ <NNP (Mr.) NNP>
VP→ <VBD ADVP>

2.2 Reordering Model

In Figure 1, we observe that the dots (·) between English words can be utilized to represent anchor points for reordering two consecutive constituents to fit the word orientations of Chinese. Take Figure 1 and Figure 3 for instance. In Figure 1, the first dot whose associated grammar rule is PP→IN NP represents the Chinese choice in ordering corresponding IN and NP syntactic constituents, containing Chinese transla- tion of "after" and "the meeting", respectively. The fifth one whose related rule is NP→NNP NNP denotes the orientation choice of NNP and NNP counterparts in Chinese; The seventh one whose associated rule is VP→VBD ADVP represents the reordering anchor of corresponding Chinese VBD and ADVP constituents. Figure 3, on the other hand, shows the reordered tree by choosing to reverse neighboring phrases of the first, fifth and seventh anchor point in Figure 1.

Mathematically, given a SL parse tree π, reordering models search for π^*, satisfying $\arg\max_{\pi'} \Pr(\pi'|\pi,\lambda)$ where λ is the set of system parameters to make syntactically reshuffled π^* more in tune with grammar in target language. In this paper, by using tree- to-string transformation algorithm illustrated below, we first transform the parse tree π into a string representation s with syntactic information encoded in the artificial anchor points denoted by '·'. Then, the problem of searching for most probable transformed tree (π^*) can be recast as one of finding best (linear) reordering label sequence for anchor points in s. In other words, provided with the representation s and the system parameter set $\lambda = \{\lambda_j\}$, our model looks for the most likely reordering label sequence y^*

$$y^* = \arg\max_y p(y|s,\lambda) = \arg\max_y \frac{1}{z(s)} \exp\left(\sum_j \lambda_j F_j(y,s)\right). \tag{1}$$

where $z(s)$ is a normalization factor and λ_j is the weight of the syntactic feature func- tion F_j. Equation (1) is in line with the conditional nature of conditional random fields. Therefore, we feed the SL string into the probabilistic sequential labeler of conditional random fields (CRFs) to find the best label sequence, upon which most probable reordered tree are based.

Tree-to-String Transformation Algorithm
Input: source-language sentence e and its parse tree π
Output: string representation s
INSERT '·' between words in e // as reordering anchor points
FOR each word w IN e
   IF w is '·'
   Lw=the word immediate to the left of the · in e
   Rw=the word immediate to the right of the · in e
   Along π, find the closest common ancestor node P for words Lw and Rw
   LHS=the immediate descendent of node P along the path from P to Lw in π
   RHS=the immediate descendent of node P along the path from P to Rw in π
      ASSOCIATE the grammatical rule P→LHS RHS, Lw, and Rw WITH this dot
         and ROCORD this information IN s
OUTPUT s

Table 2. String representation of tree in Figure 1

Dot	P	LHS	Lw	RHS	Rw
$\cdot_1$	PP	IN	After	NP	the
$\cdot_2$	NP	DT	the	NN	meeting
$\cdot_3$	S	PP	meeting	,	,
$\cdot_4$	S	,	,	NP	Mr.
$\cdot_5$	NP	NNP	Mr.	NNP	Chang
$\cdot_6$	S	NP	Chang	VP	went
$\cdot_7$	VP	VBD	went	ADVP	straight
$\cdot_8$	VP	ADVP	straight	NP	home

Table 2 summarizes the content derived from abovementioned transformation algorithm on the parse tree of Figure 1 and this information will be fed to CRFs to determine the reordering tag (in order or inversion) of the anchor points. In Table 2, **dot**
column stands for artificial anchor points in SL sentence, **Lw** and **Rw** for previous
word and successive word of the current one respectively, and **P, LHS, Lw, RHS** and
Rw constitute the syntactic reordering features of our model. Notice that, inspired by
[1] and [11], we assume SL parse trees are binarized before fed into the tree-to-string
transformation algorithm. [1] suggests binary-branching ITG rules prune seemingly
unlikely and arbitrary word permutations but yet, at the same time, accommodate most
meaningful structural reversals during translation. In [11] binarization process is reported to be beneficial to machine translation in terms of quality and speed. Therefore,
in this paper we focus on reorderings of binary trees which can be obtained by binary
syntactic parsers (e.g., Berkeley Parser) or by following the binarizing process in [11].

If, during training, probabilistic CRFs always observe inversion of the grammar rule
PP→IN NP especially with lexical "after" presenting in Lw field, and straight order of
the rule S→NP VP, CRFs model will tag the first dot as I (for inversion) and tag the sixth
as S (for straightness). Moreover, if the reordering tag of every dot is correctly determined, the SL parse tree in Figure 1 will be successfully reordered into one in Figure 3,
which abides by grammatical ordering preferences in the target language (e.g., Chinese).

Our framework leverages CRFs to train the weights of the feature functions related
to syntactic labels, syntactic rules, and lexical items provided by our tree-to-string
transformation procedure, and, at runtime, brings SL parse trees closer to TL word
order by applying lexicalized reordering grammar rules or pure grammatical rules.
Which type to choose is informed by highly-tuned feature weights in CRFs training.

2.3 Training Process of CRFs

To gain insights on how to order the corresponding SL syntactic constituents in the target
language, SL sentences are aligned to TL sentences at word level and are monolingually
parsed by some existing parser. Furthermore, based on word alignment results, firstly, the
minimum/maximum word position on target language end that SL part-of-speech tags
can cover is determined, i.e. TL spans of SL POS tags, and then the TL spans are iteratively obtained in bottom-up fashion. In the end, parse trees contain not only monolingual
grammatical labels but also bilingual information concerning the TL span of each SL tree
node, on which we work to differentiate dissimilar word ordering preferences in the two
languages from similar ones. The training process is outlined as below.

Training Procedure

Input: a sentence-aligned corpus C={(e,f)}, a word aligner *WA*, a source language parser *Par*, and a CRFs implementation *crf*

Output: system parameters of our reordering model λ

APPLY *WA* on the corpus **C** to obtain word alignment

PARSE source-language end of **C** by use of *Par*

FOR each sentence pair (e,f) IN **C**

    DENOTE π as the parse tree of e, π (*pos*) as the part-of-speech nodes in π and π (*nonT*) as the syntactic (non-terminal) nodes in π excluding nodes in π (*pos*)

    FOR each node n IN π (*pos*)

    span(n)=from min(aligned positions on TL side of n) to max(aligned positions on TL side of n)

    FOR each node n IN π (*nonT*)

    span(n)=from min(aligned positions on TL side of n's children) to max(aligned positions on TL side of n's children)

    APPLY tree-to-string transformation algorithm on e and π to obtain their string representation s

    FOR each dot d IN s

      IF span(d's LHS) <[1] span(d's RHS)

      APPEND the orientation tag 'S' to d // straight order

      IF span(d's LHS) >[2] span(d's RHS)

      APPEND the orientation tag 'I' to d // inverted order

After collecting all the string representations with ordering information, we train *crf* to determine the weights λ associated with chosen syntactic feature functions.

Take sentence pair in Figure 1 for example. The TL-end span of each label in the parse tree and the string representation with orientation information are shown in Figure 4 and in Table 3 respectively. String representations with orientation information of sentences are leverage to tune the system weights $\lambda=\{\lambda_j\}$. The weights reflect the contribution of lexical or syntactic items in determining TL word orders of a specific SL context (e.g., PP→ <IN (After) NP (the)>).

Table 3. String representation with ordering tags

Dot	P	LHS	RHS	Order
.1	PP	IN	NP	I
.2	NP	DT	NN	S[3]
.3	S	PP	,	S
.4	S	,	NP	S
.5	NP	NNP	NNP	I
.6	S	NP	VP	S
.7	VP	VBD	ADVP	I
.8	VP	ADVP	NP	S

---

[1] The min index of span of the second operand is larger than the max index of the first one.

[2] The min index of span of the first operand is larger than the max index of the second one.

[3] Intuitively, if one of the spans is NULL, straight order is adopted.

span(IN)=from 2 to 2
span(DT)=NULL
span(NN)=from 1 to 1
span(,)=from 3 to 3
span(NNP-Mr.)=from 5 to 5
span(NNP-Chang)=from 4 to 4
span(VBD)=from 7 to 7
span(RB)=from 6 to 6
span(NN)=from 8 to 8
span(NP-the meeting)=from 1 to 1
span(NP-Mr. Chang)=from 4 to 5
span(ADVP)=from 6 to 6
span(NP-home)=from 8 to 8
span(PP)=from 1 to 2
span(VP)=from 6 to 8
span(S)=from 1 to 8

Fig. 4. TL-end span of each label

3 Experiments

We start with the data sets and settings we used in experiments. Afterwards, we evaluate the impact our reordering framework has on performance of bilingual word alignment and machine translation.

3.1 Data Sets and Experimental Settings

We used the first 200,000 sentence pairs of the news portion of Hong Kong Parallel Text as our parallel corpus **C**. A MT testing data set, composed of 1035 English sentences of average 28 words randomly chosen from Hong Kong news[4] (excluding sentences in **C**), was allocated. The corresponding Chinese sentences made up of its reference translation set, that is, one reference translation per English sentence. Moreover, the English sentences in both training and testing sets were syntactically parsed by Berkeley parser[5] beforehand.

We employed CRF++[6] as the implementation of probabilistic conditional random fields to construct the proposed syntactic reordering framework. During CRFs' parameters training (Section 2.3), we deployed GIZA++ as the word aligner. Besides, to make CRF++ more accurately learn ordering choices of two languages in syntactic constituents, sentence pairs in **C** would *not* be utilized if the word alignment rate of content words (nouns, verbs and adjectives) on English end was lower than 0.8 or the

---

[4] The news portion of Hong Kong Parallel Text.
[5] http://nlp.cs.berkeley.edu/Main.html
[6] It is freely distributed in http://crfpp.sourceforge.net/

length of the English sentence was shorter than 20. In other words, CRF++ was dedicated to search for significant lexicalized or non-lexicalized reordering rules from highly-aligned and potentially long-range distorted sentence pairs. After filtering, approximately 23,000 parallel sentences of C were retained to tune CRF++.

At runtime translation, on the other hand, our framework exploited Pharaoh ([12]) as the phrase-based MT decoder. The language model Pharaoh needs was trained on the Chinese part of the whole Hong Kong news, 739,919 sentences in total, using SRI language modeling toolkit, while phrase translation table was built upon C after word aligned using GIZA++.

3.2 Evaluation

We are interested in examining whether our methodology captures meaningful syntactic relationships between the source and target languages, thus boosting the accuracy in word alignment and decoding. We experimented different ways of introducing source sentence reordering to the phrase-based machine translation system (i.e., Pharaoh). First, we performed word alignment on the original and reordered source sentences to derive two sorts of phrase translation table used in MT decoder. Then decoder was run on the unaltered test sentences as well as reordered test sentences. Therefore, there are four sets of translation results where the source sentences in the training data and test data are either unaltered or reordered. The translation quality using these four data sets was measured by BLEU scores ([13]) and summarized in a contingency matrix in Table 4.

Table 4. Results of translation quality

	original training data	reordered training data
original testing data	23.43	24.16
reordered testing data	24.76	25.71

As suggested by Table 4, when using the reordered sentences to perform word alignment and decoding, the translation quality improved by more than 0.7 BLEU point. If we left the training data unchanged and simply reordered the test sentences, we get a significant improvement of 1.3 BLEU points over translating the original test sentences. One can find that test sentence reordering resulted in greater improvement (6% relative) over training sentence reordering (3% relative). There might be two reasons for this difference. Firstly, our result is consistent with the observation presented by [14]: it is, sometimes, difficult to propagate improvements in word alignment to translation. Additionally, GIZA++, a word aligner modeling distortion in languages, is much more capable of capturing distortion of words than Pharaoh, a decoder exhibiting global reordering problems. As a result, there were about 3% improvement gap between these two different settings of data sets.

Encouragingly, if both the training and test sentences were pre-reordered, our method outperformed baseline by more than 2 BLEU points. Overall, it is safe to say that our automated reordering framework improves translation quality for disparate language pair such as English and Chinese.

4 Conclusion and Future Work

This paper has introduced a syntactic reordering framework which automatically learns reordering rules from a parallel corpus using conditional random fields. In experiments, these reordering rules, if necessary, accompanied with lexical information, are proved to be conducive to relieving the pressure of distortion modeling off word aligners and MT systems alike.

As for future work, we would like to examine whether integrating more syntactic features (e.g. the height of a tree node, the head of the phrase and etc.) into the framework further boosts the performance. We also like to inspect the performance of our methodology in other distantly-related language pairs such as English and Arabic.

References

1. Wu, D.: Stochastic inversion transduction grammars and bilingual parsing of parallel corpora. Computational Linguistics 23(3), 377–403 (1997)
2. Zens, R., Ney, H.: A comparative study on reordering constraints in statistical machine translation. In: ACL, pp. 144–151 (2003)
3. Yamada, K., Knight, K.: A syntax-based statistical translation model. In: ACL, pp. 523–530 (2001)
4. Chiang, D.: A hierarchical phrase-based model for statistical machine translation. In: ACL, pp. 263–270 (2005)
5. Galley, M., Graehl, J., Knight, K., Marcu, D., DeNeefe, S., Wang, W., Thayer, I.: Scalable Inference and Training of Context-Rich Syntactic Translation Models. In: ACL, pp. 961–968 (2006)
6. Zhang, D., Li, M., Li, C.-h., Zhou, M.: Phrase reordering model integrating syntactic knowledge for SMT. In: EMNLP/CoNLL, pp. 533–540 (2007)
7. Liu, Y., Huang, Y., Liu, Q., Lin, S.: Forest-to-string statistical translation rules. In: ACL, pp. 704–711 (2007)
8. Wang, C., Collins, M., Koehn, P.: Chinese syntactic reordering for statistical machine translation. In: EMNLP/CoNLL, pp. 737–745 (2007)
9. Xiong, D., Liu, Q., Lin, S.: Maximum entropy based phrase reordering model for statistical machine translation. In: ACL/COLING, pp. 521–528 (2006)
10. Zhang, H., Gildea, D.: Stochastic lexicalized inversion transduction grammar for alignment. In: ACL, pp. 475–482 (2005)
11. Zhang, H., Huang, L., Gildea, D., Knight, K.: Synchronous binarization for machine translation. In: NAACL/HLT, pp. 256–263 (2006)
12. Koehn, P., Och, F., Marcu, D.: Statistical phrase-based translation. In: NAACL/HLT, pp. 48–54 (2003)
13. Papineni, K., Roukos, S., Ward, T., Zhu, W.-j.: BLEU: a method for automatic evaluation of machine translation. In: ACL, pp. 311–318 (2002)
14. Ayan, N.F., Dorr, B.J.: Going beyond AER: an extensive analysis of word alignments and their impact on MT. In: ACL, pp. 9–16 (2006)

Found in Translation: Conveying Subjectivity of a Lexicon of One Language into Another Using a Bilingual Dictionary and a Link Analysis Algorithm

Jungi Kim, Hun-Young Jung, Sang-Hyob Nam, Yeha Lee, and Jong-Hyeok Lee

Division of Electrical and Computer Engineering
Pohang University of Science and Technology
San 31, Hyoja-Dong, Nam-Gu, Pohang, 790–784, Republic of Korea
{yangpa,blesshy,namsang,sion,jhlee}@postech.ac.kr

Abstract. This paper proposes a method that automatically creates a subjectivity lexicon in a new language using a subjectivity lexicon in a resource–rich language with only a bilingual dictionary. We resolve some of the difficulties in selecting appropriate senses when translating lexicon, and present a framework that sequentially applies an iterative link analysis algorithm to enhance the quality of lexicons of both the source and target languages. The experimental results have empirically shown to improve the subjectivity lexicon in the source language as well as create a good quality lexicon in a new language.

Keywords: Opinion Analysis, Sentiment Lexicon, Lexicon Translation.

1 Introduction

With the recent pursuit of study in subjectivity analysis tasks such as sentiment classification, opinion holder extraction, and opinion summarization, much research effort has been spent on automating such tasks using various natural language processing approaches. Most previous researches, from constructing language resources [1,2,3,4,5,6,7,8] and sentiment analysis [9,10,11,12] to a variety of applications [13,14,15], have targeted English language only, and naturally many language resources in subjectivity analysis have been created in English.

While a number of languages such as Japanese, Chinese, and German are directly employed in recent studies [16,17,18], some works [19,12] have explored utilizing language resources in English to develop language resources and subjectivity analysis tools in other languages.

Motivated by the latter approach, this paper presents a method for automatically creating a subjectivity lexicon in a new language using a subjectivity lexicon in a resource–rich language with the aids of 1) a bilingual dictionary of the two languages for translating the lexicon and 2) a link analysis algorithm for refining the relative rankings of the entries in the new lexicon, as well as the original lexicon. Translating subjectivity lexicon using a bilingual dictionary

W. Li and D. Mollá-Aliod (Eds.): ICCPOL 2009, LNAI 5459, pp. 112–121, 2009.

faces several problems [12]: processing the inflected forms of entries without loosing its subjective meaning, translating multi–word entries in the dictionary, and selecting the correct sense to translate among many candidates in an entry. Of the challenges mentioned, we address the problem of handling various senses in an entry, while leaving the rest as future work. Link analysis models have shown successful results in its recent applications to NLP tasks [11,8]. Especially, [8] constructed a graph of WordNet synsets using glosses to create edges among the synsets, and learn opinion–related properties (ORPs) of synsets using PageRank, a popular random–walk model widely used in web searches, that ranks all the WordNet synsets in the graph according to the evidences collected from its neighbors. The approach has shown to discern the ORPs of the synsets more accurately, especially when given an appropriate initial ORP value of the synsets. Adapting a similar framework, we have created a bipartite graph of lexicon entries, with entries of one language forming a cluster and the other language another, and applied a link analysis algorithm that is similar to both PageRank and HITS. The details of our link analysis model will be discussed in Section 3.2 of this paper.

Our work focuses on creating a subjectivity lexicon in Korean utilizing subjectivity lexicons in English; Korean is a relatively understudied language in subjectivity analysis, and it is in urgent need of resources to jump–start its study. However, our work does not rely on any language–specific information but only requires a bilingual dictionary between the source and the target languages, making it easily applicable to other language pairs.

2 Related Work

Various subjectivity lexicons have been used in many subjectivity analysis tasks. Some lexicons are manually created [20,21,14] while others are the outcomes of the research efforts on automatically learning subjectivity from dictionary and thesaurus [3,13,9,5,12,5,7,8] or raw corpus [1,2,17].

There also has been efforts to utilize the language resources created in English for analyzing the subjectivity in other languages; although in very limited fashion, [19] are first to use English resources in German sentiment analysis, by translating a German e–mail into English, then applying English sentiment classifiers to the translated text. [12] was the first genuine multilingual work in subjectivity analysis, in which subjectivity analysis resources developed for English are used for developing resources in Romanian, by translating the subjectivity lexicon and creating a subjectivity corpus through projection using a parallel corpus between English and Romanian and a subjectivity classifier in English. Similar to the approach in [12], our work directly translates the subjectivity lexicon in English to a target language. However, while they use a naive translation approach namely choosing the first sense of the translation candidates because dictionaries list the senses in order of the common usages hence the first sense being the most probable one, our work focuses on how to reduce the ambiguity errors while still maintaining a good number of translations.

[8] uses a graph representation of WordNet synsets and a random–walk model to simulate the dynamics of the vertices that have similar ORPs. While [8] obtains the clues for the edges from glosses of WordNet entries, our work creates more secure and reliable edges between vertices exploiting the bilingual dictionary such that a foreign word being the direct translation of a source word creates an edge between the two words.

3   Learning Subjectivity Lexicon

To create a subjectivity lexicon in Korean using an English subjectivity lexicon, we adopt a two step approach; first, translate the English lexicon into Korean using a bilingual dictionary, then refine the resulting lexicon using a link analysis model.

Subjectivity lexicons vary in what information (*subjective/objective, positive/negative*) is tagged on which level of lexicon entries (word, POS–tagged word, sense) and how their strengths are measured (*weak/strong*, probability score (0.0 ∼ 1.0)). We assume that our English subjectivity lexicon contains English words with POS tags and sentiment orientation with some measure of its strength (e.g. {abandon, verb, weak negative}, or {harm, verb, positive 0.0, negative 0.5, neutral 0.5}), and the Korean subjectivity lexicon in similar format. However, our method could also be used to learn not only sentiment orientation but any ORPs whose strengths can be numerically transformed into scores to be used within our link analysis model.

3.1   Translating Subjectivity Lexicon

Translating a subjectivity lexicon into another language using a bilingual dictionary is a very challenging task. Much of the subjective meaning of a lexicon can be lost when translating words that have different subjectivity in inflected forms, there are many multi–words that are not listed in the bilingual dictionary, and there are words that have various senses and different subjectivity associated with them [12].

[12] relies on a heuristic method that translates only the first sense, since bilingual dictionaries usually order the translations such that more frequently used senses are listed before the less frequently used ones. Such a scheme would probably result in a lexicon with better quality in the sense of conveying subjectivity. However, it also reduces the size of the translated lexicon, limiting its application usages.

We present several naive heuristics that have different effects on the size and quality of the resulting lexicon, in a belief that a more sophisticated heuristic would result in creating a lexicon with higher quality while maintaining a good number of entries. We assume that for each English word and its POS, our bilingual dictionary has multiple senses, with its rank in the reverse order of the usage frequency, and each sense also containing a number of translation candidates, whose rank is also ordered in reverse of its usage frequency.

First Word (FW). This approach assigns the sentiment scores of the English word to only the first word of the first sense. This translation scheme filters uncertain candidates, the size of the resulting lexicon being the smallest.

First Sense (FS). The approach taken in **FS** is similar to the one used in [12]. All the words in the first sense are assigned the sentiment scores of the English word, implying that different translation words with the same sense are equally likely to be translated.

All Senses (AS). AS assigns the sentiment scores of the English word to all the words in its translation candidates. This scheme produces the maximum number of Korean words, allowing unreliable words in the lexicon.

Sense Rank (SR). Korean words are assigned different scores by their sense ranks; words with higher sense ranks are assigned high sentiment scores, and vice versa. A simple formula of $\frac{NumSenses(w_e) - SenseRank(w_e) + 1}{NumSenses(w_e)}$ is used.

Although these heuristics are very simple, they effectively control the size and reliability of the final translated lexicon, allowing us to observe the quality of the resulting lexicons in the evaluation process.

3.2   Refining the Lexicon with a Link Analysis Algorithm

Similarly to [8], our approach uses a graph built from the words with ORPs as vertices, and the relations among the words as edges connecting the vertices. While [8] used gloss of WordNet synsets to create some semantic relations among the synsets, with the hypothesis that gloss of a synset will usually contain terms belonging to synsets with similar ORPs, our approach utilizes the bilingual dictionary so that nodes connected by edges are direct translations of each other. These types of edges are more suited for building a much more semantically tight graph structure than the one using synset glosses.

Naturally, edges of direct translations connect English words to Korean words only, and Korean words only to English words. This type of graph is called a bipartite graph, where vertices are partitioned into two disjoint sets with no edges connecting any two vertices in the same set.

HITS is a link analysis algorithm that rates vertices of a graph by determining their "hubness" (connectedness to vertices with high "authoritativeness") and "authoritativeness" (connectedness to vertices with high "hubness") values, iteratively and recursively computing the centrality of a vertex within the graph structure [22].

Considering the hubness of an English vertex as its sentiment score, and a authoritativeness of a Korean vertex as the vertex with connectedness to English vertices with high hubness, HITS algorithm applied to the bipartite graph of bilingual dictionary entries can effectively learn the refined sentiment scores of a Korean lexicon, given that English lexicon holds its hubness in the process of learning the authoritativeness of Korean lexicon. Since the sentiment (authoritativeness) scores of a Korean lexicon are not reliable in the initial iterations of the algorithm, it is necessary to lower the variability of the hubness scores of English lexicon while raising the variability of authoritativeness when learning the sentiment scores of a Korean lexicon. Damping factor in PageRank algorithm [23] has similar effects on variability of the graph structure. The prior knowledge from English sentiment lexicon and its translation to Korean provides good candidates for prior scores (referred to as *internal source* in [8], e_k and e_e in equation 1).

Combining the ideas results in equation 1 where $TC(w)$ is the set of translation candidates of a word w, α and β are damping factors for Korean and English vertices.

$$AUTH(w_k) = (1 - \alpha) * e_k + \alpha * \sum_{w_e \in TC(w_k)} HUB(w_e),$$

$$HUB(w_e) = (1 - \beta) * e_e + \beta * \sum_{w_k \in TC(w_e)} AUTH(w_k) \qquad (1)$$

Larger α indicates higher variability of authoritativeness of Korean vertices, that hubness of English vertices are trustworthy and actively affect the authoritativeness of Korean vertices, and vice versa for β.

Once the sentiment scores of a Korean lexicon is refined, the sentiment scores of Korean and English lexicons can be re–learned using the same algorithm to maximize the quality of the English lexicon as well, using the equation 2.

$$AUTH(W_e) = (1 - \alpha) * e_e + \alpha * \sum_{W_k \in TC(W_e)} HUB(W_k),$$

$$HUB(W_k) = (1 - \beta) * e_k + \beta * \sum_{W_e \in TC(W_k)} AUTH(W_e) \qquad (2)$$

In summary, refining the subjectivity lexicons in English and Korean is carried out on our two phase link analysis framework: first, running HITS with Korean words as "authorities" and English words as "hubs" to learn the authoritativeness of Korean words, and secondly, running HITS again with English words as "authorities" and Korean words as "hubs" to re–learn the authoritativeness of English words. The link analysis model in each phase should take different values for α and β to adjust the variability of vertices accordingly.

Our framework runs on positive and negative sentiment independently, producing separate rankings of lexicons for positive and negative sentiment scores.

4   Experiments

4.1   Setup

The English lexicons we use in our experiments are the subjectivity lexicon used in OpinionFinder (**OF**) [10][1] and SentiWordNet 1.0.1 (**SentiWN**) [7][2].

---

[1] http://www.cs.pitt.edu/mpqa/
[2] http://sentiwordnet.isti.cnr.it/

OF is a set of English words and sentiment annotations collected from a number of sources of which some are manually developed while others automatically gathered. Each word in **OF** has a POS tag and categories of *Positive/Negative* and *Weak/Strong*. *Weak* subjectivity words were assigned the score of 0.5, and *Strong* words with 1.0.

SentiWN is a set of WordNet synsets with automatically assigned positive, negative, and neutral probability scores. In our experiments, each word in a synset is treated separately with the sentiment scores of the synset as its own, ignoring the synonym information provided by WordNet synsets.

We use an online bilingual dictionary provided by a portal website[3]. For our experiments, a total of $63,001$ English entries were accessed, corresponding to $142,791$ translated words in Korean.

Using different translation schemes in section 3.1, both English lexicons are translated into Korean. The link analysis algorithm in section 3.2 is then tested with various sets of initial scores: uniform weight **UW** ($\frac{1}{\lceil NumberofVertices\rceil}$), and every combination of English lexicons (**OF** and **SentiWN**) translation schemes (**FW, FS, AS,** and **SR**).

The parameters α and β in equations 1 and 2 are optimized on a held–out data using values from 0.1 to 0.9 with a step of 0.1.

4.2   Evaluation Method

We followed the evaluation scheme in [8], which uses a Micro–WNOp corpus [24][4] as a gold standard and the *p–normalized Kendall τ distance* (τ_p) [25] as the evaluation measure.

Micro–WNOp is a subset of WordNet that are tagged with ORPs by the number of English majoring MSc students. Divided into three sections (*Common, Group1, Group2*), each section contains a number of synsets with its positive and negative scores. For our research, we use *Group1* as a held–out data and *Group2* as a test data. We extract one positive and one negative scores by averaging all scores of evaluators. For optimizing and evaluating Korean subjectivity lexicon, 496 synsets in *Group1* and 499 synsets in *Group2* of Micro–WNOp was translated into Korean by a knowledgeable evaluator, fluent both in English and Korean. Korean words not appearing in any of the lexicons in our experiments were removed, resulting in 87 words and their associated sentiment scores as the gold standard.

The *p–normalized Kendall τ distance* is a measure of how much two ranked lists of items agree with each other. Given a set of items $\{o_1...o_n\}$, all possible pairs of items are tested, such that the agreements of their partial orders are compared in each list, counting discordant and tied pairs for penalization, the distance is defined as

$$\tau_p = \frac{n_d + \frac{1}{2} \times n_u}{Z} \tag{3}$$

---

[3] http://endic.naver.com/
[4] http://www.unipv.it/wnop/

where n_d is the number of discordant pairs (pairs differently ordered in each list), n_u is the number of pairs ordered in the gold standard but tied in the prediction, and Z is the number of pairs ordered in the gold standard.

The measure for a predicted list whose items are ranked in the same order as the gold standard is 0, indicating that there is no discordant or undecided pair of items. In the opposite case, if items in a list are in reverse order of the items in the gold standard, then τ_p equals 1. If a list does not order items but rather returns an unordered list, then the measure becomes 0.5.

5   Results

The experimental results show our proposed translation heuristics worked as we had expected: heuristics that translate only reliable words tend to have smaller τ_p and a lower number of translated words, while heuristics that translate more words have a bigger translated τ_p. Direct evaluation of **OF** lexicon results in poor scores (Table 1). It is due to the initialization where all *Strong* subjective words have the sentiment score of 1.0, and *Weak*, 0.5, arising many tied pairs that are penalized in our evaluation measure. Once translated, however, the quality of the lexicon is better than the ones translated from **SentiWN** because when translated, scores are averaged so that the words now have different values than 0.0, 0.5 or 1.0, and **OF** contains some manually–developed resources while **SentiWN** is created in completely automatic fashion.

The proposed framework with two link analysis models has a compensating effect in each phase that the lexicons mutually complement each other in turn (Table 2 and Table 3). The quality of the lexicons in every approach has shown to range from slightly negative (+1.29%) to exceptional (−41.3%).

Table 1. *p–normalized Kendall τ distance (τ_p)* and lexicon size for English lexicons and Korean translations

	EN						
	SentiWN				OF		
POS	0.365				0.490		
NEG	0.310				0.494		
Size	10, 631				8, 221		
	KR						
	SentiWN				OF		
	FW	FS	AS	SR	FW	FS	AS	SR
POS	0.301	0.278	0.312	0.312	0.179	0.142	0.122	0.122
NEG	0.300	0.304	0.261	0.261	0.214	0.167	0.192	0.192
Size	37, 812	68, 382	142, 791	142, 791	4, 270	10, 558	32, 322	32, 322

Table 2. Changes in *p–normalized Kendall τ distance* (τ_p) and lexicon size, after the execution of the first phase of the proposed link analysis model framework, using Korean Words as authorities and English words as hubs

	KR as authority, $\alpha = 0.6, \beta = 0.9$							
	POSITIVE							
	SentiWN				OF			
	FW	FS	AS	SR	FW	FS	AS	SR
Before	0.301	0.278	0.312	0.312	0.179	0.142	0.122	0.122
After	0.285	0.273	0.293	0.293	0.132	0.117	0.110	0.112
Diff	−5.32%	−1.80%	−6.09%	−6.09%	−26.3%	−17.6%	−9.84%	−8.20%
	NEGATIVE							
	SentiWN				OF			
	FW	FS	AS	SR	FW	FS	AS	SR
Before	0.300	0.304	0.261	0.261	0.214	0.167	0.192	0.192
After	0.291	0.293	0.254	0.254	0.202	0.160	0.186	0.190
Diff	−3.00%	−3.62%	−2.68%	−2.68%	−5.61%	−4.19%	−3.13%	−1.04%
Size	9,199	39,228	39,335	39,335	39,184	39,184	39,191	39,191

Table 3. Changes in *p–normalized Kendall τ distance* (τ_p) and lexicon size, after the execution of the second phase of the proposed link analysis model framework, using English Words as authorities and Korean words as hubs

	EN as authority, $\alpha = 0.1, \beta = 0.1$							
	POSITIVE							
	SentiWN				OF			
	FW	FS	AS	SR	FW	FS	AS	SR
Before	0.365				0.490			
After	0.340	0.338	0.342	0.342	0.355	0.335	0.335	0.333
Diff	−6.85%	−7.40%	−6.30%	−6.30%	−27.6%	−31.6%	−31.6%	−32.0%
	NEGATIVE							
	SentiWN				OF			
	FW	FS	AS	SR	FW	FS	AS	SR
Before	0.310				0.494			
After	0.309	0.305	0.313	0.314	0.290	0.298	0.306	0.304
Diff	−0.323%	−1.61%	+0.968%	+1.29%	−41.3%	−39.7%	−38.1%	−38.5%
Size	73,931	73,931	73,935	73,935	73,931	73,931	73,931	73,931

6 Conclusions

This paper investigated the feasibility of exploiting a subjectivity lexicon in one language to developing a subjectivity lexicon in another language with a bilingual dictionary as the only available language resource. Our proposed method of first translating the lexicon using the bilingual dictionary with several translation heuristics, then applying a framework that sequentially applies an iterative link analysis algorithm to enhance the quality of lexicons of both the source and the target languages has been empirically shown to create good quality lexicons.

Unlike previous work, we have explored the possibility of regarding a language translation process as a subjectivity projection operation. We have also attempted to draw compensation interactions using a graph structure as a medium.

Our future work includes incorporating word sense into the translation process and extending to different language pairs.

Acknowledgments

This work was supported in part by MKE & IITA through IT Leading R&D Support Project and also in part by the BK 21 Project in 2008.

References

1. Hatzivassiloglou, V., Mckeown, K.R.: Predicting the semantic orientation of adjectives. In: Proceedings of the 35th Annual Meeting of the Association for Computational Linguistics (ACL 1997), madrid, ES, pp. 174–181 (1997)
2. Turney, P.D., Littman, M.L.: Measuring praise and criticism: Inference of semantic orientation from association. ACM Transactions on Information Systems 21(4), 315–346 (2003)
3. Kamps, J., Marx, M., Mokken, R.J., Rijke, M.D.: Using wordnet to measure semantic orientation of adjectives. In: Proceedings of the 4th International Conference on Language Resources and Evaluation (LREC 2004), Lisbon, PT, pp. 1115–1118 (2004)
4. Takamura, H., Inui, T., Okumura, M.: Extracting semantic orientations of words using spin model. In: Proceedings of the 43rd Annual Meeting of the Association for Computational Linguistics (ACL 2005), Ann Arbor, USA, pp. 133–140 (2005)
5. Esuli, A., Sebastiani, F.: Determining the semantic orientation of terms through gloss analysis. In: Proceedings of the 14th ACM International Conference on Information and Knowledge Management (CIKM 2005), Bremen, DE, pp. 617–624 (2005)
6. Andreevskaia, A., Bergler, S.: Mining wordnet for fuzzy sentiment: Sentiment tag extraction from wordnet glosses. In: Proceedings of the 11th Conference of the European Chapter of the Association for Computational Linguistics (EACL 2006), Trento, IT, pp. 209–216 (2007)
7. Esuli, A., Sebastiani, F.: Sentiwordnet: A publicly available lexical resource for opinion mining. In: Proceedings of the 5th Conference on Language Resources and Evaluation (LREC 2006), Geneva, IT, pp. 417–422 (2006)
8. Esuli, A., Sebastiani, F.: Pageranking wordnet synsets: An application to opinion mining. In: Proceedings of the 45th Annual Meeting of the Association for Computational Linguistics (ACL 2007), Prague, CZ, pp. 424–431 (2007)
9. Kim, S.M., Hovy, E.: Determining the sentiment of opinions. In: Proceedings of 20th International Conference on Computational Linguistics (COLING 2004), Geneva,CH, pp. 1367–1373 (2004)
10. Wilson, T., Wiebe, J., Hoffmann, P.: Recognizing contextual polarity in phrase-level sentiment analysis. In: Proceedings of the Conference on Human Language Technology and Empirical Methods in Natural Language Processing (HLT-EMNLP 2005), Vancouver, CA, pp. 347–354 (2005)

11. Mihalcea, R.: Random walks on text structures. In: Gelbukh, A. (ed.) CICLing 2006. LNCS, vol. 3878, pp. 249–262. Springer, Heidelberg (2006)
12. Mihalcea, R., Banea, C., Wiebe, J.: Learning multilingual subjective language via cross-lingual projections. In: Proceedings of the 45th Annual Meeting of the Association of Computational Linguistics (ACL 2007), Prague, CZ, pp. 976–983 (2007)
13. Hu, M., Liu, B.: Mining and summarizing customer reviews. In: Proceedings of the 10th ACM SIGKDD international conference on Knowledge discovery and data mining (KDD 2004), New York, USA, pp. 168–177 (2004)
14. Wiebe, J., Mihalcea, R.: Word sense and subjectivity. In: Proceedings of the 44th Annual Meeting of the Association for Computational Linguistics (ACL 2006), Sydney, AU, pp. 1065–1072 (2006)
15. Yu, H., Hatzivassiloglou, V.: Towards answering opinion questions: Separating facts from opinions and identifying the polarity of opinion sentences. In: Proceedings of 2003 Conference on the Empirical Methods in Natural Language Processing (EMNLP 2003), Sapporo, JP, pp. 129–136 (2003)
16. Takamura, H., Inui, T., Okumura, M.: Latent variable models for semantic orientations of phrases. In: Proceedings of the 11th Conference of the European Chapter of the Association for Computational Linguistics (EACL 2006), Trento, IT, pp. 201–208 (2006)
17. Kanayama, H., Nasukawa, T.: Fully automatic lexicon expansion for domain-oriented sentiment analysis. In: Proceedings of the 2006 Conference on Empirical Methods in Natural Language Processing (EMNLP 2006), Sydney, AU, pp. 355–363 (2006)
18. Hu, Y., Duan, J., Chen, X., Pei, B., Lu, R.: A new method for sentiment classification in text retrieval. In: Dale, R., Wong, K.-F., Su, J., Kwong, O.Y. (eds.) IJCNLP 2005. LNCS, vol. 3651, pp. 1–9. Springer, Heidelberg (2005)
19. Kim, S.M., Hovy, E.: Identifying and analyzing judgment opinions. In: Proceedings of the Human Language Technology Conference of the NAACL (HLT/NAACL 2006), New York, USA, pp. 200–207 (2006)
20. Stone, P.J., Dunphy, D.C., Smith, M.S., Ogilvie, D.M.: The General Inquirer: A Computer Approach to Content Analysis. MIT Press, Cambridge (1966)
21. Whitelaw, C., Garg, N., Argamon, S.: Using appraisal groups for sentiment analysis. In: Proceedings of the 14th ACM international conference on Information and knowledge management (CIKM 2005), Bremen, DE, pp. 625–631 (2005)
22. Kleinberg, J.M.: Authoritative sources in a hyperlinked environment. J. ACM 46(5), 604–632 (1999)
23. Brin, S., Page, L.: The anatomy of a large-scale hypertextual web search engine. In: Computer Networks and ISDN Systems, pp. 107–117 (1998)
24. Cerini, S., Compagnoni, V., Demontis, A., Formentelli, M., Gandini, C.: Micrownop: A gold standard for the evaluation of automatically compiled lexical resources for opinion mining. In: Language resources and linguistic theory: Typology, second language acquisition, English linguistics, Milano, IT (2007)
25. Fagin, R., Kumar, R., Mahdian, M., Sivakumar, D., Vee, E.: Comparing and aggregating rankings with ties. In: Proceedings of the ACM International Conference on Principles of Database Systems (PODS 2004), Paris, FR, pp. 47–58 (2004)

Transliteration Based Text Input Methods for Telugu

V.B. Sowmya and Vasudeva Varma

Language Technologies Research Center,
International Institute of Information Technology, Hyderabad, India
sowmya_vb@research.iiit.ac.in, vv@.iiit.ac.in

Abstract. Telugu is the third most spoken language in India and one of the fifteen most spoken languages in the world. But, there is no standardized input method for Telugu, which has a widespread use. Since majority of users of Telugu typing tools on the computers are familiar with English, we propose a transliteration based text input method in which the users type Telugu using Roman script. We have shown that simple edit-distance based approach can give a light-weight system with good efficiency for a text input method. We have tested the approach with three datasets – general data, countries and places and person names. The approach has worked considerably well for all the datasets and holds promise as an efficient text input method.

Keywords: Telugu, Text input methods, Transliteration, Levenshtein, edit-distance.

1 Introduction

Transliteration is the process of mapping text written in one language in to another by means of a pre-defined mapping. It is useful when a user knows a language but does not know how to write its script. It is also useful in case of unavailability of a direct method to input data in a given language. Hence, transliteration can be understood as the process of entering data in one language using the script of the another language. In general, the mapping between the alphabet of one language and the other in a transliteration scheme will be as close as possible to the pronunciation of the word. English transliterated text has found widespread use with the growth of internet usage, in the form of chats, mails, blogs and other forms of individual online writing. This kind of transliterated text is often referred by the words formed by a combination of English and the language in which transliteration is performed, like - Arabish (Arabic + English), Hinglish (Hindi + English) etc. Depending on various factors like mapping, language pair etc, a word in one language can have more than one possible transliterations in the other language. This is more frequently seen in case of transliteration of proper nouns and other named entities. In this paper, we deal with the problem of transliteration of text from Roman script to Telugu. Transliteration can also mean a back transliteration from Telugu to English. However, we discuss only English to Telugu transliteration throughout this work.

W. Li and D. Mollá-Aliod (Eds.): ICCPOL 2009, LNAI 5459, pp. 122–132, 2009.

Telugu is the third most spoken language in India and one of the fifteen most spoken languages in the world. It is the official language of the state of Andhra Pradesh. Telugu has 56 alphabets (18 vowels and 38 consonants), two of which are not in use now. There are 16 additional Unicode characters to represent the phonetic variants of each consonant. Telugu wikipedia is one of the largest of the Indian language wikipedias. However, Telugu still does not have a user friendly and efficient text input method, which is widely accepted and used. Many tools and applications have been designed for Indian language text input. But, an evaluation of the existing methods has not been performed in a structured manner yet, to standardize on an efficient input method.

Most of the Indian language users on the internet are those who are familiar with typing using an English keyboard. Hence, instead of introducing them to a new keyboard designed for Indian languages, it is easier to let them type their language words using Roman script. In this paper, we deal with text input as a transliteration problem. We attempted to solve this problem by trying out different ways to exploit a large word list which is available to us from the crawl data of an Indian language search engine. Amongst the different methods tried out, an edit distance based approach worked most efficiently for the problem. We have performed these experiments on Telugu. But, the idea can be generalized to other Indian languages as well. This approach is not restricted to Indian languages, though. It can be used with other non-roman script based languages too. Further, the technique will also help transliterating text offline. There is a huge amount of data in the form of Romanized Telugu or any other language, used in various sites on the internet. Lyrics sites and discussion boards are the best examples for this kind of a scenario. Our technique can be applied in converting this text to Unicode. We describe our design and subsequent experiments conducted to verify the efficiency of the system in this paper.

The rest of this paper is organized as follows - Section 2 describes the related work. Section 3 explains some of the approaches we have tried out in the process of designing an effective text input method for Telugu. Section 4 explains our final design methodology. Section 5 presents our experiments and results. Section 6 presents our conclusions and outlines the future work.

2   Related Work

Many applications concerning text input for Indian languages have been designed in the recent past. Keyboard layouts like Inscript [7] and Keylekh [3] have been developed for Indian languages. There are also online applications like Quillpad[1] and *Google's Indic transliteration*[2], which facilitate typing in Telugu through Roman script, without any previous learning on the part of the user. There are also mapping schemes to map Roman character sequences to Telugu characters. Some of them include ITRANS[3], RTS (Rice Transliteration Scheme)[4] and Wx[5]. Softkeyboards are also designed for Indian languages by Google (gadget on iGoogle),

---

[1] http://www.quillpad.com/telugu/

[2] http://www.google.co.in/transliterate/indic/Telugu

[3] http://en.wikipedia.org/wiki/ITRANS

[4] http://members.tripod.com/RKSanka/telugu/rts.html

[5] http://tdil.mit.gov.in/TelugulScriptDetailsApr02.pdf

Guruji.com[6] and Telugulipi.net[7] among several others. However, our discussion in this work is limited to the Roman script based typing interfaces for Telugu language.

Edit distances have been used for a variety of matching tasks. They have been used widely for the purpose of detecting spelling variations in named entities. Freeman et.al. [1] used an extension of Levenshtein edit distance algorithm for Cross-linguistic name mapping task in English to Arabic transliteration. Cohen et.al. [12] have performed a comparison of different string distance metrics for name matching tasks. They have also implemented a toolkit of string matching methods for general purpose application. Mauricia et.a. [11] proposed a method to build Indo-European languages tree by using Levenshtein distance[8]. Makin et.al. [6] applied string matching techniques in the context of Cross Lingual Information Retrieval among Indian languages, to identify cognates between two Indian languages. Nayan et.al. [2] used Levenshtein distance, Soundex[9] and Editex [1] for the purpose of Named Entity Recognition in Indian languages. Pingali et.al. [5] also have mentioned about the usage of Fuzzy string matching techniques for Word normalization in Indian languages.

However, though all the above approaches have used edit-distance and other string matching based approaches widely, this work differs from them in the application scenario. While all of them have used those methods for name-matching tasks in mono-lingual as well as cross-lingual retrieval, we used those methods to develop an input method for Telugu language. Hence, we have used them to build an input method for Telugu through transliteration of the Roman script.

3   Experiments in English to Telugu Transliteration

We have considered text input as a transliteration problem in this work. Hence, we have worked on evolving approaches which consider text input from this point of view. Since we had access to a 1,600,000 strong word list for Telugu, collected from a crawl data index of an Indian language search engine, we have made attempts to exploit it. Further, lack of a parallel corpus for this kind of data came in the way of using any Machine Learning based techniques. Hence, we have come up with several approaches to text input, which involved the usage of this word list. The word list in Telugu was first stored in Roman script, by following a pre-defined mapping. This mapping was formed by performing an *Ease of remembrance* experiment on the existing mapping schemes for Indian languages.

Ease of remembrance
This experiment was performed based on a similar experiment by Goonetilleke et.al. [8], which was performed to estimate the ease of remembrance of a particular romanized mapping compared to other. They have performed it for Sinhalese. We have asked a group of 9 users to romanize the alphabets of Telugu language. Users were given a 2-column table. First column contains the Telugu alphabet . Second column is vacant and the user was asked to fill it the spelling of the Telugu alphabet according to their intuition. It is followed by the following procedure:

---

[6] http://www.guruji.com/te/
[7] http://www.telugulipi.net
[8] http://en.wikipedia.org/wiki/Levenshtein_Distance
[9] http://en.wikipedia.org/wiki/Soundex

- For a given encoding scheme, calculate the average edit distance between the user's roman transliteration and the encoding scheme's roman transliteration.
- The scheme with the lowest average edit distance is the easiest to remember.

We performed the experiment with three popular mapping schemes for Indian languages (RTS, Wx and ITRANS). The results are tabulated below:

Table 1. Ease of remembrance experiment

Mapping Scheme	Average edit distance per word
RTS	0.37
Wx	0.92
ITRANS	0.54

Since RTS had a better ease of remembrance as proved by this experiment, we have used a near RTS notation to convert our word list to Roman notation. After converting the Telugu word list in to Roman script, we have utilized it in different approaches for forming a data input method. Though we have finally concluded that Levenshtein distance based approach works the best of all, we are presenting the different approaches we have tried in the process of forming an efficient text input method for Telugu. The experimented approaches are explained below.

3.1 Generating Combinations

In this method, the input word is split in to individual phonemes. For example: *bharat* is split as *bha-ra-t*. An input mapping table is created, which has two columns. The first column contains the phoneme and the second column contains possible alternatives to that phoneme. For example, the phoneme *bha* can have its variations as *ba,baa,bha,bhaa (బ,బా,భ,భా)*. The second column is filled using the data obtained by performing the *"ease of remembrance"* experiment. This approach is similar to that performed by Sandeva et.al [9], who also tried a word list based approach for building a Sinhalese language prediction system. Finally, using this mapping table, all possible combinations of words that can be formed from the input word are generated. Valid words from the generated combinations are returned as predictions. However, as the length of the word increases, lakhs of combinations need to be generated, which slows down the whole process. Further, the method has to search through the word list to give only valid words as output, which again involves the usage of the large word list. This makes the search extremely slow owing to the size of the word list. Hence, an improvement over this idea was implemented, which involves converting the existing word list in to a mapping table.

3.2 Building a Mapping Table from the Word List

In this approach, we have re-arranged the Romanized word list to form a key-value data structure. The roman-mapping was case sensitive. Hence, we have formed a new data structure in which the key is a lower-cased word and its value had all the possible case-variated words to the key word, which existed in the dictionary. For example, against an entry *kavali*, the entries will be: *{kAvAlI;kAvAli;kAvali;kavAli;khavAlI}* (కావాలి;కావాలి;కావలి;కవాలి;ఖవాలి), which are the various words that exist in the word list, that are case-variated versions of the entered word. Though this approach was better than the previous one, it had one drawback. It works only if all the vowels and consonants entered were correctly spelt by the user, which is not always the case. For example, the word *Burma* (another name for the country -Myanmar) is actually pronounced *barma* and hence written so in Telugu. But, since this approach does not save those variations in its data structure, it fails to transliterate in this case. This obviously resulted in a less efficient system since this is a common problem in text input for Indian languages.

3.3 Fuzzy String Matching Based Approaches

Since the above mentioned approaches have not proved to be efficient enough for the task, we have tried out some experiments with string similarity metrics and other fuzzy string matching approaches. First, we have experimented with *Jaro-Winkler distance*, which has been explained in detail in [4]. Our procedure is based on the assumption that the first letter entered is the correct letter. We calculate similarity between the words in the word list starting with that letter and the input word. All the words, which cross a certain threshold level are given as predictions for the input word. The approach scaled well and was fast enough. However, as mentioned by Winkler in [13], the Jaro-Winkler similarity works well for proper names. Its initial purpose was to get the spelling variations of first names and last names. But our dataset is a generalized data set, which has both named entities as well as non-named entities, since this is the problem of a general purpose text input. Hence, this approach did not give a good efficiency to provide a better text input method.

Hence, we have tried to experiment with normalization methods like Soundex. Originally designed to get the spelling variations of names, Soundex achieves its purpose by grouping the letters in to respective classes. The Soundex algorithm is explained to some extent in Freeman et.al. [1]. In essence, it assigns a code to the given word based on its grouping. Similar names will possess the same Soundex code to a large extent. We have customized the Soundex grouping of letters as per the needs of a transliteration approach. We have altered the grouping of classes to some extent and extended the "Alphabet+3 digit code" of Soundex to "Alphabet+N digit code" where N is dependent on the length of the input word, since there will be so many words that have a similar 3 digit code as the input word. However, this did not improve the efficiency much.

Hence, we have tried using *edit-distance* as a method to devise an efficient text input method for Indian languages. We have used *Levenshtein distance* for this purpose because it calculates the cost involved in converting one word in to another by considering the number of insertions, deletions and substitutions required for the source word to be converted to the target word. Typically, insertions/deletions/substitutions are the three common factors involved in typing one language using the script of the other language. This approach has worked well and was proved to be very efficient. Our approach is explained below.

4 Levenshtein Distance Based Transliteration

Levenshtein distance between two strings is defined as the minimum number of operations (which comprise of insertion, deletion or substitution of a single character) required to transform a string to another. In the scenario of transliteration based text input, the intended string differs from entered string typically in one or many of the above mentioned operations. Hence, Levenshtein distance is a suitable metric to experiment with, in the development of a text input method. The following are the steps involved in our approach:

Step 1-Pre-processing the input word: The preprocessing step involves applying a few heuristics on the input word to make it as close as possible to the internal mapping. For example, say a user enters the input word as "raamaayanam" (రామాయణం), which is one of the Indian epics. The word list actually saves such a word as "rAmA-yaNaM" according to its mapping. Hence, one of the rules applied in the preprocessing step is to replace "aa" by "a". Since we compare the edit distance between two words only after converting the words in to lower case, the two words match. This is a simple example. Such rules are written to do some pre-processing on the input word to convert it in to the required form.

Step 2-Prediction: As mentioned before, based on the intuition that the first letter entered by the user is the correct letter, we search through only the words starting with that alphabet in the word list. The words which satisfy the requirements are returned as suggestions. In a couple of experiments, we have considered that the last character should also match. However, this is not a mandatory requirement. The requirements also include calculation of three Levenshtein distances. They are:

1. Levenshtein distance between the two words (i)
2. Levenshtein distance between the consonant sets of the two words (j)
3. Levenshtein distance between the vowel sets of the two words (k)

Here, the terms *consonant set* and *vowel set* refers to the concatenation of all consonants and all vowels in the word respectively.

Step 3-Conversion to Unicode:
Finally, we have to convert the Romanized predictions back to *Unicode* notation. This is done by reversing the process followed to convert the word list in to a Roman notation, which was performed in the initial stage.

We have conducted several experiments by varying the Levenshtein distance thresholds of the three distances mentioned above. Our experiments and the results are explained in the following section.

5 Experiments and Results

We have performed some experiments by varying the threshold levels of the three Levenshtein distances we have considered in designing the system. We have tested this approach on three types of datasets, to estimate the efficiency of this system in offering good predictions. The datasets are explained below.

1. A general dataset of 500 words, which contains Telugu text typed in general. It includes Telugu words typed in Roman script, named entities like place names and country names and English words adapted in to Telugu. This data was collected from some Telugu websites on the web. This included Telugu Wikipedia, News sites and blog pages. Since the data was collected from a free-text rather than a collection of words, the text in this dataset is the representative of a real word scenario .
2. A dataset of country/place names, which had around 200 words. This was collected from Telugu Wikipedia pages on the respective places.
3. A dataset of person names. This was again collected from Wikipedia pages on famous people. It had 150 words. Some Indian names were also included in the dataset, which mostly consisted of sportsmen, politicians and writers.

There might have been some overlap of the last two datasets with the first dataset since it is a general dataset which encompassed the other two categories.

The results are summarized in the following tables. The first column indicates the experiment number, the second, third and fourth columns indicate the different Levenshtein distances explained in the previous section and the last column shows the efficiency. Efficiency is calculated as the number of words for which the system gave correct predictions for a given input word.

General Observations:
1. The system has not been very efficient with an exclusively named entity dataset compared to the generalized dataset.
2. The person list had the largest accuracy for a particular experiment, more than the generalized dataset.
3. The accuracy with the general dataset has been considerably good.

The second column in the table *word Levenshtein distance (i)* refers to the Levenshtein distance between the two words being compared. As expected, the system performed efficiently with an increasing value of *i*. But, since there should be some limit

Table 2. Accuracy with Dataset-1

Expt No.	Word Levenshtein distance(i)	Consonant set Levenshtein distance (j)	Vowel set Levenshtein distance (k)	Accuracy (%)
1	5	2	1	90.6%
2	4	2	1	90.6%
3	3	2	2	91.0%
4	4	2	2	91.8%
5	6	2	2	92%
6*	4	2	2	92.4%
7	4	2	-	92.6%
8	6	2	-	93.2%

Table 3. Accuracy with Dataset-2

Expt No.	Word Levenshtein distance(i)	Consonant set Levenshtein distance (j)	Vowel set Levenshtein distance (k)	Accuracy (%)
1	5	2	1	75%
2	4	2	1	75.29%
3	3	2	2	79.25%
4	4	2	2	79.25%
5	6	2	2	79.25%
6*	4	2	2	83.27%
7	4	2	-	79.24%
8	6	2	-	84.69%

Table 4. Accuracy with Dataset-3

Expt No.	Word Levenshtein distance(i)	Consonant set Levenshtein distance (j)	Vowel set Levenshtein distance (k)	Accuracy (%)
1	5	2	1	88.11%
2	4	2	1	88.11%
3	3	2	2	89.10%
4	4	2	2	89.5%
5	6	2	2	91.10%
6*	4	2	2	96.0%
7	4	2	-	91.10%
8	6	2	-	96.09%

*: Difference between experiment 4 and experiment 6 lies in the fact that while experiment 4 considers the last character matching condition, experiment 6 does not.

on the increasing value, we stopped at i=6. For words of length smaller than 8, we have limited the i value to 3. However, the third column *consonant set Levenshtein distance (j)* refers to the difference between consonant sets of the two words. We have decided to use this as a parameter in getting the transliterated output since there will be a lot of words within the threshold i, which may not be related to the source word in any way, but have the same Levenshtein distance. It is kept 2 throughout all the experiments because, it is very unlikely that more than two words which differ in more than two consonants will be representing the same source word. The fourth column refers to *vowel set Levenshtein distance(k),* which represents the difference in vowels of the two words. This has been varied as either 1 or 2 in most of the experiments we have conducted. This factor has been totally ignored in the last two experiments, to verify its influence on the overall system efficiency.

As it can be seen from the results, the system performed very well with the generalized test data, which proved that this can be an efficient solution to text input for Telugu. This approach is language independent and hence can be applied to any other Indian language, owing to the similarity between Indian languages. The success of the system with the Levenshtein distance approach can be attributed the relationship between the nature of Levenshtein distance and the process of typing Telugu in English, as mentioned in the previous section.

The failure of this system with Named Entities can be owing to the fact that the way they are written is different from the way they are spelt. But, our approach is based on how the words are spelt since the dictionary is converted to a Roman mapping based on the same factor. But, the system worked better with Indian named entities i.e., places, person names which are of Indian origin. It can be attributed to the same reason; since Indian words are spelt in English in the same way as they are pronounced, to a large extent. It is natural that the system will not perform very efficiently with named entities compared to generalized test data, since our purpose is not named entity transliteration but a general purpose text input system. We did not work on specifically transliterating named entities in this approach. Hence, in this perspective, the results on the named entity datasets are encouraging enough. However, the results prove that using Levenshtein distance is a workable approach to build a text input method for Indian languages. Possible alternatives to improve efficiency with named entities can be trying with a different metric, using a combination of metrics or using some heuristics in the existing method.

The variation of accuracy of the system with word Levenshtein distance threshold has been plotted in the graph below:

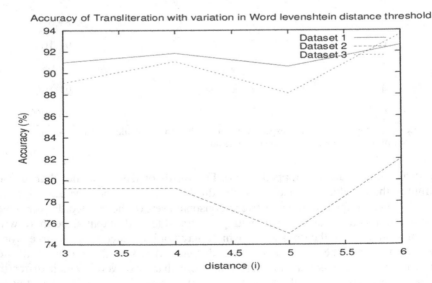

Fig. 1. Accuracy of the system

As it can be noticed from the graph, though the system did not perform well with an exclusively Named Entities based dataset, it performed considerably well with the general purpose dataset, which is a better representation of a general purpose data input needs of the user. Hence, we can claim that *Levenshtein distance* based transliteration method can provide an efficient data input system for Telugu as well as other Indian languages.

6 Conclusions and Future Work

In this paper, we have proposed a simple, yet efficient technique for text input in Telugu, which can be easily extended to other non-Roman script based languages. Since it does not involve any *learning* on the part of the system, it does not put heavy weight on the system. In this approach, we have exploited the availability of a large word list for the language to design a new text input method. Having tried out different approaches in using this word list, we have finally concluded that a Levenshtein distance based approach is most efficient of all. This is because of the relation between Levenshtein distance and the nature of typing Telugu through English. The approach offers only valid words as suggestions and it gives the results instantaneously.

We have to work on further improving the approach so as to make it work better with named entities too, since it will also help in creating gazetteers of named entities in Telugu. We have to test the system on larger datasets before making a full fledged application which uses this system. We plan to explore other distance metrics and/or using a combination of distance metrics to achieve a good working system. The system offers too many suggestions for words of smaller length. We have to look at alternative methods to deal with this problem. A proper ranking function needs to be designed to rank the results in an optimal order.

References

1. Andrew, T.F., Sherri, L.C., Christopher, M.A.: Cross Linguistic Name Matching in English and Arabic: A One to Many Mapping Extension of the Levenshtein Edit Distance Algorithm. In: Human Language Technology Conference of the North American Chapter of the ACL, pp. 471–478 (2006)
2. Animesh, N., Ravi Kiran Rao, B., Pawandeep, S., Sudip, S., Ratna, S.: Named Entity Recognition for Indian Languages. In: Workshop on NER for South and South East Asian Languages (NERSSEA), International Joint Conference on Natural Language Processing (IJCNLP) (2008)
3. Anirudha, J., Ashish, G., Aditya, C., Vikram, P., Gaurav, M.: Keylekh: A keyboard for text entry in Indic scripts. In: Proc. Computer Human Interaction (CHI) (2004)
4. Elmagarmid, A.K., Ipeirotis, P.G., Verykios, V.S.: Duplicate Record Detection: A Survey. IEEE Transactions on Knowledge and Data Engineering 19(1), 1–16 (2007)
5. Prasad, P., Vasudeva, V.: Word normalization in Indian languages. In: 4th International Conference on Natural Language Processing (ICON) (2005)
6. Ranbeer, M., Nikita, P., Prasad, P., Vasudeva, V.: Experiments in Cross-lingual IR among Indian Languages. In: International Workshop on Cross Language Information Processing (CLIP 2007) (2007)

7. Report of the Committee for Standardization of Keyboard Layout for Indian Script Based Computers. Electronics Information & Planning Journal 14(1) (October 1986)
8. Sandeva, G., Yoshihiko, H., Yuichi, I., Fumio, K.: An Efficient and User Friendly Sinhala Input method based on Phonetic Transcription. Journal of Natural Language Processing 14(5) (October 2007)
9. Sandeva, G., Yoshihiko, H., Yuichi, I., Fumio, K.: SriShell Primo: A Predictive Sinhala Text Input System. In: Workshop on NLP for Less Privileged Languages (NLPLPL), International Joint Conference on Natural Language Processing (IJCNLP) (2008)
10. Serva, M., Petroni, F.: Indo-European languages tree by Levenshtein distance. Exploring the Frontiers of Physics (EPL) (6) (2008)
11. William, W.C., Pradeep, R., Stephen, E.F.: A Comparison of String Distance Metrics for Name-Matching Tasks. In: Proceedings of Association for the Advancement of Artificial Intelligence (AAAI) (2003)
12. Winkler, W.E.: The State of Record Linkage and Current Research Problems. In: Statistics of Income Division, Internal Revenue Service Publication, R99/04

Harvesting Regional Transliteration Variants with Guided Search

Jin-Shea Kuo[1], Haizhou Li[2], and Chih-Lung Lin[3]

[1] Chung-Hwa Telecomm. Labs., Taoyuan, Taiwan
d8807302@gmail.com
[2] Institute for Infocomm Research, Singapore
hli@i2r.a-star.edu.sg
[3] Chung Yuan Christian University, Taoyuan, Taiwan
linclr@gmail.com

Abstract. This paper proposes a method to harvest regional transliteration variants with guided search. We first study how to incorporate transliteration knowledge into query formulation so as to significantly increase the chance of desired transliteration returns. Then, we study a cross-training algorithm, which explores valuable information across different regional corpora for the learning of transliteration models to in turn improve the overall extraction performance. The experimental results show that the proposed method not only effectively harvests a lexicon of regional transliteration variants but also mitigates the need of manual data labeling for transliteration modeling. We also conduct an inquiry into the underlying characteristics of regional transliterations that motivate the cross-training algorithm.

Keywords: transliteration, regional transliteration variants, cross-training algorithm, guided search, constraint-based exploration.

1 Introduction

Same foreign words are translated into Chinese with regional variants, such as Taxi becomes "計程車/Ji-Cheng-Che/[1]" in Taiwan, and "德士/De-Shi/" in Singapore. It has been an active research topic to study translation variants [1][2]. However, little work has been reported on the same problem in transliteration. Transliteration is a process of translating a foreign word into the native language by preserving its pronunciation in the original language, otherwise known as *translation-by-sound*. It not only maintains the pronunciations, but sometimes also carries forward certain meaning that can be appreciated by native people [3]. It is common that an English word is usually transliterated into different Chinese variants in different Chinese-speaking communities or regions. For example, the movie *Shrek* becomes "史瑞克/Shi-Rui-Ke/" in Taiwan and "史莱克/Shi-Lai-Ke/" in China. In many natural language processing applications, we have to deal with such regional transliteration variants. A big

---

[1] Hanyu pinyin is used for Chinese romanization.

W. Li and D. Mollá-Aliod (Eds.): ICCPOL 2009, LNAI 5459, pp. 133–144, 2009.
© Springer-Verlag Berlin Heidelberg 2009

transliteration lexicon would help us address this problem. However, new words emerge every day and it is not trivial to compile such a lexicon composed of the English words and all their regional variants. One of the possible solutions is to automatically construct a transliteration lexicon of regional variants from the Web, which is a live source of new words.

Many studies on transliteration are focused on the generative transliteration models [4][5][6] which re-write a foreign word into the native alphabets. The generative modeling technique is found useful in handling out-of-vocabulary (OOV) words, such as personal names, place names and technical terms, in tasks such as machine translation [7], and cross-lingual information retrieval [8]. However, the learning of generative models hinges on a manually validated bilingual lexicon, which is not easily available.

The Web is one of the largest text databases for OOV named entities. It is also multilingual in nature and offers real world transliterations every day. The challenge here is that these transliterations are not well-organized in a structured manner and at the same time they are artifacts created by many individuals across the globe, which inherently manifest regional variation as a result of cultural difference. The question is how to harvest these transliterations. Many efforts have been devoted to acquiring transliterations from the Web for a single language pair, such as English-Japanese [9], English-Korean [6] and English-Chinese (*E-C*) [10]. However, to our best knowledge, there are not many studies on automatically constructing transliteration lexicons of regional variants or regional lexicons in short. In a regional lexicon, an entry called a tuple includes an English word and its regional variants, such as *Shrek*, "史瑞克/Shi-Rui-Ke/" (Taiwan) and "史莱克/Shi-Lai-Ke/" (China).

The Web domain names, such as ".cn" and ".tw", provide us with a natural labeling of geographical division, also referred to as language regions. In theory, one can extract transliterations from one regional Web, and then simply use English words as the pivot to construct a lexicon of transliteration variants. The performance achieved by this approach can be considered as a baseline. In addition to this basic approach, in this paper, we approach this extraction problem from a different angle by exploiting domain knowledge encoded in a transliteration model to guide the Web search.

This paper is organized as follows. In Section 2, we briefly introduce related work. In Section 3, we present how to apply knowledge to query formulation so as to guide the search. In Section 4, we propose a cross-training strategy, which exploits regional corpora, for phonetic similarity model training and transliteration extraction. In Section 5, we conduct experiments to validate the effectiveness of the proposed algorithms. In Section 6, we discuss some observations from the databases themselves. Finally, we conclude in Section 7.

2 Related Work

Learning regional transliteration lexicons involves both transliteration modeling and extraction. The former allows us to establish a similarity metric between bilingual words to ensure the quality of extraction, while the latter studies the effective retrieval techniques to provide the quantity of extraction. The grapheme-based [5], phoneme-based [4] and hybrid [6] approaches represent typical transliteration modeling techniques. In this paper, we focus on the retrieval techniques and adopt the phonetic similarity model (PSM) [10] to validate each extracted transliteration pair. PSM is also called transliteration model in the rest of this paper. Next we briefly introduce the prior work related to transliteration extraction.

There have been many attempts to extract translations or transliterations from the Web, for example, by exploring query logs [9] and parallel [11] or comparable corpora [12]. However, most of them are for terms of a single language pair. On the other hand, Cheng et al. [1] proposed a transitive translation method by exploiting forward-backward collocation information and using English as a pivot language to construct a regional translation lexicon. However, this method relies completely on collocation information which is more suitable for the extraction of translation variants than that for transliteration.

Some recent studies use information retrieval (IR) techniques for transliteration extraction. Sproat et al. [12] exploited both phonetic similarity and temporal distribution to identify named entities in comparable corpora. Kuo et al. [10] and Lin et al. [13] advocated a method to explore English appositive words in the proximity of Chinese proper nouns in mixed code text, also known as parenthetical translation. Phonetic similarity, temporal correlation and parenthetical translation are shown to be informative clues for finding transliterations. Searching for transliterations from the Web, transliteration extraction is also known as transliteration retrieval. To work towards this end effectively, we propose a method for guiding the search of target transliterations in this paper.

3 Guided Search

Constraint-based learning algorithms [14], which impose constraints or introduce domain knowledge into the selection of candidates, have been successfully used in information extraction. The idea can also be applied to harvest regional transliteration variants to obtain quality candidates. In Web-based information retrieval, many documents are indexed by search engines; however, search queries are usually too short to reflect users' intentions. It remains a challenge to construct adequate queries for effective search. We propose to introduce constraints that incorporate knowledge to formulate the queries. Now the problem is what kind of knowledge is useful and how to include them. Transliteration modeling represented by the phonetic similarity models encoding knowledge and deducing mapping rules of basic pronunciation units from the transliteration samples in the training pool is an excellent candidate.

Taking an English word, "Abby", as input, the generative model outputs Chinese transliteration candidates, "阿布比", "阿比", "艾布比", "艾比" and "阿布贝," referred to as quasi transliterations as opposed to validated real-world transliterations, by adopting the joint source channel model [5] (http://hlt.i2r.a-star.edu.sg/transliteration/). Then, the queries are formed by augmenting the English word with each of the candidates to favor the desired returns. We expect that such a *constraint-based exploration* (CBE) will bring us benefits towards finding target transliteration. In terms of query style, if we consider the baseline as using the English words as the queries and the *E-C* word pairs as the expanded queries, we expect to leverage the search of genuine transliterations using expanded queries, which consists of quasi transliterations to be validated as search constraints.

4 Cross-Training Learning Framework

It is common that in Chinese/Japanese/Korean (CJK) predominant webpages, English words are used in parentheses near to the CJK transliterations to serve as appositive in a sentence as in Fig. 1. We adopt the strategy, known as *recognition followed by validation* [10], to use such translation clue and the phonetic similarity to extract Chinese transliteration entries. In this strategy, we first identify a transliteration pair in the proximity of English and Chinese collocation. Then, we validate each candidate by using phonetic similarity clue in a hypothesis test.

```
:: 曾對中國有偏見"理性預期"大師今首次訪華::
記者鐘心報道：記者今天獲悉，諾貝爾經濟獎得主羅伯特·盧卡斯（ROBERT
LUCAS）16日下午3：30分在武漢大學舉行首場講座，講座 ... 羅伯特·盧卡斯
（ROBERT LUCAS）美國人，1937年出生，他倡導和發展了理性預期與宏觀
經濟學研究的運用理論，深化了人們對經濟 ...
big5.xinhuanet.com/gate/big5/news.xinhuanet.com/
world/2004-06/16/content_1529176.htm - 38k - 頁庫存檔 - 類似網頁

美中自由貿易促進會籌備委員會就商人遭打強烈抗議
美中自由貿易促進會籌備委員會認為，羅斯顯然在為自己的犯罪行為進行狡
辯，我們從美聯社報道裏已經看到："目擊者說，當時正在執行任務的羅伯特·
羅斯(Robert Rhodes)，誤以為附近站著的婦女也捲入走私大麻，便向她噴射
胡椒劑，隨後把她推向墙，並按倒在 ...
big5.xinhuanet.com/gate/big5/news.xinhuanet.com/
world/2004-07/25/content_1642949.htm - 40k - 頁庫存檔 - 類似網頁
```

Fig. 1. Snippets returns for a query "Robert"

The learning of PSM transliteration model takes place as we extract transliterations. Let's recap how it works for a single language pair in Fig. 2. This algorithm works in an unsupervised manner with minimum human intervention. Now let's extend the algorithm in Fig. 2 to account for regional variation of transliterations. We carry out unsupervised learning over the regional division of the snippet databases – query returns from China and query returns from Taiwan. The transliterations which share the common English words form transliteration tuples.

Given
a). An initial PSM trained on a small set of seed pairs;
b). A snippet database;

Learning transliterations
c). Validate the transliteration candidates in the snippet database using PSM;
d). Collect the automatically validated transliterations;
e). Re-estimate the PSM from the validated transliterations with EM algorithm;
f). Repeat Steps c), d) and e) until no new transliterations are found.

Fig. 2. Unsupervised learning of PSM and transliterations from a snippet database

4.1 Cross-Training

Cross-training [15] was proposed for learning classifiers for *partially overlapped* or *correlated* classes. It considers each data set as a view to the problem to let classifiers help each other. Cross-training was used successfully in creating an integrated directory from multiple Web directories, such as Yahoo! Directory (http://dir.yahoo.com/) and Open Directory (http://www.dmoz.org/). It was also studied in the classification of Web pages [16].

Given an *E-C* regional lexicon, we would like to use cross-training to exploit the information available in different regional data sets to boost the learning. Specifically, we expect the PSM learning from China corpus will help boost the PSM learning of Taiwan corpus, and vice versa, as shown in Fig. 3.

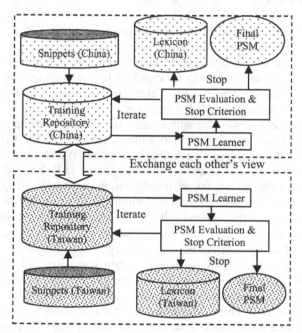

Fig. 3. Diagram of cross-training algorithm with two regional Web data sets

Given
a). A small set of labeled samples, L, two sets of unlabeled samples, U_A and U_B, and two learners A and B.
b). Learner A is trained on L to predict the labels of U_A.

Loop for *k* iterations
c). Learner B is trained on data labeled by Learner A to predict the labels of U_B;
d). Learner A is trained on data labeled by Learner B to predict the labels of U_A;

A final PSM model is obtained from Learners A and B.

Fig. 4. Cross-training with two learners for regional transliterations variants

We propose a cross-training algorithm that employs two learners (see the upper and lower panels in Fig. 3) with two data sets for simplification. Each learner can learn from a regional data set and run in an unsupervised manner as in Fig. 2. The cross-training allows the two learners to exchange their *correlated* information over the problem in a collaborative learning process. It can be seen as an extension of the unsupervised learning, as summarized in Fig. 4.

5 Experiments

To construct a regional lexicon from the Web, we need to obtain a collection of snippets that are rich in transliterations of interest. This process is also referred to as crawling. We explore two different crawling techniques: the *autonomous exploration* (AE), which is the basic approach for crawling in a random surfing manner, and the *constraint-based exploration* (CBE), which exploits domain knowledge encoded in the transliteration model to guide the crawling.

In the AE procedure, we start with a small set of transliteration pairs as seed pairs to bootstrap the initial phonetic similarity model (PSM). The PSM is used to measure the phonetic similarity between an *E-C* pair of words. We also use the English words in the seed pairs as the initial queries for Web search [17]. From the returning snippets as shown in Fig. 1, we extract transliteration candidates using the initial PSM. The validated transliterations are further submitted as queries for the new Web search. In this way, we submit queries and validate the extraction returns with the PSM. This process allows us to discover new transliteration pairs, such as "Lucas-盧卡斯/Lu-Ka-Si/" in Fig. 1 as the return of the search query "Robert".

Note that the retrieved snippets may contain both true and false transliteration pairs. The PSM model acts as a filter to screen out the false pairs. As AE procedure searches the space in a random walk manner, the retrieved results may not relate to the seed query after a while. Therefore, the AE crawler is seen as an autonomous agent. To retrieve transliteration variants, we can launch AE crawlers at different regional Web divisions independently. The returns that share the common English word form tuples of transliteration variants.

The independent AE-based crawling results from different crawlers do not guarantee anchoring at the same set of English words. To increase the possibility of desired query returns, we suggest generating transliteration candidates for a foreign word to expand the query so as to search towards the genuine transliterations. In this way, we first generate the quasi transliterations for different regions which then serve as the hints for CBE-based crawling. The idea is that a hint resulting from a reasonably good transliteration model [5] is better than no hint at all and helps find the target. We expand the common set of English words with generated regional transliterations to serve as queries. Then we launch the search in regional Web divisions to collect a database that share common English words.

Note that there are differences between AE and CBE. For example, AE procedure involves a PSM that is trained on the seed pairs, while CBE involves an additional step of query expansion. Once a snippet database is so created by either the AE or CBE procedure, we can now move on with learning the PSM model and construction of regional lexicons.

With the AE procedure, we first create a snippet database D_{AE} consisting of two data sets: TW_{AE} from .tw domain, which consists of 335,010 files in traditional Chinese amounting to 22.5 GB in size; and CN_{AE} from .cn domain, which has 450,150 files in simplified Chinese, and 44.0 GB in size. Each of these files has at most 100 snippets. Most of them are Chinese words mixed with English ones, as seen in Fig. 1.

With the CBE procedure, we select top-1,000 boy's and girl's names of year 2006 from American Social Security Online[2]. There are 1,942 unique names in total. Then, we generate top-20 Chinese candidates for each English name. In this way, we obtain about 77,680 *E-C* pairs and 6.65 GB in size. In practice, each pair is submitted to regional Web through a search engine. We obtain 38,840 returning files in traditional Chinese from .tw domain also called $TW_{CBE(20)}$ and 2.50 GB in size; 38,840 returning files in simplified Chinese from .cn domain also called $CN_{CBE(20)}$ and 4.15 GB in size. Each file has at most 100 snippets in this corpus. This database is called $D_{CBE(20)}$.

To establish the ground truth for performance evaluation, we only select first 500 files from each data set for manual labeling. This results in a reduced data set of 123.8 MB, D_{AE-500}, from the AE data; and a reduced data set of 259.0 MB, $D_{CBE-500(3)}$, with top-3 candidates, from CBE-collected data. For ease of reference, we summarize the statistics of the corpora in Table 1. Note that D_{AE-500} is a condensed corpus consisting of two respective data sets, TW_{AE-500} and CN_{AE-500}, and $D_{CBE-500(3)}$, which is a reduced version of $D_{CBE(20)}$. $D_{CBE-500(3)}$ also consists of two data sets, $TW_{CBE-500(3)}$ from .tw domain and $CN_{CBE-500(3)}$ from .cn domain. The labeling suggests 6,176 and 76,850 valid pairs, with 3,118 and 22,330 distinct pairs, for D_{AE-500} and $D_{CBE-500(3)}$, respectively.

Table 1. Statistics of regional databases

	Database	#Files	Size
D_{AE}	TW_{AE}	335,010	22.5 GB
	CN_{AE}	450,150	44.0 GB
$D_{CBE(20)}$	$TW_{CBE(20)}$	38,840	2.50 GB
	$CN_{CBE(20)}$	38,840	4.15 GB
D_{AE-500}		1,000	123.8 MB
$D_{CBE-500(3)}$		3,000	259.0 MB

We report the performance in F-measure, which is described in Eq. (1),

$$F-measure = \frac{2 \times recall \times precision}{recall + precision},$$ (1)

where *precision* is defined as the ratio of extracted number of DQTPs (distinct qualified transliteration pairs), which have been manually labeled as correct, over that of total extracted pairs and *recall* is defined as the ratio of extracted number of DQTPs over that of total DQTPs. Eq. (1) measures the performance of learning regional variants on a pair basis similar to that in single language pair, i.e., the DQTPs from two different data sets with the same English word are pooled together.

---

[2] http://www.socialsecurity.gov/OACT/babynames/index.html

5.1 Unsupervised Learning on AE Database

As discussed at the beginning of Section 4, first, we derive an initial PSM using randomly selected 100 seed DQTPs for a learner and simulate the Web-based learning process: (i) extract E-C pairs using the initial PSM; (ii) add all of the extracted E-C pairs to the DQTP pool; (iii) re-estimate the PSM by using the updated DQTP pool. We evaluate performance on the D_{AE-500} database in section 5.1 to section 5.3.

To construct a regional lexicon, we run the extraction over each data set independently in unsupervised learning and then use English as the anchor to establish the transliteration tuples. We run multiple iterations of unsupervised learning. At 6th iteration, the F-measure is 0.475. We consider this performance as the baseline in this paper.

5.2 Cross-Training on AE Database

Mandarin Chinese has been used prevalently in Taiwan and China and people in the two regions do not follow the same rules for E-C transliteration due to different local accents and cultural preference. Note that the phonetic features of the Chinese-speaking communities are similar. We expect the phonetic features from multiple regional sets will help each other's learning as in Fig. 5.

With cross-training, we run the same procedure as in section 5.1 for each of the regional data sets in parallel. Then, we can re-estimate the PSM of each learner with the transliterations extracted by the learner itself together with those extracted by the other leaner. We also run 6 iterations to see the effectiveness of learning. The F-measure performance is reported in Fig. 5 for unsupervised learning (UL) and cross-training (CT). The results show that the collaborative cross-training attains higher F-measure (0.510) than independent unsupervised learning (0.475). This suggests that cross-training benefits from learners exchanging information with the other.

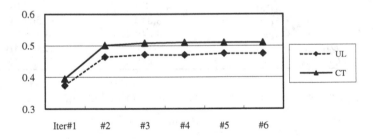

Fig. 5. Harvesting variants using unsupervised learning and cross-training from D_{AE-500}

5.3 Cross-Training on CBE Database

As discussed at the beginning of this section, the independent AE-based crawling does not guarantee the returns anchoring at the same set of English words. This will result in an inefficient process when compiling the tuples of regional variants. On the other hand, the CBE-based crawling can be considered as a kind of focused crawling

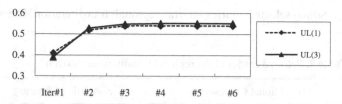

Fig. 6. Harvesting variants using unsupervised learning from $D_{CBE\text{-}500(3)}$

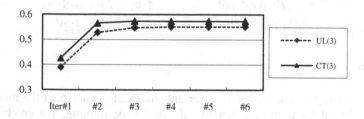

Fig. 7. Harvesting variants using unsupervised learning and cross-training from $D_{CBE\text{-}500(3)}$

[18] which is target-oriented. We conduct the unsupervised learning on $D_{CBE\text{-}500(3)}$ as shown in Fig. 6 and report the F-measure for top-1 and top-3 results. At the 6th iteration, the F-measure with top-1 candidate, denoted as UL(1), and top-3 candidates, denoted as UL(3), are 0.540 and 0.551, respectively, which outperform that on AE database.

We further conduct an experiment with cross-training and report the performance of cross-training with top-3 candidates, CT(3), in Fig. 7. At 6th iteration, the F-measure by CT(3) is 0.573, which represents the best performance.

It is observed that the experiments on CBE database show better results than those on AE database. Cross-training also consistently outperforms unsupervised learning in all cases. The performance of harvesting regional transliteration variants is inferior to that on single language pairs. This is easy to understand because the regional transliteration variants are the intersection of transliterations across two or more single language pairs that share the common English words.

5.4 Learning from the Web

We have conducted several experiments on a local database. It would be interesting to see how the proposed algorithm works directly on the Web. We conduct an experiment using the same 100 seed pairs as described in section 5.1 to train an initial PSM on $D_{CBE(20)}$, which is collected using CBE procedure with top-20 candidates. The ground truth is not available for the whole corpus, therefore, we only report the estimated precision by randomly sampling 500 tuples. There are 12,033 distinct tuples (43,369 distinct pairs) extracted, with the estimated precision of 0.834 on a tuple basis or 0.894 on a pair basis. The expected correct tuples (pairs) are 10,036 (38,768). Note that we use the full $D_{CBE(20)}$ database and run one iteration to simulate the Web learning process. Some selected entries of the regional transliteration lexicon are shown in Table 2.

Table 2. Selected entries of the regional transliteration lexicon

English	Traditional Chinese	Simplified Chinese
Archibald	阿契博得 /A-Qi-Bo-De/	阿奇巴尔德 /A-Qi-Ba-Er-De/
Torvalds	托維茲 /Tuo-Wei-Ci/	托瓦尔德斯 /Tuo-Wa-Er-De-Si/
Giono	紀沃諾 /Ji-Wo-Nuo/	季奥诺 / Ji-Ao-Nuo /
Seles	莎莉絲 /Sha-Li-Si/	塞利斯 /Sai-Li-Si/

6 Discussion

The statistics over regional transliteration variants may help understand the underlying characteristics of them and the benefits of using cross-training. We conduct an inquiry into the labeled data, D_{AE-500} and $D_{CBE-500(3)}$.

Table 3. Statistics over the manually labeled regional databases D_{AE-500} and $D_{CBE-500(3)}$

	TW_{AE-500}	CN_{AE-500}	$TW_{CBE-500(3)}$	$CN_{CBE-500(3)}$
#Trans	1.288	1.205	1.478	1.424

In the second row of Table 3, we report the average number of Chinese transliterations for an English word (#Trans). It shows that Taiwan databases that adopt traditional Chinese characters have higher numbers of transliteration variants per English word than China databases that adopt simplified Chinese characters. It suggests that transliterations are less regular in Taiwan. From Table 3, we can expect that on average we will obtain 1.247 regional variants for D_{AE} and 1.451 for D_{CBE}. It implies that we can obtain more transliterations by constraint-based exploration.

The desire to achieve semantic transliteration [3] increases number of transliteration variants. Chinese has more than 4,000 frequently-used characters representing only about 400 syllables. That means, for each syllable, there could have multiple character choices. For example, an English name "Sophia" is a girl's name. To carry its feminine association forward to Chinese, "蘇菲雅 /Su-Fei-Ya/" is used in Taiwan and "索菲娅/Suo-Fei-Ya/" is used in China. What is in common is that both choose characters of feminine connotation, except that the Taiwanese transliteration uses a Chinese surname "蘇/Su/" to start the word, while the Chinese one does not.

Despite many differences, the regional variants share many commonalities. Most of the Chinese characters carry meanings. For those that have positive or neutral connotation, there is a large overlapping between Taiwan and China databases. Table 4 lists the top-5 characters in the four data sets. It is interesting to find that the top-3 characters, i.e., "斯/Si/," "克/Ke/" and "爾/Er/," are common across the four databases. We also find that some characters are used much more often than others. The top-20 characters account for 20.234%, 24.516%, 24.012% and 29.097% of the usage in the four data sets. Note that for comparison, all transliterations in Table 4 have been converted into Traditional Chinese. Table 4 reports the usage statistics at the character level. In Table 5, we further study the correlation at whole word level in the lexicon D_{AE-500} (TW_{AE-500} and CN_{AE-500}) and $D_{CBE-500(3)}$ ($TW_{CBE-500(3)}$ and $CN_{CBE-500(3)}$). We find that 16.918% of entries in TW_{AE-500} are identical to their transliterations in CN_{AE-500}, and 24.881% of entries in CN_{AE-500} are the same as their counterparts in TW_{AE-500}. We also observe the similar overlapping between $TW_{CBE-500(3)}$ to $CN_{CBE-500(3)}$ as well.

Table 4. Top-5 character usage in regional transliteration variants

	TW_{AE-500}	CN_{AE-500}	$TW_{CBE-500(3)}$	$CN_{CBE-500(3)}$
1	斯 /Si/ (3.83%)	斯/Si/ (4.94%)	斯/Si/ (5.00%)	斯/Si/ (5.49%)
2	克 /Ke/ (2.58%)	爾 /Er/ (3.94%)	克/Ke/ (3.16%)	爾/Er/ (4.51%)
3	爾 /Er/ (2.28%)	克/Ke/ (3.03%)	爾/Er/ (2.94%)	克/Ke/ (3.21%)
4	拉 /La/ (2.05%)	特 /Te/ (2.4%)	德/De/ (2.39%)	阿 /A/ (2.77%)
5	特/Te/ (1.87%)	德 /De/ (1.97%)	特 /Te/ (2.10%)	特 /Te/ (2.72%)

Table 5. Percentage of identical transliterations across regional databases

	TW_{AE-500} to CN_{AE-500}	CN_{AE-500} to TW_{AE-500}	$TW_{CBE-500(3)}$ to $CN_{CBE-500(3)}$	$CN_{CBE-500(3)}$ to $TW_{CBE-500(3)}$
% overlap	16.918%	24.881%	20.745%	17.024%

The correlation at character and transliteration level provides consistent information that allows the cross-training to boost performance. Although the rendering of Chinese characters are different, the underlying sound equivalence warrants the phonetic exploration for the cross-training algorithm.

7 Conclusions

This paper studies two techniques for crawling Web corpora, *autonomous exploration* (AE) and *constraint-based exploration* (CBE), which exploits transliteration knowledge to guide the query search, and two learning strategies, unsupervised learning and cross-training. Experiments show that the cross-training effectively boosts the learning by exchanging correlated information across two regional learners. We find that the CBE-based crawling followed by cross-training technique is a practical method for harvesting regional transliteration variants.

We have studied transliteration variants between Taiwan and China for simplification. The same technique is applicable to deriving regional variants for Chinese transliterations of Hong Kong, Singapore and Malaysia as well. It would be an interesting work to apply the technique to other language pairs, such as North and South Korean, as well.

Acknowledgments

The research in this paper was partially supported by National Science Council, Taiwan, under the contract NSC 97-2218-E-033-002.

References

1. Cheng, P.-J., Lu, W.-H., Tien, J.-W., Chien, L.-F.: Creating Multilingual Translation Lexicons with Regional Variations Using Web Corpora. In: Proc. of 42nd ACL, pp. 534–541 (2004)
2. Kwong, O.Y., Tsou, B.K.: Regional Variation of Domain-Specific Lexical Items: Toward a Pan-Chinese Lexical Resource. In: Proc. of 5th SIGHAN Workshop on Chinese Language Processing, pp. 9–16 (2006)
3. Li, H., Sim, K.C., Kuo, J.-S., Dong, M.: Semantic Transliteration of Personal Names. In: Proc. of 45th ACL, pp. 120–127 (2007)
4. Knight, K., Graehl, J.: Machine Transliteration. Computational Linguistics 24(4), 599–612 (1998)
5. Li, H., Zhang, M., Su, J.: A Joint Source Channel Model for Machine Transliteration. In: Proc. of 42nd ACL, pp. 159–166 (2004)
6. Oh, J.-H., Choi, K.-S.: An Ensemble of Grapheme and Phoneme for Machine Transliteration. In: Proc. of 2nd IJCNLP, pp. 450–461 (2005)
7. Hermjakob, U., Knight, K., Daumé III, H.: Name Translation in Statistical Machine Translation Learning When to Transliterate. In: Proc. of 46th ACL, pp. 389–397 (2008)
8. Meng, H., Lo, W.-K., Chen, B., Tang, T.: Generate Phonetic Cognates to Handle Name Entities in English-Chinese Cross-language Spoken Document Retrieval. In: Proc. of the IEEE workshop on ASRU, pp. 311–314 (2001)
9. Brill, E., Kacmarcik, G., Brockett, C.: Automatically Harvesting Katakana-English Term Pairs from Search Engine Query Logs. In: Proc. of NLPPRS, pp. 393–399 (2001)
10. Kuo, J.-S., Li, H., Yang, Y.-K.: A Phonetic Similarity Model for Automatic Extraction of Transliteration Pairs. ACM TALIP 6(2), 1–24 (2007)
11. Nie, J.-Y., Isabelle, P., Simard, M., Durand, R.: Cross-language Information Retrieval based on Parallel Texts and Automatic Mining of Parallel Text from the Web. In: Proc. of 22nd ACM SIGIR, pp. 74–81 (1999)
12. Sproat, R., Tao, T., Zhai, C.: Named Entity Transliteration with Comparable Corpora. In: Proc. of 44th ACL, pp. 73–80 (2006)
13. Lin, D., Zhao, S., Durme, B., Pasca, M.: Mining Parenthetical Translations from the Web by Word Alignment. In: Proc. of 46th ACL, pp. 994–1002 (2008)
14. Chang, M.-W., Ratinov, L., Roth, D.: Guiding Semi-Supervision with Constraint-Driven Learning. In: Proc. of 45th ACL, pp. 280–287 (2007)
15. Sarawagi, S., Chakrabarti, S., Godboley, S.: Cross-training: Learning Probabilistic Mappings between Topics. In: Proc. of SIGKDD 2003, pp. 177–186 (2003)
16. Soonthornphisaj, N., Kijsirikul, B.: Iterative Cross-training: An Algorithm for Learning from Unlabeled Web Pages. International Journal of Intelligent Systems 19(1-2), 131–147 (2004)
17. Brin, S., Page, L.: The Anatomy of a Large-scale Hypertextual Web Search Engine. In: Proc. of 7th WWW, pp. 107–117 (1998)
18. Chakrabarti, S., Berg, M., Dom, B.: Focused Crawling: A New Approach to Topic-Specific Web Resource Discovery. In: Proc. of 8th WWW, pp. 545–562 (1999)

A Simple and Efficient Model Pruning Method for Conditional Random Fields

Hai Zhao and Chunyu Kit

Department of Chinese, Translation and Linguistics,
City University of Hong Kong,
83 Tat Chee Avenue, Kowloon, Hong Kong, China
haizhao@cityu.edu.hk, ctckit@cityu.edu.hk

Abstract. Conditional random fields (CRFs) have been quite successful in various machine learning tasks. However, as larger and larger data become acceptable for the current computational machines, trained CRFs Models for a real application quickly inflate. Recently, researchers often have to use models with tens of millions features. This paper considers pruning an existing CRFs model for storage reduction and decoding speedup. We propose a simple but efficient rank metric for feature group rather than features that previous work usually focus on. A series of experiments in two typical labeling tasks, word segmentation and named entity recognition for Chinese, are carried out to check the effectiveness of the proposed method. The results are quite positive and show that CRFs models are highly redundant, even using carefully selected label set and feature templates.

Keywords: Conditional Random Fields, Model Pruning.

1 Introduction

CRFs are a structure learning tool first introduced in [1]. CRFs often outperform maximum entropy Markov model (MEMM) [2], another popular structure learning method. The main reason is that, among directed graphical models, CRFs do not suffer from the label bias problem as much as MEMM and other conditional Markov models do [1]. So far, CRFs have been successful in a good number of applications, especially in natural language processing [3].

As any other general-purpose machine learning tool, feature engineering is also a central part in CRFs learning. Typically, selecting good and sufficient features from auto constructed candidate set is an open problem since [1]. However, most existing work is only concerned with feature refinement in training stage for training speedup or performance enhancement (forward feature selection) [4,5,6,7], and few existing work considers model pruning for the decoding requirement (backward feature elimination) [8]. We will consider the latter in this paper. Because of rapid progress of modern computer manufacture technology, larger and larger data are fed into machine learning to build larger and

W. Li and D. Mollá-Aliod (Eds.): ICCPOL 2009, LNAI 5459, pp. 145–155, 2009.

larger models. For example, tens of millions features will be encountered in recent research move, but it is not always convenient to carry a model with so many features. In this study, we will consider to prune an existing CRFs model for storage reduction and decoding speedup. Our purpose is to reduce the given CRFs model as much as possible without or with least performance loss. Namely, we try to indicate those most necessary part in the model.

The most difference between our idea and previous work, either forward or backward feature pruning, is that structural factor is involved in our consideration. Thus a simple criterion is proposed to rank feature groups rather than features that previous work usually focused on.

The remainder of the paper is organized as follows. Section 2 proposes a criterion to ranking all groups of features in a given CRFs model. Section 3 presents our experimental results. Related work is discussed in Section 4. Section 5 concludes the paper and discusses future work.

2   The Proposed Method

2.1   CRFs

Given an input (observation) $\mathbf{x} \in X$ and parameter vector $\lambda = \lambda_1, ..., \lambda_M$, CRFs define the conditional probability $p(y|x)$ of a particular output $\mathbf{y} \in Y$ as being proportional to a product of potential functions on the cliques (namely, x) of a graph, which represents the interdependency of $\mathbf{y}$ and $\mathbf{x}$.

$$p(\mathbf{y}|\mathbf{x}; \lambda) = Z_\lambda(\mathbf{x})^{-1} \prod_{c \in C(\mathbf{y}, \mathbf{x})} \Phi_c(\mathbf{y}, \mathbf{x}; \lambda) \tag{1}$$

where $\Phi_c(\mathbf{y}, \mathbf{x}; \lambda)$ is a non-negative real value potential function on a clique $c \in C(\mathbf{y}, \mathbf{x})$. $Z_\lambda(\mathbf{x}) = \sum_{\hat{\mathbf{y}} \in Y} \prod_{c \in C(\mathbf{y}, \mathbf{x})} \Phi_c(\hat{\mathbf{y}}, \mathbf{x}; \lambda)$ is a normalization factor over all output values, Y.

A log-linear combination of weighted features,

$$\Phi_c(\mathbf{y}, \mathbf{x}; \lambda) = \exp(\lambda \mathbf{f}_c(\mathbf{y}, \mathbf{x})), \tag{2}$$

is often used as individual potential functions, where $\mathbf{f}_c$ represents a feature vector obtained from the corresponding clique c. It has been proved that the form in equation (2) is a sufficient and necessary condition to guarantee the probability distribution over the graph Markovian. That is, $\prod_{c \in C(\mathbf{y}, \mathbf{x})} \Phi_c(y, x) = \exp(\lambda F(y, x))$, where $F(\mathbf{y}, \mathbf{x}) = \sum_c \mathbf{f}_c(\mathbf{y}, \mathbf{x})$ is the CRF's global feature vector for $\mathbf{x}$ and $\mathbf{y}$.

The most probable output $\hat{\mathbf{y}}$ is given by $\hat{\mathbf{y}} = \arg \max_{\mathbf{y} \in Y} p(\mathbf{y}|\mathbf{x}; \lambda)$. However $Z_\lambda(\mathbf{x})$ never affects the decision of $\hat{\mathbf{y}}$ since $Z_\lambda(\mathbf{x})$ does not depend on $\mathbf{y}$. Thus, we can obtain the following discriminant function for CRFs:

$$\hat{\mathbf{y}} = \arg \max_{\mathbf{y} \in Y} \lambda F(\mathbf{y}, \mathbf{x}) \tag{3}$$

2.2   Pruning via Ranking Feature Groups

In equations (1) and (2), $\Phi_c(\mathbf{y}, \mathbf{x}; \lambda)$ is often rewritten as two parts,

$$\Phi_c(\mathbf{y}, \mathbf{x}; \lambda) = \Phi_{c1}(\mathbf{y}, \mathbf{x}; \lambda)\Phi_{c2}(y, \mathbf{x}; \lambda), \tag{4}$$

where

$$\Phi_{c1}(\mathbf{y}, \mathbf{x}; \lambda) = \exp(\sum_k \lambda'_k f'_k(\mathbf{y}, x)), \tag{5}$$

$$\Phi_{c2}(y, \mathbf{x}; \lambda) = \exp(\sum_k \lambda_k f_k(y, x)).$$

In above equations, $f_k(y, x))$ is a state feature function that uses only the label at a particular position, and $f'_k(\mathbf{y}, x))$ is a transition feature function that depends on the current and the previous labels. Consider that state and transition features play quite different roles in decoding, the pruning will be respectively performed on them. In practice, state features often covers the most part of all ones in a given model. Thus, the pruning mostly aims at state features.

Prevailingly, a feature function, either state- or transition-, can be written as binary form,

$$f_H(y') = \begin{cases} 1, & \text{if } H \text{ holds and } y = y' \\ 0, & \text{otherwise}, \end{cases} \tag{6}$$

where H is a predefined condition (rule) around the current clique. Incorporated with their corresponding weight (score) λ, all features f consist of the model after training is completed.

Two natural ways are considered for the model pruning. One is based on the condition H that determines the feature. Feature count cut-off according to its occurrence in the training data is such a method.The other is based on feature weight statistics. In theory, λ value may range from negative infinite to positive infinite. The larger this value is, the more significant the respective feature is. It seems that we can rank all features simply according to λ value. However, decoding structural object is more sophisticated than multi-class classification procedure over a single clique because structure characteristics are additionally involved for the former. For example, Markovian characteristics should be often considered in structure learning, which cannot be effectively handled by most multi-classification algorithms. Without considering structural loss, direct filtering those low scored features in CRFs learning and decoding will inevitably lead to a dramatic decrease of performance in most cases.

Having sequence labeling task as an example, we may regard the decoding over the given structure defined by CRFs approximately as two-stage procedure. The first stage is to compute all boundary probabilities for each clique, namely, the probability distribution to output all possible labels over a clique. The second stage will find a series of labels with the maximal joint probability through searching a path over the matrix constructed by these boundary probabilities.

We will focus on the first stage since its output consists of the basis of the search in the second stage. As we cannot determine the exact label for a clique before the decoding is completed, we have to consider a groups of activated features $f_H(y)$, for all $y \in Y$. Hereafter, we also call these features, $\{f_H(y), \forall y \in Y\}$ w.r.t some H, a feature group[1]. Here feature group pruning rather than feature pruning means that all features activated according to the predefined condition H over x will be discarded in decoding. When two groups of features, f_{H1} and f_{H2}, are activated for a clique c, our question will be, which one will be more informative? The answer is the one which can help us more confidently to predict a label to c. So, the group of features with more unbalanced weight scores can be more informative for the further prediction during search optimization. We take the variance of these scores as ranking metric of every groups of features,

$$v(\lambda_H) = N^{-1} \sum_y (\lambda_H(y) - \text{avg}(\lambda_H))^2, \qquad (7)$$

where $\lambda_H(y)$ is the corresponding weight for feature $f_H(y)$, and $\text{avg}(\lambda_H) = N^{-1} \sum_y \lambda_H(y)$ and N is the number of $f_H(y)$ in the given feature group, it should not be larger than the number of label set, $|Y|$, because not all $f_H(y, x)$, $\forall y \in Y$ must occur in the training data. We hereafter will keep those groups of features with the highest scores (variance values) according to the pruning criterion formula (7) in the reduced model.

3   Experiments

3.1   Settings

A series of experiments are performed to check the effectiveness of the proposed pruning method through learning and decoding in order-1 linear-chain CRFs. Gaussian prior is adopted in all CRFs training to avoid overfitting[2]. Two typical sequence labeling tasks in Chinese, word segmentation (WS) and named entity

---

[1] We take an example to explain what a feature group is. Assume that the label set is $\{A0, A1, A2\}$. $H = \{previous\_word = 'fire'\}$, a feature group about H contains three features, $f_H(A0)$, $f_H(A1)$, and $f_H(A2)$, if all of them occur in the training corpus. Note that in some literatures a feature group defined here is also identified as a single feature [4]. Since CRFs model will assign three different weight scores for $f_H(A0)$, $f_H(A1)$, and $f_H(A2)$, respectively, we regard them three different features, and call the set, $\{f_H(A0), f_H(A1), f_H(A2)\}$, a feature group.

[2] We choose the best Gaussian prior according to a series of cross-validation experiments in the original model, and the corresponding values will be kept unchanged as pruning. Though some existing studies show that L_1 regularization is effective in producing a more sparse model than L_2 regularization, our empirical study shows that L_1 regularization cannot provide satisfied performance for these two labeling tasks as L_2 regularization does.

Table 1. Corpora Statistics

Corpus	WS		NER	
	AS	MSRA	CityU	MSRA
Training(M)	8.39	4.05	2.71	2.17
Test(K)	198	184	364	173

recognition (NER), are evaluated. Two data sets of word segmentation, AS and MSRA, are from shared task Bakeoff-2[3], and two data sets of named entity recognition, CityU and MSRA, are from Bakeoff-3 [4], as summarized in Table 1 with corpus size in number of characters (tokens). The performance of both WS and NER is measured in terms of the F-measure $F = 2RP/(R + P)$, where R and P are the recall and precision of segmentation or NER.

Existing work shows that both WS and NER for Chinese can be effectively formulated as character tagging task [9,10,11,12]. According to these results, especially from the latter, we use a set of carefully selected label set and corresponding feature sets to train model for these two tasks, respectively. We will show that the model pruning is still effective even in these models that can bring up state-of-the-art performance. 6-tag set that represents character position in a word is kept using for word segmentation task as in [11,12]. We have show that 6-tag set can bring state-of-the-art performance since our previous work in [10,11]. Its six tags are B, B_2, B_3, M, E and S. For NER, we need to tell apart three types of NEs, namely, *person*, *location* and *organization* names. Correspondingly, the six tags are also adapted for characters in these NEs but distinguished by the prefixes Per-, Loc- and Org-. Plus an additional tag "O" for none NE characters, altogether we have 19 tags for NER. The following example illustrates how characters in words of various lengths are tagged in a sequence for word segmentation learning.

他 / 来自 / 阿根廷 / 首都 / 布宜诺斯艾利斯 /。
he / is from / Argentine / capital / Buenos Aires /.
S   B E   B B_2 E   B E   B$B_2$$B_3$MM M E S

And this is an example for NE tagging.

[马   拉   多   纳]/Per / 来 / 自 /[阿   根   廷]/Loc /。
Maradona / is from / Argentine /.
Per-B Per-B_2 Per-B_3 Per-E   O   O   Loc-B Loc-B_2 Loc-E   O

Six n-grams, C_{-1}, C_0, C_1, $C_{-1}C_0$, C_0C_1, and $C_{-1}C_1$, are selected as features for both tasks. As for NER, five unsupervised segmentation features generated by accessor variety criterion with respect to n-grams of different lengths are also introduced as in [12].

---

[3] http://www.sighan.org/bakeoff2005
[4] http://www.sighan.org/bakeoff2006

Table 2. Performance comparison and number of feature groups

Participant	WS		NER	
	AS	MSRA	CityU	MSRA
Bakeoff Best	.952	.964	.8903	.8651
Zhang et al. [13]	.951	.971		
Ours	.953	.973	.8918	.8630
#Feature group	2.60M	1.55M	1.46M	1.10M

A performance comparison of our trained model (without any pruning) and other best existing results is given in Table 2. This comparison shows that we will start the model pruning experiments based on a system with state-of-the-art performance.

3.2   Pruning Results

The numbers of feature groups in four models are given at the bottom of Table 2. Note that all these models contain millions of feature groups.

According to the ranking metric in (7), we remove the model step by step and observe how the performance changes. Our experimental results show that any performance loss is not encountered until pruning rate is larger than 65% for two WS tasks and 90% for two NER tasks. These results are shown in Figure 1(a). This indicates that these models are highly redundant.

In Figure 1(b), we keep few feature groups with top scores and observe how the performance varies. Still, we find few features help a great deal in performance. 1/50 features can give above 97% performance in all tasks. The value 97% and F-score rate in Figure 1(b) are computed in this way: divide F-score with 1/50 or some other amount of features by F-score with full features.

As a comparison, we compare the proposed method with feature count cut-off[5]. We prune the model according to the proposed ranking metric with the same rate as cut-off thresholds are set to 2, 3, 4, and 5, respectively. The pruning rates of each cut-off thresholds are given in Table 3. The performance comparison between our method and cut-off method are illustrated in Figures 2. We find that the simple cut-off according to the occurrence times of features may cause serious performance loss, while our pruning method only cause little for the same pruning rate.

The experimental results have shown that the proposed method is effective and CRFs models that we adopt at least are highly redundant. We don't give the results about decoding speedup after model pruning, because decoding speed

---

[5] Here, the term, 'feature count', aims at feature group. Thus it actually means the sum of feature count within a feature group. For example, as for a feature group, $f_H = \{f_H(A0), f_H(A1), f_H(A2)\}$, if three features, $f_H(A0)$, $f_H(A1)$, and $f_H(A2)$, occur 8, 6, and 5 times, respectively, then feature count for f_H should be 19. If cut-off threshold is set to 20, then this feature group will be discarded.

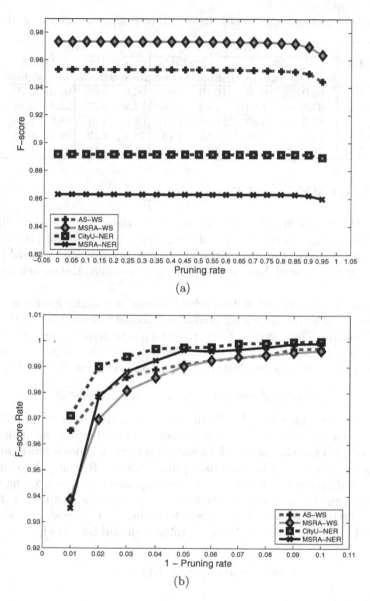

Fig. 1. Performance with different model pruning rates (F-score rate in (b) is obtained through divided by the F-score without any model pruning)

is highly sensitive detailed decoding algorithm. However, feature reduction in a model surely helps speedup decoding since the search space for decoding is narrowed.

Table 3. The rates and number of Pruned feature groups for each cut-off thresholds

Cut-off	WS				NER			
	AS		MSRA		CityU		MSRA	
	Rate(%)	#group(M)	Rate	#group	Rate	#group	Rate	#group
≥ 1	00.0	0.00	00.0	0.00	00.0	0.00	00.0	0.00
≥ 2	47.5	1.24	49.2	0.76	52.8	0.77	52.8	0.58
≥ 3	63.3	1.65	65.0	1.01	68.9	1.01	68.6	0.75
≥ 4	71.3	1.85	72.9	1.13	76.8	1.12	76.3	0.84
≥ 5	76.3	1.98	77.8	1.21	81.5	1.19	81.0	0.89

4   Related Work and Discussions

Basically, the proposed method is different from those mentioned in [8]. In our scheme, not a single feature but a feature group is picked up for pruning. As to our best knowledge, little existing work is concerned with CRFs model pruning, either, though some work has carefully discussed so-called feature selection issue [4,14].

Both model pruning and feature selection need a ranking metric to evaluate which feature is better among all candidates, so both of them share the similar idea in this sense. The differences, according to our understanding, are what rank metric is chosen and which kind of knowledge, posterior- or prior-, is adopted. In [4], the gain score of a new feature f_H with associated weight λ_H is given by:

$$G_\lambda(f_H) = \max_{\lambda_H} L_{\lambda + f_H \lambda_H} - L_\lambda - (\lambda_H^2/2\sigma^2), \tag{8}$$

where L_λ is the conditional log-likelihood for training, and σ^2 is a Gaussian prior. In order to make the gain computations tractable, the likelihood is approximated by a pseudo likelihood. In feature selection, those feature candidates with highest gain are added into the optimal subset. Recently, boosting techniques are paid more and more attention and applied to CRFs training speedup [6,7]. [6] proposes a method that simultaneously performs feature selection and parameter estimation for CRFs. In their formulation, to choose a good feature, a weighted least-square-error (WLSE) problem should be solved,

$$f_m(\mathbf{x}) = \operatorname{argmin}_f \sum_{i=1}^{N} w_i E(f(\mathbf{x}_i) - z_i)^2, \tag{9}$$

where w_i and z_i are two parameters that can be computed as in LogitBoost algorithm. Our ranking metric is some similar to [6] in formulation though quite different from the latter. In addition, the feature candidate of the latter is implicitly derived rather than explicitly ranking all possible features according to a metric score.

CRFs learning is not often an easy computational job in many cases as we need to train larger and larger labeled data. Feature selection, namely, to find an optimal feature subset for CRFs is even harder task than CRFs training itself. For example, in [4], sophisticated techniques are used to make feature selection tractable

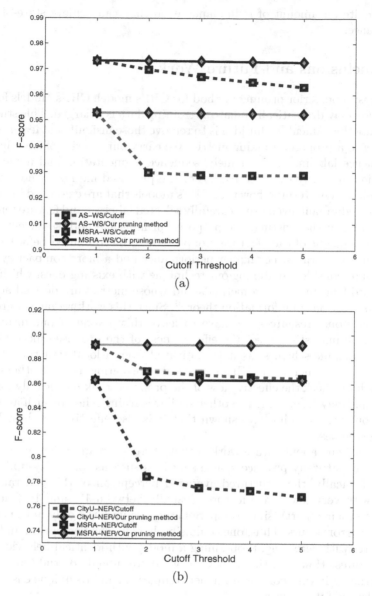

Fig. 2. Comparison of our pruning method and count cut-off method, (a) WS (b) NER

in computation. Thus, we can regard pruning an existing model with millions of features more practical than feature selection task defined by [1] in current computational machine settings. Especially, we start our work based on models obtained through training with carefully selected label set and feature template set by human observation, which is surely a tractable computational task.

Our results shows that a few features contribute a great deal to the performance and existing CRFs models that we have examined in this work at least contain quite an amount of redundancy even they can achieve state-of-the-art performance.

5   Conclusions and Future Work

We propose a posterior pruning method for CRFs model. CRFs Models for a real application may dramatically inflate as training data is enlarged. This study tries to alleviate this difficulty. Our idea is to remove those insignificant feature groups according to a proposed ranking metric. We carry out a series of experiments in two sequence labeling tasks, namely, sequence segmentation and named entity recognition, to verify the effectiveness of the proposed method. The results are quite positive. Our results show that CRFs models that are examined in this work are highly redundant, even using carefully selected label set and feature templates.

Compared to the existing, the proposed pruning method is efficient because only a local metric of each feature group needs to be computed before a sorting operation is performed. For higher performance and a more compact system, it is natural to consider combining our technique with existing ones, which mostly are forward feature selection methods and whose metrics are derived according to the observations in information theory[6]. Since this work requires a great deal of computational resources, we have to leave this as one of our future work. However, we may still expect the effectiveness of the proposed metric in these possible ensemble schemes, as it is motivated from a local structural factor of CRFs learning rather than global statistical information as most others.

Though we check the effectiveness of the proposed rank metric only for CRFs, its principle may be extended to other similar learning schemes such as MEMM. In fact, our early results have shown that it is also effective for these kinds of learning schemes.

Another issue about future work is that there are many other learning techniques that naturally produce sparse solutions such as some lazy-update algorithms. Typically, the structured averaged perceptron of [15] generally yields models with very few active features (usually between 1% and 10% active according to their report), since the parameters are updated only in the case that a training error occurs. Thus, one could simply train the perceptron and discard all features with zero weight, obtaining a model with identical behavior and far fewer features. However, this is beyond what we intend to study about CRFs model pruning in this work, and further comparison and technique ensemble will be also left as future work.

References

1. Lafferty, J.D., McCallum, A., Pereira, F.C.N.: Conditional random fields: Probabilistic models for segmenting and labeling sequence data. In: ICML 2001: Proceedings of the Eighteenth International Conference on Machine Learning, San Francisco, CA, USA, pp. 282–289 (2001)

---

[6] Apparently, [6] should be an exception.

2. Rosenfeld, B., Feldman, R., Fresko, M.: A systematic cross-comparison of sequence classifiers. In: SDM 2006, Bethesda, Maryland, pp. 563–567 (2006)
3. Sha, F., Pereira, F.: Shallow parsing with conditional random fields. In: Proceedings of the 2003 Conference of the North American Chapter of the Association for Computational Linguistics on Human Language Technology, Edmonton, Canada, vol. 1, pp. 134–141 (2003)
4. McCallum, A.: Efficiently inducing features of conditional random fields. In: Proceedings of the 19th Conference in Uncertainty in Articifical Intelligence (UAI 2003), Acapulco, Mexico, August 7-10 (2003)
5. Qi, Y., Szummer, M., Minka, T.P.: Diagram structure recognition by bayesian conditional random fields. In: Proceedings of the 2005 IEEE Computer Society Conference on Computer Vision and Pattern Recognition (CVPR 2005), San Diego, CA, USA, June 20-25, 2005, pp. 191–196 (2005)
6. Liao, L., Choudhury, T., Fox, D., Kautz, H.: Training conditional random fields using virtual evidence boosting. In: The Twentieth International Joint Conferfence on Artificial Intelligence (IJCAI 2007), Hyderabad, India, pp. 2530–2535, January 6-12 (2007)
7. Gutmann, B., Kersting, K.: Stratified gradient boosting for fast training of confidi-tional random fields. In: Malerba, D., Appice, A., Ceci, M. (eds.) Proceedings of the 6th International Workshop on Multi-Relational Data Mining, Warsaw, Poland, pp. 56–68, September 17 (2007)
8. Guyon, I., Elisseeff, A.: An introduction to variable and feature selection. Journal of Machine Learning Research 3, 1157–1182 (2003)
9. Peng, F., Feng, F., McCallum, A.: Chinese segmentation and new word detection using conditional random fields. In: COLING 2004, Geneva, Switzerland, pp. 562–568, August 23-27 (2004)
10. Zhao, H., Huang, C.-N., Li, M.: An improved Chinese word segmentation system with conditional random field. In: Proceedings of the Fifth SIGHAN Workshop on Chinese Language Processing, Sydney, Australia, pp. 162–165, July 22-23 (2006)
11. Zhao, H., Huang, C.-N., Li, M., Lu, B.-L.: Effective tag set selection in Chinese word segmentation via conditional random field modeling. In: Proceedings of the 20th Asian Pacific Conference on Language, Information and Computation, Wuhan, China, pp. 87–94, November 1-3 (2006)
12. Zhao, H., Kit, C.: Unsupervised segmentation helps supervised learning of char-acter tagging for word segmentation and named entity recognition. In: The Sixth SIGHAN Workshop on Chinese Language Processing, Hyderabad, India, pp. 106–111, January 11-12 (2008)
13. Zhang, R., Kikui, G., Sumita, E.: Subword-based tagging by conditional random fields for Chinese word segmentation. In: Proceedings of Human Language Tech-nology Conference/North American chapter of the Association for Computational Linguistics annual meeting (HLT/NAACL-2006), New York, pp. 193–196 (2006)
14. Pietra, S.D., Pietra, V.D., Lafferty, J.: Inducing features of random fields. IEEE Transactions on Pattern Analysis and Machine Intelligence 19, 380–393 (1997)
15. Collins, M.: Discriminative training methods for hidden markov models: Theory and experiments with perceptron algorithms. In: Proceedings of the 2002 Con-ference on Empirical Methods in Natural Language Processing (EMNLP 2002), University of Pennsylvania, Philadelphia, PA, USA, pp. 1–8, July 6-7 (2002)

Query-Oriented Summarization Based on Neighborhood Graph Model

Furu Wei[1,2], Yanxiang He[1], Wenjie Li[2], and Lei Huang[1]

[1] Department of Computer Science and Technology
Wuhan University, China
{frwei,yxhe}@whu.edu.cn
[2] Department of Computing
The Hong Kong Polytechnic University, Hong Kong
{cswjli}@comp.polyu.edu.hk

Abstract. In this paper, we investigate how to combine the *link-aware* and *link-free* information in sentence ranking for query-oriented summarization. Although the link structure has been emphasized in the existing graph-based summarization models, there is lack of pertinent analysis on how to use the links. By contrasting the text graph with the web graph, we propose to evaluate significance of sentences based on neighborhood graph model. Taking the advantage of the link information provided on the graph, each sentence is evaluated according to its own value as well as the cumulative impacts from its neighbors. For a task like query-oriented summarization, it is critical to explore how to reflect the influence of the query. To better incorporate query information into the model, we further design a query-sensitive similarity measure to estimate the association between a pair of sentences. When evaluated on DUC 2005 dataset, the results of the pro-posed approach are promising.

Keywords: Query-Oriented Summarization, Neighborhood Graph, Query-Sensitive Similarity.

1 Introduction

Query-oriented summarization is promoted by the Document Understanding Conferences (DUC). It aims to produce a brief and well-organized summary for a cluster of relevant documents according to a given query that describes a user's information need. A variety of models have been proposed in the literature. Most of them concentrate on evaluating the relevance of the sentence to the query by elaborately designing the features that characterize different aspects of the sentence and/or developing evaluation methods that can effectively calculate the combinational effects of the features. The most significant sentences are often picked out to produce a summary. We call this sort of models feature-based models. While feature-based models evaluate the sentences relying on the individual sentences themselves, in the recent past, there is growing interest in graph-based models where the links among the sentences are also taken into account and thereby the information embodied in the

W. Li and D. Mollá-Aliod (Eds.): ICCPOL 2009, LNAI 5459, pp. 156–167, 2009.
© Springer-Verlag Berlin Heidelberg 2009

entire graph can be utilized. In other words, the graph-based models emphasize and explore the link structure information (i.e. they are *link-aware*) in contrast with the feature-based models which are normally *link-free*.

Existing graph-based approaches to query-oriented summarization basically model the documents as a weighted text graph by taking the sentences measured by their relevance to the query as the nodes and the connection between the sentences measured by sentence similarity or association as the edges. The graph-based ranking algorithms such as PageRank are then applied to identify the most significant sentences. These approaches are inspired by the idea behind web graph models which have been successfully used by current search engines. In web graph models, the web is considered as a directed graph, namely web graph, where the web pages are regarded as the nodes and the hyperlinks among the web pages as the edges. Intuitively, graph-based summarization models work well because it takes into account global information recursively computed from the entire text graph rather than only relying on the local context of a single sentence. However, we argue that we need a critical investigation on the difference between the web graph and the text graph before we directly adapt the PageRank algorithm from web graph models to text graph models. We think the text graph is in essence different from the web graph in the following two aspects.

First, the meaning of the links and the paths through the links are different. The links on the web graph are certain. They are determined by the hyperlinks and can be changed when the hyperlinks are inserted, modified or removed. Even though the two web pages may not be directly linked, it is still possible for one to reach the other by traveling through some intermediate pages and the links among them. Traditional PageRank propagates page importance through the links in the paths. In contrast, the links on the text graph are artificial in the sense that they are added only if the similarity of a sentence pair is significant enough and they are no longer changed once the graph has been constructed. Accordingly, any two sentences must be evaluated for potential connections in the text graph. This makes the indirect paths between two sentences makes less (or even no) sense than the indirect paths between two web pages. Say, for example, importance would be repeatedly propagated if there are a direct link and many indirect links between the sentences. Propagation to neighbors only would be more reasonable. Second, the weights of the links are interpreted differently. The (normalized) edge weight in the web graph can be naturally interpreted as the transition probability between the two web pages. In contrast, the edge weight in the text graph is defined by a sentence distance or similarity measure, yet there are many different ways to define the similarity or the distance.

We highly support the idea of combining both the *link-aware* and *link-free* information for sentence ranking and investigate its application in the task of query-oriented summarization in this paper. Based on the difference between the text graph and the web graph discussed previously, we suggest evaluating sentence significance based on the neighborhood graph. The significance of a sentence is evaluated according to its own value and the propagation effects from its near neighbors. Compared with the iterative PageRank algorithm, this neighborhood based one-time propagation algorithm is of higher computing efficiency and meanwhile it also allows both the link information and the individual sentence features well used. Based on the neighborhood graph model, we pay special attentions to how to deign the distance function and study different approaches to convert the existing similarity measures to the distance measures. More important, in order to better incorporate query influence in the graph, we design a query-sensitive similarity measure to replace the commonly used query-unaware similarity measure.

The remainder of this paper is organized as follows. Section 2 reviews existing graph-based summarization models and the corresponding ranking algorithms. Section 3 introduces the proposed sentence ranking algorithm and the query-sensitive similarity. After that, Section 4 reports experiments and evaluation results. Finally, Section 5 concludes the paper.

2 Related Work

Graph-based ranking algorithms such as Google's PageRank [1] have been successfully used in the analysis of the link structure of the WWW. Now they are springing up in the community of document summarization. The major concerns in graph-based summarization researches include how to model the documents using text graph and how to transform existing page ranking algorithms to their variations that could accommodate various summarization requirements.

Erkan and Radev [2] [3] represented the documents as a weighted undirected graph by taking sentences as vertices and cosine similarity between sentences as the edge weight function. An algorithm called LexRank, adapted from PageRank, was applied to calculate sentence significance, which was then used as the criterion to rank and select summary sentences. Meanwhile, Mihalcea and Tarau [8] [9] presented their PageRank variation, called TextRank, in the same year.

Likewise, the use of PageRank family was also very popular in event-based summarization approaches [4] [5] [13] [15]. In contrast to conventional sentence-based approaches, newly emerged event-based approaches took event terms, such as verbs and action nouns and their associated named entities as graph nodes, and connected nodes according to their co-occurrence information or semantic dependency relations. They were able to provide finer text representation and thus could be in favor of sentence compression which was targeted to include more informative contents in a fixed-length summary. Nevertheless, these advantages lied on appropriately defining and selecting event terms.

All above-mentioned representative work was concerned with generic summarization. Later on, graph-based ranking algorithms were introduced in query-oriented summarization too when this new challenge became a hot research topic recently. For example, a topic-sensitive version of PageRank was proposed in [10]. The same idea was followed by Wan et al. [14] and Lin et al. [7]. Given three sets of chronologically ordered documents, Lin et al [7] proposed to construct timestamp graph for the update summary task by incrementally adding the sentences to the graph. Different from generic summarization, query-oriented summarization is necessarily driven by queries. Although the query effects can be modeled in a text graph in different ways, to our knowledge, they were confined to the graph nodes in terms of sentence relevance to a given query in all current published work. We argue that the query effects on the edges are equally if not more important than on the nodes. Sentence similarity should be a measure not only replying on the content of the two sentences involved, but also conditioned on query requirement.

Measuring similarities between two text units, such as documents, sentences, or terms, has been one of the most fundamental issues in information retrieval. While a large amount of related work was found in literature, little of them considered measuring the similarity with respect to a specified context, e.g. a query from the user. Tombros and Rijsbergen [11] [12] pioneered in development of query-sensitive similarity functions. They combined the traditional cosine similarity between the pair of documents with the collective similarity of the two documents and the query together, which was defined as the cosine similarity between the centroid of the two documents and the query. Later, Zhou and Dai [16] proposed a query-sensitive similarity measure for content-based image retrieval based on Euclidean distance which was widely used in image processing.

3   Neighborhood Graph Based Query-Oriented Summarization Model

The task of query-oriented summarization defined in DUC is to generate a summary from a query q that reflects a user's information need and a cluster of relevant documents D. The query usually consists of one or more interrogative and/or narrative sentences. The generated summary is restricted to a given length in words. So far, extractive summarization has been the predominant technique in query-oriented summarization, in which the most critical process involved is sentence ranking. We will introduction our sentence ranking strategy in the following sections.

3.1   Neighborhood Graph Based Sentence Ranking

Given a query q and a cluster of relevant documents D consisting of a set of sentences $\{s_1, s_2, ..., s_n\}$ and each sentence s_i is associated with a weight $w(s_i)$,

$$w(s_i) = rel(s_i \mid q) = \frac{\vec{s}_i \cdot \vec{q}}{|\vec{s}_i| \cdot |\vec{q}|} \tag{1}$$

We start with the following definitions and then discuss weight propagation among them.

Definition 1 (Eps-Neighborhood of a sentence): The Eps-Neighborhood of a sentence s_i (indicated by $N_\varepsilon(s_i)$) is defined as $N_\varepsilon(s_i) = \{s_{j \neq i} \in D \mid dist(s_i, s_j) \leq \varepsilon\}$, where $dist(s_i, s_j)$ is the distance between s_i and s_j.

Definition 2 (Neighborhood Graph for a sentence set): The neighborhood graph for a set of sentences D (indicated by G_ε), is a undirected graph that satisfies (1) each node in G_ε corresponds to a sentence in D; (2) each edge $e_{ij} = (s_i, s_j) \in G_\varepsilon$ iff $s_j \in N_\varepsilon(s_i)$

and its length varies in the proportion of the distance between the two sentences that the edge connects. The Eps-Neighborhood is a symmetric relation according to Definition 1. So $s_i \in N_\varepsilon(s_j)$ holds as well.

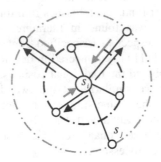

Fig. 1. Neighborhood Graph

In a neighborhood graph, as seen in Figure 1, sentences are connected to their neighbors within the defined distance. Connections bring along influence on one another. The influence in turn changes the weight of each individual sentence to some extend by the collective effects from its neighbors. Intuitively, the influence can be determined based on two factors. One is the distance between s_i and s_j. The other is the weight of s_j. The higher weighed s_j that is closer to s_i would exert greater influence on s_i. The influence between s_i and s_j is bi-directional. However, it is asymmetrical. The degree of the influence between them in the two directions may not equal when s_i and s_j are of different weights.

Definition 3 (Influence Damping Factor): Given $s_i \in N_\varepsilon(s_j)$ and $s_j \in N_\varepsilon(s_i)$, their influence on each other in terms of distance is a symmetric distance damping function defined by

$$f(s_i, s_j, \sigma) = \exp\left(-\frac{1}{\sigma^2} \cdot dist^2(s_i, s_j)\right) \tag{2}$$

where σ is a parameter to smooth the distance. We can imagine that the weight $w(s_j)$ spread out from s_j to s_i and its influence is damped with $f(s_i, s_j, \sigma)$ during it traveling along the connection of s_i and s_j. When it arrives at s_i, the remaining weight influence becomes $f(s_i, s_j, \sigma)w(s_j)$.

As a result, the entire weight of s_i (normally called sentence significance $SIG(s_i)$) is adjusted by adding the cumulative influence from all the sentences in its Eps-Neighborhood to the original weight of itself. The following equation is deduced.

$$SIG(s_i) = w(s_i) + \sum_{s_j \in N_\varepsilon(s_i)} \left(f(s_i, s_j, \sigma)w(s_j)\right) \tag{3}$$

We obtain the distance function required in equation (2) from the similarity function according to geometrical relation instead of liner relation. More precisely, the distance dist(s_i, s_j) is defined as the sine of the angle of s_i and s_j. (indicated by $\angle(s_i, s_j)$).

$$dist(s_i, s_j) = \sin(\angle(s_i, s_j)) = \sqrt{1 - \cos^2(\angle(s_i, s_j))}$$

$$= \sqrt{1 - sim^2(s_i, s_j)} \qquad (4)$$

where $sim(s_i, s_j) = \dfrac{\vec{s}_i \cdot \vec{s}_j}{\|\vec{s}_i\| \cdot \|\vec{s}_j\|}$.

3.2 Query-Sensitive Similarity

Existing similarity measures produce static and constant scores. However, we believe that similarity between the two sentences s_i and s_j should be adjusted when the query q is involved. This observation is extremely important for studying query-oriented summarization models.

Intuitively, the query-sensitive similarity measure should consist of two parts, i.e. the query-independent part and the query-dependent part. The query-independent part concerns the dedication of query-unaware similarity, while the query-dependent part further highlights the contribution of the terms in common not only in s_i and s_j but also in q. Formally, the query-sensitive similarity can be formulated as $sim(s_i, s_j \mid q) = f(sim(s_i, s_j \mid \in q), sim(s_i, s_j \mid \notin q))$

Let $s_i = \{t_{i1}, t_{i2}, ..., t_{in}\}$, $s_j = (s_{j1}, s_{j2}, ..., s_{jn})$ and $q = \{q_1, q_2, ..., q_n\}$ be three n-dimensional word vectors. $\mu = \max(q_k)$ and $\eta = \min(q_k)$ where $1 \le k \le n$ and $q_k \ne 0$. We define the following weight coefficient function

$$S(q_k) = \begin{cases} \xi, q_k = 0 \\ \xi + \left(\theta_1 + \dfrac{q_k - \eta}{\mu - \eta} \cdot (\theta_2 - \theta_1) \right), q_k \ne 0 \end{cases} \qquad (5)$$

where $0 < \theta_1 < \theta_2 < \xi < 1$. Notice that there is a special case that the above function can not cope with, i.e., $\mu = \eta$. In this case

$$S(q_k) = \begin{cases} \xi, q_k = 0 \\ \xi + \left(\dfrac{\theta_2 - \theta_1}{2} \right), q_k \ne 0 \end{cases} \qquad (6)$$

Then, we define the query-sensitive similarity function as

$$sim(s_i, s_j \mid q) = \dfrac{\sum\limits_{k=1}^{n} S(q_k) \cdot t_{ik} \cdot t_{jk}}{\sqrt{\sum\limits_{k=1}^{n} t_{ik}^2} \cdot \sqrt{\sum\limits_{k=1}^{n} t_{jk}^2}} \qquad (7)$$

When we move from query-unaware similarity $sim(o_i, o_j)$ to query-sensitive similarity $sim(o_i, o_j | q)$, the range of the adjustment is subject to the certain constraints by equation (6).

Proposition 1. The query-sensitive similarity defined by equation (7) ranges from $\xi \cdot sim(o_1, o_2)$ to $(\xi + \theta_2) sim(o_1, o_2)$, more precisely from $\xi \cdot sim(o_1, o_2) + \theta_1 \cdot sim'(o_1, o_2)$ to $\xi \cdot sim(o_1, o_2) + \theta_2 \cdot sim'(o_1, o_2)$. $sim(o_1, o_2)$ is defined as the cosine similarity between the two corresponding vectors.

$sim'(o_1, o_2)$ is contributed from the query- dependent part.

Proof: Let $n^q = \{ k \mid q_k \neq 0 \}$, then

$$sim(o_i, o_j | q) = \frac{\xi \cdot \sum_{k=1}^{n} o_{ik} \cdot o_{jk}}{\sqrt{\sum_{k=1}^{n} o_{ik}^2} \cdot \sqrt{\sum_{k=1}^{n} o_{jk}^2}} + \frac{\left(\theta_1 + \frac{q_k - \eta}{\mu - \eta} \cdot (\theta_2 - \theta_1) \right) \cdot \sum_{k \in n^q} o_{ik} \cdot o_{jk}}{\sqrt{\sum_{k=1}^{n} o_{ik}^2} \cdot \sqrt{\sum_{k=1}^{n} o_{jk}^2}} \tag{8}$$

Then,

$$sim(o_i, o_j, q) \geq \frac{\xi \cdot \sum_{k=1}^{n} o_{ik} \cdot o_{jk}}{\sqrt{\sum_{k=1}^{n} o_{ik}^2} \cdot \sqrt{\sum_{k=1}^{n} o_{jk}^2}} + \frac{\theta_1 \cdot \sum_{k \in n^q} o_{ik} \cdot o_{jk}}{\sqrt{\sum_{k=1}^{n} o_{ik}^2} \cdot \sqrt{\sum_{k=1}^{n} o_{jk}^2}}$$

$$= \xi \cdot sim(o_i, o_j) + \theta_1 \cdot sim'(o_i, o_j) \geq \xi \cdot sim(o_i, o_j) \tag{9}$$

$$sim(o_i, o_j | q) \leq \frac{\xi \cdot \sum_{k=1}^{n} o_{ik} \cdot o_{jk}}{\sqrt{\sum_{k=1}^{n} o_{ik}^2} \cdot \sqrt{\sum_{k=1}^{n} o_{jk}^2}} + \frac{\theta_2 \cdot \sum_{k \in n^q} o_{ik} \cdot o_{jk}}{\sqrt{\sum_{k=1}^{n} o_{ik}^2} \cdot \sqrt{\sum_{k=1}^{n} o_{jk}^2}}$$

$$= \xi \cdot sim(o_i, o_j) + \theta_2 \cdot sim'(o_i, o_j) \leq (\xi + \theta_2) \cdot sim(o_i, o_j) \tag{10}$$

$\square$

There are three parameters in Proposition 1, i.e. ξ, θ_1 and θ_2. They are all meaningful and can be appropriately determined according to the practical application requirements. ξ is the contribution degree of the original query-unaware similarity $sim(o_i, o_j)$ in the query-sensitive similarity function. θ_1 and θ_2 can be viewed as the lower and upper bounds of the contribution from the query-dependent part. The advantage of making the proposed query-sensitive similarity bounded is that we can determine the degree of the influence from the query by means of setting the three mentioned parameters with appropriate values. Note that, these values are usually pre-assigned according to the specified applications.

Now, we integrate the query-sensitive similarity into the neighborhood graph based sentence ranking algorithm introduced before. Equation (2) and (3) are re-formulated as

$$f(s, s_i, q, \sigma) = \exp\left(-\frac{1}{2\sigma^2} \cdot \left(1 - sim^2(s, s_i \mid q)\right)\right) \qquad (11)$$

$$SIG(s_i) = w(s_i) + \left(\sum_{s_j \in N_e(s)} \left(f(s_i, s_j, q, \sigma) \cdot w(s_j)\right)\right) \qquad (12)$$

4 Experiments

Experiments are conducted on the DUC 2005 50 document clusters. Each cluster of documents is accompanied with a query description representing a user's information need. Stop-words in both documents and queries are removed[1] and the remaining words are stemmed by Porter Stemmer[2]. According to the task definition, system-generated summaries are strictly limited to 250 English words in length. We incrementally add into a summary the highest ranked sentence of concern if it doesn't significantly repeat the information already included in the summary until the word limitation is reached. Like the other researchers, we use ROUGE[3] [6] which has been officially adopted for DUC automatic evaluations since 2005, as the evaluation metric.

In the following experiments, the sentences and the queries are represented as the vectors of words. The relevance of a sentence to the query is calculated by cosine similarity. The sentence-level inverse sentence frequency (ISF) rather than document-level IDF is used when dealing with sentence-level text processing.

4.1 Experiments on Ranking Strategy

We first evaluate the proposed neighborhood-based weight propagation ranking strategy (denoted by NM). For comparison purpose, we also present the results of another two widely used ranking strategies. One is to simply rank the sentences based on their relevance to the query (denoted by QR). The other is the PageRank deduced iterative ranking algorithm (denoted by PR). The damping factor used here is set to 0.85 according to the previous literature. Table 1 below shows the results of average recall scores of ROUGE-1, ROUGE-2 and ROUGE -SU4 along with their 95% confidence intervals within square brackets. In these experiments, the distance

Table 1. Different Models and Ranking Strategies

	ROUGE-1	ROUGE-2	ROUGE-SU4
NM	**0.3796** [0.3729, 0.3860]	**0.0770** [0.0735, 0.0804]	**0.1350** [0.1312, 0.1385]
PR	0.3702 [0.3672, 0.3772]	0.0725 [0.0704, 0.0766]	0.1306 [0.1274, 0.1341]
QR	0.3597 [0.3540, 0.3654]	0.0664 [0.0630, 0.0697]	0.1229 [0.1196, 0.1261]

---

[1] A list of 199 words is used to filter stop-words.
[2] http://www.tartarus.org/~martin/PorterStemmer
[3] ROUGE version 1.5.5 is used.

threshold used to define the neighborhood is set to 0.95 and the distance smoothing parameter is set to 1.

As shown in Table 1, both NM and PR are able to produce much better results than QR. In particular, NM outperforms QR by 5.53% of the improvement in ROUGE-1, 15.96% in ROUGE-2, and 9.85% in ROUGE-SU4. The contribution of link-aware weight is remarkable. Besides, it is also observed that NM outperforms PR by 2.54% of the increase in ROUGE-1, 6.21% in ROUGE-2 and 3.37% on ROUGE-SU4. The improvement is very encouraging to us.

4.2   Experiments on Query-Sensitive Similarity

Table 2 below compares the results of NM with query-unaware (i.e. NM) and query-sensitive similarity (called QsS-NM) measures. The three parameters in the query-sensitive similarity measure are set to ξ =0.8, θ_1 =0.1 and θ_2 =0.2.

Table 2. Query-Unaware and Query-Sensitive Similarity

	ROUGE-1	ROUGE-2	ROUGE-SU4
QsS-NM	**0.3815** [0.3749, 0.3879]	**0.0782** [0.0746, 0.0817]	**0.1357** [0.1319, 0.1392]
NM	0.3796 [0.3729, 0.3860]	0.0770 [0.0735, 0.0804]	0.1350 [0.1312, 0.1385]

We are happy to see that the improvements from the query sensitive similarity in NM indeed exist. The performance raised is consistent though not quite significant. This is not surprised at all. Given the facts that NM has already achieved notable results and the similarity measure itself only functions as a part of significance evaluation, the further improvement based on NM may become much hard-earned. We can conclude that the query-sensitive similarity is a direction worth further extensive study. More important, it can be applied in many applications other than query-oriented summarization.

4.3   Experiments on Distance Measure

The distance measure required in Influence Damping Factor needs to be calculated from the similarity measure. The cosine similarity has been recognized as a remarkably versatile and popular similarity measure in text processing. However, there is no canonical best conversion between the similarity and distance functions. In the following table, we examine three different approaches. They are (1) our proposed Sine of the angle between the two vectors (i.e. SIN) which can be regarded as a geometry conversion; (2) a simple linear conversion (i.e. LIN), and (3) the Euclidean distance on unit vectors (i.e. UED), which is a natural integration of the Euclidean distance (normally used in pattern recognition and data mining applications) and the cosine similarity (normally used in information retrieval and text mining applications).

Notation	Description
Sine (SIN)	$dist(a,b) = \sqrt{1 - sim^2(a,b)}$
Liner (LIN)	$dist(a,b) = 1 - sim(a,b)$
Euclidean Distance (UED)[4]	$dist(a,b) = \sqrt{2 - 2 \cdot sim(a,b)}$

The parameter settings here are the same as those in Section 4.1 and 4.2. We can see in Table 3 that SIN is favorable in both NM and QsS-NM although the difference between the three distance functions is not significant enough. This observation is interesting and motivates us to further investigate.

Table 3. Different Distance Measures

	ROUGE-1	ROUGE-2	ROUGE-SU4
QsS-NM (SIN)	**0.3815** [0.37493, 0.3879]	**0.0782** [0.0746, 0.0817]	**0.1357** [0.1319, 0.1392]
QsS-NM (LIN)	0.3801 [0.3734, 0.3866]	0.0779 [0.0743, 0.0815]	0.1348 [0.1310, 0.1383]
QsS-NM (UED)	0.3794 [0.3724, 0.3857]	0.0770 [0.0730, 0.0804]	0.1347 [0.1308, 0.1384]
NM (SIN)	**0.3796** [0.3729, 0.3860]	**0.0770** [0.0735, 0.0804]	**0.1350** [0.1312, 0.1385]
NM (LIN)	0.3797 [0.3734, 0.3859]	0.0760 [0.0725, 0.0793]	0.1344 [0.1309, 0.1376]
NM (UED)	0.3795 [0.3728, 0.3856]	0.0764 [0.0728, 0.0797]	0.1347 [0.1311, 0.1380]

4.4 Comparison with DUC Systems

Thirty-one systems have been submitted to DUC for evaluation in 2005. Table 4 compares neighborhood models with them. To provide a global picture, we present the following representative ROUGE results of (1) the worst-performed human summary (i.e. H), which reflects the margin between the machine-generated summaries and the human summaries; (2) the top five and worst participating systems according to ROUGE-2; (3) the average ROUGE scores (i.e. AVG); and (4) the NIST baseline which simply selects the first sentences in the documents. We can then easily locate the positions of the proposed models among them.

It clearly shows in Table 4 that both QsS-NM and NM outperform the first-ranked system (i.e. S15). QsS-NM is above S15 by 7.86% in ROUGE-2 and 3.12% in

---

[4] Let a, b be two unit vectors, the Euclidean distance,

$dist(a,b) = \sqrt{\sum_i (a_i - b_i)^2} = \sqrt{\sum_i a_i^2 + \sum_i b_i^2 - 2\sum_i (a_i \cdot b_i)} = \sqrt{2 - 2 \cdot \langle a \bullet b \rangle}$. In UED, we will first $= \sqrt{2 - 2 \cdot \cos(a,b)} = \sqrt{2 - 2 \cdot sim(a,b)}$

normalize the sentence vectors into unit vectors.

ROUGE-SU4. Even NM can also have 6.21% increase in ROUGE-2 and 2.58% in ROUGE-SU4. These are definitely exciting achievements since the best system (i.e. S15) is only 1.12% above the second-best system (i.e. S17) on ROUGE-2 and 1.46% on ROUGE-SU4.

Table 4. System Comparison

	ROUGE-1[5]	ROUGE-2	ROUGE-SU4
H	-	0.0897	0.1510
...			
QsS-NM	**0.3815**	**0.0782**	**0.1357**
NM	**0.3796**	**0.0770**	**0.1350**
...			
S15	-	0.0725	0.1316
S17	-	0.0717	0.1297
S10	-	0.0698	0.1253
S8	-	0.0696	0.1279
S4	-	0.0686	0.1277
...			
S23	-	0.0256	0.0557
AVG		0.0584	0.1121
NIST Baseline	-	0.0403	0.0872

5 Conclusion

Graph based models and algorithms have been an interesting and promising research topic in text mining. In this work, we develop a novel sentence ranking algorithm based on neighborhood graph models for query-oriented summarization. The main contributions are (1) examining the problems in the existing graph-based summarization methods, and then proposing a new ranking algorithm based on neighborhood weight propagation; (2) designing a query-sensitive similarity measure that incorporates the query information into graph edges. The ROUGE evaluations on DUC 2005 dataset show that the proposed method is workable which can outperform the best participating system in DUC competitions.

Acknowledgments

The research work presented in this paper was partially supported by the grants from NSF of Hubei, China (Project No: 2008CDB343), NSF of China (Project No: 60703008), RGC of HKSAR (Project No: PolyU5217/07E) and the Hong Kong Polytechnic University (Project No: A-PA6L).

---

[5] The ROUGE-1 scores and all the 95% confidential intervals are not officially released by DUC.

References

1. Brin, S., Page, L.: The Anatomy of a Large-scale Hypertextual Web Search Engine. Computer Networks and ISDN Systems 30(1-7), 107–117 (1998)
2. Erkan, G., Radev, D.R.: LexPageRank: Prestige in Multi-Document Text Summarization. In: Proceedings of EMNLP, pp. 365–371 (2004a)
3. Erkan, G., Radev, D.R.: LexRank: Graph-based Centrality as Salience in Text Summarization. Journal of Artificial Intelligence Research 22, 457–479 (2004b)
4. Leskovec, J., Grobelnik, M., Milic-Frayling, N.: Learning Sub-structures of Document Semantic Graphs for Document Summarization. In: Proceedings of LinkKDD Workshop, pp. 133–138 (2004)
5. Li, W., Wu, M., Lu, Q., Xu, W., Yuan, C.: Extractive Summarization using Intra- and Inter-Event Relevance. In: Proceedings of ACL/COLING, pp. 369–376 (2006)
6. Lin, C.Y., Hovy, E.: Automatic Evaluation of Summaries Using N-gram Co-occurrence Statistics. In: Proceedings of HLT-NAACL, pp. 71–78 (2003)
7. Lin, Z., Chua, T.S., Kan, M.Y., Lee, W.S., Qiu, L., Ye, S.: NUS at DUC 2007: Using Evolutionary Models for Text. In: Proceedings of Document Understanding Conference (DUC) (2007)
8. Mihalcea, R., Tarau, P.: TextRank - Bringing Order into Text. In: Proceedings of EMNLP, pp. 404–411 (2004)
9. Mihalcea, R.: Graph-based Ranking Algorithms for Sentence Extraction, Applied to Text Summarization. In: Proceedings of ACL (Companion Volume) (2004)
10. OtterBacher, J., Erkan, G., Radev, D.R.: Using Random Walks for Question-focused Sentence Retrieval. In: Proceedings of HLT/EMNLP, pp. 915–922 (2005)
11. Tombros, A., van Rijsbergen, C.J.: Query-Sensitive Similarity Measures for Information Retrieval. Knowledge and Information Systems 6, 617–642 (2004)
12. Tombros, A., van Rijsbergen, C.J.: Query-Sensitive Similarity Measures for the Calculation of Interdocument Relationships. In: Proceedings of CIKM, pp. 17–24 (2001)
13. Vanderwende, L., Banko, M., Menezes, A.: Event-Centric Summary Generation. In: Working Notes of DUC 2004 (2004)
14. Wan, X., Yang, J., Xiao, J.: Using Cross-Document Random Walks for Topic-Focused Multi-Document Summarization. In: Proceedings of the 2006 IEEE/WIC/ACM International Conference on Web Intelligence, pp. 1012–1018 (2006)
15. Yoshioka, M., Haraguchi, M.: Multiple News Articles Summarization based on Event Reference Information. In: Working Notes of NTCIR-4 (2004)
16. Zhou, Z.H., Dai, H.B.: Query-Sensitive Similarity Measure for Content-Based Image Retrieval. In: Proceedings of ICDM, pp. 1211–1215 (2006)

An Extractive Text Summarizer Based on Significant Words

Xiaoyue Liu, Jonathan J. Webster, and Chunyu Kit

Department of Chinese, Translation and Linguistics
City University of Hong Kong, Tat Chee Ave., Kowloon, Hong Kong
{xyliu0,ctjjw,ctckit}@cityu.edu.hk

Abstract. Document summarization can be viewed as a reductive distilling of source text through content condensation, while words with high quantities of information are believed to carry more content and thereby importance. In this paper, we propose a new quantification measure for word significance used in natural language processing (NLP) tasks, and successfully apply it to an extractive text summarization approach. In a query-based summarization setting, the correlation between user queries and sentences to be scored is established from both the micro (i.e. at the word level) and the macro (i.e. at the sentence level) perspectives, resulting in an effective ranking formula. The experiments, both on a generic single document summarization evaluation, and on a query-based multi-document evaluation, verify the effectiveness of the proposed measures and show that the proposed approach achieves a state-of-the-art performance.

1 Introduction

With the rapid development of research and technology in various fields, and the information explosion on the Internet, there are more and more documents covering the same topic. When a person wants to get a comprehensive review about a topic, he has to read as many as possible related documents in order not to omit any valuable points. When reading a document, he generally reads paragraph by paragraph in order to capture the main points of the authors. All of this is labor-intensive and time-consuming. With automatic text summarization, people can avoid this problem, thereby acquiring more information leading to more effective decisions in less time. Besides, summarization can also benefit other NLP tasks. For example, search engines can achieve a higher retrieval performance by filtering retrieved results according to their summaries. Also, summarization and several other NLP tasks (e.g., information extraction and question answering) can reciprocally boost each other's performance.

With text as the default material medium, summarization is defined as a reductive transformation of source text to summary text through content condensation by selection and/or generalization of what is considered important in the source [20]. So summarization focuses on getting the main meaning of a document. Which set of text segments, more concretely, which set of sentences or

W. Li and D. Mollá-Aliod (Eds.): ICCPOL 2009, LNAI 5459, pp. 168–178, 2009.

content-bearing words can achieve this objective? This question naturally recalls another closely-related concept in NLP, namely, information. Although information bears a variety of meanings in different contexts, the information in a word represents one piece of the message (or knowledge) transmitted in writing or in conversation. Each document is equivalent to a network of information, and each piece of information is associated with one content-bearing word or words. Based on this assumption, the issue of summarizing a text becomes the issue of finding the set of text segments with the largest quantity of information under a particular length constraint. Therefore, we propose an automatic document summarization approach using a new word significance measure based on word information.

The rest of the paper is organized as follows. Section 2 presents a review of related work on summarization, providing readers with a comprehensive scenario. The proposed approach is described in Section 3, followed by evaluations both on a generic single document setting, and on a query-based multi-document setting in Section 4. Section 5 concludes this paper and points out the possibilities for future work.

2   Related Work

Research on summarization can be traced back to Luhn [13] in which word frequencies and distributions were utilized to compute sentences' significance for summary creation. In the past half century, with the increasing need for automatic document summarization, more and more researchers have paid attention to it, resulting in a large body of literatures. Document summarization can be categorized as either extractive or abstractive. The latter utilizes new text which does not appear in the source. In addition, a system is referred to as generic summarization when its purpose is to capture the key meaning of input sources without special stress on any direction. By contrast, those producing summaries relevant to user queries are called query-based summarization. Both Afantenos et al. [1] and Sparck Jones [21] give a detailed survey of the existing research in this area.

Here, we focus on reviewing those approaches which share a common framework following a sentence extraction mode. In this mode, each sentence is ranked according to a scoring formula, and the highest ranked sentences will be extracted to produce a summary. Normally, the formula assigns a score to each sentence to represent its significance based on a set of features such as sentence position, sentence length, rhetorical structure [14], significance of keywords[1], etc. For most of these features, the calculation methods are similar in different formulations, whereas with regard to keywords, all kinds of measures are utilized to score a candidate, thereby making keywords play a special role in such scorings. The investigated measures include tf·idf score [8,22], information [6,10], occurrence

---

[1] Keywords refer to those words which are believed to carry key contents. The alternative sayings include "cue phrase", "significant word", "topic signature", etc. in the existing approaches.

probability [16], frequency [24], log-likelihood ratio [5,11], etc. In addition, an iterative reinforcement schema is applied to simultaneously extract summary and keywords in Wan et al. [23]. A new word significance measure is proposed in this paper.

To sum up, a generic summary aims to distill the overall meaning of a document, and extractive summarization reaches this objective by selecting the most important sentences from the document. Accordingly, a ranking formula plays a vital role in such sentence selection.

3   The Proposed Approach

The basic idea of our approach is to take advantage of the intrinsic relationship between summarization and word information to propose a new sentence ranking formula. The importance of each component word of a sentence is measured using a proposed quantification measure. Word information and entropy models have been explored in summarization and related research [17,18]. Our proposed approach is close in sprit to Cruz and Urrea's [6] work. They calculate a word's information using $log_2(p_i)$ where p_i represents word i's relative frequency in a document to be summarized, then rank each sentence using the combination of its position and component words' information. A simple evaluation on seven documents is conducted to show that word information is a promising measure for summarization.

3.1   Measure for Word Significance

In NLP tasks, a language is represented by a huge general corpus in that language. All of the words from that corpus form a harmonious system where each word plays its specific role. The information of a word in the language is viewed as the piece of message it carries to be transmitted in writing or in conversation. Generally, it is quantifiable using (1) where $p(w)$ is word w's occurrence probability (also called relative frequency) in the general corpus.

$$info(w) = -log_2 p(w) \qquad (1)$$

In our approach, for a word's information[2] used in NLP tasks, we propose a new formula to redefine its quantification using (2).

$$info(w) = p_d(w) * (-log_2 p_G(w)) \qquad (2)$$

Where $p_d(w)$ and $p_G(w)$ denote word w's relative frequency in a document to be summarized and in the general corpus G, respectively, and "$-log_2 p_G(w)$" represents a word's information in the general corpus.

In order to create an appropriate summary, our objective is to extract the most significant sentences by measuring their component words' importance via

---

[2] Note that we didn't mean to change or challenge the traditional information definition in the field of information theory.

(2). If using "$-log_2p_G(w)$" as the unique metric, that is, word w is scored in the general corpus alone, then it has an identical score no matter in which document or even in which genre of documents. It means that a word plays a uniform role in different documents. Important words are always important, and unimportant ones are always unimportant. The consequent conclusion is that all the summaries for different documents are composed of similar word sets. This is undoubtedly unreasonable. In order to tackle this problem, $p_d(w)$ is exploited to reinforce the information metric from the perspective of a word's role in a specific document. What if we consider here a word's role in a specific document alone without its information in the general corpus? Generally, a document to be summarized is a normal length text such as a scientific article, a news report, etc. Even if it is composed of a set of documents, the number of word tokens it contains is much smaller than that of the general corpus. Accordingly, the reliability of statistical calculations based on a document is not comparable to that on a language.

The proposed measure given in (2) seems similar in form to the cross entropy. In information theory, the cross entropy between two discrete probability distributions p and q is defined as (3), which measures the average number of bits needed to identify an event from a set of possibilities.

$$H(p, q) = -\sum_{x} p(x) * log_2 q(x) \qquad (3)$$

However, its essential difference from (2) lies in that the two involved possibilities p and q must distribute over the same probability space. Another measure taking the similar form with ours is tf·idf as (4), where w is a word in question, tf(w) is w's frequency in its domain document, N the total number of documents in a collection, and $d(w)$ the number of documents containing w.

$$\text{tf·idf}(w) = tf(w) * log\frac{N}{d(w)} \qquad (4)$$

Comparing formulas (2) and (4), their first components both refer to a word w's importance in a domain document represented by its frequency (or relative frequency). The second element of (2) measures w's information in a language, while the counterpart of (4) illustrates the capability of w differentiating documents in a collection. It seems that there is no correspondence between a word's information and its differentiating capability. However, we'll compare these two metrics in the following evaluations.

3.2   Sentence Ranking Formula

Based on this proposed word information quantification measure, a sentence's significance value for a generic summarization is computed using (5) where m is the number of words in sentence s, $I(w)$ is set to 1 when w is a keyword, otherwise 0, info$'(w)$ is equivalent to info(w) in (2) when w is a keyword, otherwise 0. When the documents to be processed are news articles, a feature about sentence

position will be added to the formula, resulted in (6), based on the observation
that to briefly generalize the main event at the beginning is a typical writing
style of a news report.

$$V(s) = \sum_{i=1}^{m} \text{info}'(w_i) * \frac{\sum_{i=1}^{m} I(w_i)}{m} \tag{5}$$

$$V(s) = \sum_{i=1}^{m} \text{info}'(w_i) * \frac{\sum_{i=1}^{m} I(w_i)}{m} * \frac{1}{sentPostion} \tag{6}$$

For a query-based summarizer, queries play a directive role in summary production. An expanded sentence ranking formula (7) is proposed to establish the
correlation between sentences and queries at two levels. One is at sentence level
via $simi(s, Q)$ which computes a similarity using the ratio of the double number
of common unigrams between s and Q over the total number of unigrams in s
and Q; the other is at word level with the introduction of $corr(w, Q)$ which refers
to the maximized mutual information [3] score computed from a word pair list
in which each pair is composed of w and each component word of query Q. A
MI score is calculated in a document to be summarized with a word window of
size 10 as the co-occurrence scope.

$$V(s) = \sum_{i=1}^{m} \text{info}_{corr}(w_i) * \frac{\sum_{i=1}^{m} I(w_i)}{m} * simi(s, Q) \tag{7}$$

$$\text{info}_{corr}(w_i) = \text{info}'(w_i) * corr(w_i, Q)$$

$$corr(w_i, Q) = max\{MI(w_i, w_j)|w_j \in Q\}$$

$$MI(w_i, w_j) = \frac{p(w_i, w_j)}{p(w_i) * p(w_j)}$$

3.3   The Preprocessing and Sentence Selection

During a complete summary creation process, besides the above mentioned key
step of sentence ranking, there is a preprocessing module preceding it, and a sentence selection module following it. The preprocessing operations in our approach
include: (a) Segment a text into individual sentences; (b) Tokenize sentences into
word tokens, assign parts-of-speech (POS) to each token, and then lemmatize
them; (c) Exclude stop words (function words such as "the", "but", etc) from
the text. A crucial problem in the sentence selection phase is how to eliminate
information redundancy between sentences to be included in a summary, which
is especially important in a multi-document summarization system. High information redundancy means lower content coverage. Our solution to this problem
is to calculate the string similarity between a sentence to be selected and each
of the sentences already selected, respectively. The sentence in question will be
excluded from the final summary whenever any calculated similarity score larger
than a threshold value.

4   Evaluation

4.1   Evaluation Tasks and Measures

The experiments have been conducted along two different dimensions: generic single document summarization and query-based multi-document summarization. Document Understanding Conference (DUC)[3] is aimed at providing a text summarization and evaluation platform with large-scale document sets available and enabling more researchers to participate in and to make further progress in this area. In order to make the performance comparison with other existing approaches more feasible, our evaluations are carried out by following the tasks given in DUC. The general corpus used in our approach is the BNC [2].

ROUGE (Recall-Oriented Understudy for Gisting Evaluation)[12], is a package widely used in recent document summarization evaluations such as DUC. ROUGE scores have been shown to correlate very well with manual evaluations, at least in the news article domain [7,12]. They determine the quality of a summary by counting the number of overlapping units between it and ideal summaries created by humans. It includes four different measures (ROUGE-N, ROUGE-L, ROUGE-W, and ROUGE-S) to return a recall score on N-gram, the longest common sequence (LCS), weighted LCS, and skip bigrams[4], respectively, by comparing the summary to be evaluated with the ideal summaries. Several measures of ROUGE are applied as evaluation measures in our experiments.

4.2   Generic Single Document Summarization

The generic single document summarizer based on (6) is compared with the one in Wan et al. [23]. They assume that salient sentences (or words) will be heavily linked with other salient sentences (or words) in the form of co-occurring, containing, or being contained. Based on this assumption, three graphs are built to describe the relationships of sentence-to-sentence, word-to-word, or sentence-to-word. Then, an iterative reinforcement approach is employed to simultaneously conduct document summarization and keyword extraction. The system is reported to outperform sentence rank approach [15] and mutual rank approach [25]. More importantly, it also involves "keywords". The above mentioned tf·idf metric, which has similar form with ours, also takes part in this comparison.

The comparison experiments are carried out following the task 1 of DUC02. Provided 567 English news articles, task 1 aims to create a generic summary for each document with a length of approximately 100 words. Besides the same data, we adopt the same ROUGE measures as well as a set of identical running parameters for ROUGE in the comparison because the performance of ROUGE measures is sensitive to some running parameters. For example, the "-l" option means that only the first n words in a system-generated summary are used for

---

[3] A series of summarization evaluations run by the National Institute of Standards and Technology since 2001, available at http://www-nlpir.nist.gov/projects/duc/

[4] Pairs of words having intervening word gaps no larger than a certain number of words.

Table 1. Comparison: our approach vs. the other two approaches without redundancy elimination

	Our approach	tf·idf approach	Wan et al.'s approach
ROUGE-1	0.48153	0.47772	0.47100
ROUGE-2	0.22374	0.22000	0.20424
ROUGE-W	0.16937	0.16849	0.16336

Table 2. Comparison: our approach vs. the other two approaches with redundancy elimination

	Our approach	tf·idf approach	Wan et al.'s approach
ROUGE-1	0.48218	0.47784	0.47329
ROUGE-2	0.22425	0.22005	0.20281
ROUGE-W	0.16965	0.16847	0.16373

the evaluation and thus those evaluations not adopting this option are likely to overestimate the ROUGE scores. The official ROUGE result of the task 1 of DUC02 is not available. Table 1 and 2 show the comparison results without/with redundancy elimination processing, respectively, illustrating that our approach outperforms the other two approaches with an observable improvement which is distinguishable enough for ROUGE scores.

4.3   Query-Based Multi-document Summarization

People are becoming more and more interested in customized information when facing overwhelming data overload. Therefore, query-based multi-document summarization has become a popular topic in current summarization research. Compared to a generic single document summarizer, two more modules are added to this kind of summarizer, namely, sentence compression and query expansion.

Sentence Compression. In general, the length of a produced summary is limited to a fixed word number in DUC tasks, so long sentences with extraneous text units will reduce a summary's content coverage. Our sentence compression is implemented in a similar way as Conory et al. [4]. A sentence is viewed as a set of segments separated by commas[5]. According to their positions, these segments are further classified into three sets: "B" for those at the beginning, "M" for those in the middle, and "E" for those at the end. Each part corresponds to an extraneous word unit list. If a segment is matched in a corresponding list, it will be removed from the sentence in question. Typical extraneous word units include reporting location, date lines, editor's comments, phrases like "at the same time," and "after all," etc., relative clauses led by "when", "while", and "where" under certain circumstances, text units beginning with "known as" and "namely". Actually, the size of each list is small for un-appropriate or over trimming will cause performance lowered instead of improved.

---

[5] Sentences not containing any comma will not be compressed in our approach.

Query Expansion. In DUC, each query used to describe a question on certain topic only contains about one or two sentences. The information we can acquire from it is very limited. For the purpose of obtaining more knowledge from a query, we try to extend it using an existing ontology named WordNet [9] as follows: (a) Select nouns from a POS tagged query as the expanding seeds and acquire the definition and the synonyms of each noun seed from the WordNet; (b) Tokenize and lemmatize the output from step (a); (c) Only non-stop noun words will be used to enrich the query.

Experiments. The proposed approach to query-based multi-document summarization is evaluated by following the main task of DUC07. Given a topic and a set of 25 relevant documents, the task is to synthesize a fluent, well-organized 250-word summary of the documents that answers the question(s) in the topic statement. There are 45 topics in the test data. Each topic is accompanied by four ideal summaries created by humans. The running parameters officially specified in DUC07 for ROUGE have been adopted.

A variety of experiments are conducted to check the contribution of each component of formula (7) and to compare the performances with different sentence ranking formulas. The results are presented in Table 3 where Q means an original query statement and Q' represents an expanded one. As illustrated in Table 3, by comparing the performances of ranking formulas of "1.", "2.", and "3.", or those of "4.", "5.", and "6.", we can see that the proposed word

Table 3. Performances with different ranking formulas

	ROUGE-2	ROUGE-SU4
1. $\sum_{i=1}^{m} -log_2 p_G(w_i)$	0.06678	0.12501
2. $\sum_{i=1}^{m} -log_2 p_d(w_i)$	0.08685	0.14320
3. $\sum_{i=1}^{m} info'(w_i)$	0.10245	0.15757
4. $\sum_{i=1}^{m} -log_2 p_G(w_i) * \frac{\sum_{i=1}^{m} I(w_i)}{m} * simi(s,Q)$	0.08066	0.13615
5. $\sum_{i=1}^{m} -log_2 p_d(w_i) * \frac{\sum_{i=1}^{m} I(w_i)}{m} * simi(s,Q)$	0.10560	0.15906
6. $\sum_{i=1}^{m} info'(w_i) * \frac{\sum_{i=1}^{m} I(w_i)}{m} * simi(s,Q)$	0.11172	0.16585
7. $\sum_{i=1}^{m} (info'(w_i) * corr(w_i,Q)) * \frac{\sum_{i=1}^{m} I(w_i)}{m} * simi(s,Q)$	0.11353	0.16710
8. $\sum_{i=1}^{m} (info'(w_i) * corr(w_i,Q')) * \frac{\sum_{i=1}^{m} I(w_i)}{m}$	0.10809	0.15969
9. $\sum_{i=1}^{m} (info'(w_i) * corr(w_i,Q')) * \frac{\sum_{i=1}^{m} I(w_i)}{m} * simi(s,Q)$	0.11595	0.16841

Table 4. Comparison: our approach vs. DUC07's top 5 highest scored systems

RunID	ROUGE-2	ROUGE-SU4
15	0.1245	0.1772
29	0.1203	0.1708
4	0.1189	0.1701
24	0.1180	0.1760
Our approach	0.1160	0.1684
13	0.1118	0.1645

significance measure works better than the traditional word information metric which measures a word's importance only using statistical information from a document or a general corpus alone. The performance difference between formulas "6." and "7." shows the effectiveness of the correlation between sentences and user queries established at the word level. The contribution of correlation at the sentence level is illustrated by the performance improvement in formula "9.".'s output compared with that of "8.". In addition, it seems that either absence of the two kinds of correlations, no matter at which level, will cause the performance drop based on the observation of performances' of formulas "6.", "8." and "9.". Finally, the performance comparisons between ranking formula "7." and "9." verify the effectiveness of the proposed query expansion method.

There are 30 groups participating in the DUC07 competition. According to an ANOVA test carried out by the DUC organizers, the top six highest scored systems are significantly better than the remaining 24 systems and two baseline systems [19]. Our best result ranks 5th among the top systems as presented in Table 4. One thing to mention is that the top 5 highest scored systems ranked by ROUGE-2 score have the highest ROUGE-SU4 scores as well. The system ranked second outperforms our approach only by 0.4% and the top one system does by 0.85% in ROUGE-2 score. Similar phenomena are observed in ROUGE-SU4 score. It can be said that our approach has achieved a state-of-the-art performance in query-based multi-document summarizations.

5   Conclusion and Future Work

Automatic text summarization can save people time and effort in acquiring knowledge from a single document or a collection of texts. Especially with the rapid development of the Internet, the need for automatic document summarization has increased significantly. Summarization is the condensed content of a document or a set of documents. In NLP tasks, a word's information is quantified as the quantification of the piece of message it carries in writing or conversation. So we believe that a word with high quantities of information is more helpful in creating a summary. Based on this assumption, we propose a new word significance measure and further present novel sentence ranking formulas for extractive summarization. The experiments, both on the task 1 of DUC02 which focuses on generic single document summarizing, and on the main task of DUC07 whose goal is to produce a query-based summary for a set of related documents, illustrate that our proposed approaches achieve a state-of-the-art performance.

Particularly noteworthy about our approach are the following points: (a) We redefine a new quantification measure of word importance in NLP tasks, and successfully apply it to document summarization; (b) We have proposed a novel solution to the issue of correlating sentences to be ranked with user queries: from the micro perspective - at word level, and from the macro perspective - at sentence level (or at word string level), either absence will cause the performance drop; and (c) We have incorporated linguistic knowledge, and presented a query expansion method based on an existing ontology, achieving an observable performance improvement in the proposed summarization approach.

For the future work, two possibilities are considered. One is to apply the proposed new technologies in similar research topics (e.g., question answering). The other is to pay more attention to sentence compression given its role in summary creation.

Acknowledgments

The research described in this paper was supported by City University of Hong Kong through the Strategic Research Grant 7001879.

References

1. Afantenos, S., Karkaletsis, V., Stamatopoulos, P.: Summarization from medical documents: A survey. Artificial Intelligence in Medicine 33(2), 157–177 (2005)
2. Aston, G., Burnard, L.: The BNC Handbook: Exploring the British National Corpus with SARA. Edinburgh University Press, UK (1998)
3. Church, K.W., Hanks, P.: Word association norms, mutual information, and lexicography. Computational Linguistics 16(1), 22–29 (1990)
4. Conroy, J.M., Schlesinger, J.D., O'Leary, D.P., Goldstein, J.: Back to basics: Classy 2006. In: Proceedings of DUC 2006, New York City, NY (2006)
5. Conroy, J.M., Schlesinger, J.D., O'Leary, D.P.: CLASSY 2007 at DUC 2007. In: Proceedings of DUC 2007, New York (2007)
6. Cruz, C.M., Urrea, A.M.: Extractive summarization based on word information and sentence position. In: Gelbukh, A. (ed.) CICLing 2005. LNCS, vol. 3406, pp. 653–656. Springer, Heidelberg (2005)
7. Dang, H.T.: Overview of DUC 2005. In: Proceedings of DUC 2005, Vancouver, B.C., Canada (2005)
8. Díaz, A., Gervás, P.: User-model based personalized summarization. Information Processing and Management: An International Journal 43(6), 1715–1734 (2007)
9. Fellbaum, C.: WordNet: An Electronic Lexical Database. MIT Press, Cambridge (1998)
10. Jagarlamudi, J., Pingali, P., Varma, V.: Query independent sentence scoring approach to DUC 2006. In: Proceedings of DUC 2006, New York City, NY (2006)
11. Lin, C.Y., Hovy, E.: The automated acquisition of topic signatures for text summarization. In: Proceedings of COLING 2000, Morristown, NJ, USA, pp. 495–501 (2000)
12. Lin, C.Y.: ROUGE: A package for automatic evaluation of summaries. In: Moens, M.-F., Szpakowicz, S. (eds.) Text Summarization Branches Out: Proceedings of the ACL 2004 Workshop, Barcelona, Spain, pp. 74–81 (2004)
13. Luhn, H.P.: The automatic creation of literature abstracts. IBM Journal of Research and Development (1958)
14. Marcu, D.: From discourse structures to text summaries. In: Proceedings of the ACL 1997/EACL 1997 Workshop on Intelligent Scalable Text Summarization, Madrid, Spain, pp. 82–88 (1997)
15. Mihalcea, R., Tarau, P.: Text Rank: Bringing order into texts. In: Lin, D., Wu, D. (eds.) Proceedings of EMNLP 2004, Barcelona, Spain, pp. 404–411 (2004)
16. Nenkova, A., Vanderwende, L.: The impact of frequency on summarization. In: MSR-TR-2005-101 (2005)

17. Park, H.R., Han, Y.S., Kim, T.H.: Heuristic algorithms for automatic summarization of Korean texts. In: Online Proceedings of ICCS/JCSS 1999 (1999), http://www.jcss.gr.jp/iccs990LP/p3-11/p3-11.htm
18. Ravindra, G., Balakrishnan, N., Ramakrishnan, K.R.: Multi-document automatic text summarization using entropy estimates. In: Van Emde Boas, P., Pokorný, J., Bieliková, M., Štuller, J. (eds.) SOFSEM 2004. LNCS, vol. 2932, pp. 73–82. Springer, Heidelberg (2004)
19. Schilder, F., Kondadadi, R.: Fast Sum: Fast and accurate query-based multi-document summarization. In: Proceedings of ACL 2008: HLT, Short Papers, Columbus, Ohio, USA, pp. 205–208 (2008)
20. Sparck-Jones, K.: Automatic summarising: Factors and directions. In: Mani, I., Maybury, M. (eds.) Advances in Automatic Text Summarization, pp. 1–12. MIT Press, London (1999)
21. Sparck-Jones, K.: Automatic summarising: The state of the art. Information Processing and Management: An International Journal 43(6), 1449–1481 (2007)
22. Teufel, S., Moens, M.: Summarizing scientific articles: Experiments with relevance and rhetorical status. Computational Linguistics 28(4), 409–445 (2002)
23. Wan, X., Yang, J., Xiao, J.: Towards an iterative reinforcement approach for simultaneous document summarization and keyword extraction. In: Proceedings of ACL 2007, Prague, pp. 552–559 (2007)
24. Yih, W.T., Goodman, J., Vanderwende, L., Suzuki, H.: Multi-document summarization by maximizing informative content-words. In: Proceedings of IJCAI 2007, pp. 1776–1782 (2007)
25. Zha, H.: Generic summarization and keyphrase extraction using mutual reinforcement principle and sentence clustering. In: Proceedings of SIGIR 2002, Tampere, Finland, pp. 113–120 (2002)

Using Proximity in Query Focused Multi-document Extractive Summarization

Sujian Li, Yu Zhang, Wei Wang, and Chen Wang

Institute of Computational Linguistics, Peking University,
100871 Beijing, China
{lisujian,sdrzy,wwei,goldeneagle}@pku.edu.cn

Abstract. The query focused multi-document summarization tasks usually tend to answer the queries in the summary. In this paper, we suggest introducing an effective feature which can represent the relation of key terms in the query. Here, we adopt the feature of term proximity commonly used in the field of information retrieval, which has improved the retrieval performance according to the relative position of terms. To resolve the problem of data sparseness and to represent the proximity in the semantic level, concept expansion is conducted based on WordNet. By leveraging the term importance, the proximity feature is further improved and weighted according to the inverse term frequency of terms. The experimental results show that our proposed feature can contribute to improving the summarization performance.

Keywords: weighted term proximity, multi-document summarization, query expansion.

1 Introduction

Multi-document summarization aims at giving readers a quick view to their particular interests through generating a brief, well-organized, fluent summary from multiple documents. Also, most current multi-document summarization tasks provide a specific description in the form of user queries, which serve as heuristic information to help systems produce a summary. A variety of methods have been developed, which can be either extractive or abstractive summarization. Extractive summarization involves assigning scores to some units (e.g. sentences, keywords) of the documents and extracting the sentences with highest scores, while abstractive summarization usually needs robust techniques of language generation such as sentence compression and generation. Here we mainly focus on extractive summarization, which assigned scores to sentences according to the user query and the document content.

For extractive summarization task, selection of appropriate features highly influences the system performance. Many current summarization systems have devoted much effort to exploring effective features. Kupiec et al. [1] developed a trainable summarization system which adopts various features, such as sentence length cut-off feature, fixed-phrase feature, paragraph feature and so on, and then concluded that the

W. Li and D. Mollá-Aliod (Eds.): ICCPOL 2009, LNAI 5459, pp. 179–188, 2009.

system performed better than any other system using only a single feature. Nenkova and Vanderwende [2] examined the impact of word frequency on summarization. It is remarkable that the system simply based on frequency features could perform unexpectedly well in MSE (Multilingual Summarization Evaluation) 2005. The well known summarization system MEAD has explored an effective feature based on cluster centroid[3], which is a group of words that statistically represent a cluster of documents. In addition, the features based on sentence position, sentence length ([4], [5]) are also widely used in various summarization systems. Ouyang et al [5] has used in their system the feature based on semantic relations and named entity feature.

So far, most summarization systems focus on exploring n-gram features based on consecutive terms. However, with n increasing, the summarization method will be time and space consuming. Thus, n-gram(with n>3) feature is seriously sparse and some useful discontinuous term sequences are also ignored. In fact, there are so many phrases and fixed collocations with term distance spanning more than 2 terms, which are usually important for summarization systems. To solve this problem, we need locate all phrases and fixed collocations, but still drop the information which stands between them. For example, in sentence "I'd like to go to china, if your parents permitted, with you.", the relationship between "go to china" and "with you" would be ignored, if using n-gram(n<5). The same problem also exists in the field of information retrieval. To leverage the full information of the relative position between terms, term proximity [6] and query expansion [7] [8] have been used in the information retrieval field for a long time, both improving the result of search engine. Because the query guides how to select sentences under the framework of extractive summarization, we can borrow term proximity and query expansion in our query focused summarization system.

First, we introduce the term proximity feature, based on which we further define weighted proximity to measure the effect of spanning distance on terms. At the same time, to remedy the sparseness of term sequences, we utilize WordNet[9] to conduct concept expansion.

The remainder of this paper is organized as follows. Section 2 will introduce the framework of our summarization system which is based on exploring various features. At the same time, the commonly used features are also presented. Section 3 details the proximity feature. In order to reasonably measure the proximity between terms and remedy the sparseness of term pairs, we further present the weighting method of proximity and query expansion. Section 4 illustrates experiments and evaluations. Section 5 finally concludes the paper.

2 Overview of Summarization Framework

2.1 Background

The task of DUC query focused summarization requires creating from a set of relevant documents (most set contain 25 documents) a brief, well-organized and fluent summary to the information seeking need which is indicated by the queries in the topic description. Here is an example of the topic description.

```
<topic>
<num> D0601A </num>
<title> Native American Reservation System - pros
and cons </title>
<narr>
Discuss conditions on American Indian reservations
or among Native American communities. Include the
benefits and drawbacks of the reservation system.
Include legal privileges and problems.
</narr>
</topic>
```

Fig. 1. Example of a topic description

For each topic, four human summarizers are asked to provide a summary with limited length (no more than 250 words) from the 25 related documents for the automatic evaluation.

2.2 Feature Based Scoring System

As described in section 1, most summarization systems adopt an extractive summarization framework, under which various features are explored. We mainly aim at verifying the effect the proximity feature on selecting sentences in this paper. Here we rank the sentences with a linear combination of features. That is, each sentence is assigned a score which cumulating the impacts of the features used. The impact of each feature is represented by its weight, which are tuned manually. The formula is as follows.

$$Score_s = \sum w_i f_i \qquad (1)$$

Where s means a sentence, f_i means the feature value while w_i indicates the weight of the feature f_i set experimentally. With the extractive framework, we can easily verify whether each feature can work on the summary performance, through adding a new feature into the summarization system. At the same time, by tuning the feature weight, we can know to what extent a feature improves the performance.

In order to verify our proposed features, we generate a summary using the MEAD[1] system whose basic features include centroid, position and length. In addition, we introduce two query focused features - a word matching feature and a name entity matching feature - to reflect the guidance of the query in our summarization system.

(1) Centroid feature

$$f_{centroid}(s) = \sum_{t_j \in s} tfidf(t_j) \qquad (2)$$

Where $tfidf(t_j)$ is the tf-idf score of t_j in the whole data set.

---

[1] http://www.summarization.com/mead/

(2) Sentence Position Feature

$$f_{position}(s) = 1 - \frac{i-1}{n} \tag{3}$$

where n is the total number of the sentences and s is the ith sentence in the document.

(3) Sentence length feature is used to cut off too long or too short sentences. Usually we set a threshold value K, when the length is greater than K, the sentence is reserved. Otherwise, the sentence is excluded for extracting.

(4) Word Matching (WM) Feature

$$f_{word}(s) = \sum_{t_j \in s} \sum_{t_i \in q} same(t_i, t_j) \tag{4}$$

where f_{word} is the feature value, q is the topic description. The function $same(t_i, t_j) = 1$ if $t_i = t_j$, and 0 otherwise.

(5) Name Entity Matching (NEM) Feature

$$f_{entity}(s) = | entity(s) \cap entity(q) | \tag{5}$$

where $| entity(s) \cap entity(q) |$ is the number of the named entities in both s and q. A named entity is usually defined as a word, or a sequence of words that can be classified as a person name, organization, location, date, time, percentage or quantity. Here only four classes (person, organization, location, date) are involved.

3 Weighted Proximity in Sentence Ranking

In the feature based extractive summarization systems, each sentence is scored to judge whether it should be extracted. The score should present the importance of the sentence itself in a cluster of documents, which are well represented by centroid feature. The guidance of the topic description is also important in query focused summarization systems. Here we propose the proximity feature to improve the action of the query on summarization performance. Each sentence is assigned a normalized proximity feature whose value is proportional to the cumulation of the proximity of the term pairs. We will introduce the proximity of term pairs and its improvement as the following subsections.

3.1 Proximity

We use proximity to represent the relative position of two terms. With proximity, we can comprehensively describe the meaning of a sentence, further to strengthen the impact of the query on the summary. Detailedly, for each sentence in the cluster of one topic, the proximity value is computed. First we locate the instance of each term pair in the query sentence, every two terms within a maximal distance of ten (or having a maximal of nine terms between the keyword pair) form a term pair instance (t_i, t_j)., And we compute a term pair instance (tpi) proximity as follows:

$$tpi(t_i, t_j) = \frac{1}{d(t_i, t_j)^2} \qquad (6)$$

where $d(t_i,\ t_j) = \left| d_{query}(t_i,\ t_j) - d_{doc}(t_i,\ t_j) \right|$

where $d_{query}(t_i,\ t_j)$ is the distance expressed in the number of terms between term t_i and t_j in a query, and $d_{doc}(t_i,\ t_j)$ is the distance between term t_i and t_j in the documents.

3.2 Query Expansion

WordNet is a large lexical database organized by sets of cognitive synonyms (synsets), each representing a distinct concept. Because WordNet is freely and publicly available, it is widely used for concept expansion.

The raw proximity computation will be improved by concept expansion based on WordNet. One reason is that term pairs are sparse in the corpus with medium size, which seriously affected the raw proximity value. And another is that there are always many expressions for one concept, such as "U.S.A." and "America" both stand for the concept of United States of America. To solve this problem, we expand the query by expanding each component term to a cluster of terms with similar meaning. For efficiency, here we adopt a simple strategy by getting only one synset according to the part of speech of the term. After query expansion, the term pair instance evolved to be a concept pair instance, and the formula is as follows.

$$tpi(t_i, t_j) = \frac{1}{d(c_i, c_j)^2} \qquad (7)$$

where $d(c_i,\ c_j) = \left| d_{query}(c_i,\ c_j) - d_{doc}(c_i,\ c_j) \right|$

where $d_{query}(c_i,\ c_j)$ is the distance between concept c_i expanded by term t_i and concept c_j expanded by term t_j in a query, and $d_{doc}(c_i,\ c_j)$ is the distance between concept c_i and c_j in the documents.

3.3 Weighted Proximity

Because each term in a document may have different importance, we propose that different term pairs even with the same spanning distance should have different degree of proximity, with the consideration of the relative importance of terms in the documents. Usually the importance of a term can be represented by the inverted document frequency (idf). And the formulation is further improved as follows.

$$tpi(t_i, t_j) = \frac{1}{d(c_i, c_j)^2} \times IDF_{t_i} \times IDF_{t_j} \qquad (8)$$

Where IDF_{ti} and IDF_{tj} respectively mean the inverted document frequency of term t_i and term t_j.

4 Experiments and Results

4.1 Experiment Design

We set up our experiments on the data set of DUC 2006[10]. The baseline system we use is the mead system with the limited features: position, sentence length and centroid. All documents are pre-processed by removing stop words and stemming remains. According to the task definition, system generated summaries are strictly limited to the 250 English words in length. After sentence scoring, we conduct a reranking process, called Maximal Marginal Relevance (MMR)[11]. That is, when we select a sentence with the highest score, the sentence needs also be compared to the sentences already in the summary. If the sentence is similar to any sentence already in the summary, the sentence will not be considered into the summary. The process is repeated until the length of the summary reach the upper limit.

To verify the effect of our proposed feature in summarization system, we design two sets of experiments. In the first experiment, we observe the impact of the proximity feature and its improvement on the summarization performance by tuning the feature weights. The second experiment designs whether the proximity feature works with WM and NEM features added. Because WM and NEM features are two important features to reflect the guidance of the query in generating summaries.

4.2 Evaluation Metrics

ROUGE (Recall Oriented Understudy for Gisting Evaluation) toolkit has been working well for evaluating summarization systems. It adopts a variety of n-gram matching approaches to evaluate

$$R_n(X) = \frac{\sum_{j=1}^{h} \sum_{i \in N_n} \min(X_n(i), M_n(i, j))}{\sum_{j=1}^{h} \sum_{i \in N_n} M_n(i, j)} \tag{9}$$

Where N_n represents the set of all n-grams and i is one member from N_n. $X_n(i)$ is the number of times the n-gram i occurred in the summary and $M_n(i,j)$ is the number of times the n-gram i ocurred in the j-th model reference(human) summary. There are totally h human summaries. When computing ROGUE score for a summarization system, human summaries must be created in advance. In our experiments, for each topic set, there are four human summaries for evaluation. ROUGE-1, ROUGE-2 and ROUGE-SU4, the DUC automatic evaluation criteria [12], are used to compare our systems built upon the proposed approaches. ROUGE-2 evaluates a system summary by matching its bigrams against the model summaries. ROUGE-SU4 matches unigrams and skip-bigrams of a summary against model summaries. A skip-bigram is a pair of words in their sentence order, allowing for gaps within a limited size.

4.3 Experiment 1: Weight Tuning

The design of this experiment aims at proving that the proximity works in improving summarization performance and at the same time illustrates the changed performance with weight changing. The baseline system we used is MEAD with three basic features: the sentence length threshold and the centroid weight are both set to be 10 by experience. Then we set the weight of the proximity feature to be 2, 5, 10 or 20 respectively. Table.1 gives the results: the average ROUGE-1, ROUGE-2 and ROUGE-SU4 value and corresponding 95% confidential intervals of all systems are all proposed.

Table 1. Result of experiments (Prox short of proximity, WProx short for weighted proxity, and QE short for query expansion. R-1 short for Rouge-1, R-2 short for Rouge-2, R-SU4 short for ROUGE-SU4).

Method	Feature weight	Average R-1 and CI	Average R-2 and CI	Average R-SU4 and CI
Baseline		0.37870(0.36630, 0.39245)	0.07708(0.07052, 0.08441)	0.13141(0.12450, 0.13894)
+ Prox	2	0.38030(0.36578, 0.39515)	**0.07864(0.07165, 0.08656)**	0.13281(0.12499, 0.14116)
	5	**0.38654(0.37341, 0.39936)**	0.07852(0.07136, 0.08619)	**0.13368(0.12654, 0.14084)**
	10	0.38043(0.36832, 0.39286)	0.07612(0.06923, 0.08357)	0.13036(0.12362, 0.13739)
	20	0.38110(0.36808, 0.39510)	0.07527(0.06845, 0.08300)	0.13045(0.12323, 0.13809)
+ Prox + QE	2	0.38311(0.36905, 0.39782)	0.07939(0.07238, 0.08690)	0.13384(0.12623, 0.14181)
	5	**0.38959(0.37661, 0.40300)**	**0.08039(0.07332, 0.08785)**	**0.13528(0.12802, 0.14244)**
	10	0.38298(0.37126, 0.39565)	0.07784(0.07103, 0.08515)	0.13170(0.12511, 0.13854)
	20	0.38467(0.37276, 0.39730)	0.07816(0.07128, 0.08562)	0.13229(0.12558, 0.13911)
+ WProx + QE	2	0.38136(0.36708, 0.39636)	0.07883(0.07207, 0.08640)	0.13286(0.12573, 0.14097)
	5	**0.39050(0.37675, 0.40437)**	**0.08095(0.07372, 0.08833)**	**0.13562(0.12842, 0.14281)**
	10	0.38034(0.36832, 0.39286)	0.07612(0.06923, 0.08357)	0.13036(0.12362, 0.13739)
	20	0.38329(0.37196, 0.39556)	0.07734(0.07063, 0.08478)	0.13190(0.12533, 0.13868)

In the table, the "+" symbol means that a feature is added to the baseline system. For example, "+ Prox" means that the system includes the proximity feature except the three basic features. The figures are boldfaced for the highest performance of each system with a different set of features. Fig. 2 illustrates the Rouge-2 values of each system with weight tuning. From the results we can see that the effect of the proximity feature, producing a significant raise. While appropriately applying query expansion and weighted proximity, the improvement continues. Also, we can conclude the best weight for the proximity feature is about 5, at which the three systems all nearly achieve their best, as Fig. 2 shows.

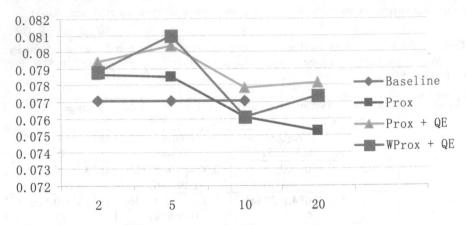

Fig. 2. Rouge-2 values with weight tuning

4.4　Experiment 2: Query Focused Features

In this experiment our goal is not to conclude which feature can improve the query-focused summarization more. We mean to present that the proximity feature can further improve the summarization performance with other query focused features available. Word match (WM) feature and name entity match (NEM) feature are two important query relevant features, which work in query focused summarization systems. These experiments are still implemented based on the baseline system. With WM and NEM features added respectively or simultaneously, the performance is further improved when the improved proximity feature is used. Table 2 gives the results and the boldfaced figures clearly demonstrate that the proximity feature is effective.

Table 2. Results of systems with different query focused features

Method	Rouge-1	ROUGE-2	Rouge-Su4
+ WM	0.38964(0.37733, 0.40351)	0.08128(0.07456, 0.08832)	0.13771(0.13008, 0.14460)
+ WM + WProx + QE	**0.39084(0.37988, 0.40256)**	**0.08193(0.07542, 0.08896)**	**0.13656(0.13061, 0.14313)**
+ WM + NEM	0.39175(0.37811, 0.40613)	0.08101(0.07373, 0.08878)	0.13750 (0.12996, 0.14511)
+ WM + NEM + WProx + QE	**0.39334(0.38296, 0.40487)**	**0.08200(0.07562, 0.08908)**	**0.13715(0.13135, 0.14375)**

5 Conclusion and Future Work

In this paper, we propose an effective feature which can represent the relation of key terms for the query focused multi-document summarization systems. First, we introduce the feature of term proximity commonly used in the field of information retrieval, which can comprehensively represent the meaning of a query according to the relative position of terms. To resolve the problem of data sparseness and to represent the proximity in the semantic level, concept expansion is conducted based on Word-Net. By leveraging the term importance, the proximity feature is further improved and weighted according to the inverse term frequency of terms. The experimental results show that the proximity feature and its improvement can contribute to improving the summarization performance.

In this work, concept expansion is conducted simply by expanding one term to its synset. We will explore more complex semantic relations to conduct further concept expansion for improving the proximity feature. In addition, now we manually tune the feature weight and only a few features are used with the proximity feature. Our future work will adopt machine learning methods to tune the feature weights and employ the proximity feature more appropriately.

Acknowledgement

We would like to thank the anonymous reviewers for their detailed comments. This work is supported by NSFC programs (No: 60603093 and 60875042), and 973 National Basic Research Program of China (2004CB318102).

References

1. Kupiec, J.M., Pedersen, J., Chen, F.: A Trainable Document Summarizer. In: Proceedings of the 18th Annual International ACM SIGIR Conference on Research and Development in Information Retrieval, Seattle, Washington, pp. 68–73 (1995)
2. Nenkova, A., Vanderwende, L.: The Impact of Frequency on Summarization. MSR-TR-2005-101. Microsoft Research Technical Report (2005)
3. Radev, D.R., Jing, H.Y., Stys, M., Tam, D.: Centroid-based summarization of multiple documents: sentence extraction, utility-based evaluation, and user studies. Information processing&management 40(6), 919–938 (2004)
4. Radev, D.R., Teufel, S.: Evaluation challenges in large-scale multi-document summarization: the MEAD project. In: Johns Hopkins University CLSP Workshop Final Report (2001)
5. OuYang, Y., Li, S.J., Li, W.J.: Developing Learning Strategies for Topic-based Summarization. In: ACM Conference on Information and Knowledge Management (CIKM 2007), Lisboa, Portugal, pp. 79–86 (2007)
6. Hawking, D., Thistlewaite, P.: Proximity operators – So near and yet so far. In: Proceedings of TREC-4, Gaithersburg, MD, pp. 131–143 (1995)
7. Qiu, Y., Frei, H.P.: Concept based query expansion. In: Proceedings of the 16th annual international ACM SIGIR, Pittsburgh, United States (1993)

8. Rasolofo, Y., Savoy, J.: Term proximity scoring for keyword-based retrieval systems. In: Sebastiani, F. (ed.) ECIR 2003. LNCS, vol. 2633, pp. 207–218. Springer, Heidelberg (2003)
9. Miller, G.A., Beckwith, R., Felbaum, C., Gross, D., Miller, K.: Introduction to WordNet: An On-line Lexical Database (1993)
10. Hoa, T.D.: Overview of DUC 2006. In: Document Understanding Conference 2006 (2006), http://duc.nist.gov
11. Carbonell, J.G., Goldstein, J.: The use of MMR, diversity-based reranking for reordering documents and producing summaries. In: Proceedings of the 21st ACM SIGIR conference on Research and development in information retrieval, Melbourne, Australia, pp. 335–336 (1998)
12. Lin, C.Y., Hovy, E.: Manual and Automatic Evaluation of Summaries. In: Document Understanding Conference (2002), http://duc.nist.gov

Learning Similarity Functions in Graph-Based Document Summarization

You Ouyang, Wenjie Li, Furu Wei, and Qin Lu

Department of computing, the Hong Kong Polytechinc University, Hong Kong
{csyouyang,cswjli,csfuwei,csluqin}@comp.polyu.edu.hk

Abstract. Graph-based models have been extensively explored in document summarization in recent years. Compared with traditional feature-based models, graph-based models incorporate interrelated information into the ranking process. Thus, potentially they can do a better job in retrieving the important contents from documents. In this paper, we investigate the problem of how to measure sentence similarity which is a crucial issue in graph-based summarization models but in our belief has not been well defined in the past. We propose a supervised learning approach that brings together multiple similarity measures and makes use of human-generated summaries to guide the combination process. Therefore, it can be expected to provide more accurate estimation than a single cosine similarity measure. Experiments conducted on the DUC2005 and DUC2006 data sets show that the proposed learning approach is successful in measuring similarity. Its competitiveness and adaptability are also demonstrated.

Keywords: Document summarization, graph-based ranking, sentence similarity calculation, support vector machine.

1 Introduction

A text summarization task requires creating short and concise summaries from long and redundant text data. Since the nature of original data varies, lots of specified summarization tasks have been defined and studied in the literature. The goal of document summarization, in particular, is to compress (sets of) long documents to short summaries which are anticipated to preserve as much information as possible. That is to say, summaries should contain the most important concepts conveyed in original documents.

Within the general framework of extractive summarization, the concepts in original documents are first ranked by their importance. The highest ranked ones are then picked up to form the summary. Judging the importance of the concepts is a crucial but complicated problem which needs to consider multiple aspects according to the variety of tasks. In previous studies, a number of local and global factors have been studied and examined. Most factors, usually indicated by features, are based on statistical and syntactic analysis of the original text. In recent years, graph-based ranking algorithms, such as PageRank or HITS which have been very successful in ranking web pages, are introduced to the text ranking area. The graph-based ranking approaches consider the intrinsic structure of the texts instead of treating texts as simple aggregations of terms.

W. Li and D. Mollá-Aliod (Eds.): ICCPOL 2009, LNAI 5459, pp. 189–200, 2009.

Thus it is able to capture and express richer information in determining important concepts.

The two basic elements in a graph model are the nodes and the edges. In text ranking applications, the nodes can be of various granularities of text fragments like terms, sentences, documents and etc. Here we focus on sentence ranking and thereby take sentences as nodes. Then the remaining issue regarding to graph construction is how to define the edges that establish the connection between the nodes. Unlike in a web graph where the linkage information between the two pages is explicit, the edges in text graphs are not provided beforehand. A typical way adopted in existing graph-based summarization models is to calculate the similarity between the sentences and then establish the edges if the two sentences are believed similar enough. Therefore, similarity calculation plays an important role in graph construction and it directly affects the ranking results. However, the problem of how to measure the similarity between the sentences is neglected in most existing graph-based summarization approaches, which simply apply the cosine similarity. In this study, we explore machine learning of similarity functions which allows synthetical and efficient scaling of sentence linkage in a document graph.

The main evaluation forum providing benchmarks for researchers working on document summarization to exchange their ideas and experiences is the Document Understanding Conferences (DUC). Since nowadays researchers pay more and more attention to the tasks which model the real-world problems, the DUC defines a query-focused multi-document summarization task in 2005 which is motivated by modeling complex question answering. The task requires creating a brief, well-organized and fluent summary from a set of relevant documents according to a given query that describes a user's information need. We choose this task as the platform to study how to develop a good similarity function to measure the relations between the sentences. To this end, we first define several similarity measures from different points of views on the relations between the sentences, including one query-dependent and three query-independent measures. Then we conduct a preliminary study to investigate the feasibility of learning similarity functions. The primary objective is to examine if we can make use of the given human-generated "golden" summaries to learn a reliable similarity function from a set of pre-defined similarity measures.

The reminder of the paper is organized as follows. Section 2 briefly introduces the related work. Sections 3 then details the proposed supervised similarity learning approach and its application in document summarization. It is followed by Section 4 which presents experiments and evaluations. Finally, Section 5 concludes the paper.

2 Related Work

Document summarization has attracted much attention since the initial work by Luhn [1]. Summarization approaches can be roughly classified into two categories: abstractive summarization and extractive summarization [2]. Abstractive summarization writes a concise abstract that truly summarizes documents. However, due to the limitation of current nature language understanding and generation techniques, abstractive approaches are still confined in specified domains [3, 4]. In contrast, extractive summarization, which selects a number of indicative text fragments from the original documents to form a summary instead of rewriting an abstract, are much easier to implement. In a particular summarization system, the selected text fragments can be phrases [5], sentences [1, 6, 8], or paragraphs [7] etc. Currently, many successful systems adopt the sentences considering the tradeoff between content richness and grammar correctness. They extract the most salient sentences from original documents to compose a summary. For these systems, the sentence ranking algorithm that determines which sentences are more important than others is crucial.

In fact, measuring the importance of the sentences is a complicated problem. . Existing studies examined many factors such as TFIDF, key phrase, position and etc. A traditional feature-based ranking algorithm uses multiple features to reflect these factors and calculate the importance of sentences based on the combination effect of them. Machine learning approaches are usually introduced to improve the feature combination process [6, 8]. A common problem with these summarization approaches is that they just consider the characteristics of sentences themselves but ignore the relations between sentences. Motivated by incorporating the inter-sentence information, currently there is a trend to introduce graph-based models to the sentence ranking in order to obtain more accurate estimation of sentence importance. TextRank [9] and LexRank [10], which are inspired by PageRank, are good examples. Erkan and Radev [10] used weighted undirected graphs to represent documents by taking sentences as vertices and the cosine similarity between sentences as the edge weight function. PageRank-like iterative ranking algorithms were then applied to calculate sentence importance scores. In contrast, following the idea of HITS, Zha [11] built a bipartite graph of terms and sentences to capture the interactions between terms and sentences for ranking sentences and terms simultaneously. In [12], Mihalcea and Tarau presented a comparative study of different graph-based ranking methods. Three algorithms, namely HITS, Positional Power Function and PageRank were examined. They found out that when the same similarity function was used to construct the graphs, the performances of the different algorithms were very close to one another. The above works are conducted on generic summarization. To query-focused summarization, it has been well acknowledged that query information should be taken into account when ranking sentences. OtterBacher et al [13] proposed a query-sensitive version of TextRank in a query-based random walking model. Their idea was followed by Wan et al. [14] who further differentiated between inter-document and intra-document relationships. Addressing the issue of measuring similarity with respect to a specified context, Tombros and Rijsbergen [15] pioneered the development of the query-sensitive similarity functions. In fact, the model in [13] can be equally transferred by matrix notation transformation to a general graph-based model which measures sentence relations with a query-sensitive similarity function. Therefore, we think that the key issue of the graph models is indeed the similarity functions which measure the relations between the nodes. Thus we regard designing similarity measures as the basic problem in this study.

3   Graph-Based Summarization Model Based on Similarity Function Learning

In this section, we start with giving several similarity measures which measure the relations between the sentences from different aspects. Then we propose a learning-based strategy which can combine these measures (called features in machine learning) in order to obtain more accurate estimations. Finally, we introduce a graph-based sentence ranking algorithm.

3.1 Similarity Measures

Most graph-based approaches use the cosine similarity to scale the relations between two sentences. The cosine similarity mainly reflects the extent of overlap between the word vectors of the two sentences. However, the cosine similarity measure may not sufficiently reflect the relations in the context of query-focused summarization. In our belief, sentence relations should be determined by multiple factors. Here are some examples selected from the DUC 2006 data set.

[D0601A] Native American Reservation System - pros and cons
(A) Aside from that, only 63 percent of **Indians** are high **school** graduates.
(B) President Clinton turned the attention of his national poverty tour today to arguably the poorest, most forgotten U.S. citizens of them all: American **Indians**.
(C) We're still behind, which is affecting our **schools**, our students.

We can see that "Indians" is a common word in (A) and (B), but meanwhile (A) also overlaps (C) with the word "school". Given that the query of this topic is to discuss conditions on American Indian reservations or among Native American communities, a proper similarity measure should be able to recognize that (A) actually is more related to (B) than to (C). The following is another example.

[D0604D] Anticipation of and reaction to the premier of Star Wars Episode I
(D) Most **expect** it to go over well with the **Japanese** audience.
(E) For many **Japanese** fans, that's just too much to ask.
(F) We **expect** this to be a busy night.

The same word in sentences (D) and (E) is "Japanese" while the same word in sentences (D) and (F) is "expect". Obviously, sentences (D) and (E) are much more related to each other with or even without the given query. This rests with the difference of the content overlapped. A named entity such as "Japanese" is surely more informative than a common word such as "expect".

A common problem is exhibited in the above illustrative examples. The sentence pairs with equal number of overlapping words have different relations between them. Such situations, however, can hardly be identified by the cosine similarity alone. Indeed, the cosine similarity comes up with the wrong decisions in the two given examples. Therefore, it is reasonable to believe that the relations are not only concerned with the number (or the extent) of the overlapped words, but also depend on queries, name entities and many other factors. In this work, we examine a number of potential factors and conclude four different similarity measures for scaling the sentence relations.

The first similarity measure we use is the traditional cosine similarity. For the calculation of the cosine similarity, sentences are first represented by sentence vectors. The entries in the vectors are the TFISF scores of the words, where TF is the word frequency and ISF is the inversed sentence frequency in the documents. The similarity is then calculated by the cosine value of the angle between the two sentence vectors.

$$sim_{cosine}(s_i, s_j) = \frac{\sum_{w \in s_i, s_j} tf(w, s_i) \cdot tf(w, s_j) \cdot isf^2(w)}{|s_i| \cdot |s_j|} \tag{1}$$

where w indicates a word in the documents, $tf(w, s_i)$ is the frequency of w in s_i, $isf(w)$ is the inversed sentence frequency of w in the documents.

Name entities, such as persons, locations and organizations, contain rich semantic information. Therefore, we consider the entity overlapping as well and derive the entity-based similarity measure as

$$sim_{entity}(s_i, s_j) = \frac{\sum_{e \in s_i, s_j} tf(e, s_i) \cdot tf(e, s_j)}{|s_i| \cdot |s_j|} \tag{2}$$

where e indicates a named entity in a sentence.

The position of a sentence is a common-used indicator to judge whether a sentence is important. For example, traditional approaches often select the first sentences in the documents. This is a reasonable idea since usually many writers would like to give a brief introductions or reviews at the very beginning of the documents in order to give readers a general impression of what the documents are going to tell. For the problem of relation scaling, we make a basic assumption that the adjacent sentences are more related than the separated sentences because the adjacent sentences are probably talking about the same thing. Based on this assumption, the position similarity measure is defined according to the relative distance of the two sentences,

$$sim_{position}(s_i, s_j) = \frac{1}{|pos(s_i) - pos(s_j)|} \tag{3}$$

where $pos(s)$ is the position of a sentence s in a document.

To emphasize the role of query, we also define a query-sensitive similarity, which is considered more suitable for query-focused summarization. In the calculation, the modified cosine similarity only counts the words which appear in the query.

$$sim_{query}(s_i, s_j) = \frac{\sum_{w \in Q} tf(w, s_i) \cdot tf(w, s_j) \cdot isf^2(w)}{|s_i| \cdot |s_j|} \tag{4}$$

where Q is the query.

3.2 Supervised Similarity Function Learning

The similarity measures represent different points of views to measure the relations between the sentences. Since the task is related to all the factors, using one single view alone is not sufficient to scale the relation indeed. A simple and straightforward solution is to use the similarity measures as a set of features and then combine the features to obtain a composite measure, e.g. by using a linear combination function.

$$sim_{compsite}(s_i, s_j) = \lambda_1 \cdot sim_{cosine}(s_i, s_j) + \lambda_2 \cdot sim_{query}(s_i, s_j)$$
$$+ \lambda_3 \cdot sim_{entity}(s_i, s_j) + \lambda_4 \cdot sim_{postion}(s_i, s_j) \tag{5}$$

The composite similarity function covers the effect of multiple factors, therefore it can be expected to be more accurate and reliable. The feature weights λ_i in the linear combination can be either assigned manually or tuned by conducting exhaustive experiments. However, manually assigning feature weights relies on human knowledge. The performance is not predictable. Repeating experiments may find the optimum weights, but it is time-consuming when the number of features increases. As a better solution, we develop a supervised learning approach which can combine the features automatically by utilizing human generated "golden" summaries. This approach makes it potentially possible to automatically search for the best similarity function.

The training data used to learn the composite similarity function is generated automatically with reference to human generated "golden" summaries. This idea comes from the assumption that the human summaries should contain the most important contents in original documents. Based on this assumption, the similarity between the two sentences in training data is assigned as

$$sim_{train}(s_i, s_j) = sim(s_i, s_j \mid H) = \frac{\sum_{w \in H} tf(w, s_i) \cdot tf(w, s_j) \cdot isf^2(w)}{|s_i| \cdot |s_j|} \tag{6}$$

where H is a collection of human summaries. Notice that unlike the training data used in information extraction that provides standard answers, the training data constructed in this way is somewhat "pseudo" standard in the sense that it provides useful information though may not be completely accurate. But it is practical. In fact, it is almost impossible even for human to assign an accurate similarity value to each pair of sentences.

Given the document sets D whose corresponding human summaries H are given, the training data is constructed as $\{(sim_{train}(s_i, s_j), V_{s_i, s_j}) \mid s_i, s_j \in D\}$, where V_{s_i, s_j} is the four dimensional feature vectors of the sentence pair (s_i, s_j). A regression model is then used to learn a scoring function $f : V_{s_i, s_j} \rightarrow sim_{train}(s_i, s_j)$ that maps from feature vectors to a real similarity value. In this paper we adopt the linear v-SVR model [16] which finds the optimum function f_0 from a set of candidate functions $\{w \cdot x + b \mid w \in R^n, b \in R\}$ by minimizing the structure risk function

$$\Phi(w, b, \varepsilon) = \frac{1}{2} \| w \|^2 + C \left(\frac{1}{|D|} \sum_{s_i, s_j \in D} L(sim_{train}(s_i, s_j) - (w \cdot V_{s_i, s_j} + b)) + v\varepsilon \right) \tag{7}$$

where $L(x)$ is the loss function, C and v are the weights to balance the factors.

Once the regression function f_0 is learned, the similarity of any two sentences s'_i and s'_j in the new document sets D' can be predicted as:

$$sim_{predict}(s'_i, s'_j) = f_0(V_{s_i, s_j}) = w_0 \cdot V_{s_i, s_j} + b_0 \tag{8}$$

3.3 Graph-Based Sentence Ranking Algorithm

Once the similarity measure is defined, the document graph can be easily built based on sentence relations, and then a graph-based ranking algorithm derived from the famous PageRank [17] is applied to rank and select the summary sentences. The details of the algorithm are given below.

We denote the document set to be summarized as $D = \{s_i, i=1, 2, ..., N\}$ where s_i indicates a sentence in D and N is the total sentence number in D. The ranking algorithm will assign an important score $score(s_i)$ for each sentence s_i. Let the initial sentence scores be $1/N$, the target importance scores are calculated recursively by using the formula given below.

$$score_{n+1}(s_i) = (1-d) \cdot \frac{1}{N} + d \cdot \sum_{s_j} \left(score_n(s_j) \cdot \frac{sim(s_i, s_j)}{\sum_{s_k} sim(s_i, s_k)} \right) \qquad (9)$$

where d is set to 0.85, $sim(\ ,\ )$ is the similarity measure that scales the relation between the two sentences s_i and s_j. The final scores are obtained when the calculation is converged.

The graph-based ranking algorithm works on a relation graph where the sentences in the documents are connected. It allows the importance of each sentence to be calculated from the importance of all the other sentences in each iterating step. Like PageRank, the convergence of the algorithm is ensured by the random walk factor d. Through the interaction between the sentences and the iterative process, we could reach a final sentence ranking result which has taken into account the structural information of documents.

4   Experiment and Evaluation

4.1   Evaluation Data Set

The experiments are conducted on the query-focused summarization data sets from DUC 2005 and 2006. Each data set includes 50 document sets, and each document set contains a query and 25-50 relevant news documents. For each document set, several human summarizers are asked to provide a 250-word summary for automatic evaluation. The following table gives some information of the data sets.

Table 1. Information of the data sets

Year	No. of Documents per Set	No. of Sentence per Set	Total No. of Documents	News resources
2005	25-50	387-1931	1593	*Los Angeles Times, Financial Times of London*
2006	25	191-1572	1250	*Associated Press, New York Times, Xinhua Newswire*

The DUCs evaluate machine generated summaries with several manual and automatic evaluation metrics [18]. In this paper, we use ROUGE [19] to compare our systems with human summarizers and top performing DUC systems. ROUGE (Recall Oriented Understudy for Gisting Evaluation) is a state-of-art automatic summarization evaluation method based upon N-gram comparison. For example, ROUGE-2 evaluates a system summary by matching its Bi-grams against the model summaries.

$$R_n(s) = \frac{\sum_{j=1}^{h}\sum_{t_i \in S} Count(t_i \mid S, H_j)}{\sum_{j=1}^{h}\sum_{t_i \in S} Count(t_i \mid H_j)} \tag{10}$$

where S is the summary to be evaluated, H_j ($j=1, 2, ..., h$) is h model human summaries as golden standards. t_i indicates all the Bi-grams in the summary S, $Count(t_i \mid H_j)$ is the number of times that the Bi-gram t_i occurs in the j-th model human summary H_j and $Count(t_i \mid S, H_j)$ is the number of times that t_i occurs in both summary S and H_j.

Though ROUGE is based on simple N-gram matching, and argued by quite a number of people for its fitness, it has been working well. For example, in DUC 2005, ROUGE-2 has a Spearman correlation of 0.95 and a Pearson correlation of 0.97 compared with human evaluation, while ROUGE-SU4 has correlations of 0.94 and 0.96 respectively [18]. In the following experiments, we provide three commonly referenced ROUGE scores for the purpose of comparison, including ROUGE-1, ROUGE-2 and ROUGE-SU4.

4.2 Experiment Set-Up

The initial step of our summarization system is splitting the documents into the sentences. The sentences are then ranked by the proposed graph-based ranking approach. Top sentences are selected into the summary until the word (actually the sentence) limitation is reached. According to the task definition, the generated summaries are strictly limited to 250 English words in length. During sentence selection, we apply the MMR method [20] to alleviate the problem of information redundancy. Each time the candidate sentence currently under concerned is compared with the sentences that are already picked up into the summary. If the sentence is not considered significantly similar to any sentence already in the summary, it is then selected into the summary. The similarity between sentences is calculated by the cosine similarity measure.

All documents are pre-processed by removing stop words and stemming. Named entities including person and organization names, location and time are automatically tagged by GATE[1]. The regression models are implemented by LIBSVM [21]. Two-fold cross-validation is applied to the summarization systems with the supervised similarity functions to conduct open tests. The 50 document sets of one year are divided into two 25-document groups. Each time, we use one group to generate training data and test on the other. The scores are averaged as the final overall scores.

4.3 Experimental Result

In the experiments we first compare the efficiency of different similarity functions in document graph construction. Table 2 and Table 3 report the average ROUGE-1, ROUGE-2 and ROUGE-SU4 scores of six different approaches which all follow the graph-based algorithm introduced in section 3.3 but use different similarity functions, including four individual sentence similarity measures (labeled as "**Cosine**", "**Query**", "**Entity**", and "**Position**" respectively), the linear combination of multiple similarities with manually assigned weights (labeled as "**Linear**")[2] and the supervised similarity learning function (labeled as "**Learning**").

---

[1] It is publicly available from http://gate.ac.uk/.
[2] The feature weight used in the experiments is Cosine:Query:Entity:Position = 1:2:2:0.1.

Several things can be observed from the results. First of all we can see that the query-sensitive similarity performs better compared to the original cosine similarity for a query-focused summarization task. This illuminates the importance of designing corresponding similarity measures for specified tasks. However, the entity-based and position-based measures do not perform well in both years. We attribute the reason to the data sparseness problem. To the entity measure, the problem is that only a few sentences contain name entities. The problem of the position measure is that it only considers the sentence pairs in the same documents. Consequently, they both can only reflect a small portion of the sentence relations in the whole document collection. Table 4 shows the percentages of the sentence pairs whose similarity values do not equal zero among all the pairs. It is clear that only a few sentence pairs have none-zero similarity values under the entity-based measure or the position-based measure. This unavoidably affects their efficiency on measuring the relevance between sentences.

Although none of the single similarity functions can ideally measure the relevance between sentences, on the other hand, the linear combination of these similarities achieves better results. It improves the performance remarkably compared to the single measures. This proves that the combination similarity function which synthesizes multiple points of views on the relations is more effective and precise on scaling the relevance. The results also show that the supervised similarity learning algorithm can further boost the performance by optimizing the combination function. However, to our surprise, the improvement brought by the learning process is not significant. We attribute the unexpected result to the fact that we only include four similarity measures in our system. When the combination process only involves a few numbers of measures, manual search can also find reasonably good feature weights. In future work, we intend to design more appropriate measures to see if we can benefit more from the advantages of supervised learning.

Table 2. Results of Different Similarity Functions on the DUC2005

Similarity Function	Rouge-1	Rouge-2	Rouge-SU4
Position	0.2886	0.0328	0.0849
Entity	0.3325	0.0486	0.1055
Cosine	0.3635	0.0615	0.1206
Query	0.3641	0.0621	0.1219
Linear	0.3719	0.0708	0.1280
Learning	0.3819	0.0730	0.1325

Table 3. Results of Different Similarity Functions on the DUC2006

Similarity Function	Rouge-1	Rouge-2	Rouge-SU4
Position	0.3410	0.0509	0.1071
Entity	0.3550	0.0772	0.1337
Cosine	0.3926	0.0828	0.1390
Query	0.3925	0.0854	0.1411
Linear	0.4016	0.0885	0.1445
Learning	0.4083	0.0911	0.1485

Table 4. Percent of sentence pairs with none-zero similarities under different measures

	Cosine	Query	Entity	Position
05	35.73%	24.84%	0.048%	4.59%
06	42.44%	35.01%	0.119%	5.29%

We then compare our summarization system to current state-of-the-art systems. We select the top three DUC systems in 2005 and 2006 respectively. Tables 5 and 6 report the average ROUGE-1, ROUGE-2 and ROUGE-SU4 scores of a DUC human summarizer (labeled as "H", or "A"), a lead-based baseline provided by the DUC (labeled as "**Baseline**"), top-three performing systems (labeled as "**24**" or "**15**" etc.), average of all DUC participating systems in each year (labeled as "**Average**") and our learning-based approach (labeled as "**Learning**"). It is shown that our summarization system performs better than all the submitted systems in the DUC 2005, and ranks the second in the DUC 2006. These results suggest that the proposed approach is very competent.

Table 5. Performance of Different Approaches on the DUC2005

System	Rouge-1[3]	Rouge-2	Rouge-SU4
H	-	0.0897	0.1510
Learning	0.3822	0.0730	0.1325
15	-	0.0725	0.1316
17	-	0.0717	0.1297
8	-	0.0696	0.1279
Average	-	0.0617	0.1158
Baseline	-	0.0403	0.0872

Table 6. Performance of Different Approaches on the DUC2006

System	Rouge-1	Rouge-2	Rouge-SU4
A	-	0.1036	0.1683
24	-	0.0956	0.1553
Learning	0.4083	0.0911	0.1485
15	-	0.0910	0.1473
12	-	0.0899	0.1476
Average	-	0.0746	0.1302
Baseline	-	0.0495	0.0979

Finally we examine the stability of the learning algorithm by conducting a comparison on using different training data to learn the similarity function. Table 7 below presents the results when training and testing supervised similarity function on different data sets. In the results, the performances are very close when the similarity function is trained on the different data sets but tested on the same data set. This proves that the learning algorithm is stable.

---

[3] Rouge-1 scores are not officially reported in DUC reports.

Table 7. Results on Different Training / Testing Sets

	Rouge-1	Rouge-2	Rouge-SU4
Train: 05 / Test: 05	0.3819	0.0730	0.1325
Train: 06 / Test: 05	0.3819	0.0729	0.1310
Train: 05 / Test: 06	0.4045	0.0901	0.1453
Train: 06 / Test: 06	0.4083	0.0911	0.1485

5 Conclusion

In the study of this paper, we investigated the problem of how to scale sentence relations in graph-based summarization. We defined several similarity measures from different points of view of the relations and proposed a supervised learning algorithm to effectively combine the features. We then apply the learned similarity functions to a graph-based ranking approach. Results show that the proposed method is efficient and stable. The resulting system can perform as well as state-of-the-art systems when evaluated by ROUGE on the data sets from the DUC 2005 and the DUC 2006.

Acknowledgments. The work described in this paper was supported by Hong Kong RGC Projects (No. PolyU5217/07E and No. PolyU5230/08E).

References

1. Luhn, H.P.: The automatic creation of literature abstracts. IBM J. of R. and D. 2(2) (1958)
2. Radev, D.R., Hovy, E., McKeown, K.: Introduction to special issue on summarization. Computational Linguistics 28(4), 399–408 (2002)
3. Barzilay, R., McKeown, K., Elhadad, M.: Information fusion in the context of multi-document Summarization. In: Proceedings of ACL 1999. College Park, MD (1999)
4. Zajic, D., B. Dorr.: Automatic headline generation for newspaper stories. In: Proceedings of the ACL workshop on Automatic Summarization/Document Understanding Conference (2002)
5. Ercan, G., Cicekli, I.: Using lexical chains for keyword extraction. Information Processing & Management 43, 1705–1714 (2007)
6. Kupiec, J.M., Pedersen, J., Chen, F.: A Trainable Document Summarizer. In: Fox, E.A., Ingwersen, P., Fidel, R. (eds.) Proceedings of the 18th Annual International ACM SIGIR Conference on Research and Development in Information Retrieval, pp. 68–73 (1995)
7. Mitra, M., Singhal, A., Buckley, C.: Automatic text summarization by paragraph extraction. In: Proceedings of the ACL 1997 VEACL 1997 Workshop on Intelligent Scalable Text Summarization, Madrid (1997)
8. Ouyang, Y., Li, S., Li, W.: Developing learning strategies for topic-based summarization. In: Proceedings of the sixteenth ACM conference on Conference on information and knowledge management, Lisbon, Portugal, pp. 79–86 (2007)
9. Mihalcea, R., Tarau, P.: TextRank – bringing order into texts. In: Proceedings of the 2004 Conference on Empirical Methods in Natural Language Processing (2004)
10. Erkan, G., Radev, D.R.: LexPageRank: Prestige in Multi-Document Text Summarization. In: Proceedings of EMNLP, pp. 365–371 (2004)

11. Zha, H.: Generic Summarization and Key Phrase Extraction using Mutual Reinforcement Principlae and Sentence Clustering. In: Proceedings of ACM SIGIR, pp. 113–120 (2002)
12. Mihalcea, R., Tarau, P.: An Algorithm for Language Independent Single and Multiple Document Summarization. In: Proceedings of IJCNLP (2005)
13. OtterBacher, J., Erkan, G., Radev, D.R.: Using Random Walks for Question-focused Sentence Retrieval. In: Proceedings of HLT/EMNLP, pp. 915–922 (2005)
14. Wan, X., Yang, J., Xiao, J.: Using Cross-Document Random Walks for Topic-Focused Multi-Document Summarization. In: Proceedings of the IEEE/WIC/ACM International Conference on Web Intelligence, pp. 1012–1018 (2006)
15. Tombros, A., van Rijsbergen, C.J.: Query-Sensitive Similarity Measures for Information Retrieval. Knowledge and Information Systems 6, 617–642 (2004)
16. Schölkopf, B., Smola, A., Williamson, R., Bartlett, P.L.: New Support Vector Algorithms. Neural Computation 12, 1207–1245 (2000)
17. Brin, S., Page, L.: The Anatomy of a Large-scale Hypertextual Web Search Engine. Computer Networks and ISDN Systems 30(1-7), 107–117 (1998)
18. Dang, H.T.: Overview of DUC 2005. In: Document Understanding Conference 2005 (2005), http://duc.nist.gov
19. Lin, C.-Y., Hovy, E.: Automatic Evaluation of Summaries Using N-gram Co-occurrence Statistics. In: Proceedings of HLT-NAACL, pp. 71–78 (2003)
20. Carbonell, J., Goldstein, J.: The use of MMR and diversity-based reranking for reordering documents and producing summaries. In: Proceedings of the 21st Annual International ACM-SIGIR Conference on Research and Development in Information Retrieval (1998)
21. Chang, C.-C., Lin, C.-J.: LIBSVM: A Library for Support Vector Machines, http://www.csie.ntu.edu.tw/~cjlin/libsvm

Extracting Domain-Dependent Semantic Orientations of Latent Variables for Sentiment Classification

Yeha Lee, Jungi Kim, and Jong-Hyeok Lee

Division of Electrical and Computer Engineering
Pohang University of Science and Technology
San 31, Hyoja-Dong, Nam-Gu, Pohang, 790–784, Republic of Korea
{sion,yangpa,jhlee}@postech.ac.kr

Abstract. Sentiment analysis of weblogs is a challenging problem. Most previous work utilized semantic orientations of words or phrases to classify sentiments of weblogs. The problem with this approach is that semantic orientations of words or phrases are investigated without considering the domain of weblogs. Weblogs contain the author's various opinions about multifaceted topics. Therefore, we have to treat a semantic orientation domain-dependently. In this paper, we present an unsupervised learning model based on aspect model to classify sentiments of weblogs. Our model utilizes domain-dependent semantic orientations of latent variables instead of words or phrases, and uses them to classify sentiments of weblogs. Experiments on several domains confirm that our model assigns domain-dependent semantic orientations to latent variables correctly, and classifies sentiments of weblogs effectively.

Keywords: sentiment classification, sentiment analysis, information extraction, text mining.

1 Introduction

An increasing number of internet users are expressing not only factual data but also their subjective thoughts and opinions on various topics in weblogs. A lot of recent research tries to access the author's opinions and sentiments hidden in the weblogs. There are many applications that can be exploited when we can access weblogs' opinions or sentiments. For instance, information extraction and question-answering systems could flag statements and queries regarding opinions rather than facts [1]. Also, it has proven useful for companies, recommender systems and editorial sites to create summaries of people's experiences and opinions that consist of subjective expressions extracted from reviews (as is commonly done in movie ads) or even just a review's *polarity* – positive ("thumbs up") or negative ("thumbs down") [2].

Most previous work [3,4,5,6] investigated semantic orientations of words or phrases to analyze sentiments of sentences or documents. However, semantic orientations of words or phrases are investigated without reflecting properties of the domain in which documents are included. Weblogs deal with various topics, and they contain both facts

W. Li and D. Mollá-Aliod (Eds.): ICCPOL 2009, LNAI 5459, pp. 201–212, 2009.

and opinions, and the same word might possess different semantic orientations in different domains. Therefore, we have to assign different semantic orientations of words or phrases according to the domain of the weblogs.

In this paper, we present an unsupervised learning model to classify sentiments of weblogs. Therefore our model does not require sentiment tagged corpus to be trained. Our model, which is based on an aspect model, assigns semantic orientations of latent factors depending on the domain of the weblogs. Our model uncovers semantic orientations of latent factors, which are domain dependent, and use them for sentiment classification. The experiments on three domains (movie, automobiles and digital cameras) show that our model is effective at accessing a domain dependent semantic orientation and classifying weblogs' sentiments.

The paper is organized as follows. Section 2 introduces related work. In Section 3, we formulate the sentiment classification problem of the weblogs and show the detail of our approach. The experimental results are presented in Section 4. Finally, we conclude the paper and discuss future work in Section 5.

2 Related Work

In the case of opinion analysis, there has been a lot of previous research such as the development of linguistic resource, subjectivity detection and sentiment classification.

In developing linguistic resources, some previous works have focused on learning adjectives or adjectival phrases [3,4,5]. Riloff et al. [7] developed a system that can distinguish subjective sentences from objective sentences using lists of subjective nouns learned by bootstrapping algorithms. Wilson et al. [8] presented a two-step contextual polarity classification to analyze phrase–level sentiment. Kamps et al. [9] proposed measures that determine the semantic orientation of adjectives using WordNet's synonymy relation. Takamura et al. [10] used latent variables to find semantic orientations of phrases. Their approach is similar to our model in that it uses latent variables. However our approach is different from Takamura et al. in that our approach finds semantic orientations of latent variables and uses them to classify the sentiments of the weblogs.

Turney [5] classified the sentiment of a document using the average semantic orientation of phrases that was assigned using the PMI method. Pang et al. [11] employed three standard machine learning techniques (Naive Bayes, Maximum Entropy, and SVM) to classify the sentiment of a document. Pang and Lee [2] presented cut-based classification. In their approach, sentences in a document are labeled as either subjective or objective, and a standard machine learning classifier that classifies document-level sentiment is applied to subjective sentences. Whitelaw et al. [12] presented a method for sentiment classification which is based on analysis of appraisal groups.

Applications using sentiment analysis of weblogs or news have been proposed [13, 14]. Mei et al. [15] proposed a probabilistic model to capture the mixture of topics and sentiments simultaneously. Liu et al. [16] investigated ways to use sentiment information from blogs for predicting product sales performance. In order to mine sentiment information from blogs, they presented a S-PLSA model based on PLSA. They used sentiment information captured by S-PLSA as features of an auto regression model. Our approach, on the other hand, presents a general framework to classify sentiments of the weblogs using semantic orientations of latent variables.

3   Weblogs Classification

In this section, we propose a novel probabilistic approach to classify the sentiments of weblogs, which is an unsupervised learning model.

The weblogs contain various opinions of the author about many fields. This property of the weblog causes a word to have different semantic orientations according to the domain in which it is used. For example, the adjective "unpredictable" may have a negative orientation in an automotive review in a phrase such as "unpredictable steering", but it could have a positive orientation in a movie review in a phrase such as "unpredictable plot" [5]. This problem results from the use of domain-independent semantic orientations of words or phrases without considering the properties of the domain in which they are used. In general, the semantic orientation of a word is affected by the surrounding context as well as the domain. For example, words following a negation word can have the opposite semantic orientation. However, in this study, we deal with the problem that results from the property of the weblogs, exemplified in the above case. In order to analyze complicated properties of weblogs, we regard them as results generated by the mixture model of the latent factors. We expect that those latent factors would correspond to the author's sentiments presented in the weblogs. We use semantic orientations of latent factors, instead of words or phrases, to classify the sentiments of weblogs.

To this end, we present a Sentiment Aspect Model (SentiAM) based on the aspect model. Aspect model [17] is a latent variable model for co-occurrence data which associates an unobserved class variable $z \in Z = \{z_1, \cdots, z_K\}$ with each observation. SentiAM adds a semantic orientation factor to the aspect model. We regard the semantic orientation factor as having a dependency relationship with the latent variable. Figure 1 (a) shows a graphical representation of the statistical dependencies of SentiAM. If our model can capture domain-dependent semantic orientations of latent variables, it will yield better sentiment classification accuracy compared to the model that uses domain-independent semantic orientations of words or phrases.

3.1   Sentiment Aspect Model

In this section, we formally present SentiAM to classify sentiments of weblogs.

Let $D = \{d_1, d_2, \cdots, d_N\}$ be a set of weblogs, with words from a vocabulary $W = \{w_1, w_2, \cdots, w_M\}$. The weblog data set can be represented as a $M \times N$ matrix $R = (n(d_i, w_j))_{ij}$, where $n(d_i, w_j)$ denotes the number of times w_j occurs in weblog d_i. And

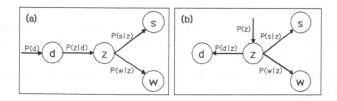

Fig. 1. Graphical model representation of the Sentiment Aspect Model. S: semantic orientation factor.

let $S = \{P, N, F\}$ be a set of semantic orientations. P, N and F represent positive, negative and neutral orientations respectively. Let $Z = \{z_1, z_2, \cdots, z_K\}$ be a set of latent variables.

Suppose that the weblog d, the semantic orientation s and the word w are conditionally independent given the latent variable z (corresponding graphical model representation is depicted in Figure 1 (b)). Then, we can view the problem of classifying the sentiment of the weblog d as follows:

$$S^* = \arg\max_{s \in \{P,N\}} P(s|d) = \arg\max_{s \in \{P,N\}} \sum_{z_k \in Z} P(s|z_k)P(z_k|d) \tag{1}$$

Because probability $P(d)$ does not have any effect on the decision of the weblog's sentiment, we can transform the equation (1) by using Bayes rule to the following:

$$S^* = \arg\max_{s \in \{P,N\}} \sum_{z_k \in Z} P(s|z_k)P(d|z_k)P(z_k) \tag{2}$$

In equation (1), $P(z|d)$ represents how much a latent variable z occupies in the sentiment of a weblog d, intuitively, and $P(s|z)$ represents a semantic orientation of a latent variable z.

For the sentiment classification of the weblogs, the parameters of SentiAM are learnt through two steps. In the first step, the generative probabilities ($P(d|z)$, $P(w|z)$ and $P(z)$) are calculated based on the aspect model. Next step finds the probabilities of semantic orientations $P(s|z)$ of latent variables.

3.2   Generative Probabilities

According to Figure 1 (b), assuming that the weblog d and the word w are conditionally independent given the latent variable z, the generative process of weblog-word pair (d, w) is defined by the mixture:

$$P(d,w) = \sum_{z \in Z} P(z)P(d|z)P(w|z) \tag{3}$$

We use Expectation-Maximization [18] algorithm to estimate the parameters, $P(d|z)$, $P(w|z)$ and $P(z)$, which maximizes the below likelihood function.

$$P(D,W) = \prod_{d \in D} \prod_{w \in W} P(d,w)^{n(d,w)} \tag{4}$$

EM algorithm involves an iterative process with alternating steps, expectation step and maximization step, in order to learn the parameters which maximize complete likelihood.

In the expectation step (E-Step), the posterior probabilities are computed for the latent variables:

$$P(z|d,w) = \frac{P(z)P(d|z)P(w|z)}{\sum_{z' \in Z} P(z')P(d|z')P(w|z')} \tag{5}$$

In the maximization step (M-Step), the parameters are updated:

$$P(w|z) = \frac{\sum_{d \in D} n(d,w)P(z|d,w)}{\sum_{d \in D} \sum_{w' \in W} n(d,w')P(z|d,w')} \quad (6)$$

$$P(d|z) = \frac{\sum_{w \in W} n(d,w)P(z|d,w)}{\sum_{d' \in D} \sum_{w \in W} n(d',w)P(z|d',w)} \quad (7)$$

$$P(z) = \frac{\sum_{d \in D} \sum_{w \in W} n(d,w)P(z|d,w)}{\sum_{d \in D} \sum_{w \in W} n(d,w)} \quad (8)$$

The parameters, $P(d|z)$ and $P(z)$, learnt by the EM algorithm are used to classify sentiments of the weblogs, and the parameter $P(w|z)$ is used to find the probabilities of semantic orientations of latent variables $P(s|z)$.

3.3   Finding Domain-Dependent Semantic Orientations of Latent Variables

We use a lexicon resource tagged with positive and negative semantic orientations in order to find domain-dependent semantic orientations of the latent variables.

In our approach, SentiWordNet [19] is used as a polarity tagged lexicon. SentiWordNet is a lexical resource in which each synset of WORDNET (version 2.0) is associated to three numerical scores $Obj(s)$, $Pos(s)$ and $Neg(s)$. And it describes how Objective, Positive and Negative the terms contained in the synset are. For each word in SentiWordNet, positive, negative and neutral scores are defined as probabilities ($Obj + Pos + Neg = 1$). Therefore we can readily find probabilities of semantic orientations of words, and we use them to find semantic orientations of latent variables.

The semantic orientations of the latent variables are calculated as the following:

$$P(S = P|z) = \sum_{w \in W} P_{IND}(S = P|w)P(w|z) \quad (9)$$

$$P(S = N|z) = \sum_{w \in W} P_{IND}(S = N|w)P(w|z) \quad (10)$$

Given a word, $P_{IND}(\cdot|w)$ represents probability of domain-independent semantic orientation defined in SentiWordNet. SentiWordNet defines semantic orientation of a word according to its sense. Therefore, semantic orientation of a word could become different if its sense is changed. We use the first sense of the word to simplify the experiment, because WSD (Word Sense Disambiguation) is another issue and out of the scope of this paper.

In equation (9) and (10), the probability of semantic orientation of latent variable z is the expectation of the probabilities of semantic orientations of all words which are generated by the latent variable z. The expectation makes the semantic orientation of the latent variable to be domain-dependent.

In the aspect model, different latent factors correspond with different topics, and words generated with high probability by a particular latent factor are related with topics captured by the latent factor. Due to these properties, different meanings (dependent on the context) of a polysemous word are identified by different latent factors. Similarly, different latent variables of SentiAM correspond with different opinions and sentiments contained in weblogs, and words generated with high probability by a particular latent factor have similar semantic orientations. For example, "unpredictable" is defined as negative semantic orientation with 0.625 probability by SentiWordNet. On the other hand, "unpredictable" is used with positive semantic orientation in the movie domain. Therefore a latent variable which generates "unpredictable" with high probability also generates many other words which have positive semantic orientation. Finally, the use of the expectation of semantic orientations of words makes the latent variable to assign the semantic orientation domain-dependently. Through experimenting on several different domains, we can verify the effect of the expectation of the semantic orientations.

3.4 Features Selection

In reality, SentiAM gives poor results when we use all words in the weblogs to train parameters of SentiAM. Weblogs contain not only the writers' opinions but also factual descriptions, and this damages the effectiveness of the modeling. This is because the opinionated words and non-opinionated words may co-occur with each other, thus they will not be separated by the EM algorithm. This inhibits latent variables from properly modeling weblogs' opinions. We consider feature selection to solve the problem. Instead of considering all words present in the weblogs, we attempt to seek out appraisal words to describe weblogs.

To this end, we choose subjective words in SentiWordNet $(Pos + Neg > 0.0)$ as candidate words. To investigate the influence of feature selection on sentiment classification accuracy, we make four feature types using candidate words.

Type A consists of adjectives only. **Type B** is comprised of adjectives and verbs. **Type C** consists of adjectives and adverbs. **Type D** is comprised of all feature candidates, ie. nouns, verbs, adjectives and adverbs.

4   Experiments and Results

We conducted several experiments on three different domains. We tried to verify that latent variables are able to model domain-dependent semantic orientation correctly in each domain and that the use of the latent variables are effective for sentiment classification of the weblogs.

4.1   Data Sets

We used reviews in the domains of Movie, Automobiles and Digital Cameras. As a movie review dataset, the polarity dataset of Pang and Lee [2] was used. It contains 1000 positive and 1000 negative reviews all written before 2002 with a cap of 20 reviews per author per category. For an automobile review dataset, Epinion's[1] result set from "Cars & Motorsports" section for a keyword automobile was used. For a digital cameras dataset, Epinion's result set from "Digital Cameras" section for keywords Canon, Nikon and Pentax was used. Among the reviews, short reviews with less than 50 words were excluded. Epinions review system displays authors' rating with five stars.

---

[1] http://epinions.com

Table 1. Test Data Sets. # Type A: the number of Type A (adjectives); # Type B: the number of Type B (adjectives+verbs); # Type C: the number of Type C (adjectives+adverbs); # Type D: the number of Type D (nouns+verbs+adjectives+adverbs); Auto.: Automobiles domain; Dig. Cam.: Digital Cameras domain.

Domain	# Pos.	# Neg.	# Avg. words	# Type A	# Type B	# Type C	# Type D
Movie	1000	1000	746.33	4174	5391	5406	9721
Auto.	130	130	613.28	1114	1528	1511	2616
Dig. Cam.	200	200	131.78	518	706	704	1213

We regard reviews with more than 3 stars (≥ 4) as positive reviews and reviews with less than 3 stars (≤ 2) as negative reviews. The number of positive reviews obtained from epinions significantly outnumbers the number of negative reviews. Therefore, we randomly chose positive reviews to match the number of negative reviews. In general, the use of a different number of positive and negative reviews as test dataset can lead to a biased result. Once the two groups are selected in equal numbers, the reviews are parsed for html-tags removal and POS tagging by Stanford Tagger. No stemming and stopword lists were used. All feature words between a negation word ("not", "isn't", etc.) and the first punctuation mark following the negation word is marked with NOT tag [11]. Table 1 shows information of the dataset which we used for experiment.

4.2   Baseline

For the baseline of the experiment, we classified weblogs' sentiments using semantic orientations of subjective words within SentiWordNet. For each word, SentiWordNet defines its semantic orientation as a score (probability). We regard a review as a positive review when the sum of positive scores of subjective words within a review is greater than that of negative scores, otherwise we regard it as a negative review.

The baseline precisions of the movie domain, the automobile domain and the digital camera domain are 0.44, 0.63 and 0.62, respectively. We can see that the precision was worse than that of random selection in movie domain. This result shows the difficulty of sentiment classification in the movie domain. This result is because there are many words that have a different semantic orientation compared to domain-independent semantic orientation defined at SentiWordNet such as "unpredictable" in the movie domain. This result shows the problem when using domain-independent semantic orientations of words or phrases. Therefore domain-dependent semantic orientation of latent variables can remedy this problem.

4.3   Semantic Orientation of Latent Variables

We wanted to verify that latent variables capture domain-dependent semantic orientation correctly. To do this, we used words such as "unpredictable" that have different semantic orientations depending on the domain where they are used. In SentiWordNet, "unpredictable" has a negative semantic orientation with its 0.625 score. For each domain, we verified semantic orientations of latent variables which generate "unpredictable" with high probability. Table 2 shows semantic orientations of two

Table 2. Semantic orientation of the two latent variables that produces the word "unpredictable" with the highest probability

		Movie	Auto.	Dig. Cam.
1st	$P(Pos|z)$	0.27	0.23	0.23
	$P(Neg|z)$	0.23	0.27	0.23
2nd	$P(Pos|z)$	0.26	0.23	0.23
	$P(Neg|z)$	0.24	0.24	0.22

latent variables which generate "unpredictable" with the highest probability. The results of movie and automobile datasets correspond to our expectation. Even though the domain-independent semantic orientation of the word "unpredictable" is negative, the two latent variables that generate the word the most have positive semantic orientations in the movie domain.

We expected that latent variables generating the word "unpredictable" with high probability would have a negative semantic orientation in the digital cameras dataset. To the contrary of our expectation, positive semantic orientation is higher or equal to negative semantic orientation. We think this is due to the small size we had for SentiAM to learn parameters $P(z)$, $P(d|z)$, $P(w|z)$ and $P(s|z)$ through the EM algorithm. As shown in the Table 1, the size of the digital cameras dataset is noticeably smaller than the other two. In fact the word, "unpredictable", occurs only once in 400 reviews in the digital cameras dataset upon a closer inspection. This might lead to improper parameter training of SentiAM.

Table 3. Words with different semantic orientations in the movie domain. IND. SO: (positive/negative) semantic orientation pair defined at SentiWordNet; DEP. SO: (positive/negative) semantic orientation pair of latent variables which generate the word with the highest probability; CONTEXT: a segment of text in which the word appears.

WORD	IND. SO	DEP. SO	CONTEXT
otherwordly	0.00/0.88	0.31/0.21	was a striking mood piece with an otherworldly feel
unconventional	0.00/0.88	0.27/0.23	that movie worked because it took an unconventional story
ad-lib	0.00/0.75	0.31/0.21	by people with little gift for ad-lib
sarcastic	0.00/0.75	0.27/0.23	succeeds in giving his character a sarcastic sense of humor
unexpected	0.00/0.63	0.26/0.23	there is plenty of action and an unexpected dose of humour
unpredictable	0.00/0.63	0.27/0.23	the ending is unpredictable and incredibly satisfying

We found words in the movie domain with semantic orientations different to domain-independent ones. Table 3 lists some of them with their semantic orientations and contexts.

The experiment shows that SentiAM assigns domain-dependent semantic orientation to latent variables correctly. The experiment presented in the next section shows that these latent variables also outperform other types of features such as words and phrases in the sentiment classification of the weblogs.

Table 4. Best Overall Precision. Prec.: precision; Rec.: recall.

Domain	Type	Prec.	Rec.	Feature
Movie	Positive	0.67	0.91	
	Negative	0.85	0.56	Type A
	Overall	0.74	0.74	
Auto.	Positive	0.61	0.85	
	Negative	0.75	0.45	Type A
	Overall	0.65	0.65	
Dig. Cam.	Positive	0.59	0.80	
	Negative	0.62	0.42	Type A
	Overall	0.62	0.61	

4.4 Sentiment Classification

In this section, we investigate the influence of various feature sets (Type A, Type B, Type C, and Type D) and the number of latent variables on accuracy of weblogs' sentiment classification.

We used the same number of positive reviews as negative reviews. Therefore, a random guessing sentiment of the reviews will have 50% accuracy.

Table 4 shows the best performance we achieved for each domain and the feature set used. In the movie domain, we obtained 24% higher precision than random guessing and 30% higher precision than the baseline. In the automobile domain, we also obtained 15% and 2% higher precision than random guessing and the baseline. In the digital camera domain, we obtained 12% better precision than random guessing but the same precision with the baseline.

We think that the small improvement of accuracy in automobiles and digital cameras compared to that in the movie domain is due to the small size of the two domains' test corpora. As we saw in section 4.3, the bigger the size of the dataset, the better SentiAM assigns domain-dependent semantic orientations of latent variables, thus resulting in higher accuracy.

Feature Type A which consists of adjectives only, resulted in the best accuracy in all domains. Many previous works [5, 20, 3] related to sentiment analysis dealt with adjectives heavily. Adjectives are less ambiguous with respect to sentiment than other word classes. Therefore, they can convey the author's opinion more correctly than any other parts of speech.

Figure 2 (a) shows the influence of varying feature types on sentiment classification of the weblogs in the movie domain. The two other domains yield similar results and the following analysis on the movie domain also applies to them.

Type A and Type B produced results with higher accuracy than the others. This is because adjectives and verbs reflect the authors' opinions less ambiguously with respect to sentiment than other word classes. We obtained the worst accuracy when using Type D which includes nouns. Nouns are likely to be non-opinionated or less-opinionated. Thus including them in the feature set might generate noise when latent variables separate the different opinions and sentiments of the weblogs. We have not yet investigated the influence of nouns on sentiment classification. We leave this issue for future work.

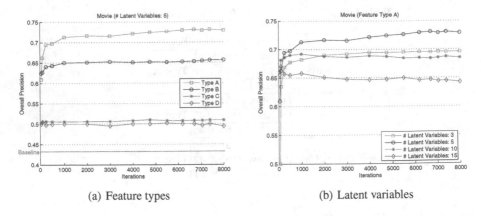

(a) Feature types   (b) Latent variables

Fig. 2. In the movie doman, overall precision according to feature types and latent variables

Figure 2 (b) shows the accuracy of sentiment classification according to different numbers of latent variables, $z = 3, 5, 10, 15$. We obtained the best accuracy using five latent variables, the worst accuracy using fifteen latent variables. Too many latent variables overfits the data set and does not produce either positive or negative polarity. On the other hand, too few latent variables might not be able to capture semantic orientation with enough accuracy and thus reduces the accuracy of sentiment classifier as well.

5   Conclusions and Future Work

In this paper, we have presented a novel probabilistic approach to classify sentiments of weblogs. Our model, SentiAM, is an unsupervised learning model based on the aspect model. SentiAM assigns domain-dependent semantic orientations to latent variables using resources in which semantic orientations of words or phrases are tagged domain-independently. Experimental results confirm that semantic orientations of latent variables are effective at classifying the sentiments of weblogs.

We have presented a general framework to capture domain-dependent semantic orientations of latent variables. Though we used SentiWordNet as a polarity tagged lexicon resource, any resource can be applied. Therefore, semantic orientations of lexicons exploited by previous work can be also used by our framework.

We used semantic orientation of the first sense of a word in SentiWordNet. Knowledge about word sense can improve accuracy of sentiment classification. We could use WSD or any means to improve word sense detection, thus improving the accuracy of sentiment classification.

We use semantic orientations of latent variables to classify sentiments of weblogs. Our framework could, of course, also be applied to analyzing semantic orientations of more fine units such as sentences and words. We leave this issue for our future work.

Acknowledgement. This work was supported in part by MKE & IITA through IT Leading R&D Support Project and also in part by the BK 21 Project in 2008.

References

1. Cardie, C., Wiebe, J., Wilson, T., Litman, D.: Combining low-level and summary representations of opinions for multiperspective question answering. In: Working Notes of the 2003 AAAI Spring Symposium on New Directions in Question Answering, pp. 20–27 (2003)
2. Pang, B., Lee, L.: A sentimental education: Sentiment analysis using subjectivity summarization based on minimum cuts. In: Proceedings of the 42nd Meeting of the Association for Computational Linguistics (ACL 2004), Barcelona, Spain, pp. 271–278 (July 2004)
3. Hatzivassiloglou, V., McKeown, K.R.: Predicting the semantic orientation of adjectives. In: Proceedings of the 35th Annual Meeting of the Association for Computational Linguistics, Madrid, Spain, pp. 174–181. Association for Computational Linguistics (July 1997)
4. Wiebe, J.M.: Learning subjective adjectives from corpora. In: Proceedings of AAAI 2000, pp. 735–740 (2000)
5. Turney, P.: Thumbs up or thumbs down? semantic orientation applied to unsupervised classification of reviews. In: Proceedings of 40th Annual Meeting of the Association for Computational Linguistics, Philadelphia, Pennsylvania, USA, pp. 417–424. Association for Computational Linguistics (July 2002)
6. Kim, S.M., Hovy, E.: Automatic detection of opinion bearing words and sentence. In: Proceedings of IJCNLP 2005, pp. 61–66 (2005)
7. Riloff, E., Wiebe, J., Wilson, T.: Learning subjective nouns using extraction pattern bootstrapping. In: Proceedings of CoNLL 2003, pp. 25–32 (2003)
8. Wilson, T., Wiebe, J., Hoffmann, P.: Recognizing contextual polarity in phrase-level sentiment analysis. In: Proceedings of Human Language Technology Conference and Conference on Empirical Methods in Natural Language Processing, Vancouver, British Columbia, Canada, pp. 347–354. Association for Computational Linguistics (October 2005)
9. Kamps, J., Marx, M., Mokken, R.J., de Rijke, M.: Using wordnet to measure semantic orientations of adjectives. In: Proceedings of LREC 2004, pp. 1115–1118 (2004)
10. Takamura, H., Inui, T., Okumura, M.: Latent variables models for semantic orientations of phrase. In: Proceedings of EACL 2006, pp. 201–208 (2006)
11. Pang, B., Lee, L., Vaithyanathan, S.: Thumbs up? sentiment classification using machine learning techniques. In: Proceedings of the 2002 Conference on Empirical Methods in Natural Language Processing, pp. 79–86. Association for Computational Linguistics (July 2002)
12. Whitelaw, C., Garg, N., Argamon, S.: Using appraisal groups for sentiment analysis. In: Proceedings of CIKM 2005, pp. 625–631. ACM, New York (2005)
13. Morinaga, S., Yamanishi, K., Tateishi, K., Fukushima, T.: Mining product reputations on the web. In: KDD 2002: Proceedings of the eighth ACM SIGKDD international conference on Knowledge discovery and data mining, pp. 341–349. ACM, New York (2002)
14. Devitt, A., Ahmad, K.: Sentiment polarity identification in financial news: A cohesion-based approach. In: Proceedings of the 45th Annual Meeting of the Association of Computational Linguistics, Prague, Czech Republic, pp. 984–991. Association for Computational Linguistics (June 2007)
15. Mei, Q., Ling, X., Wondra, M., Su, H., Zhai, C.: Topic sentiment mixture: modeling facets and opinions in weblogs. In: WWW 2007: Proceedings of the 16th international conference on World Wide Web, pp. 171–180. ACM, New York (2007)
16. Liu, Y., Huang, X., An, A., Yu, X.: Arsa: a sentiment-aware model for predicting sales performance using blogs. In: Proceedings of SIGIR 2007, pp. 607–614. ACM, New York (2007)

17. Hofmann, T., Puzicha, J., Jordan, M.I.: Unsupervised learning from dyadic data. In: Advances in Neural Information Processing Systems (1999)
18. Dempster, A.P., Laird, N., Rubin, D.: Maximum likelihood from incomplete data via the em algorithm. Journal of the Royal Statistical Society 39(B), 1–38 (1997)
19. Esuli, A., Sebastiani, F.: Sentwordnet: A publicly available lexical resource for opinion mining. In: Proceedings of LREC 2006, pp. 417–422 (2006)
20. Hatzivassiloglou, V., Wiebe, J.: Effects of adjective orientation and gradability on sentence subjectivity. In: Proceedings of COLING 2000, pp. 299–305 (2000)

Mining Cross-Lingual/Cross-Cultural Differences in Concerns and Opinions in Blogs

Hiroyuki Nakasaki[1], Mariko Kawaba[1], Takehito Utsuro[1],
and Tomohiro Fukuhara[2]

[1] Graduate School of Systems and Information Engineering, University of Tsukuba,
1-1-1, Tennodai, Tsukuba, 305-8573, Japan
[2] Research into Artifacts, Center for Engineering, University of Tokyo,
Kashiwa 277-8568, Japan
{nakasaki,kawaba,utsuro}@nlp.iit.tsukuba.ac.jp

Abstract. The goal of this paper is to cross-lingually analyze multilingual blogs collected with a topic keyword. The framework of collecting multilingual blogs with a topic keyword is designed as the blog feed retrieval procedure. Mulitlingual queries for retrieving blog feeds are created from *Wikipedia* entries. Finally, we cross-lingually and cross-culturally compare less well known facts and opinions that are closely related to a given topic. Preliminary evaluation results support the effectiveness of the proposed framework.

Keywords: blog, topic analysis, cultural gaps, Wikipedia, CLIR.

1 Introduction

Weblogs or blogs are considered to be one of personal journals, market or product commentaries. There are several previous works and services on blog analysis systems (e.g., [1]). With respect to blog analysis services on the Internet, there are several commercial and non-commercial services such as *Technorati, BlogPulse, kizasi.jp,* and *blogWatcher*. With respect to multilingual blog services, *Globe of Blogs, Best Blogs in Asia Directory,* and *Blogwise* can be listed.

The goal of this paper is to cross-lingually analyze multilingual blogs collected with a topic keyword. First, the framework of collecting multilingual blogs with a topic keyword is designed as the blog feed retrieval procedure recently studied in TREC 2007 Blog track as one of its task [2]. In this paper, we take an approach of collecting blog feeds rather than blog posts, mainly because we regard the former as a larger information unit in the blogosphere and prefer it as the information source for cross-lingual blog analysis. Second, multilingual queries for retrieving blog feeds are created from *Wikipedia* (English and Japanese versions[1]) entries, where interlanguage links are used for linking English and Japanese translated entries. Here, the underlying motivation of employing Wikipedia is in linking a knowledge base of well known facts and relatively neutral opinions with rather

---

[1] http://en,ja.wikipedia.org/

W. Li and D. Mollá-Aliod (Eds.): ICCPOL 2009, LNAI 5459, pp. 213–224, 2009.

raw, user generated media like blogs, which include less well known facts and much more radical opinions. We regard Wikipedia as a large scale ontological knowledge base for conceptually indexing the blogosphere. Finally, we use such multilingual blog feed retrieval framework in higher level application of cross-lingual blog analysis. Here, we cross-lingually and cross-culturally compare less well known facts and much more radical opinions that are closely related to a given topic.

In addition to proposing the overall framework of cross-lingual and cross-cultural comparison of concerns and opinions in blogs in two languages, this paper shows the effectiveness of the proposed framework with detailed examples of efficiently mining and comparing cross-lingual differences in concerns and opinions.

2   Overall Framework of Cross-Lingual Blog Analysis

Overview of the proposed framework is shown in Figure 1. First, multilingual queries for retrieving blog feeds on a topic (in this case "whaling") are created from *Wikipedia* entries. Next, from the collected blog feeds, terms that are characteristic only in one language or in both languages are automatically extracted. Here, we apply a statistical measure for mining cross-lingual differences between

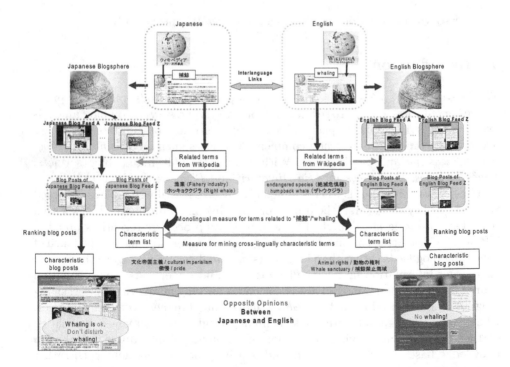

Fig. 1. Overall Framework of Cross-Lingual Blog Analysis

terms in two languages, as well as a monolingual measure for terms related to the given topic. Then, by counting occurrences of the topic name and the related terms extracted from the Wikipedia entry in blog posts in both languages, characteristic blog posts are ranked. Finally, by manually analyzing top ranked blog posts, we can efficiently discover cross-lingual differences in concerns and opinions of blog posts in two languages.

3   Sample Topics

We first selected about fifty topic keywords from Wikipedia entries, where each of them has both Japanese and English entries in Wikipedia, and sufficient number of Japanese and English blog feeds can be found. Then, we manually examine both Japanese and English blog posts for each of those topic keywords. For a preliminary evaluation of this paper, we selected four topic keywords in Table 1, where, for each topic, the table shows their short descriptions, and characteristic cross-lingual differences in facts / opinions included in the retrieved blogs. Those four topic keywords are closely related to political issues and cross-lingual differences are to some extent related to differences in opinions.

Table 1. Sample Topics used in the Evaluation and their Descriptions

Topic — Short Description	
Differences in Facts/Opinions	
(Japanese Blogs)	(English Blogs)
Whaling — There are arguments *for* and *against* whaling.	
Most blogs are *for* whaling. Some of them are nationalistic.	Most blogs are *against* whaling, especially, whaling in Japan. Some are blogs for whale watching.
Organ transplant — A medical operation for the purpose of replacing damaged organ with a working one from the donor's body.	
Many blogs point out that Organ Transplant Law of Japan should be revised. Some blogs are picking up the news about transplant by the Japanese doctor using diseased kidney.	Many blogs strongly recommend donor registration because of shortage of organs for patients. Some blogs are criticizing Chinese illegal transplant.
Tobacco smoking — The fact that smoking does harm to health is mostly argued.	
Although most bloggers are *against* smoking, one or two blogger(s) are *for* smoking.	Most bloggers are *against* smoking because it may cause lung cancer.
Subprime lending — Beginning in late 2006, the U.S. subprime mortgage industry entered what many observers have begun to refer to as a meltdown.	
Most bloggers argue influences of the U.S. subprime problem on Japanese economy.	Financial analysts argue issues of subprime problems, housing bubble, and the resulting financial crisis.

4 Procedure of Cross-Lingual Blog Analysis

4.1 Blog Feed Retrieval

For the purpose of cross-lingual blog analysis, in our framework, multilingual queries for retrieving blog feeds are created from Wikipedia entries. This section briefly describes how to retrieve blog feeds given a query for each language (in this paper, English and Japanese).

First, in order to collect candidates of blog feeds for a given query, in this paper, we use existing Web search engine APIs, which return a ranked list of blog posts, given a topic keyword. We use the search engine "Yahoo!" API[2] for English, and the Japanese search engine "Yahoo! Japan" API[3] for Japanese. Blog hosts are limited to major ones, namely, 12 for English[4] and 11 for Japanese[5].

Next, we employ the following procedure for the blog distillation:

i) Given a topic keyword, a ranked list of blog posts are returned by a Web search engine API.
ii) A list of blog feeds is generated from the returned ranked list of blog posts by simply removing duplicated feeds.
iii) Re-rank the list of blog feeds according to the number of hits of the topic keyword in each blog feed. The number of hits for a topic keyword in each blog feed is simply measured by the search engine API used for collecting blog posts above in i), restricting the domain of the URL to each blog feed.

Table 2. Statistics of # (Japanese/English) of terms used for collecting blog feeds/posts, blog feeds/posts, words/morphemes

Topic	# of topic-related terms from Wikipedia	# of blog feeds	# of blog posts	# of total words/morphemes
Whaling	162 / 174	121 / 239	2232 / 6532	5024966 / 2611942
Organ transplant	100 / 231	89 / 206	696 / 1301	995927 / 781476
Tobacco smoking	399 / 276	86 / 252	1481 / 400	1323767 / 492727
Subprime lending	39 / 68	134 / 205	1088 / 1216	980552 / 883450

4.2 Blog Post Retrieval

We automatically select blog posts that are closely related to a topic, which is given as a title of an Wikipedia entry. To do this, we first automatically extract

---

[2] http://www.yahoo.com/

[3] http://www.yahoo.co.jp/ (in Japanese).

[4] blogspot.com,msnblogs.net,spaces.live.com,livejournal.com,vox.com, multiply.com,typepad.com,aol.com,blogsome.com,wordpress.com,blog-king. net,blogster.com

[5] FC2.com,yahoo.co.jp,rakuten.ne.jp,ameblo.jp,goo.ne.jp,livedoor.jp, Seesaa.net,jugem.jp,yaplog.jp,webry.info.jp,hatena.ne.jp

terms that are closely related to each Wikipedia entry. More specifically, from the body text of each Wikipedia entry, we extract bold-faced terms, anchor texts of hyperlinks, and the title of a *redirect*, which is a synonymous term of the title of the target page. Then, blog posts which contain the topic name or at least one of the extracted related terms are automatically selected.

For each topic, Table 2 shows the numbers of terms that are closely related to the topic and are extracted from each Wikipedia entry. Then, according to the above procedure, blog posts which contain the topic name or at least one of the extracted related terms are automatically selected. Table 2 also shows the numbers of the selected blog posts, as well as those of blog feeds for those posts and the total numbers of words/morphemes contained in those posts.

4.3   Extracting Characteristic Terms

Next, this section gives the procedure of how to extract characteristic terms from the blog posts retrieved according to the procedure described in the previous section. First, candidate terms are automatically extracted from the selected blog posts. Here, for Japanese, noun phrases are extracted as candidate terms, while for English, sequences of one word, two words, and three words are extracted as candidate terms. Then, those candidate terms are ranked according to the following two measures, so that terms that are characteristic only in one language or in both languages are selected:

a) Total frequency of each term in the whole selected blog posts. This measure is used for filtering out low frequency terms.

b) Cross-lingual rates $R_J(X_J, X_E)$ and of $R_E(Y_E, Y_J)$ term probabilities below, where term probabilities P_J and P_E are measured against the whole selected blog posts:

$$R_J(X_J, X_E) = \frac{P_J(X_J)}{P_E(X_E)}, \quad R_E(Y_E, Y_J) = \frac{P_E(Y_E)}{P_J(Y_J)}$$

Here, the pairs X_J and X_E, Y_E and Y_J are translation pairs found through interlanguage links of Wikipedia, or those found in an English-Japanese translation lexicon Eijiro[6]. This measure is especially for mining cross-lingually characteristic terms for each language.

Certain number of terms do not have translation into the other language, or even if they have translation in Wikipedia or Eijiro, the translation does not appear in the whole selected blog posts in the other language. Here, although some of such terms without translation or with zero frequency translation are extremely characteristic only for one language, most of other terms are noises that should be ignored here. Among such terms, those which are extremely characteristic only for one language tend to have high frequencies, and thus are ranked high in the ranking a) according to their total frequencies. Therefore, we consider their monolingual frequencies together with their cross-lingual rates and judge whether they are characteristic terms or noises.

---

[6] http://www.eijiro.jp/, Ver.79, with 1.6M translation pairs.

Table 3. Samples of Characteristic Terms Extracted from Japanese/English Blog Posts

(a) Whaling

JP Term	Freq. in JP blogs	EN Term	Freq. in EN blogs	$R_J(X_J,X_E)$	JP Term	Freq. in JP blogs	EN Term	Freq. in EN blogs	$R_E(X_E,X_J)$
反捕鯨国	136	antiwhaling country	0	∞	動物の権利	0	animal rights	233	∞
調査捕鯨	620	scientific whaling	116	2.78	捕鯨禁止海域	2	whale sanctuary	101	97.15
—	—	—	—	—	絶滅危惧種	47	endangered species	303	12.40
—	—	—	—	—	ザトウクジラ	98	humpback whales	266	5.22
—	—	—	—	—	絶滅	236	extinction	299	2.44

(b) Organ transplant

JP Term	Freq. in JP blogs	EN Term	Freq. in EN blogs	$R_J(X_J,X_E)$	JP Term	Freq. in JP blogs	EN Term	Freq. in EN blogs	$R_E(X_E,X_J)$
日本移植学会	75	No Translation (The Japan Society for Transplantation)	0	∞	No Translation	0	organ harvesting	270	∞
病気腎移植	442	No Translation (transplant using diseased kidney)	0	∞	人権	9	human rights	508	71.93
脳死移植	366	brain-dead transplant	0	∞	ドナーカード	27	donor card	124	5.85
臓器移植法	123	organ transplant law	3	32.17	臓器提供	200	organ donation	673	4.29

(c) Tobacco smoking

JP Term	Freq. in JP blogs	EN Term	Freq. in EN blogs	$R_J(X_J,X_E)$	JP Term	Freq. in JP blogs	EN Term	Freq. in EN blogs	$R_E(X_E,X_J)$
マナー	127	manners	1	47.27	肺癌	18	lung cancer	637	95.08
禁煙	520	smoking cessation	59	3.28	乳癌	6	breast cancer	339	151.79
—	—	—	—	—	受動喫煙	136	secondhand smoke	95	1.88

(d) Subprime lending

JP Term	Freq. in JP blogs	EN Term	Freq. in EN blogs	$R_J(X_J,X_E)$	JP Term	Freq. in JP blogs	EN Term	Freq. in EN blogs	$R_E(X_E,X_J)$
日本経済	96	economy of Japan	0	∞	ウォールストリート	11	Wall Street	474	47.83
日経平均	100	Nikkei 225	1	90.10	経営危機	3	financial crisis	55	20.35
株価	451	stock prices	30	13.54	不動産	100	real estate	637	7.07
—	—	—	—	—	住宅バブル	32	housing bubble	189	6.56

Table 3 shows excerpts of manually selected characteristic terms, as well as their ranking with respect to frequencies or cross-lingual rates $R_J(X_J, X_E)$ and $R_E(Y_E, Y_J)$. Here, most of them are characteristic only in one language, while some are characteristic in both languages. As we show in section 4.5, those terms as well as their frequencies and cross-lingual rates are useful signals for estimating differences in concerns and opinions in English and Japanese.

Table 4. Top 10 Ranked Japanese/English Blog Posts ("Whaling" and "Organ transplant")

Topic	
Japanese	English
rank of posts / author ID as feed rank / description	rank of posts / author ID as feed rank / description
Whaling	
(posts) 1st, 3rd, 5th, 6th, 8th / (feeds) 1st / *for* whaling. Criticizing anti-whaling groups.	(posts) 1st, 3rd, 4th, 5th, 10th / (feeds) 2nd / *neutral* with respect to whaling. Author lives in Japan for 30 years.
(posts) 4th / (feeds) 6th / *for* whaling. Author lives in US for 12 years.	(posts) 6th / (feeds) 3rd / *against* whaling. Animal rights activist.
(posts) 7th, 9th / (feeds) 4th / *for* whaling. Another blog of 1st ranked author.	(posts) 8th / (feeds) 10th / *against* whaling. Support Sea Shepherd, but against Greenpeace.
Organ transplant	
(posts) 2nd, 3rd, 4th, 6th, 9th / (feeds) 1st / Picking up news about kidney transplant using diseased kidney. Criticizing The Japan Society for Transplantation.	(posts) 2nd, 6th / (feeds) 8th / Quoting an article *against* Chinese illegal organ transplant.
(posts) 7th / (feeds) 14th / *against* brain-dead transplant. Organ transplant law should be carefully revised.	(posts) 3rd / (feeds) 2nd / Quoting an article *against* illegal organ transplant.
(posts) 8th, 10th / (feeds) 7th / *against* kidney transplant using diseased kidney.	(posts) 8th / (feeds) 7th / Picking up news article related to organ donation. Recommend blog readers to be an organ donor.

4.4 Ranking Blog Feeds/Posts

Finally, we rank the blog feeds/posts in terms of the topic name and the related terms extracted from the Wikipedia entry (as described in section 4.2)[7]. Here, only the blog posts that are retrieved in section 4.2 are ranked, and only the blog feeds that contain such blog posts are ranked. Ranking criteria are given below:

- Blog posts are ranked according to the following score, which is defined as a weighted sum of frequencies of the topic name and the related terms.

$$\sum_t weight(t) \times freq(t)$$

Here, $weight(t)$ is defined as 3 when t is the topic name or the title of a *redirect*, as 2 when t is a bold-faced term, and as 0.5 when t is an anchor text of hyperlinks.

---

[7] An alternative here is to rank the blog feeds/posts in terms of cross-lingually characteristic terms extracted in the previous section. However, compared with the related terms extracted from Wikipedia entries, certain number of terms automatically extracted from blog posts may be noises, and hence damage the results of ranking blog feeds/posts.

Table 5. Top 10 Ranked Japanese/English Blog Posts ("Tobacco smoking" and "Subprime lending")

| Topic | |
Japanese	English
rank of posts / author ID as feed rank / description	rank of posts / author ID as feed rank / description
Tobacco smoking	
(posts) 1st / (feeds) 7th / There is a conflict between smokers and anti-smoking people. Smokers and anti-smoking people have different cultures.	(posts) 2nd / (feeds) 6th / Comparing smoking rate in northern US and southern US. Tobacco is one of the large agricultural products in US.
(posts) 2nd, 5th, 10th / (feeds) 10th / *against* smoking. Smokers should observe some smoking manners while they are smoking.	(posts) 5th / (feeds) 1st / Strongly recommending smoking cessation. Smoking is just harmful to human's body.
(posts) 9th / (feeds) 14th / Warning smokers that smoking may increase a risk of dementia.	(posts) 9th / (feeds) 9th / Not smoking cigarette is the best way to prevent the development of lung cancer.
Subprime lending	
(posts) 1st, 4th, 6th, 9th / (feeds) 2nd / Japanese finance professor's blog. He points out that Japanese market couldn't response subprime problem in early time.	(posts) 1st, 4th / (feeds) 3rd / Author indicates that Federal Reserve Bank is thinking subprime issues are not that serious problems.
(posts) 3rd / (feeds) 17th / Japanese financial analyst blog. Author indicates that because no one thought price of real estate decline, subprime problem had expanded for long time.	(posts) 3rd / (feeds) 1st / Author indicates that subprime borrowers can't do anything. Lenders screwed up borrowers' life.
(posts) 10th / (feeds) 18th / Criticizing Federal Reserve Board as a cause of recent crisis, including subprime problem and financial crisis.	(posts) 5th / (feeds) 19th / Housing bubble made people buy new house, using subprime lending program, even though many people knew burst bubble is inevitable.

- Blog feeds are ranked according to the total frequencies for all the blog posts ranked above, where the total frequency for each blog post is calculated as above, in terms of the topic name and the related terms.

Tables 4 and 5 list excerpts of top 10 ranked blog posts, along with total frequencies of characteristic terms in each post, blog author identity as its rank in blog feed ranking. Although a few posts are not on the given topic, most other posts are deeply concerned with the given topic, and furthermore, some of them represent clear opinions on *for* or *against* the issue of the given topic[8].

---

[8] For the topic "Whaling", among bloggers whose blog is in English, only one blogger is rather neutral, where his blog is full of comments opposing the claim that anti-whaling against Japan is a kind of racism.

(a) Whaling

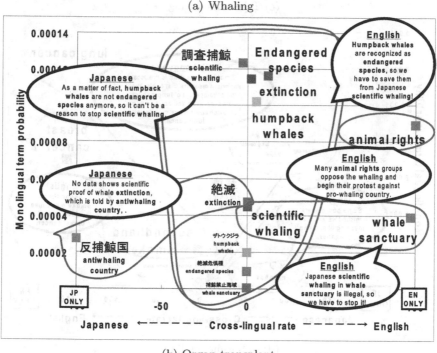

(b) Organ transplant

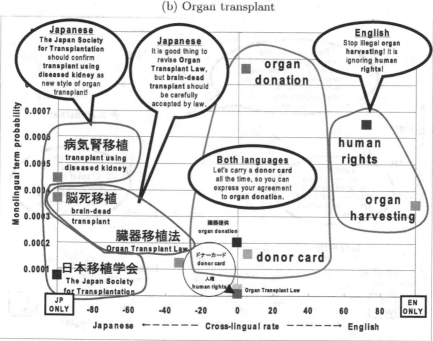

Fig. 2. Maps of Characteristic Terms for Visually Mining Cross-Lingual/Cross-Cultural Differences ("Whaling" and "Organ transplant")

(c) Tobacco smoking

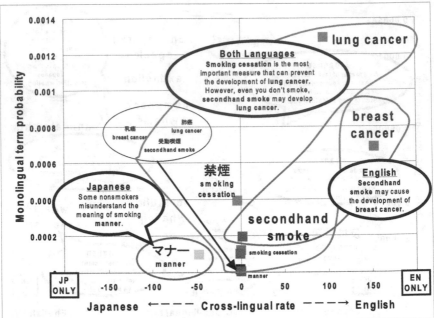

(d) Subprime lending

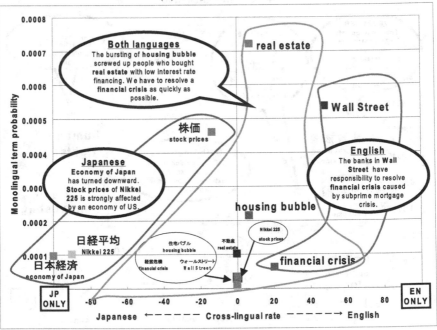

Fig. 3. Maps of Characteristic Terms for Visually Mining Cross-Lingual/Cross-Cultural Differences ("Tobacco smoking" and "Subprime lending")

4.5 A Map of Characteristic Terms for Visually Mining Cross-Lingual/Cross-Cultural Differences

In order to visually mine cross-lingual/cross-cultural differences in concerns and opinions in blog posts, we design a map of characteristic terms extracted from Japnese/English blog posts as shown in Figures 2 and 3. In this map, a Japanese term X_J with the English translation X_E is plotted at the coordinate $(-R_J(X_J, X_E), P_J(X_J))$ or at $(-(\text{maximum rate in the map}), P_J(X_J))$ (when $P(X_E) = 0$). Similarly, an English term X_E with the Japanese translation X_J is plotted at the coordinate $(R_E(X_E, X_J), P_E(X_E))$ or at (maximum rate in the map, $P_E(X_E)$) (when $P(X_J) = 0$). In the map, several terms which have relatively high point-wise mutual information are grouped together along with an excerpt from typical posts including those terms. Terms that are characteristic only in one language tend to be plotted apart from Y-axis, together with excerpts typical only in one language. On the other hand, terms that are characteristic in both languages tend to be plotted close to Y-axis, together with excerpts typical in both languages.

The followings roughly summarize the findings for some of the four topics. For the topic "Whaling", almost all the terms which are characteristic in English blogs represent against-whaling opinion. On the other hand, almost all the terms which are characteristic in Japanese blogs are those for expressing criticism against anti-whaling activities in Australia. For the topic "Organ transplant", many terms which are characteristic in English blogs represent opinions against Chinese illegal organ transplant. On the other hand, many terms which are characteristic in Japanese blogs are closely related to kidney transplant using diseased kidney.

Based on those obserbation results, we can argue that major contribution of this paper is that we successfully invent a framework of mining cross-lingual differences of opinions and cultural concerns in blogs of two languages. It can be obviously seen from the results shown in this section that one of most important near future works is to incorporate multilingual sentiment analysis techniques such as those previously studied in [3,4]. Then, it will become for us to easily classify those top ranked blog posts and feeds into *for*, *neutral*, and *against* with respect to the issue of the given topic.

5 Conclusion

This paper proposed how to cross-lingually analyze multilingual blogs collected with a topic keyword. In addition to proposing the overall framework of cross-lingual and cross-cultural comparison of concerns and opinions in blogs in two languages, this paper showed the effectiveness of the proposed framework with detailed examples of efficiently mining and comparing cross-lingual differences in concerns and opinions. There exist several works on studying cross-lingual analysis of sentiment and concerns in multilingual news [5,6,7,8]. [5] studied how to combine reports on epidemic threats from over 1,000 portals in 32 languages. [6] studied how to combine name mentions in news articles of 32 languages. [7]

also studied mining comparative differences of concerns in news streams from multiple sources. [8] studied how to analyze sentiment distribution in news articles across 9 languages. Those previous works mainly focus on news streams and documents other than blogs. Future works for cross-lingual blog analysis on facts and opinions include incorporating multilingual sentiment analysis techniques.

References

1. Fukuhara, T., Utsuro, T., Nakagawa, H.: Cross-Lingual Concern Analysis from Multilingual Weblog Articles. In: Proc. 6th Inter. Workshop on Social Intelligence Design, pp. 55–64 (2007)
2. Macdonald, C., Ounis, I., Soboroff, I.: Overview of the TREC-2007 Blog Track. In: Proc. TREC 2007 (Notebook), pp. 31–43 (2007)
3. Evans, D.K., Ku, L.W., Seki, Y., Chen, H.H., Kando, N.: Opinion Analysis across Languages: An Overview of and Observations from the NTCIR6 Opinion Analysis Pilot Task. In: Proc. 3rd Inter. Cross-Language Information Processing Workshop (CLIP 2007), pp. 456–463 (2007)
4. Wiebe, J., Wilson, T., Cardie, C.: Annotating Expressions of Opinions and Emotions in Language. Language Resources and Evaluation 39, 165–210 (2005)
5. Yangarber, R., Best, C., von Etter, P., Fuart, F., Horby, D., Steinberger, R.: Combining Information about Epidemic Threats from Multiple Sources. In: Proc. Workshop: Multi-source, Multilingual Information Extraction and Summarization, pp. 41–48 (2007)
6. Pouliquen, B., Steinberger, R., Belyaeva, J.: Multilingual Multi-document Continuously-updated Social Networks. In: Proc. Workshop: Multi-source, Multilingual Information Extraction and Summarization, pp. 25–32 (2007)
7. Yoshioka, M.: IR interface for contrasting multiple news sites. In: Li, H., Liu, T., Ma, W.-Y., Sakai, T., Wong, K.-F., Zhou, G. (eds.) AIRS 2008. LNCS, vol. 4993, pp. 508–513. Springer, Heidelberg (2008)
8. Bautin, M., Vijayarenu, L., Skiena, S.: International Sentiment Analysis for News and Blogs. In: Proc. ICWSM, pp. 19–26 (2008)

Partially Supervised Phrase-Level Sentiment Classification

Sang-Hyob Nam, Seung-Hoon Na, Jungi Kim, Yeha Lee, and Jong-Hyeok Lee

Division of Electrical and Computer Engineering
Pohang University of Science and Technology
San 31, Hyoja-Dong, Nam-Gu, Pohang, 790–784, Republic of Korea
{namsang,nsh1979,yangpa,sion,jhlee}@postech.ac.kr

Abstract. This paper presents a new partially supervised approach to phrase-level sentiment analysis that first automatically constructs a polarity-tagged corpus and then learns sequential sentiment tag from the corpus. This approach uses only sentiment sentences which are readily available on the Internet and does not use a polarity-tagged corpus which is hard to construct manually. With this approach, the system is able to automatically classify phrase-level sentiment. The result shows that a system can learn sentiment expressions without a polarity-tagged corpus.

Keywords: sentiment classification, sentiment analysis, information extraction, text mining.

1 Introduction

Sentiment analysis is the process of extracting opinions from written documents and determining whether they are positive or negative expressions. In recent years, the Internet usage has increased and many people have used it to publish their opinions about various topics, such as movies or the quality of various goods. The amount of published opinion has increased rapidly, so automatic sentiment extraction is desirable.

Much previous works on sentiment analysis has focused on document-level sentiment classification. Pang and Lee [1] [2] use a machine learning technique with minimum cuts algorithm and Turney [3] extracts polarity of phrases using the pair-wise mutual information(PMI) between the phrases and seed words. However, document-level sentiment classification is too coarse for many sentiment tasks such as opinion search and opinion tracking, reputation survey and opinion-oriented information extraction. Document-level sentiment classification incorrectly assumes that subject of all sentiment expression is same with the subject of a document. Therefore, these applications need phrase-level sentiment analysis.

Recently, many researchers have focused on the phrase-level sentiment analysis. Nasukawa [4] constructs a sentiment lexicon, and patterns manually with polarity and POS of a word. Zhongchao [5] also manually defines sentiment patterns and learn a polarity scores using document frequencies of each pattern in positive and negative documents. Wilson [6] uses these previous sentiment resources and a polarity-tagged corpus and

W. Li and D. Mollá-Aliod (Eds.): ICCPOL 2009, LNAI 5459, pp. 225–235, 2009.

tried to identify contextual polarity in phrase-level sentiment analysis. Breck [7] also uses polarity-tagged corpus to identify opinion phrases in a sentence.

Polarity-tagged corpus contains sentences whose opinion expressions are tagged with positive and negative labels. However such corpus is hard to construct manually and not readily available in various domains. Our experiment result shows that it is hard to achieve high recall with small amount of a polarity-tagged corpus in a supervised approach.

However, we can get a sufficient sentiment sentences such as movie reviews on the Internet. We use these sentences to train our phrase-level sentiment classification system instead of using a polarity-tagged corpus. Sentiment sentences are marked by users as positive or negative. We construct a positive phrase corpus and a negative phrase corpus from the sentiment sentences. Those phrases are used to construct polarity-tagged corpus automatically. Our system does not require a manual polarity-tagged corpus. We call this approach a partially supervised approach, because our system learns sentiment tags with automatically constructed polarity-tagged corpus. We views the problem of sentiment labeling at phrase-level as a sequential tagging. Therefore our approach uses Hidden Markov Model (HMM) and Conditional Random Fields(CRF) which is used frequently in tagging problem.

This paper presents a new partially supervised approach to phrase-level sentiment classification. Beginning with a large sentence-level sentiment resource, we calculate sentiment orientation of each phrases, then we get a positive phrase set and a negative phrase set. With these subjectivity clues, we automatically construct polarity-tagged corpus by marking subjectivity clue as positive in positive sentences and negative in negative sentences. Our partially supervised approach learns from the automatically constructed polarity-tagged corpus. Experiment at results show that partially supervised approach is a feasible approach in the phrase-level sentiment classification.

2 Approach

2.1 Sentiment Resources

There are several approaches to automatic sentiment resource construction such as the conjunction method [8], the PMI method [9] and the gloss use method [10]. Turney [3] uses only phrases that contain adjectives or adverbs. Those methods construct useful sentiment resources, but they have some limitations.

Those methods can not extract the sentiment of phrases which are dependent on specific domains. There are also many phrases in corpora which are not correctly spelled, such as movie reviews or goods reviews on the Internet. They do not work well on jargons or idioms, which are difficult to find in the dictionary or to analyze using a parser or a tagger. Such approaches also use rich English sentiment resources which are not available in other languages. Therefore we propose an automatic sentiment resource construction approach which works well in such environments. In this paper we construct sentiment resources using positive or negative sentences. Those sentences have polarity scores between 1 and 10. A value of 10 is the most positive sentimental score and 1 is the most negative sentimental score. We can use the average score of a word if the size of each score set is the same.

$$AvgScore(w_j) = \frac{\sum_{s_i \in S} Score(s_i) \times Freq(w_j, s_i)}{Freq(w_j)} \tag{1}$$

However, the size of each score set is not the same in most of cases. Therefor we normalize each score.

$$NormScore(w_j) = \frac{\sum_{s_i \in S} Score(s_i) \times \frac{Freq(w_j, s_i)}{\sum_{w_k \in W} Freq(w_k, s_i)}}{\frac{Freq(w_j)}{\sum_{w_k \in W} Freq(w_k)}} \tag{2}$$

$$NormScore(w_j) = \frac{\sum_{s_i \in S} Score(s_i) \times P(w_j | s_i)}{P(w_j)} \tag{3}$$

s_i is a score set between 1 and 10. S is a set of all scores and W is a set of all words. $Score(s_i)$ is constant value of a score set s_i. If s_i is s_9, $Score(s_9)$ is 9. We can determine the polarity of each phrase using this approach. This approach can be easily applied to all language and domains.

2.2 Features of Phrases

Unigrams and bigrams are good features in sentiment document classification [1], indicating that unigram and bigram are appropriate features for identifying the sentiment of phrases. We also used trigram. The experimental data used in this paper is in Korean which is an agglutinative language. We applied Korean segmentation to the training and test data set, which segments auxiliary words and compound nouns. We get follow positive and negative unigrams, bigrams and trigram by using Section 2.1 approach (Table 1, 2).

'discount-card' was the most negative unigram in Korean movie review, because people said that even 'discount-card' was wasteful for the movie. 'discount-card' has domain specific polarity. And there are some named entity word such as 'Sparrow', 'Depp', 'ut-dae', and 'an Emergency Action Number'. Negative bigram 'ho rul' is a part of negative trigram 'gin-gup-jo-chi ho rul'. Table 1 and Table 2 show that unigram, bigram and trigram appropriate for sentiment phrase feature and Section 2.1 works well for extracting semantic orientation of word.

2.3 Automatic Construction of Tagged Sentiment Resource

The Sentiment resource construction approach presented in Section 2.1 is not error prone. However this method is good enough for automatically constructing a polarity-tagged corpus. We calculate semantic orientation of phrase using sentence-level resources. While constructing semantic resources, we identified semantic orientation scores of phrases between 1 and 4 as negative, between 6 and 10 as positive and others as neutral. After constructing the semantic resources, we labeled the sentiment of each phrase in the sentence-level sentiment resource. We tagged subjectivity phrases as positive in the positive sentence set, and tagged them as negative in the negative sentence

Table 1. Semantic resource result of most positve phrases

	Positive	
unit	word	score
unigram	jjang-jjang('good-good')	9.908
unigram	Sparrow('Sparrow')	9.879
bigram	jin-jja jaemiteuyo('really funny')	9.936
bigram	choi-go imnida('This is the best')	9.911
trigram	nermu jaemi iteuyo('It's a lot of fun')	9.904
trigram	Depp eui maeryuk('charm of Depp')	9.880

Table 2. Semantic resource result of most negative phrases

	Positive	
unit	word	score
unigram	hal-in-card('discount-card')	1.031
unigram	ut-dae('Humor University/Korean humor site')	1.068
bigram	ho rul('a number')	1.031
bigram	jugido aggapda('wasteful to')	1.071
trigram	gin-gup-jo-chi ho rul('a Emergency Action number')	1.072
trigram	gut do yong-hwa('disappointing movie')	1.099

set. Other phrases were tagged as neutral. We shows this procedure by example. jjang-jjang('good-good') is a positive word (Table 1). Although it is a positive word, negative sentence can have the word. Following sentence is a negative sentence.

- jjang-jjang ha-nun nom-dul da alba. ("All people who say good-good to the movie are employee of the movie company")

We labeled subjectivity word in this sentence by polarity of the sentence. Polarity of the sentence is negative, therefore we labeled subjectivity word 'jjang-jjang' as negative.

- jjang-jjang/**Negative** ha-nun/Neutral nom-dul/Neutral da/Neutral alba/Neutral ./ Neutral

Following sentence is a positive sentence.

- scenario ga jjang-jjang ha da("scenario is good-good")

We labeled subjectivity as,

- scenario/Neutral ga/Neutral jjang-jjang/**Positive** ha/Neutral da/Neutral

Positive or negative sentiment phrases can represent opposite senses by their context. We followed the sense of the context rather than the sense of the sentiment phrase itself. We confirmed that this assumption is correct in the experiment. We used these automatically constructed tagged sentiment resource in the learning of HMM and CRF.

2.4 Opinion Tagging with Conditional Random Fields

Similar to our approach Breck [7] use CRF to identify sources of opinion phrases. They defined the problem of opinion source identification as one of sequential tagging. Given a sequence of tokens, $x = x_1 x_2...x_n$, we need to generate a sequence of tags, $y = y_1 y_2...y_n$. The tag is a polarity label which can be positive or negative or neutral. There are three kinds of labels that are positive, negative or neutral. A detailed description of CRFs can be found in Lafferty [11]. For our sequence tagging problem, we create a linear-chain CRF based on an undirected graph $G = (V, E)$, where V is the set of random variables $Y = \{Y_i | 1 \leq i \leq n\}$, one for each of n tokens in an input sentence. And $E = \{(Y_{i-1}, Y_i) | 1 < i \leq n\}$ is the set of $n-1$ edges forming a linear chain. For each sentence x, we define a non-negative clique potential $exp(\sum_{k=1}^{K} \lambda_k f_k(y_{i-1}, y_i, x))$ for each edge, and $exp(\sum_{k=1}^{K'} \lambda'_k f'_k(y_i, x))$ for each node, where $f_k(...)$ is a binary feature indicator function, λ_k is a weight assigned for each feature function, and K and K' are the number of features defined for edges and nodes respectively. Following Lafferty [11], the conditional probability of a sequence of labels y given a sequence of tokens x is

$$P(y|x) = \frac{1}{Z_x} exp(\sum_{i,k} \lambda_k f_k(y_{i-1}, y_i, x) + \sum_{i,k} \lambda'_k f'_k(y_i, x)) \qquad (4)$$

$$Z_x = \sum_{y} exp(\sum_{i,k} \lambda_k f_k(y_{i-1}, y_i, x) + \sum_{i,k} \lambda'_k f'_k(y_i, x)) \qquad (5)$$

where Z_x is a normalization constant for each x, and given training data D, a set of sentences paired with their correct positive, negative, neutral tag sequences, the parameters of the model are trained to maximize the conditional log-likelihood $\prod_{(x,y) \in D} P(y|x)$. For inference, given a sentence x in the test data, the tagging sequence y is given by $argmax_{y'} P(y'|x)$. We used word features between the -4 and 4 window in the CRF model.

2.5 Opinion Tagging with Hidden Markov Model

We use the HMM which is usually used in the tagging problem. There are three states in our HMM model: positive, negative and neutral. Observations of our HMM model are word. HMM model predicts state of each observations. We get initial probability, emission probability and transition probability from the automatically constructed polarity-tagged corpus. We use the Viterbi algorithm to encode the test data using those probabilities.

2.6 Opinion Tagging with Hidden Markov Model and Conditional Random Fields Together

We automatically constructed a tagged sentiment resource that is only partially correct. As a result, it is difficult to expect excellent precision performance with such an incomplete resource. Instead of using tagged sentiment resource directly to label sentiment phrases in the training data, we can refine the data using HMM or CRF. We select the HMM to refine the tagged sentiment resource.

It is important to revise the polarity of the tagged sentiment resource which is refined by HMM, because HMM is trained by automatically constructed tagged sentiment resource. The system revise the labeling error of the tagged sentiment resource, because we know the polarity of the sentence.

For example, HMM sometimes marks negative sentence "We fully grasped inversion story of the movie" as "We/Neutral fully/Neutral grasped/Neutral inversion/**Positive** story/**Positive** of/Neutral the/Neutral movie/Neutral". The system revises the result to "We/Neutral fully/Neutral grasped/Neutral inversion/**Negative** story/**Negative** of/ Neutral the/Neutral movie/Neutral" by using the sentence polarity. Then CRF learns the tag with the neighborhood words.

The system considers all subjectivity tags in the positive sentence set as positive tags and we also consider all subjectivity tags in negative sentence set as negatives. We can expect better precision performance than when using the automatically constructed sentiment resource directly. CRF model is trained by the tagged sentiment resource refined by HMM. We refer to this combination of HMM and CRF as the HMM+CRF model.

3   Experiments

3.1   Training Data

Training data are composed of movie reviews from naver movie review[1] that are scored at the sentence level. Training data are scored from 1 to 10. We used the scores which are in the *Pos* (7-10), *Neg*(1-4) ranges. The number of points in each score set is 20,000, so the total number of training data is 160,000. The data contains some sentences that have doubtful scores, because sometimes people set movie reviews wrong. We use the *Pos* and *Neg* sets when we construct the sentiment resource. We only use *Neg*(1, 2, 3) and *Pos*(8, 9, 10) scores when we construct tagged sentiment resource to get more explicitly expressed resources.

3.2   Test Data

The test data set was also extracted from naver movie review. These data are comprised of more recent review sentences than the training data set. We asked two annotators to classify and label the data set with scores of 1, 2, 3 (900 negative sentences) and 8, 9, 10 (900 positive sentences) scores. They tagged each sentimental phrase in the sentence as positive, negative or neutral. We want to evaluate consistency and agreement between human evaluators. Polarity tag boundary is not exactly same between annotators. Therefore we use a CRF model trained by the sentiment tag sequence assigned by each human to evaluate consistency and agreement. The two humans assigned consistent tags to test data (Table 3, Table 4). Agreement between Human1 and Human2 was reasonable enough to use them as test data, because precision and recall are high enough to believe that there are shared sentimental common sense between the humans (Table 3, Table 4). The CRF model that was trained by sentiment tag sequences of Human2 is better than Human1 (Table 3, Table 4). So we selected the test data of Human2 as our experiment test data.

---

[1] http://movie.naver.com

Table 3. sentimental phrase Human-Human Agreement via CRF model (%). Higher percentage indicates higher agreement between human in positive or negative phrase tagging.

Test	exact				overlap			
	Human1		Human2		Human1		Human2	
	Recall	Precision	Recall	Precision	Recall	Precision	Recall	Precision
Human1	98.10	98.45	73.38	72.74	95.00	100.00	82.74	84.55
Human2	70.55	73.16	98.31	99.06	75.75	87.93	95.28	99.96

Table 4. subjectivity phrase Human-Human Agreement via CRF model (%). Higher percentage indicates higher agreement between human in subjectivity phrase extraction.

Test	exact				overlap			
	Human1		Human2		Human1		Human2	
	Recall	Precision	Recall	Precision	Recall	Precision	Recall	Precision
Human1	98.12	98.47	74.12	73.48	95.00	100.00	83.38	85.20
Human2	71.49	74.13	98.45	99.20	76.34	88.61	95.28	99.96

3.3 Evaluation

As with other information extraction tasks, we use precision, recall and f-measure to evaluate the performance of our approach. Precision is $\frac{|C \cap P|}{|P|}$ and recall is $\frac{|C \cap P|}{|C|}$, where C and P are the sets of correct and predicted expression spans, respectively. F_1 is the harmonic mean of precision and recall, $\frac{2 \times P \times R}{P+R}$. Evaluation is done on the sentimental phrase in the sentence. It was tagged as positive or negative in the sentence. Our method often identifies expressions that are close to, but not precisely the same as, the manually identified expressions. For example, for the expression "roundly criticized" our method might only identify "criticized". We therefore introduced softened variants of precision and recall as follows. We define soft precision as $SP^a = \frac{|\{p | p \in P \wedge \exists c \in C s.t. a(c,p)\}|}{|P|}$ and soft recall as $SR^a = \frac{|\{c | c \in C \wedge \exists p \in P s.t. a(c,p)\}|}{|C|}$, where $a(c, p)$ is a predicate that is true only when expression c 'assigns' to expression p in a sense defined by a . We report results according to two predicates: *exact* and *overlap*. $exact(c, p)$ is true only when c and p in $exact(c, p)$ are the same spans - this yields the usual notions of precision and recall. A softer notion is produced by the predicate, which is true when the spans of c and p overlap [7].

3.4 Baseline

Sentiword resource baseline marks a phrase as positive when it belongs to an automatically constructed positive phrase set in Section 2.1 and marks a phrase as negative when it belongs to a negative phrase set.

We run the 10-fold cross validation test using only tagged test data (1800 sentences). Supervised CRF (S-CRF) and Supervised HMM (S-HMM) are used in the test. We used that result as our baselines as well, we compared supervised approaches and our partially supervised approaches. Features of supervised CRF are the same as the partially supervised CRF.

Table 5. Results for identifying sentiment of phrases in n-gram model (%)

	exact			overlap		
Method	Recall	Precision	F_1	Recall	Precision	F_1
unigram	11.79	38.38	18.04	36.42	55.79	44.07
bigram	35.31	41.42	38.12	51.35	49.25	50.28
trigram	14.90	**45.90**	22.50	19.69	**62.07**	29.90
bigram + trigram	36.65	40.44	38.45	52.31	49.91	51.08
bigram + unigram	**41.71**	40.27	**40.98**	66.05	46.12	54.31
all	41.44	38.57	39.95	**66.72**	45.89	**54.34**

Table 6. Results for identifying sentiment of phrases in various models (%)

	exact			overlap		
Method	Recall	Precision	F_1	Recall	Precision	F_1
Sentiword resource	41.44	38.57	39.95	**66.72**	45.89	54.34
Suvervised-CRF	41.56	**61.72**	49.67	45.59	83.38	58.95
Suvervised-HMM	51.30	53.92	**52.58**	58.77	76.44	66.45
Partially-Supervised-HMM	**56.48**	41.15	47.61	59.68	76.01	**66.86**
Partially-Supervised-CRF	44.39	43.10	43.74	57.82	62.78	60.20
Partially-Supervised-HMM+CRF	53.55	44.88	48.83	51.16	**86.91**	64.41

Table 7. Results for identifying subjectivity phrases in various models (%)

	exact			overlap		
Method	Recall	Precision	F_1	Recall	Precision	F_1
Sentiword resource	46.62	56.65	51.14	**70.85**	48.80	57.80
Suvervised-CRF	50.75	**72.38**	59.66	51.91	**94.31**	66.96
Suvervised-HMM	**64.29**	62.62	**63.44**	65.77	89.49	**75.82**
Partially-Supervised-HMM	60.98	51.63	55.91	64.38	82.16	72.19
Partially-Supervised-CRF	47.36	55.20	50.98	61.53	66.77	64.04
Partially-Supervised-HMM+CRF	57.44	51.44	54.27	53.88	91.44	67.80

3.5   Results

Bigram model performs better than the trigram or the unigram model. Trigram and unigram models outperform the recall of bigram in the sentiment resources, because unigram and trigram can determine the polarity bigram can not determine. Unigram improves performance more than trigram when it was used with bigram (Table 5). These models show better performance on the overlap evaluation than the exact evaluation (Table 5, 6).

Partially supervised HMM, CRF and HMM+CRF outperforms the performance of the models that use only sentiment resources, especially the precision. Supervised HMM perform better than other model in exact evaluation. Its f-measure is 52.58% in exact evaluation. f-measure difference between supervised HMM and partially supervised HMM is 4.97% in exact evaluation. But, partially supervised HMM shows better overall performance than other models in overlap evaluation. Its f-measure is 0.41% higher than supervised HMM in overlap evaluation.

Precision of partially supervised CRF is high in exact evaluation, but recall of this model is not so good. Training data of the partially supervised CRF is not completely correct. The data was generated automatically by sentiment resources constructed by our approach. The sentiment resources which generate the training data of CRF have a 66.72% recall in overlap evaluation. This performance affects the recall of CRF. 45.89% precision of training data also affects the precision of CRF. But we improved the precision by using the polarity of a sentence.

Partially supervised HMM improved recall, but its precision is not high. We can use HMM+CRF to overcome weak precision of partially superived HMM and weak recall of supervised CRF.

Table 7 shows the performance of identifying source of subjectivity phrases. Supervised HMM performs well in the exact evaluation.

4 Discussion

4.1 Subjectivity Labeling Problem

The most important part of identifying sentiment of phrases is subjectivity tagging. Breck [7] identified subjectivity phrases using the various features and CRF as a supervised learning in the MPQA. It is difficult to compare directly with the evaluation result of the experiment, because we do not use the same dataset(MPQA) and the language is also different. In spite of these difference, we know that from their results, their f-measure of identifying subjectivity phrase is 73.05% in overlap evaluations [7]. It shows that it is not an easy problem to identify subjectivity phrases even if we use various features and supervised learning.

Many subjectivity errors come from the negative sentimental phrase. There are data sparseness problems in identifying the negative sentiment of phrases, because there are many ironic, cynical, and metaphoric and simile expressions in the negative expressions. These affect the overall performance in identifying the sentiment of phrases.

4.2 Necessary Characteristics of Training Data

We used the partially supervised approach to overcome the problem of insufficient polarity-tagged corpus. Our approach used tagged sentiment of phrases automatically generated by sentiment resources. These sentiment resources are automatically extracted from sentence-level sentiment resource. Our approach also needs sentence-level sentiment training data. Such data sets are more plentiful than tagged sentimental phrase data sets. However in these data sets, there are more polarity annotations at the document level than at the sentence level. We need to select sentiment sentences in sentences when we use those data sets. In this case, this process unavoidably carries some error in selecting sentiment sentences.

5 Summary and Conclusion

We compared the sentiment phrase (positive, negative or neutral) tagging performance between various models (Table 6). We also compared the subjectivity phrase (sentimental or neutral) tagging performance (Table 7). One interesting result is the difference in performance in identifying sentiment (Table 6) and subjectivity (Table 7). Subjectivity includes positive and negative sentiment. Therefore, it is simpler to label subjectivity phrases than to label sentiment phrases. In spite of the fact that identifying subjectivity phrases is a simpler task than identifying the sentiment of phrases, precisions in identifying subjectivity and sentiment are within 10% in both the exact and the overlap evaluations. This suggests that errors between positive and negative labels are minor. In other words, the overall performance is more heavily affected by the performance of subjectivity classification than by the performance of sentiment classification. The difficulty observed in identifying subjectivity phrases implies some ambiguity, even between human decisions (Table 4). So the most important part of identifying sentiment of phrases is subjectivity tagging. Many subjectivity errors occurred when identifying negative sentimental phrases.

Our model solved the phrase-level sentiment classification problem by using partially supervised tagging approaches. That approach only used the sentence-level sentiment resource. Its precision is 76.01% and its f-meausre is 66.86%. Its f-measure is higher than the supervised approaches in the overlap evaluation. We found that the sentiment phrase tagging problem can be solved by a partially supervised approach.

Acknowledgement. This work was supported in part by MKE & IITA through IT Leading R&D Support Project and also in part by the BK 21 Project in 2008.

References

1. Pang, B., Lee, L.: A sentimental education: Sentiment analysis using subjectivity summarization based on minimum cuts. In: ACL, pp. 271–278 (2004)
2. Pang, B., Lee, L., Vaithyanathan, S.: Thumbs up?: sentiment classification using machine learning techniques. In: EMNLP 2002: Proceedings of the ACL 2002 conference on Empirical methods in natural language processing, Morristown, NJ, USA, pp. 79–86. Association for Computational Linguistics (2002)
3. Turney, P.D.: Thumbs up or thumbs down?: semantic orientation applied to unsupervised classification of reviews. In: ACL 2002: Proceedings of the 40th Annual Meeting on Association for Computational Linguistics, Morristown, NJ, USA, pp. 417–424. Association for Computational Linguistics (2001)
4. Nasukawa, T., Yi, J.: Sentiment analysis: capturing favorability using natural language processing. In: K-CAP 2003: Proceedings of the 2nd international conference on Knowledge capture, pp. 70–77. ACM, New York (2003)
5. Fei, Z., Liu, J., Wu, G.: Sentiment classification using phrase patterns, pp. 1147–1152. IEEE Computer Society, Los Alamitos (2004)

6. Wilson, T., Wiebe, J., Hoffmann, P.: Recognizing contextual polarity in phrase-level sentiment analysis. In: HLT 2005: Proceedings of the conference on Human Language Technology and Empirical Methods in Natural Language Processing, Morristown, NJ, USA, pp. 347–354. Association for Computational Linguistics (2005)
7. Breck, E., Choi, Y., Cardie, C.: Identifying expressions of opinion in contenxt. In: Proceedings of the Twentieth International Join Conference on Artificial Intelligence (2007)
8. Hatzivassiloglou, V., McKeown, K.R.: Predicting the semantic orientation of adjectives. In: Proceedings of the eighth conference on European chapter of the Association for Computational Linguistics, Morristown, NJ, USA, pp. 174–181. Association for Computational Linguistics (1997)
9. Turney, P.D., Littman, M.L.: Measuring praise and criticism: Inference of semantic orientation from association, vol. 21, pp. 315–346. ACM Press, New York (2003)
10. Esuli, A., Sebastiani, F.: Determining the semantic orientation of terms through gloss classification. In: CIKM 2005: Proceedings of the 14th ACM international conference on Information and knowledge management, pp. 617–624. ACM, New York (2005)
11. John, L., McCallum, A., Pereira, F.: Conditional random fields:probabilistic models for segmenting and labeling sequence data. In: 18th International Conference on Machine Learning (2001)

A Novel Composite Kernel Approach to Chinese Entity Relation Extraction

Ji Zhang[1,2], You Ouyang[1], Wenjie Li[1], and Yuexian Hou[2]

[1] Department of Computing, The Hong Kong Polytechnic University, Hong Kong
{csjizhang,csyouyang,cswjli}@comp.polyu.edu.hk
[2] School of Computer Science and Technology, Tianjin University, China
yxhou@tju.edu.cn

Abstract. Relation extraction is the task of finding semantic relations between two entities from the text. In this paper, we propose a novel composite kernel for Chinese relation extraction. The composite kernel is defined as the combination of two independent kernels. One is the entity kernel built upon the non-content-related features. The other is the string semantic similarity kernel concerning the content information. Three combinations, namely linear combination, semi-polynomial combination and polynomial combination are investigated. When evaluated on the ACE 2005 Chinese data set, the results show that the proposed approach is effective.

Keywords: Kernel-based Chinese Relation Extraction, Composite Kernel, Entity Kernel, String Semantic Similarity Kernel.

1 Introduction

Relation extraction is the task of finding predefined semantic relations between pairs of entities from the text. The research on relation extraction has been promoted by the Message Understanding Conferences (MUCs) and Automatic Content Extraction (ACE) program. According to the ACE program, an entity is an object or a set of objects in the world and a relation is an explicitly or implicitly stated relationship between entities. For example, the sentence "Bill Gates is the chairman and chief software architect of Microsoft Corporation" conveys the ACE-style relation "ORG-AFFILIATION" between the two entities "Bill Gates (PER)" and "Microsoft Corporation (ORG)".

The problem of relation extraction is typically cast as a classification problem. When learning a classification model, one important issue that has to be addressed is how to scale the similarity between the two relation instances. Existing approaches include feature-based and kernel-based approaches. Feature-based approaches transform a relation instance into a linear vector of carefully selected linguistic features, varying from entity semantic information to lexical and syntactic features of the relation context. Kernel-based approaches, on the other hand, explore the structured representation such as parse tree or dependency tree, and compute the similarity between the structured contexts. In fact, feature-based approaches can be deemed as a specific case of kernel-based approaches by using the dot-product as a kernel function.

W. Li and D. Mollá-Aliod (Eds.): ICCPOL 2009, LNAI 5459, pp. 236–247, 2009.
© Springer-Verlag Berlin Heidelberg 2009

Therefore, although feature-based approaches are easier to implement and achieve much success, kernel-based approaches still attract much interest from researchers due to their ability of exploring complex structured features through various kinds of representation of objects.

In contrast to the significant achievements concerning English and other Western languages, research progress in Chinese relation extraction is quite limited. This may be attributed to the different characteristic of Chinese language, e.g. no word boundaries and lack of morphological variations, etc. Especially, the widespread tree-kernel based approaches in English relation extraction do not adapt to Chinese well since the quality of the available Chinese syntactic analysis tools are not as reliable as English tools. Motivated by this, we investigate in this paper how to design useful kernels for Chinese entity relation extraction, which will not be restrained by the unsatisfied Chinese parsing results. We propose to use a composite kernel which consists of two individual kernels. The first kernel is a linear kernel formulating the non-content characteristics of the relation instances, including position structure features, entity type features and entity subtype features. The second kernel explores the content information in the contexts of the relation instances. Instead of tree-based kernels, we introduce a novel string-based kernel which can avoid the errors propagated from the incorrect parsing results. With these two kernels, we examine several combination functions to search for a near "optimum" composite kernel. Experiments on the ACE 2005 data set show that the polynomial combination is more effective in capturing the information of the entities and their contexts.

The reminder of the paper is organized as follows. Section 2 briefly introduces the related work. Section 3 details our proposed approach. Section 4 presents experiments and evaluations and Section 5 concludes the paper.

2 Related Work

Lots of approaches have been proposed in the literature of relation extraction, including rule-based, feature-based and kernel-based approaches.

Rule-based approaches employ a number of linguistic rules to capture various relation patterns for identifying the relations. For example, Miller et al. [1] addressed the task of relation extraction from the statistical parsing viewpoint. The result essentially depended on the quality of the entire full parse trees.

Feature-based approaches utilize a set of carefully selected features obtained from different levels of text analysis, from part-of-speech (POS) tagging to full parsing and dependency parsing. For example, Kambhatla [2] employed Maximum Entropy models to combine diverse lexical, syntactic and semantic features derived from the text for relation extraction. Zhao and Grishman [3] explored a large set of features that are potentially useful for relation extraction. Zhou et al. [4] explored various features in relation extraction using SVM. They conducted exhaustive experiments to investigate the incorporation and the individual contribution of diverse features and reported that chunking information contributes to most of the performance improvement from the syntactic aspect. Jiang and Zhai [5] systematically explored features of different levels of complexity in three subspaces and evaluated the effectiveness of different feature subspaces. They reported that using basic unit features was generally sufficient to achieve state-of-art performance, while over-inclusion of complex features might hurt the performance.

Kernel-based approaches design kernel functions on the structured representation (sequences or trees) of the relation instances to capture the similarity between the two relation instances. For example, Zelenko et al. [6] proposed extracting relations by computing kernel functions based on two parsing trees. Culotta and Sorensen [7] used augmented dependency tree kernel, which is context-sensitive. The above two work was further advanced by Bunescu and Mooney [8] who argued that the information to extract a relation between two entities can be typically captured by the shortest path between them in the dependency graph. Zhang et al. [9] explored the use of the syntactic features in convolution tree kernels for relation extraction. It revealed that the syntactic structure features embedded in a parse tree are very effective for relation extraction and these features can be well captured by the convolution tree kernel. Zhou et al. [10] proposed a tree kernel based on context-sensitive structured parse trees and combined the tree kernel with a feature-based kernel. Evaluation on the ACE RDC corpora showed that feature-based and tree-kernel based approaches complemented each other. They thus reached the conclusion that a composite kernel which could integrate both flat and structured features was preferred.

The previous approaches mainly focused on English relation extraction task. Although Chinese processing is as important as English and other Western language processing, only a little work has been published on Chinese relation extraction. Zhang et al. [11] exploited a feature-based approach by modeling the position structure between two entities and using them along with entity type features and context features in classification. Later Li et al. [12] proposed a further study which introduced several novel wordlist features and some correction mechanisms based on relation hierarchy and co-reference information. Their system achieved very good performance. There were also some kernel-based approaches proposed for Chinese relation extraction. Che et al. [13] defined an improved edit distance kernel over the original Chinese string representation around particular entities. But their study was limited to the PERSON-AFFLIATION relation type only. Huang et al. [14] examined the performance of the tree kernel and shortest path dependency kernel for Chinese relation extraction. It outperformed the traditional feature-based approaches on non-nested relations, but unfortunately the overall performance was not satisfying.

3   A Composite Kernel Approach to Chinese Relation Extraction

In this section, we introduce a composite kernel for Chinese relation extraction. The composite kernel consists of an entity kernel and a string semantic similarity kernel.

3.1   Entity Kernel

The entity kernel considers the non-content characteristics of the entities in the relation instances. The kernel is constructed by two kinds of features. The first kind of features is the position features which depict the position structure of a relation instance. Structure information is an important factor for judging the relation. For example, many entity pairs with a relation type "Employment" have the nested position structure, such as "俄罗斯总统" (Russian president) and "俄罗斯" (Russia).

In this paper we defined six position features which depict both the internal and external structures of a relation instance. Given a named entity mention nem, let $nem.start$ and $nem.end$ denote the start and end positions of nem in a sentence respectively. Let $nem_i \supset nem_j$ denotes $(nem_i.start, nem_i.end) \supset (nem_j.start, nem_j.end)$ and $(nem_i.start, nem_i.end) \neq (nem_j.start, nem_j.end)$, and let $nem_k \perp (nem_1, nem_2)$ denotes $nem_1.end < nem_k.start$ and $nem_k.end < nem_2.start$.

The internal position features are defined by the relevant position between the two entities of the relation instance, including nested, adjacent and separated. On the other hand, the external features represent whether the two entities of the instance are embedded in some other entities, including none-embedded, one-embedded and both-embedded. The definition of the internal and external features is expressed in Table 1 and Table 2 respectively. Making use of symmetrical expression, for any entity pair nem_1 and nem_2, we assume $nem_1 \supset nem_2$ or nem_1 precedes nem_2 to simplify the expressions. By combining 3 internal and 3 external features, a total of 9 different position structures can be denoted, which are illustrated in Appendix A.

Table 1. The internal postion structure features between two named entities

Type	Condition	Label
Nested	$nem_1 \supset nem_2$	(a)
Adjacent	$nem_1.end < nem_2.start \wedge \neg\exists\,(nem_j)(nem_j \perp (nem_1, nem_2))$	(b)
Separated	$nem_1.end < nem_2.start \wedge \exists\,(nem_j)(nem_j \perp (nem_1, nem_2))$	(c)

Table 2. The external position structure features between two named entities

Type	Condition	Label
None-embeded	$\neg\exists\,(nem_i)(nem_i \supset nem_1) \wedge \neg\exists\,(nem_i)(nem_i \supset nem_2)$	(d)
One-Embedded	$(\exists\,(nem_i)(nem_i \supset nem_1) \wedge \neg\exists\,(nem_j)(nem_j \supset nem_2)) \vee$ $(\neg\exists\,(nem_i)(nem_i \supset nem_1) \wedge \exists\,(nem_j)(nem_j \supset nem_2))$	(e)
Both-Embedded	$\exists\,(nem_i)(nem_i \supset nem_1) \wedge \exists\,(nem_j)(nem_j \supset nem_2)$	(f)

A position-based kernel is then defined by the 6 position features as

$$K_p(P_1, P_2) = \sum_{i=1..6} C(P_1.f_i, P_2.f_i)$$

where P_1 and P_2 indicate the position structures of two relation instances respectively, $P.f_i$ is the i-th position feature of the position structure P. The function $C(.,.)$ returns 1 if the two feature values are identical and 0 otherwise.

Another kind of features is the entity type attributes features which are defined as the types and subtypes of the two entities in a relation instance. The entity types and subtypes also impose a strong constraint on the relation types. For example, if there is a relation between the two entities with entity types "Person" and "Weapon", the relation type will has a large probability to be the "User-Owner-Inventor-Manufacturer" relation. In this paper, we use binary features to depict the type and subtype information of an entity.

A type-based kernel is then defined by these type features as

$$K_e(E_1, E_2) = \sum_i C(E_1.f_i, E_2.f_i)$$

where E_1 and E_2 are two name entities, $E.f_i$ represents the i-th type feature of the entity E.

Finally, the entity kernel is defined by combining the position-based and type-based kernels together as:

$$K_L(R_1, R_2) = K_p(R_1.P, R_2.P) + \sum_{i=1,2} K_e(R_1.E_i, R_2.E_i)$$

where R_1 and R_2 stand for two relation instances, $R.P$ and $R.E_{1,2}$ indicate the position structure and the two entities of the relation instance R respectively.

In the above equation, $K_p(.,.)$ returns the number of position feature values in common, and $K_e(.,.)$ returns the number of type feature values in common. Thus the whole entity kernel can be viewed as a reflection of the non-content characteristic of the two relation instances.

3.2 String Semantic Similarity Kernel

In our belief, besides the non-content information, the content information in contexts of the two relation instances is also very important to their similarity. However, as mentioned in the introduction, the tree-based kernel which was widely used in English relation extraction did not work well in Chinese relation extraction due to the constraints of the Chinese parsing tools. So in our study we aim to develop a kernel which does not rely on any complicated text structure like parsing trees. In [15], Islam and Inkpen proposed a string-based similarity which simply represented the texts as strings instead of trees. Following their idea, we develop a string semantic similarity kernel to capture the content information.

In the kernel definition, we choose the characters as the basic string units rather than the words, considering Chinese word-based models may be heavily affected by word segmentation errors. We start with the estimation of the semantic similarity of the two characters by Point-wise Mutual Information (PMI) which is a popular method for calculating corpus-based similarities between the words.

$$f^{pmi}(w_1, w_2) = \log_2 \frac{f^b(w_1, w_2) \times M}{f^t(w_1)f^t(w_2)}$$

where $f^t(w)$ is the frequency of the character w appearing in the entire corpus, $f^b(w_1, w_2)$ stands for the frequency of the characters w_1 and w_2 appearing together in a sentence and M is total number of the tokens in the corpus. After the similarities of all the character pairs are calculated, they are divided by the maximum one to obtain the normalized values between 0 and 1.

Based on the PMI similarity between the two characters, we use the following way to calculate the semantic similarity between the two text strings. Consider a text string T_1 which has m characters $\{p_1, p_2, ..., p_m\}$ and another text string T_2 which has n characters $\{r_1, r_2, ..., r_n\}$, where n is assumed to be greater than or equal to m. We first construct an $m*n$ similarity matrix M with the pairwise similarities between all the characters of the two strings by putting β_{ij} ($\beta_{ij} \leftarrow PMI(p_i, r_j)$) into the position of i-th row and j-th column in the matrix. After constructing the similarity matrix M, we iteratively select a set of indicative elements from the matrix. Each round we find out the maximum-valued element γ_{ij} in M and add this element to an output list ρ if $\gamma_{ij} \geq 0$. Then we remove all the matrix elements of i-th row and j-th column from M and then repeat the finding and adding steps. The iteration is repeated until either $\gamma_{ij} = 0$, or $m - |\rho| = 0$. At the end of the above process, the list ρ will consist of the most similar character pairs between the two text strings without repeating characters. The elements in ρ are then summed up and the sum is regarded as the similarity between the two strings. Finally we multiply the similarity by the reciprocal harmonic mean of m and n to obtain a balanced similarity value between 0 and 1.

In conclusion, the similarity between T_1 and T_2 is calculated as:

$$Sim(T_1, T_2) = \frac{\sum_{i=1}^{|\rho|} \rho_i \times (m+n)}{2mn}$$

The string semantic similarity kernel is defined as:

$$K_S(R_1, R_2) = Sim(R_1.T, R_2.T)$$

where $R_1.T$ and $R_2.T$ indicate the contents of the two relation instances respectively. Here the content of a relation instance is defined as the characters between the two entities and the surrounding characters in a given window size. In later experiments, the window size is set to 4.

3.3 Composite Kernel

Since the entity kernel and the string kernel depict the non-content and content information of the relation instances respectively, a nature thought is that the two kernels can well complement each other. Therefore a combination of them should yield more accurate estimation of the relevance between the two relation instances. In this paper, we try several different functions to combine the two kernels:

1) Linear Combination

$$K_1(R_1, R_2) = a \cdot K_L(R_1, R_2) + (1-a) \cdot K_S(R_1, R_2)$$

Here the sub-kernels $K(.,.)$ are normalized first and a is the coefficient to balance the two kernels. a is set to 0.5 experimentally.

2) Semi-Polynomial Combination

$$K_1(R_1, R_2) = a \cdot K_L^P(R_1, R_2) + (1-a) \cdot K_S(R_1, R_2)$$

Here $K^P(\cdot, \cdot)$ is the polynomial expansion of $K(\cdot, \cdot)$ with degree $d=2$, i.e. $K^P(\cdot, \cdot) = (K(\cdot, \cdot) + 1)^2$.

3) Polynomial Combination

$$K_1(R_1, R_2) = a \cdot K_L^P(R_1, R_2) + (1 - a) \cdot K_S^P(R_1, R_2)$$

Here the definition of $K(\cdot, \cdot)$ is the same as above.

Essentially, the combination functions imply different views of the structure between the kernels. Generally, if a view is more coincident with actual situation, it can lead to the better kernels.

4 Experiments

4.1 Experiment Setting

The experiments are set up on the data set of the ACE 2005 Chinese Relation Detection and Characterization task provided by Linguistic Data Consortium (LDC). The 633 documents are manually annotated with 9278 instances of relations. 6 relation types and 18 subtypes are pre-defined. We use 75% of the total data set to train the SVM classifiers and the remaining to evaluate. Precision (P), Recall (R) and F-measure (F) are adopted to evaluate the performance.

In the implement, we use SVMlight [17] as the binary classification tool and chose the one-vs-other multi-class classification strategy. For all the classifiers, we add a "NONE" class when there is no any predefined relation between the two entities. We apply our approach on a subset of all the possible entity pairs. First, only pairs of entities in the same sentences are regarded as the relation candidates. Moreover, we only label the entity pairs with nested internal position type, or with both adjacent internal type and none-embedded external type. The reason of this consideration is that in the actual data the ratios of positive to negative class of the other position types are so imbalanced that the learning method is very inefficient on them. So we would rather just label all the entity pairs with the other position types as negative to preserve the precision. On the other hand, in actual the data almost 90% of the relation instances belong to the chosen types so the harm to the recall caused by ignoring the other position types is within the acceptable range. Table 3 gives the detailed statistics, and the chosen types are indicated in bold.

Table 3. The ratios of positive to negative entity pairs with different internal position types

Position Type	Positive Class	Negative Class	Ratio
Nested + None-embedded	**4853**	**2512**	**1:0.52**
Nested + One-embedded	**354**	**1810**	**1:5.11**
Nested + Both-embedded	**1105**	**706**	**1:0.64**
Adjacent + None-embedded	**1976**	**17102**	**1:8.65**
Adjacent + One-embedded	0	10863	1:INF
Adjacent + Both-embedded	50	3966	1:79.32
Separated + None-embedded	928	45564	1:49.10
Separated + One-embedded	1	34873	1:34873
Separated + Both-embedded	11	10618	1:965.3
Total	9278	128014	1:13.80

4.2 Experimental Results

The first set of experiments is set up to examine the role of the two sub-kernels. We compare the three kernels: (1) only the entity kernel (K_L); (2) only the string semantic similarity kernel (K_S); (3) the linear composite kernel combining both entity kernel and string semantic similarity kernel (K_S+K_L). Table 4 reports the precisions, recalls and F-measures. We can see that the performance is low when the string similarity kernel is used alone. In contrast, the performance is much higher when only the entity kernel is used. It seems to indicate that the non-content information is much more important than the content information. In fact, most relation types have their conventional structures and entity types. Therefore, the non-content information is essential and decisive in exploring the relations between two entities. This means that we can not use the string kernel to substitute the entity kernel. On the other hand, the content information may play the role as a complement of the non-content information. The result that the performance is improved by integrating the two kernels supports this idea, though the improvement is not very significant. However, at least we can expect that a combination of the two kernels which explore the relation from different points of views can lead to the better kernels.

Table 4. Results of the sub-kernels and linear composite kernel

Type	Precision	Recall	F-measure
K_L	0.679181	0.474035	0.558361
K_S	0.273585	0.124345	0.170979
K_L+K_S	0.679295	0.495474	0.573003

In the second set of experiments, we intend to further study the effect of kernel combination by comparing the performance of several different composite kernels introduced in Section 3.3. An additional quadratic entity kernel (KL^2) is also included. Table 5 reports the performance of all the kernels. From the experiments, we observe that:

1) The best composite kernel achieves 6% improvement over the entity kernel. This further proves that the two individual kernels are complementary and the combination surely makes sense. Also, it clearly states the importance of selecting appropriate combination functions.

2) Among our composite kernels, the polynomial combination yields the best composite kernel, and the semi-polynomial combination outperforms the linear combination. These results suggest that in this problem the internal structures between the kernels are more likely to be quadratic. Another evidence of this conclusion is that when using the entity kernel alone, the quadratic form also performs better than the linear form.

Table 5. Results of different composite kernels

Type	Precision	Recall	F-measure
K_L	0.679181	0.474035	0.558361
K_L^2	0.790769	0.489757	0.604884
Linear Kernel	0.679295	0.495474	0.573003
Semi-Polynomial Kernel	0.786617	0.504050	0.614402
Polynomial Kernel	0.818324	0.497856	0.619076

In the third set of experiments, we compare our kernel-based approach to the approach introduced in [11]. They propose a sophisticated feature-based approach which includes both entity-based features and context-based features. Notice that their entity-based and context-based features are not defined exactly the same as ours. Results are reported in Table 6. The performance of our proposed kernel-based approach is remarkably better than the performance of their proposed feature-based approach.

Table 6. Results of the feature-based and kernel-based approaches

Type	Precision	Recall	F-measure
Feature-based Approach	0.701260	0.457767	0.553937
Kernel-based Approach	0.818324	0.497856	0.619076

5   Conclusion

In this paper, we propose a composite kernel for Chinese relation extraction. Two kernels concerning the roles of both the content and non-content information in similarity calculation are defined and combined to obtain the composite kernel. Several combination functions are compared in experiments to find the good composite kernel. Experiments on the ACE 2005 data set show that the proposed approach is effective.

Acknowledgements

The work described in this paper was supported by HK RGC (CERG PolyU5211/05E) and China NSF (60603027).

References

1. Miller, S., Fox, H., Ramshaw, L., Weischedel, R.: A novel use of statistical parsing to extract information from text. In: NAACL 2000 (2000)
2. Kambhatla, N.: Combining lexical, syntactic and semantic features with Maximun Entropy models for extracting relations. In: ACL 2004 (2004)

3. Zhao, S.B., Grishman, R.: Extracting relations with integrated information using kernel kernel methods. In: ACL 2005, Univ of Michigan-Ann Arbor USA, 25-30 June 2005, pp. 419–426 (2005)
4. Zhou, G.D., Su, J., Zhang, J., Zhang, M.: Exploring Various Knowledge in Relation Extraction. In: ACL 2005 (2005)
5. Jiang, J., Zhai, C.: A Systematic Exploration of the Feature Space for Relation Extraction. In: Proceedings of NAACL/HLT, pp. 113–120 (2007)
6. Zelenko, D., Aone, C., Richardella, A.: Kernel Methods for Relation Extraction. Journal of Machine Learning Research 2003(2), 1083–1106 (2003)
7. Culotta, A., Sorensen, J.: Dependency Tree Kernel for Relation Extraction. In: ACL 2004 (2004)
8. Bunescu, R., Mooney, R.: A shortest Path Dependency Tree kernel for Relation Extraction. In: Proceedings of HLT/EMNLP, pp. 724–731 (2005)
9. Zhang, M., Zhang, J., Su, J., Zhou, G.D.: A Composite Kernel to Extract Relations between Entities with both Flat and Structured Features. In: COLING-ACL 2006, Sydney, Australia, pp. 825–832 (2006)
10. Zhou, G., Zhang, M., Ji, D., Zhu, Q.: Tree Kernel-based Relation Extraction with Context-Sensitive Structured Parse Tree Information. In: Proceedings of EMNLP, pp. 728–736 (2007)
11. Zhang, P., Li, W.J., Wei, F.R., Lu, Q., Hou, Y.X.: Exploiting the Role of Position Feature in Chinese Relation Extraction. In: Proceedings of the 6th International Conference on Language Resources and Evaluation (LREC) (to appear, 2008)
12. Li, W.J., Zhang, P., Wei, F.R., Hou, Y.X., Lu, Q.: A Novel Feature-based Approach to Chinese Entity Relation Extraction. In: Proceeding of ACL 2008: HLT, Short Papers (Companion Volume), Columbus, Ohio, USA, pp. 89–92 (June 2008)
13. Che, W.X.: Improved-Edit-Distance Kernel for Chinese Relation Extraction. In: Dale, R., Wong, K.-F., Su, J., Kwong, O.Y. (eds.) IJCNLP 2005. LNCS(LNAI), vol. 2651. Springer, Heidelberg (2005)
14. Huang, R.H., Sun, L., Feng, Y.Y.: Study of kernel-based methods for chinese relation extraction. In: Li, H., Liu, T., Ma, W.-Y., Sakai, T., Wong, K.-F., Zhou, G. (eds.) AIRS 2008. LNCS, vol. 4993, pp. 598–604. Springer, Heidelberg (2008)
15. Islam, A., Inkpen, D.: Semantic Text Similarity Using Corpus-Based Word Similarity and String Similarity. ACM Transactions on Knowledge Discovery from Data 2(2), Article 10 (July 2008)
16. Turney, P.: Mining the web for synonyms: PMI-IR versus LSA on TOEFL. In: Flach, P.A., De Raedt, L. (eds.) ECML 2001. LNCS, vol. 2167, p. 491. Springer, Heidelberg (2001)
17. Joachims, T.: Text categorization with Support Vector Machines: Learning with many relevant features. In: Proceedings of European Conference on Machine Learning (1998)

Appendix A

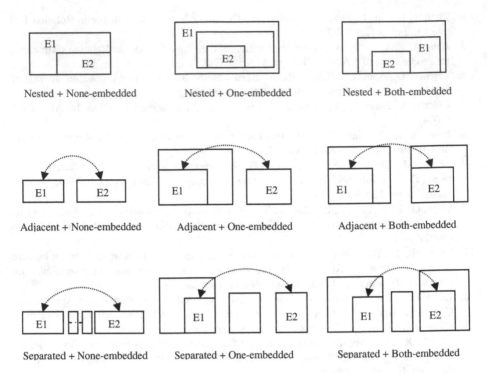

Fig. 1. The position structures (internal position types + external position types)

Appendix B

Table 7. List of ACE relation types and subtypes

Relation Type	Relation Subtype	Frequency
ART (Total No: 630)	User-Owner-Inventor -Manufacturer	630
GEN-AFF (Total No: 1937)	Citizen-Resident- Religion-Ethnicity	746
	Org-Location	1191
ORG-AFF (Total No: 2198)	Employment	1584
	Founder	17
	Ownership	25
	Student-Alum	72
	Sports-Affiliation	69
	Investor-Shareholder	85

	Membership	346
PART-WHOLE	Artifact	14
(Total No: 2286)	Geographical	1289
	Subsidiary	983
	Business	188
PER-SOC	Family	384
(Total No: 660)	Lasting-Personal	88
PHYS (Physical)	Located	1358
(Total No: 1588)	Near	230

Automatic Acquisition of Attributes
for Ontology Construction

Gaoying Cui, Qin Lu, Wenjie Li, and Yirong Chen

Department of Computing, The Hong Kong Polytechnic University,
Hong Kong, China
{csgycui,csluqin,cswjli,csyrchen}@comp.polyu.edu.hk

Abstract. An ontology can be seen as an organized structure of concepts according to their relations. A concept is associated with a set of attributes that themselves are also concepts in the ontology. Consequently, ontology construction is the acquisition of concepts and their associated attributes through relations. Manual ontology construction is time-consuming and difficult to maintain. Corpus-based ontology construction methods must be able to distinguish concepts themselves from concept instances. In this paper, a novel and simple method is proposed for automatically identifying concept attributes through the use of Wikipedia as the corpus. The built-in {{Infobox}} in Wiki is used to acquire concept attributes and identify semantic types of the attributes. Two simple induction rules are applied to improve the performance. Experimental results show precisions of 92.5% for attribute acquisition and 80% for attribute type identification. This is a very promising result for automatic ontology construction.

Keywords: Attribute acquisition, ontology construction, Wikipedia as resource source.

1 Introduction

An ontology can be seen as an organized structure of concepts according to their relations. Usually, a concept C has a set of associated attributes which uniquely describes C. For instance, the concept {software} should be associated with a manufacturer and a release date, among other things. As attributes themselves are also concepts, an attribute of a concept C can also be defined by a relation between C and another concept C_i. Some researchers formally view concepts as vectors of relations or attributes, which are extracted from syntactic structures [1-5]. Most current ontologies are constructed manually by domain experts, some with assistive tools. However, manual construction is time-consuming and timely update is always difficult [6-7].

Automatic ontology construction can take either a top-down approach or a bottom-up approach. In the top-down approach, some upper-level ontology is given and algorithms are developed to expand it from the most general concepts downwards to reach the leaf nodes where instances of concepts can be attached as leaves [8]. On the other hand, in the bottom-up approach, some domain corpus is used to extract concepts, attributes and relations without prior ontological knowledge. Most corpus-based ontology construction assumes that the set of concept terms are known first. Thus, the

W. Li and D. Mollá-Aliod (Eds.): ICCPOL 2009, LNAI 5459, pp. 248–259, 2009.
© Springer-Verlag Berlin Heidelberg 2009

work is to identify relations among the concept terms [9-10]. In a truly corpus-based approach, one important issue is the ability to distinguish concepts from concept instances, which are the intents and extents of the concepts, respectively. It should be pointed out that instances of concepts are normally not considered a part of ontology. If they are appended in an ontology, they should appear only as leaf nodes. There are methods to identify relations between concepts assuming that concept terms are given. In real corpora, concepts and their instances are inter-mixed. In some cases, concept instances appear even more than their corresponding concepts. For example, [[Internet Explorer]] and [[Microsoft Excel]] are instances of the concept {software}, and in a general corpus, such instances may occur more. The association between instances and their corresponding concepts must be identified. Otherwise the constructed ontology would be a confusing network of links without distinction of concepts and their instances. However, for ontology construction using the corpus based approach, there is a natural gap between the ontology as a concept-level structure and the corpus as an instance-rich resource. For example, there are more sentences like "Nokia N73 has two cameras and a powerful CPU" rather than "A mobile phone can has one or more cameras and a CPU" in a real corpus. Thus it is a very challenging work to acquire concepts and their associated attributes using a bottom-up approach.

Wikipedia (Wiki for short), the world's largest online encyclopedia, serves as the corpus with definitions and descriptive information. Its tags and constructs defined through XML also supply semantic rich information for text mining and information extraction. This paper proposes a simple method to identify the set of instances of the same concept through the {{Infobox}} structure supplied in Wiki for instances with reference to the concept they belong to. Furthermore, attributes of a concept can be identified through a simple identification scheme which identifies the most appropriate set of attributes of a concept by ranking the attributes linking different instances to the same concept. As each acquired attribute may have different semantic classifications, the algorithm also identifies the most appropriate semantic type with the help of category information in Wiki articles. These categories roughly give a topic of given attribute according to its values indicating the attribute's semantic nature. For example, "category: people" will be given to the {name} attribute of concept {writer}, denoted as {name}$_{writer}$, so it would not be qualified as a software or a server in computer science domain. Simple rules are applied to the identification algorithm to improve the performance.

The rest of the paper is organized as follows. Section 2 presents some related works. Section 3 describes the proposed model and the algorithm for acquiring concept-level attributes and identifying attribute types. Section 4 shows the evaluation details along with some analyses. Section 5 concludes the paper with future directions.

2 Related Works

Many efforts have been made to acquire attributes for ontology construction. For top-down methods, it is hard for algorithms to define attributes or give a comprehensive list of attributes for the most general concepts. Thus, most top level ontologies and relations between their general concepts are usually defined by linguists or domain experts. The suggested upper merged ontology (SUMO) is such kind of ontology, which was built by a working group with collaborators from the fields of engineering, philosophy, and information science [7]. Efforts are also made to use automatic methods to roughly classify concept attributes. The work in [15] proposed a classification of concept attributes and developed two supervised classifiers to identify concept attributes from candidates extracted from the Web. The classifiers used four types of information: morphological information, clustering information, a question model and an attribute-usage model which is based on text patterns such as "what is\are the A of the C", where A is an attribute and C is a concept. The proposed 5-way automatic attribute classification is as follows: "activity", "part & related object", "quality", "related agent", and "non-attribute".

For bottom-up ontology construction, most of the efforts focused on automatic methods to acquire attributes from a given corpus. Therefore, the methods need to bridge the gap between instance-rich resource and concept-level target, an ontology. Clustering is one of the natural ideas to solve this problem. Attribute-based and value-based (instances of attributes) clustering were compared in [1] to evaluate whether attributes can lead to better lexical descriptions of concepts. Simple text patterns were used to automatically extract both value-based and attribute-based descriptions of concepts for clustering purposes. The conclusion is that even though there are less occurrences of attributes in a corpus than the values of them, attributes still can describe concepts as well as or even better than attribute values do. On the other hand, the best descriptions of concepts include attributes with more general attribute values. Both clustering and pattern-based fuzzy inferences were used in [9] to acquire concepts, attributes, associations and new instances for a Chinese domain ontology. An unsupervised neural network algorithm was used for clustering concepts and defining taxonomic relationships. Then the attributes and associations were extracted based on episodes, which are triples with parallel or serial structures or their combinations. These episodes indicate subject-verb-object or parallel or descriptive relations. However, this clustering and shallow semantic analyzing method does not perform well in the area with rapid changing terms and concepts or with complex semantics. Pattern based methods are also tried by many researchers on semi-structured texts or more efficiency resources such as tables and query logs [11-12]. The work of [11] proposed a pattern based method which acquired attribute-value pairs for given objects from tables in HTML documents. The proposed method acquired attributes for objects from 620 given class-object pairs collected from definition sentences in Japanese Wiki. The approach in [12] exploited both web documents and query logs to acquire class instances and class attributes. It started from a set of 40 manually-assembled classes and 5 seed attributes. Patterns were used to find instances for classes and attributes adopting on these instances, so the instances linked attributes to classes. However, the precision is considerable only on small-scale manually-assembled classes. These approaches for attribute acquisition are complicated in method or limited in effectiveness and coverage.

Wiki is an open-content and collaboratively, it has expanded from around 1 million articles (November, 2006) to more than 2 millions till now [13]. Wiki is an information-rich resource with internal and external hyperlinks and relevant classification declared by contributors manually, which makes it a good resource for concept, attribute, and relation extraction. However, Wiki is also an instance-concept mixed corpus, which means some Wiki pages describe concept instances, while others describe concepts. For example, a page on the subject {Company} is a concept page. In this paper, several notations are defined to identify different kinds of objects. The notation {C} is for concept **C**. Yet, a page on the subject of [[Microsoft]] is actually an instance page. The notation [[**I**]] indicates an instance or a value of an attribute. As attributes themselves are also concepts, the notation {location}$_{company}$ indicates that {location} is an attribute of the concept {company}. The notation [**AT**] labels attribute types. In this work, a method is proposed to identify concept attributes with the help of instance description information supplied by Wiki infoboxes among the ways Wiki links instances to concepts.

3 Algorithm Design

An {{Infobox}} in Wiki is a consistently-formatted table which is mostly present in articles with a common subject (*concepts*) to provide summary information and help to improve navigation to closely related articles (*instances and attribute values*) in that subject. In fact, an {{Infobox}} is a generalization of a taxobox (from taxonomy) which summarizes information for a subject or subjects [14].

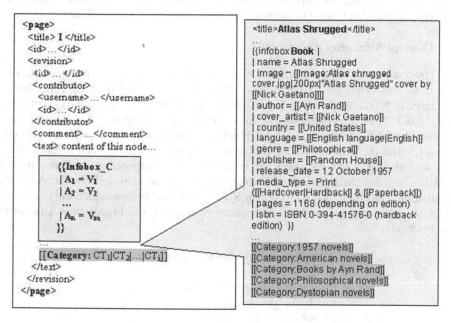

Fig. 1. An Example of a Wiki Page with {{Infobox}} and Category Information

Fig. 1 shows the syntax of {{Infobox}} in a Wiki article page and an example of an {{Infobox}}. The left part of Fig. 1 illustrates the syntax of a Wiki instance page with {{Infobox}} and Category List. The right part gives an example of {{Infobox}} contents and categories. It shows an instance article page with the name [[Atlas Shrugged]], which is the name of a novel and the related information according to predefined {{Infobox}} syntax. The first line of an {{Infobox}} provides {book} as the concept which the instance [[Atlas Shrugged]] belongs to. The subsequent list defined using "=" are attributes of {book} which are associated with the instance [[Atlas Shrugged]]. The terms or phrases on the right part are values of the corresponding attribute on the left hand side. For instance, in the entry *author=[[Ayn Rand]]*, author can be considered an attribute of {book}, denoted by {author}$_{book}$, and [[Ayn Rand]] is an instance of {author}$_{book}$.

Consequently, {{Infobox}} can be used for two purposes. Firstly, it can be used to extract attributes for a given concept. Secondly, it can be used to estimate appropriate semantic type for each attribute. It should be pointed out that even though each {{infobox}} contains a list of attributes, a different {{infobox}} as instance of the same concept may use a different list of attributes. Therefore, there is the issue of how to identify a common set of attributes which are considered most appropriate for a concept. In Wiki, an additional list of category information is contained in a page in the form of "*[[Category:CT$_1$|CT$_2$| ...|CT$_i$]]*" as shown in Fig. 1 where CT_1 to CT_i are total i number of categories the page editor considers to be related to this page. They are used to classify articles in Wiki and serve as the table of contents for the whole Wiki structure. An article's categories should reflect the classes to which the subject of the article belongs, or topics to which it is related to [14]. In this work, Wiki category information is used to estimate the semantic type of the attributes.

3.1 Concept Attributes Acquisition

As {{Infobox}} structures in instance pages denote corresponding concepts, the first step is to collect all the instance pages through the identification of {{Infobox}} structures in Wiki. As shown in Fig. 1, the format of Wiki and {{Infobox}} are relatively fixed. Thus the corresponding information can be acquired by patterns. Each attribute *A* of different instances(*Is*) belonging to one concept *C* is collected into one set $S_A(C)$ with the help of two 2-level hash tables, one for concept and instance mapping named $H_I(C)$ and the other for instance and corresponding attributes named $H_A(C)$. Then the attribute identification process can be achieved by the Attribute Acquisition Algorithm (AAA) to obtain $S_A(C)$ as shown bellow which only selects a set of attributes whose number of appearances in $H_A(C)$ is bigger than a majority threshold value.

```
Attribute Acquisition Algorithm (AAA)
{ for each C in H_I(C)
       {    Count_of_Ins = scalar(H_I(C));
            for each I in H_I(C)
            {  for each A in H_A(I)
               {
                   H_A(C)->{A}++;
               }endfor
            }endfor
       }endfor
    for each C in H_A(C)
       {
            Freq= H_A(C)->{A};
```

```
        if(Freq>=THRE*Count_of_Ins)
        {put A into S_A(C)}endif
    }endfor
}endalgorithm AAA
```

AAA can be divided into two parts. The first part is the counting of appearances for each attribute for C. The second part is the selection of qualified attributes according to the majority threshold value, named **THRE**, which is an experimentally determined algorithm parameter. In algorithm AAA, all the appearance count stored in a 2-level hash $H_A(C)$ with first level of keys as concepts and the second level as attributes. The attributes associated with more than a threshold of instances for the same concept will be selected as qualified concept attributes. All the qualified attributes are stored into the set $S_A(C)$.

3.2 Attribute Type Identification

The conclusion of [1] has mentioned that concepts can be described better if both attributes and attribute values are supplied. Generally speaking, in ontology construction, the same attribute name can be used for concepts of an ontology in the same domain or concepts in ontologies of different domains. One way to identify a specific attribute is by identifying the distinct semantic type of its attribute. For example, the concept {Airliner accident} has an associated {site}$_{Airliner\ accident}$ attribute to indicate the location of an accident whereas for organizations such as {UKschool}, an associated attribute {site}$_{UKschool}$ can be the website address of this organization. This example shows that if the *domain of the attribute value range* (called the *attribute type*) is identified, it can further qualify the semantic type of the attribute.

Attribute values can be stated in different formats such as words, sentences and tables. Identifying attribute type is not straight forward because they are quite arbitrary in its presentation form. This work proposes to use the frequency of Wiki article names as instances to indicate the implicit inclination of attribute types. This is based on two considerations. First, the attribute value descriptions contain useful information but are usually not well-formed. So, the use of NLP tools such as parsers are not quite suitable for this task. Second, attribute values do contain related Wiki article names using pre-defined form so it is easy to acquire these Wiki articles. In fact, these article names can be considered as named entities marked in attribute value descriptions. Consequently, these Wiki article names are taken as key words of attribute value descriptions for attribute type analysis. For example, attribute {developer}$_{software}$ of [[REXX]](a programming language) has a value "Mike Cowlishaw & [[IBM]]" which format indicates that there is a Wiki article entitled "IBM". Thus the article page is identified. If there is no Wiki article name marked in an attribute value description, the substrings of the attribute values will be used as keywords to look for homonymic Wiki article names. Then, the category information in matched Wiki pages can be used to identify the type for each attribute of a concept. For example, {developer}$_{software}$ of [[ICQ]] takes [[AOL]](American online) and {developer}$_{software}$ of [[Internet Explorer]] takes [[Microsoft]] as values. Then a 2-level hash mapping Wiki article names to corresponding categories [13] can be used to obtain categories of Wiki pages named [[Mike Cowlishaw]], [[IBM]], [[AOL]], and [[Microsoft]], such as "Category:Computer Programmers", "Category:Software companies of the United

States" and "Category:Companies listed on NASDAQ". The most frequently used categories will be selected as the attribute type of a given attribute. Two 2-level hash tables are used in Type Identification Algorithm (**TIA**). One is $\mathbf{H_V(A)}$ mapping attributes to key words in their values. The other is the category hash mapping article names to corresponding gram list, referred to as $\mathbf{H_{CAT}(V)}$.

```
Type Identification Algorithm (TIA)
{ for each A in H_V(A)
    {    MAX=0;
        for each V in H_CAT(V)
        {  for each CAT in H_CAT(V)
            {
                Freq = H_CAT(A)->{CAT}++;
                If (Freq>= MAX)
                {MAX=Freq;}endif
            }endfor
        }endfor
    }endfor
    for each A in H_CAT(A)
    {
        F = H_CAT(A)->{CAT};
        if(F==MAX)
        {put CAT into S_CAT(A);}endif
    }endfor
}endalgorithm TIA
```

The structure of algorithm TIA also contains two parts similar to AAA. The first part is to collect candidates of an attribute type. The second is to select the most appropriate semantic type if an attribute. In algorithm TIA, *A* is an attribute, *V* is a key word in attribute value and *CAT* is a category linking to one key word *V*. *Freq* records the number of instances linking to the same category. *MAX* records the maximum vote number for each attribute. The first part of algorithm TIA is to collect the categories with key word values directly linking to them and record the categories with *Freq*. The candidates are considered as possible attribute type of attributes and stored in $\mathbf{H_{CAT}(A)}$. In the second part, all the qualified attribute types with highest *Freq* will be stored into the result set, namely $\mathbf{S_{CAT}(A)}$.

As Wiki is an open-content and collaboratively edited encyclopedia, some categories are not formal enough to be considered as attribute types. For example, categories of dates are too specific, such as "category:1980" for the year 1980. The semantic type induced from this value should be DATE rather than a specific date value. In the experiment, TIA has also integrated some pre-processing and post-processing steps to handle these special cases which will be discussed in Section 4.2.

4   Experiment and Evaluation

The experiments are implemented using the English Wiki with the cut off date of November 30th, 2006 containing about 1.1 million article and category pages. After applying {{Infobox}} extraction patterns, 111,408 {{Infobox}} have been extracted for 110,572 article names, which are considered as instance pages of Wiki. The difference between the number of {{Infobox}} and article name is due to the fact that the same instance page can be linked to different concepts through multiple {{infobox}} structures. For example, [[Arnold Schwarzenegger]] is an instance of {Actor} and also an instance of {Governor}, which contains different attributes. In the algorithm, an instance is allowed to be associated with more than one concept term. There are 1,558 concepts relevant to the 110,572 instances. For example, concept {company} has 2,585 instances, such as [[Microsoft]] and [[Bank of China]].

4.1 Evaluation for Algorithm AAA

There are two measures in the evaluation of AAA on the extracted attributes. The first measure is to examine how many of the extracted attributes are in fact commonly accepted as attributes for the corresponding concepts. This measure is referred to as the attribute precision, p. The commonly used measure of recall for acquired attributes in this work is trivial because the union of the attributes of all instances belonging to one concept defines the whole set of attributes of this concept. It is not really the scope of this work to judge their appropriateness as a whole because there is no uniformed agreement on the completeness of attributes which is a subjective issue and depends on the level of details needed. On the other hand, different threshold values in AAA can result in different sets of extracted attributes and also different number of concepts with respect to the total number of concept pages (total of 1,558) in Wiki. So, the second measure is to examine how many concepts are identified with attributes. In other words, the measure is the recall of concepts, r.

Experiments are conducted to see how different values of **THRE**, the algorithm parameter, can affect the performance in terms of attribute precision and concept recall. The value of **THRE** ranges from 0.0 to 1.0 by taking 0.1 as increment for each value. So, a total of 11 sets of data are produced. The commonly used f-measure for a balanced recall and precision cannot be directly applied in this work because the recall and the precision are not on the same objects, one for concepts and the other for attributes. However, we can use a so called f-factor which takes consideration of both the attribute precision and concept recall to find a good threshold value which gives a balanced consideration of both measures. The f-factor, f_i, is defined in a similar way as the commonly used f-factor as follows:

$$f_i = 2 * r_i * p_i / (r_i + p_i) \tag{1}$$

where r_i and p_i are concept recall and attribute precision of the ith data set.

For actually evaluation, a sampling method is used to estimate both the precision and recall because the sizes of the results are very large. For evaluation, 40 samples that are evenly distributed concept-attribute pairs in each data set are evaluated. For the total 11 sets of data, a total of 440 concept-attribute pairs are evaluated manually.

Fig. 2 shows the evaluation result. It can be seen that the attribute precision ranges from 52.5% to 92.5% with an optimal point at around 0.9. On the other hand, the recall of concepts decreases from 100% when **THRE** is 0.0 to 80.0% when **THRE** is 1.0. For example, if the threshold is set as 1, 311 concepts out of 1,558 would have no attributes because there is no attribute shared by all instances. The highest value of

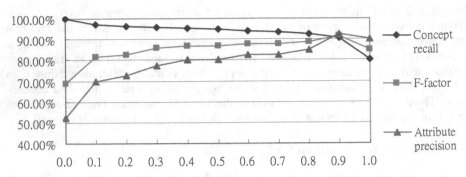

Fig. 2. Performance of Attribute Precision and Concept Recall

f-factor is reached when the threshold is set to 0.9. At this point, the concept recall is 90.7% and attribute precision reaches 91.6% and f-factor as 92.5%. To explain more on the effect of different ***THRE***, take the concept node {company} as an example. There are a total of 2,585 instances of {company}. When ***THRE*** is set to 1.0, it means that an attribute would qualify if it appears in all the instances. In fact, for {company}, there is no qualified attributes under threshold 1.0. When ***THRE*** is reduced to 0.9, nine attributes that are common to 90% of the instances are identified including {company name}$_{company}$, {company type}$_{company}$, {location}$_{company}$, {foundation}$_{company}$, {company logo}$_{company}$, {homepage}$_{company}${key people}$_{company}$, {industry}$_{company}$, and {products}$_{company}$. But if the threshold is set to 0.2, attributes such as {net-income}$_{company}$ and {parent}$_{company}$ would also be included. According to the experiments, the threshold value around 0.9 is a good choice.

4.2   Evaluation for Algorithm TIA

To evaluate TIA for attribute type identification, the optimal threshold value ***THRE*** of 0.9 is fixed. The evaluation of TIA examines the precision of acquired attribute types and how many concepts/attributes can be covered by TIA, referred to as the recall of concepts/attributes.

Initial evaluation of TIA uses 100 evenly distributed samples of <*concepts, attributes, attribute values*> by manual examination. The recall of typed concepts is less than 50% and attribute recall is also too low. Further analysis is then made to find the reason to such a low performance. As Wiki is a collaborative online encyclopedia, some editors list attributes with only names in the {{Infobox}} without supplying values which give rise to data sparseness. Also, the formats of attribute values are not uniform making it difficult to extract them even if they are present. Besides, some of the categories present in the Wiki pages are actual instance level values rather than concept level category names as mentioned in section 3.2. Thus, the proposed method cannot acquire categories for all attributes nor select the most appropriate attribute type. For example, the semantic type of {clubs}$_{football player}$ should be [football clubs], not instances of football clubs. However, most Wiki categories list the actual country names such as "category: Spanish football clubs" and "category: Italian football clubs". So, the issue is to remove the instance information.

In fact, simple preprocessing and post-processing to attribute values and categories can resolve the problem in some degree.

The preprocessing is to eliminate the reference to named entities such as countries, cities, etc.. An n-gram collection (n=1, 2 here) is applied to attribute values and categories. Unigrams and bigrams of these category strings are extracted as substitutes of categories and those with highest product of frequency and length will be considered as attribute type. That is to use the components of a category instead of the category itself. As a result, [football clubs] will be extracted as category.

The post-processing handles the errors caused by numeric values and hyperlinks. Some of the categories in Wiki pages are actual attribute values rather than attribute types. For example, the attribute type of year 1200 should be [year] rather than "Category:1200" containing the actual attribute value of year 1200. There are also cases where the categories of attribute values, such as value 8,514,877 of $\{area\}_{country}$ for instance {Brazil}is not defined as a Wiki article name. Some attributes are listed without given any attribute value, such as attribute $\{awards\}_{architect}$ is empty for all instances of {architect} in the Wiki version used here. According to the analysis, two simple induction rules are applied as post-processing. They are listed as follows:

R1: If the text of an attribute contain only years or months or other date measurement words, its attribute type is labeled [DATE]. Otherwise, if they contain only numbers and delimiters, its attribute type is labeled [NUMBER]. All hyperlinks are labeled [LINKS].

R2: If an attribute has no attribute values, its attribute type is labeled by the name of this attribute.

Table 1. Comparison of Attribute Types Using Different TIAs

	AT Precision	Recall for Concepts	Recall for Attributes
TIA	16.7%	47.0%	14.0%
TIA_{Ngram}	28.2%	100%	67.0%
TIA_{Rules}	80.0%	100%	76.0%

Table 1 shows the evaluation result of the original TIA (*TIA*), TIA+Preprocessing (TIA_{Ngram}), and TIA+Preprocessing+Post-processing(TIA_{Rules}). It can be seen that the original TIA covers less than half of the concepts. Also, less than one quarter of the attribute types are correctly identified. After adding the pre-process part, coverages of concepts and attributes reach 100% and 67%, respectively. However, the precision is still no more than 30%, which means only category information is not enough. By applying two simple induction rules, the precision of TIA reaches 80% and the recall of attributes also near 80%. As the performance is improved quite significantly after applying n-grams and induction rules, further analysis is made to look for reasonable explanations. The Table 2 shows the contributions of original TIA, the n-gram preprocessing and post-processing rules in identifying attribute types.

Table 2. Attribute Type Distribution

Attribute types	TIA	n-gram	NUMBER	DATE	LINKS	Attribute names	Uncovered
Percentage	16.3%	17.1%	17.7%	9.1%	2.2%	13.5%	24.1%

Table 2 shows that pre-processing by using n-grams contributes to an additional 17.1% attribute type identification and post-processing contribute to 42.5% of the attribute types including numbers, dates, links and attribute names. This explains why the performance of pre-processing and post-processing can significantly improve the performance so that many more attributes can be correctly categorized. However there is still about one quarter of the attribute types which cannot be identified by the algorithm, which means that category information is not sufficient for attribute type identification. The unvalued attributes also limit the precision of algorithm. Other information in Wiki may be used in the future to improve the performance of TIA.

5   Conclusion and Future Works

In this paper, a novel approach is proposed for acquiring concept attributes. As an association between instances and concepts, {{Infobox}} tables in Wiki are used to acquire essential attributes for concepts and category information are used to identify attribute types to complement the descriptions of concepts. A simple substring handling and two simple induction rules can effectively improve the precision and coverage of attribute type identification. The f-factor of concept attribute acquisition reached 91.6%. The precision of attribute type identification reached 80%. The advantage of the proposed method is that it only uses information supplied by Wiki. There is no need for complex algorithm or training. Although the coverage of infobox cannot cover all pages, the method is completely automatic and the acquired instances and concept attributes are enough for bootstrapping ontology construction and can be directly used for automatic ontology construction and extension.

More information from Wiki can be used to improve the precision of concept attributes acquisition and attribute type identification. For example, the absolute number of instances for one concept can be considered as an influence factor for concept attribute identification. Also, the context of the pages containing infoboxes can be used for finding more potential attribute values to enhance the precision of attribute type identification. Other work can also be explored to apply the proposed method in a selected domain for domain ontology construction.

Acknowledgments. This project is partially supported by CERG grants (PolyU 5190/04E and PolyU 5225/05E), B-Q941 (Acquisition of New Domain Specific Concepts and Ontology Update), and G-YE66 (An Intelligent Risk Assessment System for International Maritime Safety and Security Law in HK and China).

References

1. Almuhareb, A., Poesio, M.: Attribute-Based and Value-Based Clustering: An Evaluation. In: Proceedings of Conference on Empirical Methods in Natural Language Processing (EMNLP), Barcelona, Spain (2004)
2. Grefenstette, G.: SEXTANT: Extracting semantics from raw text implementation details. Heuristics: The Journal of Knowledge Engineering (1993)
3. Lin, D.: Automatic retrieval and clustering of similar words. In: Proceedings of the 17th International Conference on Computational Linguistics and 36th Annual Meeting of the Association for Computational Linguistics (COLING-ACL), Montreal, pp. 768–774 (1998)
4. Curran, J.R., Moens, M.: Improvements in automatic thesaurus extraction. In: Proceedings of the ACL-SIGLEX Workshop on Unsupervised Lexical Acquisition, Philadelphia, PA, USA, pp. 59–66 (2002)
5. Kilgarriff, A.: Thesauruses for Natural Language Processing. In: Proceedings of the IEEE 2003 International Conference on Natural Language Processing and Knowledge Engineering (NLPKE 2003), Beijing (2003)
6. Natalya, F., Noy, Deborah, L.: McGuinness: Ontology Development 101: A Guide to Creating Your First Ontology (2001) (last visited September 20th, 2008),
http://protege.stanford.edu/publications/ontology_development/ontology101-noy-mcguinness.html
7. Niles, I., Pease, A.: Towards a Standard Upper Ontology. In: Proceedings of the Second International Conference on Formal Ontology in Information Systems (FOIS 2001) (2001) (last   visited   September   20th,   2008),
http://home.earthlink.net/~adampease/professional/FOIS.pdf
8. Chen, Y., Lu, Q., Li, W., Li, W., Ji, L., Cui, G.: Automatic Construction of a Chinese Core Ontology from an English-Chinese Term Bank. In: Proceeding of ISWC 2007 Workshop OntoLex 2007 - From Text to Knowledge: The Lexicon/Ontology Interface, Busan, Korea, pp. 78–87 (2007)
9. Lee, C.S., Kao, Y.F., Kuo, Y.H., Wang, M.H.: Automated ontology construction for unstructured text documents. Data & Knowledge Engineering 60, 547–566 (2007)
10. Yang, Y., Lu, Q., Zhao, T.: A Clustering Based Approach for Domain Relevant Relation Extraction. In: Proceedings of the 2008 IEEE International Conference on Natural Language Processing and Knowledge Engineering (IEEE NLP-KE 2008), Beijing, China, October 19-22 (2008)
11. Yoshinaga, N., Torisawa, K.: Open-Domain Attribute-Value Acquisition from Semi-Structured Texts. In: Proceedings of the OntoLex 2007 - From Text to Knowledge: The Lexicon/Ontology Interface, Busan, South-Korea, November 11th (2007)
12. Pasca, M., Durme, B.V.: Weakly-supervised Acquisition of Open-domain Classes and Class Attributes from Web Documents and Query Logs. In: Proceedings of ACL 2008: HLT, Columbus, Ohio, USA, pp. 19–27 (2008)
13. Cui, G., Lu, Q., Li, W., Chen, Y.: Corpus Exploitation from Wikipedia. In: Proceedings of the International Conference on Language Resources and Evaluation (LREC 2008), Marrakech, Morocco, May 28-30 (2008)
14. Wikipedia (English version), http://en.Wikipedia.org
15. Poesio, M., Almuhareb, A.: Identifying Concept Attributes Using a Classifier. In: Proceedings of the ACL-SIGLEX Workshop on Deep Lexical Acquisition, Ann Arbor, pp. 18–27 (2005)

Speech Synthesis for Error Training Models in CALL

Xin Zhang[1], Qin Lu[2], Jiping Wan[1], Guangguang Ma[1], Tin Shing Chiu[2],
Weiping Ye[1], Wenli Zhou[1], and Qiao Li[1]

[1] Department of Electronics, Beijing Normal University
yeweiping@bnu.edu.cn
[2] Department of Computing, Hong Kong Polytechnic University

Abstract. A computer assisted pronunciation teaching system (CAPT) is a fundamental component in a computer assisted language learning system (CALL). A speech recognition based CAPT system often requires a large amount of speech data to train the incorrect phone models in its speech recognizer. But collecting incorrectly pronounced speech data is a labor intensive and costly work. This paper reports an effort on training the incorrect phone models by making use of synthesized speech data. A special formant speech synthesizer is designed to filter the correctly pronounced phones into incorrect phones by modifying the formant frequencies. In a Chinese Putonghua CALL system for native Cantonese speakers to learn Mandarin, a small experimental CAPT system is built with a synthetic speech data trained recognizer. Evaluation shows that a CAPT system using synthesized data can perform as good as or even better than that using real data provided that the size of the synthetic data are large enough.

Keywords: training data preparation, computer aided language learning, Speech synthesis, formant modification.

1 Introduction

With the rapid development of computing technology such as speech processing, multimedia and internet, computer-assisted language learning (CALL) systems are getting more comprehensive [1]. A computer assisted pronunciation teaching (CAPT) system, as the basic component of a CALL system, can give feedbacks to a learner's mis-pronunciation in order to improve his pronunciation. In addition to an embedded automatic speech recognizer, a CAPT is able to score the pronunciation quality of the learner. A simple CAPT system, which gives one evaluation score based on different speech features, can only tell how good a learner performs, but not how he can improve. More complicated error model based CAPT systems can give suggestions on how to improve learner's pronunciations [2][3][4].

A more comprehensive speech recognizer in CAPT needs acoustic models for both the correctly pronounced phones and the incorrectly pronounced ones. Consider a native Chinese learning the English word "flag" ([flæg]). Since [æ] is not a Chinese phone, the learner is most likely to utter it either as [fleg] or [flag]. Having both two error phone models and the correct model, the recognizer can tell not only how wrong

W. Li and D. Mollá-Aliod (Eds.): ICCPOL 2009, LNAI 5459, pp. 260–269, 2009.

the actual pronunciation is as a score, but also which actual error model is most likely pronounced. As a result, the system can give more concrete suggestions to a learner such as "put your tongue a little downward" to improve learner's pronunciation from [fleg] to "flag" ([flæg]). Obviously, a comprehensive CAPT system like this is much better than those which can only give a simple score without specific suggestions. Yet a comprehensive CAPT needs a large amount of incorrectly pronounced speech data to train the error models through a large amount of recording followed by error type clustering using either a manual or an automatic classification method. Without enough training data, error models can face data sparseness problem. Collecting incorrectly pronounced speech data is a labor intensive and costly work. And incorrectly pronounced speech data is much more difficult to obtain than the correct ones [5].

Instead of exhaustive manual recording and classification to minimize the effect of data sparseness problem, this paper proposes an alternative method to produce incorrect speech data through a formant speech synthesis. Analysis of a small set of samples of correct/incorrect phone pairs suggests the formant relationships between these pairs. According to the obtained formant relationships, the formant frequencies in the vocal tract filter of the correct phone are mapped into that of the incorrect ones. In this way, all the incorrect speech data are obtained from their correct counterparts. The characteristics of the speakers and other environmental variations of original correct speech are unchanged by keeping the original formant bandwidths and the LPC residual.

A small experimental system is built for demonstration and evaluation of the proposed method. Experiment shows that the synthetic incorrect speech trained model performs as good as its prerecorded counterpart and with enough generated synthetic data, it can actually out-perform the pre-recorded counterpart.

The rest of the paper is organized as follows. The basic design idea and methodology are explained in Section 2. Experiments and results are detailed in section 3. Section 4 is the conclusion.

2 Design and Methodology

2.1 Basic Design Idea of the Formant Synthesizer

Fig. 1 shows a general speech synthesizer. The synthesis process can be modeled as a linear combination of a vocal tract filter as a linear time-invariant system and the glottal sound as an input signal to the system. The vocal tract filter can be characterized by formant frequencies and formant bandwidths. $\hat{s}(n)$ is the synthesized speech. The synthesizer for error phone production in this work uses a vocal tract filter specified by the first four formant frequencies F_1 to F_4 and the first four bandwidths B_1 to B_4.

To excite any vocal tract, a sound source is needed. In this paper, the linear prediction (LPC) residual is used as the sound source. By extracting the LPC residual from the prerecorded speech material, the pitch and voice of the speaker remain the same.

The following is a brief description of linear prediction analysis. A more detailed treatment can be found elsewhere in literature [9]. The sampled speech waveform $s(n)$ can be approximated by another sequence $\hat{s}(n)$ through linear prediction of the past p samples of $s(n)$:

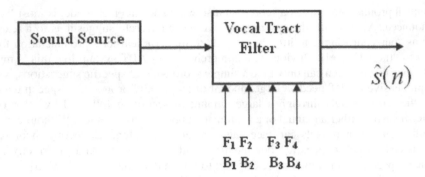

Fig. 1. The basic structure for speech synthesizer

$$\hat{s}(n) = \sum_{k=1}^{p} a_k s(n-k) \qquad (1)$$

p is prediction order. The linear prediction coefficients a_k can be determined by minimizing the mean squared differences. The LPC residual is:

$$e(n) = s(n) - \hat{s}(n) \qquad (2)$$

Formants are the resonances of the vocal tract. they are manifested in the spectral domain by energy maxima at the resonant frequencies. The frequencies at which the formants occur are primarily dependent upon the shape of the vocal tract, which is determined by the positions of the articulators (tongue, lips, jaw, etc). The relationship or ratio of adjacent formants is called formant structure.

Former researches demonstrate that the quality (correct or incorrect) of a phone is mainly determined by formant frequency structure whereas sound source, formant bandwidths, absolute values of formant frequencies and other speech parameters are mostly depend on different speaker, speaker's different state and emotion, and different environmental conditions [6]. A reasonable inference is that by modifying only formant structure, a correct phone can be synthesized into an incorrect phone, yet other speech characteristics can be kept unchanged. Consequently, the phone model trained by the synthesized incorrect speech data is likely to be the same robust to variations on speaker and other conditions as its correct counterpart.

Table 1 shows the first four formant frequency values of two different phones [a:] and [e], read by two different speakers, A and B. The ratios of the corresponding formant frequencies between different phones are also listed. Table 1 shows that the formant structures by both speakers are very similar for the same phonemes even though they have very different absolute formant values. In fact, the ratios of the two phonemes from the two speakers are almost the same. This suggests that the formant frequency ratio of different phones from a small set of speech data can be applied to generate a larger set of speech data.

Table 1. The first 4 formants frequency values of different vowels [a:] and [e] recorded by two speakers, ratio is $F_i([e])/F_i([a:])$, i=1,2,3,4.

	A				B			
	F_1	F_2	F_3	F_4	F_1	F_2	F_3	F_4
[a:]	802	1126	2933	3483	1128	1632	3453	4520
[e]	588.4	1970	2893	3500	800	2213	3143	4345
Ratio	0.734	1.749	0.986	1.005	0.71	1.36	0.91	0.96

This invariant of formant ratio is meaningful to build the incorrect speech synthesizer. Scaling formant frequencies by the ratio of the incorrect to the correct, a correct phone can be synthesized into an incorrect one. The principle in this work is synthesis large amount of incorrect speech data from correct speech data using the ratios obtained from a much smaller set of sample data. The characteristics of speakers, emotions and other variations are kept unchanged as the original correct speech data.

2.2 Auto-synthesis Program Procedures

Some preparations need to be done before auto-synthesis. Firstly, the common types of pronunciation errors are identified through expert analysis and summarization. This requires good understanding of the two dialects and the phonetic differences so that conceptual error models can be established. Based on the analysis result, correct and incorrect speech data are then compared to each other to identify the relationships between the first four formant frequencies of correct and incorrect speech data. As a result, the modification ratio of each formant can be determined.

After the preparation, the prerecorded correct speech data and the corresponding formant ratios can be input to the auto-synthesizer to generate the incorrect speech data one by one as shown in the block diagram in Fig.2.

The proposed auto-synthesis has three steps. Step One is the LPC analysis. The LPC coefficients of the prerecorded correct speech data are computed by the autocorrelation method. The LPC residual of the prerecorded correct speech data is extracted by inverse filtering. And the first four formant frequencies of the same data are decided by solving the LPC equation [7]. Here the prediction order p=18.

Step Two is the formant frequency modification. The formant frequencies of the prerecorded correct speech data are multiplied by the pre-decided ratios to obtain the modified formant frequencies for incorrect synthetic speech data. A new vocal tract filter for the incorrect synthetic speech is built using the modified formant frequency values.

Step Three is the synthesis. The LPC residual is used to excite the vocal tract filter, and then the new synthesized incorrectly pronounced speech data are obtained.

The proposed method has two main advantages. Firstly, it can maintain the characteristics of the speakers used in the training data by keeping the original LPC residual and formant bandwidth. Multiplying the formant frequencies only by a ratio can also keep the difference of formant location caused by different vocal tract sizes. Secondly, the relationship between formant frequencies and the type of incorrectly pronounced error concluded by a small set of speech data can be used to modify other speech data which is not from this small set.

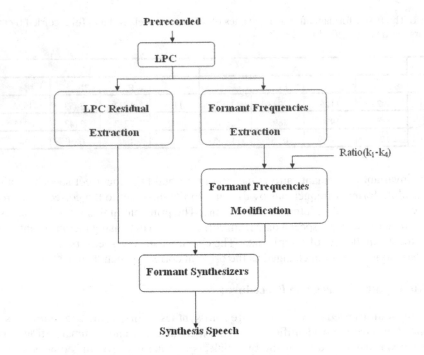

Fig. 2. Block-diagram of auto-synthesis program

3   Experiment and Results

The incorrectly pronounced speech data synthesized in this experiment is used in a Chinese Putonghua CAPT system rEcho [4] to teach native Cantonese speakers to speak Mandarin. Three typical syllables/characters confusing to native Cantonese speakers "ge[kɤ]", "he[xɤ]", and "xi[ɕi]" are chosen for the experiment [8]. The types of incorrectly pronounced syllables for each choice are showed in Table 2.

The corresponding syllables/characters are constructed into some carefully chosen sentences for the purpose of pronunciation error detection. Table 3 shows the 3 sentences containing these phones (1) "李大[哥]卖面包(li3 da4 ge1 mai4 mian4 bao1)" with [kɤ] in it, (2) "阿力[喝]咖啡 (a1 li4 he1 ka1 fei1)" with [xɤ]，and (3) "阿美有[习]题答案 (a1 mei3 you3 xi2 ti2 da2 an4)" with [ɕi]. Another 6 sentences with the incorrect pronunciations showed in Table 2 can then be constructed.

Table 2. Types of incorrectly pronounced syllables

Syllable	[kɤ]	[xɤ]	[ɕi]
Error type 1	[kɛ]	[xɛ]	[ʂi]
Error type 2	[kɔ]	[xɔ]	[si]

Table 3. Sentences and modification ratios

Formant Ratio		K_1	K_2	K_3	K_4
李大哥卖面包	[kɤ]-⟩ [kɛ]	1	1.5	1.5	1
li da ge mai mian bao	[kɤ]-⟩ [kɔ]	0.9	0.8	2	0.9
阿力喝咖啡	[xɤ]-⟩ [xɛ]	1	1.5	1.5	1
a li he ka fei	[xɤ]-⟩ [xɔ]	0.9	0.8	2	0.9
阿美有习题答案	[ɕi]-⟩ [ʂi]	0.67	0.7	1	1
a mei you xi ti da an	[ɕi]-⟩ [si]	1.4	1.2	1	1

The aim of the experiments is to examine the performance of the synthesized incorrect speech data when applied to the CAPT system. Two speech training databases are used for comparison the synthesized data training acoustic models to the prerecorded data training ones. The prerecorded speech database is from a group of 20 male and 20 female speakers who are native mandarin speakers and can imitate Cantonese. They are requested to utter each of the 9 sentences twice. When they are asked to pronounce the incorrect phones, they are instructed to follow the error models and types summarized by expert. The synthetic speech database is obtained by modifying the correct speech data in the prerecorded database. In other words, the prerecorded database contains 9 sentences in all, 3 with correct pronunciations and 6 with incorrect pronunciations whereas the synthetic database contains only the 6 sentences with incorrect phonemes. There are 80 samples for each of the sentences in both databases. The modification ratio used by the algorithm to generate the synthesized database is showed in Table 3 where K_1~K_4 are the modification ratio of F_1~F_4, respectively.

3.1 Evaluation by Open Test

In this section, the performances of the CAPT using both the prerecorded and the synthesized speech data are evaluated by prerecorded testing data. For each sentence, the training set of prerecorded and synthesized model comprises 60 sentences, which are randomly selected from the prerecorded and synthesized database. The test sets for the two models are the same, comprising 20 prerecorded sentences which are not contained in the training set. Fig. 3 shows the evaluation result expressed by character error rate(*cer*). [kɤ], [kɛ] and [kɔ] represent the 1 correct and 2 synthetic incorrect sentences of the 1st sentence "李大哥卖面包(li3 da4 ge1 mai4 mian4 bao1)". [xɤ], [xɛ], [xɔ] and [ɕi], [ʂi], [si] represent the 2nd and 3rd sentences respectively.

From Fig.3, it can be seen that with equal amount of training sentences, the synthetic sentence training models perform worse than their prerecorded counterparts as a whole. Among the 3 sentences, [xɤ] and [ɕi] in the 2nd and the 3rd sentence are relatively more difficult to synthesize with fricative consonants in them. Therefore, the 2nd and the 3rd sentences have lower *cer* than the 1st sentence.

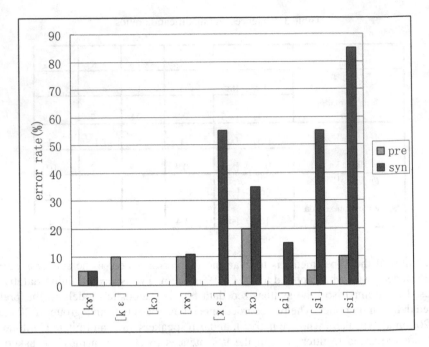

Fig. 3. Error rates using prerecorded data for testing

It is understandable that the CAPT performs better using prerecorded real data for training compared to the system using equal amount of synthesized data. However, synthetic phones are artificially synthesized with a ratio. By deliberately changing the ratio, more synthesized sentences can be generated to enlarge the training size whereas using prerecorded data does not have that liberty.

To further investigate the size of the synthesized data to the performance of CAPT, another set of experiment is conducted using the sentence "阿力喝咖啡(a1 li4 he1 ka1 fei1)" with different sizes of synthesized data. Results are listed in Fig.4. Fig. 4 shows that the system trained by 80 synthesized sentences gives a *cer* of 55% for the error phone [xɛ]. Yet when the synthesized data size is increased to 640, the *cer* is reduced to 11.1% which is basically the same as the pre-recorded data. In the case of [xɔ], the synthetic *cer* is decreased from 33% with 80 training sentences to 10% with 640 sentences, which is even better than the prerecorded counterpart of 20%. Generally speaking, the more synthesized data are used, the better the *cer* values are. In fact, *cer* decreases quite rapidly as the number of synthetic training sentences increases. The results also indicate that in a system with limited real speech data for training, synthesized speech data is not only useful, it can even perform better than system using real data provided that there are sufficient synthesized data used.

The additional synthesized data are obtained by adjusting up to 10% of the formant ratio in both directions.

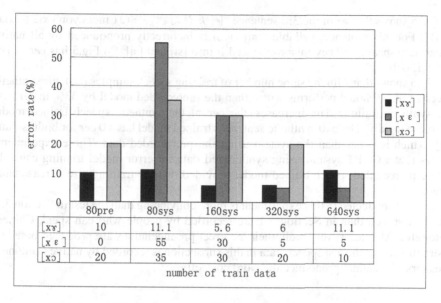

Fig. 4. *cer* of the 2nd sentence with more synthetic training sentences

3.2   Test by Native Cantonese Speakers

In this section, the prerecorded and synthesized data are used to train the CAPT system, respectively.   The test data set is recorded by 4 male and 3 female who are native Cantonese speakers and cannot speak Chinese Putonghua well. This is very much like the real working condition of CAPT.

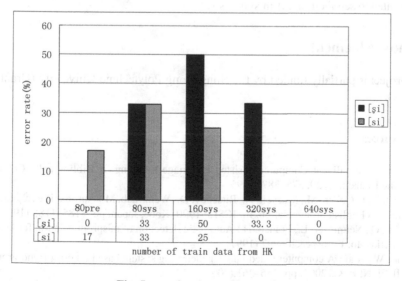

Fig. 5. *cer* of native speaker testing

Fig.5 shows the *cer* of the 3rd sentence "阿美有习题答案(a1 mei3 you3 xi2 ti2 da2 an4)". For this sentence, syllable "[ɕi]" (习) is incorrectly pronounced by all native Cantonese speakers. They mispronounced it into [si] and [ʂi]. So Fig.5 has *cer* of [si] and [ʂi] only.

Fig.5 shows that with the same number of training speech samples (80), the synthetic speech trained model performs worse than the prerecorded model by 33% in *cer*. As the synthetic training data increases, the *cer* of the synthetic speech trained model decrease rapidly. The 640 synthetic sentences trained model has a 0 *cer* for both [si] and [ʂi], which is better than the system using the prerecorded data. These experiments shows that a CAPT system using synthesized data for error model training can substitute prerecorded speech trained model provided that the training size is reasonably large.

The test conducted in this experiment is more convincing than the test in Section 3.1. The test speech data in Section 3.1 are recorded by people who can speak Chinese Putonghua(Manderin) very well, their incorrect pronunciations are produced based on instructions. But the test speech data in this subsection is recorded by native Cantonese speakers who cannot pronounce the word correctly.

4 Conclusion

This paper presented a novel work to use synthesized data for error model training in the CAPT system. Results show that with reasonably large number of synthesized speech data based on correct and incorrect speech data, a CAPT system can give comparably performances as its prerecorded counterpart. This gives light to the availability of more comprehensive CAPT systems which requires a large amount of training data, especially incorrectly pronounced data. More experiments can be conducted on the appropriate size of the synthetic data. Other phonetic features may also be investigated to see their effect in synthesis.

Acknowledgement

This project is partially funded by the Hong Kong Polytechnic University (Grant No.: A-PF84).

References

1. Bailin, A.: Intelligent Computer-Assisted Language Learning. A Bibliography Computers and the Humanities 29, 375–387 (1995)
2. Bernstein, J., Cohen, M., Murveit, H., Ritschev, D., Weintraub, M.: Automatic evaluation and training in English pronunciation. In: ICSLP 1990, Kobe, Japan, pp. 1185–1188 (1990)
3. Ronen, O., Neumeyer, L., Franco, H.: Automatic detection of mispronunciation for language instruction. In: Eurospeech 1997 (1997)
4. Zhou, W., et al.: A computer aided language learning system based on error trend grouping. In: IEEE NLP-KE 2007, pp. 256–261 (2007)

5. Anderson, O., Dalsgaard, P., Barry, W.: On the use of data-driven clustering technique for identificationof poly- and mono-phonemes for four European languages, Acoustics, Speech, and Signal Processing (1994)
6. Klatt, D.H.: Software for a cascade/parallel formant synthesizer, Massachusetts Institute of Technology, Cambridge, Massachusetts 02139 (October 1979)
7. McCandless, S.S.: An algorithm for automatic formant extraction using linear prediction spectra. IEEE transactions on acoustics, speech, and signal processing assp-22(2) (April 1974)
8. Wang, L.: Cantonese how to learn speaking Chinese mandarin(广东人怎样学习普通话). Peking university press (1997)
9. Rabiner, L., Juang, B.-H.: Fundamentals of Speech Recognition. Prentice-Hall International, Inc., Englewood Cliffs

Probabilistic Methods for a
Japanese Syllable Cipher

Sujith Ravi and Kevin Knight

Information Sciences Institute
Computer Science Department
University of Southern California
Marina del Rey, California 90292
{sravi,knight}@isi.edu

Abstract. This paper attacks a Japanese syllable-substitution cipher. We use a probabilistic, noisy-channel framework, exploiting various Japanese language models to drive the decipherment. We describe several innovations, including a new objective function for searching for the highest-scoring decipherment. We include empirical studies of the relevant phenomena, and we give improved decipherment accuracy rates.

Keywords: Substitution cipher, decipherment, language modeling.

1 Introduction

In this paper, we use natural language processing techniques to attack a Japanese substitution cipher. In a substitution cipher, every token of a natural language (plaintext) sequence is replaced by a cipher token, according to some substitution key.

For example, an English plaintext:

"HELLO WORLD ..."

may be enciphered as:

"NOEEI TIMEL ..."

according to the key:

P: ABCDEFGHIJKLMNOPQRSTUVWXYZ
C: XYZLOHANBCDEFGIJKMPQRSTUVW

If the recipients of the ciphertext message have the substitution key, they can use it (in reverse) to recover the original plaintext. Interestingly, a third party who intercepts the message may be able to guess the original plaintext by analyzing the repetition patterns in the ciphertext.

From a natural language perspective, we can view this cryptanalysis task as a kind of unsupervised tagging problem [1]. We must tag each ciphertext token with some element of the plaintext vocabulary. The resulting tag sequence must make sense, so we use language modeling (LM) techniques to rank proposed decipherments. We also need search techniques to find high-ranking decipherments quickly.

W. Li and D. Mollá-Aliod (Eds.): ICCPOL 2009, LNAI 5459, pp. 270–281, 2009.

	1	2	3	4	5	6	7
1	i	ro	ha	ni	ho	he	to
2	ti	ri	nu	ru	wo	wa	ka
3	yo	ta	re	so	tu	ne	na
4	ra	mu	u	<>	no	o	ku
5	ya	ma	ke	hu	ko	e	te
6	a	sa	ki	yu	me	mi	si
7	<>	hi	mo	se	su	n	<>

Fig. 1. Original Uesugi cipher key in Japanese

Fig. 2. Transliterated version of the checkerboard-style key used for encrypting the Uesugi cipher

In this paper, we attack a particular Japanese syllable-substitution cipher from the Warring States Period, said to be employed by General Uesugi Kenshin.[1] The cipher employs the checkerboard-style key shown in Figures 1 and 2. The key is filled out according to the *i-ro-ha* alphabet, which uses each Japanese syllable exactly once. To encode a message, we look up each syllable in the key, and we replace it with a two-digit number. The first digit is the column index, and the second digit is the row index.

For example, the plaintext:

"wa ta ku si ..."

is enciphered as:

"62 23 74 76 ..."

Note that the key contains *ka* but not *ga*. In this system, plaintext *ga* is enciphered in the same way as *ka*, i.e., as 72. Likewise, *go* is enciphered the same as *ko*, and *gu* is enciphered the same as *ku*, and so forth. Note that this means the recipient may generate several readings from the cipher and must use common sense to determine which reading is most sensible. Alternatively, the sender can try to rephrase the original message in order to avoid unintended ambiguity.

Variations of the system exist. For example, instead of two digits, two characters can be used, so that the ciphertext has the outward appearance of written language. Also, the key can be scrambled periodically to increase security.

The goal of cryptanalysis is to take an intercepted number sequence and guess a plaintext for it, without the benefit of the key. In this paper, we investigate the number sequence in Figure 3.

---

[1] http://www.samurai-archives.com/kenshin.html
http://en.wikipedia.org/wiki/Cryptography_in_Japan
http://global.mitsubishielectric.com/misty/tour/stage2/index.html

11 53 33 54 64 51 67 71 36 41 72 67 13 34 55 72 34 11 16 25 23 26 45 14 27 23 25 27 35 42 73 72 41
11 71 11 16 67 55 71 73 36 36 31 41 31 16 14 32 72 57 74 33 75 71 36 56 36 23 25 45 16 22 35 22
31 76 56 13 22 62 33 31 71 64 37 27 16 72 22 23 25 61 42 64 51 67 72 23 72 23 56 26 25 76 36
37 54 41 64 71 76 56 43 63 66 23 25 45 64 73 76 51 71 43 33 13 22 35 14 45 54 72 34 11 23 12 31
25 76 75 11 16 57 72 14 57 16 26 46 45 54 66 11 16 53 72 61 41 53 35 75 37 27 71 54 55 55 21 52
54 66 34 55 72 76 34 14 66 52 64 45 53 37 22 41 11 16 16 22 35 67 11 71 16 53 76 74 73 22 46 36 37 54
55 55 21 51 43 35 41 26 71 72 12 73 42 52 11 13 11 13 16 72 57 16 31 33 73 42 37 54 41
64 37 51 76 75 27 71 54 43 76 22 52 37 65 31 31 72 14 47 23 25 31 57 13 54 23 56 76 41 37
73 22 32 61 36 64 51 67 37 75 73 76 73 22
72 67 23 12 56 34 61 27 71 73 71 37 16 11 73 74 56 52 43 31 56 53 53 11 71 25 31 46 36 27 71
54 64 51 37 51 11 65 73 22 37 21 55 76 41 37 72 72 42 55 71 54 64 55 22 41 55 43 13 37
66 23 33 16 76 72 22 35 33 71 11 16 34 11 16 34 16 56 54 76 23 41 37 16 12 36 73 34 27 71 54
37 75 73 11 16 66 74 26 41 73 22 75 11 16 34 36 27 54 23 56 76 37 27 36 11 75 53 61 74 73 22 46 74
41 11 71 31 76 23 73 36 55 71 64 51 72 33 71 72 23 76 35 73 36 66 55 55 21 31 61 54 23 74 27
73 36 52 23 54 66 41 75 25 76 14 27 23 25 45
12 12 54 23 11 73 55 67 31 73 74 73 22 75 31 31 36 23 54 72 23 73 67 11 41 76 61 54 13 76 16 42
41 75 64 11 16 34 12 74 76 26 76 16 23 22 75 13 54 64 51 11 65 31 73 11 16 72 73 42 64 51 67 72 23 72 23
41 37 11 23 34 64 71 14 57 73 41 55 71 54 36 76 36 52 37 37 75 73 76 23 25 27 35 33 71
71 22 23 75 75 31 72 31 72 76 36 34 76 21 66 76 73 35 33 31 55 71 16 42 71 36 31 73 51
13 22 71 55 21 73 74 55 55 21 51 43 35 73 22

Fig. 3. Encrypted Uesugi cipher sequence containing 577 syllables

2   Previous Work

In the past, researchers have explored many strategies for attacking decipherment problems [2,3,4]. We follow a probabilistic approach, as suggested by Knight et al. [5]. That paper proposes a noisy-channel model of ciphertext production. First, a plaintext e is produced according to probability $P(e)$. Then, the plaintext is encoded as ciphertext c, according to probability $P(c|e)$. We estimate an n-gram model for $P(e)$ on separate plaintext data. We then adjust the $P(c|e)$ parameter values in order to maximize the probability of the observed (ciphertext) data. This probability can be written:

$$P(c) = \sum_e P(e) \cdot P(c|e) \tag{1}$$

The $P(c|e)$ quantity is the product of the probabilities of the individual token substitutions that transform e into c, i.e., the substitution probabilities make up the guessed key. Knight et al. [5] propose the EM algorithm [6] as a method to guess the best probabilistic values for the key. Once the key is settled on, the Viterbi algorithm can search for the best decipherment:

$$argmax_e P(e|c) = argmax_e P(e) \cdot P(c|e) \tag{2}$$

Knight et al. [5] also develop a novel technique for improving decipherment accuracy. Prior to decoding, they stretch out the channel model probabilities, using the Viterbi algorithm to instead search for:

$$argmax_e P(e|c) = argmax_e P(e) \cdot P(c|e)^3 \tag{3}$$

Finally, they provide an evaluation metric (number of guessed plaintext tokens that match the original message), and they report results on English letter substitution decipherment.

3 Present Contributions

The novel contributions of this paper are:

- We attack a more difficult cipher system. The Uesugi cipher has more characters than English, it has no word boundaries, and even the correct key yields multiple decipherment candidates. (This last feature makes it unsuitable for methods such as [7]).
- We attack cipher lengths that are not solved by low-order language models. We present an empirical study of training sizes, perplexities, and memory requirements for n-gram language models, and we relate language-model perplexity to decipherment accuracy.
- We find that higher-order n-gram models paradoxically generate worse decipherments, according to the method of [5]. We invent an adjustment to the EM objective function that solves this problem. This method allows much more accurate decipherment of shorter ciphers.
- We study the impact of random restarts for EM (not employed by [5] for letter substitution ciphers), and we find additional significant effects on accuracy.

4 Experimental Set-Up

In order to train language models over Japanese syllable sequences, we obtain a *roomaji* version[2] of the book *Tale of Genji* (c. 1021 AD). We process the roomaji into syllables and remove typographical errors. The final sequence contains approximately one million syllables and 65 unique syllable types. We split this data into three parts:

- LM training data (900,012 syllables).
- LM smoothing data (1419 syllables).
- Plaintext messages (various sizes).

We encipher the plaintext messages by first replacing *ga* with *ka*, and so forth, and then making substitutions according to the hidden i-ro-ha table 2. Our ciphertexts contain 46 unique types. Three of the cells in the 7×7 i-ro-ha table are unused in the cipher system.

Our evaluation metric for decipherment is the same as [5]—we count the number of matches between the guessed decipherment sequence and the original message. Note that a successful decipherment must not only re-create the correct key, but it must determine (using plaintext context alone) whether a cipher token should be decoded as *ka* or *ga*, etc.

The most common syllable in our data is *to*. The baseline of replacing every ciphertext token with *to* yields an accuracy of 4%.

---

[2] http://etext.virginia.edu/japanese/genji/roman.html

5   Experiments

To recap (from Equation 1), we search for values of the probabilistic substitution table P($c|e$) that maximize P(c):

$$P(c) = \sum_e P(e) \cdot P(c|e)$$

P($c|e$) is a 65 x 46 table. We begin with uniform probabilities, so that each of the 65 plaintext characters maps to any of the 46 ciphertext numbers with probability 1/ 46.

5.1   Language Models

Decipherment requires knowledge about the general plaintext language (in our case, Japanese), and this is captured in the P(e) language model. In our experiments, we create n-gram models (at various orders) out of plaintext training data (of various sizes). In collecting n-gram counts, we drop singletons when n>3. We smooth by interpolating with lower-order n-grams. We estimate one smoothing λ per n-gram order.

We represent LMs as weighted finite-state acceptors (WFSAs). For each LM, we measure its memory size (number of WFSA transitions) and its perplexity on held-out data. We measure perplexity on the plaintext messages, though of course, these messages are not used in the construction of any LMs. Figure 4 shows the relationship between memory requirements and LM entropy in bits/character (perplexity = $2^{entropy}$) of various LMs. Note that for any particular memory size a machine may have, we can select the LM order that gives the best perplexity.

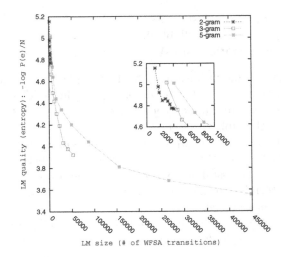

Fig. 4. Relationship between LM memory size and LM entropy. Plotted points represent language models trained on different amounts of data and different n-gram orders.

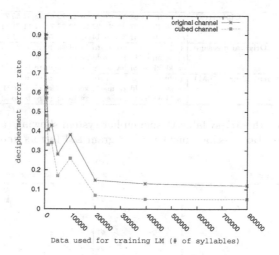

Fig. 5. Effect of LM training data size on decipherment error for the Uesugi cipher using 3-gram LM with (a) original channel decoding (b) cubing the channel probabilities before decoding (Knight et al. [5])

We use EM to search for the best table $P(c|e)$. EM is an iterative algorithm that improves $P(c)$ from one iteration to the next, until convergence. Because exact convergence is typically not reached, we terminate when the iteration-over-iteration change in $P(c)$ falls below a set threshold. We terminate early if 200 iterations are reached.

Figure 5 shows decipherment results when we use a 3-gram LM trained on various amounts of data. We can see that more LM data (i.e., more knowledge about the Japanese language) leads to better decipherment. Figure 5 also confirms that maximizing Equation 3:

$$argmax_e P(e|c) = argmax_e P(e) \cdot P(c|e)^3$$

is better than maximizing Equation 2:

$$argmax_e P(e|c) = argmax_e P(e) \cdot P(c|e)$$

Figure 6 shows the ciphertext, original message, and best decipherment obtained from using the 3-gram LM.

5.2   Random Restarts

The results so far employ a uniform starting condition for $P(c|e)$. We were surprised to find that different starting points result in radically different decipherment strings and accuracies. Figure 7 and 8 shows the result of the uniform starting condition along with 29 random restarts using the 2-gram and 3-gram LMs, respectively. Each point in the scatter-plot represents the results of EM

Ciphertext	11 53 33 54 64 51 67 71 36 41 72 67 13 34 55 72 34 11 16 25 23 26 45 14 27 23 25 27 35 42 73 72 41 11 71 11 16 67 55 71 73 36 36 31 41 31 16 14 32 72 57 74 33 75 71 36 56 36 23 ...
Original message	i du re no o ho n to ki ni ka n yo u go ka u i a ma ta sa bu ra hi ta ma hi ke ru na ka ni i to i a n go to na ki ki ha ni ha a ra nu ga su gu re te to ki me ki ta ...
Best decipherment (3-gram LM)	i du re no o ho n to ki ni ka n yo u go ka u i a ma ta sa bu ra hi ta ma hi ke ru na ka ni i to i a n go to na ki ki ha ni ha a ra _zu_ _ka_ su gu re te to ki me ki ta ...

Fig. 6. Sample from the 577-syllable Uesugi cipher system showing (a) Ciphertext (b) Original message (c) Best decipherment using 3-gram LM (errors underlined)

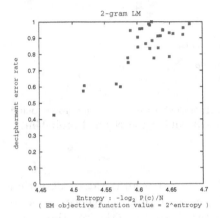

Fig. 7. Effect of random restarts on decipherment with a 2-gram model. Each point measures the result of a single EM run, in terms of EM's objective function (x-axis) and decipherment error (y-axis).

Fig. 8. Effect of random restarts on decipherment with a 3-gram model

from one starting point. The x-axis gives the entropy in bits/character obtained at the end of an EM run, and the y-axis gives the accuracy of the resulting decipherment. We observe a general trend—when we locate a model with a good $P(c)$, that model also tends to generate a more accurate decipherment. This is good, because it means that EM is maximizing something that is of extrinsic value. Figure 8 shows two distinct clusters. In one cluster, EM finds a very bad $P(c)$, and it returns a nonsense decipherment. In the other cluster, EM finds something much more reasonable. It is interesting that human cryptanalysts experience much the same phenomenon. When one has mentally committed to the correctness of a small set of substitutions (e.g., "72 must be *ro*!"), it can be very hard to escape during subsequent analysis.

Figure 9 shows the learnt substitution table from the best 3-gram decipherment with correct entries marked with *.

When we use random restarts for decipherment, we cannot simply pick the string with the best accuracy, as this would entail looking at the answer. Instead,

a	16* 1.00	e	65* 1.00		74* 0.71	o	64* 1.00		23* 0.90
	31* 0.77	ga	72* 1.00	ku	36 0.15		14* 0.79	ta	43 0.07
ba	45 0.16		35* 0.80		63 0.09	ra	61 0.12		41 0.03
	71 0.07	ge	23 0.20		67 0.05		72 0.10		75* 0.98
be	61* 0.67	gi	13 1.00		25* 0.87		33* 0.91	te	65 0.01
	71 0.32	go	55* 1.00		74 0.06	re	14 0.09	ti	12* 1.00
	76 0.47	gu	74* 1.00	ma	53 0.04		22* 0.96	to	71* 1.00
bi	73 0.46		31* 0.93		12 0.03	ri	56 0.04		53* 0.72
	13 0.06	ha	76 0.07	me	56* 1.00	ro	21* 1.00	tu	76 0.15
bo	51* 0.83	he	61* 1.00		66* 0.82		42* 0.90		12 0.13
	45 0.17	hi	27* 1.00	mi	75 0.10	ru	36 0.09		34* 0.93
bu	45* 0.56		51* 0.92		22 0.08		26* 0.78	u	12 0.07
	53 0.44	ho	31 0.08	mo	37* 1.00	sa	72 0.22		31 0.76
da	23* 1.00		45* 0.91		34 0.99		27 0.39	wa	54 0.24
	75* 0.54	hu	27 0.09	mu	31 0.01	se	47* 0.31	wo	52* 1.00
de	52 0.46	i	11* 1.00	na	73* 1.00		26 0.30		13* 0.83
di	12* 0.79	ka	72* 1.00		67* 0.94	si	76* 1.00	yo	66 0.09
	46 0.21	ke	36 0.09	n	54 0.06	so	43* 1.00		37 0.08
	71* 0.66		36* 0.97	ne	56 1.00		57* 0.34	yu	46* 1.00
do	76 0.21	ki	34 0.03	ni	41* 1.00		66 0.18	za	73 1.00
	36 0.12		55* 0.97	no	54* 1.00	su	53 0.17	ze	61 1.00
	31 0.53	ko	51 0.03		32* 0.54		34 0.17	zi	⋆ 1.00
du	53* 0.24			nu	62 0.45		71 0.14		51 0.86
	34 0.22							zo	12 0.09
									37 0.05
									57* 0.70
								zu	16 0.16
									32 0.15

Fig. 9. Substitution table learnt from best 3-gram decipherment showing P(c|e) values. Correct entries are marked by *.

we pick the string that results from the model with the best P(c). As seen in Figure 8, the best P(c) does not guarantee the best accuracy. However, we are able to significantly improve on the uniform-start decipherment through random restarts. Because of this, the rest of the experimental runs in this paper employ 30 random restarts.

5.3 Objective Function

We intuitively feel that more knowledge of Japanese will lead to better decipherments. This is true for long ciphers like the one we have seen so far. What about shorter ciphers? How do the different n-gram LMs perform when used for deciphering shorter ciphers? We split the original 577-syllable cipher in half to create a shorter 298-syllable cipher, and apply the same decipherment strategy. Table 1 shows best decipherment error rates associated with different LM orders (trained on the same data) for the two ciphers (longer and shorter versions). We observe that we can get better accuracies with higher n-gram LMs for the longer cipher (577 syllables). However on the shorter cipher (298 syllables), when we increase the n-gram order of the LM, we find that decipherment surprisingly gets worse. Inspection reveals that the 5-gram decipherment contains many more actual Japanese words. While the text is nonsense, from a certain distance it appears more Japanese-like than the 2-gram decipherment. When we take measurements, we find that the 5-gram LM strongly prefers the (nonsense) string from its decipherment over the (sensible) correct answer, in terms of P(e).

Table 1. Decipherment error rates with different LMs on long/short ciphers

LM model	Long Cipher (577 syllables)	Short Cipher (298 syllables)
2-gram	0.46	0.89
3-gram	0.12	0.96
5-gram	0.09	0.95

Table 2. Decipherment error rates on two different Uesugi ciphers using (a) Original EM objective function (b) New objective function (square-rooting LM)

LM model	Long Cipher (577 syllables)		Short Cipher (298 syllables)	
	EM(original)	EM(new objective fn.)	EM(originial)	EM(new objective fn.)
2-gram	0.46	0.29	0.89	0.78
3-gram	0.12	0.05	0.96	0.78
5-gram	0.09	0.02	0.95	0.61

It is therefore quite opinionated in the wrong direction. We find that the 2-gram LM is less opinionated—it still prefers its decipherment over the correct answer, but not to such a degree.

The consequence of the 5-gram model being so wrongly opinionated is that the substitution model probabilities learn to become more fuzzy than usual, in order to accommodate the LM's desire to produce certain strings. The learnt substitution table is much more non-deterministic than the true substitution table (key).

We remedy this. Recall from Equation 1 that EM's objective function is:

$$P(c) = \sum_e P(e) \cdot P(c|e)$$

Here, the P(e) factor carries too much weight, so in order to reduce the "vote" that the LM contributes to EM's objective function, we create a new objective function:

$$P(c) = \sum_e P(e)^{0.5} \cdot P(c|e) \tag{4}$$

Note that this is substantially different from the proposal of [5] to stretch out the substitution probabilities after decipherment has finished. Instead, we actually modify the objective function EM uses during decipherment itself.

Table 2 shows the improvements we get from the new objective function at various n-gram orders for the two ciphers. The results are much more in accord with what we believe should happen, and gets us to where better n-gram models give us better decipherment error on short ciphers. In addition, the new objective function substantially improves long-cipher decipherment error over the methods of [5].

To sum up our experiments on the Uesugi cipher, Figure 10 shows a nice correlation between LM entropy and end-to-end decipherment accuracy.

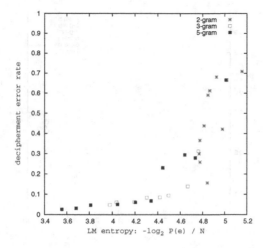

Fig. 10. LM entropy vs. decipherment error rate (using various n-gram order LMs on the 577-syllable Uesugi cipher)

6   English Results

For direct comparison with [5], we include graphs with English letter-substitution results. Figures 11-13 give the results.

Table 3 shows improvements achieved on a 98-letter English cipher when using the new objective function introduced in Section 5.3. For the graphs in Figures 12 and 13, we also improve LM smoothing and thereby obtain further

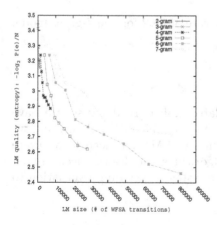

Fig. 11. Relationship between LM memory size and LM entropy for English letter-substitution decipherment

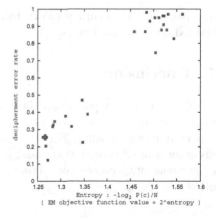

Fig. 12. Effect of random restarts on EM decipherment for a 98-letter English cipher using 2-gram model

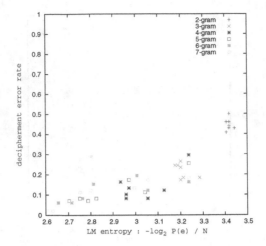

Fig. 13. LM entropy vs. decipherment error rate (using various n-gram order LMs on a 98-letter English cipher)

Table 3. Decipherment error rates on a 98-letter English cipher using (a) Original EM objective function (Knight et al. [5]) (b) New objective function (square-rooting LM). All the LMs are trained on 1.4 million letters of English data, and use 10 random restarts per point.

LM model	EM(original) error-rate	EM(new objective fn.) error-rate
2-gram	0.41	0.43
3-gram	0.59	0.16
5-gram	0.53	0.11
7-gram	0.65	0.11

improvements in accuracy (down to an error-rate of 0.02 for the 7-gram model trained on 7 million letters).

7   Conclusion

We have studied a particular Japanese syllable cipher. In doing so, we have made several novel improvements over previous probabilistic methods, and we report improved results. Further improvements in LMs may lead to accurate decipherment of shorter texts, and further algorithms may lead to accurate decipherment of more complex Japanese cipher systems, including translation to other languages.

Acknowledgements

This research was supported by the Defense Advanced Research Projects Agency under SRI International's prime Contract Number NBCHD040058.

References

1. Merialdo, B.: Tagging English text with a probabilistic model. Computational Linguistics 20(2), 155–171 (1994)
2. Peleg, S., Rosenfeld, A.: Breaking substitution ciphers using a relaxation algorithm. Comm. ACM 22(11), 598–605 (1979)
3. Olson, E.: Robust dictionary attack of short simple substitution ciphers. Cryptologia 31(4), 332–342 (2007)
4. Knight, K., Yamada, K.: A computational approach to deciphering unknown scripts. In: Proceedings of the ACL Workshop on Unsupervised Learning in Natural Language Processing (1999)
5. Knight, K., Nair, A., Rathod, N., Yamada, K.: Unsupervised analysis for decipherment problems. In: Proceedings of the COLING/ACL (2006)
6. Dempster, A.P., Laird, N.M., Rubin, D.B.: Maximum likelihood from incomplete data via the EM algorithm. Journal of the Royal Statistical Society Series 39(4), 1–38 (1977)
7. Ravi, S., Knight, K.: Attacking decipherment problems optimally with low-order n-gram models. In: Proceedings of the EMNLP (2008)

Dialogue Strategies to Overcome Speech Recognition Errors in Form-Filling Dialogue

Sangwoo Kang[1], Songwook Lee[2], and Jungyun Seo[3]

[1] Department of Computer Science, Sogang University, Korea
[2] Department of Computer Science, Chungju National University, Korea
[3] Department of Computer Science & Interdisciplinary Program of Integrated Biotechnology, Sogang University, Korea
swkang@sogang.ac.kr, leesw@cjnu.ac.kr, seojy@sogang.ac.kr

Abstract. In a spoken dialogue system, the speech recognition performance accounts for the largest part of the overall system performance. Yet spontaneous speech recognition has an unstable performance. The proposed postprocessing method solves this problem. The state of a legacy DB can be used as an important factor for recognizing a user's intention because form-filling dialogues tend to depend on the legacy DB. Our system uses the legacy DB and ASR result to infer the user's intention, and the validity of the current user's intention is verified using the inferred user's intention. With a plan-based dialogue model, the proposed system corrected 27% of the incomplete tasks, and achieved an 89% overall task completion rate.

Keywords: dialogue, strategy, speech recognition, word error rate, form-filling dialogue, sub-dialogue, generation.

1 Introduction

A dialogue system is an efficient interface for human-computer interaction that helps users achieve their goals using natural language. Recent research on dialogue systems has focused on spoken dialogue systems that combine a text-based dialogue system with automatic speech recognition (ASR) system. ASR is classified as either isolated speech recognition or continuous speech recognition, based on the recognition unit. A dialogue system requires spontaneous speech recognition technology, which is a type of continuous speech recognition. However spontaneous speech recognition systems have not exceeded an accuracy of 70% in a laboratory environment [1]. One reason for this is that ASR system and dialogue system have been unable to utilize mutual feedback because of being independently studied. However, more recently, a design that integrated the two systems was tried, but was limited to a small working area [2].

We propose a postprocessing method that uses the domain knowledge after ASR process to overcome the performance problems of ASR system in a spoken dialogue system. The language processing analyzes the speech recognition result, or sentence, as a speech-act, action, named entity, etc. The speech-act is used as the most important information for recognizing a user's intention, and for Dialogue management. In the proposed method, we use information from the legacy database to infer the current

W. Li and D. Mollá-Aliod (Eds.): ICCPOL 2009, LNAI 5459, pp. 282–289, 2009.
© Springer-Verlag Berlin Heidelberg 2009

speech-act. The validity of the user's analyzed intention can then be verified using the inferred speech act. The proposed system has to generate system responses dynamically for erroneous ASR results.

2 Related Works

2.1 Effects of Speech Recognition Errors on Speech-Act

It is difficult to analyze the intention of a user when the data is contaminated with speech recognition errors. Specifically, an erroneous speech-act may result in misunderstanding the user's goal. Speech-acts are the most important factor when determining a task goal. Thus, speech-act analysis should work robustly throughout the entire dialogue system.

The following examples by Cavazza [3] show how to process a dialogue between a system and user, where speech-acts are mis-recognized. Fig. 1 shows the system generating an incorrect response, because the system recognizes the user's speech-act "reject" as "accept."

> U1: Do you have any movies?
> S1 : I found 22 programs for your request.
> I would suggest: "Twelve Monkeys."
> U2: Good if I mean anything for long.
> (Could you find me anything funny)
> S2: Here is "Twelve Monkeys," then. Goodbye!

Fig. 1. Example about generating an incorrect response

2.2 Researches for Correction of Speech Recognition Errors in a Dialogue System

Studies on methods for correcting speech recognition errors have mostly focused on the language model or acoustic model in ASR system. Recently, researchers have been making efforts to use dialogue knowledge in these studies. Gorrell [4] divided the system's answers into twelve categories according to the patterns of speech recognition errors, and then chose the most correct answer using Latent Semantic Analysis (LSA).

This paper proposes dialogue strategies that are adoptable in the field of *form-filling dialogues*. Form-filling dialogues use a form to allow the system to share knowledge with a user during a dialogue. The user's goal is achieved through inserting, deleting, modifying, or searching the form. Most task-oriented dialogues have a bias toward form-filling [5]. Litman and Allen [6] introduced a plan theory into a dialogue model. A plan-based dialogue model uses discourse and domain knowledge, which is called a recipe. This recipe consists of constraints, applicable conditions, sub-actions, and effects, and is governed by inference rules. The user's intention is recognized by a plan tree that links the user's intentions with the recipes. The system can process a mixed initiative dialogue using an obligation stack, which arranges the system's responses and belief space [7]. Oh [8] applied a plan-based model in Korean. However the performance of those models was not guaranteed in the spoken dialogue system, because they assumed that there were no errors in the input data from ASR and Natural Language Understanding (NLU) systems. Therefore, it is necessary to devise methods to overcome the errors from ASR and NLU systems in the application of a spoken dialogue system.

3   System Architecture

A traditional spoken dialogue system consists of ASR system, NLU system, and dialogue manager. ASR system transforms a user's speech into text. The NLU system analyzes the speech-act, the action, and named-entities related to the action to determine the user's intention, and then delivers them to the dialogue manager [9]. The performance of the NLU system cannot be trusted when ASR results are incorrect. Therefore, a scheme is needed to determine whether or not the results of ASR and NLU systems are correct, as well as a system that can manage the dialogue dynamically according to the verified results. Fig. 2 shows the architecture of the proposed system. The error detection module verifies the NLU output. When the output of this module is valid, it is delivered to the dialogue manager. A system initiative negotiation sub-dialogue strategy is tried if the module is invalid.

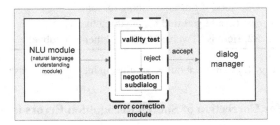

Fig. 2. Dialogue system with error correction module

The next section will explain this negotiation sub-dialogue strategy in detail.

4   Dialogue Strategy for Overcoming Speech Recognition Errors

In a *form-filling dialogue*, the words spoken by the user are used as commands for managing the form, such as for *insertion, deletion, modification,* and *searching,* and each command corresponds with an action and a speech-act. When the system fails to analyze the user's command, it tries to infer the user's command based on the above four commands. For inference, the system manages a sub-dialogue for negotiation using a user's database and knowledge. Confirmation strategies are divided into implicit confirmation and explicit confirmation. Explicit confirmation is a method where the system directly asks whether the results of ASR are correct or not, whereas implicit confirmation is a method where the system confirms the accuracy by watching the user's reaction to the system's utterance.

We propose strategies for generating a negotiation sub-dialogue for speech recognition errors. Each was devised based on recognition error patterns. The first strategy deals with an unknown user action and unknown speech-act for a given utterance. The second applies to a pattern where the speech-act is determined to be a *"wh-question,"* but the *target* is unknown. Each strategy has its own inference and confirmation-generation rules. These will be explained in the next sub-section.

4.1 Pattern with Unknown Speech-Act and Unknown Action

The system may not be able to determine the speech-act of the user's current utterance when ASR fails to recognize the predicate related to both the speech-act and action (shown in Fig. 3). In this case, the system does not manage the dialogue further, because it does not know the user's intention. However, in the proposed method, we can continue the dialogue by inferring the user's intention using the user's database and some recognized words.

We use the *domain object* to represent the state of a task. For example, as illustrated in Fig. 3, the recognized words are *"today," "one hour"* and *"Hong Gildong"* each of which is used to fill a corresponding property of the domain object. The domain object is used as the condition for a database search. Then, based on the result of the database search, the system continues the dialogue using the three proposed strategies.

Pattern with Unknown Speech-act and Unknown Action

Result of database search		Applying strategy
1. No tuple	→	Strategy #1
2. One tuple	→	Strategy #2
3. More than one tuple	→	Strategy #3

recognized words by ASR system :
today, one, p.m., Hong gildong

domain object

date	time	location	person	content
today	1		Hong Gildong	

user database

date	time	location	person	content
today	1	cafeteria	Hong Gildong	lunch meeting
today	2	K Hall	Park Chanho	seminar
today	6	C Hall	Lee Seungyup	lunch meeting

Fig. 3. Database search procedure in strategy #2

Strategy #1 guesses at the insertion of data for the user's intention, because the system found nothing in its search using the given properties, which are composed of recognized words. In strategy #2, the system infers the modification or deletion of data, except for that inserted, to determine the user's intention, because only one tuple is searched. The system uses explicit or implicit confirmation to determine the correct intention from among all the candidates. In strategy #3, because more than one tuple is searched, the system should ask the user for additional knowledge, and should add the given knowledge into the previous properties. With the updated properties, the system searches the database again and continues the dialogue using strategies #1, #2, and #3 recursively. Fig. 4 shows the processes of the three strategies, where both the

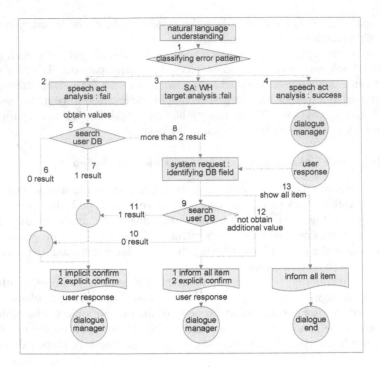

Execution process
1. Classification of error pattern. 2. Pattern with unknown speech-act and unknown action. 3. Pattern with "wh-question" and unknown target. 4. Pattern with known speech-act and known action. 5. Searching user's DB using recognized words. 6. Applying strategy #1. 7. Applying strategy #2. 8. Applying strategy #3: Acquiring additional properties. 9. Re-searching user's DB. 10. Applying strategy #1. 11. Applying strategy #2. 12., 13. Exceptional handling.

Fig. 4. Execution process in pattern with unknown speech-act and unknown action

speech-act and action are unknown. The next paragraph will explain details of strategy #2 using an example.

Fig. 5 shows the candidate list of user utterances for the recognized words. The system guesses at the user's utterance from among seven utterances based on the recognized properties. To respond to every possible intention of the user, the system uses explicit and implicit confirmation. If only one tuple was discovered after searching the user's DB using the recognized properties, it is possible for the utterance to involve a modification or deletion of the tuple. To deal with this situation, the system seeks an answer to user system utterance #2 in Fig. 6, which is confirmed explicitly. Utterance #2 is used to confirm whether or not the inferred intention of the user is correct. In other cases, the user's utterance may be a question concerned with properties (utterance #3 ~ #6). In addition, utterance #7 is a case where the user's knowledge conflicts with the system's knowledge. To solve this conflict, the system generates system utterance #1, which is a kind of implicit confirmation as shown in Fig. 6. Utterance #1 implicitly informs the user that they have the wrong information. Consequently, the system can satisfy every candidate intention.

```
Recognized properties
today, one, lunch, meeting

Candidate utterance
1. Change the lunch meeting at one PM today.
2. Cancel the lunch meeting at one PM today.
3. Inform the lunch meeting at one PM today.
4. Who have I the lunch meeting at one PM today?
5. Where have I the lunch meeting at one PM today.
6. Do I have the lunch meeting at one PM today?
7. Resister the lunch meeting at one PM today.
```

```
user  : 오늘  오후 한시에  식사  약속
         ( lunch meeting one PM today )

system 1: I find one schedule to have a lunch
          with Mr. Hong in cafeteria.
system 2: Which task do you want
          a deletion or modification ?
```

Fig. 5. The candidate list of user utterances   **Fig. 6.** Dialogue example of strategy #2

4.2 Pattern with "wh-question" and Unknown Target

A "wh-question" is a kind of speech-act. However, it is different from other speech-acts in that it requires an additional property: the *target* of the question. The *target* is what the user wants to know through the "wh-question" utterance. If the system cannot determine the *"target"* of a user's question, the system may give the user wrong information.

Let us explain how to process this pattern where the speech-act is a "wh-question" and the *target* is unknown. This pattern is classified by the following three detailed cases.

Pattern with *"wh-question"* and unknown target

Result of database search		Applying strategy
1. No tuple	→	Strategy #4
2. One tuple	→	Strategy #5
3. More than one tuple	→	Strategy #6

Strategy #4 is used to solve the case where there is no tuple after the DB search with recognized properties. Although the system does not recognize the word for the *target*, the system can give an answer that says that "there is no information." Therefore, this is implicit confirmation, because the system implicitly informs the user that he/she has the wrong information. In strategy #5, the system infers that the user wants to know a specific property. Although the system searches the tuple containing what the user wants to know, the system cannot give the user a correct answer, because the system does not know *the target* yet. Our choice is to give an answer that contains enough properties to include the correct answer, using recognized words. Strategy #6 is similar to strategy #3, as the system acquires additional properties though more questions. The system updates the domain object using additional properties, then searches the user's database again. Based on the results of the DB search, the system continues the dialogue recursively using the strategies.

5 Experiments and Results

The proposed dialogue strategies were adopted in the field of form-filling dialogues. We experimented with strategy #2 using a plan-based dialogue system dealing with form-filling dialogue.

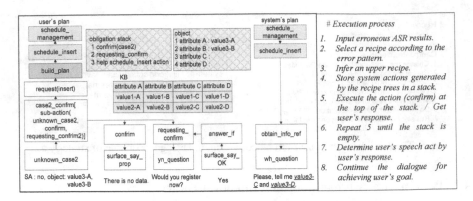

Fig. 7. General plan-based model using proposed method

For the purpose of our experiments, we expanded the plan-based dialogue system used by Oh [12]. Our system constructed a discourse structure using *recipes*. So, additional recipes were built for the proposed dialogue strategies. *"case2_confirm"* is the upper recipe of *"surface_unknown_case2,"* and initiates a negotiation sub-dialogue by strategy #2. This recipe can generate implicit and explicit conformation, and the user's intention is determined based on the user's response.

Fig. 7 shows how to expand the proposed method into a general plan-based model. Our proposed method has high portability, with only a minimum effort needed to modify the confirmation representation.

5.1 Results

We used the ASR system of Ahn and Jung [10] for the spoken dialogue recognition. In the experiments, we used a confidence level of 0.8 for the ASR results. Therefore, when the confidence value was higher than 0.8, the system regarded the recognition of the word as successful. However, if the confidence value was lower than 0.8, the recognition had failed, and the system entered the negotiation sub-dialogue. In our experiments, 200 dialogues were used. We measured the task completion rate when the confidence value of a word was lower than 0.8.

As shown in Table 1, the performance of the base system not using the proposed strategies was 85%. However, the performance of our system using the proposed strategies was 89%, 4% higher than the base system. Consequently, our system corrected 27% of the overall errors.

Table 1. Experiment results

	Base system	Proposed system	Error Recovery Rate
Task completion rate	85%	89%	27%

6 Conclusion and Future Work

We proposed dialogue strategies to overcome speech recognition errors. When the system cannot determine the speech-act of an utterance due to speech recognition errors, it confirms the user's intention by gathering additional knowledge with negotiation sub-dialogue strategies. Users can achieve their goal through this sub-dialogue even if speech recognition errors occur.

The proposed system corrected 27% of the incomplete tasks. When a system fails to understand a user's command, most dialogue systems retry from the beginning of the dialogue. This is inefficient, and the performance of a dialogue system may be undervalued. However, our system attempts to use a negotiation sub-dialogue to achieve the goal of the user, which will lead to increased confidence in the system. The task completion rate of the proposed system was improved by 4%, but the user-sensed improvement would be higher than 4% because rather than start over from the beginning of the dialogue, the system continues with an efficient sub-dialogue.

In the future, we will try to devise a robust model that covers various dialogue phenomena and study aspects of cognitive science besides linguistic approaches. We will also continue to work on resolving error propagation problems from ASR system.

Reference

1. Hain, T.: Implicit modelling of pronunciation variation in automatic speech recognition. Speech Communication 46, 171–188 (2005)
2. Kim, K., Lee, C., Jung, S., Lee, G.G.: A Frame-Based Probabilistic Framework for Spoken Dialog Management Using Dialog Examples. In: 9th SIGdial Workshop on Discourse and Dialogue, pp. 120–127. Association for Computational Linguistics, USA (2008)
3. Cavazza, M.: An Empirical Study of Speech Recognition Errors in a Task-oriented Dialogue System. In: 2th SIGdial Workshop on Discourse and Dialogue, pp. 98–105. Association for Computational Linguistics, Denmark (2001)
4. Gorrell, G.: Language Modelling and Error Handling in Spoken Dialogue System. Licentiate thesis, Linköping University, Sweden (2003)
5. Goddeau, D., Meng, H., Polifroni, J., Seneff, S., Busayapongchai, S.: A Form-Based Dialog Manager for Spoken Language Applications. In: 4th International Conference on Spoken Language, pp. 701–705. IEEE Press, USA (1996)
6. Litman, D., Allen, J.: A Plan Recognition Model for Subdialogue in Conversations. Cognitive Science 11, 163–200 (1987)
7. Chu-Carroll, J., Carberry, S.: Generating information-sharing sub- dialogues in expert-user consultation. In: 14th International Conference on Artificial Intelligence, pp. 1234–1250. AAAI, UK (1995)
8. Oh, J.: The Design of Plan-based Dialogue System In Task Execution Domain. M.S. thesis, Sogang University, Korea (1999)
9. Walker, M., Passonneau, R., Boland, J.: Quantitative and Qualitative Evaluation of Darpa Communicator Spoken Dialogue Systems. In: 39th Annual Meeting of the Association for Computational Linguistics, pp. 512–522. Association for Computational Linguistics, France (2001)
10. Ahn, D., Chung, M.: One-pass Semi-dynamic Network Decoding Using a Subnetwork Caching Model for Large Vocabulary Continuous Speech Recognition. IEICE Transaction. Information and Systems E87-D(5) 5, 1164–1174 (2004)

Research on Domain Term Extraction Based on Conditional Random Fields

Dequan Zheng, Tiejun Zhao, and Jing Yang

MOE-MS Key Laboratory of NLP and Speech,
Harbin Institute of Technology, 150001 Harbin, China
{dqzheng,tjzhao,yangjing}@gmail.com

Abstract. Domain Term Extraction has an important significance in natural language processing, and it is widely applied in information retrieval, information extraction, data mining, machine translation and other information processing fields. In this paper, an automatic domain term extraction method is proposed based on condition random fields. We treat domain terms extraction as a sequence labeling problem, and terms' distribution characteristics as features of the CRF model. Then we used the CRF tool to train a template for the term extraction. Experimental results showed that the method is simple, with common domains, and good results were achieved. In the open test, the precision rate achieved was 79.63 %, recall rate was 73.54%, and F-measure was 76.46%.

Keywords: Term Extraction, CRF Model, Unithood, Termhood.

1 Introduction

Terms are the most fundamental units used to represent and encapsulate a concept in any specific domain [1]. Automatic domain term extraction (ADTE) has important significance and practical value in natural language processing. It is the key step in automatic domain ontology construction, and is widely used in information retrieval, information extraction, data mining, machine translation and other information processing fields. Algorithms for automatic term extraction compute at least two indexes. One called domain index, and the other is unit index [2]. Kage introduced Unithood and Termhood[3]. Unithood refers to the degree of strength or stability of syntagmatic combination or collocation. Termhood refers to the degree that a linguistic unit related to domain-specific concepts [4].

Generally, there are two kinds of measures for estimating the unithood. One is the internal measure [5,6,7], the other kind of measure is the contextual measure [8,9]. In this paper, we computed the mutual information and the left/right entropy of a term candidate. The most commonly used measurement for termhood is the TF/IDF, it calculates the termhood by combining word frequency with a document and word occurrence within a set of documents.

W. Li and D. Mollá-Aliod (Eds.): ICCPOL 2009, LNAI 5459, pp. 290–296, 2009.
© Springer-Verlag Berlin Heidelberg 2009

2 Related Works

The research on terms extraction is mainly based on corpus, ADTE is further classified terms into related fields' terminology. Terms extraction involves two steps, the first step extracts term candidates which have high unithood and the second step verifies them as terminology measured by their termhood. Nakagawa limited the term candidates in compound nouns and single-nouns, and his works only focused on the relationship between single-nouns and compound nouns, his method cannot deal with non-compound terms [10]. Eide Frank focused on domain-specific key phrase extraction, he considered only two attributes for discriminating between key phrases and non-key phrases, i.e. the TF/IDF score of a phrase, and the position of the phrase's first appearance in the whole document [11]. Frank mainly focused on key phrases of a document, the second feature may not help much in extracting terms. Chan proposed a statistical model for finding domain specific words (DSW). He defined Inter-Domain Entropy (IDE) as acquiring normalized relative frequencies of occurrence of terms in various domains. Terms whose IDE are above a threshold are unlikely to be associated with any certain domain. Then the top-k% candidates can be determined as the domain specific words of the domain.

At present, in Chinese ADTE, Computational Linguistics Institute of Peking University in conjunction with the Chinese standards Research Center did a project, they developed an information technology and technology building standards, extracted related term candidates from the corpus, and then they filtered it using context information and chapter structure. Jing-Shin Chang used bootstrapping method to extract domain vocabulary automatically [12]. Sung-chen Lin extracted domain terms automatically using topic words [13], he thought that terms always appear at the same time with topic words, and these terms with high frequency are domain terms.

3 Domain Term Extraction Method

The most important factors for CRF model are that, suitable features can be chosen according to the special task and the use of simple features to express the complex natural language phenomenon. In this paper, in order to make the method be domain independent, we use as less domain knowledge as possible. We adopted several common features, which are the words themselves, the POS of the word, semantic information, left information entropy, right information entropy, mutual information and TF/IDF. Compared with our previous works, we have added the semantic information as a new feature in this paper.

Among the seven features, the words themselves provide some domain knowledge, for example, some words, such as "枪", "机","舰", "弹", can be suffix of terms in military domain. The POS of the words is another important feature of the term. In general terms are single-nouns and compound nouns, and also include some verbs. Semantic information is tagged based on HowNet. Left and right entropies are important measures for judging if a word is the borderline of a term, so it can be said to be a term's unithood. Left and right entropies can measure the uncertainty of a word's collection with its adjacent words. For example, if the left word of a word w varies, we can treat w as the left border of a term. The formula below can be used to estimate the left information entropy of a word.

$$E_l(w) = -\sum_{a \in A} p(w_{la}/w) \log(p(w_{la}/w))$$ (1)

In formula (1), $E_l(w)$ is the left information entropy of word w, A is the word set which appears to the left of the word w。 w_{la} is the string composed of the word w and the word to the left of w. $p(w_{la}/w)$ is, given w, the probability of the word to the left of w is a . In the same way, we can get the right information entropy formula。

In CRF model, the token is the largest sequential component. It is composed of non-separators. Generally speaking the token is the basic unit in CRF, and it has a different meaning according to different tasks. In this paper a token refers to a word, so we can't calculate the term candidates' mutual information and TF/IDF. We adopted the words' information entropy, mutual information and TF/IDF. The formula of mutual information of words w_1 and w_2 is as show below:

$$M(w_1, w_2) = \frac{p(w_1, w_2)}{p(w_1) \times p(w_2)}$$ (2)

In formula (2) , $p(w_1, w_2)$ is a coherent-probability of words w_1 and w_2.

We supposed that the TF/IDF of the words composing terms helps to estimate the TF/IDF of terms, so we treat the words' TF/IDF as a feature of CRF model. The TF/IDF formula is:

$$\text{TF/IDF}(w) = 1 - \frac{\text{Doc\_count}(w)}{\text{count}(w)}$$ (3)

Doc_count(w) is the number of the file in which a word w appears, and count(w)is total number of word w that appears in all the files。 The value of TF/IDF is in the range of 0 and 1. The larger the TF/IDF is, the more domain knowledge w carries。

As far as we know, CRF model treats the features' value as a tag. But the value of left and right information entropy, mutual information and TF/IDF are float numbers, so they can't be used directly as features. We used K-Means clustering to classify these values. In this paper the features have been divided into 10 grades according to their values, and each grade represents a class. How many classes to be divided for the best results can not be determined in this paper because experiments were only done for 10 grades.

4   Experiments and Evaluation

In this paper, the tool for POS tagging was designed by HIT [14], and the tag sets can be found in "HIT Chinese tree tagging sets". We use the symbols B, I, and O to label the terms. B is the beginning of a term, I is the other part of a term., and O are the other words.

4.1 Experimental Sets

The Experiment was divided into three groups. We used POS, left and right informa-tion entropy and TF/IDF as features in group1, added mutual information into the model in group 2, and added semantic information in group 3. Different templates were used in group 1, group 2 and group 3. The scale of the corpus was measured by the number of words.

4.2 Evaluation Index

Generally speaking, there are four indexes to evaluate in domain term extraction. The four indexes are precision, recall, F-measure, and coverage,

(1) Precision for term extraction

$$C = \frac{the\ number\ of\ correct\ terms}{the\ total\ mumber\ of\ terms\ that\ extracted\ from\ the\ corpus} \qquad (4)$$

(2) Recall for term extraction

$$C = \frac{the\ number\ of\ correct\ terms}{the\ mumber\ of\ terms\ that\ the\ corpus\ contains} \qquad (5)$$

(3) Coverage for term extraction

$$C = \frac{the\ number\ of\ correct\ terms}{the\ total\ mumber\ of\ terms\ that\ the\ domain\ has} \qquad (6)$$

(4) F-term measure

$$F = \frac{2 \times P \times R}{P + R} \times 100\% \qquad (7)$$

To compute the term coverage we need a domain terminology. But now there is only one IT terminology which is supplied by the Institute of Computational Linguis-tics, Peking University and we don't have a military terminology, so we can't calcu-late the coverage in our experiment. We just used precision, recall, and F-measure, to evaluate the results.

4.3 Experiments Results and Analysis

Our training data came from the military news of Sohu network. And we did experi-ments with varying sizes of training data. The test data was the articles from the magazine "Modern Military" 2007, volumes 1 to 8. Due to the large number of terms, it will be time consuming to calculate the precision and the recall rate. This paper only calculated the relative precision and recall rate of terms extracted only from Vol.3 of "Modern Military" 2007 magazine. Figure 1 shows the results using different features. In group 1, we used five features, i.e. word itself, POS, left and right infor-mation entropy and TF/IDF; in group 2, we added mutual information into the model; in group 3, we also added the semantic information as feature.

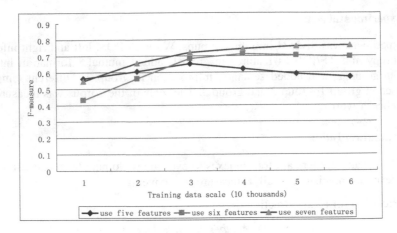

Fig. 1. Experiment results

In figure 1, the vertical unit represents 10,000 words. It can be seen in figure 1, that the F-measure improved with a certain degree after we added the mutual information as feature in training the CRF model. But it was not significantly improved when the training data achieved 30,000 words. The best result in figure 2 is that the precision rate achieves 73.24 %, recall rate is 69.57%, and F-measure is 71.36%. In group 3, we also added the semantic information as feature, the F-measure is improved with the training data scale. When the training data achieved 60,000 words, the best results in figure 2 is that the precision rate achieves 79.63 %, recall rate is 73.54%, and F-measure is 76.46%.

To further verify the correctness of our method, we made detailed analysis of the terms we extracted. Table 1 illustrates some terms that appeared in corpus with high frequency, while table 2 illustrates some terms that only appeared once in the corpus.

Table 1. Terms with high frequency

NO.	terms	NO.	terms	NO.	terms	NO.	terms
1	武器	6	空军	11	作战	16	美军
2	战斗	7	海军	12	雷达	17	战争
3	军事	8	陆军	13	攻击	18	指挥
4	部队	9	战斗机	14	航母		
5	国防	10	无人机	15	联合军演		

In table 1, it can be seen that most of terms with high frequency are single words. When we added POS and words features in training CRF template, the features related to the frequency were not dominant. As a result, we could extract some terms that appeared with lower frequency.

Table 2. Terms only appearing one time

NO.	terms	NO.	terms
1	LAM巡弋攻击导弹	6	IN-SAT）系列地球同步通信卫星
2	A-10攻击机	7	发动机演示器
3	AGM-65 "小牛" 空地导弹	8	国家安全综合体
4	"捕食者B"（MQ-9）无人机	9	实验卫星系列
5	M270/M270A1多管火箭炮	10	1234E型轻型护卫舰

There are no standard test data and evaluation for term extraction in Chinese, so we can not compare our results to other experiments. But the following are some of other evaluations done by others like, JianZhou Liu from Huazhong Normal University automatic extracted terms from open corpus, and the precision of the first 10,000 terms was 75.4% [15]. In the literature [16], Wenliang Chen extracted domain terms from classified corpus including financial, military, sports and legal fields. He got different results in different domains. The highest precision rate he achieved was 94.87% in the sport fields, while the lowest was 74.95%. He pointed out that if we only relied on domain corpus the highest precision would be 43.40%. Tingting He used Proton string decomposition method to extract terms. The precision of terms which were composed by more than three words was 72.54% [17].

5   Conclusion

This paper presented a new method to extract domain terms. According to the experimental results, our method based on CRF model performed well. We got good results using only six features. If we had added other features into the model, the results may have been even better. For example, we could get the best grade number and best templates for the model through experiments. Of course, what is more important is that we can add some domain features such as keywords feature, dictionary feature etc. There are several methods to make our proposal achieve optimum performance. In future works, we will experiment in various domains, and improve on our proposal.

Acknowledgement. This work is supported by the national natural science foundation of China (No. 60736044) and the National High-Tech Development 863 Program of China (No. 2006AA010108).

References

1. Zhifang, S.U.I., Chen, Y.: The Research on the Automatic Term Extraction in the Domain of Information Science and Technology. In: Proceedings of the 5th East Asia Forum of the Terminology
2. Luo, S., Sun, M.: Two-Character Chinese Word Extraction Based on Hybrid of Internal and Contextual Measures. In: Proceedings of the Second SIGHAN Workshop on Chinese Language Processing, pp. 24–30 (July 2003)

3. Kageura, K., Umino, B.: Methods of automatic term recognition. A review Terminology 3(2), 259–289
4. Chen, Y.: The Research on Automatic Chinese Term Extraction Integrated with Unithood and Domain Feature, Master Thesis in Beijing, Peking University, p. 4
5. Dunning, T.: Accurate Method for the Statistics of Surprise and Coincidence. Computational Linguistics 19(1), 61–74
6. Cohen, J.D.: Highlights: Language- and Domain-independent Automatic Indexing Terms for Abstracting. Journal of American Soc. for Information Science 46(3), 162–174
7. Schone, P., Jurafsky, D.: Is knowledge-free induction of multiword unit dictionary headwords a solved problem? In: Proceedings of EMNLP (2001)
8. Sornlertlamvanich, V., Potipiti, T., Charoenporn, T.: Automatic corpus-based Thai word extraction with the C4.5 learning algorithm. In: Proceedings of COLING 2000 (2000)
9. Chien, L.F.: Pat-tree-based adaptive keyphrase extraction for intelligent Chinese information retrieval. Information Processing and Management 35, 501–521
10. Nakagawa, H., Mori, T.: A simple but powerful automatic term extraction method. In: COMPUTERM 2002 Proceedings of the 2nd International Workshop on Computational Terminology, Taipei,Taiwan, August 31, 2002, pp. 29–35 (2002)
11. Frank, E., Paynter, G.W., Witten, I.H., Gutwin, C., Nevill-Manning, C.G.: Domain-specific keyphrase Extraction. In: Proceedings of 16th International Joint Conference on Artificial Intelligence IJCAI 1999, pp. 668–673 (1999)
12. Chang, J.: Domain Specific Word Extraction from Hierarchical Web Documents: A First Step Toward Building Lexicon Trees from Web Corpora. In: Proceedings of the Fourth SIGHAN Workshop on Chinese Language Learning, pp. 64–71
13. Lin, S.: Topic Extraction Based on Techniques of Term Extraction and Term Clustering. Computational Linguistics and Chinese Language Processing 1(9), 97–112 (2004)
14. Mitlab, http://mitlab.hit.edu.cn
15. Liu, J., He, T., Ji, D.: Extracting Chinese Term Based on Open Corpus. In: The 20th International Conference on Computer Processing of Oriental Languages, Shengyang, pp. 43–49 (2003)
16. Chen, W., Zhu, J.: Automatic Learing Field Words by Bootstrpping. In: Proceedings of the 7th National Conference On Computational Linguistics, pp. 67–72. Tsinghua university press, Bingjing (2003)
17. He, T., Zhang, Y.: Automatic Chinese Term Extraction Base on Decomposition of Prime String. Computer Engineering (December 2006)

PKUNEI – A Knowledge–Based Approach for Chinese Product Named Entity Semantic Identification

Wenyuan Yu, Cheng Wang, Wenxin Li, and Zhuoqun Xu

Key Laboratory of Machine Perception,
Peking University, 100871, Beijing, China
{yuwy,cici,lwx,zqxu}@pku.edu.cn

Abstract. We present the idea of Named Entity Semantic Identification that is identifying the named entity in a knowledge base and give a definition of this idea. Then we introduced PKUNEI - an approach for Chinese product named entity semantic identification. This approach divided the whole process into 2 separate phases: a role-model based NER phase and a query-driven semantic identification phase. We describe the model of NER phase, the automatically building of knowledge base and the implementation of semantic identification phase. The experimental results demonstrate that our approach is effective for the semantic identification task.

Keywords: named entity, semantic identification.

1 Introduction and Background

In the domain of business information extraction (IE), there is a strong need of the named entity recognition of the product names known as the task of product NER. Whereas some realistic business IE applications call for more semantic information from the text of named entities, such as to semantically identify which product the product name actually stands for in a knowledge base of products. For instance, if we want to search articles about certain product, we need to identify all the product names in the article text representing this product. There is still a gap between product NER and the further requirements of semantic information extraction. Thus, we would like to introduce a new task called Named Entity Semantic Identification to solve the problem. Compared with the traditional NER, the task of Named Entity Semantic Identification is to find out the exact entity which the text that recognized as named entity really stands for. Figure 1 is an example which demonstrates the task of named entity semantic identification: the term "JoyBook S52" was recognized as a product named entity and finally identified as the No.86091 Entity in the knowledge base.

This paper describes the definition of product named entity semantic identification and an approach for the product named entity semantic identification, in which a class-based language model and a query-based identification mechanism were employed. This system is divided into 2 phases. At first phase, we use the class-based Markov model to tag all the potential named entity in the given text. At the second

W. Li and D. Mollá-Aliod (Eds.): ICCPOL 2009, LNAI 5459, pp. 297–304, 2009.

phase, we use a query-based identification mechanism to find out which entities in the knowledge-base match the product named entities in the given text. Experimental results show that this system performs well in the domain of IT products.

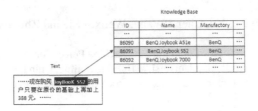

Fig. 1. An Example of Product Named Entity Semantic Identification. "JoyBook S52" was recognized as product named entity and identified as the No.86091 Entity in the knowledge base.

2 PKU NEI (Peking University Named Entity Identification)

2.1 Consideration

PKU NEI (Peking University Named Entity Identification) is an approach that solved the Product Named Entity Semantic Identification task using an automated generated knowledge-base. And a series of experiments shows its high reliability and high accuracy.

The pipeline of task of Product Named Entity Identification could be intuitively divided into 2 phases: Named Entity Recognition Phase and the Semantic Identification Phase. Generally, at the Named Entity Recognition Phase, we first do a product NER job to detect the potential named entities appeared in the input text. At the Semantic Identification Phase, based on the result of the NER Phase, we identify corresponding entities to the entities detected by the NER phase. Different from the concerns of traditional NER, in the Named Entity Recognition Phase of Product Named Entity Semantic Identification, we do not care much about the exact words in the named entities, because it is just an intermediate result, we could refine it in the second phase. Instead, the recall-measure of the NER means much more, and it is the bottleneck of the whole system's recall performance, because in the process describe above, the recall could not be promoted in the second Semantic Identification Phase.

The Semantic Identification Phase has different concerns from the first phase. It requires a knowledge base. The key problem is how to deal the ambiguity problem and how to identify the entity accurately in a short time.

2.2 Named Entity Recognition Phase

2.2.1 Method
PKU NEI adopts an algorithm to do the NER task based on a role-model [9]'s variant. As we discussed in Section 2.1, the task of this phase is different from general NER tasks, so we designed a new process to deal with the problem with new observation set, new role set and new procedure.

Similar as the H. Zhang *et al.* [9]'s algorithm, our algorithm uses the result of the segmentation and POS-tagging task as features. Moreover, as we can use knowledge base, we classify the tokens with more categories besides their POS tag: potential company/organization/brand name and potential model names.

We tag the token as potential company/organization/brand name (CN) by detecting if the token matches the company/organization/brand name in the knowledge base.

We tag tokens as potential model names (MN) when they composed only in non-Chinese characters or digits.

We tag tokens as potential limitation attributes (LA) when they in a manually maintained list contains product catalog names such as "笔记本电脑", "手机", "显示器" or some attributes product usually have, such as "超薄" "智能". It depends on the domains. These words usually play a different role from those words that have same POS-tag.

And we tag the tokens by usual POS-tagging, if these tokens could not be tagged as CN, MN or LA. We adopt the POS tagging system called PKU-POS set which is defined by Peking University. Tokens are tagged like "nr" "v" "u"...

And we define a set OB as:

$$OB : \{o \mid o \in PKU\text{-}POS \lor o = CN \lor o = MN \lor o = LA \}$$

Besides, taking account of the task's feature, we defined a set of roles for product NER phase as following.

Table 1. Roles set of Product NER task

Roles	Significance	Examples
S1	Brand Name in NE	现在有商家对*方正*S650N再次进行调价
S2	Limiting attribute in NE, including the series name of NE.	联想 Thinkpad x300*超薄*笔记本电脑
S3	Model name in NE	DELL XPS *M1330*是戴尔第一款13.3寸屏幕的笔记本电脑
S4	Neighboring token in front of NE	*这款*同方火影N3000外形设计时尚、豪华
S5	Neighboring token in following NE	神舟天运F525S*配备*了读卡器
S6	Others	盈通G8800GS-384GD3标准版*显卡又狂降了一百元*

So we have set ROLES defined as:

$$ROLES : \{S1, S2, S3, S4, S5, S6\}$$

To simplify the problem, we consider the problem as a HMM task. Given a sequence of text $W_1W_2...W_n$, we could generate a observation sequence of HMM by tagging them in set OB. After that we got the observation sequence of HMM :

$o_1o_2...o_n$. And the state set is just the same as the role set ROLES. After we trained the parameters using maximum-likehood method, we have a HMM built. After we calculate the most likely sequence of hidden states, we can using the templates demonstrated in Table 2 for matching the sequence, and find out the potential NEs.

Table 2. Templates for Product NE (for IT hardware passages)

Templates	Examples
(S1 +…) S1 + S3	这款*联想 天逸 F31A-ST*配备的250GB硬盘
S2 + S3 + S5	走进中关村网站收到了索尼今年推出的新一代直联式*刻录机 VRD-MC3 并*进行了简单的试用
S1 + S3 + S2	Diamond 对世人发出它们怪兽般的怒吼——*Monster MX200 声卡*诞生了
S4 + S3 + S5	*购买176S 的*消费者
S4 + S3 + S2	现代 *的Q15N 液晶显示器*悄悄升级了

2.3   Semantic Identification Phase

2.3.1   Overview

The PKU NEI uses a query based method to identify the entity names to the entry in knowledge base.

The knowledge base contains the following information for entities: entity's standard name and its variants, entity's catalog, entity's manufactory, the segmentation the entity's name into tokens and a weight of each part. The performance of this phase is highly depended on the quality of the knowledge base. In the section 3.3.2, we would emphases the method to build the knowledge base automatically. The method of determining named entities' entries (like finding out Enity_ID) in knowledge base could be summarized as 2 parts: query and score. Task of query calls for finding out all the entities contains at least one token in the knowledge base. Task of score is that for all entities match at least one token, we calculate a score, and the score is determined by the matching-degree. The most matching one is the result entity.

Besides taking account of the matched tokens' weight in knowledge base, context information about the catalog and manufactory is also important. In section 3.3.3, we will describe our method.

2.3.2   Construction of Knowledge Base in IT Hardware Domain

Based on the structured information in some hardware related website, we designed a method to construct a knowledge base with 82839 entities in the area of IT hardware without much participating of human. To design the method to construct the knowledge base, we would take several concerns into consideration. First, the method should be automatic. Even with in a specific domain, there are still thousands kinds of product could be found. Starting to construct a knowledge base from scratch manually is not possible. Fortunately, there are usually data source we could use for helping us to construct a knowledge base. Second, we need high quality of estimating the weight-value of each token of entity names, because the semantic identification uses the weight-values to identify the entities.

There are a lot of hardware websites on the internet which provide the news about the hardware products and benchmarks between products. The hardware website usually maintains a structured information bases to help the visitors to find the related information about a specific product (Fig.2 is typical sample). In the webpage, we can retrieve the information about the entities' names, aliases, manufactories and the related articles in the website. We crawl all page of product information base in this website like Fig.2 and we exploit this information to construct the knowledge base.

After tokenizing each product's name and its aliases, the remaining problem is to determine the weight of each token.

Let t is a token appeared in product e's name, V(t | e) is the weight of t in entity e.

$$V(t \mid e) = P(e \mid t) = \frac{P(e)}{\sum_{e' \; contains \; token \; t} P(e')} \quad (1)$$

We use the V(t | e) to estimate the importance of the token t in identifying the product entity e.

And in practice, we assume that the text frequency of entity is linear related with document frequency of entity, so we let N is the total number of articles, and we use the C(e) / N to estimate P(e), where C(e) is the count of e's related articles(Fig.2 (2)). We storage each token t in each entity e's weight V(t | e) in the knowledge base. Table.3 is an example of the generated knowledge base's entry.

Table 3. An example entry in the generated knowledge base

Standard Name	惠普 Compaq Presario V2000
Aliases:	hp compaq presario v2000
Manufactory	惠普 hp
Tokens & Weights:	(惠普, 0.057) (compaq, 0.161) (presario, 0.266) (v2000, 0.516) (hp, 0.059)
...	...

2.3.3 Query and Score

With the knowledge base like Table.3, we could identify the potential entities in NER phase to the knowledge base by querying like what search engine usually does.

(1) provides a way to evaluate the importance of a token for certain entity. The matching-degree in PKU NEI is the sum of V(t | e) for all matching token t. In addition, we considered the context information in this phase. If an entity's manufactory is appeared near the recognized entity name (by NER Phase), there would be a good chance that the entity is the product of this manufactory. So we would add a factor to the matching-degree. With the consideration of all these factors, we suppose the entity in the knowledge base with the highest matching-degree is the result we want.

Fig. 2. The screen shot of the webpage which providing the information about Canon EOS 50D. (1) Area No.1 framed in red rectangle in the picture is the manufactory, product name and aliases. (2) Area No.2 framed in red rectangle in the picture is the list of the related articles.

For identifying the entity effectively, we use the tokens in knowledge base's entries to create an inverted index table. And for the potential entity names $W_iW_{i+1}\ldots W_j$ in the text $W_1W_2\ldots W_n$, we query the tokens W_k, $W_{k+1}\ldots W_l$ in the knowledge base using the inverted table, and we get the a series sets of entities R_k, $R_{k+1}\ldots R_l$, where R_i is the set of entity which contains the token W_i, Let $R = \bigcup_{k \leq i \leq l} Ri$. Then for each e in the set R, calculate the

$$M_e = \sum_{k \leq i \leq l \wedge e \ containsWi} wi + \begin{cases} \dfrac{1.0}{d+4}, & \text{the token } W_{k-d} \text{ identicating the } e's \text{ manufactory} \\ 0, & \text{no tokens indicating } e's \text{ manufactories before} \end{cases}$$

"1.0/(d + 4)" is the factor of context manufactory information. It would be a enhancement when the manufactory information is located near the recognized named entity.

And e with $M_e = max(M_{e'})$, is the entity we want.

3   Experiments

We have tested our approach in hardware product domains. For testing the algorithm of NER phase, we selected 1000 paragraphs containing IT hardware product entities in many catalog from http://www.intozgc.com/, and we tag these paragraphs manually. We selected randomly for training set in size of 100 and 500 paragraphs. And the rest of paragraphs are used for testing. Compared with [4], our method has a higher F-Measure. Different corpus and test data might be an important cause to consider. Our usage of knowledge might be another cause, like the work of tagging CN and LA in NER phase provide a more precise observation description. Another reason may be the easier standard of judging the result. If NER result could provide enough information for the process of semantic identification phase, we suppose that it is OK.

Table 4. Comparision results between NER with 100-size trainingdata and NER with 500-size training data

Method	Recall	Precision	F-Measure
100-size	0.84	0.79	0.819
500-size	0.93	0.85	0.890

For training data of 100 paragraphs, its result is much worse than the 500 case. I think efficient training data is crucial.

For determining the knowledge base using by the second phase, we spidered the website of http://product.zol.com.cn/ and calculate the weight for the entities. Finally we got an entity knowledge base containing 82839 entities covering many catalogs.

Table 5 is illustrating the overall performance in our experiments.

Table 5. Recall and precision of the task (with 500 training cases)

Phase	Recall	Precision	F-Measure
NER Phase	0.93	0.85	0.890
Semantic Identification Phase	1.00	0.98	0.990
All	0.93	0.83	0.880

Because the Semantic Identification Phase accepts the NER phase's potential NE unconditionally, so the Semantic Identification Phase got a recall 1.00. The performance of precision of this phase got a good result when the input potential NE is correct.

4 Conclusion and Future Work

In this research, our main contributions are:

1. We proposed the concept of Named Entity Semantic Identification for helping the Information Extraction tasks. It focuses on identifying the named entities in text. And we developed a system named PKU NEI for this task.
2. In NER Phase of PKU NEI, we proposed a refinement of a role-model-variant which applicable to the Chinese Product Named Entity Recognition.
3. In Semantic Identification Phase of PKU NEI, we provide a systematic way of building required knowledge base automatically. And based on this knowledge base, we provide an approach to semantically identify the recognized entity names in text.

The weakness of role-model was responsible for the failure of some cases. The performance of this phase is the bottleneck of the whole system. In the future, our research should put more attention on the refinement of the NER phases and try to drive this approach for practical system.

Acknowledgements

This research is sponsored by the National Grand Fundamental Research 973 Program of China under Grant No.2007CB310900, National Innovation Program for Undergraduates and the Supertool Inc.

References

1. Pierre, J.M.: Mining Knowledge from Text Collections Using Automatically Generated Metadata. In: Karagiannis, D., Reimer, U. (eds.) PAKM 2002. LNCS, vol. 2569, pp. 537–548. Springer, Heidelberg (2002)
2. Bick, E.: A Named Entity Recognizer for Danish. In: Lino, et al. (eds.) Proc. of 4th International Conf. on Language Resources and Evaluation (LREC 2004), Lisbon, pp. 305–308 (2004)
3. Niu, C., Li, W., Ding, J.h., Srihari, R.K.: A Bootstrapping Approach to Named Entity Classification Using Successive Learners. In: Proceedings of the 41st ACL, Sapporo, Japan, pp. 335–342 (2003)
4. Liu, F., Liu, J., Lv, B., Xu, B., Yu, H.: Product Named Entity Recognition Based on Hierarchical Hidden Markov Model. In: Proceedings of Forurth SIGHAN Workshop on Chinese Language Processing, pp. 40–47. Juje, Korea (2005)
5. Bikel, D.M., Miller, S., Schwartz, R., Weischedel, R.: Nymble.: a High-Performance Learning Name-finder. In: Fifth Conference on Applied Natural Language Processing, pp. 194–201 (1997)
6. Isozaki, H., Kazawa, H.: Efficient supportvector classifiers for named entity recognition. In: Proceedings of the COLING 2002, pp. 390–396 (2002)
7. Paliouras, G., Karkaletsis, V., Petasis, G., Spyropoulos, C.D.: Learning decision trees for named-entity recognition and classification. In: Proceedings of the 14th European Conference on Artificial Intelligence, Berlin, Germany (2000)
8. Sun, J., Zhou, M., Gao, J.: A Class-based Language Model Approach to Chinese Named Entity Identification. Computational Linguistics and Chinese Language Processing 8(2), 1–28 (2003)
9. Zhang, H., Liu, Q., Yu, H., Cheng, X., Bai, S.: Chinese Named Entity Recognition Using Role Model. Special issue Word Formation and Chinese Language processing of the International Journal of Computational Linguistics and Chinese Language Processing 8(2), 29–60 (2003)
10. Zhao, J., Liu, F.: Product named entity recognition in Chinese text. Lang. Resources & Evaluation 42, 197–217 (2008)

Experiment Research on Feature Selection and Learning Method in Keyphrase Extraction

Chen Wang, Sujian Li, and Wei Wang

Institute of Computational Linguistics, Peking University
100871 Beijing, China
wangchen386@gmail.com, lisujian@pku.edu.cn, pierro@126.com

Abstract. Keyphrases can provide a brief summary of documents. Keyphrase extraction, defined as automatic selection of important phrases within the body of a document, is important in some fields. Generally the keyphrase extraction process is seen as a classification task, where feature selection and learning model are the key problems. In this paper, different shallow features are surveyed and the commonly used learning methods are compared. The experimental results demonstrate that the detailed survey of shallow features plus a simpler method can more enhance the extraction performance.

Keywords: Keyphrase extraction, Feature selection, Learning method.

1 Introduction

Usually the main idea of the documents is expressed by one or more words, named keyphrases. With keyphrases, the readers can rapidly catch the important content of the documents. Moreover, keyphrases can be used as the index, through which users can find the documents they want. For example, when a search engine searches the documents with keyphrases as indexes, it can give the results more precisely. However, most of the keyphrases are indexed manually, which cost a huge amount of labor and time. Thus, automatically indexing keyphrases is a significant work.

Keyphrase extraction and keyphrase assignment are two general approaches of automatically keyphrase indexing. Keyphrase assignment, in despite of its better performance, is difficult to accomplish. As most of keyphrases appear in the documents and these keyphrases capture the main topic, the keyphrases extraction techniques are commonly used.

Our research focuses on keyphrase extraction from Chinese news in People Daily. Here we treat the keyphrase extraction process as a supervised learning task. First, we collect all of the phrases from the documents and labeled them as either positive or negative examples. The positive phrases mean that they can serve as the keyphrases, while the negative ones are those which cannot serve keyphrases. At the same times, we extract some shallow features from the samples and used learning method to build the model. When we run the model on the test documents, the examples marked positive are considered as keyphrases.

The remainder of this paper is organized as follows. Section 2 discusses related work. Section 3 describes our system architecture. Various shallow features are

W. Li and D. Mollá-Aliod (Eds.): ICCPOL 2009, LNAI 5459, pp. 305–312, 2009.

introduced in Section 4. Section 5 illustrates the experiment results and Section 6 presents our conclusion and future work.

2 Related Work

Turney (1999) implemented a system for keyphrase extraction called GenEx, with parameterized heuristic rules and a genetic algorithm [1]. He used some frequency features and some position features [2]. Frank et al. (1999) implemented another system named Kea with the Bayesian approach [3]. He used only two features: TF×IDF and first occurrence. A lot of experiments have been done which proved the performances of Kea and GenEx are statistically equivalent. These two systems are simple and robust. However, limited by their performance, it's still unpractical to use these original systems to replace manual work.

Based on these two works above, many new systems have been brought forward. Mo Chen (2005) presented a practical system of automatic keyphrase extraction for Web pages [4]. They used the structure information in a Web page and the query log data associated with a Web page collected by a search engine server. They added some features about structure extracted from html documents. Since they treated a Web page as a special text and promoted the performance in the area of Web page processing, it's not a general model of text processing.

Olena Medelyan (2006) improved the Kea system by using the thesaurus and adding semantic information on terms and phrases [5]. The new system, named Kea++, can sometimes double the performance of Kea. Basing on Kea, Kea++ adds two features: the length of the phrase in words and a feature related to thesaurus. However, the performance of this system highly depends on the quality of the thesaurus, which is not public available.

In this paper, we try to survey more shallow features to describe the characteristic of keyphrases more precisely and more comprehensively. We hope the new system is a general model of text processing and don't rely on the thesaurus. We experiment on several popular learning models, such as decision tree, Naïve Bayes, SVM and CRF, to compare the performance of these systems.

3 System Overview

Keyphrase extraction is seen here as a classification task. First we collected some documents indexed with keyphrases. All the word sequences with length less than 6 are extracted from the documents and serve as the input of next modules. Because many of the word sequences are meaningless and inappropriate for being keyphrases, we apply some filter rules to acquire a set of candidate keyphrases. The filter rules will be introduced below. The indexed keyphrase can be seen as positive samples, and the other candidate keyphrases are labeled as negative samples. Each candidate keyphrase is represented by a feature vector x_i. Then whether a candidate is a keyphrase or not will be $y_i \in \{Yes, No\}$, Yes means a keyphrase, and No means not being a keyphrase. Then, all the candidate phrases composed of the training set $\{<x_i, y_i>\}$. According to the training data, we can approximately learn a function $f:X \rightarrow Y$, where X means the set of feature vectors, and Y is {*Yes, No*}. When a new article comes, we also use the filter rules to get all the candidate keyphrases, and generate a feature vector for each candidate phrase. With the function f, we can acquire the corresponding result whether a candidate phrase belongs to keyphrases. This process is illustrated in Figure 1.

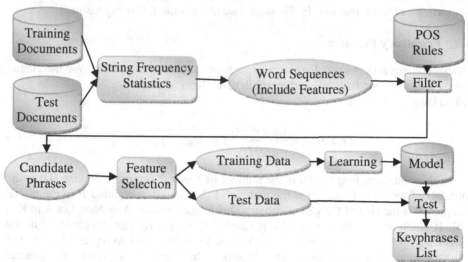

Fig. 1. System Architecture

The acquisition of candidate keyphrases is the foundation of our work. We hope to obtain all the phrases as the candidate keyphrases which are included in the collection of word sequence. We assume that a word sequence with higher frequency and specific syntactic structures is preferred to be a phrase.

Filter Rules 1: $\forall S = w_1 w_2 \ldots w_n$ is a Chinese word sequences. If freq $(S) < 2$, then S $\notin$ { x | x is a keyphrase}.

We filter the word sequences which occur less than two times and get the set of keyphrase candidates because most of keyphrases appear in article more than once.

Filter Rules 2: $\forall S = w_1 w_2 \ldots w_n$ is a Chinese word sequences. PS $= p_1 p_2 \ldots p_n$ is the POS sequences of S. If PS $\notin$ { x | x is a POS sequence of training data}, then S $\notin$ { x | x is a keyphrase}.

With the training data, we got most of the meaning combination of POS. Using these POS sequences, we can filter the meaningless word sequences.

When obtaining the shallow statistical features of the phrase set, we select several ones. The details will be discussed in flowing section. Then we choose several supervised leaning method to build the model. After scoring the candidate phrases, the phrases with high score are tagged as keyphrases. We use cross-validation to evaluate the performance of our system.

4 Feature Design

Through feature designing, we use several features which were proposed in the former papers and add some new features. Some of these features are statistic trend of the keyphrases. Other features are intuitively designed. We also evaluate the importance of these features .In this paper, we discuss the following features.

4.1 Frequency Features

These features reflect some frequency aspects of candidate keyphrases. We use Nagao string frequency statistics algorithm to calculate these features.
TF×IDF

$$TF \times IDF = \frac{\text{freq}(P, D)}{\text{size}(D)} \times (-\log_2^{\frac{\text{df}(P)}{N}})$$ (1)

In this equation, freq (P, D) is the number of times P occurs in D. size (D) is the number of words in D. df (P) is the number of documents containing P in the global corpus. N is the size of the global corpus. This feature was used by Nevill.et.al in Kea [6]. It combines the frequency of a phrase's use in a particular document with the frequency of that phrase in general use. We use term frequency to represent the use of phrases in particular document and document frequency to represent the general usage. Because some leaning algorithms are linear, we add TF and IDF as other 2 features independently.
ISF

$$ISF = -\log_2^{\frac{\text{sf}(P)}{N}}$$ (2)

ISF stands for Inverse Sentence Frequency. In this equation, sf(P) is the number of sentences containing P in the global corpus. N is the size of the global corpus. Like IDF, a phrase's sentence frequency indicates how common it is. A phrases which is less appears often contain especial and important meaning. We present this features to estimate the importance of sentence difference in keyphrase extraction.

4.2 Position Feature

First Occurrence

$$First\ Occurrence = \frac{\text{numbefore}(P, D)}{\text{size}(D)}$$ (3)

In the equation, numbefore (P, D) is the number of word that precede the phrase's first appearance in D. size(D) is the number of words in D. This feature represents the position of the phrase's first appearance. It was also used by Nevill.et al. in Kea [6]. This feature represents how much of the document precedes first appearance of the phrase.

4.3 Features Combining the Frequency and the Position

Number in Title
Title is the most concise abstract of a document. This feature was used by Mo Chen in Kex [4].

Rate in First Paragraph

$$Rate\ in\ First\ Paragraph = \frac{freqFirstPara(P, D)}{freq(P, D)} \tag{4}$$

In the equation, freqFirstPara (P,D) is the number of times P occurs in the first paragraph of D. freq(P,D) is the number of times P occurs in D. Authors often present their topic in the earliest paragraph. Thus, phrases which appear in the first paragraph may be the keyphrases. We define this feature to estimate the importance of the phrases in this special paragraph.

Rate in First Sentence

$$Rate\ in\ First\ Sentence = \frac{freqFirstStc(P, D)}{freq(P, D)} \tag{5}$$

In the equation, freqFirstStc (P,D) is the number of times P occurs in the first sentences of every paragraph in D. First sentence always include the critical point of the whole paragraph. We propose this feature to estimate the importance of topic sentence and the phrases in this particular sentence.

4.4 Phrases Length

This feature was used by Olena Medelyan in Kea++ [5]. Length indicates how much words the phrase include. It's a good feature to filter long and meaningless phrases. This feature is independent with the context of article, so we classify it specially.

4.5 Documents Features

Word Number
This is the number of words in document.

Keyphrase Number
This is an approximate number of keyphrases. We can estimate this feature using the feature *Word Number* discussed before.

Keyphrase Rate
This feature is calculated as *Keyphrase Number* divided by *Word Number*. It indicates how we estimate the number of keyphrases. Higher keyphrase rate maybe also show higher possibility of positive examples.

5 Experiments

5.1 Sample Filter

In our document collection, there are 392 documents with 2,118 keyphrases. 780 keyphrases appear somewhere in the body of the corresponding documents. The first step is extracting phrases from documents. We extracted all of the word strings whose length is not greater than 5 words. There are 69,064 negative examples but only 780 positive examples. Secondly, we calculate the term frequency and filter out the word string which appears only once. We accomplish this filter because we can filter out lots of useless phrases both in the training data and the test data. Then we got 17807 negative examples and 683 positive examples. The ratio of positive examples ascends from 1.12% to 3.83%. Because of the low ratio of positive examples, we try to use POS Rules to filter out the negative examples. The result, however, is not very ideal. While we filter a number of negative examples, we also filter nearly half of the positive examples at the same time. Due to the lack of keyphrases (not more than 2118), we add some manual work on POS filter.

5.2 Feature Evaluation

We evaluate the features to choose the important ones. Using information gain attribute evaluation (in Weka 3.5[1] attribute selection module) and ranker search method, we got the importance order of the features. Table 1 shows the importance of each feature.

Table 1. Rank of the Features

Rank	Feature	Importance
1	TF	0.03264
2	TF×IDF	0.02578
3	ISF	0.02576
4	Number in Title	0.02332
5	Length	0.01719
6	Word Number	0.01435
7	IDF	0.01117
8	Keyphrase Rate	0.0087
9	Keyphrase Number	0.00725
10	First Occurrence	0.00515
11	Rate in First Paragraph	0.00429
12	Rate in First Sentence	0

Using TF×IDF and First Occurrence, Kea learns with Naïve Bayes method. Kea++ adds Length and another feature which is related to the thesaurus. Because the lack of thesaurus data, we list the original data here. In the first row and the second row of Table 2, the data shows the performance of these systems in original document collection (in English) [5].

---

[1] Weka 3: Data Mining Software in Java, http://www.cs.waikato.ac.nz/ml/weka.

In the third row and the fourth row of Table 2, the data shows the experiments on our document collection (in Chinese). From the result of Kea (in the first row of Table 2 and the third row of Table 2), we can draw a conclusion that the performance of extraction techniques is less dependent on languages. According to the rank of features in Table 1, we establish a system which is temporarily called "our system". In our system, we chose some appropriate features (TF ×IDF, First Occurrence, TF, ISF, IDF, Number in Title, Length and Keyphrase Number) and learn the training data with Naïve Bayes method. We could easily find out that appropriate shallow features bring the improvement of the performance. The performance of our system is better than Kea's and our system maybe enhance the performance of Kea more than Kea++.

Table 2. The performance of Kea and Kea++ in English Documents and the performance of Kea and Our System in Chinese Documents

System	Precision	Recall	F
Kea(English)	13.3	12.4	12.0
Kea++(English)	28.3	26.1	25.2
Kea(Chinese)	46.2	7.2	12.4
Our System(Chinese)	28.1	40	33

5.3 Leaning Model

To solve this learning problem, we use C4.5, Naïve Bayes, SVM, CRF algorithm to accomplish the classifier. We still choose TF ×IDF, First Occurrence, TF, ISF, IDF, Number in Title, Length and Keyphrase Number as the features. The results are showed in Table 3.

Table 3. Result of Learning Models

Algorithm	Precision	Recall	F
C4.5	74.5	6	11.1
SVM	76.3	6.6	12.1
CRF	24.44	9.48	13.66
Naïve Bayes	28.1	40	33

C4.5 is a kind of decision tree. We use J48 (in Weka 3.5) as an accomplishment of C4.5. This model can be generated rapidly and get the capability of processing continual data. But this model will excessively depend on one main feature and ignore the others.

In the experiment of SVM, we use SMO algorithm (in Weka 3.5). SVM is a great classifying algorithm, especially a small sample. This algorithm can find the global optimization model. A main disadvantage of SVMs is the complexity of the decision rule, which requires the evaluation of the kernel function for each support vector. This linear model does not fit the task very well.

CRF is the most popular algorithm these years. It's powerful in sequence labeling tasks, such as Named Entity Reorganization, Information Extraction and Text

Chunking. CRF model could overcome the data sparseness and solve the "Label Bias" problem. Unfortunately, this model could not suit the tasks which are not sequential.

Naïve Bayes is a simple model, but it gets a high quality in classifying problem, especially when the features are independent with each other. From the result above, we could draw the conclusion that Naïve Bayes method can suit to the task of keyphrase extraction.

6 Conclusion

This paper discusses the feature selection and learning methods through a lot of experiments of keyphrase extraction. With the appropriate features and learning algorithm, we can improve the performance of keyphrase extraction system, even better than thesaurus based system. However, there's a long way to reach the ideal result. In the future work, we will consider adding some semantic knowledge as heuristics, such as thesaurus and topic word, to improve the system in some specific area.

Acknowledgement

This work is supported by NSFC programs (No: 60603093 and 60875042), and 973 National Basic Research Program of China (2004CB318102).

References

1. Turney, P.D.: Learning to Extract Keyphrases from Text. Technical Report ERB-1057, National Research Council, Institute for Information Technology (1999)
2. Turney, P.D.: Learning Algorithms for Keyphrase Extraction. Information Retrieval 2, 303–336 (2000)
3. Witten, I.H., Paynter, G.W., Frank, E., Gutwin, C., Nevill-Manning, C.G.: Kea: Practical Automatic Keyphrase Extraction. In: Proc. of the 4th ACM Conference on Digital Libraries (1999)
4. Chen, M.: A Practical System of Keyphrase Extraction for Web Pages. In: CIKM 2005, Bremen, Germany, October 31-November 5 (2005)
5. Medelyan, O., Witten, I.H.: Thesaurus Based Automatic Keyphrase Indexing. In: JCDL 2006, Chapel Hill, North Carolina, USA, June 11–15 (2006)
6. Frank, E., Paynter, G.W., Witten, I.H., Gutwin, C., Nevill-Manning, C.G.: Domain-Specific Keyphrase Extraction. In: Proceedings of the Sixteenth International Joint Conference on Artificial Intelligence, July 31-August 2006, pp. 668–673 (1999)

Korean-Chinese Machine Translation Using Three-Stage Verb Pattern Matching

Chang Hao Yin, Young Ae Seo, and Young-Gil Kim

NLP Team, Electronics and Telecommunications
Research Institute, 161 Gajeong-Dong, Yuseong-Gu Daejon, 305-350, Korea
{yustian,yaseo,kimyk}@etri.re.kr

Abstract. In this paper, we describe three-stage pattern matching approach and an effective pattern construction process in the Korean-Chinese Machine Translation System for technical documents. We automatically extracted about 100,000 default verb patterns and about 10,000 default ordering patterns from the existing patterns. With the new three-stage approach, additionally using default verb and ordering patterns, the matching hit rate increases 3.8% , comparing with one-stage approach.

Keywords: Korean-Chinese machine translation, verb pattern, pattern construction.

1 Introduction

Recently some Korean global companies promote the localization policy in Chinese market. To break the language barrier we developed a Korean-Chinese machine translation system focusing on the technical domain. We adopt pattern-based approach, which simplifies traditional three-stage rule-based MT system to 2 stages - analysis and verb pattern matching part. Verb pattern plays the most important role in our system. Syntactic transformation and verb sense disambiguation almost depends on the verb patterns. In our system, each Korean verb pattern exactly leads to one Chinese verb pattern. Intuitively the size of verb pattern is the bigger the better, so manual construction is the main drawback of pattern-based approach, but in comparison with the manual rule design, it is much more reasonable for the robust MT system. Furthermore pattern addition guarantees performance improvement progressively with much lower side effects. In this framework the key issues are two: The first is how to effectively construct verb patterns which implies which patterns contribute to the system mostly. The second is how to increase the hit rate of verb pattern utilizing the existing patterns, when transferring to other domain. Our pattern-based system originates from Korean-Chinese TV news caption MT system. For the couple of years' development in news domain, we constructed over 300,000 verb patterns, which leading to progressive improvement. But we found, at the certain point, the addition of pattern dose not take much effect any more, which means the newly added patterns actually have no impact any more for news system. But, we found in technical documents, there are still many matching failures, it means existing patterns are still insufficient for the new domain, so we need some criterion to extract the most

W. Li and D. Mollá-Aliod (Eds.): ICCPOL 2009, LNAI 5459, pp. 313–320, 2009.

proper patterns from the numerous candidates. It is also hard to estimate how many patterns we need in new domain and how to reuse the existing patterns. In section 2, we briefly introduce system overview, and in section 3, describe 3-stage verb pattern matching approach and the process of pattern construction. In section 4, shows how the hit rate of matching changes with the increase of pattern size and, using the three-stage pattern matching.

2   System Overview

Fig. 1 shows the structure of our Korean-Chinese MT system. There are two main parts in our architecture. One is analysis part the other is patterns matching one. The analysis part consists of Korean morphological analysis module, and parsing module. Korean input is separated into several simple sentences. After parsing, the simple sentences are converted into the proper format, which includes noun chunking, verb restoration of some duel POS noun, attachment of semantic features.

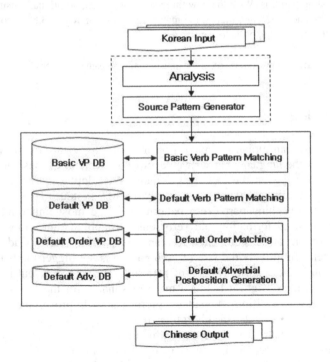

Fig. 1. Korean-Chinese MT System Overview

In our previous system, we use only one stage verb pattern matching approach, if it hits the pattern, then it generates Chinese according to the Chinese pattern linked with Korean pattern. If it fails, Chinese generator arranges the word order by rules. Unfortunately in this case most of long inputs leads to the Chinese outputs are in disorder. In our new system we extend previous standalone matching process to three-stage structure. If it fails in the basic verb pattern matching stage, then it tries default verb matching in the second stage. Default verb pattern is automatically extracted from basic verb patterns. If it also fails in second stage, then it tries the default ordering pattern in third stage. Default ordering pattern is automatically extracted from default verb patterns. In the default ordering pattern there is no exact Korean verb and Chinese verb, but generalized with symbol KVERB and CVERB, so if it hits the pattern, then generates Chinese verb through partial verb pattern matching in stage one or two. Some of Korean adverbial postpositions have semantic ambiguities. We use disambiguation database of adverbial postposition to resolve this kind of problem occurred in the third stage. If it fails in the last stage, then has to arrange the word order by rules as in the previous system did. We strive to improve the pattern hit rate and avoid the default generation by rules.

3 Three–Stage Verb Pattern Matching

3.1 Basic Verb Pattern

In our system verb patterns consists of two parts. Korean pattern is linked with Chinese pattern by symbol ">", and uses postpositions like "가(GA: subject case marker)", "에서(ESEO: adverbial case marker)" to express syntactic relation. We use about 200 semantic features to express the Korean pattern. In the following verb pattern example, it uses semantic features like "concrete place, symbol" to disambiguate the multi-sense Korean verb "뜨다(DE-DA). The Korean verb "뜨다(DE-DA) has over 20 senses according to the change of the following arguments. In this case, using semantic feature is the effective solution for disambiguation.

Verb Pattern: A=concrete place!에 B=symbol!가 뜨(display)!다 > 在 A 上 ㄱ 示:v B

We can see semantic code or word is a necessary feature in the technical domain, and we call patterns using such features are basic verb patterns. We've constructed over 300,000 basic verb patterns for about 20,000 Korean verbs. It is about 15 patterns per one verb, and we can see the improvement with the increase of patterns. In section 4, we show the evaluation result. Using the existing basic patterns, we've manually tested 400 sentences of technical documents. We focused on the results of 50 sentences, which was under the 40 point (the perfect translation is 100 point.). The result was that, among theses 50 low-point outputs, 46% error was caused by the insufficiency of verb patterns, which means the system is still hungry for patterns. The problem is there are tremendous patterns are waiting for be constructed. For more effective construction of patterns and utilization of existing patterns, we analyzed the 150,000 existing patterns for about 20,000 Korean verbs. We focused on the divergence of the Chinese verbs, which linked with Korean verbs. As a result, we've constructed 16, 000 patterns for about 8,000 verbs. We found, these verbs are monosense verbs. From the lexical disambiguation point of view, it means some patterns are duplicated. The root of the following Korean frequent verbs originates from Chinese verbs, and most of these verbs have the unique Chinese translation. Over 50% of frequent Korean verbs are in this category. We define them as A-class verbs, and should pay attention to the duplicated construction. About 4,000 verbs have two senses in average, and in the most of cases, they are biased to a unique Chinese trans-lations. Some are Chinese-root verbs and others are pure Korean verbs. We define them as B-class verbs. For A, B class verbs, we should focus on the syntactic diver-gence between Korean and Chinese instead of the lexical transformation. About 8,000 verbs have 5 senses in average, and most of them are pure Korean verbs. We define them as C-class verbs. The Korean verb "뜨다" has more than 20 senses with the change of semantic feature of argument, like "float, fly, rise, become stale, be distant, move, scoop up...". For this class verb, we should focus on the disambiguation of lexical divergence. Through the above analysis, the current basic verb pattern using semantic features is reasonable for some verbs, especially for C-class verb. For A, B class verb, it is inefficient that continuously adding patterns without a certain con-struction criterion.

3.2 Default Verb Pattern

For A, B class verb, we constructed patterns by length of them. The length represents with the number of arguments in patterns. We only constructed the unique structure of patterns comparing with the existing patterns for these class verbs. For verb "개발하다(develop)", we've constructed over 80 verb patterns with the same struc-ture of "A=SEM1!가(SBJ-MARKER) B=SEM2!를 (OBJ-MARKER) 개발하!다 > A 开发:v B"

We extract one default pattern from these 80 existing patterns for the above struc-ture, using default argument marker "*". We sort the existing patterns by Korean verb and the structure of Korean pattern, and squeeze them to one default pattern by the frequency of Chinese verbs and translation of Korean postpositions. We automatically extract 100,000 default patterns, from the existing basic patterns, which will cover the most of A, B class verb patterns. The followings are the example of default patterns.

Default pattern: A=*!가(SBJ-MAKER) B=*!를통해 (VIA) C=*!로부터(FROM) D=*!를(OBJ-MARKER) 구입하!다(buy) > A 通过 B 从 C 购买:v D.

In the pattern matching module, we add the default pattern matching function. Af-ter failure of the basic pattern matching, it tries the default matching. In the section 4, it shows the pattern hit rate and translation performance comparison between two versions.

3.3 Default Ordering Pattern

We use default verb patterns to improve the hit rate. The evaluation result shows it works, but still it fails in some cases. In the following example, we extract a default verb pattern from the basic pattern.

Basic verb pattern: A=*!가(SBJ-MAKER) B=제도(system)!에서(IN) C=범위 (range)!에따라(according to) 결정되!다(be decided) > A 在 B 中 由 C 而 确定:v

Default Verb Pattern: A=*!가(SBJ-MAKER) B=*!에서(IN) C=*!에따라 (accord-ing to) 결정되!다(decide) > A 在 B 中 由 C 而 确定:

If the Korean input sentence is "송신주파수가 무선 통신 규약에서 주파수대에 따라서 결정되다(The transmitting frequency is decided by the band of wireless communication protocol)", then it hits the basic or default verb patterns. But in the above Korean input, if the verb be changed from "결정되다(be decided)" to "정해지다(be decided)", which is the synonym of original verb, then unfortunately it fails the matching, because of the pattern insufficiency of substitution verb "정해지다(be decided)". For this case we try another approach to utilize the existing patterns without the new manual construction. We automatically squeezed 100,000 default verb patterns to the 10,000 default ordering patterns. We sort them by the structure of patterns, generalizing the concrete Korean verbs with abstract symbol KVERB, and Chinese verbs with abstract symbol CVERB. The main role of default ordering patterns is arranging the Chinese word in right order.

Default ordering pattern: A=*!가(SBJ-MAKER) B=*!에서(IN) C=*!에 따라(according to) KVERB > A 在 B 中 由 C 而 CVERB:v

For default ordering matching, we add another function, which is called after default verb pattern failure. We can see from the above example, default ordering pattern has no exact verb to generate and the translation of Korean postposition is also not disambiguated. For verb generation, we use the partly matched arguments to select the most highly scored patterns and take the Chinese verb in that pattern. For post position generation, we make reference to the default postposition data, which described in section 3.4. We strive to utilize the existing verb patterns as possible as we can, on the basis of without downgrading of translation performance. The relevant evaluation shows in section 4.

3.4 Default Adverbial Postposition Generation

The default adverbial postposition data is used in the default generation or when default ordering pattern get hits.

The Korean postposition like "까지(to, also)" has two senses. We extracted the disambiguation data from the basic verb patterns. It uses semantic code of the argument and the collocation of verb as features. The following is the format of data.

[까지] *!까지 @Chn1-Frq1,Chn2-Frq2...
[까지] $장소(place)!까지_가다(go)@ 到(to) 10
[까지] $가치(value)!까지_기록하다(record)@ 连(also) 4

3.5 The Process of Pattern Construction

Fig. 2 shows the process of pattern construction. We use our analyzer to get pattern matching log data in volume, and use the Korean pattern generator to automatically reformat the candidates. First, we classify these verbs as three classes, introduced in section 3.1.We define the verb class with the following criterion through the analysis of the existing verb patterns. If the proportion of the most frequently used Chinese verb is under 50%, then it is C-class verb, or it is A, B class. The A-class verb pattern like "A=*!가(SBJ-MARKER) B=*!를(OBJ-MARKER) 개발하다(develop)" has only two arguments without adverbial arguments, so there is a strong probability that it is hit by existing verb patterns or default patterns. For about 15,000 verbs in A, B class we've manually constructed only 20,000 unique patterns from the 200,000 candidates. For the high frequent 5,000 C-class verb, we've constructed the whole candidates about 30,000 patterns, which have over two arguments. Default verb patterns and default adverbial postposition data are automatically extracted from the basic verb patterns, and default ordering patterns are automatically extracted from the default verb patterns. If we add new basic verb patterns, then it will automatically enlarge the default verb and ordering patterns.

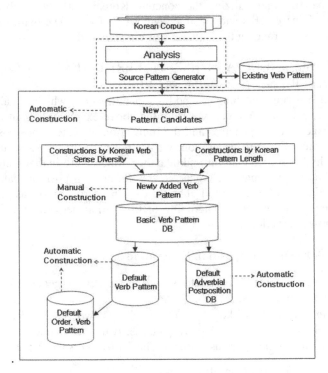

Fig. 2. Process of the Pattern Construction

4   Evaluation

Fig.3 shows the hit rate and the number of matching failure with the addition of new basic patterns for 2,000 sentences of technical domain. We use the existing 150,000 basic patterns as a base system. With the increase of 50,000 basic patterns, the hit rate only increases 0.6%.

The next two bunches of patterns are the newly constructed patterns, which are followed the criterion of three verb classes. As a result, the third bunch of 25,000 basic patterns leads to the increase of 11.1% and the third bunch of 25,000 basic patterns leads to the increase of 11.3% hit rate. Comparing with the previous addition of 50,000 patterns, it has a significant improvement.

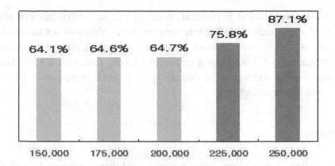

Fig. 3. Change of Verb Pattern Hit Rate

Fig. 4 shows the hit rate change with the addition of default verb pattern and default ordering pattern. Using 100,000 default verb patterns, the hit rate increases 2.9%, and with the 10,000 default ordering patterns, the hit rate increases 0.9%. Using three-stage verb pattern matching, the hit rate totally increases 3.8%, comparing with the basic one-stage system.

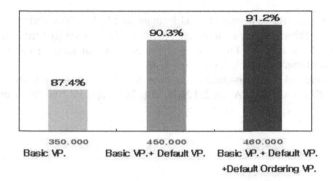

Fig. 4. Change of Verb Pattern Hit Rate

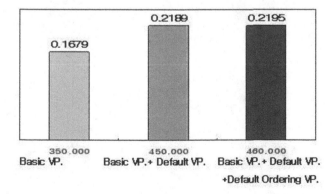

Fig. 5. Change of BLEU score

Fig. 5 shows the translation performance using the new verb pattern approach. We use 400 technical sentences with 4 references as the evaluation set to check the BLEU score. The result is similar with the one showed in Fig. 5. Using default verb patterns, BLUE score increases 5.1% and using default ordering patterns, BLEU score increase 0.1%. Using three-stage verb pattern matching, the score increases 5.16%, comparing with the basic one-stage system.

5 Conclusion

This paper described three-stage verb pattern matching approach and the relevant process of pattern construction in our Korean-Chinese machine translation system in technical domain. With this approach, we made promising improvement of pattern matching performance. In the next phase, we will try the recombination technique to automatically construct default ordering patterns, and adopt this approach to Korean-English system to see the feasibility.

References

1. Takeda, K.: Pattern-Based Context-Free Grammars for Machine Translation
2. Watanabe, H., Takeda, K.: A Pattern-based Machine Translation System Extended by Example-based Processing. In: Proceedings of the 36th annual meeting on Association for Computational Linguistics, vol. 2, pp. 1369–1373
3. Kim, C., Hong, M.: Korean-chinese machine translation based on verb patterns. In: Richardson, S.D. (ed.) AMTA 2002. LNCS, vol. 2499, pp. 94–103. Springer, Heidelberg (2002)

Domain Adaptation for English–Korean MT System: From Patent Domain to IT Web News Domain

Ki-Young Lee, Sung-Kwon Choi, Oh-Woog Kwon, Yoon-Hyung Roh,
and Young-Gil Kim

Natural Language Processing Team,
Electronics and Telecommunications Research Institute,
161 Gajeong-dong, Yuseong-gu
Daejeon, Korea, 305-350
{leeky,choisk,ohwoog,yhnog,kimyk}@etri.re.kr

Abstract. This paper addresses a method to adapt an existing machine translation (MT) system for a newly targeted translation domain. Especially, we give detailed descriptions of customizing a patent specific English-Korean machine translation system for IT web news domain. The proposed method includes the followings: constructing a corpus from documents of IT web news domain, analyzing characteristics of IT web news sentences according to each viewpoint of MT system modules (tagger, parser, transfer) and translation knowledge, and adapting each MT system modules and translation knowledge considering characteristics of IT web news domain. To evaluate our domain adaptation method, we conducted a human evaluation and an automatic evaluation. The experiment showed promising results for diverse sentences extracted from IT Web News documents.

Keywords: machine translation, domain adaptation.

1 Introduction

Generally, we can get satisfactory performance of machine translation system by narrowing translation target domain. Recently, some MT systems achieved great performance in specific domain and could be successful in commercial market. So, it is very important to restrict target domain of MT system for its practicality.

These facts being given, changing target domain of an existing MT system is also another important issue. There have been studies on domain adaptation in MT communities [1,2,3]. This paper presents a method to adapt an existing MT system for changing its translation target domain. The process of domain adaptation includes adaptation of each module of MT system and customization of translation knowledge, such as dictionary, transfer patterns, analysis rules. In this paper, we give an explanation of the steps for customizing the existing patent specific MT system for newly targeted IT web news domain.

We already developed an English-Korean MT system for patent. Also, using the patent MT system, the online translation service for English patent documents has

W. Li and D. Mollá-Aliod (Eds.): ICCPOL 2009, LNAI 5459, pp. 321–328, 2009.

been provided at IPAC (International Patent Assistance Center) under MOCIE (Ministry of Commerce, Industry and Energy) in Korea. Now, as another challenge, based on the patent specific English-Korean MT system, we are developing an English-Korean MT system for IT web news. So, our focus is how to tune an existing MT system for new target domain.

The English-Korean MT system for IT web news consists of analysis module including tagging and syntactic analysis, transfer module and generation module. The English-Korean MT system for IT web news employs dictionary, parsing rules, transfer patterns, lexical rules and so on as main knowledge. Syntactic analyzer (or Parser) parses English sentences using parsing rules which is linked to transfer patterns. After syntactic analysis, English-Korean transfer is performed to convert English syntactic structure to Korean syntactic structure using the transfer patterns and to select Korean target words of English source words. Finally, Korean generator generates Korean sentences.

The detailed explanation about the domain adaptation method for each MT system modules and translation knowledge will be described in the section 2. The section 3 describes experimental results and discussions. In the section 4, we sum up the discussion and show the future research direction.

2 Domain Adaptation Method

This section gives the detailed description about how to adapt each module of the MT system and knowledge like dictionary and patterns.

2.1 POS Tagging Module

POS tagging module carried out the adaptation based on early mentioned analysis results for the characteristics of IT web news domain from the perspective of POS tagging. Considering that the customization from the patent domain to the IT web news domain is a shift to a little bit broad domain, the main customization of POS tagging module focused to release its restriction. The domain adaptation approaches by tagging module are described below:

- Adjust lexical probabilities to IT web news domain: We coordinated probabilities of the words with the distinctive difference between the lexical probabilities built from the IT web news corpus and the existing lexical probabilities.
- Add sparse contextual probabilities: N-gram data which did not found in the patent domain were added to cover the IT web news domain.
- Improvements in performance of morphological analysis

    - The algorithm for unknown hyphen words was devised for the IT web news domain.
    - The recognition performance for proper nouns which appear at first position in the sentence was improved.
    - The chunking mechanism for time/number were improved

2.2 Syntactic Analysis Module

The main process for the adaptation of syntactic analysis module includes the followings:

- The process for coordinate NP structure: To deal with various types of coordinate NP structure, additional parsing rules were introduced.
- The improvement in recognition accuracy for time-related NP structures and number-related ADVP.
- Tuning for interrogative sentences: There were many interrogative sentences in IT web news domain. Especially, introducing ADJP gap, we improved the ability to parse WHADJP sentences.
- Tuning for sentences including varied expressions like inversion, ellipsis: We allocated more weights to related parsing rules to cover the various expressions.
- The use of IT web news domain specific patterns: We applied patent-specific patterns before parsing to reduce parsing complexities.
- Base NP chunking
- Improvement in performance of base NP chunking: We devised the mechanism to resolve ambiguities between 'BNP' and 'BNP BNP'.

2.3 Transfer Module

As mentioned above, many semantically ambiguous words are used in the IT web news domain. This means that a target word selection according to context would play important role for improving translation accuracy. At the same time, it means that a refinement of target words of each entry in the dictionary is a prerequisite for target word selection. So we introduced a target word selection function for frequently used nouns and verbs.

In the case of nouns, we defined co-occurring words as the words which is located at the position to modify the ambiguous head word within noun phrase. First, frequent noun phrases were extracted from the English IT web news corpus. Second, for the noun phrases extracted from the English corpus, corresponding Korean noun phrases were extracted from the Korean comparable corpus. Third, English co-occurring words to be used to resolve target word selection ambiguities were extracted from the English noun phrase aligned to Korean noun phrase. In the case of verbs, we used the words located at argument positions of verbs as clues for selecting proper target word for ambiguous verbs. Similarly, we extracted frequent verb frames from the English IT web news corpus and the comparable Korean IT web news corpus. After aligning verb frames, clues to resolve translation ambiguities of verbs were extracted at the argument position of English verb frames [4, 5].

2.4 Translation Knowledge

Knowledge adaptation includes the construction of unknown 'words/compound words' and corresponding target words, the adaptation of target words of existing words for the IT web news domain and the construction of patterns used frequently in the IT web news domain.

We extracted unknown words and unknown compound words from the IT web news corpus and then added to dictionary attaching their target words. Table 1 shows the number of unknown words and unknown compound words registered newly in this process.

Table 1. The number of unknown words and unknown compound words

Category	Number of words
Added unknown words	29,000
Added unknown compound words	55,000

We also performed the domain adaptation for target words of nouns, verbs and adjectives of dictionary. For this, using the English-Korean comparable corpus, we refined target words of source words semi-automatically and added IT web news domain specific contents for each entry of dictionary. Fig. 1 illustrates IT web news domain specific contents of example words. In Fig. 1, word 'circumference' has contents for IT web news domain and contents for patent domain. In Fig. 1, we can see the feature name, such as 'ETYPE', 'KPOS', 'WSEM', 'KROOT', etc, and their feature values. For example, 'KROOT' means the Korean target word feature.

```
[KEY]
circumference@NOUN
[CONTENT]
{변환:NEWS
[(ETYPE COMM)(KPOS NOUN)(WSEM )(SEM )(KROOT 주변)(KCODE NN00001)]
[(ETYPE COMM)(KPOS NOUN)(WSEM )(SEM )(KROOT 영역)(KCODE NN00001)]
}
{변환:PAT
[(ETYPE COMM)(KPOS NOUN)(WSEM circumference#2)(SEM length#1)(KROOT
원주)(KCODE NN00001)(KCOUNT 개)(KCCODE UU00601)(SOURCE KEDICT)]
[(ETYPE COMM)(KPOS NOUN)(WSEM )(SEM )(KROOT 원주둘레)(KCODE
NN00001)(SOURCE KEDICT)]
}
```

Fig. 1. The example of domain specific content of dictionary

```
[KEY]
VP_VERB_ADV
[CONTENT]
{ NP0 VERB1:[eroot ** [be do have]] ADV1 } -> { ADV1 VERB1!:[kroot := [그렇],
kcode := [VV00019]] }

{ NP0 VERB1:[etype == [i0]] ADV1 } -> { ADV1 VERB1! }
{ NP0 VERB1 ADV1 } -> { ADV1 VERB1! }

[KEY]
NP_SBAR
[CONTENT]
{ SBAR1 } -> { SBAR1!:[kend := [ㄴ지], kecode := [EN00401]] }
```

Fig. 2. The example of transfer patterns

Transfer patterns and lexical rules which are employed for the structural transfer were extracted from the IT web news corpus automatically, and then corresponding Korean translation parts were added by hands. We present the example of transfer patterns and lexical rules in Fig. 2 and Fig. 3 respectively. Transfer pattern and lexical rule have same format. They consist of a source part and a target part. A source part contains the condition on which the pattern can be matched.

```
[KEY]
@VERB_become_distanced_from
[CONTENT]
{ become! distanced from } -> { 소원해지!:[kflex2:=[에서], kfcode2:=[JJ00202]] }

[KEY]
@VERB_take_DET_picture
[CONTENT]
{ take! DET1 picture } -> { DET1:[의] 사진을_찍! }

[KEY]
@PP_for_dear_life
[CONTENT]
{ for! dear life } -> { 죽을_힘을_다하여! }
```

Fig. 3. The example of lexical rules

Table 2 presents the number of transfer patterns and lexical rules which were additionally introduced for IT web news domain.

Table 2. Number of transfer patterns and lexical rules constructed for IT web news domain

Category	Number of rule & patterns
Transfer patterns	1,200
Lexical rules	34,800

3 Experiments

3.1 Human Evaluation

To evaluate proposed domain adaptation method, we conducted a human evaluation and a automatic evaluation. First, a detailed description about the human evaluation is the followings:

- Test set: The test set for the experiment consists of 400 sentences extracted from various articles of the zdnet news site and the mercury news site. And its average sentence length is about 17.05 words.
- Test set configuration:

Table 3. Test set

Category	Number of sentences
News	170 sentences
Blogs	70 sentences
Whitepapers	30 sentences
Reviews	30 sentences
Opinion	50 sentences
Special reports	50 sentences

● Evaluation criterion:

Table 4. Scoring criterion for translation accuracy

Score	Criterion
4	The meaning of a sentence is perfectly conveyed
3.5	The meaning of a sentence is almost perfectly conveyed except for some minor errors (e.g. wrong article, stylistic errors)
3	The meaning of a sentence is almost conveyed (e.g. some errors in target word selection)
2.5	A simple sentence in a complex sentence is correctly translated
2	A sentence is translated phrase-wise
1	Only some words are translated
0	No translation

● Evaluation: After instruction about the evaluation criterion, 5 professional translators evaluated translation results. Ruling out the highest and the lowest score, the rest 3 scores were used for measuring average translation accuracy.

Table 5. The comparison of translation accuracy

Category	Translation accuracy	Translation accuracy higher than 3 scores
MT system for patent	74.02%	54.25%
Customized MT system for IT web news	79.41%	74.0%

For comparison, we evaluated two MT systems (the existing patent specific English-Korean MT system and the customized English-Korean MT system for IT web news domain). The results are shown in Table 5.

After applying the domain customization process, there was an remarkable improvement in translation accuracy. The number of the sentences that were rated equal to or higher than 3 points was 296. It means that about 74.0% of all translations were understandable.

3.2 Automatic Evaluation

We also conducted automatic evaluation. The test set for the automatic evaluation consists of 1,000 sentences. For each sentence, a set of 5 references was produced by hands in advance. Table 6 presents the Bleu scores for two English-Korean MT systems. In Table 6, BLEU-MA column represents the Bleu score measured at morpheme level.

Table 6. Automatic evaluation results

Category	BLEU-MA
MT system for patent	0.2856
Customized MT system for IT web news	0.3306

3.3 Evaluation for Each MT System Module

We evaluated performance of each module of two MT systems. The results are shown in Table 7. In table 7, ERR means error reduction rate. The improvements in each module can be seen. Especially, ERR of the target word selection module is higher than ERR of other modules. The reason is caused by the customization of knowledge, such as dictionary, patterns, as well as the introduction of target word selection function. In table 7, the tagging accuracy was measured in the word level and the syntactic analysis accuracy and the target word selection accuracy were measured in the sentence level.

Table 7. Evaluation results for each MT system module

Category	Tagging accuracy (words)	Syntactic analysis accuracy (sentences)	Target word selection accuracy (sentences)
MT system for patent	98.40%	55.3%	49.8%
Customized MT system For IT web news	99.07%	77.9%	85.8%
ERR	40%	50.6%	71.7%

4 Conclusion

In this paper, we presented the domain adaptation method from the patent domain to the IT web news domain for an English-Korean MT system. This method includes the customization of each MT system module as well as knowledge. Of course, the proposed domain adaptation method can be generalized and be applied to other domain and to other MT systems. We have demonstrated the effectiveness of the proposed method by conducting human evaluation and automatic evaluation. Because some processes of the proposed method require human hands, our next research topic is about how to customize MT system automatically.

References

1. Hong, M.P., Kim, Y.G., Kim, C.H., Yang, S.I., Seo, Y.A., Ryu, C., Park, S.K.: Customizing a Korean-English MT System for Patent Translation, MT Summit X, pp. 181–187 (2005)
2. Ayan, N.F., Dorr, B.J., Kolak, O.: Domain Tuning of Bilingual Lexicons for MT, Technical Reports of UMIACS (2003)
3. Zajac, R.: MT Customziation. In: MT Summit IX Workshop (2003)
4. Hong, M., Kim, Y.-K., Park, S.-K., Lee, Y.-J.: Semi-Automatic Construction of Korean-Chinese Verb Patterns Based on Translation Equivalency. In: COLING 2004 Workshop on Multilingual Linguistic Resources (2004)
5. Lee, K.Y., Park, S.K., Kim, H.W.: A Method for English-Korean Target Word Selection Using Multiple Knowledge Sources. IEICE Trans. Fundamentals E89-A(6) (2006)

Constructing Parallel Corpus from Movie Subtitles

Han Xiao[1] and Xiaojie Wang[2]

[1] School of Information Engineering, Beijing University of Post and Telecommunications
artex.xh@gmail.com
[2] CISTR, Beijing University of Post and Telecommunications
xjwang@bupt.edu.cn

Abstract. This paper describes a methodology for constructing aligned German-Chinese corpora from movie subtitles. The corpora will be used to train a special machine translation system with intention to automatically translate the subtitles between German and Chinese. Since the common length-based algorithm for alignment shows weakness on short spoken sentences, especially on those from different language families, this paper studies to use dynamic programming based on time-shift information in subtitles, and extends it with statistical lexical cues to align the subtitle. In our experiment with around 4,000 Chinese and German sentences, the proposed alignment approach yields 83.8% precision. Furthermore, it is unrelated to languages, and leads to a general method of parallel corpora building between different language families.

Keywords: sentence alignment, parallel corpora, lexical cues.

1 Introduction

Text alignment is an important task in Natural Language Processing (NLP). It can be used to support many other NLP tasks. Lots of researches have been done on bilingual alignment [1,2,3,13], and some specific kinds of corpora have gained more and more focus. One of the typical examples is the movie subtitles, it is free available and has rich semantic. [4] showed that a Machine Translation(MT) system gave a slightly better result when training on subtitles compared to Europarl (Europarl Parallel Corpus). [4] also argued that the text genre of "file subtitles" is well suited for MT, in particular for statistical MT.

A subtitle file in a movie is a textual data corresponding to: a set of dialogues, a description of an event or sounds, noises and music (that is often called as hearing impaired subtitle). The popular subtitle formats are based on the time [6]. They are characterized by an identifier, a time frame and finally a sequence of words. Usually each text piece consists of one or two short sentences shown on screen with an average seconds [7]. [8] mentioned that the readers for subtitles have only a limited time to perceive and understand a given subtitle so the internal understanding complexity is small. The linguistic subtitle structure is closer to oral language with great variability. As a result the language of subtitling covers a broad variety of any conceivable topic, even with exaggerated modern youth language. Still, [5] pointed out widespread unknown words in subtitles. They comprise proper names of people and products,

W. Li and D. Mollá-Aliod (Eds.): ICCPOL 2009, LNAI 5459, pp. 329–336, 2009.

rare-word forms and foreign words. One must notice the fact that different language versions of subtitles for a same movie are not necessarily written by the same person. Still, the amount of compression and re-phrasing is different for various languages, and it also depends on cultural differences and subtitle traditions. The Fig. 1 shows a short example of German subtitles and their Chinese correspondences in SubRip format.

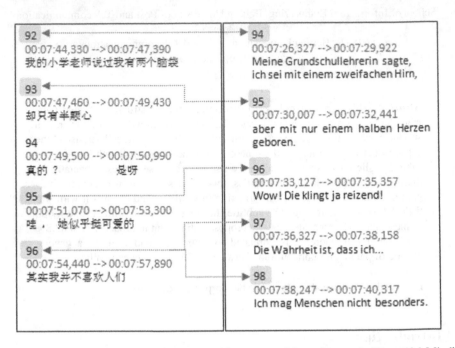

Fig. 1. A piece of Chinese and German subtitles extracted from the movie "Beautiful Mind". The Chinese subtitle 96 is divided into two subtitles 97 and 98 in its corresponding German translation, and Chinese subtitle 94 does not occur in German version.

Sentence alignment is an almost obligatory first step for making use of German-Chinese subtitles. It consists of finding a mapping between source and target language sentences allowing for deletions, insertions and some n:m alignments, but it restricts crossing dependencies. Most works on automatic alignment of film subtitles are still in its infancy. [6] handled the alignments on time with a variation by empirically fixing the global time-shifting at 500 milliseconds. [11] showed that the alignment approach based on time overlap combined with cognate recognition is clearly superior to pure length-based alignment. The results of [11] are of 82.5% correct alignments for Dutch-English and 78.1% correct alignments for Dutch-German. The approach of [11] is entirely based on time information, thus, it often requires the subtitles to be equally synchronized to the original movie. A method named Dynamic Time Warping (DTW) for aligning the French-English subtitles was obtained from Internet [10]. The approach of [10] requires a special bilingual dictionary to compute subtitle correspondences, and [10] reports 94% correct alignments when turning recall down to 66%. However, the corresponding lexical resources in [10] cannot be easily accessed.

In this paper, we propose a new language-independent approach considered both time frames and lexical content of subtitles, which automatically aligns the subtitle pairs. The purpose is to extract the 1:1 alignment from German and Chinese subtitles for our subtitle translation. Section 2 dedicates to the method presented by us for subtitle alignments, and our improvement by using lexical anchors. The evaluations of result with comparison to traditional length-based approach are discussed in Section 3.

2 Alignment Solution

Before alignment can be applied, the subtitle corpus needs to undergo a few preprocessing steps. Each German subtitle file has been tokenized and corresponding Chinese subtitle has been segmented, which are crucial for the success of selecting corresponded word. We intend to combine stemming, which has been demonstrated to improve statistical word alignment [9]. For German, a light stemmer (removing inflections only for noun and adjectives) presents some advantages. Despite its in flexional complexities, German has a quite simple suffix structure, so that, if one ignores the almost intractable problems of compound words, separable verb prefixes, and prefixed and infixed "ge", an algorithmic stemmer can be made quite short and effective. The umlaut in German is a regular feature of plural formation, so its removal is a natural feature of stemming, but this leads to certain false conflations (for example, schön, beautiful; schon, already). In future work, we would like to improve the stemmer especially for the irregular morphological variations used by verbs and nouns. We expect that the effect of combining these morphological operations will reduce the sparse data problem and speed up the computation of correspondence pairs.

2.1 Dynamic Time Warping

A considerable number of papers [1-3] have examined the aligning sentences in parallel texts between various languages. These works define a distance based on length or lexical content, which involves the use of dynamic programming. Since the time information is explicitly given in subtitle file, intuitively, corresponding segments in different translations should be shown at roughly the same time. However, this case does not occur very often. Every subtitle file is built independently from others even for the original video track. This result in growing time gaps between corresponding beans. The time span is never identical at the millisecond level.

In order to handle this problem, we apply dynamic programming to calculate the best path between two subtitle files. This algorithm uses the interval of the start time from two subtitles to evaluate how likely an alignment between them. Two subtitles are not considered as an aligned pair if their start times are far away from each other. To make it easily find the most probable subtitle alignment, the possible alignments in our approach are empirically limited to {1:1, 1:0, 0:1, 2:1, 1:2, 2:2}. Initially, the German and Chinese subtitles are asynchronous. The cost of all possible alignments, which are measured by time differences, has been considered from the beginning to the end of the subtitle file.

Let $T(i,j)$ be the lowest cost alignment between subtitle $1, \dots, i$ and $1, \dots, j$ where i is the index of Chinese and j is the index of German subtitle. Previously the $T(0,0)$ is set to 0. Then one can define and recursively calculate $T(i,j)$ as follows:

$$T(i,j) = \min \begin{cases} T(i,j-1) + \lambda_{0:1}cost(i,j+1) \\ T(i-1,j) + \lambda_{1:0}cost(i+1,j) \\ T(i-1,j-1) + \lambda_{1:1}cost(i,j) \\ T(i-1,j-2) + \lambda_{1:2}cost(i,j-1) \\ T(i-2,j-1) + \lambda_{2:1}cost(i-1,j) \\ T(i-2,j-2) + \lambda_{2:2}cost(i-1,j-1) \end{cases}, \tag{1}$$

where λ is the inverse of priori probability in order to give a lower cost to more frequency match types.

This leaves determining the cost function, $cost(i,j)$ as follow:

$$cost(i,j) = \left[\delta_{cur}(i,j) - \delta_{prev}(i,j)\right]^2, \tag{2}$$

$$\delta_{cur}(i,j) = i_{start} - j_{start}, \tag{3}$$

where $\delta_{cur}(i,j)$ calculates the start time delay between i and j. One may notice that the previous delay may cause growing delay for the following subtitles. In order to solve this problem, the previous delay δ_{prev} must be subtracted from the current delay. According to the different align mode, δ_{prev} is selected as follows:

$$\delta_{prev}(i,j) = \begin{cases} \Delta(i,j-1), & align\ 0:1 \\ \Delta(i-1,j), & align\ 1:0 \\ \Delta(i-1,j-1), & align\ 1:1 \\ \Delta(i-1,j-2), & align\ 1:2 \\ \Delta(i-2,j-1), & align\ 2:1 \\ \Delta(i-2,j-2), & align\ 2:2 \end{cases} \tag{4}$$

So, in essence, Δ is a matrix that gives the delay caused by each possible alignment. For each step, once the align mode of i and j is determined by (1), $\Delta(i,j)$ must be set to $\delta_{cur}(i,j)$ of the selected mode. That is to say, the matrix Δ is built dynamically in the procedure.

2.2 Lexical Cues Extension

Since the previous algorithm is based on the purely time information, it ignores the richer information available in the text. To obtain an improvement in alignment accuracy, the lexical content must be considered. Intuitively, the lexical content could be used to find reliable anchor points. Previous work [2,9,11] focused on using bilingual dictionary to find anchor points in the subtitle pairs, or using string similarity measures [11] such as the longest common subsequences to decide the most relevant candidate pairs. Here, we apply the approach based on measures of association on roughly parallel texts, which has been processed by dynamic programming in Section 3, to derive the bilingual dictionary automatically. Then we find the anchor points by means of this dictionary. It's assumed that the aligned region is the terms from 1:1, 2:1, 1:2 and 2:1 matches. Though the validity of the co-occurrence clue is obvious for parallel corpora, it also holds for comparable corpora and unrelated corpora [12]. The χ^2 test used by [13] is efficient way of identifying word correspondence, it has a simple form as follow:

$$\chi^2 = \frac{N(O_{11}O_{22} - O_{12}O_{21})^2}{(O_{11}+O_{12})(O_{11}+O_{21})(O_{12}+O_{22})(O_{21}+O_{22})}, \qquad (5)$$

where N is the number of all roughly alignments except 1:0 and 0:1 mode. For a selected German word G and a Chinese word C, the two-by-two contingency tables are built for them. O_{11} counts the number aligned pairs which co-occurrence G and C, O_{12} is the count of pairs that have G in German subtitles, but lost C in the correspondence Chinese subtitle. O_{21} is the count of pairs in which Chinese subtitle have C, but the aligned German subtitle misses G. O_{22} counts the number of pairs that have neither G nor C.

For each Chinese word and word in current subtitles, we use (1) to calculate their χ^2 score. Using the confidence level of $\alpha = 0.05$ and the critical value $\chi^2 = 3.845$, we can decide whether C and G are good candidate for translation pair or not. Note that all entries belonging to the words are not found in the German stop list and Chinese stop list. Since the size of each subtitle file is limited, the word C may have several correspondent words G with the same score. For them, the pairs which score the highest are remained. Table 1 shows the result for 6 Chinese words and their correspondent German translations in 685 results totally.

Table 1. 6 Results for Chinese words and their corresponding German translations. Bold words are accepted translations.

Chinese word	Expected translation	Candidate German translations automatically generated			
啤酒	Bier	**bier**			
五角大楼	Pentagon	**pentagon**			
恭喜	gluckwunsch	**gluckwunsch**			
安排	arrangieren	**arrangi**	gebet	treffenmit	wiederholt
女孩子	Mädel	atomphysik	erzahlt	heisse	**madel**
全世界	Welt	erklart	**global**	kommunismus	sowjetsist

As the Table 1 illustrated, in many cases our program predicts the expected word with other typical associates mixed. Since a number of reliable word correspondences have been found, we can use them to predict anchor points by some simple heuristics. We count a score that indicates the number of words to match between the Chinese subtitle C and German subtitle G as follows

$$(C, G) = \frac{1}{n} \sum_{i=1}^{n} \delta\big(tr(C_i), G_j\big) \, \forall j, \qquad (6)$$

$$\delta(x, y) = \begin{cases} 1, & y \in x \\ 0, & y \notin x \end{cases} \qquad (7)$$

where $tr(C_i)$ is the translation of word C_i in Chinese subtitle C based on the previous bilingual dictionary. Since our dictionary may provide several candidate German translations for a Chinese word, and $tr(C_i)$ can be a word or a collection. Therefore a Kronecker $\delta(x, y)$ is given to check the matches. Assuming that an alignment should mainly consist of match translations, we can use a threshold σ for this score to decide whether an alignment is likely to be correct or not, thus, to be an anchor point.

3 Evaluation

We examine the pure-length based approach [13] and the DTW based on time-delay with its lexical extension that we proposed in this paper. The evaluation has been conducted on a corpus extracted from randomly selected 10 movies. For each movie, we take out randomly around 400 Chinese and their German corresponding subtitles, which result in 4,128 aligned sentence pairs. Our selection is based on the principle that the sentence pairs are at initial of the movie and consecutive within each movie. All of t sentence pairs hese pairs are manually aligned. When conducting some previous evaluations, most of them limited their test to few dozens for each movie, which obviously facilitates the task. We separated 1,000 sentence pairs from all this manually aligned pairs as a training set. We then used relative frequencies of each occurring alignment mode in training set to estimate the parameter λ. For efficiency reasons we round them into integers as shown in Table 2.

Table 2. Adjusted priors for various alignment types

Parameters	Value
$\lambda_{0:1}$	30
$\lambda_{1:0}$	56
$\lambda_{1:1}$	1
$\lambda_{1:2}$	23
$\lambda_{2:1}$	11
$\lambda_{2:2}$	79

Therefore it will cause the algorithm to give 1:1 match for a priority, which is most common. These parameters will be shared in the three approaches we evaluated. For the length-based approach, the number of German characters generated by each Chinese character is also calculated in our training set, the mean $c = 2.667$, with a standard deviation $\sigma = 1.040$.

The result of time-based dynamic programming and its lexical extension are listed in Table 3. The threshold σ as mentioned above was set to 0.05 previously. To be able to compare our results with other work, the evaluations are presented in terms of recall and precision. However, in some cases the count of exact matches is somewhat arbitrary. We count partially correct alignments, which have some overlap with

Table 3. Performance of different alignment approaches

Approach	Recall	Precision	F-measure	Add partially correct		
				Recall	Precision	F-measure
Len	30.8%	30.1%	30.4%	38.2%	37.3%	37.7%
Len+ Lexi	37.5%	50.6%	43.1%	45.8%	61.8%	52.6%
Time	73.4%	67.8%	70.5%	83.0%	76.7%	79.7%
Time+ Lexi	66.4%	72.4%	69.3%	76.8%	83.8%	80.1%

correct alignments in both Chinese and German beads. In order to make it easier to compare and uniform, the partial correct is defined as 50% correct, and we added it accordingly to the recall and precision.

The pure length-based approach showed their weakness being compared to other approaches on sentence alignment of subtitles. The possible reason could be the inaccurate Gaussian assumption of $l_2 - l_1 c$ in this specific domain, where l_2 and l_1 are the length of potential aligned sentences in German and Chinese. Since the linguistic structure of subtitle is closer to the oral language with great variability, this leads the translators of this sort of material to use informal and incompatible translations. The translations may drop some elements for cultural reasons. The correlation coefficient of German and Chinese sentence length in subtitles is 0.813, which indicates the sentence lengths between these two languages are not perfectly correlated. It results the poor performance of length based approach.

The score showed that the dynamic programming with lexical extension yields better precision, which could be expected due to the anchor points, since the lexical extension actually finds the translation pairs from the coarse aligned sentences. These reliable word alignments limit the search space for local minima. While we only allow the 1:1 alignments to be anchors, the original 1:2, 2:1 and 2:2 alignments will be divided into several pairs, which results more retrieved pairs than actual ones and leads the low recall. Our purpose is not to align all subtitles, but just to produce an aligned the subset of the corpus for further research. The developed alignment method on the total Chinese and German subtitle corpus retrieved only 1:1 and 1:2 alignments, for which there is a correct rate of 88.4%.

4 Conclusions

A sentence alignment method for movie subtitles is proposed in this paper. The proposed approach is based on the time-shift information in subtitles and it uses dynamic programming to minimize the global delay. The statistical lexical cues are also introduced to find word correspondence. As we have shown in the evaluation in Section 3, this additional technique yields better performance, it enhances about 7% of precision. Future work will be based on IBM Word Alignment Model to retrieve translation pairs instead of using co-occurrence statistic. The subtitle alignment is a novel and broad domain, and it may give a true picture of the translation quality and a useful system. The results of this paper may boost the research towards a practical MT system between German and Chinese.

References

1. Brown, P., Lai, J.C., Mercer, R.: Aligning Sentences in Parallel Corpora. In: Proceedings of the 29th annual meeting on Association for Computational Linguistics, Berkeley, California, pp. 169–176 (1991)
2. Wu, D.K.: Aligning a Parallel English-Chinese Corpus Statistically with Lexical Criteria. In: Proceedings of the 32th Annual Conference of the Association for Computational Linguistics, Las Cruces, New Mexico, pp. 80–87 (1994)
3. Shemtov, H.: Text Aligment in a Tool for Translating Revised Documents. In: Proceedings of the 6th Conference on European Chapter of the Association for Computational Linguistics, Utrecht, The Netherlands, pp. 449–453 (1993)
4. Armstrong, S., Way, A., Caffrey, C., Flanagan, M., Kenny, D., O'Hagan, M.: Improving the Quality of Automated DVD Subtitles via Example-based Machine Translation. In: Proceedings of Translating and the Computer, Aslib, London, vol. 28 (2006)
5. Martin, V.: The Automatic Translation of Film Subtitles. A Machine Translation Success Story? In: Resourceful Language Technology: Festschrift in Honor of Anna, vol. 7. Uppsala University (2008)
6. Mathieu, M., Emmanuel, G.: Multilingual Aligned Corpora from Movie Subtitles. Rapport interne LISTIC, p. 6 (2005)
7. Vandeghinste, V., Sang, E.K.: Using a Parallel Transcript/Subtitle Corpus for Sentence Compression. In: LREC, Lisbon, Portugal (2004)
8. Popowich, F., McFetridge, P., Turcato, D., Toole, J.: Machine translation of Closed Captions. Machine Translation 15, 311–341 (2000)
9. Och, F., Ney, H.: Improved Statistical Alignment Models. In: Proceedings of the 38th Annual Meeting of the Association for Computational Linguistics, pp. 440–447 (2000)
10. Lavecchia, C., Smaïli, K., Langlois, D.: Building Parallel Corpora from Movies. In: 5th International Workshop on Natural Language Processing and Cognitive Science, Funchal, Portugal (2007)
11. Tiedemann, J.: Improved Sentence Alignment for Movie Subtitles. In: Proceedings of the 12th Recent Advances in Natural Language Processing, Borovets, Bulgaria, pp. 582–588 (2007)
12. Reinhard, R.: Automatic Identification of Word Translations from Unrelated English and German Corpora. In: Proceedings of the 37th annual meeting of the Association for Computational Linguistics on Computational Linguistics, College Park, Maryland, pp. 519–526 (1999)
13. Gale, W.A., Church, K.W.: A Program for Aligning Sentences in Bilingual Corpora. Computational Linguistics 19(1), 75–102 (1993)

Meta-evaluation of Machine Translation Using Parallel Legal Texts

Billy Tak-Ming Wong and Chunyu Kit

Department of Chinese, Translation and Linguistics
City University of Hong Kong, Tat Chee Avenue, Kowloon, Hong Kong
{ctbwong,ctckit}@cityu.edu.hk

Abstract. In this paper we report our recent work on the evaluation of a number of popular automatic evaluation metrics for machine translation using parallel legal texts. The evaluation is carried out, following a recognized evaluation protocol, to assess the reliability, the strengths and weaknesses of these evaluation metrics in terms of their correlation with human judgment of translation quality. The evaluation results confirm the reliability of the well-known evaluation metrics, BLEU and NIST for English-to-Chinese translation, and also show that our evaluation metric ATEC outperforms all others for Chinese-to-English translation. We also demonstrate the remarkable impact of different evaluation metrics on the ranking of online machine translation systems for legal translation.

Keywords: Machine Translation Evaluation, Legal Text, BLIS, BLEU, ATEC.

1 Introduction

Evaluation is one of the central concerns in the field of machine translation (MT). Along with the development of MT technology, various evaluation approaches have been proposed to examine different facets of the quality of MT output, for instances, assessing fluency, accuracy and informativeness on a 5-point scale [1], testing understandability via comprehension exercises [2], checking grammatical test points in the form of a test suite [3], and many others.

In recent years, MT evaluation has undergone a paradigm shift from human judgment to automatic measurement. As defined in Papineni et al. [4], an MT output is better than others if it is closer to professional human translation. This turns MT evaluation into a matter of assessing text similarity between MT output and human translation. Since, a number of evaluation metrics have been proposed along this line of exploration, including BLEU [4], NIST [5], TER [6], and METEOR [7], to provide a fast, cost-effective and objective way to compare the performance of different MT systems on the same basis. They have been widely adopted by MTers as *de facto* standards for MT evaluation for various purposes, in particular, system comparison and development.

In practice, however, these metrics are not intended to directly measure the translation quality of a given MT system. Rather, it measures how similar a piece of MT output is to a human translation. However, theoretical support is still to be found for

W. Li and D. Mollá-Aliod (Eds.): ICCPOL 2009, LNAI 5459, pp. 337–344, 2009.

the relation between such similarity and the quality of the output. It is based on experimental evidences that we claim that these two variables tend to correlate with each other. It is therefore a question to ask whether such correlation remains constant across different languages and text genera.

This kind of uncertainty inevitably leads to the works on meta-evaluation for MT, i.e., the evaluation of MT evaluation metrics. This has been one of the major themes in a number of recent MT evaluation campaigns, including HTRDP [8], TC-STAR [9], NIST open MT evaluation [10] and the shared task of MT evaluation in ACL workshop on statistical MT [11]. Different text genera are covered, such as news, business, dialog, travel, technology, etc. In most cases, the evaluation metrics correlate with human judgments reliably, but still there are discordant cases. Culy and Riehemann [12] show that the two evaluation metrics BLEU and NIST perform poorly to assess the quality of MT outputs and human translation of literary texts, and some MT outputs even outscore professional human translations. Callison-Burch et al. [13] raise an example in 2005 NIST MT evaluation that the system ranked at the top in the human evaluation section is ranked only the sixth by BLEU. Babych et al. [14] comment that these evaluation metrics cannot give a "universal" prediction of human perception towards translation quality, and their predictive power may be "local" to particular languages or text types. For a new language pair and text genre, human evaluation of the performance of a given metric is necessary in order to prove its reliability.

In this paper we present our recent work on the evaluation of a number of MT evaluation metrics using legal texts in Chinese and English. Our previous work [15] on evaluating the use of online MT in legal domain has shown the potential of MT evaluation metrics in helping lay users to select appropriate MT systems for their translation needs. We now take a further step to explore different evaluation metrics in search of the most reliable ones for this task. In Section 2, the development of evaluation data is described in detail, including the retrieval, preprocessing and translation of legal texts, and their human evaluation, followed by a recognized evaluation protocol. Section 3 reports the automatic evaluation on these texts with different popular evaluation metrics, and the correlation between metric scores and human judgments. Section 4 concludes this paper, highlighting the value of this kind of meta-evaluation, particularly from the user perspective.

2 Development of Evaluation Data

The basic resource required for our evaluation is a set of parallel texts aligned at sentence level. Instead of developing such a resource from scratch, we used an existing parallel corpus, namely BLIS [16], for our work. It is the most authoritative and comprehensive legal text collection in Hong Kong with high quality translation and complete coverage of all Hong Kong laws. The stylistic features of legal texts, i.e., the complex structures of long sentences and the use of special terminologies, however, pose a challenge not only for MT systems but also for the evaluation metrics in use, a huge challenge to differentiate between the subtle quality differences of their human translations and MT outputs.

Two phases of work were involved in turning the BLIS corpus into the evaluation data we need. The first is to identify a representative subset of parallel sentences for translation by different MT systems and the second to evaluate the translation quality of these MT outputs by human evaluators.

2.1 Retrieval, Preprocessing and Translation of Parallel Sentences

To retrieve a representative sub-corpus from BLIS, all its documents were randomly picked out with a constraint of 20 sentences in length. This is to ensure that the evaluation dataset were not dominated by a small number of long documents. In total, 40 Chinese-English bilingual documents were selected in this way.

The necessary preprocessing was then performed on these selected texts, including removal of identical sentence pairs and special characters (e.g., $= \leqq \geqq$ ※↑↓▲△●☆) that were not to be handled by MT. The sentence alignment for the selected texts, which had been automatically performed by machine, was manually double-checked in order to ensure its correctness. Finally, the dataset consisted of 269 pairs of unique parallel sentences. This data size was proved adequate to provide reliable evaluation results, as shown in Estrella et al. [17]. Each of these sentences was translated into the other language by four commercial off-the-shelf MT systems, comprising both transfer-based and statistical systems. A program was developed for submitting the source texts sentence by sentence to each MT system and then collecting their translation outputs in an automatic manner. Two sets of MT outputs, i.e., both the English-to-Chinese (EC) and Chinese-to-English (CE) translations, were subsequently retrieved.

2.2 Evaluation by Human Evaluators

The human evaluation of these MT outputs was carried out following the protocol of NIST open MT evaluation [18]. It focused on two essential features of translation quality, i.e., adequacy and fluency. The former refers to the degree to which the translation conveys the information of its source text or reference translation, whereas the latter to the degree to which the translation is grammatical, readable and understandable. Totally 70 evaluators participated in this evaluation, including 48 undergraduates and 22 postgraduates. All of them are Hong Kong students with Chinese as their mother tongue and English as a second language. About half of them major in language-related subjects such as linguistics, translation, and English communication, and the other half in various other subjects.

For each sentence of MT output, the evaluators were first asked to judge its fluency and, afterwards, its adequacy by comparing it with a reference translation. A 5-point scale (Table 1) was used for the rating of both. As defined in the guideline of NIST's MT assessment [18], the fluency refers to a sentence that is "well-formed grammatically, contains correct spellings, adheres to common use of terms, titles and names, is intuitively acceptable and can be sensibly interpreted", and the adequacy to "the degree to which information present in the original (i.e., the reference translation) is also communicated in the translation".

Table 1. The 5-point scale for fluency and adequacy judgment

Fluency: How do you judge the fluency of this translation?		Adequacy: How much of the meaning of the reference translation is expressed in this translation?	
5	Perfect	5	All
4	Good	4	Most
3	Non-native	3	Much
2	Disfluent	2	Little
1	Incomprehensible	1	None

The evaluators were encouraged to follow their intuitive reactions to make each judgment and not to ponder their decisions. For each sentence, they were instructed to spend, on average, no more than 10 seconds on fluency and 30 seconds on adequacy. The evaluation was conducted via an online web interface. Each evaluator was randomly assigned roughly the same number of questions, with a restriction that candidate translations from the same source document were not evaluated by the same evaluator. In other words, no evaluator would work on different translations of the same source document by different MT systems. There were 35 sets of translations in total, and each set was handled by two evaluators.

3   Evaluation of Automatic MT Evaluation Metrics

The MT outputs assessed by human evaluators were then evaluated again with different automatic evaluation metrics. The reliability of an evaluation metric is determined by how consistent its evaluation results agree with human judgment on the same piece of MT output.

Five evaluation metrics were examined in this evaluation, including BLEU [4], NIST [5], METEOR [7], TER [6], and ATEC [19] (see Appendix). The first three were used in 2008 NIST open MT evaluation [10] and the last was developed by us. The MT outputs were divided into two groups, i.e., the EC and CE translations, and then evaluated with these metrics using a single reference translation. For EC translation, only BLEU and NIST metrics applied, as they were the only two applicable to Chinese texts. The evaluation was conducted at both the character and word levels, with the aid of a word segmentation program from Zhao et al. [20]. For CE translation, all five metrics were applied.

To determine the closeness of evaluation metric scores to human judgment of translation adequacy and fluency, the Pearson correlation coefficient was used. For CE translation, the correlation was measured at both the sentence and system levels. The former is measured in terms of the difference between human ratings and metric scores for each candidate translation sentence, while the latter for a whole set of translation sentences. For EC translation, the correlation measurement was carried out at the system level only, as BLEU and NIST are not designed to work at the sentence level.

Table 2. Correlations between automatic evaluation metrics and human judgments

| | English-to-Chinese Translation | | | |
	$BLEU_{char}$	$BLEU_{word}$	$NIST_{char}$	$NIST_{word}$
Fluency system	.848	.847	.519	.849
Adequacy system	.978	.990	.864	.991

| | Chinese-to-English Translation | | | | |
	BLEU	NIST	METEOR	TER	ATEC
Fluency system	.823	.831	.845	.893	.980
Adequacy system	.773	.783	.797	.857	.960
Fluency sentence	-	-	.361	.349	.199
Adequacy sentence	-	-	.436	.304	.305

Table 2 reports the correlation results for each evaluation metric. For EC translation, it shows that both BLEU and NIST can attain a higher correlation with the aid of word segmentation than without. Both of them perform better at the word level than at character level. Especially for NIST, working on words improves its correlation on fluency from .519 to .849, and achieves a very strong correlation of .991 on adequacy, nearly equivalent to human judgment. BLEU also presents a mild correlation improvement at the word level, but not as significant as NIST. In this sense, BLEU is more stable in providing consistent evaluation results at both the character and word levels.

For CE translation, all the other evaluation metrics outperform better than BLEU at the system level, demonstrating a higher correlation on both fluency and adequacy. Among these metrics, our ATEC is the best at modeling human judgment of translation quality, showing correlations of .98 and .96 on fluency and adequacy, respectively. At the sentence level, however, all the three metrics in use show rather weak correlations. METEOR is the best, but its correlations around .40 are still far below a reliable standard. In a practical sense, this implies that these evaluation metrics can compare the performance of various MT systems in a quite credible manner given enough evaluation data, but cannot tell which sentence is better translated by which MT system.

Finally, an interesting observation is that at system level, all the evaluation metrics show a higher correlation on adequacy than on fluency in EC translation. However, a sharp contrast can be found in CE translation, that is, the metrics correlate with human judgments better on fluency rather than on adequacy. It is an interesting point to start further study of the behaviors of evaluation metrics on different languages.

To have a better understanding on how evaluation metrics would affect the results of MT evaluation, we have repeated our previous evaluation of online MT systems on translating legal documents from various languages into English [15]. This time the evaluation metric ATEC is used to compare with BLEU that was used in [15]. ATEC is shown above to have achieved the highest correlation on English translation. Table 3 presents the resulted rankings of the online MT systems according to BLEU and ATEC scores for various language pairs. About half of the ranks, as highlighted

Table 3. Rankings of online MT systems by BLEU and ATEC (Notation: BLEU → ATEC)

	BabelFish	Google	PROMT	SDL	Systran	WorldLingo
Dutch	1 → 2	-	-	4 → 4	2 → 1	3 → 3
French	2 → 2	1 → 4	5 → 3	6 → 6	3 → 1	4 → 5
German	5 → 6	2 → 2	6 → 4	4 → 5	1 → 1	3 → 3
Greek	1 → 1	-	-	-	2 → 3	3 → 2
Italian	3 → 5	2 → 3	4 → 1	6 → 6	1 → 2	5 → 4
Portuguese	1 → 1	3 → 4	5 → 3	6 → 6	1 → 1	4 → 5
Russian	1 → 1	-	2 → 4	-	4 → 3	3 → 2
Spanish	2 → 4	3 → 3	5 → 1	1 → 2	3 → 4	6 → 6
Swedish	-	-	-	-	2 → 2	1 → 1
Arabic	-	1 → 1	-	-	2 → 2	3 → 3
Chinese	3 → 4	1 → 1	-	-	4 → 3	2 → 2
Japanese	1 → 1	4 → 4	-	-	1 → 1	1 → 3
Korean	2 → 1	3 → 3	-	-	1 → 1	4 → 4

in grey color, are changed due to the different scores by the two metrics. This shows that the choice of evaluation metric can have a significant impact on system comparison. Hence, a proper selection of evaluation metrics is critical to this end. It needs to be based on careful evaluation and analysis of the strengths and weaknesses of each evaluation metric.

4   Conclusion

We have presented our recent work on the evaluation of a number of popular scoring metrics for automatic MT evaluation using parallel texts from the legal domain. As so many evaluation metrics are available for measuring different features of MT outputs and each of them has its own strengths and weaknesses on various text types as well as language pairs, this evaluation has explored the basic methodology to guide us to opt for a proper choice of evaluation metric for our particular situation. It also serves as a complement to other related evaluations on other text genera and languages, in the hope of a more comprehensive understanding of the evaluation metrics in use.

Our evaluation shows that the pioneering evaluation metrics BLEU and its variant NIST demonstrate their high reliability in evaluating EC translation, especially with the aid of Chinese word segmentation. For CE translation, however, our own metric ATEC achieves a higher correlation with human judgments of translation quality. The impact of such difference in the correlation is further exemplified by the huge variance of the system rankings of online MT systems on different language pairs. The high correlations obtained by BLEU, ATEC and other evaluation metrics, however, are retainable only at the system level. The correlations at the sentence level are still rather low for all evaluation metrics. This suggests an inadequacy of our understanding of the elements that constitute the notion of translation quality and how they contribute to the quality. Our future work will concentrate on further exploration in this direction. The evaluation data generated in our work reported above, including the system translations, human judgments and scores of evaluation metrics, has been made publicly available at `http://144.214.20.216:8080/ctbwong/ LegalMetaEval/` for research purpose.

References

1. Doyon, J., Taylor, K., White, J.: The DARPA Machine Translation Evaluation Methodology: Past and Present. In: AMTA 1998, Philadelphia, PA (1998)
2. Tomita, M., Shirai, M., Tsutsumi, J., Matsumura, M., Yoshikawa, Y.: Evaluation of MT Systems by TOEFL. In: TMI 1993: The Fifth International Conference on Theoretical and Methodological Issues in Machine Translation, Kyoto, Japan, pp. 252–265 (1993)
3. Yu, S.: Automatic Evaluation of Quality for Machine Translation Systems. Machine Translation 8, 117–126 (1993)
4. Papineni, K., Roukos, S., Ward, T., Zhu, W.-J.: Bleu: a Method for Automatic Evaluation of Machine Translation. IBM Research Report, RC22176 (2001)
5. Doddington, G.: Automatic Evaluation of Machine Translation Quality Using N-gram Co-occurrence Statistics. In: Second International Conference on Human Language Technology Research, San Diego, California, pp. 138–145 (2002)
6. Snover, M., Dorr, B., Schwartz, R., Micciulla, L., Makhoul, J.: A Study of Translation Edit Rate with Targeted Human Annotation. In: AMTA 2006, Cambridge, Massachusetts, USA, pp. 223–231 (2006)
7. Banerjee, S., Lavie, A.: METEOR· an Automatic Metric for MT Evaluation with Improved Correlation with Human Judgments. In: ACL 2005: Workshop on Intrinsic and Extrinsic Evaluation Measures for Machine Translation and/or Summarization, pp. 65–72. University of Michigan, Ann Arbor (2005)
8. Liu, Q., Hou, H., Lin, S., Qian, Y., Zhang, Y., Isahara, H.: Introduction to China's HTRDP Machine Translation Evaluation. In: MT Summit X, pp. 18–22. Phuket, Thailand (2005)
9. Choukri, K., Hamon, O., Mostefa, D.: MT evaluation & TC-STAR. In: MT Summit XI Workshop: Automatic Procedures in MT Evaluation, Copenhagen, Denmark (2007)
10. NIST Open MT Evaluation, `http://www.nist.gov/speech/tests/mt/`
11. Callison-Burch, C., Fordyce, C., Koehn, P., Monz, C., Schroeder, J.: Further Meta-evaluation of Machine Translation. In: ACL 2008: HLT - Third Workshop on Statistical Machine Translation, pp. 70–106. Ohio State University, Columbus (2008)
12. Culy, C., Riehemann, S.Z.: The Limits of N-gram Translation Evaluation Metrics. In: MT Summit IX, New Orleans, USA (2003)
13. Callison-Burch, C., Osborne, M., Koehn, P.: Re-evaluating the Role of Bleu in Machine Translation Research. In: EACL 2006, Trento, Italy, pp. 249–256 (2006)
14. Babych, B., Hartley, A., Elliott, D.: Estimating the Predictive Power of N-gram MT Evaluation Metrics across Language and Text Types. In: MT Summit X, Phuket, Thailand, pp. 412–418 (2005)
15. Kit, C., Wong, T.M.: Comparative Evaluation of Online Machine Translation Systems with Legal Texts. Law Library Journal 100-2, 299–321 (2008)
16. Kit, C., Liu, X., Sin, K.K., Webster, J.J.: Harvesting the Bitexts of the Laws of Hong Kong from the Web. In: 5th Workshop on Asian Language Resources, Jeju Island, pp. 71–78 (2005)

17. Estrella, P., Hamon, O., Popescu-Belis, A.: How much Data is Needed for Reliable MT Evaluation? Using Bootstrapping to Study Human and Automatic Metrics. In: MT Summit XI, Copenhagen, Denmark, pp. 167–174 (2007)
18. NIST's Guideline of Machine Translation Assessment, http:// projects.ldc.upenn.edu/TIDES/Translation/TransAssess04.pdf
19. Wong, T.M., Kit, C.: Word Choice and Word Position for Automatic MT Evaluation. In: AMTA 2008 Workshop: Metrics for Machine Translation Challenge, Waikiki, Hawaii (2008)
20. Zhao, H., Huang, C.N., Li, M.: An Improved Chinese Word Segmentation System with Conditional Random Field. In: Fifth SIGHAN Workshop on Chinese Language Processing, Sydney, Australia, pp. 162–165 (2006)

Appendix: Introduction of ATEC

ATEC evaluates MT outputs in terms of two essential features of translation quality, namely, word choice and word position. The word choice of a translation is measured by the conventional measures precision (P), recall (R) and their average F-measure (F), in terms of the unigram matching rate between a candidate translation (c) and a reference translation (r), which is defined as follows in (1):

$$F(c,r) = \frac{2P(c,r)R(c,r)}{P(c,r)+R(c,r)} \tag{1}$$

To account for the variances of word position between the candidate and the reference, we add a penalty to the formula to sum up the word position differences of each matched unigram as follows in (2), where w is a weighting factor empirically set to 4.

$$Penalty = 1 - w * \sum_{match(c,r)} PosDiff(c,r) \tag{2}$$

The ATEC score for each candidate sentence is computed by combining the unigram F-measure and the penalty of word position difference in the following formula. The final score for a system is obtained by averaging the sentence scores.

$$ATEC = F(c,r) * Penalty \tag{3}$$

Flattened Syntactical Phrase-Based Translation Model for SMT

Qing Chen and Tianshun Yao

Natural Language Processing Lab, Northeastern University,
Shenyang, Liaoning, P.R. China
chenqing@ics.neu.edu.cn, tsyao@mail.neu.edu.cn

Abstract. This paper proposed a flattened syntactical phrase-based translation model for Statistical Machine Translation (SMT) learned from bilingual parallel parsed texts. The flattened syntactical phrases are sets of ordered leaf nodes with their father nodes of single syntax trees or forests ignoring the inner structure, containing lexicalized terminals and non-terminals as variable nodes. Constraints over the variable nodes in target side guarantee correct syntactical structures of translations in accordant to the syntactical knowledge learned from parallel texts. The experiments based on Chinese-to-English translation show us a predictable result that our model achieves 1.87% and 4.76% relative improvements, over Pharaoh, the state-of-art phrase-based translation system, and the system of traditional tree-to-tree model based on STSG.

Keywords: flattened syntactical phrase; synchronous grammar; syntactical structure.

1 Introduction

There have been several popular models for SMT in recent years, since the state-of-art word-based model [1] again received attentions last century. Among all these models, phrase-based models are most popular, due to theirs simplicity and powerful mechanism for well modeling local reorderings and multi-word translations. While due to the fact that phrase-based models cannot handle long-distance reorderings, discontinuous phrases and linguistic information, such as syntactical structure, syntax-based models are then proposed. There are two alternative ways to make use of syntactical information: one is to use additional non-linguistic structures or grammars to describe real syntactical structures of languages [4,5]; the other way is to directly model syntactical structure(s) of languages [6,7,8,9,10,12,13].

Although good models and advancements has been proposed already, there are still several fundamental issues for SMT to be investigated, such as how to properly transfer non-isomorphic trees between languages , and reorderings models based on structures and so on.

In this paper, we propose a translation model based on flattened syntactical phrases, which are designed to reduce the complicity and sparseness of original tree-to-tree models by ignoring the inner structures of aligned trees or forests, and

W. Li and D. Mollá-Aliod (Eds.): ICCPOL 2009, LNAI 5459, pp. 345–353, 2009.

somehow to relieve the negative influence of the errors companied with syntactical analysis. In additional, for flattened syntactical phrase, $\{V_i\}$, non-terminals indexed by i, where i is the start position of aligned nodes in the other side, are introduced to make translation more flexible, and we find that some invalid translations can be firstly filtered in accordance to the syntactical context of V_i.

2   Related Work

For phrase-based models, a French (source) sentence f is always segmented into various different phrase combinations, where each phrase has several English (destination) translations learned from bilingual parallel texts; then in each phrase combination, the translations of phrases are then permutated to be candidate English translations; finally, by using certain ranking methods, one or more most higher-score English sentence(s) e would be selected as the best translation(s) of f from all English candidate sentences generated by model.

The noisy-channel model [2] is firstly introduced for modeling the translation by assuming that the inputted f is encoded from e, and the aim of translation is to find a decoder to encode e into f. By Bayesian rule, this procedure can be formalized as:

$$e^* = \underset{e}{\mathrm{argmax}}\, P(e|f) = \underset{e}{\mathrm{argmax}}\, P(e)P(f|e)$$

where we call $P(e)$ and $P(f|e)$ as language model and translation model respectively. One more flexible model is then proposed by Och and Ney [3], a log-linear model using Maximum Entropy framework:

$$P(e|f)\frac{1}{z(e)}\exp\left(\sum_{m=1}^{M} \lambda_m h_m(f,e)\right)$$

where $h_m(f,e)$ is defined as the mth feature function over f and e, and λ_m is its weight; $z(e)$ is a factor for normalization. Under this framework, any traditional models mentioned above and any relevant knowledge can be easily taken into account as feature functions. It has been a standard framework for SMT.

Much efforts have been carried out to improve reordering models for phrase-based models, including the basic distance-based distortion model [14,15], flat reordering model [16], lexicalized reordering model [17,18], phrase reordering model [19], and syntactical reordering models [20,21] for global reorderings.

There already exist several syntax-based tree-to-tree translation models sharing similar idea in mapping between syntactical trees of both languages, such as Cowan's tree adjoining grammar (TAG) [7], and dependency grammars [9,22,23]. It seems to be hard and complicate that these models leave syntactical structures unchanged for modeling. A tree sequence alignment-based model proposed in [24], captures both non-syntactical phrases and discontinuous phrases with linguistic features.

To avoid the weaknesses of syntactical information, synchronous grammar based translation models are proposed by defining a non-syntactical structures to denote the real structures of languages, such as Inversion Transduction Grammar (ITG) [4], where syntactical trees are restructured as binary trees, and then the reordering problem turns to be ordered or reversed; for hierarchical phrase-based model [5], hierarchical structures are only determined by word alignments, but to some extent, they always could capture syntactical information in a flat form.

3 Motivation

Considering the translation example and their syntactical trees shown in Fig. 1, the syntactical structures of both language completely different, but we still could find possible mappings for translation by word alignments, such as:

Source: $VP \rightarrow PP(P(与_1)NR(北韩_2))VP\ (VE(有_3)\ NN(邦交_4))$,

Target: $VP \rightarrow VBP(have_3)\ NP(NP(diplomatic\ relations_4)\ PP(IN(with_1)\ NP(North\ Korea_2)))$

where the words with same subscript in both languages are connected, and nodes with brackets indicate their structures, a tree-to-tree model can extract syntactical rules as:

$$< VP \rightarrow PP(P(与)\ NR_1)\ VP(VE(有)\ NN_2),$$
$$VP \rightarrow VBP(have)\ NP(NP_2\ PP(IN(with)\ NP_1)) > \qquad (1)$$

which require full structure matching in source side and then the possible translations are also limited to the ones rooted by NP. In fact, a suitable translation may not be rooted by NP, but be rooted by the nodes equaling to NP in syntactical form.

And for hierarchical phrase-based model, a possible rule is shown:

$$< 与X_1\ 有\ X_2 \rightarrow have\ X_2\ with\ X_1 > \qquad (2)$$

this rule seems to be clearly and flat, any content matching this hierarchical phrase [与 X_1 有 X_2] could be translated into [$have\ X_2\ with\ X_1$], regardless of what the

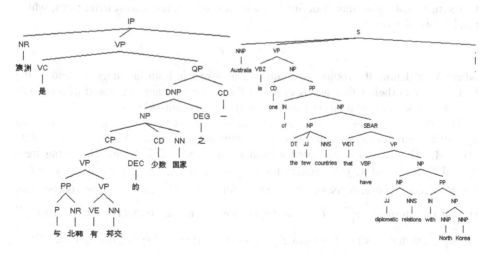

Fig. 1. Bilingual syntactical trees of translation example

contents of X_1 and X_2 really are, even their structures. One sample as $[X_1 \text{ 的 } X_2]$, its translations include $[X_2 \text{ that } X_1]$, $[X_1 X_2]$, $[X_2 \text{ of } X_1]$, etc. There are two issues to be noticed: first, how to determine the boundaries of X_1 and X_2 because different boundaries may lead to different translations, and they share the same probabilities in hierarchical phrase-based model; second, even the boundaries of X_1 and X_2 are determined, the selection of its translation rules can only be determined by the probabilities estimated in training data, regardless of the syntactical structure it really contains. These sometimes occur simultaneous, for example, Chinese strings [削[苹果 的皮]] and [[削苹果]的刀], where symbols [and] are used to indicate the real syntactical structures, share the same form $[X_1 \text{ 的 } X_2]$, but in fact, their syntactical structures and translations are completely different.

As above mentioned, our flattened syntactical phrases are then proposed to handle them. By the definition in section 4, above translation pair can be rewrite as:

$$< VP \rightarrow X_1 \, VP(X_2), VP \rightarrow have \, X_2|_{R2+PP \rightarrow NP} \, X_1|_{NP+R1 \rightarrow NP}) > \quad (3)$$

where $R1$ and $R2$ refer to the root of X_1 and X_2 respectively; on source side, only root(s) and leaf nodes with their father nodes are for searching procedure; and on target side, syntactical constraints on variable nodes are given, according to its syntactical context, such as $X_1|_{NP+R1 \rightarrow NP}$, which means whatever the translations of X_1 are, $R1$ should always form a syntactical structure NP with the previous node NP.

There are also lexical phrases similar to that in phrase-based models, except for syntactical context, such as:

$$< CD \, NN \rightarrow \text{少数国家}, NP \rightarrow the \, few \, countries > \quad (4)$$

4 Synchronous Grammar

Our synchronous grammar is defined as a serious of synchronous rewrite rules, which can be formalized as:

$$< X \rightarrow \alpha, Y \rightarrow \beta >$$

where X, Y denote the root(s) of a sub-tree or forest in both languages; α and β, the leaf nodes and their father nodes of X and Y respectively, are composed of terminals (lexicons) and non-terminals (variable nodes) in each right-side.

The rule extraction method in our model use word alignment and bilingual syntactical structures to determine the boundaries of rules. Given training data $\{[f, e, A, D]\}$, where A is the word alignment of f and e, D is bilingual parsing trees T_f and T_e for f and e, f_i^{i+M} stands for a syntactical phrase in f from position i to $i + M$, $T_{f_i^{i+M}}$ represents as the sub-tree or forest of f_i^{i+M} and X as its root(s); and similar definitions to e_j^{j+N}, $T_{e_j^{j+N}}$ and Y in target; a is the connections between f_i^{i+M} and e_j^{j+N}, then we call $< X \rightarrow T_{f_i^{i+M}}, Y \rightarrow T_{e_j^{j+N}}, a >$ a flattened syntactical phrase, iff:

1. **1.** $\forall f_k \sim e_k \in a$, $f_k \in f_i^{i+M}$ and $e_k \in e_j^{j+N}$; **2.** $\forall f_k \in T_{f_i^{i+M}}, f_k \in f_i^{i+M}$ or f_k is non-aligned; **3.** $\forall e_k \in T_{e_j^{j+N}}, e_k \in e_j^{j+N}$ or e_k is non-aligned; **4.**   non-aligned f_k at either sides of $T_{f_i^{i+M}}$, makes $f_i^{i+M} - f_k \Rightarrow T_{f_i^{i+M}-f_k}$; **5.**   non-aligned e_k at either sides of $T_{e_j^{j+N}}$, makes $e_j^{j+N} - e_k \Rightarrow T_{e_j^{j+N}-e_k}$.

More formally, the set of rules is the ones derived from flattened syntactical phrase or composed with other rules, which are satisfied with:

1. **1.**   If $< X \to T_{f_i^{i+M}}, Y \to T_{e_j^{j+N}}, a >$ is a syntactical phrase pair, then $< X \to f_i^{i+M}, Y \to e_j^{j+N} >$ is a initial rule of $[f, e, A, D]$;

2. **2.** If $< X \to \alpha, Y \to \beta >$ is a rule of $[f, e, A, D]$, and $< X \to T_{f_i^{i+M}}, Y \to T_{e_j^{j+N}}, a >$, here $\alpha = \alpha_1 N \alpha_2$ and $\beta = \beta_1 V \beta_2$, then $< X \to \alpha_1 N_k \alpha_2, Y \to \beta_1 V_k \beta_2 >$ is a composed rule of $[f, e, A, D]$, k is index for connecting terminals and non-terminals in both sides.

Large amount of rules would be extracted by above definitions. To avoid some of them which contain too many nodes or complicated structures slowing down training and decoding procedures, we filter the extracted rules by: the number of non-terminals and terminals in source side is limited to $N(=4)$, due to the statistics that the percentage of nodes with 2-4 children is more than 95%; the depth of source right-side structure is limited to $H(=N-2)$, where 2 is the minimal number of children that non-terminals contains; only $V(-2)$ non-terminals are allowed in single rule; fully non-terminals rules are the special ones with only 1 depth allowed.

5 Translation Model

Done as in [3,5] , we use a log-linear model over derivations to denote our model, instead of the traditional noisy-channel model:

$$\Pr(D, e|f) = \exp(\sum_I \lambda_i h_i(D)) / \sum_D (\exp\left(\sum_I \lambda_i h_i(D)\right)) \tag{5}$$

where $\Pr(D, e|f)$ is the probability of derivation D, which is proportional to that of D conditioned on f; $h_i(D)$ is a feature function defined on derivation D with weight λ_i.

A derivation always contains many ordered rules, so we could decompose above feature functions on rules as following:

$$h_i(D) = \prod_{<\cdot> \in D} h_i(< X \to \alpha, Y \to \beta >) \tag{6}$$

$<\cdot>$ is each single rule of D, then if we treat these features as the weight of rules:

$$w(< X \to \alpha, Y \to \beta >) = \prod_i h_i(< X \to \alpha, Y \to \beta >)^{\lambda_i} \tag{7}$$

then the translation model can be final written as:

$$Pr(D, e|f) = \frac{\exp(\lambda_{LM} h_{LM}(e) + w(D))}{\sum_D (\lambda_{LM} h_{LM}(e) + w(D))} \tag{8}$$

where $h_{LM}(e)$ is defined as a feature of n-gram language model with weight λ_{LM}.

5.1 Features

The features used in our model can be divided into two parts, one is the default feature set as in phrase-based models, and the rests are the syntactical features:

- $Pr(\alpha|\beta)$, $Pr(\beta|\alpha)$, $leaf(\alpha|\beta)$, $leaf(\beta|\alpha)$, similar to the traditional translation probability as that of phrase-based model;
- $Pr(T_e|e)$, $Pr(e|T_e)$, the probabilities e generated by T_e and e parsed to T_e;
- Rule Penalties: Rule number penalty, allows to model the prefer rule number in derivation; Depth penalty, allow to model the prefer structures, more flat or sharp; Penalty for null translated words;
- Traditional features, the 5-gram language model and word penalty.

6 Decoder

Our decoder is based on a redefined algorithm based on Cocke-Kasami-Younger (CKY) algorithm with beam search, for mapping derivations of languages:

$$A \overset{R}{\to} < A_1, A_2, ..., A_N > \tag{9}$$

where R is the rule covering the sequence of $A_1, A_2, ..., A_l$, and $< A_1, A_2, ..., A_l >$ is the translation of $A_1, A_2, ..., A_l$ by R. Clearly, we can find that when $N = 2$, it return to original CKY algorithm. So given a French string f, our decoder is to find a best derivation D that yields $\hat{e}$ making:

$$\hat{e} = \underset{D \to f}{\text{argmax}} \ P(D, e|f) \tag{10}$$

7 Experiments

In this section, experiments on Chinese-to-English translation are applied, and three models are used: **Helix**, the implementation of our model; Pharaoh, the state-of-art phrase-based system; and the traditional tree-to-tree model using STSG. Two 5-gram language models trained respectively on training set and English Gigaword corpus containing 2.8 billion words are used in models, and Stanford lexicalized parser[1] for parsing Chinese sentences, Berkeley parser[2] for English sentences. The statistics of data sets are listed in Table 1 in detail.

---

[1] Free toolkit available on http://nlp.stanford.edu/software/lex-parser.shtml
[2] Free toolkit available on http://nlp.cs.berkeley.edu/pages/Parsing.html

Table 1. Statistics of Data Sets for Experiments

Data Set	Corpus	#Sentence
Training Set	FBIS	12.8M
Testing Set	NIST 06 test	1,048
Dev. Set	NIST 05 test	1,082

7.1 Baseline Systems

For baseline system one, Pharaoh, the state-of-art phrase-based model, all the parameters remain default as those in Pharaoh. The length for source phrases is limited to 3, and 5 for target phrases. The features not relating to syntax are also added for fair comparison; and baseline two is a traditional tree-to-tree model using STSG applied similar limitations of syntactical structures mentioned in 4.1.

7.2 Helix

In *Helix* system, the input is source sentence and its syntax tree. A preprocess that removing non-terminals with one single child, subcategorizing some node annotations with various context, such as *VP* into *VP, VPD, VPG, VPN, VPP, VPZ* by their annotations, are implemented firstly. According to the rule extraction method, we totally extracted 5.48M rules, and by limitations, finally get 2.58M rules, of which 1.22M are lexicon rules and 93.3K fully non-terminal rules. Following is the number of each rule type used in developing and testing data sets:

Table 2. The number of rules for Dev and Testing Sets

Data	Lexicon Rules	Total Rules
Dev Set	117.9K	243.3K
Testing Set	103.4K	234.9K

7.3 Evaluation

The evaluation metric for these experiments is a case insensitive BLEU-4. The parameters of feature functions in both systems are firstly trained by minimal error rate training method proposed by, and then are used in corresponding translation models. The final performance of the three systems shows in table 3.

Table 3. BLEU Scores of systems

System	Dev Set	Testing Set
Pharaoh	0.2610	0.2530
STSG	0.2332	0.2247
Helix	0.2758	0.2723

Our system achieves 1.87% and 4.76% relative improvements over two baseline systems on testing set, which shows that our model can better modeling translation, and compared to STSG, our model is more competitive in handling syntactical structures by flattening syntactical structures into syntactical phrases.

For some complicate and long-range syntactical structures, our model performs much better than STSG, but there are still some syntactical structures not modeling well for both systems, such as the most simple sequence or structure of similar words separated by Chinese punctuation "、", because we could not count on the models to generate a single powerful rule to cover all these samples with different number of words, not to say Pharaoh.

8 Conclusion and Future Work

In this paper, we proposed a flattened syntactical phrase-based translation model, and experimental results indicate our model outperform over the state-of-art phrase-based model, Pharaoh and traditional tree-to-tree model using STSG. Our method managed to make traditional tree-to-tree model more flexible by turn syntactical structures into flattened syntactical phrases only containing the key nodes as the root, leaf nodes and their father nodes for translation. Flattened syntactical phrases not only function like hierarchical phrases, but also can incorporate syntactical information for guidance.

The conflicts between word alignment and syntactical structures in rule extraction cause many losses of rules compared to non-tree-to-tree models, a possible way is by using a loosely aligning model or cross-validation on them to allow more possible translation rule to be extracted.

Acknowledgments

This work was supported in part by the National 863 High-tech Project (2006AA01Z154), the Program for New Century Excellent Talents in University (NCET-05-0287), MSRA research grant(FY08-RES-THEME-227), and National Science Foundation of China(60873091).

References

1. Brown, P.F., Cocke, J., Della Pietra, S.A., Della Pietra, V.J., Jelinek, F., Lafferty, J.D., Mercer, R.L., Roossin, P.S.: A statistical approach to machine translation. Computational Linguistics 16(2), 79–85 (1990)
2. Brown, P.F., Cocke, J., Della Pietra, S.A., Della Pietra, V.J., Mercer, R.L.: The mathematics of machine translation: Parameter estimation. Computational Linguistics 19, 263–312 (1993)
3. Och, F.J., Ney, H.: Discriminative training and maximum entropy models for statistical machine translation. In: Proceedings of the 40th Annual Meeting of the ACL, pp. 295–302 (2002)
4. Wu, D.: Stochastic inversion transduction grammars and bilingual parsing of parallel corpora. Computational Linguistics 23, 377–404 (1997)
5. Chiang, D.: A hierarchical phrase-based model for statistical machine translation. In: Proceedings of the 43rd Annual Meeting of the ACL, pp. 263–270 (2005)

6. Gildea, D.: Loosely tree-based alignment for machine translation. In: Proceedings of the 41st Annual Meeting of the ACL, companion volume (2003)
7. Cowan, B., Kucerova, I., Collins, M.: A discriminative model for tree-to-tree translation. In: Proceedings of the 2006 Conference on Empirical Methods in Natural Language Processing, pp. 232–241 (2006)
8. Quirk, C., Menezes, A., Cherry, C.: Dependency Treelet Translation: Syntactically Informed Phrasal SMT. In: Proceedings of the 43rd Annual Meeting of the ACL, pp. 271–279 (2005)
9. Liu, Y., Liu, Q., Lin, S.: Tree-to-string Alignment Template for Statistical Machine Translation. In: Proceedings of the 44th Annual Meeting of the ACL, pp. 609–616 (2006)
10. Huang, L., Knight, K., Joshi, A.: Statistical syntax-directed translation with extended domain of locality. In: Proceedings of the 7th Biennial Conference of the Association for Machine Translation in the Americas (AMTA), pp. 66–73 (2006)
11. Yamada, K., Knight, K.: A syntax-based statistical translation model. In: Proceedings of the 39th Annual Meeting of the ACL (2001)
12. Marcu, D., Wang, W., Echihabi, A., Knight, K.: SPMT: Statistical Machine Translation with syntactified target language phrases. In: Proceedings of the 2006 Conference on Empirical Methods in Natural Language Processing, pp. 44–52 (2006)
13. Koehn, P., Och, F.J., Marcu, D.: Statistical Phrase-based Translation. In: HLT/NAACL 2003, pp. 127–133 (2003)
14. Och, F.J., Ney, H.: The alignment template approach to statistical machine translation. Computational linguistics 30, 417–449 (2004)
15. Koehn, P., Och, F.J., Marcu, D.: Statistical phrase-based translation. In: Proceeding of HLT-MAACL, pp. 127–133 (2003)
16. Kumar, S., Byrne, W.: Local phrase reordering models for statistical machine translation. In: Proceedings of Human Language Technology Conference and Conference on Empirical Methods in Natural Language processing (HLT/EMNLP), Vancouver, Canada, pp. 161–168 (2005)
17. Kumar, S., Byrne, W.: Local phrase reordering models for statistical machine translation. In: HLT-EMNLP 2005 (2005)
18. Koehn, P., Axelrod, A., Birch, A., Mayne, Callison-Burch, C.: Edinburgh system description. In: IWSLT 2005 Speech Translation Evaluation (2005)
19. Xiong, D., Liu, Q., Lin, S.: Maximum Entropy Based Phrase Reordering Model for Statistical Machine Translation. In: Proceedings of the 21st International Conference on Computational Linguistics and 44th ACL, Sydney, Australia, pp. 521–528 (2006)
20. Li, C.-H., Zhang, D., Li, M., Zhou, M., Guan, Y.: A Probabilistic Approach to Syntax-based Reordering for Statistical Machine Translation. In: Proceedings of the 45th Annual Meeting of the ACL (2007)
21. Wang, C., Collins, M., Koehn, P.: Chinese Syntactic Reordering for Statistical Machine Translation. In: EMNLP-CNLL 2007, pp. 737–745 (2007)
22. Lin, D.: A path-based transfer model for machine translation. In: Proceedings of COLING (2004)
23. Ding, Y., Palmer, M.: Machine Translation Using Probabilistic Synchronous Dependency Insertion Grammars. In: Proceedings of the 43rd Annual Meeting of the ACL (2005)
24. Zhang, M., Jiang, H., Aw, A., Li, H., Tan, C.L., Li, S.: A Tree Sequence Alignment-based Tree-to-Tree Translation Model. In: Proceedings of the 46th Annual Meeting of the ACL (2008)

An Integrated Approach for Concept Learning and Relation Extraction

Qingliang Zhao and Zhifang Sui

Institute of Computational Linguistics, Peking University
Beijing, PRC
{zhaoqingliang,szf}@pku.edu.cn

Abstract. Concept learning and hierarchical relations extraction are core tasks of ontology automatic construction. In the current research, the two tasks are carried out separately, which separates the natural association between them. This paper proposes an integrated approach to do the two tasks together. The attribute values of concepts are used to evaluate the extracted hierarchical relations. On the other hand, the extracted hierarchical relations are used to expand and evaluate the attribute values of concepts. Since the interaction is based on the inaccurate result that extracted automatically, we introduce the weight of intermediate results of both tasks into the iteration to ensure the accuracy of results. Experiments have been carried out to compare the integrated approach with the separated ones for concept learning and hierarchical relations. Our experiments show performance improvements in both tasks.

Keywords: Ontology, Integrated Approach, Concept Learning, Attribute Values Extraction, Hierarchical Relations Extraction.

1 Introduction

Ontology is a kind of concept models that could describe system at the level of semantics and knowledge. It aims to access knowledge of a domain in a general way and provides a common understanding for concepts in the domain so as to realize knowledge sharing and reuse among different application programs and organizations [1].At the beginning, most of ontologies are constructed entirely by hand, which had to spend a great deal money, material, manpower and time. Automatic or semi-automatic means have been proposed for the last 30 years and many achievements have been made.

Researches on ontology automatic construction are substantially as follows: term extraction [2] [3], concept extraction including: definition of terms and attributes of terms [4], relations between terms extraction [5], concept hierarchies clustering [6].

Automatic extraction of attributes values for a concept is one of the most important tasks of concept learning. Named-Entity Recognition and Information Extraction are currently used in this task. Hierarchical relation is among the most important relations about concepts and is a fundamental way to organize the knowledge. Lexico-syntactic patterns, Distributional Similarity & Clustering, Document-subsumption and Linguistic

W. Li and D. Mollá-Aliod (Eds.): ICCPOL 2009, LNAI 5459, pp. 354–361, 2009.

Approaches and so on are currently used to extract the hierarchical relations automatically[7][8].

In the current research, concept learning and hierarchical relations extraction are carried out separately, however there are interrelated to each other. On the one hand, the attribute values of concepts are very helpful to judge if they have a "is-a" relationship. On the other hand, we say a concept is the hypernym of some concepts because it has the common attribute values of these concepts. Thus the two tasks can be integrated into one to guide each other.

The remainder of this paper is organized as follows: in section 2, we introduce our basic idea. While in section 3, we present the core algorithm. And then, in section 4, we describe the experiments and do several result analyses. Finally, we conclude and provide avenues for further research.

2 Basic Idea

2.1 Inference of Attributes Values through Hierarchical Relations

If concept A is a hyponymy of concept B, concept A has all the attribute values of concept B.

$$\text{Hyponym}(A, B) \wedge \text{Attribute}(ATTR\_VALUE, \ ATTR\_NAME, \ B) \Rightarrow \qquad (1)$$
$$\text{Attribute}(ATTR\_VALUE, \ ATTR\_NAME, \ A)$$

2.2 Inference of Hierarchical Relations through Attributes Values

If the attribute value set of concept A is the subset of that of concept B, concept A is very likely to be a hypernym of concept B.

$$\text{Attributes}(A) \subset \text{Attributes}(B) \not\Rightarrow \text{Hyponym}(B, A) \qquad (2)$$

2.3 Integration of the Two Approaches

In the integration of the concept learning and hierarchical relations extraction, we can use Hypothesis (1) and hierarchical relations extracted to guide attribute values extraction. Also, we can use Hypothesis (2) and attribute values to guide hierarchical relations extraction. However, as the attribute values extraction and hierarchical relations extraction are completed automatically, the result is not accurate. "Bad" intermediate results may result in even more wrong results in the next iteration. To prevent this, two strategies are introduced to make up.

Strategy 1: Bootstrap based on WWW
Strategy 2: To introduce the weight of premise into the inference

3 Key Technology

3.1 Main Framework

The inputs of the method of integrated approach of concept learning and hierarchical relations extraction based on WWW are concepts, a seed collection of the attributes values and a seed collection of hierarchical relations. The collection of candidates for attributes values and hierarchical relations is gained through the attributes values extraction, hierarchical relations extraction and the interaction between them.

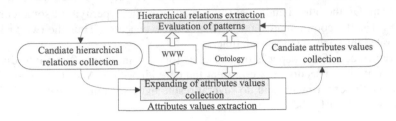

Fig. 1. The figure shows the overview frame of the system

3.2   Extract Hierarchical Relations Guided by Attribute Values

In this section, we present a Bootstrap system (Fig 2), which develops the key component of the hierarchical relations extraction. This system presents a technique to generate patterns from HTML documents (Section 3.2.1). More specially, this system presents a new strategy to evaluate the quality of patterns (Section 3.2.2). Finally, we use the patterns to extract hierarchical relations.

3.2.1   Generate Patterns

The pattern is defined as *<left, A, middle, B, right, weight>*. The *left, middle, right* are the left, middle and right context of both concept A and concept B. The *weight* is the associating weight with the relationship, which can be used to evaluate it.

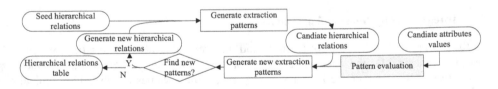

Fig. 2. Extract hierarchical relations

3.2.2   Evaluate Patterns

The evaluation of the candidate pattern is the key part of our system. We evaluate the patterns following the two strategies. One is that the maximal similarity between the pattern to be evaluated and seed patterns is greater than the threshold τ. The other is that the collection of attributes values of concept A and B has a include-relationship.

For the first strategy, the similarity between two patterns P_1 and P_2 is defined as:

$$Sim(P_1, P_2) = \begin{cases} left_{P_1} \square left_{P_2} + middle_{P_1} \square middle_{P_2} + right_{P_1} \square right_{P_2} & if\ the\ Sim(P_1, P_2) \geq \tau \\ 0 & else \end{cases} \quad (3)$$

For the second strategy, the collection of attributes values of concept A and B has a include-relationship is defined as:

$$Include(A,B) = \frac{\sum_i \sum_j Attribute(attrs(A)[i], ATTR\_NAME[j], B) \times weight(attrs(A)[i])}{count(attrs(A))}$$

attrs(A) is the candiate attributes values collection of concept A   (4)

weight(value) is the confidence of attribute value "value".

Integrated formula is as below:

$$Score(P) = Max_i(Sim(P, P_i)) \times Include(A, B) \quad P_i \in Seed\ Patterns \quad (5)$$

The whole process will end when no new candidate relations are generated.

3.3   Extract Attribute Values Guided by Hierarchical Relations

In this section, we present Snowball systems (Figure 3), which develops the function of attribute values extract of each concept. More specially, we present a method to expand seed set through coordinate construction (3.3.1); then we present a method to expand seed set through hierarchical relations extracted by 3.2 (3.3.2).

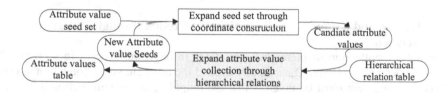

Fig. 3. Extract attribute values

3.3.1   Expand Attribute Value Collection through Coordinate Construction
Our goal is to extract the attribute values of a class with a seeds set from WWW. HTML document is too large scale to be treated as the basic unit. So we can not only retain the necessary context information but also ensure the particle size is suitable. Then the task of attribute values extraction will be divided into two steps as follow:

Step 1: Select the relevant sentences including attribute values;
Step 2: Extract the attribute values from those sentences.

We choose the sentences following the two conditions. The first one is that the sentence contains a coordinate construction. The second one is that the sentence contains at least one attribute value seed. One reason why the coordinate construction is used is that it is the simplest construction. Another reason is that the phrases in the coordinate construction have the same characteristics.

In the case of giving attribute values seeds as few as possible, in order to get adequate relevant sentences and eventually obtain accurate comprehensive aggregation of attribute values, we conclude the strategy of choosing sentences and distilling attributes interactively. The whole process will end until no new candidate attribute value emerges. As below graph, the frame is the part of choosing sentences and distilling attributes interactively.

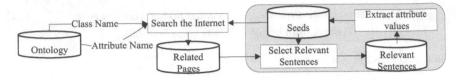

Fig. 4. The interaction between choosing relevant sentences and distilling attributes

If a phrase is in a coordinate construction with another one with high weight, it should also have a high weight too.

$$weight_{phrase} = weight_{phrase} + \sum_{0}^{m} weight_{phrase_m} \qquad (6)$$

$\sum_{0}^{m} weight_{word_m}$ is the sum of the weight of the phrases in the same coordinate construction with the target phrase. Complete algorithm of 3.3.1 is as below:

3.3.2 Expand and Evaluate Attribute Value Collection through Hierarchical Relations

We can get a collection of hierarchical relations through the process in section 3.2, which we denote by *HRSet*. Thus we can expand the attribute value collection via the *HRSet*. One problem must be noted is that the output of process in section 3.2 is not an accurate one. So the attribute values generated through it will be given a weight.

if Hyponym(A, B)
    *Add Attribute (A, ATTR _ NAME, Attr(B)[i], weight(Attr(B)[i]) * weight(Hyponym(A, B)));*
else
    do nothing

If we have extracted that concept A has the attribute value *Attr(B)[i]*, we increase the weight of this attribute value by the product of weight of *Attr(B)[i]* and *Hyponym(A, B)*; else, we create a new attribute value *Attr(B)[i]* for concept A, and set the product of weight of *Attr(B)[i]* and *Hyponym(A, B)* as the weight of it.

4   Experiment

4.1   Experiment Settings

We use Attribute values extraction based on WWW as our baseline 1 and *DIPRE* as our baseline2. *DIPRE* is a method presented by Alex Mayers.This paper choose ontology in modern medicine domain which bases on Medical Subject Headings (MeSH) compiled by U.S. National Library of Medicine. There are 20,000 classes in the ontology and each class has attributes: Name, Definition, Code, Symptom, Laboratory examination, Pathogeny and so on. We choose 100 classes as our test set.We retrieve from the WWW related to an ontology concept via Google API. Only the first 100 documents are used for the attribute values extraction.

4.2 Results

4.2.1 Baseline 1: Attribute Values Extraction Based on WWW
The attribute value extraction task is carried out separately.

Table 1. Manually computed precision estimate, derived from a random sample of 10 concepts

Concept	Seeds	Precision	Recall	F-value
感冒(Cold)	{咳嗽(Cough)}	73.31%	100%	0.8460
慢性咽炎(Chronic pharyngitis)	{咽痛(Pharyngodynia)}	67.33%	100%	0.8048
肺炎(Pneumonia)	{咳嗽(Cough)}	80.19%	73.34%	0.7661
过敏性鼻炎(Allergic rhinitis)	{打喷嚏(Sneezing)}	73.83%	100%	0.8495
非典型性肺炎(SARS)	{发热(Fever)}	87.61%	83.31%	0.8541
浅表性胃炎(Superficial gastritis)	{腹胀(Distension)}	80.09%	88.12%	0.8391
病毒性心肌炎(Viral myocarditis)	{心悸(Palpitation)}	73.23%	88.17%	0.8001
哮喘(Asthma)	{喘息(Breathing)}	67.12%	100%	0.8033
尿毒症(Uremia)	{恶心(Nausea)}	73.31%	83.37%	0.7802
结膜炎(Conjunctivitis)	{眼红(Red Eyes)}	53.31%	83.37%	0.6503
Average		72.93%	90.00%	0.7993

4.2.2 Baseline 2: *DIPRE*
The hierarchical relations extraction task is carried out separately.

Table 2. Use only the strategy I in table 1, and set $\tau =0.80$. Manually computed precision estimate, derived from a random sample of 10 concepts.

	Correct	*Incorrect*	*Precision*
DIPRE	142	76	65.14%

4.2.3 Integrated Approach
The two tasks are done together in an integrated approach.

Table 3. Manually computed precision estimate, derived from a random sample of 10 concepts

Concept	Seeds	Precision	Recall	F-value
感冒(Cold)	{咳嗽(Cough)}	75.19%	100%	0.8584
慢性咽炎(Chronic pharyngitis)	{咽痛(Pharyngodynia)}	73.36%	100%	0.8463
肺炎(Pneumonia)	{咳嗽(Cough)}	86.15%	86.20%	0.8617
过敏性鼻炎(Allergic rhinitis)	{打喷嚏(Sneezing)}	78.51%	100%	0.8796
非典型性肺炎(SARS)	{发热(Fever)}	84.59%	90.72%	0.8755
浅表性胃炎(Superficial gastritis)	{腹胀(Distension)}	80.84%	88.21%	0.8436
病毒性心肌炎(Viral myocarditis)	{心悸(Palpitation)}	70.71%	93.14%	0.8039
哮喘(Asthma)	{喘息(Breathing)}	72.92%	100%	0.8434
尿毒症(Uremia)	{恶心(Nausea)}	73.36%	82.83%	0.7781
结膜炎(Conjunctivitis)	{眼红(Red Eyes)}	53.31%	78.36%	0.6345
Average		74.89%	92.00%	0.8225

The result shows that our approach improves the F-value by 2.32% from the Baseline 1.

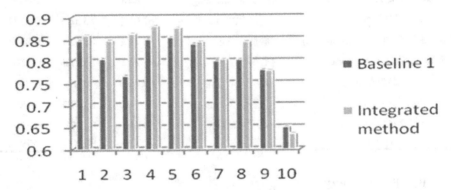

Fig. 5. Compare of Baseline 1 and Integrated method. We can see our approach works better than Baseline 1 at almost all the samples.

Table 4. Use only the strategy I in table 1, and set τ =0.75. Manually computed precision estimate, derived from a random sample of 10 concepts.

	Correct	Incorrect	Precision
DIPRE(τ =0.80)	142	76	65.14%
Our Approach(τ =0.80)	156	62	71.56%
Our Approach(τ =0.75)	169	49	77.52%
Our Approach(τ =0.40)	103	115	47.25%

The result shows that our approach improves the Precision by 12.38% from the Baseline 2.

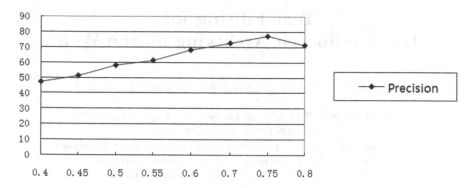

Fig. 6. The precision with different values of the parameter τ

We get the best result when τ given the value 0.75.

5 Conclusions and Further Research

This paper proposes an integrated approach. The candidate attribute values of concepts are used to evaluate the extracted hierarchical relations. The hierarchical relations are used to expand the candidate attribute values of concepts. We introduce the weight into the iteration to ensure the accuracy of results. Our experiments show performance improvements in both tasks.

Acknowledgments. This work is supported by NSFC Project 60503071, 60873156, 863 High Technology Project of China 2006AA01Z144 and 973 Natural Basic Research Program of China 2004CB318102.

References

1. Liu, Y.: On Automatic Construction of Domain Ontology, Post-Doctor thesis, Peking University (2007)
2. Sato, S., Sasaki, Y.: Automatic collection of related terms from the web. IPSJ SIG Notes 2003(4), 57–64, 20030120 (2003)
3. Buitelaar, P., Cimiano, P., Grobelnik, M., Sintek, M.: Ontology Learning from Text. In: Tutorial at ECML/PKDD 2005 (2005)
4. Cimiano, P., Staab, S.: Learning Concept Hierarchies from Text with a Guided Agglomerative Clustering Algorithm. In: Proceedings of the ICML 2005 Workshop on Learning and Extending Lexical Ontologies with Machine Learning Methods (2005)
5. Cimiano, P.: Ontology Learning and Population: Algorithms, Evaluation and Applications. PhD thesis, University of Karlsruhe (forthcoming, 2005)
6. Agichtein, E., Gravano, L.: Snowball: Extracting Relations from Large Plain-Text Collections. In: ACM DL (2000)
7. Cimiano, P., Hotho, A., Staab, S.: Learning concept hierarchies from text corpora using formal concept analysis. J. Artificial Intelligence Research 24, 305–339 (2005)
8. Maedche, A.: Ontology Learning for the Semantic Web. Kluwer Academic Publishers, Boston (2002)

Text Editing for
Lecture Speech Archiving on the Web

Masashi Ito[1], Tomohiro Ohno[2], and Shigeki Matsubara[3]

[1] Graduate School of Information Science, Nagoya University
masashi@el.itc.nagoya-u.ac.jp
[2] Graduate School of International Development, Nagoya University
[3] Information Technology Center, Nagoya University
Furo-cho, Chikusa-ku, Nagoya, 464-8601, Japan

Abstract. It is very significant in the knowledge society to accumulate spoken documents on the web. However, because of the high redundancy of spontaneous speech, the transcribed text in itself is not readable on an Internet browser, and therefore not suitable as a web document. This paper proposes a technique for converting spoken documents into web documents for the purpose of building a speech archiving system. The technique edits automatically transcribed texts and improves its readability on the browser. The readable text can be generated by applying technology such as paraphrasing, segmentation and structuring to the transcribed texts. An edit experiment using lecture data showed the feasibility of the technique. A prototype system of spoken document archiving was implemented to confirm its effectiveness.

Keywords: spoken language processing, digital archiving, web contents, paraphrasing, sentence segmentation.

1 Introduction

The enormous amount of information on the web have been forming an infrastructure for the so-called knowledge society. Most of such the information is expressed in text at the present time. Hereafter, it is expected that not only texts but also audio, video or other mixed media will be utilized as the knowledge resources. Above all, speech is a kind of language media, and produced daily. In fact, the amount of spoken documents being produced is overwhelmingly more than that of written documents. If the speech such as discourse, lecture, monologue, conversation and discussion are accumulated on the web, the amount of sharable information in the knowledge society would get much larger.

Several styles for archiving the spoken documents on the web can be considered. Though a style of uploading speech data would be very simple and would have high feasibility, its significance from a viewpoint of reusability is not so large. If the transcribed text is also archived in addition to the speech data, its effectiveness would be increased in terms of accessibility. On the other hand, because of high redundancy of spontaneous speech, the transcribed text in itself is not readable on an Internet browser, and therefore not suitable as a web document.

W. Li and D. Mollá-Aliod (Eds.): ICCPOL 2009, LNAI 5459, pp. 362–369, 2009.

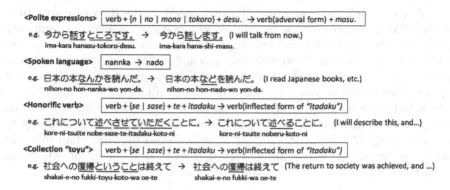

Fig. 1. Examples of the paraphrase rules and their applications

This paper proposes a technique for converting spoken documents into web documents for the purpose of building a speech archiving system. The technique edits automatically transcribed texts and improves its readability on the browser. The readable texts can be generated by applying language technologies such as paraphrasing, segmentation and structuring to the transcribed texts. An edit experiment was conducted by using lecture speech data, and the result has shown the feasibility of the technique. Furthermore, a prototype system of spoken document archiving was implemented in order to confirm its effectiveness.

This paper is organized as follows: Section 2 discusses spoken document archiving on the web. Section 3 describes an edit technique of spoken documents. Section 4 reports evaluation of the technique. Section 5 describes our speech archiving system.

2   Spoken Document Archiving on the Web

We have aimed at constructing an environment where spoken documents are archived as web documents. In general, a web document is described by the markup language such as HTML, and created in consideration of the readability on a browser. In that sense, a spoken document is not suitable for being read with an Internet browser. Therefore, a transcribed text needs to be converted into an HTML text.

As a research on speech archiving for Web contents creation, Bain et al. have constructed a system named ViaScribe in order to improve accessibility of speech data [1]. ViaScribe targets lecture environments and creates a learning material into which audio, video, slides and transcribed texts are integrated. The learning material is uploaded to the Web, then the participants can access it with a Internet browser. ViaScribe inserts linefeeds into the transcribed text at places where pauses occur in order to improve the readability. Although Bain et al. target English speech, redundancy in spoken documents is larger in Japanese speech. Therefore only the linefeed insertion cannot achieve enough readability.

Aiming at improving readability of a text based on the discourse structure, Shibata et al. have proposed a method of automatically generating summary slides from a text [2]. They have clearly specified the relations between sentences or clauses by itemization. However, their research differ from ours in that the units such as words or phrases are not targets. Furthermore, treating the written language, they do not consider the features of spoken language.

As a technique for converting the transcribed text, there exists research on automatic summarization [3, 4, 5, 6] and conversion from spoken language to written language [7]. However, they are all conversions between plain texts. In contrast, we propose a method for converting it into a web document, which can be utilized as a fundamental technology in the archiving system.

3   Text Editing of Spoken Document

The conversion of spoken documents into web documents is executed by editing spoken sentences so that they become easy to read. The conversion is realized by performing paraphrasing of expressions, segmentation into short sentences and structuring of a sentence in sequence.

3.1   Paraphrasing

In spoken language, there are a lot of expressions which are not proper as written language expressions. Such expressions can be converted into readable expressions by paraphrasing them into other expressions.

Paraphrasing is classified into three types: deletion, replacement and insertion, according to the kind of target expressions. In *deletion*, redundant expressions particular to spoken language are removed. There exists not only fillers (uh, er etc.) and hesitations but also other redundant expressions.
(1) 正常化 ということ が行われた (the thing which is called normalization is performed)
"ということ (the thing which is called)" is redundant, and the readability is improved by removing it. In *replacement*, expressions which are not proper as written language are replaced with other expressions. For example, in the case of
(2) 日本の本 なんか を読みました (I read Japanese books, etc.)
"なんか (etc.)" is an expression particular to spoken language. By replacing "なんか (etc.)" with "など (etc.)", it becomes a proper expression. Furthermore, in honorific expressions, polite expressions, and so on, there are several cases where replacement is needed. In *insertion*, expressions which do not appear in spoken language are added.

In order to realize the three types of paraphrasing mentioned above, we created paraphrasing rules by using the actual lecture speech data [8]. Fig. 1 shows examples of the rules and their applications. Here, in insertion, since considering the meaning is required, it is difficult to create the rules by only surface information. Therefore, the target of this paper is limited to deletion and replacement.

Though I think that you may see what Suzuki will say, I'm adopted , so I will talk by the fell of doing a kick-off.

鈴木が何を言うかはご察知と思います。(I think that you may see what Suzuki will say.)
ご指名ですのでキックオフをするという感じで話します。 (I'm adopted, so I will talk by the fell of doing a kick-off.)

Fig. 2. Example of sentence segmentation

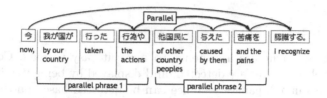

Fig. 3. Detection of the parallel phrases

3.2   Segmentation

In sentence segmentation, one sentence is divided into two or more sentences. In the case of a long sentence, the structure of the sentence is simplified and thus it becomes easy to read. In segmentation, a sentence is divided at any of word boundaries, and the final *bunsetsu*[1] of each divided sentence is transformed into a proper expression as the sentence-end bunsetsu. Fig. 2 shows an example of sentence segmentation.

(3) 鈴木が何を言うかはご察知と思いますがご指名ですのでキックオフをするとい
    う感じで話します。 (Though I think that you may see what Suzuki will say,
    I'm adopted, so I will talk by the feel of doing a kick-off.)

In this example, by inserting a sentence boundary between "思いますが (Though I think that)" and "ご指名ですので (I'm adopted, so)" and transforming "思いますが" into "思います (I think that)", the following sentence is generated:

(4) 鈴木が何を言うかはご察知と思います。ご指名ですのでキックオフをするとい
    う感じで話します。 (I think you may see what Suzuki will say. I'm adopted,
    so I will talk by the feel of doing a kick-off.)

The place into which a sentence boundary should be inserted is limited. For analysis about the place, we divided sentences in the transcribed lecture speech text by hand. About 89% of 299 sentence divisions are performed just after a conjunctive particle *"keredomo"*, *"ga"*, *"node"*, *"shi"*, *"to"*, *"kara"*, or *renyou-tyuushi* bunsetsu. Here, *renyou-tyuushi* bunsetsu is a bunsetsu of which the morphological information is one of the following two cases: adverbial form (e.g. "食べ," "訳で") and adverbial form + conjunctive particle *"te"* (e.g. "食べ て," "書いて") .

---

[1] *Bunsetsu* is a linguistic unit in Japanese that roughly corresponds to a basic phrase in English. A bunsetsu consists of one independent word and zero or more ancillary words.

Since the above-mentioned conjunctive particles and *renyou-tyushi* bunsetsu correspond to a predicate, they often become the ends of semantically meaningful units. In our research, these are considered to be the candidates of sentence boundaries. However, a sentence can not necessarily be divided at all the candidates of division points. In some cases, the meaning of the original sentence may be lost by dividing at the candidate. Therefore, we established the condition of sentence segmentation based on dependency structure. That is, a sentence is segmented at a division point if no bunsetsu, except for a bunsetsu located just before the point, depends on some bunsetsu located after the point.

3.3   Structuring

In our research, we structure a sentence to make it easy to read. Concretely speaking, parallel structures are detected, and displayed by being itemized. The parallel structures in a Japanese sentence can be detected based on the dependency structure. We use JUMAN [10] as morphological analysis and KNP [9] as dependency parsing.

Fig. 3 shows the detection of the parallel phrases in the following sentence:
(5) 今我が国が行った行為や他国民に与えた苦痛を認識する. (Now, I recognize the actions taken by our country and the pains of other country peoples caused by them.)

In this sentence, noun phrase "我が国が行った行為や (the actions taken by our country)" and "他国民に与えた苦痛を (the pains of other country peoples caused by them)" have a parallel relation with each other.

3.4   Example of Sentence Conversion

As an example of text edit by our technique, we describe the edit process of the following sentence:
(6) 西半球には米州機構というのがありますし欧州ヨーロッパには皆様ご承知のようなEUとか全欧州安保協力機構というのがありますしアフリカにはアフリカ統一機構というのがあるわけです。 (In the Western Hemisphere, the Organization of American States exists, and in Europe, the EU and Organization for Security and Cooperation in Europe exist, and in Africa, the Organization of African Unity exists.)

First, in paraphrasing processing, paraphrasing rules are applied to the underlined parts.
(7) 西半球には米州機構 というの がありますし欧州ヨーロッパには皆様ご承知のようなEUとか全欧州安保協力機構 というの がありますしアフリカにはアフリカ統一機構 というの が あるわけです。

Second, in segmentation processing, the sentence is divided into three sentences by slashes right after the underlined bunsetsus.
(8) 西半球には米州機構が ありますし//欧州ヨーロッパには皆様ご承知の EU とか全欧州安保協力機構が ありますし//アフリカにはアフリカ統一機構があります。

Last, in structuring processing, our technique identifies the parallel phrases by

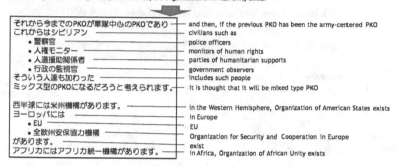

Fig. 4. Conversion of the transcribed text into the edited text

detecting bunsetsus which have parallel relation with each other, based on the dependency structure of the second sentence, and then, the parallel phrases are itemized and displayed.

(9) 欧州ヨーロッパには皆様ご承知の EU とか全欧州安保協力機構が あります。

Fig. 4 shows the conversion of the transcribed text into the edited text. We can see that it becomes easy to read by the conversion.

4   Evaluation

To evaluate our method, we conducted an experiment on text conversion. As the experimental data, we used the transcribed data of five Japanese lectures in the simultaneous interpretation database [8]. We created the correct data of text conversion by editing each sentence in the above-mentioned data by hand. Evaluation is conducted based on each precision and recall for paraphrasing, segmentation and structuring. In addition, the precision is defined as the ratio of the correctly edited places to the places edited by our method, and the recall is defined as the ratio of the correctly edited places to the manually edited places in the correct data.

Fig. 5 shows an example of successful conversions. A total of 1452 places were paraphrased. The precision and recall were 72.5% and 66.5%, respectively. As the result of error analysis, we found out that redundant expressions were not fully deleted. This is because the paraphrasing rules for sentence-end expressions which contain redundant expressions are not fully created.

Next, segmentation was performed at a total of 598 places. The precision and recall of segmentation were 50.5% and 59.3%, respectively. Our segmentation technique does not take into account the length of a sentence. Therefore, even if an original sentence is short or each sentence generated by dividing the original

Fig. 5. Example of a success of the sentence edit

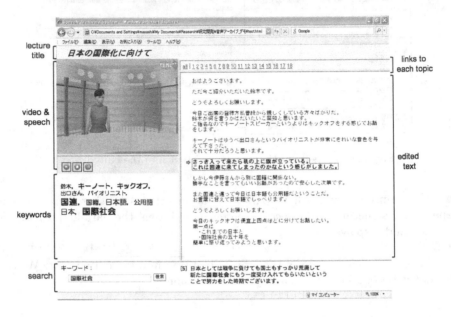

Fig. 6. Speech archiving system RISA

one becomes too short, our method segments the original one. In that case, the readability is not necessarily improved by our segmentation.

Finally, structuring was performed at a total of 201 places. The precision and recall were 32.0% and 25.9%, respectively, both were low. A possible reason is the problem with the accuracy of morphological and dependency analysis. Especially the dependency accuracy on a sentence including parallel structures was not high, and then it materially affected the performance of structuring.

5   Speech Archiving System

We implemented a speech archiving system named RISA according to our technique which has been explained in section 3. The system converts recorded spoken documents into web content for the purpose of their circulation on the Internet. The content consists of five components: text, sound, video, keyword, and search interface (as shown in Fig. 6). The texts are created by executing linefeed insertion and topic segmentation after text editing. They are saved as HTML files. We used the speech synthesis software HitVoice [11] for generating sound content, and TVML (TV program Making Language) [12], which is provided by NHK Science & Technical Research Laboratories, for video content generation. The users can directly access to the subcontents because text, sound and video are aligned in a fine-grained fashion. The important words in the text are presented as keywords. The search component outputs the corresponding topic to the query input. The set of keywords enables broad viewing of the content of a spoken document. The links of each topic enable topic-by-topic browsing and are suitable for selective reuse.

6 Conclusion

This paper has proposed a technique for converting speech transcripts into Web texts for lecture contents archiving. The technique recognizes speech and edits the transcribed text. Paraphrasing, segmentation, and structuring enable removal of unsuitable phrases and redundant expressions in written language. The experiment using lecture speech has shown the effectiveness of the technique. The speech archiving system was implemented to confirm its feasibility.

Acknowledgements. This research was partially supported by the Grant-in-Aid for Scientific Research (B) of JSPS and by The Asahi Glass Foundation.

References

1. Bain, K., Basson, S., Faisman, A., Kanevsky, D.: Accessibility, transcription, and access everywhere. IBM System Journal 44(3), 589–603 (2005)
2. Shibata, T., Kurohashi, S.: Automatic Slide Generation Based on Discourse Structure Analysis. In: Dale, R., Wong, K.-F., Su, J., Kwong, O.Y. (eds.) IJCNLP 2005. LNCS, vol. 3651, pp. 754–766. Springer, Heidelberg (2005)
3. Chatain, P., Whittaker, E.W.D., Mmzinski, J.A., Furui, S.: Topic and Stylistic Adaptation for Speech Summarisation. In: Proc. IEEE ICASSP (2006)
4. James, C., Mirella, L.: Models for Sentence Compression: a Comparison Across Domains, Training Requirements and Evaluation Measures. In: Proc. ACL/COLING 2006, pp. 377–384 (2006)
5. Zhu, X., Penn, G.: Summarization of Spontaneous Conversations. In: Proc. 9th ICSLP, pp. 1531–1534 (2006)
6. Murray, G., Renals, S., Carletta, J., Moore, J.: Incorporating Speaker and Discourse Features into Speech Summarization. In: Proc. HLT, pp. 367–374 (2006)
7. Shitaoka, K., Nanjo, H., Kawahara, T.: Automatic Transformation of Lecture Transcription into Document Style Using Statistical Framework. In: Proc. 8th ICSLP, pp. 2169–2172 (2004)
8. Matsubara, S., Takagi, A., Kawaguchi, N., Inagaki, Y.: Bilingual Spoken Monologue Corpus for Simultaneous Machine Interpretation Research. In: Proc. 3rd LREC, pp. 153–159 (2002)
9. http://nlp.kuee.kyoto-u.ac.jp/nl-resource/knp.html
10. http://nlp.kuee.kyoto-u.ac.jp/nl-resource/juman.html
11. http://www.hke.jp/products/voice/voice_index.htm
12. http://www.nhk.or.jp/strl/tvml/english/player2/index.html

Document Clustering Description Extraction and Its Application

Chengzhi Zhang[1,2], Huilin Wang[2], Yao Liu[2], and Hongjiao Xu[2]

[1] Department of Information Management, Nanjing University of Science & Technology,
Nanjing 210093, China
[2] Institute of Scientific & Technical Information of China, Beijing 100038, China
{zhangchz,wanghl,liuy}@istic.ac.cn, xuhongjiao_1111@163.com

Abstract. Document clustering description is a problem of labeling the clustering results of document collection clustering. It can help users determine whether one of the clusters is relevant to their information requirements or not. To resolve the problem of the weak readability of document clustering results, a method of automatic labeling document clusters based on machine learning is put forward. Clustering description extraction in application to topic digital library construction is introduced firstly. Then, the descriptive results of five models are analyzed respectively, and their performances are compared.

Keywords: clustering description, document clustering, machine learning, topic digital library.

1 Introduction

Clustering description is one of the key issues in document clustering application. The traditional clustering algorithm can cluster the objects, but it can not give concept description for the clustered results. Therefore, it's necessary to find a method to solve the problem of document clustering description and to meet the users' special needs. Document clustering description is to label the clustered results of document collections. It can help users determine whether the clusters are relevant to users' information requirements or not. Therefore, labeling a clustered set of documents is an important and challenging work in document clustering applications.

To resolve the problem of the weak readability of the traditional document clustering results, a method of automatic labeling document clusters based on machine learning is put forward. The authors introduce clustering description extraction in application to topic digital library building firstly. Then, they analyze descriptive results of five models respectively, and compare their performance.

The rest of this paper is organized as follows. The next section reviews some related work on extraction of document clustering description. In section 3, a detailed description of the proposed approach is presented. Subsequently in section 4, the authors introduce clustering description extraction in application to topic digital

W. Li and D. Mollá-Aliod (Eds.): ICCPOL 2009, LNAI 5459, pp. 370–377, 2009.

library building firstly. The proposed approach is then evaluated. The paper is concluded with the conclusion and future wok in section 5.

2 Related Work

Clustering description algorithms can be divided into two categories which are manual description methods and automatic description methods. Glenisson & Glänzel [1], Lai & Wu [2] extracted clustering description manually. Automatic methods mainly extract important words from the clustering set of documents. Different clustering algorithms employ different ways to calculate the importance of words [3].

Cutting & Karger used term frequency as the weight of word and select words with high weight as clustering description [4] [5]. Muller and Dorre used the top N words as clustering description [6]. Anton & Croft [7] used key phrase as classification description. In their opinion, phrase-based cluster representations are superior compared to individual terms-based ones. Zamir & Etzioni [8], Lawrie and Croft [9] set the maximal-length phrases with high frequency and phrases with the highest TF*IDF value in the clustering set to be clustering description respectively. Glover & Pennock [10] used statistical model based on parent, child and self features.

Tseng & Lin [3] used WordNet as an external resource to extract category words to be clustering description symbols. Pucktada & Jamie [11] used statistical information of descriptive words in cluster, super cluster and document set comprehensively to score the descriptive ability of descriptive words and get label of every cluster. Dawid [12] proposed that DCF (*Description Comes First*□can be applied to solve the problem of weak readability and interpretability.

3 Clustering Description Algorithms Based on Machine Learning

To solve the problem of the weak readability of document clustering result, the requirement of clustering description is analyzed. Some methods are used to extract the clustering description. In this paper, clustering description problem is transformed into classification problem, which need to classify or rank candidate category description words. Then, these words can be separated into clustering description words and non-description words. Three machine learning methods i.e. support vector machine model (SVM), multiple linear regression model (MLR) and Logistical regression model (Logit), are used to solve clustering description problem.

3.1 Basic Requirements of Clustering Description

The basic requirements of clustering description should include the following contents:

(1) Conciseness. Conciseness means that clustering description should be as short as possible, but sufficient enough to convey the topic of the cluster [12]. The simplest measurement of conciseness of descriptive words is the length. It can be measured by the number of characters or words in descriptive words. Byron & Martin [13] put forward that the conciseness problem of clustering description can be solved by

combing minimum description length principle and maximum description accuracy principle.

(2) Comprehensibility. Comprehensibility indicates ability to map clustering description to content of clusters. This ability of clustering description is called transparency by Dawid [12], while Krishna [14] calls it the productiveness of labels.

(3) Accuracy. Accuracy means that clustering description should reflect the topic of the corresponding cluster. Different from keyword extraction, object of clustering description is not individual document but multiple documents in the cluster with the same subject. Tseng & Lin [3] use correlation coefficient and its variation to measure the correlation degree between descriptive words and cluster.

(4) Distinctiveness. Distinctiveness means that descriptive words must frequently appear in clusters it represents and rarely appear in other clusters. Hanan & Mohamed [15] propose a modified TF*IDF method to compute the distinctiveness of descriptive words. Pucktada & Jamie [11] also propose a similar method to measure the distinctiveness of descriptive.

Some global features (e.g. frequency of descriptive words in current cluster, a modified TF*IDF and average value of first position of descriptive words appeared in current cluster) are used to measure accuracy and distinctiveness of descriptive words.

3.2 Two Benchmark Models

To compare the performance of clustering description algorithms based on machine learning, two benchmark models, i.e. BaseLine1 (denoted as BL1) and BaseLine2 (denoted as BL2) are proposed respectively.

The first benchmark model uses center vector (which is also called Concept Vector) of clusters as descriptive words. In this paper, top 5 words with the high weights in concept vector will be selected.

The second model is based on a heuristic method. According to the requirements of clustering description, the importance of candidate descriptive words is evaluated with several features which are Document Frequency (DF), Inverse Cluster Frequency (ICF) and length of words (LEN).

3.3 Machine Learning Models

In this paper, three statistical machine learning models, i.e. multiple linear regression model (denoted as MLR), Logistical regression model (denoted as Logit), and support vector machine model (denoted as SVM) will be applied in clustering description extraction respectively. Vapnik proposed support vector model in 1995 to solve the problem of binary classification [16]. In this paper, training and testing of SVM are all based on SVM^{light} [17].

3.4 Feature Selection of Clustering Description

According to the requirements of clustering description, features used in the process of clustering description extraction are shown in table 1.

Table 1. Features of clustering description sample

	Feature denotation	Computation method
Word	Descriptive word	Word
LEN	Length of descriptive word	$\dfrac{Len\ (Word\ )}{Max\ \_\ Len}$
POS	Part-of speech of descriptive word and according to whether single word in descriptive word is a noun, value is 0 or 1.	$\sum_{k} POS(Word_{jk})$
DF*ICF	Product of document frequency and inverse cluster frequency of descriptive word in current cluster	$\dfrac{DF(Word)}{|C_i|} \times \log_2 \dfrac{N+1}{n_i+1}$
$\overline{TF*IDF}$	Average value of TF*IDF (before clustering) of descriptive words in current cluster	$\sum_{j=1}^{|C_i|} TF*IDF(Word) \Big/ |C_i|$
$\overline{DEP}$	Average value of first position of descriptive words in current cluster	$\sum_{j=1}^{|C_i|} \dfrac{\#(word)}{\sum word_j} \Big/ |C_i|$
$\overline{Title}$	Document ratio of descriptive word appeared in title in current cluster, and value of Title (j) is 0 or 1.	$\sum_{j=1}^{|C_i|} Title(j) \Big/ |C_i|$
$\overline{Abstract}$	Document ratio of descriptive word appeared in abstract in current cluster, and value of Abstract (j) is 0 or 1.	$\sum_{j=1}^{|C_i|} Abstract(j) \Big/ |C_i|$
$\overline{Heading}$	Document ratio of descriptive word appeared in heading in current cluster, and value of Heading (j) is 0 or 1.	$\sum_{j=1}^{|C_i|} Heading(j) \Big/ |C_i|$
$\overline{First\_Para}$	Document ratio of descriptive word appeared in first paragraph in current cluster, and value of First_Para (j) is 0 or 1.	$\sum_{j=1}^{|C_i|} First\_Para(j) \Big/ |C_i|$
$\overline{Last\_Para}$	Document ratio of descriptive word appeared in last paragraph in current cluster, and value of Last_Para (j) is 0 or 1.	$\sum_{j=1}^{|C_i|} Last\_Para(j) \Big/ |C_i|$
$\overline{Reference}$	Document ratio of descriptive word appeared in reference in current cluster, and value of Reference (j) is 0 or 1.	$\sum_{j=1}^{|C_i|} Reference(j) \Big/ |C_i|$

Word denotes descriptive word itself. *LEN* is length of descriptive word and *POS* is the part-of-speech of it. *DF*ICF* is document frequency multiplies inverse cluster frequency of descriptive word. $\overline{TF*IDF}(t_{ij})$ is average value *TF*IDF* (before clustering) of descriptive word t_{ij} in C_i. $\overline{DEP}$ is average value of first position of t_{ij} in current cluster. Position_global denotes global position feature, namely document ratio of descriptive word appearing in title, abstract, heading, and first paragraph and last paragraph in current cluster.

Table 1 shows 12 features and their normalized computation methods used in the model of BL1、 BL2、 MLR、 Logit and SVM respectively

3.5 Training and Testing of Model

3.5.1 The Construction of Model Training Set

In this section, training sets are built for MLR、Logit and SVM respectively. For there is no manually annotated sample of clustering description, the clustered results is labeled manually and use the labeling results as clustering description data set to verify the three models with 10-fold cross-validation. In this paper, training and testing of SVM are all based on SVM^{light} [17]. Table 2 shows a sample of training data for SVM model.

Table 2. Sample of training data for SVM model

Lable	DF*ICF	LEN	POS	TF*IDF	DEP	$\overline{T}$	$\overline{A}$	$\overline{R}$	Candidate phrase
-1	0.1438	0.4000	1.0000	0.0808	0.6642	0.3721	0.3488	0.0698	企业档案(enterprise archives)
+1	0.1237	0.4000	1.0000	0.1064	0.5913	0.3488	0.3721	0.3023	档案工作(archives work)
-1	0.0783	0.2000	1.0000	0.0157	0.9722	0.0000	0.0465	0.0000	名字(name)
-1	0.0710	0.3000	1.0000	0.0129	0.9020	0.0465	0.0930	0.0000	管理体制(management system)
+1	0.0597	0.4000	1.0000	0.0145	0.8141	0.0233	0.1163	0.1628	档案管理(archives management)
-1	0.0588	0.6000	1.0000	0.0176	0.9607	0.0465	0.0233	0.0000	会员代表大会(member congress)

3.5.2 Testing the Model

For BaseLine1, we use top 5 words in concept vector as clustering description words. For BaseLine2, we use top 5 words as clustering description words. We use training set of MLR, Logit and SVM model to train them and get training models respectively. Then, we calculate the weight of every descriptive word in test cluster using the training model and top 5 words to be cluster description words.

4 Experimental Results

In this section, we apply clustering description extraction into topic digital library construction firstly. Then, we analyze descriptive results of BL1、BL2、MLR、Logit and SVM respectively, and compare their performance.

4.1 Application of Clustering Description Extraction

We use document clustering and clustering description extraction to build topic digital library. The hierarchical structure is generated after clustering documents in each cluster. The clustering result is the taxonomy of document set, and it is modified to the hierarchical structure for user navigation after manual adjustments. Figure 1 shows the hierarchical structure and navigation result of the realty domain. The online version of topic digital library system based on clustering description extraction is open and the website address is http://topic.cnki.net.

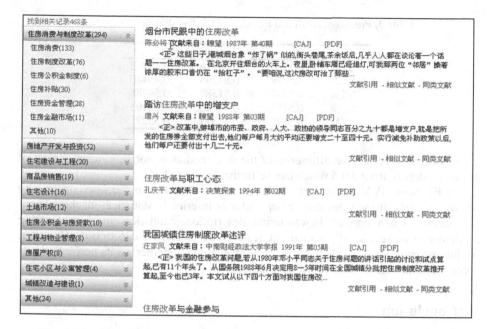

Fig. 1. Hierarchical Structure and Clustering Navigation Result of the Realty Domain

4.2 Data Sets and Evaluation Method of Clustering Description

In this study, we collect documents from database of 'Information Center for Social Sciences of RUC', which is available at http://art.zlzx.org. We randomly choose 2,000 academic documents from the database. Each document includes the title, abstract, keywords, full-text, heading of paragraph or sections, boundary information of paragraphs or sections, references, etc. Then we annotate clustered results (the number of cluster is 20), and set the category label and its corresponding cluster to be the training set and test set separately. Data set includes clustering description and its corresponding cluster. We adopt 10-fold cross-validation to evaluate clustering description models. Precision, recall and F1 value, which are classic evaluation methods in the field of information retrieval, will be applied to evaluate the performance of the method of clustering description.

4.3 Experiment Result and Analysis

4.3.1 Performance of Models
Table 3 shows precision, recall and F1 value of clustering results of these five models.

As shown in Table 3, performance of statistical machine learning is superior to benchmark model in term of precision. Moreover, SVM model is better than MLR model which is superior to Logistic model. This indicates that SVM model can perform effective classification, and extract effective clustering description in the task of clustering description. BaseLine1 is superior to BaseLine2 which selects cluster descriptive words combining *DF*, *ICF* and *LEN*.

Table 3. Precision, recall and F1 value of the five description models

	P	R	F1
BL1	0.37202	0.50276	0.42762
BL2	0.40782	0.51298	0.45440
MLR	0.58671	0.51387	0.54788
Logit	0.57836	0.50822	0.54103
SVM	0.61973	0.49877	0.55271

According to recall, the difference of the five models is not significant. Recall of all the models is around 0.5 which can be further improved.

For F1 value, SVM model performs the best, and Baseline1 is the worst one among the five models. It indicates that center vector is inferior to statistical machine learning method when applied in clustering description. Statistical machine learning method can make use of all kinds of features of clustering description. However, traditional methods can only assemble several features together, so its performance is worse than statistical machine learning method.

5 Conclusion

We study the readability of result of document clustering and try to solve this problem. Machine learning models are applied to clustering description and the experimental results show that the performance of SVM model is the best. There are two problems to solve in document clustering description extraction: (1) There are few existing human labeled clustering description corpus. At the same time, manually labeling clustering description corpus is costly and time-consuming. (2) Models we discussed in this paper can not obtain satisfying precision and recall, so it's necessary to find more effective clustering description features to enhance the quality of clustering description. Therefore, we'll study how to select more effective clustering description features in future.

Acknowledgments. This research was partially supported by National Key Project of Scientific and Technical Supporting Programs (No.2006BAH03B02), Project of the Education Ministry's Humanities and Social Science funded by Ministry of Education of China (No.08JC870007).

References

1. Glenisson, P., Glänzel, W., Janssens, F., De Moor, B.: Combining Full Text and Bibliometric Information in Mapping Scientific Disciplines. Information Processing & Management 41(6), 1548–1572 (2005)
2. Lai, K.K., Wu, S.J.: Using the Patent Co-citation Approach to Establish a New Patent Classification System. Information Processing & Management 41(2), 313–330 (2005)
3. Tseng, Y.-H., Lin, C.-J., Chen, H.-H., Lin, Y.-I.: Toward generic title generation for clustered documents. In: Ng, H.T., Leong, M.-K., Kan, M.-Y., Ji, D. (eds.) AIRS 2006. LNCS, vol. 4182, pp. 145–157. Springer, Heidelberg (2006)

4. Cutting, D.R., Karger, D.R., Pedersen, J.O., Tukey, J.W.: Scatter/Gather: A Cluster-based Approach to Browsing Large Document Collections. In: 15th International ACM SIGIR Conference on Research and Development in Information Retrieval, pp. 318–329. ACM Press, New York (1992)
5. Cutting, D.R., Karger, D.R., Pedersen, J.O.: Constant Interaction-time Scatter/Gather Browsing of Large Document Collections. In: 16th International ACM SIGIR Conference on Research and Development in Information Retrieval, pp. 126–135. ACM Press, New York (1993)
6. Muller, A., Dorre, J., Gerstl, P., Seiffert, R.: The TaxGen Framework: Automating the Generation of a Taxonomy for a Large Document Collection. In: 32nd Hawaii International Conference on System Sciences, pp. 2034–2042. IEEE Press, New York (1999)
7. Anton, V.L., Croft, W.B.: An Evaluation of Techniques for Clustering Search Results. Technical Report, Department of Computer Science, University of Massachusetts, Amherst (1996)
8. Zamir, O., Etzioni, O.: Web Document Clustering: A Feasibility Demonstration. In: 19th International ACM SIGIR Conference on Research and Development in Information Retrieval, pp. 46–54. ACM Press, New York (1998)
9. Lawrie, D., Croft, W.B., Rosenberg, A.L.: Finding Topic Words for Hierarchical Summarization. In: 24th Annual International ACM SIGIR Conference on Research and Development in Information Retrieval, pp. 249–357. ACM Press, New York (2001)
10. Glover, E., Pennock, D.M., Lawrence, S., Krovetz, R.: Inferring Hierarchical Descriptions. In: 11th International Conference on Information and Knowledge Management, pp. 4–9. McLean, VA (2002)
11. Pucktada, T., Jamie, C.: Automatically Labeling Hierarchical Clusters. In: 2006 International Conference on Digital government research, pp. 167–176. ACM Press, New York (2006)
12. Dawid, W.: Descriptive Clustering as a Method for Exploring Text Collections. Ph.D Thesis. Poznan University of Technology, Poznań, Poland (2006)
13. Gao, B.J., Ester, M.: Clustering description Formats, Problems and Algorithms. In: 6th SIAM International Conference on Data Mining. ACM Press, New York (2006)
14. Kummamuru, K., Lotlikar, R., Roy, S., Singal, K., Krishnapuram, R.: A Hierarchical Monothetic Document Clustering Algorithm for Summarization and Browsing Search Results. In: 13th International WWW Conference, pp. 658–665. ACM Press, New York (2004)
15. Ayad, H.G., Kamel, M.S.: Topic discovery from text using aggregation of different clustering methods. In: Cohen, R., Spencer, B. (eds.) Canadian AI 2002. LNCS (LNAI), vol. 2338, pp. 161–175. Springer, Heidelberg (2002)
16. Vapnik, V.: The Nature of Statistical Learning Theory. Springer, New York (1995)
17. SVM-light Support Vector Machine, http://svmlight.joachims.org

Event-Based Summarization
Using Critical Temporal Event Term Chain

Maofu Liu[1,2], Wenjie Li[2], Xiaolong Zhang[1], and Ji Zhang[2]

[1] College of Computer Science and Technology, Wuhan University of Science and Technology,
Wuhan, P.R. China
liumaofu@wust.edu.cn
[2] Department of Computing, The Hong Kong Polytechnic University, Kowloon, Hong Kong
{csmfliu,cswjli,csjizhang}@comp.polyu.edu.hk

Abstract. In this paper, we investigate whether temporal relations among event terms can help improve event-based summarization and text cohesion of final summaries. By connecting event terms with happens-before relations, we build a temporal event term graph for source documents. The event terms in the critical temporal event term chain identified from the maximal weakly connected component are used to evaluate the sentences in source documents. The most significant sentences are included in final summaries. Experiments conducted on the DUC 2001 corpus show that event-based summarization using the critical temporal event term chain is able to organize final summaries in a more coherent way and make improvement over the well-known tf*idf-based and PageRank-based summarization approaches.

Keywords: Event-Based Summarization, Event Term Graph, Temporal Event Term Chain, Depth-First Search Algorithm.

1 Introduction

Event has been regarded as an effective concept representation in recently emerged event-based summarization. With regard to the definition of events, in conjunction with the common agreement that event contains a series of happenings, we formulate events as "[Who] did [What] to [Whom] [When] and [Where]" at sentence level. In this paper, we focus on "did [What]" and define verbs and action nouns in source documents as *event terms* that characterize or partially characterize event occurrences.

Notice that in addition to the quality and quantity of the informative contents conveyed by the extracted sentences, the relations among the extracted sentences, such as temporal relations in news articles, and structure of the final summary text should also be a matter of concern. Sentence relation in source and summary text, if appropriately defined and identified, is a good means to reflect text cohesion, the way of getting the source and extracted text to "hang together" as a whole and the indicator of text unity. In the literature, text cohesion has been modeled by lexical cohesion in terms of the semantic relations existing between not only pairs of words but also over a succession of a number of nearby related words spanning a topical unit of the text. These

W. Li and D. Mollá-Aliod (Eds.): ICCPOL 2009, LNAI 5459, pp. 378–385, 2009.

sequences of related words are called lexical chains and tend to delineate portions of the text that have a strong unity of meaning.

Lexical chains have been investigated for extractive text summarization in the past. They are regarded as a direct result of units of text being "about the same thing" and having a correspondence to the structure of the text. Normally, nouns or noun compounds are used to denote the things and compute lexical chains (i.e. lexical chains are normally noun chains). In this paper, we assume that the source text describes a series of events via the set of sentences and take both informative content and structure of the source text into consideration. We look for the *critical temporal chain* of event terms and use it to represent the source text and to generate the final summary. We concentrate on verb chains, other than noun chains, aiming to improve event-based summarization and lexical cohesion of the generated summary. Here, event terms and event term chain represent informative content and text cohesion, respectively.

To compute the critical temporal chain, event terms are connected to construct a *temporal event term graph* based on the *happens-before* relation provided in VerbOcean. This relation indicates that the two verbs refer to two temporally disjoint intervals or instances [1]. The DFS-based (Depth-First Search) algorithm is applied in searching the critical chain. Then the event terms on the critical temporal chain are used to evaluate sentences. Sentences with the highest significance scores are extracted to form the final summary.

The remainder of this paper is organized as follows. Section 2 reviews related work. Section 3 introduces the proposed event-based summarization approach using critical temporal event term chain. Section 4 then presents experiments and discussions. Finally, Section 5 concludes the paper and suggests the future work.

2   Related Work

Daniel et al. [2] pilot the study of event-based summarization. Filatova and Hatzivassiloglou [3] then define the concept of atomic events as a feature that can be automatically extracted. Atomic events are defined as the relationships between the important named entities. Allan et al. [4] present a list of events within the topic in the order those events are reported and produce a revised up-to-date summary at regular time intervals. Lim et al. [5] group source documents on time slots by the time information given by newspaper articles or publication dates. They build the local or global term cluster of each time slot and use it to identify a topical sentence as the representative for the time slot.

The concept of lexical chain is originally proposed to represent the discourse structure of a document by Morris and Hirst [6]. Barzilay and Elhadad [7] first introduce lexical chain in single document summarization. The lexical chains are computed using relatedness of nouns determined in terms of the distance between their occurrences and the shape of the path connecting them in the WordNet thesaurus. Following the same line of thought, Silber and McCoy [8] employ lexical chains to extract important concepts from the source document and make lexical chains a computationally feasible candidate as an intermediate representation. Reeve et al. [9] apply lexical chain based summarization approach to biomedical text. The concepts were not derived from WordNet but domain-specific semantic resources, UMLS Metathesaurus and semantic network.

At present, the applications of temporal information in summarization are mostly based on time information in the source document or publication date. The lexical chains mentioned above are all based on nouns, derived from WordNet or domain specific knowledge base. In this paper, we derive temporal information from the temporal relations among event terms and regard the temporal event term chains as the immediate representation of the source document.

3   Summarization Using Critical Temporal Event Term Chain

3.1   Temporal Event Term Graph Construction

In this paper, we introduce VerbOcean, a broad-coverage repository of semantic verb relations, into event-based summarization. Different from other thesaurus like Word-Net, VerbOcean provides five types of semantic verb relations at finer level. In this paper, only the *happens-before* temporal relation is explored. When two events happen, one may happen before the other. This is defined as the *happens-before* temporal relation in VerbOcean.

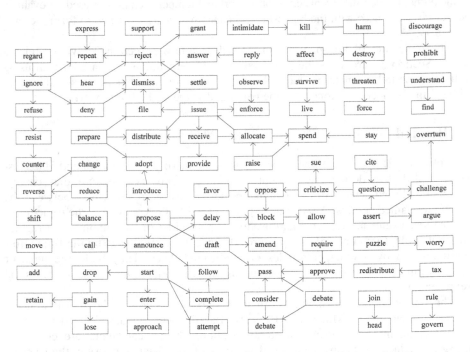

Fig. 1. Temporal event term graph based on the *happens-before* relation

The *happens-before* temporal relations on a set of event terms can be naturally represented by a graph, called temporal event term graph. We formally define the temporal event term graph connected by temporal relation as $G=(V, E)$, where V is a set of event term vertices and E is a set of edges temporally connecting event terms.

Fig. 1 above shows a sample of temporal event term graph built from a DUC 2001 document set.

The temporal event term graph is a directed graph because the *happens-before* relation in VerbOcean clearly exhibits the conspicuous anti-symmetric property. For example, we may have some "question" with something and then decide to "criticize" it for some reason. The event represented by the term "question" *happens-before* the one represented by the term "criticize". That is why a directed edge from "question" to "criticize" appears in Fig. 1.

3.2 Critical Temporal Event Term Chain Identification

The temporal event term graph based on the *happens-before* relation is not a fully connected graph. For example, there are eight sub-graphs or components in the graph illustrated in Fig. 1. Among them, a maximal weakly connected component, which contains the maximal number of the event terms, can be found. We assume that the event terms in the maximal weakly connected component reflect the main topic of original documents since such a component normally involves much more connected (i.e. relevant) event terms than any other components on the graph. Referring back to Fig. 1, the maximal weakly connected component contains 118 event terms, while the second largest weakly connected component contains only 8. Note that, for illustration purpose, only a partial maximal weakly connected component is shown in Fig. 1.

Some maximal weakly connected sub-graphs are cyclic. In such a situation, the edge whose terminal term vertex has the maximal in-degree is removed in order to avoid the infinite loop in the identification of the critical temporal event term chain. Anyway, the terminal term can still be reached from other term vertices. The connection remains.

From the directed acyclic graph, we extract all the source vertices and sink vertices. The source vertex is defined as a vertex with successors but no predecessors, i.e. some edges being incident out of it but no edge being incident on it. On the contrary, the sink vertex is defined as a vertex with predecessors but no successors, i.e. some edges being incident on it but no edge being incident out of it.

All directed paths in the directed acyclic graph of the maximal weakly connected component from each source vertex to each sink vertex are computed with the DFS-based algorithm. The longest path is defined as the critical temporal event term chain and the critical temporal event term chain in Fig. 1 is "regard→ignore→refuse→resist→counter→reverse→shift→move→add".

Afterwards, we evaluate the sentences that contain the event terms in the chain and judge which ones should be extracted into the final summary based upon the critical temporal event term chain computation.

3.3 Sentence Selection

To apply the critical temporal event term chain in summarization, we need to identify the most significant sentences that best describe the event terms in the chain. Considering terms are the basic constitution of sentences, term significance is computed first. Since this paper studies event-based summarization, we only consider event terms and compute the significances of the event terms in the maximal weakly connected component of a temporal event term graph.

Two parameters can be used in the calculation of event term significance. One is the occurrence of an event term in source documents. The other is the degree of an event term in a temporal event term graph. The degree of a term vertex in the directed graph is the sum of the in-degrees and out-degrees of that term.

For each event term in the critical temporal chain, it is likely to locate more than one sentence containing this term in source documents. We only extract one sentence for each event term to represent the event to avoid repeating the same or quite similar information in the summary. For sentence selection, the sentence significance is computed according to the event terms contained in it.

Based on event term occurrences, the significance of a sentence can be calculated by the following Equation (1).

$$SC_i = \frac{TFS_i}{TFS_m} \tag{1}$$

where TFS_i and TFS_m are the sum of the term occurrences of the ith sentence and the maximum of all the sentences that contain event terms in the critical temporal chain, respectively.

Alternatively, we can use degrees of event terms to calculate the significance of a sentence.

$$SC_i = \frac{DS_i}{DS_m} \tag{2}$$

where DS_i and DS_m are the sum of the term degrees of the ith sentence and maximum of all the sentences which contain event terms in the critical temporal chain, respectively.

It should be emphasized here that in Equations (1) and (2) the event terms under concern must be the ones in the maximal weakly connected component of the temporal event term graph.

4   Experiment and Discussion

We evaluate the proposed summarization approach based on the critical temporal event term chain on the DUC 2001 corpus. The corpus contains 30 English document sets. Among them, 10 sets are observed to contain descriptions of event sequences. They are the main concern of this paper. All final summaries are generated in 200 words length.

The final summary shown in Fig. 2 is generated from the temporal event term graph and the critical temporal event term chain in Fig. 1 according to the calculation of sentence significance based on the vertex degree. The corresponding source document set is about the topic "whether to exclude illegal aliens from the decennial census and the final vote result of the Congress". We can see that the final summary indeed talks about the resident census history, the exclusion announcement, the reasons of the agreement and rejection, and the vote result. More important, the critical temporal event term chain contributes to the cohesion of the final summary. The summary has apparently shows temporal characteristic in sentence sequences, from resident

For 190 years, said Sen. Daniel Patrick Moynihan (D-N.Y.), the federal government has counted all inhabitants without regard to citizenship in accordance with the Constitution's provisions.
Groups which have filed suit to ignore the aliens contend large concentrations of them could result in some states gaining seats in the House of Representatives at the expense of other states.
Asking people about their status likely would result in people lying or refusing to participate in the count, officials say, resulting in a potential undercount of residents in many areas.
But he added that he is "optimistic, cautiously optimistic," that House conferees would resist the Senate-approved ban and not force Bush to veto the legislation.
Sen. Pete Wilson (R-Calif.) countered that excluding illegal residents from the decennial census is unfair to the states that have suffered from a huge influx of immigration beyond the legal limits.
The Senate's action was sharply criticized by Undersecretary of Commerce Michael Darby, but he voiced hope that it would be reversed by a Senate-House conference.
There could be enough of them to shift seats away from at least five states to Sun Belt states with large numbers of illegal residents.
The amendment was adopted after the Senate voted 58 to 41 against a move to reject it, and 56 to 43 against scuttling it as unconstitutional.

Fig. 2. The final summary for critical temporal chain in Fig. 1 based on vertex degree

census history, exclusion announcement and reasons for agreement and rejection to Senate vote result at the end.

To evaluate the quality of generated summaries, an automatic evaluation tool, called ROUGE [10] is used. The tool presents three ROUGE values including uni-gram-based ROUGE-1, bigram-based ROUGE-2 and ROUGE-W which is based on longest common subsequence weighted by the length.

Table 1. ROUGE scores on Term Occurrence and tf*idf

	tf*idf	Term Occurrence	Improvement
ROUGE-1	0.29222	0.36118	23.6%
ROUGE-2	0.04494	0.06254	39.2%
ROUGE-W	0.10099	0.12877	27.5%

Table 1 above shows the average ROUGE scores of event term occurrence and tf*idf approaches on the ten selected document sets. The ROUGE-2 score of the event term occurrence approach is comparatively about 39.2% better than the tf*idf approach. Our approach also shows more advantageous than the tf*idf approach on both ROUGE-1 and ROUGE-W. We highlight the ROUGE-2 scores here because we take semantic relevance between the events into account but tf*idf does not.

Google's PageRank [11] is one of the most popular ranking algorithms. It is a kind of graph-based ranking algorithm deciding on the importance of a node within a graph by taking into account the global information recursively computed from the entire graph. After constructing the temporal event term graph, we can also use the PageRank algorithm to calculate the significance of the terms in the graph. Because the calculations of sentence significance using PageRank and vertex degree are both based on the links among the vertices in the graph, we compare the ROUGE scores of the critical temporal event term chain based summarization using the vertex degree in sentences selection to those of PageRank-based approach.

Table 2. ROUGE scores on PageRank and Degree

	PageRank	Degree	Improvement
ROUGE-1	0.35645	0.36546	2.5%
ROUGE-2	0.06403	0.06490	1.6%
ROUGE-W	0.12504	0.13021	4.1%

Table 2 above compares the average ROUGE scores of the two approaches. The ROUGE-1 score of the event term degree approach is about 2.5% above the ROUGE-1 score of the PageRank algorithm while the ROUGE-2 scores of them are quite similar. This is mainly because both the degree and the PageRank approaches take the semantic relevance between event terms into consideration in the calculation of significances of event terms and sentences.

Table 3. ROUGE scores on Term Occurrence and Degree

	Term Occurrence		Degree	
	Ten Sets	Twenty Sets	Ten Sets	Twenty Sets
ROUGE-1	0.36118	0.30453	0.36546	0.30099
ROUGE-2	0.06254	0.04390	0.06490	0.04449
ROUGE-W	0.12877	0.10861	0.13021	0.10803

Table 3 finally compares the average ROUGE scores of the ten document sets selected for the experiments above and the other twenty document sets in the DUC 2001 corpus. The ROUGE-1 average scores of the twenty document sets are much worse than the average scores of the ten document sets, i.e. about 15.7% lower using term occurrence and 17.6% lower using event term degree. The similar conclusions can be drawn on ROUGE-2 and ROUGE-W. This suggests that the proposed event-based approaches indeed can handle those documents describing events or event sequences much better. But they may not suit event irrelevant topics.

5   Conclusions and Future Work

In this paper, we investigate whether temporal relation between events helps improve performance of event-based summarization. By constructing the temporal event term graph based on the semantic relations derived from the knowledge base VerbOcean and computing weakly connected components, we find that the maximal weakly connected component can often denote the main topic of the source document.

Searching in the maximal weakly connected component with DFS-based algorithm, we can discover a critical temporal event term chain. The event terms in this chain are supposed to be critical for generating the final summary. In experiments, the significance of these terms is measured by either term occurrence in source documents or the degree in the constructed graph. The ROUGE results are promising. Term occurrence significantly outperforms tf*idf and term degree is also comparative to well-known PageRank.

In the future, we will introduce the other types of VerbOcean verb semantic relations into event-based summarization. Besides the critical temporal chain in the event term graph, we will investigate the other possible temporal event term chains in the semantic computation. We also plan to combine the surface statistical features and the semantic features during the selection of representative sentences in order to generate better summaries.

Acknowledgments

The work described in this paper was supported partially by a grant from the Research Grants Council of the Hong Kong Special Administrative Region, China (Project No. CERG PolyU 5217/07E) and Research Grant from Hubei Provincial Department of Education (No. 500064).

References

1. Timothy, C., Patrick, P.: VerbOcean: Mining the Web for Fine-Grained Semantic Verb Relations. In: Proceedings of Conference on Empirical Methods in Natural Language Processing (2004)
2. Daniel, N., Radev, D., Allison, T.: Sub-event based Multi-document Summarization. In: Proceedings of the HLT-NAACL Workshop on Text Summarization, pp. 9–16 (2003)
3. Filatova, E., Hatzivassiloglou, V.: Event-based Extractive Summarization. In: Proceedings of ACL 2004 Workshop on Summarization, pp. 104–111 (2004)
4. Allan, J., Gupta, R., Khandelwal, V.: Temporal Summaries of News Topics. In: Proceedings of the 24th Annual International ACM SIGIR Conference on Research and Development in Information Retrieval, pp. 10–18 (2001)
5. Lim, J.M., Kang, I.S., Bae, J.H., Lee, J.H.: Sentence Extraction Using Time Features in Multi-document Summarization. In: Information Retrieval Technology: Asia Information Retrieval Symposium (2004)
6. Morris, J., Hirst, G.: Lexical Cohesion Computed by Thesaurus Relations as an Indicator of the Structure of Text. Computational Linguistics 17(1), 21–48 (1991)
7. Barzilay, R., Elhadad, M.: Using Lexical Chains for Text Summarization. In: Proceedings of ACL 1997/EACL 1997 Workshop on Intelligent Scalable Text Summarization, pp. 10–17 (1997)
8. Silber, H.G., McCoy, K.F.: Efficiently Computed Lexical Chains as an Intermediate Representation for Automatic Text Summarization. Computational Linguistics 28(4), 487–496 (2002)
9. Reeve, L.H., Han, H., Brooks, A.D.: The Use of Domain-Specific Concepts in Biomedical Text Summarization. Information Processing and Management 43(6), 1765–1776 (2007)
10. Lin, C.Y., Hovy, E.: Automatic Evaluation of Summaries using N-gram Cooccurrence Statistics. In: Proceedings of HLTNAACL, pp. 71–78 (2003)
11. Page, L., Brin, S., Motwani, R., Winograd, T.: The PageRank CitationRanking: Bring Order to the Web. Technical Report, Stanford University (1998)

Acquiring Verb Subcategorization Frames in Bengali from Corpora

Dipankar Das, Asif Ekbal, and Sivaji Bandyopadhyay

Department of Computer Science and Engineering,
Jadavpur University, Kolkata, India
dipankar.dipnil2005@gmail.com, asif.ekbal@gmail.com,
sivaji_cse_ju@yahoo.com

Abstract. Subcategorization frames acquisition of a phrase can be described as a mechanism to extract different types of relevant arguments that are associated with that phrase in a sentence. This paper presents the acquisition of different subcategory frames for a specific Bengali verb that has been identified from POS tagged and chunked data prepared from raw Bengali news corpus. Syntax plays the main role in the acquisition process and not the semantics like thematic roles. The output frames of the verb have been compared with the frames of its English verb that has been identified using bilingual lexicon. The frames for the English verb have been extracted using Verbnet. This system has demonstrated precision and recall values of 85.21% and 83.94% respectively on a test set of 1500 sentences.

Keywords: Subcategorization, Frames, Acquisition, Target Verb, Bilingual Lexicon, Synonymous Verb Set (SVS), VerbNet, Evaluation.

1 Introduction

Subcategorization refers to certain kinds of relations between words and phrases in a sentence. A subcategorization frame is a statement of what types of syntactic arguments a verb (or adjective) takes, such as objects, infinitives, that-clauses, participial clauses, and subcategorized prepositional phrases [1]. Several large, manually developed subcategorized lexicons are available for English, e.g. the COMLEX Syntax [2] and the ANLT [3] dictionaries. VerbNet (VN) [4] is the largest on-line verb lexicon with explicitly stated syntactic and semantic information based on Levin's verb classification [5]. It is a hierarchical domain-independent, broad-coverage verb lexicon with mappings to other lexical resources.

The collection of different subcategorization frames for other parts-of-speech phrases is also an important task. But the verb phrase of a language usually takes various types of subcategorization frames compared to other parts of speech phrases. There are several reasons for the importance of subcategorization frames for the development of a parser in that language. There are many languages that have no existing parser. So the information acquired from the subcategorization frames can improve the parsing process. Apart from parsing and dictionary preparation, we can use

W. Li and D. Mollá-Aliod (Eds.): ICCPOL 2009, LNAI 5459, pp. 386–393, 2009.
© Springer-Verlag Berlin Heidelberg 2009

the acquired subcategorization frames for Question-Answering system to retrieve predictable components of a sentence. The acquired subcategorization frames can also be used for phrase alignment in a parallel sentence level corpus to be utilized for training a statistical machine translation system.

The description of a system developed for automatically acquiring six verb subcategorization frames and their frequencies from a large corpus using rules is mentioned in [7]. Development of a mechanism for resolving verb class ambiguities using subcategrization is reported in [6]. All of these works deal with English. A cross-lingual work on learning verb-argument structure for Czech language is described in [8]. In [9], the method consists of different subcategorization issues that may be considered for the purpose of machine aided translation system for Indian languages.

The present work deals with the acquisition of verb subcategorization frames of a specific verb from a Bengali newspaper corpus. The subcategorization of verbs is an essential issue in parsing for the free phrase order languages such as Bengali that has no existing parser. In this paper, we have developed a system for acquiring subcategorization frames for a specific Bengali verb that occurs most frequently in the Bengali news corpus. Using a Bengali–English bilingual lexicon [10], the English verb meanings with its synonyms have been identified for the Bengali verb. All possible acquired frames for each of the English synonyms for the Bengali verb have been acquired from the VerbNet and these frames have been mapped to the Bengali sentences that contain the verb tagged as main verb and auxiliary. It has been experimentally shown that the accuracy of the frame acquisition process can be significantly improved by considering the occurrences of various argument phrases and relevant POS tags before and after the verb in a sentence. Evaluation results with a test set of 1500 sentences show the effectiveness of the proposed model with precision and recall values of 85.21% and 83.94% respectively.

The rest of the paper is organized as follows. Section 2 describes the framework for the acquisition of subcategory frames for a specific Bengali verb. Evaluation results of the system are discussed in section 3. Finally section 4 concludes the paper.

2   Verb Subcategorization Frames Acquisition from Corpus

We developed several modules for the acquisition of subcategorization frames from the Bengali newspaper corpus. The modules consist of POS tagged corpus preparation, Verb identification and selection, English verb determination, VerbNet frames acquisition and Bengali Verb Subcategorization Frame Acquisition.

2.1   POS Tagged Corpus Preparation

In this work, we have used a Bengali news corpus [11] developed from the web-archive of a widely read Bengali newspaper. A portion of the Bengali news corpus containing 1500 sentences have been POS tagged using a Maximum Entropy based POS tagger [12]. The POS tagger was developed with a tagset of 26 POS tags (http://shiva.iiit.ac.in/SPSAL2007/iiit_tagset_guidelines.pdf), defined for the Indian languages. The POS tagger demonstrated an accuracy of 88.2%. We have also developed a rule-based chunker to chunk the POS tagged data for identifying phrase level information during the acquisition process.

2.2 Verb Identification and Selection

We have partially analyzed the tagged and chunked data to identify the words that are tagged as main verb (VM). The identified main verbs have been enlisted and passed through a stemming process to identify their root forms. Bengali, like any other Indian languages, is morphologically very rich. Different suffixes may be attached to a verb depending on the different features such as Tense, Aspect, and Person. The stemmer uses a suffix list to identify the stem form. Another table stores the stem form and the corresponding root form for each verb.

The specific root verb that occurs most frequently in any inflected form (as main verb with VM POS tag) is taken up for fine-grained analysis of verb subcategorization frames. It is expected that the corpus will have adequate number of occurrences for each subcategorization frame of the verb. We have chosen the verb (*dekha*) (see) from the corpus that has the largest number of occurrences in the corpus.

The specific root verb, selected in the way as described above, has been considered as the target verb in our work. The sentences containing the target verb including their inflected forms are collected. We have also collected the sentences where the target verb appears as an auxiliary verb (VAUX). These sentences are kept separate for further analysis as these sentences are good candidates for subcategorization frames acquisition.

(*ami*)	(*tader*)	(*aamgulo*)	(*khete*)(VM)	(*dekhechi*)(VAUX)
I	them	mangoes	eating	have seen

2.3 English Verb Determination

The verb subcategorization frames for the equivalent English verbs (in the same sense) are the initial set of verb subcategorization frames that are considered as valid for the Bengali verb. This initial set of verb subcategorization frames are validated in the POS tagged corpus. The process described in section 2.2 already identifies the root form of the target verb. To determine equivalent English verbs, we have used the available Bengali-English bilingual dictionary that has been preprocessed for our task. Various syntactical representations of a word entry in the lexicon are analyzed to identify its synonyms and meanings with respect to verb only. The example of an entry in the bilingual lexicon for our target verb (*dekha*) is given as follows.

[*dēkhā*] v to see, to notice; to look; a. seen, noticed adv. in imitation of.

The above lexicon entry for the Bengali word shows that it can have three different POS tags: verb (v), adjective (a) and adverb (adv). We are interested with those entries that appear with the verb POS. Different synonyms for the verb having the same sense are separated using "," and different senses are separated using ";" in the lexicon. The synonyms including different senses of the target verb have been extracted from the lexicon. This yields a resulting set called Synonymous Verb Set (SVS). For example, the English synonyms (*see, notice*) and synonym with other sense (*look*) are selected for Bengali verb (*dekha*). Now, the task is to acquire all the existing possible frames for each member of the SVS from the VerbNet.

2.4 VerbNet Frames Acquisition

VerbNet associates the semantics of a verb with its syntactic frames, and combines traditional lexical semantic information such as thematic roles and semantic predicates, with syntactic frames and selectional restrictions. Verb entries in the same VerbNet class share common syntactic frames, and thus they are believed to have the same syntactic behavior. The VerbNet files contain the verbs with their possible subcategory frames and membership information is stored in XML file format.

The XML files of VerbNet have been preprocessed to build up a general list that contains all members (verbs) and their possible subcategorization frames (primary as well as secondary) information. This preprocessed list is searched to acquire the subcategorization frames for each member of the SVS of the Bengali verb (*dekha*) (identified in section 2.3). As the verbs are classified according to their semantics in the VerbNet, the frames for the particular Bengali verb are assumed to be similar to the frames obtained for the members of its SVS. It has also been observed that the members of the SVS also occur in separate classes of the VerbNet depending on their senses. The acquired frames (primary and secondary) for each member of the SVS of the verb (*dekha*) have been enlisted based on their occurrences in the VerbNet classes as shown in Table 1. Stimulus is used by verbs of perception for events or objects that elicit some response from an experiencer. This role usually imposes no restrictions. Theme is used for participants in a location or undergoing a change of location. The prepositional phrases that occur with any of these two senses, i.e., theme and stimulus, are defined as the secondary frames.

Table 1. The members and their subcategorization frames extracted from the Verbnet for the corresponding Bengali verb (*dekha*)

SVS (VerbNet classes)	Primary Frames	Secondary Frames
See (see-30.1) Notice (see-30.1-1)	Basic Transitive, S, Attribute Object Possessor-Attribute Factoring Alternation, HOW-S, WHAT-S, NP-INF-OC, NP-ING-OC, POSSING, PP	Stimulus-PP
Look (peer-30.3)	PP	Theme-PP

2.5 Bengali Verb Subcategorization Frame Acquisition

The acquired VerbNet frames have been mapped to the Bengali verb subcategorization frames by considering the position of the verb as well as its general co-existing nature with other phrases in Bengali sentences. The NNPC (Compound proper noun), NNP (Proper noun), NNC (Compound common noun) and NN (Common noun) tags help to determine the subjects, objects as well as the locative information related to verb.

In simple sentences the occurrence of the NNPC, NNP, NNC or NN tags preceded by the PRP (Pronoun) NNP, NNC, NN or NNPC tags and followed by the verb gives similar frame syntax for "Basic Transitive" frame of the VerbNet.

> (*ami*)(PRP)   (*kakatua*)(NNP)   (*dekhi*)(VM)
> I   parrot   see

The syntax of "WHAT-S" frame for a Bengali sentence has been acquired by identifying the sentential complement part of the verb (*dekha*). The target verb followed by a NP chunk that consists of another main verb and WQ tag (question word) helps to identify the "WHAT-S" kind of frames.

> (*ami*)(PRP) (*dekhlam*)(VM)   (NP)((*tara*) (PP)   (*ki*)(WQ)   (*korche*)(VM))
> I   saw   they   what   did

In order to acquire the frame of "NP-ING-OC", we have created the list of possible Bengali inflections that can appear for the English "-ING" inflection. These inflections usually occur in sentences made up of compound verbs with conjunctive participle form (-e) and infinitive form (-te). If the last word of the phrase contains any of these inflections followed by the target verb then it gives a similar description of the VerbNet frame "NP-ING-OC".

> (*ami*)(PRP)   (NP) ((*tader*)   (*haste*))   (*dekhechi*)
> I   them   laughing   have seen

The presence of JJ (Adjective) generally does not play any role in the acquisition process of verb subcategorization frames. Some frames like "Attribute Object Possessor-Attribute Factoring Alternation", "HOW-S", "Theme-PP" and "Stimulus-PP" did not have any instance in our corpus. A close linguistic analysis shows that these frames can also be acquired from the Bengali sentences.

3 Evaluation

The set of acquired subcategorization frames or the frame lexicon can be evaluated against a gold standard corpus obtained either through manual analysis of corpus data, or from subcategorization frame entries in a large dictionary or from the output of the parser made for that language. As there is no parser available for the Bengali and also no existing dictionary for Bengali that contains subcategorization frames, manual analysis from corpus data is the only method for evaluation. The sentences retrieved from the chunker (with an accuracy of 89.4%) have been evaluated manually to extract the sentences that are fully correct. These sentences have been considered as our gold standard data for evaluation of subcategorization frames.

A detailed statistics of the verb (*dekha*) is presented in Table 2. Stemming process has correctly identified 276 occurrences of the verb (*dekha*) from its 284 occurrences in the corpus with an accuracy of 97.18%. During the Bengali verb subcategorization frame acquisition process, it has been observed that the simple sentences contain most of the frames that its English verb form usually takes from VerbNet. Analysis of a simple Bengali sentence to identify the verb subcategorization frames is easier in the absence of a parser than analyzing complex and compound sentences.

The verb subcategorization frames acquisition process is evaluated using type precision, type recall and F-measure. The results have been shown in Table 3. The evaluation

Table 2. The frequency information of the verb (dekha) acquired from the corpus

No. of sentences in the corpus	1500
No. of different verbs in the corpus	45
No. of inflected forms of the verb (*dekha*) in the corpus	22
Total no. of occurrences of the verb (*dekha*) (before stemming) in the corpus	284
No. of sentences where (*dekha*) occurs as a verb	276
No. of sentences where (*dekha*) occurs as a main verb (VM)	251
No. of sentences where (*dekha*) occurs as an auxiliary verb(VAUX)	25
No. of simple sentences where (*dekha*) occurs as a verb	139
No. of simple sentences where (*dekha*) occurs as a main verb (VM)	125
No. of simple sentences where (*dekha*) occurs as an auxiliary verb (VAUX)	14

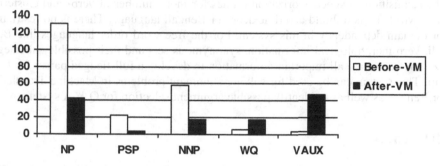

Fig. 1. Frequency of occurrence of different phrases before and after the main verb (VM)

Table 3. Average precision, recall and F-measure for 276 different sentences evaluated against the manual analysis of corpus data

Measure	Stage-1	Stage-2
Recall	83.05%	83.94%
Precision	78.50%	85.21%
F-Measure	80.71	84.57

process has been carried out in two stages. In Stage-1, we have retrieved whatever result we acquired from the corpus and have identified the frames keeping the phrases and their orderings intact. In Stage-2, we have drawn histogram type charts of different phrases as well as tags that appear as frames for a verb before and after of its occurrences in the sentence. This chart is shown in Figure 1. Based on these values, various rules have been applied. Results show that the recall value is not changed so much but there is an appreciable change in the precision values after considering the occurrences of different chunks and tags to select the arguments of the verb.

Number of different types of frames acquired is shown in Table 4. The result shows a satisfactory performance of the system.

Table 4. The frequencies of different frames acquired from corpus

Subcategory Frames	No. of occurrences in the corpus
Basic Transitive	82
S (Sentential Complements)	5
WHAT-S	3
NP-INF-OC	10
NP-ING-OC	2
POSSING	6
PP	12

4 Conclusion

The acquisition of subcategorization frames for more number of verbs and clustering them will help us to build a verb lexicon for Bengali language. There is no restriction for domain dependency in this system. For the free word order languages like Bengali, verb morphological information, synonymous sets and their possible subcategorization frames are all important information to develop a full-fledged parser for Bengali. This system can be used for solving alignment problems in Machine Translation for Bengali as well as to identify possible argument selection for Q & A system.

References

1. Manning, C.D.: Automatic Acquisition of a Large Subcategorization Dictionary from Corpora. In: Proceedings of the 31st Meeting of the ACL, pp. 235–242. ACL, Columbus (1993)
2. Grishman, R., Macleod, C., Meyers, A.: Comlex syntax: building a computational lexicon. In: Proceedings of the International Conference on Computational Linguistics, COLING 1994, Kyoto, Japan, pp. 268–272 (1994)
3. Boguraev, B.K., Briscoe, E.J.: Large lexicons for natural language processing utilizing the grammar coding system of the Longman Dictionary of Contemporary English. Computational Linguistics 13(4), 219–240 (1987)
4. Kipper-Schuler, K.: VerbNet: A broad-coverage, comprehensive verb lexicon. Ph.D. thesis, Computer and Information Science Dept., University of Pennsylvania, Philadelphia, PA (June 2005)
5. Levin, B.: English Verb Classes and Alternation: A Preliminary Investigation. The University of Chicago Press (1993)
6. Ushioda, A., Evans, D.A., Gibson, T., Waibel, A.: The Automatic Acquisition of Frequencies of Verb Subcategorization Frames from Tagged Corpora. In: Boguraev, B., Pustejovsky, J. (eds.) Proceedings of the Workshop on Acquisition of Lexical Knowledge from Text, Columbus, Ohio, pp. 95–106 (1993)
7. Lapata, M., Brew, C.: Using subcategorization to resolve verb class ambiguity. In: Fung, P., Zhou, J. (eds.) Proceedings of WVLC/EMNLP, pp. 266–274 (1999)
8. Sarkar, A., Zeman, D.: Automatic extraction of subcategorization frames for czech. In: Proceedings of COLING 2000 (2000)

9. Samantaray, S.D.: A Data mining approach for resolving cases of Multiple Parsing in Machine Aided Translation of Indian Languages. In: International Conference on Information Technology. IEEE Press, Los Alamitos (2007)
10. Samsad Bengali to English Dictionary,
    http://home.uchicago.edu/~cbs2/banglainstruction.html
11. Ekbal, A., Bandyopadhyay, S.: A Web-based Bengali News Corpus for Named Entity Recognition. Language Resources and Evaluation (LRE) Journal 42(2), 173–182 (2008)
12. Ekbal, A., Haque, R., Bandyopadhyay, S.: Maximum Entropy Based Bengali Part of Speech Tagging. In: Gelbukh, A. (ed.) Advances in Natural Language Processing and Applications, Research in Computing Science (RCS) Journal, vol. 33, pp. 67–78 (2008)

An Investigation of an Interontologia: Comparison of the Thousand-Character Text and Roget's Thesaurus

Sang-Rak Kim[1], Jae-Gun Yang[2], and Jae-Hak J. Bae[2,*]

[1] Institute of e-Vehicle Technology, University of Ulsan; ITSTAR Co., Ltd.,
Ulsan, South Korea
[2] School of Computer Engineering & Information Technology, University of Ulsan,
Ulsan, South Korea
Shem0304@itstar.co.kr, {jgyang,jhjbae}@ulsan.ac.kr

Abstract. The present study presents the lexical category analysis of the Thousand-Character Text and Roget's Thesaurus. Through preprocessing, the Thousand-Character Text and Roget's Thesaurus have been built into databases. In addition, for easier analysis and more efficient research, we have developed a system to search Roget's Thesaurus for the categories corresponding to Chinese characters in the Thousand-Character Text. According to the results of this study, most of the 39 sections of Roget's Thesaurus except the 'Creative Thought' section were relevant to Chinese characters in the Thousand-Character Text. Three sections 'Space in General', 'Dimensions' and 'Matter in General' have higher mapping rate. The correlation coefficient is also around 0.94, showing high category relevancy on the section level between the Thousand-Character Text and Roget's Thesaurus.

Keywords: Thousand-Character Text, Roget's Thesaurus, Ontology, Interontologia.

1 Introduction

With the development of the Internet, the volume of information is now incomparable with that in the past. In order to classify and manage such a large amount of information, we need standardized classification systems. A standardized classification system can be created through human cognitive ability to classify things. However, human cognitive ability is not each individual's specific ability. Everything in the world has its own unique characteristics, by which it is classified into specific categories, and we understand things more easily by associating them to related categories. In this way, we simplify information processing and understand perceived things better by classifying them systematically according to their characteristics.

The lexical classification systems covered in this study have been developed into various types according to the use of words or information. There are examples of application in the areas of artificial intelligence, computational linguistics and information technology: information retrieval, knowledge management, information system design, ontology building, machine translation, and dictionary compilation. There

---

* Corresponding author.

W. Li and D. Mollá-Aliod (Eds.): ICCPOL 2009, LNAI 5459, pp. 394–401, 2009.

are also implemented lexical classification systems related to the vocabulary resources of natural languages such as Roget's Thesaurus[1], WordNet[2], Lexical FreeNet[3], Kadokawa Thesaurus[4], and EDR[5]. Cases of ontology building include KR Ontology[6], CYC Ontology[7], Mikrokosmos Ontology[8], SENSUS Ontology[9] and HowNet[10], and there are business applications of ontology such as Enterprise Ontology[11], UMLS[12], UNSPSC[13], RosettaNet[14], ISO 2788[15] and ANSI Z39.19[16].

Lexical classification is concept classification by nature. Lexical classification systems mentioned above suggest that there are various concept classification systems today. It is said that people have the same cognition, memory, causal analysis, categorization, and reasoning process. They assume that if there is any difference, it is not from difference in cognitive process but from difference in culture or education[17]. As mentioned above, in the current situation that various concept classification systems are being used in different application areas, it is keenly required to interlock concept classification systems and intelligent information systems. In response to the demand, research is being made on ontology mapping, merge and integration, and semantic integration[18, 19]. The main research method is utilizing shared ontologies or finding mappings in ontological features.

However, if there is a general concept classification system (*interontologia*) as a reference system, it will become more systematic and easier to integrate concept classification systems semantically. Thus, as a case study on an *interontologia*, the present study examined the relevancy of lexical categorization between the Thousand-Character Text [20, 21], which is a representative Eastern classic, and Roget's Thesaurus[1], which is a famous Western classified lexicon. Through this study, we analyze similarity between the two in categorization and classification.

2 The Thousand-Character Text and Roget's Thesaurus

The Thousand-Character Text(千字文) was written by Zhou Xingsi(周興嗣) by order of Emperor Wu(武帝) in the Liang(梁) Dynasty of China in around the 6th century, and transmitted and distributed to Korea early in ancient times. This is a representative classical Chinese textbook used widely to teach children. The oldest Thousand-Character Text annotated with pronunciation and meaning in Korean is the version of Han Seok-Bong(韓石峰) published in 1583. There is also a record on an earlier version published in Gwangju, Korea in 1575. The Thousand-Character Text is old four-character verse composed of a total of 250 four-character phrases or 125 couplets and its materials are Chinese history, culture, etc. [20, 21].

Roget's Thesaurus [1] was first published in 1852 by English surgeon Peter Mark Roget. This is the first synonym/antonym dictionary. Roget's Thesaurus is not in meaningless alphabetical order. The thesaurus classifies lexical knowledge systematically. The top hierarchy is composed of 6 classes, under which are divisions. Each division is again subdivided into sections. In each hierarchy is unique entry information, and at the end of the hierarchical structure are listed a total of 1044 categories. Each category has a list of synonyms by part of speech. On the other hand, if a specific word in the list of synonyms refers to another category, the reference is expressed in the form of "Vocabulary &c. (Entry word) Entry number."

There is a study on lexical classification systems in Korean representative classics such as the Thousand-Character Text, Yuhap(類合) and Hunmongjahoi(訓蒙字會) [20]. In the study, they argue that the Thousand-Character Text is structured well and has a clear system. In addition, they emphasize the accuracy of its classification system that does not allow even a repetition of the same character among the 1000 characters. Largely according to semantic paragraphs, they classify concepts in the Thousand-Character Text as follows: astronomy, nature, royal task, moral training, loyalty and filial piety, virtuous conducts, five moral disciplines, humanity and justice, palace, meritorious retainers, feudal lords, topography, agriculture, mathematics, quiet life, comfort, miscellaneous affairs, skills, admonition, etc. They conclude that in presenting Chinese characters by semantic paragraph, the Thousand-Character Text arranges basic Chinese characters appropriately and is outstanding in terms of lexical system and the perception of basic Chinese characters.

3 Relevancy Analysis

This study has conducted analysis on concept relevancy between the Thousand-Character Text and Roget's Thesaurus through six steps as follows.

Step 1. Index the Thousand-Character Text and Roget's Thesaurus, and build databases: Sort out Chinese characters from the Thousand-Character Text, and words from Roget's Thesaurus. Then build the master databases of the Thousand-Character Text and Roget's Thesaurus.

Step 2. Collect English words similar in meaning to Chinese characters in the Thousand-Character Text and build a database: Determine English words representing meaning of Chinese characters in Thousand-Character Text, referring to Chinese-English dictionary Kingsoft2008[22], and Classical Chinese Character Frequency List[23].

Step 3. Choose English words with the closest meaning to Chinese characters in the Thousand-Character Text: Determine one English word representing meaning of each Chinese character in the Thousand-Character Text through a drop-down list.

Step 4. Map Chinese characters in the Thousand-Character Text to Roget's Thesaurus categories: Choose Roget's Thesaurus categories of the English words representing Chinese characters in the Thousand-Character Text through a drop-down list.

Step 5. Analyze the results of mapping Chinese characters in the Thousand-Character Text to Roget's Thesaurus: Verify Chinese characters in the Thousand-Character Text classified into the Roget's Thesaurus categories.

Step 6. Map Chinese characters in the Thousand-Character Text to Roget's Thesaurus sections: Classify Chinese characters in the Thousand-Character Text into Roget's Thesaurus sections, and make a correlation analysis.

4 Evaluations

Fig. 1 is the distribution chart of Chinese characters in the Thousand-Character Text mapped to Roget's Thesaurus categories. Among the 1,044 categories of Roget's

Thesaurus, 424 categories have one or more corresponding Chinese characters while 620 categories do not have any corresponding Chinese characters. Thus, the overall mapping rate is about 41%. Although the mapping rate is somewhat low, Fig. 1 shows that the mapping is distributed over the range of all categories.

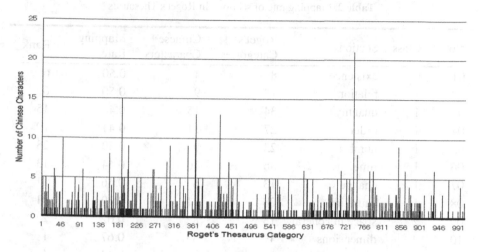

Fig. 1. Mapping of Chinese characters in the Thousand-Character Text to Roget's Thesaurus categories

We have analyzed the mapping on the section level of Roget's Thesaurus, which are higher categories in the hierarchy of the thesaurus. Fig. 2 shows the result of section level analysis. Among a total of 39 sections in Roget's Thesaurus, only one does not have any corresponding Chinese character, but 38 sections have one or more. The overall mapping rate is as high as 97%. Table 1 compares the mapping on the category level with the one on the section level of Roget's Thesaurus.

Table 1. Results of mapping by classification level

Level	Number of mapped Entries	Number of unmapped entries	Total	Mapping rate(%)
Category	424	620	1,044	41
Section	38	1	39	97

Based on the results of mapping presented above, we examine the correspondence to Chinese characters in the Thousand-Character Text on the section level. Except section 'Creative Thought', most of the 39 sections have a direct relationship to the Chinese characters in the Thousand-Character Text. The mapping rate is relatively high in three sections 'Space in General', 'Dimensions' and 'Matter in General.' The Chinese characters implying non-material and metaphysical meanings show high correspondence.

Table 2. Mapping rate of sections in Roget's Thesaurus

No	Class	Sections	Roget's Categories	Chinese Characters	Mapping Rate	Rank
01	1	existence	8	4	0.50	6
02	1	relation	18	9	0.50	6
03	1	quantity	34	15	0.44	15
04	1	order	27	11	0.41	19
05	1	number	23	9	0.39	23
06	1	time	36	16	0.44	13
07	1	change	13	6	0.46	11
08	1	causation	28	11	0.39	21
09	2	space in general	13	8	0.62	2
10	2	dimensions	49	33	0.67	1
11	2	form	25	11	0.44	16
12	2	motion	52	23	0.44	14
13	3	matter in general	5	3	0.60	3
14	3	inorganic matter	37	13	0.35	25
15	3	organic matter	100	44	0.44	16
16	4	operations of intellect in general	6	3	0.50	6
17	4	precursory conditions and operations	15	6	0.40	20
18	4	materials for reasoning	9	2	0.22	34
19	4	reasoning processes	4	1	0.25	30
20	4	results of reasoning	26	8	0.31	27
21	4	extension of thought	9	2	0.22	34
22	4	creative thought	3	0	0.00	39

Table 2. (*continued*)

No	Class	Sections	Roget's Categories	Chinese Characters	Mapping Rate	Rank
23	4	nature of ideas communicated	9	1	0.11	38
24	4	modes of communication	26	11	0.42	18
25	4	means of communicating ideas	50	17	0.34	26
26	5	volition in general	23	5	0.22	36
27	5	prospective volition	60	28	0.47	10
28	5	voluntary action	24	11	0.46	12
29	5	antagonism	25	13	0.52	5
30	5	results of voluntary action	8	3	0.38	24
31	5	general intersocial volition	25	14	0.56	4
32	5	special intersocial volition	8	2	0.25	30
33	5	conditional intersocial volition	8	2	0.25	30
34	5	possessive relations	51	20	0.39	22
35	6	affections in general	7	2	0.29	28
36	6	personal affections	62	29	0.47	9
37	6	sympathetic affections	36	10	0.28	29
38	6	moral affections	56	14	0.25	30
39	6	religious affections	26	4	0.15	37

Table 2 shows the correspondence between the Thousand-Character Text and Roget's Thesaurus on the section level. We can see that the number of Chinese characters changes as the number of Roget's Thesaurus categories does. We have obtained the correlation coefficient r_{xy} for the association between the number of Chinese characters in the Thousand-Character Text and Roget's Thesaurus categories on the section level.

$$r_{xy} = \frac{N \sum XY - (\sum X)(\sum Y)}{\sqrt{[N \sum X^2 - (\sum X)^2][N \sum Y^2 - (\sum Y)^2]}}. \tag{1}$$

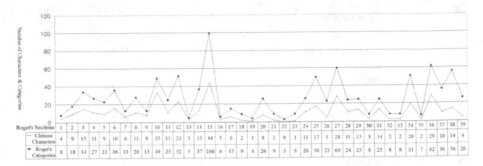

Roget's Sections	1	2	3	4	5	6	7	8	9	10	11	12	13	14	15	16	17	18	19	20	21	22	23	24	25	26	27	28	29	30	31	32	33	34	35	36	37	38	39
Chinese Characters	4	9	15	11	9	16	6	11	8	33	11	23	3	13	44	3	6	2	1	8	2	0	1	11	17	5	28	11	13	3	14	2	2	20	2	29	10	14	4
Roget's Categories	8	18	34	27	23	36	13	28	13	49	25	52	5	37	100	6	15	9	4	26	9	3	9	26	50	23	60	24	25	8	25	8	8	51	7	62	36	56	26

Fig. 2. Correspondence between the Thousand-Character Text and Roget's Thesaurus on the section level

In the correlation analysis, the number of Roget categories is defined as X, the number of mapped Chinese characters as Y, and the number of Roget sections as N. For Equation (1), the values of variables are as follows.

$$\sum X_i = 1044, \sum Y_i = 424, \sum X_i Y_i = 18629, \sum X_i^2 = 44474, \sum Y_i^2 = 8252$$

If these values are substituted for the variables in Equation (1), we obtain $r_{xy} = 0.94$, showing quite a high correlation between the Thousand-Character Text and Roget's Thesaurus on the section level.

5   Conclusions and Future Research

The present study have examined concept relevancy between the Thousand-Character Text and Roget's Thesaurus. The correlation analysis suggests that the experimental data have very high relevancy. From the result of our experiment, we may say that there is an *interontologia* behind Roget's Thesaurus and the Thousand-Character Text.

Tasks for future research include: (1) complementing omitted parts in mapping of Chinese characters in the Thousand-Character Text to Roget's Thesaurus categories with the 1800 commonly used Chinese characters in Korea and comparing the results; and (2) analyzing difference between comparison of the Thousand-Character Text and Roget's Thesaurus on the category and section levels. From these studies, we expect to have a set of Chinese characters for a refined lexical knowledge classification system. Lastly, based on the character set, we will develop a new lexical category system applicable to knowledge classification.

Acknowledgments. This work was supported by the Korea Research Foundation Grant funded by the Korean Government. (KRF-2008-313-H00009)

References

1. Roget's Thesauri, http://www.bartleby.com/thesauri/
2. WordNet, http://wordnet.princeton.edu/
3. Lexical FreeNet, http://www.cinfn.com/doc/
4. Ohno, S., Hamanishi, M.: New Synonyms Dictionary, Kadogawa Shoten, Tokyo (1981) (written in Japanese)
5. The EDR Electronic Dictionary, http://www2.nict.go.jp/r/r312/EDR/index.html
6. KR Ontology, http://www.jfsowa.com/ontology/
7. CYC Ontology, http://www.cyc.com/
8. Mikrokosmos Ontology, http://crl.nmsu.edu/Research/Projects/mikro/htmls/ontology-htmls/onto.index.html
9. SENSUS Ontology, http://www.isi.edu/natural-language/projects/ONTOLOGIES.html
10. HowNet, http://www.keenage.com/html/e_index.html
11. Enterprise Ontology, http://www.aiai.ed.ac.uk/project/enterprise/enterprise/ontology.html
12. UMLS, http://www.nlm.nih.gov/research/umls/
13. UNSPSC, http://www.unspsc.org/
14. RosettaNet, http://www.rosettanet.org
15. ISO 2788, http://www.collectionscanada.gc.ca/iso/tc46sc9/standard/2788e.htm
16. ANSI Z39.19, http://www.niso.org/standards/resources/Z39-19-2005.pdf
17. Richard, E.N.: The Geography of Thought: How Asians and Westerners Think Differently... and Why. Simon & Schuster, New York (2004)
18. Kalfoglou, Y., Schorlemmer, M.: Ontology mapping: the state of the art. The Knowledge Engineering Review 18(1), 1–31 (2003)
19. Noy, N.F.: Semantic Integration: A Survey of Ontology-Based Approaches. SIGMOD Record 33(4), 65–70 (2004)
20. Kim, J.-T., Song, C.-S.: Comparison of Vocabulary Classification Systems among Thousand-Character Text, Yuhap, and Hunmongjahoi, Korean Literature Society, Linguistics and Literature, vol. 52, pp. 159–192 (1991) (written in Korean)
21. Jin, T.-H.: Problems in the Translations and Sounds of Thousand-Character Text, Hangeul-Chinese Character Culture, vol. 104, pp. 80–82 (2008) (written in Korean)
22. Kingsoft 2008 (谷歌金山词霸), http://g.iciba.com/
23. Classical Chinese Character FrequencyList, http://lingua.mtsu.edu/chinese-computing/statistics/char/list.php?Which=CL

Author Index